I0831360

THE READERS OF *NOVYI MIR*

THE READERS OF *NOVYI MIR*

Coming to Terms with the Stalinist Past

DENIS KOZLOV

HARVARD UNIVERSITY PRESS
Cambridge, Massachusetts, and London, England
2013

Library of Congress Cataloging-in-Publication Data

Kozlov, Denis, 1973–
The readers of Novyi Mir : coming to terms with the Stalinist past / Denis Kozlov.
pages ; cm
Includes bibliographical references and index.
ISBN 978-0-674-07287-9 (alk. paper)
1. Literature and society—Soviet Union. 2. Reader-response criticism—Social aspects—Soviet Union. 3. Authors and readers—Soviet Union. 4. Novyi mir—History. 5. Russian periodicals—Soviet Union—History. 6. Russian literature—Social aspects—Soviet Union. 7. Terror in literature. 8. Terror—Soviet Union—Public opinion. 9. Soviet Union—History—Public opinion. I. Title.
PG3022.K69 2013
891.709'0044—dc23 2012044170

Посвящается моему деду, Августу Моисеевичу Шерешевскому, и бабушке, Алле Давыдовне Шерешевской, которые все это пережили.

CONTENTS

Introduction: Readers, Writers, and Soviet History 1

1 A Passion for the Printed Word: Postwar Soviet Literature 24

2 Barometer of the Epoch: Pomerantsev and the Debate on Sincerity 44

3 Naming the Social Evil: Dudintsev's Ethical Quest 88

4 Recalling the Revolution: The Pasternak Affair 110

5 Literature above Literature: Tvardovskii's Memory 134

6 Reassessing the Moral Order: Ehrenburg and the Memory of Terror 171

7 Finding New Words: Solzhenitsyn and the Experience of Terror 209

8 Discovering Human Rights: The Siniavskii-Daniel' Trial 239

9 In Search of Authenticity: The "Legends and Facts" Controversy 263

10 Last Battles: The End of Tvardovskii's *Novyi mir* 295

Epilogue: Tradition, Change, Legacies 323

Archives Consulted 333

Notes 335

Acknowledgments 419

Index 423

THE READERS OF *NOVYI MIR*

INTRODUCTION

Readers, Writers, and Soviet History

IN *SPEAK, MEMORY,* Vladimir Nabokov recalls the debates about Russian history that he, while a student at Cambridge, used to have with his college friend. Attempting, passionately and desperately, to prove his points about the nature of the Russian Revolution and its relationship to literature to "Nesbit" (one of names by which he, in various versions of the memoir, concealed his friend's identity), the young Nabokov came up with various ideas—or, as he ironically remembered them, "truths"—about his country's past. One of them was that "the history of Russia . . . could be considered from two points of view (both of which, for some reason, equally annoyed Nesbit): first, as the evolution of the police . . . ; and second, as the development of a marvelous culture."[1] In response to such grand pronouncements, Nabokov wrote, his English friend would stay safely behind the fortifications of theoretical sympathy with the socialist project, good-natured skepticism about strange Russian émigrés, understatement, and "multiple manipulations of a pipe . . . [,] horribly aggravating when you did not agree with him and delightfully soothing when you did." To Nesbit, Nabokov's truths were "mere fancies."[2]

We do not know whether his classification of Russian history worked for Nabokov himself, as he certainly knew that culture and the police, the two elements of his system, constantly overlapped.[3] Yet it is a memorable classification—not so much as a rigid taxonomy of Russia's historical phenomena, but as a delineation of two major themes that have been prominent in writings about this country's past. What is also memorable is the passion with which the young Nabokov "talked history." In his fervent monologues, which so puzzled his friend, he reflected the spirit of his contemporaries. Talking about history was common among educated Russians at the time when their country was going through unprecedented cataclysms of revolution, civil war, and terror. As an émigré, Nabokov was influenced, indeed formed, by these upheavals, and he returned to them during his Cambridge days and ever after. He wrote *Speak, Memory* about himself, but it is also about Russian history—the fruit of his autobiographical and historical reflections, inseparable from each other.

Throughout his life, Nabokov remained thoroughly skeptical of things Soviet. Yet it might have pleased Vladimir Vladimirovich to learn that, some forty years after he left his country, people there also began discussing their past. They turned to the same themes—revolution, civil war, and terror—that had captivated him. And just as Nabokov did at Cambridge, they began to talk in the same breath about history and literature. It is those discussions, which unfolded among Soviet literary audiences during the 1950s and 1960s, that this book will explore.

Modern Russia, late imperial and Soviet, has been justly described as a "literature-centered civilization"—a country where, for the lack of other mechanisms of legitimate political expression, literature served as an important venue for social commentary. From the late eighteenth and early nineteenth centuries, literature had been the principal means for elaborating both the modern Russian state ideology and the modern Russian language—two projects that went hand in hand and were often implemented by the same literary-minded statesmen, authors, and thinkers.[4] In the nineteenth century, literature became the main battleground of political ideas and beliefs, an expression of values that the educated society debated within itself and sought to inculcate in the people's minds. Ultimately, in the eyes of many Russians and in the words of Nikolai Chernyshevsky, literature became a "guide to life."[5]

Literature-centrism in Russia had emerged long before 1917, but it was in the Soviet times that it reached its peak. The doctrine of socialist realism, which sought to create an exemplary society inspired by literary and artistic images, held that writers should become the principal transmitters and disseminators of the new regime's agenda for sociopolitical change and enlightenment.[6] As it emerged in the late 1920s and early 1930s, socialist realism blurred the boundaries between literature and journalism: on the one hand, literature was mobilized for political purposes; on the other hand, journalists regularly aspired to a literary career.[7] Reading, too, was reorganized in accordance with the regime's needs. Universal literacy became a government priority, one Soviet project that certainly yielded impressive results. The figure of the reader was lionized as the embodiment of an emblematic political phenomenon: familiarity with literature, especially the classics, was now essential to the idea of the new Soviet person "becoming cultured."[8] Propagandists declared the Soviet Union a country of readers—the best-read nation on earth.

Literature was indeed widely read in Russia, and it was never the domain only of highbrow connoisseurs. Engineers, workers, teachers, doctors, students, and soldiers actively responded to reflective literary publications. The capitals, Moscow and Leningrad, generated a minority of these responses; most came from the provinces, notably from large provincial cities. Soviet social thought and polemics were thus by no means exclusively capital-centered, nor were they driven by an elite intelligentsia. The intellectual landscape was richer and broader than that, with a vast, diverse readership consistently and openly formulating opinions on socially urgent issues.

Much of this literature-inspired activism, as well as a veneration for reading, had characterized late imperial Russian culture too, and authors had crossed the border between literature and journalism before 1917—as, for example, Leo Tolstoy did in *Tales of Sevastopol.* However, the place of literature in the new society was much more prominent than before.[9] Whereas prerevolutionary literary audiences had only occasionally numbered beyond the tens of thousands, their Soviet successors routinely numbered in the millions. More important, the Soviet era witnessed an unprecedented symbiosis between government efforts and those of the intelligentsia and the literary community—a joint strategy aimed at the creation of a new consciousness and a new Soviet person. Nothing like this symbiosis had existed in Russia before.

Regulation and limitation became important forces behind the Soviet reading revolution.[10] Public libraries functioned as disciplining agencies, vigilantly pruning their collections, guarding access to printed matter, and monitoring public taste through presumably enlightening activities, such as readers' conferences.[11] The explicitly anticommercial ethos of cultural dissemination regimented the public's literary consumption, prescribing serious reading as a necessity. With the relative scarcity of other options for leisure-time entertainment, such reading was indeed one of the few recreational activities available to the average person.[12] Thus came true the dream of the nineteenth-century intelligentsia, who since Nekrasov's time had fought against cheap popular print, aspiring instead to direct the mass reader toward "serious," edifying books.[13]

However, the regulatory and policing functions of this environment should not obscure the fact that Soviet literary audiences never fit the Procrustean bed of ideology. For many people, literature indeed was a crucial element of their emotional, intellectual, and political life—a world in which they felt freer than anywhere else. Continuing the prerevolutionary tradition, the literary realm remained the principal setting in which alternative ideas emerged, dissent was voiced, and opinions were formulated and exchanged. The time-honored role of literature as the main generator of socioethical norms persisted during the Soviet decades.

If not a "guide to life," then, literature is an important guide to Russian and Soviet history. By looking at how writers, editors, and readers addressed society's problems and reflected on the human condition, historians can draw a telling portrait of the time.[14] It is from the perspective of analyzing the relationship between literature and society as intellectual, cultural, and political history that this book is written.

The book is about the readers of the most famous Soviet literary journal, *Novyi mir* (New World). Founded in 1925 and still published today, it continued the nineteenth-century tradition of "thick journals," literary periodicals that are sometimes defined as a genre in their own right.[15] A legacy of imperial Russian culture, where they had existed since the 1830s and 1840s, the thick journals functioned as major sites for public conversation and deliberately pursued a combination of literary, political, journalistic, and enlightenment aims.[16] Their self-description, which in Soviet times was commonly reproduced in a caption above the table of contents, was: "a literary-artistic and socio-political journal" *(literaturno-khudozhestvennyi i obshchestvenno-politicheskii zhurnal)*. All the elements of this definition, notably literary quality and social charge, were important to editors and to readers. Traditionally, thick journals enjoyed a degree of creative and political autonomy. Their crucial characteristic, distinguishing them from any other type of periodical, was that they had their own "line"—a well-defined worldview, literary strategy, cultural program, and aesthetic ideal that every such journal was supposed to maintain. A thick journal was to have its own voice. This is why, as a leading scholar argues, thick journals tended to flourish during moments of political liberalization in Russia, when such voices were allowed to converse in print, and to retreat into relative shadow in times of reinforced censorship.[17]

The first heyday for Russia's thick journals came in the 1860s, during the Great Reforms. In the exuberant atmosphere of government magnanimity, rising hopes, and lively discussion that characterized the early reign of Alexander II, literary periodicals came to voice widely divergent political opinions within educated society. The journals polemicized with each other, and their programs became rallying standards for like-minded editors, writers, and readers. The readers of the radical journals *Contemporary (Sovremennnik)* and *Notes of the Fatherland (Otechestvennye zapiski)* stood far apart from subscribers to the liberal *Messenger of Europe (Vestnik Evropy)* and the conservative *Russian Messenger (Russkii vestnik).*[18] It was in the latter journal, *Russian Messenger,* that in March 1862 Ivan Turgenev first published his famous novel *Fathers and Sons,* which became one of the most controversial and politically debated books in Russian history. For the next half-century the novel split Russian educated society into groups of readers hotly contesting their interpretations of its characters and ideas.[19] If literature was Russia's form of parliamentarianism, literary journals and their audiences became its first political parties.

These metaphors were less applicable after the 1880s, when, following two glorious decades at the center of intellectual life, thick journals began to lose their exclusive aura of mastery over the minds of readers. In the ever more sophisticated and commercialized culture of late imperial Russia, reading audiences were increasingly compartmentalized. At the turn of the twentieth century, political discussions moved into the domain of newspapers, while philosophical thought and creative talent found outlets in books and specialized periodicals. Illustrated magazines and other forms of popular print proliferated as well.[20]

The Russian Revolution shattered this literary landscape but did not eliminate many of its long-standing features, which revived after 1917. Thick journals reemerged in Soviet Russia to play an important role in the regime's propagandistic endeavors. Despite growing censorship and the subservience of writers to the will of the authorities, the relative intellectual permissiveness of the New Economic Policy (NEP) years, along with the impulse of revolutionary modernism inspired by the new political power of literature, made the 1920s another high point for the thick journal.[21] Perhaps an additional factor was the influx of a vast and relatively uninitiated readership that espoused the new cultural ideals but also accepted guidance in matters of literary taste. Guidance was in the very nature of a thick journal, with the editors' selection and organization of texts for their trusting, loyal audiences.[22] The 1920s saw the founding of some of the most eminent Soviet thick journals, which would for decades remain central to the country's intellectual life—*Zvezda* (1924), *Oktiabr'* (1924), and *Novyi mir* itself (1925).

From the outset *Novyi mir* was a highly prestigious periodical, but its time of glory came in the 1950s and 1960s, during the Thaw. This epoch of reforms, vibrant polemics, and tectonic sociocultural transformations marked a third high point in the history of thick journals, and perhaps a high point for all Russian literature as well. The Thaw was a moment when literature remained culturally and politically significant for the authorities and for readers, while at the same time the literary environment once again came to enjoy a considerable degree of autonomy. Accordingly, thick journals flourished. Developing their different lines, they clashed with one another over a broad spectrum of opinions. The literary-political landscape of the Thaw looked strikingly similar to that of a hundred years earlier, during the Great Reforms.[23] With the intelligentsia's expectations on the rise, and with politics hotly contested by literary means, these two epochs became the historical springtimes of Russian literature-centrism.

The prime focus of social polemics and intellectual change during the Thaw was the Stalinist past. On 4 March 1956, in the wake of Nikita Khrushchev's revelations about Stalin at the Twentieth Party Congress, the poet Anna Akhmatova pronounced her famous dictum: "Now . . . two Russias will look each other in the eye: the one that imprisoned people and the other one that was imprisoned. A new epoch has begun."[24] Indeed, the Thaw was a new epoch—a time of major evolutionary change, when the fundamental notions of the Soviet polity, the worldview, and indeed the very language that had originated in the Stalin decades began to erode.[25] The erosion was neither immediate nor unproblematic, but the official reassessment of Stalin's legacy did prompt a broader, widespread reevaluation of the country's recent past.[26] At the turn of the second half of the century, thousands of people sought to comprehend the first half, rethinking and actively debating the experiences of the Revolution, the Civil War, the forced collectivization of agriculture, World War II, and, principally, the historic tragedy that would later come to be known as the Stalin terror.

Literature became the principal medium for these reflections and conversations. During the Thaw, politics, viewed as history, was debated via established literary channels. Politics as history became the domain of readers. After Khrushchev renewed his forceful attack on Stalin at the Twenty-Second Party Congress in 1961, for several years state violence became a relatively legitimate topic in literature and the press. Brief as it was, this moment of openness had a lasting impact. The publication and intense discussion of such literary texts as Aleksandr Solzhenitsyn's *One Day in the Life of Ivan Denisovich* (1962) or Ilya Ehrenburg's monumental memoir *People, Years, Life* (1960–1963, 1965) led readers to reassess the ethical foundations of their existence and, ultimately, of the established sociopolitical order. People of diverse ages and backgrounds engaged in this epic reassessment—from college students to their fathers and grandfathers who had built and for decades defended Soviet power. The early 1960s thus created a watershed in modern Russian history. Under the impact of literature, readers began to view the Soviet past through the prism of the terror and to draw the lineage of the Soviet order not from 1917 but from 1937—that is, not so much from the Revolution as from the massive state violence that followed it.

It has been suggested on several occasions that the awareness of this violence was peripheral to twentieth-century Russian culture—that a meaningful discussion of this phenomenon failed to take place until the very last Soviet years, or even later.[27] One study branded the survivors of the terror, and by extension their posterity, as "Whisperers," implying that the fear of state repression had for a long time, if not forever, impeded the possibility of holding an open conversation about mass executions and concentration camps, that such conversations have always been limited to private, hermetic, deeply suppressed and horror-ridden settings.[28] My book challenges this view. The issue of the twentieth century's state violence and its legacy was not peripheral but absolutely central to public life and language during the Thaw, with crucial implications for the subsequent decades. Discussions of the Stalin past transcended the limits of a dissenting underground and took place in considerable openness, in and around legitimate publications. Thousands of people in the 1960s displayed great confidence in their entitlement to express political and historical views openly, and regarded the official media channels as appropriate venues for such self-expression. More than ever before, people perceived reading and responding to literature as consequential political activities.

The relatively open and public nature of these conversations compromised the established Soviet political language, notably that of the press. Although most discussions did not make it into print, they were inspired by publications in major, official press organs. As a result, linguistic legitimacy was shattered. Old journalistic devices, especially the phraseology of witch-hunting and scapegoating, now became associated with the Stalin-era repression and thus were compromised, gradually but beyond repair. Under the burden of mounting evidence about the recent extermination of human beings, the official language of endemic social strife and the images of "enemies" began to disintegrate. To be sure, this did not happen overnight after the publication of works by Ehrenburg or Solzhenitsyn. And yet, as readers debated these books that exposed the details of arrests and disappearances, fear and silence, interrogations and prison camps, the old socially exclusive mentality and vocabulary began to decline. The preoccupation with maintaining uniform standards of "Sovietness" gradually yielded to more flexible ideas of social membership, to more sophisticated and open-minded interpretations of history and contemporary problems.

Another result of the widespread discussion of the terror was an increased attention to legality.[29] Many people began to see legal "technicalities" as a safeguard against relapsing into mass violence akin to that of 1937–1938. A direct consequence of the literary revelations of the 1960s was the rise of the human rights movement, which would become so prominent later. Although ousted from print shortly after Khrushchev's fall in 1964, the theme of the terror remained the subtext of innumerable conversations and modes of behavior, underlying many if not all major polemics in late Soviet culture.

Soviet society was not the only one for which the 1950s and 1960s became a crucial time in the conceptualization of twentieth-century political violence. Beneath the obvious differences between Western Europe and the Soviet Union, there was a common set of historical problems and evolving attitudes toward the past. Post–World War II European polities nearly simultaneously came to face very similar questions—how to dismantle the repressive institutions and machinery; how to identify and prosecute the perpetrators; how to reorganize politics and rebuild trust in justice; how (if at all) to discuss repression and its legacy; what to do with the old imagery, language, and ways of thinking; and finally, how to avoid a return of the tragic past.[30]

In each nation's case, the processes of remembrance, commemoration, and, above all, retribution were neither linear nor straightforward.[31] Along with remembering, there were strong tendencies *not* to remember but instead to put the past behind. When they were taken up, the historical polemics often pursued similar courses. East and west of the Iron Curtain, the 1950s and 1960s witnessed a search for alternative legitimacies and continuities, as well as a resurgence of the language of legality, democracy, and rights, which thinkers and political activists viewed as guarantees against the return of mass violence.[32] And, if not as prominently as in the Soviet Union, in West Germany and France literature became instrumental in drawing public attention to the recent tragedies.[33] Historical agendas were thus among many others that the Soviet and Western European cultures began to share during the Thaw years. Ultimately, in Russia as elsewhere in Europe, conversations about the past played a key role in the movement away from authoritarianism.[34]

This is not a book about the collapse of the Soviet Union, and least of all would I want to propose teleological arguments shepherding the complex history of this country to its collapse. Yet in the long run the polemics I discuss here did much to undermine the foundations of the Soviet ideological, educational, ethical, linguistic, and aesthetic order. The people of the Thaw became vastly different from their early Soviet predecessors, the diarists and autobiographers of the 1920s and especially the 1930s, who had consciously and voluntarily sought to remodel themselves in accordance with their vision of the interests, ideas, and language of the new regime. Rather than this being a "totalitarian" imposition of scripts, many authors in the 1930s deliberately identified with the values of self-perfection and national modernization, traditionally shared by the Russian intelligentsia and lionized by the new order.[35] Compared with those early years, the Thaw marked a different historical process—the *unmaking* of Soviet subjectivity. The new awareness of the centrality of mass violence in the country's history urged people to dissociate themselves from the interests, scripts, and language of this regime, to seek new forms of self-expression and new grounds for intellectual stability rather than absorbing themselves in the old, now manifestly inadequate political language. During the Thaw, individuals displayed increasingly less concern about being part of any collective movement. The "purificatory zeal," so characteristic of the 1930s, began to wane. Just as people had done three decades earlier, the readers and writers of the 1950s and 1960s continued to write letters and autobiographies on their own initiative. Yet there was less and less association with the state values, less of a desire to "inscribe their life into a larger narrative of the revolutionary cause."[36] Under the weight of the growing historical reflection and social skepticism, greatly prompted by literary developments, that narrative began to disintegrate.[37]

Novyi mir and its readers were emblematic of these processes. I intentionally do not dwell on whether it was the journal's writers and editors or its readers who had the primary agency in setting the intellectual agendas of the Thaw. Singling out one group of historical actors at the expense of the other would not do justice to either of them. Instead, I propose that the relationship between literary professionals and their audience was mutual and dialogical, with the agendas emerging as a result of this dialogue.

The Thaw-era *Novyi mir* was headed by two outstanding authors, thinkers, and public figures—Konstantin Simonov (1915–1979), who was editor in chief from 1946 to 1950 and again from 1954 to 1958, and Aleksandr Tvardovskii (1910–1971), editor in chief from 1950 to 1954 and 1958 to 1970. At the time by far the most prestigious literary periodical in the country, the journal owed its success to the high professional standards that these two senior editors maintained, as well as to its independent, often semi-oppositional political stance—the "line" that, especially under Tvardovskii, became *Novyi mir*'s trademark and made its name at home and abroad. The journal had immense cultural and ethical authority that ranged far beyond literature, and it is not a major overstatement to say that it stood at the very heart of Soviet intellectual life. Its best-remembered achievement was the publication of Solzhenitsyn's *One Day in the Life of Ivan Denisovich* in November 1962. But there were other publications in the journal whose contemporary resonance, if not long-term impact, rivaled that of *One Day*. Thanks to these texts *Novyi mir* became, and remains, a Russian cultural legend.

Historians have traditionally focused on the theme of "literature and power" in the Soviet context, exploring relations between writers and editors, on the one hand, and political and ideological authorities on the other—party bureaucrats, government officials, censors, and the like. *Novyi mir,* in this respect, has always intrigued scholars with what one has termed "permitted dissent," the phenomenon of relative independence of a press organ within the admittedly oppressive regime.[38] Students of literature have explored the journal's aesthetic platform, its patterns of literary criticism, and the work of its eminent authors, frequently tying such analyses to the politics of power.[39] In particular, numerous observers have been fascinated by Solzhenitsyn, Tvardovskii, and their fateful literary relationship.[40] Simonov has also received some attention, although a thorough analysis of his ideas remains to be written.[41] Much of this early research on *Novyi mir* retains considerable value today, and although it appeared at the prearchival stage of Soviet studies, the evidence available since the archives became accessible in the 1990s has turned out to support many of the previous arguments about the journal's relations with state power. This might be so because *Novyi mir* attracted massive attention during the Cold War, when Western analysts were able to obtain information from rich sources, including eyewitnesses and firsthand participants in the journal's saga. In the late Soviet decades, the drama of literature and power in Russia—an integral part of Nabokov's "history of the police"—was watched closely, for it meant much, if for different reasons, on both sides of the Iron Curtain.[42]

To follow Nabokov's admittedly imperfect classification, though, this book is about culture rather than about police. Instead of focusing on relations between writers, authorities, and texts, I primarily explore the relationship between texts and readers. Mostly this is not a history of the journal as an institution, of its relations with the political and cultural establishment, its polemics with other journals, or the texts it published. These topics do figure prominently in the book, but mainly it is about a different, less studied yet no less important problem—literature and society. My question is: How did the reading audience change in the process of contemplating and discussing the publications that became landmarks in the country's history? Ultimately, answering this question may help to explain how ideas are disseminated and intellectual change occurs among broad audiences in a relatively closed society, something the Soviet Union remained in its late decades.

Novyi mir's archive contains an exceptionally vast and well-preserved collection of readers' letters from the late 1940s to the early 1970s—more than 600 files containing about 12,000 letters. Only a tiny fraction of the collection has been published, while the overwhelming majority of the letters—97 to 99 percent—have never seen the light of day. More than 3,000 of these unpublished letters for the years 1948 to 1970, written in response to the journal's publications and addressed to its editors and authors, constitute the main body of evidence for my work. Uniquely extensive and well organized, this archive is different from the papers of many other Soviet journals and newspapers from those years. Unlike other periodicals, *Novyi mir* did not have an editorial policy of letter disposal. The letters were preserved meticulously, especially under Tvardovskii, who viewed readers' responses as a vital part of the literary process and made it his policy to preserve all of them. Former members of the editorial board confirm that this policy was closely followed.[43] I do not know of a similar commitment by Simonov, but the numbers of readers' letters that survive from his terms of editorship, especially the second one (1954–1958), are also impressive.

Novyi mir handed some of its papers over to the Central State Archive of Literature and Art, now the Russian State Archive of Literature and Art (RGALI), in Moscow as early as the fall of 1962. Accidentally or not, Tvardovskii made this transfer on the eve of publishing *One Day in the Life of Ivan Denisovich*. Interestingly, the papers appeared incomplete to the archivists, who inquired why many editorial materials, such as protocols and stenographic records of board meetings, were missing. The journal's response was that the archive was in fact complete. Few stenographic records and written protocols had ever existed, because the editors met daily and discussed their business informally, without producing much paperwork.[44] Fortunately, they treated readers' letters with greater respect than routine bureaucratic matters.

In practice, not all the letters written to *Novyi mir* have survived, not even for the Tvardovskii years.[45] The preserved files probably reveal not only the relative popularity of the journal's publications but also the editors' interests and predilections, as well as the many predicaments *Novyi mir* faced. As a rule, the letters that have survived in largest numbers were written in response to the politically important publications that were crucial for the journal's fortunes, or (often one and the same thing) to those publications and literary discussions that the editors considered especially meaningful. For the researcher, this is an advantage rather than an obstacle. Such discussions maximally engaged all the parties—the editors, the authorities, and the readers. The surviving letters thus not only reflect editorial concerns and political controversies but also create a telling portrait of *Novyi mir*'s active audience. And although each set of letters is limited by unique circumstances of preservation and selection, examining this correspondence over the span of two decades does reveal long-term trends in language and thought.

It is true that the word "discussion" needs to be used with some caution in reference to unpublished readers' letters to literary journals. Indeed, strictly speaking, this letter writing did not constitute a direct, unmediated discussion in a public forum. And yet, as the subsequent pages will make clear, the letters were often intended as calls for action, addressed to writers and editors with copies occasionally forwarded to party and government officials. Many of the letters were also written collectively. And individually written ones often mention intense conversations among fellow readers that preceded and inspired the acts of letter writing. So while not exactly a discussion by itself, the letter writing by readers in response to literature published in the journal did manifest numerous, and turbulent, discussions that were taking place in society at the time.

Among the letter writers, of special interest to me were the victims and perpetrators of state violence. A remarkable fact of history during the Thaw is that both of these groups—Akhmatova's two Russias—avidly read literature and responded to it with amazingly little inhibition. Often, their letters would turn into long autobiographies of twenty, thirty, even fifty handwritten pages, in which the writers reflected—sometimes defensively, at other times critically and soberly—on their own life experience as part of a larger history. As they read in print about the arrests, prison camps, and executions of the recent past, these people came to confront their own past, their entrenched beliefs and values. At times they came to confront each other as well.

Can we draw a clear line between victims and perpetrators, especially in the Soviet case? And what about those who, either because of good fortune, their young age, or our elementary lack of information, seem to fall in neither category but instead belong to a third group—the bystanders? Many of those who wrote letters probably did not rush to supply future historians with exhaustive autobiographical information. What about them, those who either did not care or did not dare to speak openly about their past? How can we analyze the experience of someone whom that experience had taught to use utmost discretion in speaking and writing?

The chronic reticence of Soviet-era written sources, whether institutional or personal, is a familiar problem that has led some historians to question the value of those sources altogether.[46] I am more optimistic about the information this evidence can provide. Reticent as some of them might have been, many letter writers during the Thaw were, again, remarkably outspoken and fearless in their public statements. As I read through hundreds and hundreds of letters, I was often amazed at how *unafraid* their authors were to speak their mind—something they by no means had to do, but did nonetheless. In addition, the letters frequently reveal more than their authors intended to say. They reveal, among other things, that the "bystander" paradigm rarely endures trial by evidence. The historic tragedies of the century affected Soviet people in countless ways, sparing virtually no one. Even if they did not mention it, this impact showed in what and how they wrote. In this realm of intense, politically charged conversations, there were no bystanders.[47]

But how large was this realm? Or, to put this question in a common scholarly form, how *representative* were the readers, with their letters, of something that may be called popular opinion(s)? Over years of presenting my research to various audiences, the more I practiced responding to this question, the more apparent it became to me that a statistically faultless answer did not exist. No one will ever have a perfect, hermetic base of evidence that will conclusively demonstrate whether a certain set of ideas was or was not representative of a general climate of opinion in society. The nesting-doll set of questions about how the surviving letters reflect the original incoming correspondence, how that correspondence reveals a larger readership, and how the readership's views measured against a broader panorama of opinions at the time probably will never be resolved. As early as the 1960s and 1970s, Soviet sociologists who studied reading grappled with these very questions, and in the end they begrudgingly concluded that such indicators of representation could not be reliably measured.[48] Strictly speaking, statistically representative evidence does not exist in the social history of ideas—it is a dream rather than a practical goal.

However, numbers do not tell the whole story. Representativeness is more than a statistical category. The dissemination of ideas in society is a dynamic process that needs to be measured not so much by fixed numerical indicators as by impact over time. Ideas take a long time to be absorbed in the public mind. They often meet with resistance and rejection, and it is only gradually that they become pervasive. The fact that a concept initially evoked a limited or hostile reception does not mean that the concept was insignificant or that it would not grow on the audience as time passed. This was precisely what happened with the ideas and language of twentieth-century experience that *Novyi mir* elaborated during the Thaw. Already the center of attention among educated readers in the 1960s, over the next twenty years these ideas and this language would evolve into a genuine intellectual orthodoxy. They would emerge as a powerful force during Mikhail Gorbachev's perestroika in the late 1980s, playing a crucial role in the fortunes of the Soviet Union during its last years, and they would continue to prevail afterward in the post-Soviet literary, artistic, media, and ultimately political universe. In this sense, the line of *Novyi mir,* and the repercussions it evoked in society, was representative. In fact, it represented nothing less than the dominant intellectual vector of late twentieth- and early twenty-first-century Russia. To this day—despite the challenges of the post-Soviet years—the historical, ethical, and linguistic values formulated by *Novyi mir* remain central in Russian culture.

It is important, therefore, to examine the mechanisms by which these ideas and this language, during the first years of their public life, began to take hold of the people's minds. Responses to literature, a logical product of reading, offer one such mechanism.

Just as reading itself was a time-honored pursuit in Russia, so was the readers' correspondence with authors and literary periodicals. Nineteenth- and early twentieth-century readers eagerly wrote letters to Tolstoy, Dostoevsky, Korolenko, and Chekhov—letters that are strikingly similar to the ones we find in Soviet-era archives. They insisted that literature ought to and did represent reality accurately and authentically. Their letters often turned into autobiographies, sharing life stories and concerns of a political, personal, or even an intimate nature with a trusted author. They asked the writer whether his characters were positive or negative, and specifically requested positive heroes as examples for how they should lead their lives. They asked for continuations of stories, inquiring what had happened to the characters later.[49] They wrote collective letters.[50] At times a writer inspired them so much that they penned their responses in verse.[51] Young ladies in provincial towns would fall in love with literary characters and put novels under their pillow at night in the hope of seeing their sweetheart in dreams.[52] All these features (save perhaps the dream induction) are present in Soviet readers' letters written half a century later. Letter writers in Russia, whether before or after 1917, treated literature as a revelation of ethical and social truth, and the writer as an oracle of that truth, a moral authority of an almost religious order, capable of providing people with guidance for their lives.[53]

The writers responded, often at great length, and although their attitudes toward such correspondence varied, many perceived interaction with readers as an important part of their work. Tolstoy answered hundreds of readers' letters about *The Kreutzer Sonata* (1889) and *Resurrection* (1899). His correspondents approached him with social reflections, personal and family troubles, questions of faith, inquiries about the role of women in public and private life, reports of local injustices, and even thoughts of suicide.[54] Dostoevsky, whose serialized *Diary of a Writer* (1876–1877) elicited emotional responses from many readers, took a similar approach and even intervened on behalf of his readers or their protégés, in some cases, for instance, protecting them from litigation.[55]

The major forms and principles of communication between writers and readers that became prominent in the Soviet literary world were not invented by the ideologues of socialist realism, nor were they a result of any "Sovietization" of the literary community or the reading audience. These forms and principles were inherited from the prerevolutionary literary culture, and that inheritance was conscious and deliberate. Classical Russian literature continued to serve as a beacon, a model of writing and behavior, for its Soviet successors, who were often well versed in the literary tradition and actively sought to maintain or reestablish continuities with the past.[56]

Novyi mir was, again, the best example here. Tolstoy was Tvardovskii's favorite author and source of inspiration. Vladimir Lakshin (1933–1993), Tvardovskii's younger colleague and longtime de facto deputy at the journal, was a scholar of nineteenth-century Russian literature, an expert on Tolstoy, Ostrovsky, and Chekhov, and like Tvardovskii, he attached great importance to readers and their letters, arguing for the integral role of the audience in literature.[57] The Russian classics also inspired the *Novyi mir* editors in their political stance. During the Thaw, the civic activism and close interaction between writers and readers that had characterized nineteenth- and early twentieth-century Russian literature became a model for emulation by literary professionals. And the role of a literary journal as the herald of its epoch, the master of minds, was also purposely built on the foundation of cultural tradition.

That said, the Soviet epoch brought much that was new to the idea and practice of public letter writing, including correspondence about literature. To apply the Soviet paradigm of spontaneity versus consciousness, while in imperial Russia expressing political opinions via (readers') letters had been a spontaneous practice, after 1917 letter writing received the high-priority status of a "conscious" activity that the regime sought to encourage, organize, and direct. Letters became an important element in the new political culture, which proclaimed itself democratic and participatory. From at least the 1920s, the Bolsheviks promoted letter writing as "input from below, a manifestation of mass, democratic participation in Soviet power."[58] Authorities up to the highest level monitored letters as a source of information about the popular mood. Letters were also a tool of propaganda, an instrument of mass mobilization and opinion building. "Initiatives" or responses "from below" cast in an epistolary form figured prominently in political campaigns, including those against "enemies of the people." Newspapers selected appropriate letters for publication, or even solicited letters from targeted correspondents, using them as evidence of popular support, indignation, or other feelings, depending on the need.[59]

During the later Soviet decades, letter writing from the public continued to be an activity to which journalists ascribed great significance—some out of conviction, others out of habit. In the 1950s and 1960, editorial boards and special "departments of letters" at newspapers and journals routinely invested much time in recording, analyzing, and discussing readers' correspondence.[60] Most letters were never published, but all were officially considered important and warranting at least some kind of response. It was customary to answer most, if not all letters, no matter how briefly.[61] Underneath this mandatory formal respect, editorial attitudes varied and could be not only respectful, as at *Novyi mir,* but also sarcastic, cynical, or manipulative—here Soviet journalists were no different than their Western counterparts.[62] Nonetheless, working with readers' letters remained a political priority for the press—above all, as a mechanism of creating a climate of opinion. In February 1954 the journalist Boris Agapov (1899–1973), a senior editor of the principal literary newspaper *Literaturnaia gazeta,* eloquently formulated this approach: "Our task is not at all to reflect the opinion that we receive via readers' letters. . . . Our task is to influence this public opinion [*obshchestvennoe mnenie*], stressing what we consider correct and noting what we consider incorrect. Were we simply a mouthpiece [of readers' attitudes], that would be wrong."[63]

The political aspects of letter writing were also important for its practitioners, many of whom perceived this correspondence as a form of genuine participation in power. In her work on the 1930s, Sheila Fitzpatrick distinguished between two major categories of public letter writing (which, in her definition, meant "letters written to public figures and institutions")—supplication and civic activism. She divided letter writers into "supplicants"—humble subjects who pursued their own private and personal interests in requesting that officials act on their letters—and "citizens," who wrote, or claimed to write, in the public interest with no explicit prospect of personal gain.[64] If we adopt this interpretive framework, letters about literature appear to have been overwhelmingly acts of citizenship rather than supplication. The letter writers had little or nothing to gain from expressing their political, historical, or ethical views. In fact, they had something to lose: when discussing controversial issues, they put themselves at risk and at the mercy of their addressees, not to mention the postal authorities and other, more ominous agencies. Yet not only did they write, but they also usually signed their letters and provided a return address. Anonymous epistles did exist but were never a majority.

Perhaps one hope of gain came out of publicistic vanity: the desire to have one's letter published? But while some letters were indeed aimed at publication, most were not.[65] Letter writers frequently declared that they wrote for purely altruistic reasons—to express an opinion only for the information and further use of their trusted author or editor, but by no means for publication. Sometimes they did not even expect a full-fledged response and were content simply to know that their letter was received.

The remarkable, sometimes almost self-destructive candor and the altruistic civic charge of the letters reveal the great degree of trust that their authors placed not only in the addressee but also in their own entitlement and ability to express political views openly, and thus to have a meaningful impact on society. In this way, the letters call for a discussion of freedom and unfreedom in Soviet society, suggesting political freedom as a culture- and time-specific category, rather than an absolute one.[66]

Interestingly, the Soviet approach to letter writing as a form of participatory politics proved strikingly modern at the turn of the twenty-first century, both in Russia and in the West. Facing the advance of the Internet, influential periodicals and news channels gradually abandoned the liberal concept of the press as a platform from which intellectuals disseminate ideas on a top-down basis to uninformed audiences. The media began to merge professional and amateur journalism, incorporating Weblogs, forums, and comment pages as an integral part of reporting and analyzing events. Contributions from amateur observers became a legitimate part of media culture. Scholars began talking about a new face of political democracy—the so-called deliberative democracy, which presumes that open, informal, and emotional citizen participation is intrinsically valuable as an effective mechanism for engaging large numbers of people in political conversations. In the best-case scenario, such conversations may influence the actual decision-making process.[67]

There are certainly many differences between the modern-era cyberspace and the letter writing of the Thaw, let alone between the Soviet polity and latter-day democracies. For one thing, whereas online posts today are broadly accessible, the universe of Soviet letter writing was always an iceberg, most of it quietly submerged in institutional archives. And yet the letters were intended as a political force, an incentive for socially significant action. Readers, for instance, often meant to supply new information or ideas on the basis of which the writer would create a new text of social importance. In some cases, this worked. Not only were many writers genuinely interested in the letters they received, but some actually used them in their literary work: Solzhenitsyn's *The Gulag Archipelago* is the prime example. Beyond the realm of literature, the letter writers or their addressees often forwarded copies of letters to agencies of power—including the Central Committees of the Communist Party and the Young Communist League, Komsomol; the union and republican governments; local authorities; and major newspapers, such as *Pravda* and *Izvestiia*.

The forms of political culture cast in the early Soviet years thus had a lasting impact. By the time of the Thaw, letters had become an established mechanism for influencing politics. In that sense, despite all the limitations, the concept of deliberative democracy did apply to the idea, if not always the practice, of Soviet politics. Intended as a tool for social action and participation in power, letter writing was a form of activism that presumed the authors' high degree of identification with the existing order—their perception of themselves as its integral part. Effectively, this is what citizenship is about.

Important as politics was for the letter writers, their responses to literature cannot, of course, be interpreted only in terms of political participation. Letters are human documents that reveal the minds and personalities of their authors. The readers, after all, ignored some literary pieces but responded to others with long, emotional texts. As a rule, letter writing was a one-time activity: there were some prolific letter writers who wrote repeatedly and on various occasions, but most people wrote only one such letter—often, they said, once in their lifetime. What was it about a particular article, novel, or memoir that compelled someone to spend hours or even days putting her thoughts on paper, and then to send those thoughts far away in expectation of no recognition, no reward? It is not that the letter writers were particularly well versed in the fine points of literature. As I mentioned earlier, *Novyi mir* was never a domain of highbrow intellectuals, not anything like the *New Yorker* (although in terms of literary prestige the two were comparable). Yet, despite their often rudimentary literary education and limited proficiency in written self-expression, the intensity and eloquence with which readers responded to the literature was often impressive.

Here is where arguments about the regulated nature of Soviet reading, presumably supervised and controlled from above, reach their limits.[68] Based on a multitude of sanctioned publications, such arguments reproduce a picture of readership actively promoted by the Soviet political and cultural authorities—a picture, to use socialist realist terminology, of "life as it should have been." In actual life, readers could and did identify or disagree with a published text in myriad unexpected, unregulated ways. They could openly criticize a publication or tacitly distance themselves from it, reserving skeptical comments until safer times.[69] Readers' reactions became more visibly complex during the Thaw, as fear subsided and literature began exploring new themes, elaborating new languages, and posing increasingly complicated questions. In reality Soviet reading and intellectual history were diverse and nonlinear, reflecting the wide variety of perceptions that existed in that multifaceted and sophisticated culture.

This prompts a general observation about the relationship between the Soviet political context and the intellectual landscape. Long-term trends of thought in Soviet society were not immediately linked to short-term fluctuations in the leadership's policies. A less linear trajectory of intellectual change was at work that possessed a dynamic of its own, independent from the immediate political exigency. Despite all the influence of high politics on culture, intellectual life did exist in the Soviet Union, and it was not directly subservient to the leadership's changing attitudes.

Readers' reactions to a published text primarily depended not on any external regulating factor but on the relevance of that text to their lives. The intensity of their reactions originated in the ability of an author to stir emotions, provoke thoughts, and relate to human experiences. Reader-response theory argues that it is the readers who create meaning in literature: there is no objective meaning as such; instead, each reader builds his or her own, fully legitimate interpretation of a text based on the ideas he or she invests in the text and invokes in the act of reading.[70] This fully applies to Soviet reading audiences, including that of *Novyi mir.* It may be helpful to think in terms of "guilds" of readers—groups of people, united by similar backgrounds, who reacted intensely to the texts they perceived as addressing their experiences. Thus, many of those who responded to Vladimir Dudintsev's 1956 *Not by Bread Alone,* a novel with engineers and inventors as its main protagonists, were themselves engineers and inventors. Many of those who responded to Solzhenitsyn's *One Day in the Life of Ivan Denisovich* were former inmates, free hires, or guards of concentration camps. Such guild responses remained prominent throughout the Thaw, and they certainly revealed a perception of literature grounded in the principles of realism. And this is precisely what makes readers' letters valuable to a historian. Because they approached literature as a realistic depiction of life, the readers reacted to it by writing about life as well. Realism turned their responses to literature into autobiographies; it led people to tell their life stories and to present their experiences as relevant, indeed integral, to their country's history.

It is apt at this point to discuss the categories of experience and historical consciousness that are central to this book. My interpretation of experience differs from the one Joan Scott suggested in the early 1990s when she emphasized the socially and, above all, linguistically, constructed nature of this category. Experience is not objectively given to us, Scott argued; on the contrary, it is formulated (constructed) at particular moments, by particular subjects, and in a particular language. Experience is expressed, and therefore exists, in the terms of the one who expresses it, and so the historian's task is to pay close attention to the language and circumstances in which experience is formulated. While this interpretation is useful in stressing the power of language to shape and constitute subjectivity, Scott's emphasis on the constructed nature of experience requires a qualification. A singular focus on constructedness turns experience into a presentist category, depriving the past of any ability to influence and shape the mind. Scott advised historians to "take as their project *not* the reproduction and transmission of knowledge said to be arrived at through experience, but the analysis of the production of that knowledge itself."[71] I argue that experience works both ways, that it is about both production *and* reproduction of knowledge, and that the relationship between the past and the present in the conceptualization of experience is reciprocal and dialogical. Experiences may be constructed, but construction is not a purely rational and logical faculty that human beings possess. On the contrary, the terms of construction are themselves historical. The nature of experience is discursive, but discourse is not emancipated from its historical context.

Although the term "memory" does appear in the pages that follow, central to my argument is the category of historical consciousness. This book does not draw the radical distinction between history and memory that Pierre Nora (and earlier Maurice Halbwachs) detected in modern culture. For Nora, memory was someone's lived and living past, personally experienced and intimately known, whereas history was a detached attempt by professional scholars to reconstruct that past. In modern societies preoccupied with newness and change, he argued, memory plays an ever-diminishing role, no longer constituting an "environment" in which humans function on a daily basis, but rather relegated to a number of more or less well-maintained "sites."[72] My working assumption is that this ritualized weathering of memory is a variable that depends on the historical circumstances and the issue in question. For "sites of memory" to emerge, their forms and meanings need to be established—usually following extended, multidecade or even multicentury deliberation. Without such an establishment of meanings, memorialization as coming to terms with the past is impossible. Moreover, while issues of the past may appear resolved at certain times and in certain cultures, in others they retain or regain urgency.[73] Thus, diminution of memory certainly does not apply to how, in the second half of the twentieth century, Europeans viewed the historic cataclysms of the century's first half. Rather than a diminution, this was a time of memory production, a moment when the recent upheavals were everyone's yesterday and thousands were pondering their meaning. For contemporaries, this memory was not a cluster of "sites" but an environment saturated with universal importance.

For these reasons, I tend to side with those who suggest that the concepts of history and memory are not mutually exclusive but instead are fused together in the notion of historical consciousness. Historians, this argument goes, are not disengaged intellectuals; on the contrary, they are capable of emotional affinity with their objects of study, of "witnessing to the experience of others," a process often informed by the historian's own experience. The same fusion between a personal experience of bygone events and a capacity, indeed a willingness, to interpret their historical significance characterizes not only historians but also anyone else who ponders the past.[74]

The understanding of historical consciousness as the human ability to remember and at the same time to make sense of the past is central to this book. Important in the Western context, the notion might be of particular significance for twentieth-century Russia, where interpretations of the past proved not only politically momentous but also notably fragile.[75] In their polemics about literature, Soviet readers evoked their own individual and family backgrounds, ascribing historical interpretations to their lives in the context of the recent history they had seen unfold.

What elucidates these historically conscious conversations is, again, the paradigm of citizenship.[76] The presence of the past in the readers' letters, at once as personal background and as historical reasoning, suggests that the letter writers functioned in an "environment of memory." Yet they did so in a way that characterized their time and culture—hoping at once to explain the past for themselves and to make their explanations serve a common cause. As infinitely far away as the readers of *Novyi mir* stood from Vladimir Nabokov, for many of them, just as for Nabokov, their own lives were inseparable from their country's history. As they read, thought, and wrote, they changed—and so did the country itself.

1

A PASSION FOR THE PRINTED WORD

Postwar Soviet Literature

AT THE END of World War II, Soviet literature-centrism was at its peak. Not only was the population overwhelmingly literate, as a result of concerted campaigns back in the 1920s and especially the 1930s, but also there was a remarkable craving for the printed word in the immediate postwar years.[1] Decades later, one of the most respected Soviet writers, Yuri Trifonov (1925–1981), would reflect on the origins of this phenomenon. Trifonov became famous in 1950, when Tvardovskii's *Novyi mir* published his first novel, *Students.* This book about student life in contemporary Moscow was an immediate success. Enthusiastic responses flooded the editorial mailbox, and Stalin himself joined the admirers of the young author: in the following year the book received a Stalin Prize in literature.[2] In his memoirs, Trifonov tried to explain why the novel, unremarkable from a high literary standard and his own mature viewpoint, had once been so popular. The explanation, he concluded, must have been not so much in the book itself as in the zeitgeist—the atmosphere of heightened expectations from literature that existed among readers in the late 1940s and early 1950s. Despite the unbearable drudgery of socialist realist writing that dominated the literary landscape, he wrote,

> Readers wanted books about contemporary life, the life that was familiar to them. The quality of prose, overall, plummeted

> starkly in comparison to the 1930s, not to mention the 1920s. Giftless novels by [Fedor] Panferov and colourless prose by [Nikolai] Shpanov or [Arkadii] Perventsev came to the forefront. . . . And yet the avidity for reading, the passion for books was an enormous, all-embracing fascination—after the war, after all the misfortunes, after the rationing system, after the years when books had been sold in order to buy bread. Therefore, writings in which there flickered at least a semblance of truth were embraced with unbelievable and seemingly inexplicable delight. Discussions about the novels *Far from Moscow* by [Vasilii] Azhaev or *Kruzhilikha* by [Vera] Panova gathered thousands of people. And what was in those books to discuss? What was there to debate? Everything in them was clear and indisputable. All that commotion, all those deliberations from the podia, all those arguments and shouting, were the expressions of passionate and yearning *love for the book.*
>
> Never in the history of Russia was there a more rewarding audience of readers than after the end of the war.[3]

Trifonov's description was accurate. For all that is known about literature-centrism, one is still impressed by the significance that people ascribed to fiction during the postwar years. Literature and references to it surfaced among people in all walks of life, in places expected and unexpected. Unlike *Novyi mir,* for example, the newspaper *Komsomol'skaia Pravda* was by no means a literary periodical. It was, rather, the main press organ of the Komsomol and the declared mouthpiece of the country's youth. And yet, from 1952 to 1954, among the newspaper's twenty-three departments that covered various aspects of life for young people—"working-class youth," "studying youth," "Komsomol life," college students, the military, science, construction, propaganda, foreign affairs, and so on—the one department that consistently beat others in the amount of readers' letters received was the department of literature. In 1952, out of 53,704 letters *Komsomol'skaia Pravda* received, 12,973 came to the department of literature—compared with 1,363 to the college students' department, 1,559 to that of "working youth," 2,935 to "studying youth," 2,086 to the military department, 1,559 to agriculture, 1,502 to propaganda, 789 to foreign affairs, and 38 (only!) to science.[4] The same situation was repeated in December 1953 and January 1954, when the literary department again received more letters than any other. Many of these letters contained amateur stories, poems, and sketches sent by readers hoping for publication.[5] Very few of the letters were actually published: only 33 out of 12,973 letters in the department of literature, or about one quarter of 1 percent, saw the light of day in 1952, while just 3 out of 1,597 appeared in print in January 1954. Nonetheless, in accordance with Soviet journalistic practice, the editorial office duly responded to nearly every one of them.[6]

To be sure, many of the letters were examples of readers' graphomania, the practice of obsessive writing well known to scholars of modern Russian culture.[7] Yet the sheer volume of correspondence, and the formal respect it was granted, illustrate how much attention both literature and the practice of letter writing received at the time. Even if the huge volume of letters was partly owing to graphomania, it is remarkable how extensive the phenomenon had become: thousands of pages claiming literary status were mailed to a newspaper of a clearly nonliterary nature. Literature reached far beyond its own realm during the postwar years, becoming not simply a means of social commentary but something far greater: a lens through which an individual saw, interpreted, and interacted with the outside world.

Literature's official status contributed to its social prestige. Under Stalin, literature was a matter of state importance, and decisions about publication, circulation, appointments, awards, or reprisals against editors and authors were often given a high political priority. The Union of Soviet Writers had existed since 1934, but strategic issues of literary policy were never its prerogative. Those concerns were resolved at the very top of the power hierarchy—by the Politburo, Orgburo, or Secretariat of the Central Committee. Thick journals, in particular, as the central element in the literary edifice, occupied much of the leaders' attention. The highest party agencies were closely involved in the functioning of the journals, issuing numerous decrees with such characteristic titles as: "On the Journal *Oktiabr*'" (4 August 1939), "On the Editorial Boards of Literary Journals" (20 August 1939), "On Control over Literary Journals" (2 December 1943), "On Raising the Responsibility of Secretaries of Literary Journals" (3 December 1943), "On the Journal *Znamia*" (23 August 1944), "On the Journals *Zvezda* and *Leningrad*" (14 August 1946, the infamous one), "On the Editorial Board of the Journal *Zvezda*" (30 August 1946), "On the Journal *Znamia*" (4 October 1948 and 27 December 1948), or "On Publishing Works of Literature [Previously] Published in Journals" (12 May 1950).[8]

There was always something wrong with the journals. Either writers did not treat their own membership in journal editorial boards seriously, or the "responsible secretaries" of those boards did not ensure proper coordination among the writers-cum-editors, or the literary critics were not astute enough in their analysis, or they all made poor choices in selecting the manuscripts, or, if properly selected, the manuscripts were then poorly edited.

Different explanations exist for this remarkably tight supervision of literature by the country's leadership. It could be that literary issues served the symbolic purposes of the regime, which was demonstrating or reasserting its power during these turbulent years.[9] Literature might also have provided an outlet for inner struggles at the top, such as the one between Andrei Zhdanov and Georgii Malenkov in 1946 to 1948.[10] Personalities mattered too, especially one personality. As much as opinions on literary matters could vary, the ultimate decision belonged to Stalin, the first reader in this country of readers.[11] Konstantin Simonov, who had several opportunities to talk to Stalin in person during these years, noted the leader's keen interest in literature. Stalin impressed even the most informed writers with his nuanced knowledge of texts and characters, and his degree of involvement in literary affairs was extraordinary.[12] In one case, for example, in December 1948 Dmitrii Shepilov (1905–1995), then head of the Central Committee's department of propaganda and agitation, sought to interrupt the distribution of that month's issue of the literary journal *Oktiabr'*. He needed to halt the distribution in order to make last-minute changes to a novel by Fedor Panferov (1896–1960) about World War II, *In the Land of the Defeated,* which in Shepilov's opinion contained vulgar and "crudely naturalistic" passages belittling the Soviet war effort. Yet even the authority of a Central Committee department head was not enough to hold the distribution of the already published issue and to introduce last-minute changes—indeed a costly operation. Shepilov garnered the support of the second most powerful person in the party, Georgii Malenkov. But this proved not enough either: Malenkov then appealed to Stalin. Only at that point did a laconic resolution appear on the document requesting the hold: "Reported. The issue is resolved."[13] In such an environment, reading books was a most serious affair indeed.

Periodicals and Dissemination of the Printed Word

Given its significance, the literary habitat of the late 1940s and early 1950s looked, at least on the surface, remarkably spare. Similar to the well-known *malokartin'e*, the scarcity of new feature-film productions during the late Stalin years, those years could also be described as the time of *malozhurnal'e*—a scarcity of literary journals, especially the thick monthlies that formed the face of literature. It was customary for a major Soviet literary text, before being published in book form, to be serialized in a thick journal.[14] However, in the year of Stalin's death, 1953, there were only four thick literary journals being published in the capitals. Three were based in Moscow—*Novyi mir*, *Oktiabr'*, and *Znamia* (established, respectively, in 1925, 1924, and 1931)—and one in Leningrad, *Zvezda*, established in 1924. (The literary journal *Leningrad*, which had existed in its latest incarnation since 1940, was eliminated by a Central Committee decree in August 1946).[15] It was not until 1955 that new thick journals were launched—*Druzhba narodov*, *Iunost'*, and *Inostrannaia literatura* in Moscow, as well as *Neva* in Leningrad. In 1956, there appeared *Nash sovremennik* (previously an almanac, monthly since 1964) and *Molodaia gvardiia* (resumed after publication ceased in 1941), followed in 1957 by *Moskva* (also previously an almanac)—all three published in Moscow.[16] To these we should add several regional periodicals and, since 1969, the journal *Avrora*, published in Leningrad.[17] Mentioned in practically every important cultural conversation of the time, these journal titles became household names for any educated family, framing the landscape of Soviet literary and intellectual life for the next several decades.

Noticeably, much of this landscape took shape during the Thaw. As of the late Stalin years, not only were there few thick journals, but also their print runs were painfully small. At the end of World War II in 1945, *Novyi mir*'s nationwide circulation was only 21,000 (for both subscription and retail sales), while *Oktiabr'* had an even lower circulation rate of 12,400.[18] To show how tiny these numbers were, in 1945 Moscow, for example, a city of about 4 million people, received 2,500 yearly sets, or annual subscriptions (with twelve monthly issues per set), of *Novyi mir*. Leningrad received 700. All of postwar Ukraine, a country of at least 27.4 million people, received a paltry 2,000 sets of the journal, while Belarus, with its population of more than 7 million, got only 600.[19] The circulation of other thick journals was equally minuscule.[20]

After the war, the shortages were resolved only slowly: while print runs began to grow, they remained far from abundant. In 1947 *Novyi mir* circulated 59,800 yearly subscriptions nationwide, compared with 60,300 for *Oktiabr'*, 59,300 for *Znamia*, and 25,000 for *Zvezda*.[21] This meant that in

1947 the Republic of Belarus, for example, with its postwar population of about 7 million received only 1,000 yearly subscriptions to *Novyi mir*.[22] Two years later, in 1949, the journal's nationwide circulation rose, but only slightly, to 63,300. In that year Simonov, in his capacity as the journal's editor in chief, urged Central Committee secretary Malenkov to increase the yearly circulation to 100,000, describing the current figure as "utterly insufficient to satisfy the readers' demands." A major urban industrial and research center such as Stalino (Donetsk), he wrote, received only 102 yearly sets of *Novyi mir*, while Stalingrad got only 202—apparently even fewer than in 1945, when it had received 250. Armenia, a country with a population of about 1.3 million, received only 252 yearly sets of *Novyi mir* in 1949—a drop in the ocean, although still a fivefold improvement from 1945, when the republic received a microscopic 50 sets.[23] Yet Simonov failed to secure such a drastic increase in the journal's circulation. All the Central Committee would agree to in 1949 was an increase from 63,300 to 66,000 nationwide, and that was only because it was the amount by which subscriptions to the journal had exceeded the designated maximum print run. Characteristically, this technical issue had to be resolved at the pinnacle of power—by a special decree of the Central Committee Secretariat.[24] By May 1950, *Novyi mir*'s circulation had grown a little further, to 67,300, while *Oktiabr'* circulated an equally unimpressive 65,400 sets. *Znamia* had 61,300, and *Zvezda* 27,000.[25]

The paltry circulation of literary journals was part of the general shortage of printed matter. Like the rest of Soviet economy, press dissemination was based on the principle of the centralized allocation of resources. Readers dealt not directly with a publisher or a periodical to which they wished to subscribe, but with a government institution. The system dated back to the early Soviet years, specifically to Lenin's decree of 21 November 1918, which prescribed employing the postal service in the distribution of periodicals. Initially the mail service proved to be not up to the task, and throughout the 1920s readers continued to subscribe directly by contacting editorial offices of newspapers and journals. It was not until Stalin's "Great Turn" that the rigidly uniform state mechanism for press dissemination took shape: a government agency called Soiuzpechat' (literally "Union Press") was formed in 1930, replacing its inefficient predecessors and monopolizing subscriptions as well as, from 1937, the distribution of the press.[26]

World War II carried this regimented system to an extreme, drastically reducing opportunities for individual readers to get access to periodicals.

During the war, information, and paper on which it was printed, acquired greater strategic importance than ever before. Many newspapers and journals, including literary ones, were discontinued, while the circulation of others sharply dropped.[27] Paper was channeled toward the publication of newspapers and other print matter that more directly served the military and propaganda efforts. In place of the prewar system of subscriptions, most periodicals were now distributed according to centrally imposed limits; first priority was given to the military, and then subscriptions were allotted to various lower-priority institutions in the rear, with a fixed quota for each title per institution. After the war, much of this regimentation persisted, only gradually yielding to new peacetime practices. During the late Stalin years a system of tight quotas, imposed by the Central Committee and enforced via a hierarchy of regional party and Komsomol organs, continued to restrain subscriptions to periodicals. Under party supervision, the distribution of quotas to institutions and localities—or the "allocation of limits" *(razmeshchenie limitov)*, the contemporary term—was now the purview of Soiuzpechat'. Structurally a unit of the USSR People's Commissariat of Communications (after 1946, the Ministry of Communications), and officially known as the ministry's Central Directorate for the Distribution and Expedition of the Press, Soiuzpechat' operated a wide network of regional branches. In coordination with the postal service, it reached the population via local post offices, and it managed its own retail outlets as well.

Every year during and shortly after the war, the "allocation of limits" became a major headache for thousands of Soviet officials. In a characteristically militarized fashion, they described their yearly efforts as "subscription campaigns," drafting numerous memos to emphasize the undertaking as a matter of state importance. "The distribution of the press is not a technical but a political task. It is imperative for you to convey this idea to each and every employee," senior Soiuzpechat' bureaucrats in Omsk instructed their subordinates about subscriptions for 1945.[28] Every such campaign required complex coordination among regional departments of education, planning, the military, the police, health care, and so on, not to mention party and Komsomol committees. The institutions busily corresponded with each other about the proper allocation of press quotas to cities and villages, local soviets and collective farms, libraries and "reading huts," schools, hospitals, and even veterinary clinics. High authorities, up to the minister of communications himself, reminded their staff about strictly observing the quotas and bearing personal responsibility for exceeding them. Occasional instances of such excesses became political emergencies: heads would roll, and to satisfy the unforeseen extra subscribers, decisions to print additional copies would have to be endorsed at the topmost level of power, as was the case with *Novyi mir* in 1949.[29]

Realizing how cumbersome this procedure was, after the war administrators began pushing for reform. In October and November 1946 the head of Soiuzpechat', F. Ramsin, approached the Central Committee Directorate of Propaganda and Agitation and its head, Georgii Aleksandrov (1908–1961), with suggestions for improving the system. First of all, the notion of the subscriber was to change. State funding of institutional subscriptions was to be sharply reduced, and instead individuals would be encouraged to subscribe to periodicals on their own. Limits on circulation (and therefore subscriptions) would remain in place, but most newspapers and journals would now reach the readers directly rather than via the workplace or another institutional setting. The advantages were obvious: whereas earlier, many of the copies ended up sitting in various offices, now they could reach a far broader audience. The financial aspect of these changes was also important: individual subscriptions meant that people would be spending their own money rather than taking advantage of free periodicals bought by state enterprises, on the government's dime. For the thick literary journals in particular—*Novyi mir, Znamia, Oktiabr'*, and *Zvezda*—60 percent of their circulation would be designated for individual subscription. The numbers available for retail sale via bookstores and kiosks were to grow as well. The state thus ended up with a net financial gain and turned the dissemination of the printed word from a liability into an asset.[30]

These suggestions came into effect in the 30 November 1946 decree of the USSR Council of Ministers, "On the Order of Distribution of Newspapers and Journals." That winter, thousands of subscription outlets for individual readers opened all over the Soviet Union, at local post offices and branches of Soiuzpechat'. Factories, administrative offices, institutes, and hospitals cut their subscription allocations, while individuals indeed subscribed more actively: their share of subscriptions in the circulation of major journals and newspapers grew from between 37 and 42 percent in 1946 to anywhere from 66 to 73 percent in 1947. Over time this share would increase further: two decades later, in 1965/66, individual readers' subscriptions represented nearly 90 percent of all subscriptions to periodicals in Moscow and other regions.[31]

Problems persisted, however, as the publishing environment was an inseparable part of the Soviet economy of shortages. Print runs remained small, and subscriptions, although now largely individual, continued to be limited. Especially in big cities like Moscow, Leningrad, Kiev, and Sverdlovsk, there would always be more people who wished to subscribe to this or that newspaper or journal than the subscription quotas allowed.[32] Retail sales could not compensate for that, as they were minuscule, with few kiosks and an insufficient supply of periodicals. As of May 1950, subscriptions consumed 98.3 percent of the circulation of *Novyi mir,* 98.3 percent of *Oktiabr',* 92.8 percent of *Znamia,* and 100 percent of *Zvezda,* leaving negligible numbers of copies for retail.[33] Local Soiuzpechat' administrators often considered the batches of periodicals designated for retail simply as reserves they could tap when they ran out of subscription copies.[34] And while retail sales subsequently increased, they would always account for a minor share of circulation: in 1966, for example, retail sales represented only 20 percent of *Novyi mir*'s nationwide circulation.[35] This meant that it was often hard, if not impossible, to buy journals (and often newspapers, too) at a retail kiosk. With subscriptions limited and retail copies nearly unavailable, the authorities had to be creative and invent other means for providing broad access to the press—such as public newsboards. It was common in Soviet cities to see groups of several people standing and reading the papers posted on large sidewalk newsboards. Brought about by the shortage of the printed word, such practices of collective public reading, at the same time, promoted discussions and the exchange of opinions among readers—often right there, on the street.[36]

Shortages would plague the system of press dissemination throughout the late 1940s, the 1950s, and much of the 1960s. Official reports frequently noted that the readers' demand for periodicals exceeded supply. Literary journals were no exception and were not even prominent in this regard: from time to time shortages would emerge even for such major newspapers as *Pravda, Izvestiia,* and *Komsomol'skaia Pravda,* or for journals such as *Rabotnitsa, Krestianka,* and *Ogonek*—all of which had much larger print runs than *Novyi mir.*[37] In 1954 Soiuzpechat' recorded an excess demand for up to one million subscriptions for *Pravda*—numbers on a scale about which Simonov and Tvardovskii could not even dream.[38] In 1961 a particularly severe paper shortage forced the party leadership to contemplate reducing the circulation of central newspapers two to five times.[39] Readers sent angry letters even to Khrushchev himself, complaining, as one Evgenii Voronikin from Pskov did, that retail kiosks in the city received only five to ten copies of each central newspaper. Naturally, those would be sold out early in the morning. "Your statements and speeches, Nikita Sergeevich, inspire us," the reader remarked caustically. "Only, it is not always possible to hear them . . . on the radio. One cannot buy a central newspaper at a Soiuzpechat' kiosk after work. . . . *Pravda* and *Izvestiia* are farther away from us than the planet Saturn."[40] Indeed, in 1961 Pskov Oblast, a region populated by nearly a million people, was allowed only 14,835 subscriptions to *Pravda*, or 1 for every 67 individuals. *Novyi mir* had a mere 393 yearly subscriptions in the oblast, or 1 per 2,545 people.[41] A similar scarcity of publications existed in many other regions—Altai and Arkhangel'sk, Belgorod and Astrakhan', Vologda and Bryansk.[42]

Officials tried to improve the situation. So far as the readers' demand and the paper supply allowed, Soiuzpechat' endeavored to minimize the list of titles for which circulation was limited. It also suggested moving away from centrally imposed quotas to a system in which circulation would be established not before but after a yearly subscription campaign, on the basis of local demand. This partly worked: on 25 July 1958 the Central Committee implemented those suggestions by a special decree.[43] Overall, the trend during the late 1950s and 1960s was toward greater coordination between the press run and the actual subscription demand for a periodical. Circulation became more flexible and could go up or down each year. The number of limited-circulation titles diminished, until eventually the limits were removed entirely in October 1964, shortly after Khrushchev's downfall.[44] However, even after 1965, the first "limitless" year, subscription rates remained centrally controlled, and economic vicissitudes would occasionally force the authorities to reimpose limits, whether formally or informally. Readers would long remember the various subscription schemes that local administrators invented—such as requiring Communists to subscribe to party publications, inducing people to cast lots for the opportunity to subscribe to an interesting journal, and imposing mandatory subscription "packages," in which high-demand titles were coupled with less popular ones. It was not until 1988 and 1989, under Gorbachev, that subscription limits were finally abolished.[45]

During the Thaw, shortages became all the more acute as the readers' demand for the press skyrocketed, especially in the capital cities. Muscovites, for example, bought 2.3 million annual subscriptions to newspapers and journals in 1953, and by 1956 subscriptions in the city had jumped to

3.75 million.[46] Literature played a crucial part in the reading boom of the Thaw—to the point that a decade later, subscriptions to literary journals in the capital of the Soviet Union exceeded subscriptions to the Communist Party journals, even though the latter were imposed on readers by all means available. In 1966, Muscovites bought 246,419 annual subscriptions to party journals, but as many as 316,182 subscriptions to literary journals. As for the main national newspaper, *Pravda,* that year it circulated to 320,400 subscribers in Moscow, a number almost equal to the subscriptions to literary journals—a comparison that mortified officials at Soiuzpechat'.[47]

Readers' grumbling about not being able to obtain literary journals remained standard in the 1960s. Tellingly, demand exceeded supply not only for *Novyi mir* but also for its rival, *Oktiabr'*, a journal that occupied quite the opposite political platform. In 1965, the editor in chief of *Oktiabr'*, Vsevolod Kochetov (1912–1973) complained to the Russian Federation Bureau of the Party Central Committee about the insufficiency of his journal's current circulation (150,000 copies), in light of high demand from potential subscribers.[48]

Despite the many problems and occasional print-run fluctuations, the circulation of literary journals, and of *Novyi mir* in particular, gradually went up during the postwar decades. Under Tvardovskii, *Novyi mir*'s circulation rose to 104,000 in June 1950, 130,000 in January 1952, and 140,000 in January 1954, the level at which it would remain for a while.[49] Simonov, who returned to the journal and replaced Tvardovskii in the summer of 1954, tried increasing the circulation further, to 175,000, but failed.[50] Later, again under Tvardovskii, circulation dropped back to 100,000 in 1960 and to 85,000 in 1961 (the years of the major paper shortage in the country), but then it started growing again.[51] For 1962, when *Novyi mir* published Solzhenitsyn's *One Day in the Life of Ivan Denisovich*, the journal's circulation was up to 90,000, then to 100,000 in 1963, and by the end of that year it was apparently up to 113,000.[52] By January 1966, *Novyi mir*'s total circulation had risen to 150,000, with 120,000 annual sets going to subscribers and the rest to retail outlets. By January 1968, in the Russian Federation alone the journal had surpassed its 1966 all-union subscription figures and reached 121,000 subscriptions. As of January 1970, the last month of Tvardovskii's editorship, in the Soviet Union overall the subscription rate for *Novyi mir* (without retail) hovered at 146,000.[53]

Moneywise, in December 1945 the journal's price was 10 rubles per issue; in December 1946 it was 5 rubles.[54] From February 1948, at least, a single issue cost 7 rubles, with the yearly paperback set of twelve issues thus amounting to 84 rubles.[55] *Novyi mir* was also printed in a somewhat more expensive hardcover edition, which cost 9 rubles a month or 108 rubles a year, but most of its relatively small print run was apparently purchased by libraries, which needed to have durable copies.[56] Importantly, these prices persisted throughout the tenure of both editors, Simonov and Tvardovskii, remaining the same for almost a quarter of a century, despite inflation. The price did not change even after the tenfold currency depreciation of 1961: then it became 70 kopecks an issue, or 8 rubles 40 kopecks a year for the paperback edition and 90 kopecks per issue and 10.80 for the annual hardcover edition. These exact prices were still in effect in early 1970, at the end of Tvardovskii's editorship.[57]

How affordable was this? It appears that, from an individual reader's financial viewpoint, a subscription to *Novyi mir* was not particularly costly, although it was also not cheap. In 1950, a yearly subscription to the paperback edition (84 rubles) would cost 1.1 percent of an average urban laborer's or office employee's yearly wage of 7,668 rubles.[58] Apparently, there were dedicated readers prepared to spend that much money on a literary journal. In 1956, an average family in Moscow spent 2.3 percent of the average nationwide salary per year (or more than 200 out of 8,580 rubles) on newspapers and journals. Earnings in Moscow could be higher than in the provinces, and spending on periodicals per family in the USSR overall was generally lower—anywhere from 60 to 90 rubles in 1956, or close to 1 percent of the average yearly income.[59] If someone really wanted to subscribe to *Novyi mir*, it was financially feasible, although it could mean making choices and excluding other titles from the household's subscription diet. Later, during the 1960s, with inflation, wage increases, and fixed subscription prices, the journal slowly became more affordable. As of 1969, *Novyi mir*'s yearly subscription price of 8 rubles 40 kopecks would take up only 0.6 percent of the average yearly wage of 1,402.8 rubles.[60] To be sure, these numbers refer mostly to urban readers—the financial situation in the countryside could be worse.[61]

However, money does not tell the whole story. In addition to having the pecuniary means, one also had to obtain physical access to the journal, which was often difficult. The ever-present shortages, of course, greatly increased every time the journal published something particularly interesting. Then, long lines would form in libraries, with potential readers entering their names on special rosters and waiting weeks if not months for their turn with an issue. Consequently, sharing was a common practice. Unlike many other material objects, books and journals can be used by many people, and *Novyi mir*'s readers frequently shared copies with one another. Their letters often described how the same tattered copy of the journal had been read by dozens, even hundreds of pairs of eyes. People read it at libraries and at work. Neighbors subscribed collectively, and the more fortunate individual subscribers lent their copies to relatives, friends, friends of friends, and so on. Here figurative lines formed as well, and it was not uncommon, according to readers' accounts, for someone to borrow an issue of *Novyi mir* for one sleepless night, when they would stay up and read the piece that fascinated them. Published stories and articles were copied out on individual typewriters, and in cases of extremely popular texts, the typed copies could be sold on the black market at several times the journal's state retail price.

Thus, the available statistics cannot fully measure the readership for *Novyi mir*—nor, for that matter, for any other literary journal or text. The obverse of the economy of shortages was that the actual readership for any publication of broad interest was much larger than anything the official numbers can reveal. Modest circulation figures should not lead us to think that the reading audiences were indeed that small. While numerically inferior to the readership of the major central newspapers, or of popular illustrated magazines such as *Ogonek*, *Rabotnitsa*, or *Krest'ianka*, the literary audiences (and in particular that of *Novyi mir*) nevertheless numbered in the hundreds of thousands—and sometimes millions. Also, texts originally published in *Novyi mir* were often reprinted later and reached an even wider audience. To give one example, Solzhenitsyn's *One Day in the Life of Ivan Denisovich* came out in *Novyi mir* with a circulation of 90,000 in 1962, but next year it was reprinted separately in *Roman-gazeta*, a periodical that devoted each issue entirely to one literary piece and had a circulation of 700,000. In the same year, 1963, the novella came out in book form, from the Sovetskii pisatel' publishing house (100,000 copies), in Lithuanian and Estonian translations (15,000 and 10,000 copies, respectively), and 500 special copies were even printed for the visually impaired. Officially, then, close to a million copies of *One Day* were printed.[62] Even barring such multiple reprints, it is safe to say that when *Novyi mir* published a text that readers considered exceptionally important, its audience easily went over a million.

These were not yet the million-some print runs and multimillion-member audiences that thick journals would boast two decades later, during the perestroika years.[63] But the numbers were many times greater than the circulation of literary journals in imperial Russia. Nekrasov's *Sovremennik*, the journal often mentioned as *Novyi mir*'s predecessor and inspiration, circulated in about 7,000 copies in 1860 and 1861, its best years, and usually printed far fewer than that. The print runs of the imperial era were also quite comparable to the circulation rates of Soviet literary journals during the 1920s.[64] And even in comparison to the late Stalin years, by the mid-1960s literary journals had made major progress in reaching larger audiences. Overall, the circulation of *Novyi mir* increased sevenfold in two decades, between 1945 and 1966.[65] During the Thaw, literature came to matter in Russia as never before.

The Rise of Novyi mir

It was in this environment, where readers yearned for writers' prophetic words but had painfully limited opportunities for accessing them, that *Novyi mir* entered its finest hour. In a culture in which so many eyes were fixed upon so few publishing venues, the appearance of any high-quality and socially charged prose was destined to capture universal attention. What was necessary for such prose to appear was an editor with a keen eye for language, a vision for promoting social reflection by literary means, and enough professional and political weight to carry his ideas through. Fortunately for *Novyi mir*, during these years it had not one but two such editors: Simonov and Tvardovskii. But what was also necessary for the journal's rise was a favorable cultural and political situation. Despite the ideological rigidity of the late Stalin years, it was then that such a situation emerged.

Novyi mir had not always occupied the prestigious number-one position in Russian literature for which it is famous today. Although it was always on the very short list of the country's most important literary periodicals, for years it was perhaps the least notable among them. Founded in 1925, it had had its early moments, such as the 1926 publication of Boris Pilnyak's *Tale of the Unextinguished Moon* during the editorship of Viacheslav Polonskii (1926 to 1931). But overall, initially the journal remained in the shadow of its more illustrious peers, particularly *Krasnaia nov'*, in circulation from 1921 to 1942, and it had a reputation for solidity rather than for literary innovation and conceptual breakthroughs. One historian of literature has described the atmosphere of the early *Novyi mir* as "anesthetic," saying that authors used it as a "dustbin for their less successful efforts."[66] During and immediately after World War II the journal was not in the best shape, either. Its last editor in chief before the war, a Stalin protégé and head of the Union of Soviet Writers, Vladimir Stavskii (1900–1943; editor from 1937), had left for the front as a war correspondent and been killed in battle. From 1941 to 1946 the journal's de facto head was its "responsible secretary" Vladimir Shcherbina (1908–1989)—a fairly reputable literary scholar who, however, lacked the charisma required for leading such an important publication.

Not coincidentally then, among the thick journals *Novyi mir* was, in the 1940s, the one that drew the least of the authorities' wrath. At some point all the others received individual reprimands from the party leadership or the Writers' Union: *Oktiabr'* in 1939 and 1943, *Zvezda* and *Leningrad* in 1946, and *Znamia* in 1944 and 1948. *Novyi mir*, on the other hand, although occasionally mentioned together with the other journals, received comparatively less attention even in those instances.[67] The context of such mentions could be rather dismissive, too. When on 2 December 1943 the head of the Central Committee's board of propaganda and agitation, Georgii Aleksandrov, joined by his two deputies, informed Secretary Malenkov about the state of the thick journals, he mentioned *Novyi mir* as the least interesting of them all—not from a political standpoint but from a purely aesthetic one: "The weakest one, artistically, is the journal *Novyi mir*, which publishes many mediocre, insignificant works of literature."[68]

Stalin apparently shared this view—or, more likely, the view was originally his own. A couple of years later, on 18 April 1946, Andrei Zhdanov echoed this condescending attitude to *Novyi mir* when, in a speech before a group of Central Committee propagandists, he cited Stalin's recent "ranking" of literary periodicals. "Comrade Stalin very harshly characterized our thick journals," Zhdanov said. "Comrade Stalin named *Novyi mir* as the worst of all thick journals, while *Zvezda* is second to it from the bottom. Comrade Stalin considers *Znamia* as relatively the best or the very best journal, followed by *Oktiabr'*, *Zvezda*, and *Novyi mir*."[69]

The leader's initial lack of interest in it may explain why *Novyi mir* not only more or less escaped significant reprisals during the 1940s but even benefited from some of them. Notably, it benefited from the repressive cultural campaign that began with the attack on the Leningrad-based journals *Zvezda* and *Leningrad* in August 1946. The campaign dispelled the postwar intelligentsia's hopes for liberalization, reimposing ideological orthodoxy and leading to a restructuring of the Union of Writers along more rigid lines.[70] But although the literary crusade likely had implications for high politics (the attack on the Leningrad journals preceded by a short time the destruction of the city's party leadership in the "Leningrad Affair" of 1949–50), the criticism was phrased in aesthetic rather than only ideological terms. Always superattentive to literature, Stalin claimed that all the journals lacked both "talented" and "significant" publications, and he also resented stagnation in literary criticism. To attract new talent, a new editorial cadre was needed.[71] For "the worst of all thick journals," the reshuffling of staff took less punitive forms than for the others and proved ultimately rather beneficial. In the fall of 1946, on the crest of this repressive wave in literature, *Novyi mir* received Konstantin Simonov as its new editor in chief.

Simonov, like Tvardovskii, who would replace him in 1950, was among Stalin's favorites. The thirty-year-old laureate of three Stalin Prizes was a prolific author who had become genuinely famous thanks to his wartime journalism and, especially, his poetry. Some of his poems, such as "Wait for Me" and "You Remember, Alyosha, the Roads of Smolensk," had won the hearts of millions of readers, including numerous soldiers, who learned them by heart. In 1946, almost simultaneously with his taking the editorship of *Novyi mir,* Simonov was appointed deputy general secretary of the Writers' Union and thus became, technically speaking, second-in-command of the Soviet literary establishment. Senior to him was only Aleksandr Fadeev (1901–1956), who in the same year, 1946, became the union's general secretary, a title reminiscent of Stalin's own. No one, then, was in a better position than Simonov to add an air of importance to *Novyi mir.*

Simonov had strong opinions about literature, and they will figure later in this book when I will compare them with Tvardovskii's and discuss what both editors' strategies meant for literature and for the intellectual landscape in general. For now, it is worth looking at Simonov as a literary administrator—a pursuit in which he proved highly capable and energetic. With Stalin's personal endorsement, he secured not only the increase of *Novyi mir*'s circulation but also (on 13 May 1947) a 50-percent increase in the journal's page count, something Stalin denied to *Zvezda* in the same year.[72] *Novyi mir* thus became literally the thickest of all thick journals. Simonov also besieged the Central Committee and the Supreme Soviet (often successfully) with requests to expand the journal's editorial premises and staff, raise salaries and honoraria, acquire new furniture and even cars, and so on.[73] The material improvements were badly needed: previously, the journal's overworked and underpaid staff of eighteen people (twenty-two after 1947) had had to function in a suite devoid of furniture, and even the editor in chief lacked office space.[74] Now that situation began to improve.

As for literature proper, Simonov took his appointment as a signal that his journal should become the new leader in the literary realm. "The decision of the CC VKP(b) about the journals, against *Zvezda* and *Leningrad*," he wrote in late 1946, "has led *Novyi mir*'s editorial board to conclude, first of all, that the journal has to become one of the centers for the ideological and artistic shaping of Soviet literature."[75] He attracted new people to the editorial board—the famous writers Valentin Kataev and Boris Agapov, and also younger talents who had his trust: a wartime friend and colleague from the army newspaper *Krasnaia zvezda*, Aleksandr Krivitskii, and the hitherto unknown thirty-three-year-old theater critic from Kiev, Aleksandr Borshchagovskii. All these efforts paid off: soon enough, the journal earned a compliment from Stalin for having become "much better."[76] Capitalizing on this credit of trust and goodwill, the editor apparently felt that he could afford certain risks. Simonov obtained Stalin's personal sanction to publish (in September 1947) several stories by Mikhail Zoshchenko, who had just a year earlier received severe criticism from Zhdanov and the Central Committee and become, in effect, untouchable.[77] In November of the same year, Simonov managed to publish his own unusually candid and reflective novella on life in postwar Russia, *The Smoke of the Fatherland*, one of his works that he would later value the most.[78]

These occasional breakthroughs should not create the impression of an intellectual liberalization. They came at the expense of rigid—and on Simonov's part, also heartfelt—political discipline, as well as the tight overseeing of the journal by the high authorities. There were, quite literally, human costs too. The resurgent political repression of these years, particularly the nationwide campaign against "bourgeois cosmopolitanism," led the editor to sacrifice his friend Borshchagovskii, who became a principal target of the campaign and had to quit his editorial job in 1949. Simonov himself was not immune to criticism, either. His *Smoke of the*

Fatherland displeased Stalin and was brutally attacked in the press, leading the author to rethink his approach to writing and to produce what was expected from him: an "anti-cosmopolitan" play—*A Stranger's Shadow* (*Chuzhaia ten'*, 1948)—commissioned, again, by Stalin himself.[79] In that same year, 1948, *Novyi mir* published *Far from Moscow,* by Vasilii Azhaev (1915–1968), a major novel that became an instant classic of socialist realism. This achievement, crowned by the first-degree Stalin Prize in literature for 1949, came after weeks and weeks of the author's—and Simonov's—industrious reworking of the thousand-page manuscript. Together, and with the assistance of the journal's editorial team, they rewrote hundreds of pages, bringing the text into accordance with the socialist realist canon, and in the process perfecting the canon itself. Literature remained at the center of the intellectual and linguistic order, which, at least outwardly, appeared more firmly established than ever before.[80]

In February 1950, in a complex cadre rotation apparently inspired by Fadeev, Simonov left *Novyi mir* to become the editor of *Literaturnaia gazeta,* the country's principal literary newspaper.[81] He left behind a far stronger journal, logistically well prepared to take the leading role in literature that it indeed stepped into under Simonov's successor, Aleksandr Tvardovskii. The ideas and strategies of Tvardovskii, which I will later address in much detail, shaped *Novyi mir* as a cultural phenomenon. Among other breakthroughs, the journal began publishing socially critical prose that exposed society's hitherto barely mentionable problems. Crucial among them was the deplorable state of the countryside and the collective-farm economy, depicted in a pioneering sketch by Valentin Ovechkin (1904–1968) titled *District Routine,* which was published in September 1952.[82] Many observers have been surprised by the fact that Ovechkin's sketch came out while Stalin was still in power. This could be less paradoxical than it seems. Starting with Simonov's appointment and continuing under Tvardovskii, the rise of *Novyi mir* as the foremost literary journal happened to a great extent on Stalin's initiative and under his supervision. During the late 1940s and early 1950s, the Soviet leader repeatedly sent controversial signals about raising the aesthetic quality of literature and literary criticism. The signals reached a new height in October 1952, when, in his speech to the Nineteenth Party Congress, Georgii Malenkov (undoubtedly with Stalin's endorsement) declared that he resented the abundance of "mediocre, dull, and at times simply hackwork pieces" being published. In particular, Malenkov called for a diversification of the literary landscape and for bolder social criticism by literary means.[83] It is possible that *Novyi mir* became a platform for such experiments. Its now special status entitled the journal to a few more liberties, allowing it to be more critical than other periodicals could afford.

Eventually, though, it seems Stalin may have lost his fondness for *Novyi mir.* The winter of 1953 saw a major press campaign against the journal, owing to its publication of Vasilii Grossman's *For a Just Cause*—a novel that Simonov had initially rejected but Tvardovskii accepted and published.[84] But then Stalin died in early March, and the campaign quickly dissipated. It is not known how his literary experiments would have ended had he lived longer. However, one of their lasting results was a robust literary journal ready to play a major role in the country's intellectual life. Stalin's role in the rise of *Novyi mir* was ironic, of course, given that only a decade later the journal would be at the center of the country's critical reinterpretation of his legacy. In his eagerness to foster serious literature, the leader had forged a double-edged weapon.

In many ways, the development of the literary environment during the late Stalin years prepared the Soviet reading audience for what was to happen during the Thaw. At the same time, the theme of continuity between these two historical epochs requires a caveat. Besides Stalin's benevolence and the editors' agendas, another force that shaped literature, and *Novyi mir* as a cultural phenomenon, was the readership itself. And here, when comparing the late Stalin years with the Thaw, one cannot help but see differences.

Soviet readers were also prolific letter writers under Stalin—hundreds of letters in *Novyi mir*'s archives and others testify to that. When reacting to Azhaev's *Far from Moscow,* Trifonov's *Students,* or even Grossman's *For a Just Cause,* most often they wrote to praise the work, but occasionally readers could be quite critical. At times they even wrote to object to an opinion expressed in *Pravda.*[85] And yet for the most part the criticism, as well as the praise, did not stray far from official opinions expressed in the media. People would applaud social commentary in a published text, even something as bold as Ovechkin's *District Routine,* or they would object to a particular detail or an interpretation. But the massive, widespread, and open defiance of officially expressed viewpoints, the confrontational stance that would in a few years become central to the atmosphere of the Thaw, was not yet visible.[86] The letter writers of the late 1940s and early 1950s were also—whether out of fear or the (closely related) lack of inspiration from the contemporary media—far more reserved and less reflective in commenting on the historical, social, and ethical problems that writers like Ovechkin and Grossman exposed. Last but not least, in their open written statements, the letter writers of the late Stalin years remained firmly within the linguistic formulas and ethical values formed during the previous Soviet decades.[87]

All of this would change during the Thaw. Apprehensions about open self-expression would diminish quickly after March 1953, while criticism of officially endorsed opinions would grow visibly and increasingly bold. More important, the culture would begin to rediscover and reformulate the ethical, political, and linguistic principles on which Soviet society was based. In conjunction with and through interactions with their readers, numerous authors and editors—above all those grouped around Tvardovskii's *Novyi mir*—would start deliberately promoting a culture of moral reflection on social and historical issues, as well as a reworking of the verbal apparatus of self-expression. Undermined by these activities and many other factors, the ethos and language of Stalinist culture began their decline.

For these shifts to take effect, though, intellectual agendas had to be set. Someone had to formulate, openly and in print, not only the issues at stake but also the strategic role of literature as the principal mechanism for addressing them. It was not long before such a literary manifesto emerged.

2

BAROMETER OF THE EPOCH

Pomerantsev and the Debate on Sincerity

OF ALL THE SOVIET WRITERS who became the focus of public attention in 1953 and 1954, Vladimir Mikhailovich Pomerantsev (1907–1971) appeared the least likely to initiate any change in literature, let alone a literary Thaw. He did not possess the authorial glory of Ilya Ehrenburg, who would soon launch the very term "Thaw" into circulation, or the poetic fame of Olga Berggol'ts, who called on authors to depict the richness of human emotions with her 1953 "Conversation about the Lyric."[1] He was not a major philosopher like Mikhail Lifshits, who would stir minds with his caustic mockery of journalistic clichés in "The Diary of Marietta Shaginian" (1954).[2] Nor was he a young rising star in prose or literary criticism like Fedor Abramov or Mark Shcheglov, whose iconoclastic articles in *Novyi mir* challenged such luminaries of socialist realism as Semen Babaevskii and Leonid Leonov.[3] Pomerantsev was neither famous nor young, and few would call him brilliant. Yet it was he who provoked everyone's fascination, with hundreds of readers writing letters to him, celebrated critics and top literary officials arguing with him on the pages of the most prestigious periodicals, and the worried Central Committee functionaries monitoring the social repercussions of his ideas. All of this happened thanks to his article, which Tvardovskii's *Novyi mir* published in December 1953: "On Sincerity in Literature."[4]

Forty-six years old when the article appeared in print, Pomerantsev was still a literary beginner. He had trained in the law at Irkutsk University and spent his early years after graduation working as an investigator and a court official in Siberia and the Lower Volga region. That was during the years of collectivization, and the young Pomerantsev had to deal with many criminal cases brought against peasants. His later publications did not and could not display any principled objection to the Great Turn, but the life of the collectivized peasantry, drastically different from how the press described it, had obviously made an impression on him. In many writings, "On Sincerity in Literature" among them, he would return to this theme.

Emblematic of many a Soviet writer, his path to literature lay through journalism and was heavily influenced by World War II. The beginnings of his literary career, for which he eventually abandoned the law, dated back to the 1930s, when he worked for the antireligious newspaper *The Godless (Bezbozhnik)*.[5] During the war he served in the military: from July 1941 in a rifle regiment, and from May 1942 as a propaganda officer, first with one of the armies at the Western Front and later in the Seventh Department of the Political Directorate at the Third Belorussian Front. As were all such "seventh departments," his was charged with stirring up agitation among the Wehrmacht troops and thereby undermining their morale and inducing them to surrender. Proficient in German, Pomerantsev dealt with German POWs, prepared radio broadcasts, and wrote leaflets for the enemy "audience." It was then that he first met Aleksandr Tvardovskii, whose prewar poem *The Land of Muravia* he admired and who was now a military correspondent at the Third Belorussian Front.[6] Following the war, Pomerantsev worked in the Soviet military administration in Germany (known as SVAG) and continued his journalistic pursuits at the occupation newspaper *Tägliche Rundschau*.[7]

His first novel, the 1951 *Bookseller's Daughter (Doch' bukinista)*, was drawn from his wartime and postwar career and depicted the SVAG dream—the evolution of ordinary Germans toward socialism in postwar Berlin.[8] Although Pomerantsev displayed intimate knowledge of the city's geography and daily life, the book evoked little enthusiasm in the Soviet literary community. Discussion of it among members of the prose section of the Writers' Union had to be postponed three times because no one had read it; the few available comments from the rank-and-file audience were rather disparaging, too.[9] And so it must have been surprising for readers who opened the December 1953 issue of *Novyi mir* to find Pomerantsev's name beside the title of what became one of the earliest and most explosive publications of the Thaw.

"On Sincerity in Literature" strikes today's reader as a remarkably loosely structured piece, full of equivocations and esoteric euphemisms whose meanings are not immediately apparent. For this discussion, it is worth beginning with a brief synopsis. Although the article opened with a statement about the lack of sincerity in contemporary writing, Pomerantsev never clearly defined sincerity, and his understanding of it had to be distilled little by little from the text. He proceeded right away to describe sincerity's opposite—insincerity. Being insincere did not necessarily mean lying, he argued, but could also mean the "constructedness" *(delannost')* of a literary piece. He did not define this term either, but one could gather that constructedness denoted a writer's following of a well-worn template of standard characters, settings, and situations. Constructedness meant anything that stemmed not from the author's inner self but from a literary or social convention, whether dictated by conformity or a desire for professional success. Constructedness was about substituting craft for talent, going through the motions of textual production rather than investing one's writing with heartfelt ideas. Displaying characteristic confidence in the intellectual capacity of readers, Pomerantsev believed that they were able to distinguish between the "sincere" and the "constructed," and that they would reject the latter.[10]

A template, though, was not the worst manifestation of insincerity. A template "leaves us indifferent, but does not yet generate outright disbelief in the literary word."[11] Such disbelief, Pomerantsev suggested, originated in another kind of insincerity—the "varnishing of reality." In battling against this phantom, he continued a long tradition of Soviet literary criticism established in the 1920s and 1930s.[12] He identified three major devices employed in the varnishing of reality in literature and film—"inventing wholesale prosperity," avoiding extremes, and, the most subtle, circumventing the very topics that might allow for a controversial interpretation.[13] There was no need for such tactics, he argued. The greater truth of Soviet society's ideals and deeds was high enough to require no artificial elevation. "Why do we need idealization," he asked, "when we . . . constantly put into practice the ideal itself?"[14] The writer's duty was only to help society in this great project—not by varnishing but by being the people's conscience, by voicing ethical concerns about urgent problems. Like painful therapy, the writer's word was to be used to heal social ills.

But the therapy would heal only if administered with a firm belief in the patient's curability, the strategic righteousness of society's path. This was crucial to Pomerantsev's understanding of sincerity. "We do not need just any sincerity," he argued. A subjective opinion or misconception could be sincere, too, but that was not what he wanted. Authentic sincerity implied harmony not simply between inner belief and verbalization, but among three components: belief, text, and the greater cause. Sincerity meant a seamless merger between, on the one hand, the author's commitment to an uncompromising representation of reality and, on the other hand, his or her full identification with the socialist ideal.[15]

Although complicating the socialist realist canon, Pomerantsev's ideas were not at radical variance with it. The ideal still figured prominently in both the old (varnishing) and the new (sincere) approach, only a varnisher's path to the ideal was straight and easy, while Pomerantsev's path was programmatically winding and arduous. "The sincerity that leads to the truth of life, truth of the party [*sic*], is not a passing mood," he wrote. "Such sincerity is greater. It embraces at once reason, conscience, and inclination. . . . It requires a mental intensity not at all necessary in cases of insincerity or a passing mood. [Authorial] purpose is simple, but sincerity is always very complex."[16]

His emphasis on balancing the individual and the social in literature distinguished Pomerantsev from some other contemporary proponents of sincerity and emotionality (for example, Olga Berggol'ts), who might have included such political statements as disclaimers to preempt ideological accusations.[17] But Pomerantsev spent too many pages on the political aspect of sincerity for this to be a mere disclaimer. Sincerity as an act of citizenship, and not just an outpouring of individual emotion, was integral to his ideas.

To illustrate this, he included a long episode from the early 1930s, clearly autobiographical yet veiled as something that had happened to a friend. It describes a young law school graduate charged with investigating the ostensibly illegal activities of a chairwoman in a remote Siberian collective farm. Known as "the daredevil woman" *(boi-baba)*, she is indeed "creative" in seeking incentives for her workers and neighbors—for example, brewing moonshine to reward them. However, she does not seek personal gain, cares for the workers' well-being, and takes the ideals of socialism to heart.

On the one hand, she has clearly committed economic offenses, possibly crimes; on the other hand, her offenses were for the sake of the greater good, and the farm collective became stronger. And so, while the letter of law prescribes that the investigator prosecute the woman, his heart tells him to do otherwise. In the end, he listens to his conscience and writes a report in her defense, leading to a row with his superiors.[18]

The example suggested that sincerity meant acting at once in accordance with public good and individual conscience, and that it was possible to reach a point of harmony between the two. The same principle applied to literature: "This is how it should be in books, too. . . . Their sincerity . . . should also be firmly rooted. Their sincerity should also be courageous. . . . Do not write until you have grown incandescent. . . . Know for what you struggle. . . . Think not about prosecutors. . . . Make no ready-made conclusions. Do not admit a single line that carries no breath of life. . . . Be independent. And then your truth will merge with the truth of us all."[19]

Alas, argued Pomerantsev, that was not how contemporary authors wrote. Following this Tolstoyan literary manifesto, he returned to identifying various types of literary hackwork. The format of the article now changed from a monologue to a dialogue between the Author (aka Pomerantsev himself) and one such type, named "the Producer of Standard." The Author blamed the Producer for creating clichéd, unconvincing characters and politically correct yet absurd situations, such as a mechanic and his fiancée dreaming of how they would repair equipment for a collective farm. The Producer retorted that in the recent past (clearly implying the Stalin years), a literary career had been unthinkable without the author's conforming to these standards of representation. The crudity of the end product had always been clear to him, yet pragmatism had prevailed: whoever wanted to publish had to play by the rules of the repressive environment. For an article that came out in 1953, Pomerantsev used rather direct language to depict the repression. The Producer says, "My work brought no reviews expressing opinions and stimulating creative arguments—only court sentences [*prigovory*]."[20] Tellingly of the zeitgeist, such understandably human arguments evoke no compassion in the mercilessly righteous Author, who keeps blaming his adversary for servility, hypocrisy, cowardice, lack of ideas, and so on.

Pomerantsev then moved from abstractions to specifics. He targeted literature about the countryside—a genre that, as of late 1953, was in its prime, thanks to the Central Committee's efforts at reviving the impoverished rural economy.[21] Encouraged by these efforts, journalists and literary critics developed what one scholar has aptly called "agricultural glasnost."[22] *Novyi mir* was at the forefront and even ahead of this process: it was Tvardovskii who, as early as September 1952, published the first groundbreaking criticism of collective-farm agriculture, Ovechkin's *District Routine.*[23] Over the next few years, an avalanche of critical writings about the countryside began shaping what would later become the "village prose" of the 1960s to 1980s.[24] Pomerantsev neither pioneered nor exactly belonged to this nascent genre, but his was one of the early voices in the polemic. Like other critics (including, a few months later, *Novyi mir*'s other famous debutant, Fedor Abramov), he attacked two especially "varnished" novels about village life—*Cavalier of the Golden Star,* by Semen Babaevskii, and the somewhat subtler *Harvest,* by Galina Nikolaeva.[25] He praised Ovechkin for exposing the authorities' extractionary management of the rural economy and for creating vivid characters with authentic speech and recognizable daily concerns. To Pomerantsev, this was one of the most necessary changes in literature: even books describing production were to focus on human beings, for whose sake production was undertaken.[26]

Pomerantsev's criteria for authorial responsibility were high enough to plunge almost any writer into despair. As if in a medieval fable, before earning the right to publication a manuscript had to withstand three trials. First, the author was to give it to "people in distress" and see if the manuscript would make them happier. Then he was to give it to "the self-contented" and see if it would disrupt their blissful confidence. Finally, he was to take the manuscript on a stroll past the facades of "houses with memorial plaques," once inhabited by great writers, to see if the promenade would make him humbly recognize his text's imperfections. Only passing these tests would ensure that "people needed" the manuscript, and only then would it be publishable.[27] The article then ended without a real conclusion, instead describing a few more human character types, distilled from Pomerantsev's legal and journalistic career, which were again meant to show that the complexity of life eclipsed social conventions. Literature was to take this into account.[28]

Much of what he argued may sound strange to a modern-day reader—as it would even a few years later, in the 1960s.[29] Accustomed to the notion of texts as constructed phenomena, scholars would shrug their shoulders at Pomerantsev's objection to "constructedness" or his idea of reaching literary harmony between ethics and politics. Demands for sincerity to be "firmly rooted" or "courageous" would appear irritatingly imprecise, especially when coupled with euphemistic omissions of names, places, and titles. And references to "the greater truth of us all" could easily seem like verbal sugarcoating of some hidden "thesis." Add to that the article's extravagantly loose structure, and it seems impossible to explain why this ostensibly incoherent piece commanded such enormous attention from readers, including the highest agencies of power. "On Sincerity" was among the most influential publications of the Thaw, yet also one of its least transparent.

This is perhaps why, although its mention is de rigueur in any major study of post–World War II Russian intellectual history, Pomerantsev's article and its impact have never received a detailed analysis. Historians briefly refer to his protest against the ideological diktat for literature, his demand for writers' candid and truthful depiction of social reality, and his criticism of socialist realist distortions of that reality. Scholars agree that the article set the terms for many subsequent literary and political debates during the Thaw.[30] Some add that Pomerantsev's agenda originated in "the great ethical tradition of Russian literature, and especially the moral quests of the Russian intelligentsia, the search for truth and the meaning of life."[31] Accurate as these observations are, a closer look at the author, the text, and its repercussions is in order.

First Reactions

The first reactions to "On Sincerity" were an exhilarating surprise for Pomerantsev, who had never expected such a vast and overwhelmingly positive response. In January 1954, weeks after the article had come out, he delightedly reported to Tvardovskii that the piece was producing a "colossal resonance."[32] During the first few days, he received compliments and congratulations from fellow writers, who wrote to him, called him by telephone, or asked friends to convey their thanks. Literally overnight, the unknown and unsuccessful middle-aged beginner had entered the limelight of professional attention and fame.[33]

Letters from readers began to arrive, too. "Lieutenants, librarians, teachers, students, and engineers," as Pomerantsev described them joyfully, wrote to *Novyi mir* with their expressions of gratitude. In accordance with its usual practice, the journal forwarded typed copies of the letters to the author while keeping the originals in the editorial archive. A few more days, and it was not just a matter of individual letters: the article became the subject of exuberant polemics among thousands of people. They debated it at Komsomol and party meetings, at gatherings of artists and doctors, at research institutes of the Academy of Sciences, and at the Stalin Automobile Plant. The actors of the Pushkin Theater in Moscow discussed the article "with delight," while Aleksei Popov, director of the Red Army Theater, ecstatically read it aloud to participants in a playwrights' seminar.[34] In Leningrad, typists made money by copying "On Sincerity" and selling each typed copy on the black market for twenty-five rubles, more than three times the price of the journal issue.[35] One reader, whom Pomerantsev had never met, found his home telephone number and called him, jubilantly reporting that the article had received an enthusiastic welcome at Komsomol gatherings in Ukraine.[36]

Yet the reason Pomerantsev relayed all of this to Tvardovskii was not so much to share the joy of success as to cover himself against the ominous clouds gathering on the horizon. Despite all the congratulations, resentment against the article was building up in the literary establishment. Anatolii Surov (1910–1987), an influential dramatist who had just a few days earlier praised the article, suddenly changed his mind and at a playwrights' meeting on 15 January attacked it as "philistine, commonplace, and instigating a conflict with the state." The playwrights, few of whom respected Surov (later that year he would be scandalously expelled from the union on charges of plagiarism) disagreed and even tried hushing him. But alarmingly, at the same meeting the first secretary and de facto head of the Writers' Union, Aleksei Surkov (1899–1983), supported Surov and also cast aspersions on the article. Pomerantsev managed to reach Surkov in his office and asked directly what was wrong. Surkov's menacing reply was that this would have to be the subject of a separate, long, and serious conversation. Emboldened by the readers' support, the hot-tempered Pomerantsev flared up and dramatically replied that Surkov was making a big mistake opposing "the public opinion" *(mnenie obshchestvennosti)*, but this made no impression whatsoever on the literary magnate.[37]

Then other strange things began to happen. A well-established literary critic, Liudmila Skorino (1908–1999), to whom Pomerantsev had shown a draft of "On Sincerity," and who had originally seemed to like it, made a sudden about-face and was preparing a negative response. Flabbergasted, Pomerantsev telephoned Skorino and demanded an explanation. She responded that her initial praise had been a matter of private conversation, while the published censure would be the "mature reflection of a critic." "What, are you against discussion?" she asked with well-intoned naïveté. "What's wrong if I pick holes in your work and then you do in mine?" What was wrong was not even so much the treachery as the fact that in the recent past, similar censures had translated into court sentences, something Pomerantsev had just described. Picking holes could easily turn from metaphoric to literal. Duly assessing these signals, he asked Tvardovskii for protection.[38]

Tvardovskii could not really offer any. He tried to calm the anxious author, suggesting that critical reviews in the press were the norm in the literary world. It would have been worse, he argued, had some secret gathering of administrators adopted a resolution deciding the manuscript's and the author's fate. Publication, on the other hand, was healthy, as it placed everyone's arguments out in the open, before the readers' eyes. "This is how we will live from now on," Tvardovskii wrote optimistically. As for the colleagues' duplicity, nothing else was to be expected, and the experienced editor advised the beginning author not to waste time and nerves worrying about it. "I am shaking your hand and wishing you good health and good spirits. Just sneeze at all this."[39]

It soon became clear that "all this" was nothing to sneeze at. A week later, on 30 January 1954 *Literaturnaia gazeta* published the first major criticism of "On Sincerity." It belonged to the writer Vitalii Vasilevskii (1908–1991)—whose son Andrei, ironically, would at the turn of the next century become the editor of *Novyi mir,* which his father once stigmatized. Building a perfect straw-man argument, Vasilevskii ignored Pomerantsev's idea of a merging of the personal and the social. Pomerantsev, he said, preferred the abstract, subjective criterion of sincerity (which Vasilevskii did not discuss) to the truly important criteria of worldview and "party position." Good literature had to be well written, Vasilevskii agreed, and perhaps it needed to be sincere, but above all it had to be ideologically correct. As for Pomerantsev's examples of life's complexity, he refuted them as unrepresentative. To support his opinion, Vasilevskii cited Lenin's 1917 "Statistics and Sociology," an unfinished article much favored by Soviet commentators. In it, Lenin had made a distinction between "facts" *(fakty)* and "little facts" *(faktiki)*—between, on the one hand, the entire body of evidence bound together by various contexts and, on the other hand, isolated phenomena torn out of context to support an ill-founded theory.[40] "On Sincerity," Vasilevskii argued, was doing just that: cherry-picking "little facts," tearing isolated negative examples out of the general positive context of Soviet reality.[41]

With little variation, those were the charges Pomerantsev would face over the next few months from the press and a number of other powerful agencies. In February 1954 Liudmila Skorino published—in the journal *Znamia*, where she was a longtime member of the editorial board—her critical piece, about which Pomerantsev had been forewarned. Here, too, was the laundry list of charges: "idealism," "subjectivism," facts versus little facts, and so on. A literary scholar of considerable erudition, Skorino invoked the classics. Pomerantsev, she argued, was calling for "confessional" literature and thus going against the grain of the Russian tradition that had always merged confession with another mode of writing, the sermon, in which literary texts by definition carried a social message.[42]

These initial probes were followed by a barrage of heavy artillery. On 20 March 1954 *Literaturnaia gazeta* published a programmatic article by Boris Sergeevich Riurikov (1909–1969), the newspaper's editor in chief, future deputy head of the Central Committee Department of Culture (1955–1958), and editor (1963–1969) of the journal *Foreign Literature (Inostrannaia literatura)*. A well-educated philologist and expert tactician, Riurikov produced a masterpiece of casuistry and political sensitivity. Rather than simply accusing his opponent of neglecting literature's ideological content, he turned Pomerantsev's own arguments against him. What should guide the writer, he argued, was "the great truth of life . . . and not some little piece of it." While sounding similar to Pomerantsev's idea, this meant something very different: unquestioned political loyalty. What mattered were the fine accents. Like Pomerantsev, Riurikov cited Ovechkin's *District Routine* as an example of good literature, but he shifted the emphasis from social criticism to optimism. Riurikov's Ovechkin wrote in sanguine confidence that the problems of the countryside would be resolved and did not at all detract from the greater good of the country's strategic path. It almost sounded as if the element of social criticism was altogether absent from *District Routine*. Riurikov passed over in silence the authenticity of Ovechkin's language, an important point for Pomerantsev. As for sincerity, he was not against it, but he argued that Pomerantsev's interpretation of sincerity as emanating primarily from the writer's persona could lead to subjective misconceptions. Quite masterfully, Riurikov even linked

Pomerantsev's presumed "voluntarism" and defense of the individual with "the cult of personality," something that was increasingly criticized in the press.[43]

Pomerantsev, of course, did not advocate voluntarism, literary or any other, and as we have seen, he did pay much attention to literature's political content. Under different circumstances, he might even have agreed with some of what his critics argued. The emphasis was different, but there was no fundamental contradiction: in principle, everyone was in favor of sincerity, spoke the language of "greater truth," believed in literature's societal charge, and praised Ovechkin as an example thereof. Everyone was against "constructedness" and the "varnishing of reality." Everyone even agreed on the same infamous varnishers, Babaevskii first. If this was so, then why was such a bitter campaign waged against Pomerantsev's article and the journal that published it?

For one thing, Pomerantsev had walked a few steps further than anyone else, beyond criticizing localized phenomena and toward generalizations about literature in its entirety. His declaration of total abnormality in the profession was very radical for the winter of 1953–54, especially given the unstable and unpredictable political situation. But there was also another factor at play. Pomerantsev's manifesto would not have become so scandalous had it not inflamed a vast audience, at home and abroad.

The Schism in the Literary Guild

The Central Committee closely monitored, even if it did not swiftly respond to, all the developments around the article. On 8 February 1954, the Department of Science and Culture reported to the party's chief ideologist, Petr Pospelov (1898–1979), pointing out Pomerantsev's "subjectivism" and disregard for ideology. Dissatisfied with Vasilevskii's "toothless" response, the authors of the report recommended "more serious and harsh criticism." What troubled them was that "On Sincerity" was being "advertised and proclaimed as 'a new banner of literature' among certain literary and quasi-literary [*okololiteraturnykh*] circles."[44] The same concern sounded in other messages the leadership began receiving. In March 1954, the writer Boris Polevoi (1908–1981) reported that the articles by Pomerantsev and Lifshits led the literary community to anticipate an "intellectual NEP," a certain loosening of ideological firmness and stability, presumably similar to the results of the New Economic Policy in the 1920s. Most harmful, wrote Polevoi, was that the articles fueled Western propaganda about a weakening of Soviet literature's ideological impact.[45]

The *Novyi mir* articles also disoriented the Soviet Union's allies in Europe. Accustomed to viewing any Moscow publication as a call for action, Eastern European ideologues were puzzled by "On Sincerity" and had little idea on how to respond to it.[46] Riurikov echoed this concern when in June he told his subordinates at *Literaturnaia gazeta* about his recent trip to Poland. Writers and journalists in Warsaw, he said, had expressed "enormous, intense interest" in what was happening in Moscow—and equally enormous bewilderment: "They did not understand why the Soviet press was publishing one [such] article after another. They meant articles in the journal *Novyi mir.* And others, trying to gamble on those articles, declared: Look, don't you understand, this is Moscow's new directive, this is Moscow telling you what to do—and you object."[47] At a turbulent April meeting of the Polish Council of Culture in Warsaw there was "a most bitter discussion," Riurikov recounted, and dangerous slogans were advanced—freedom of creativity *(svoboda tvorchestva)* and freedom of speech. Similar developments were taking place in Czechoslovakia and Bulgaria. Riurikov failed to persuade his Eastern European colleagues that what was happening in the Soviet press was a normal discussion: "Comrades told me: this discussion of yours has cost us dearly." Thus, he explained, "Our confusion here is . . . perceived there as if through a large magnifying glass."[48] But the reverse was also true: Soviet observers paid close attention to any foreign repercussions of their domestic intellectual life.[49]

Riurikov's phrase about "our confusion" merits attention. The editor in chief was obviously dissatisfied with his subordinates' response to *Novyi mir,* as well as his own. "We as workers of Soviet literature, the Soviet press," he stated, "bear full responsibility for all this, because we have not rendered sufficient help to our comrades."[50] Indeed, during the spring and early summer of 1954 the Soviet press was extremely slow and haphazard in organizing a response to Pomerantsev as well as the other *Novyi mir* authors, with many journalists divided on the issue. At home, just as abroad, confusion ruled the day. Much like their Polish and East German colleagues, Latvian writers, for example, took the article's publication in Moscow as a sign of official endorsement, and the Riga-based literary journal *Karogs* reprinted it. On his trip to Latvia in the spring, another

Literaturnaia gazeta journalist had to answer unpleasant questions very similar to those his boss Riurikov had faced in Poland. "When talking to people there," he remembered, "I defended my newspaper and its line, although I felt that there was no line."[51]

Many of his colleagues agreed.[52] That their newspaper had "no line" was a common theme at *Literaturnaia gazeta*'s editorial board meetings during the first half of 1954. Apparently, for a while there was indeed no line. Vasilevskii's article, for example, was initially viewed skeptically by some at the newspaper, and even Riurikov considered the piece weak.[53] There was even talk of a "schism" *(raskol)* on the board when "a few comrades decidedly or half-decidedly began defending Pomerantsev's article."[54] Later, several journalists continued to believe that *Novyi mir* had advanced good points worth discussing seriously, and board meetings continued to devolve into heated arguments on the issue.[55]

Other periodicals added to the atmosphere of uncertainty. On 17 March 1954, three days before Riurikov's article came out, *Komsomol'skaia Pravda* published a letter that actually supported Pomerantsev: a rebuttal to Vasilevskii and Skorino. The letter writers—a schoolteacher and future professor of Russian literature, Iurii Mann, together with four students at Moscow University—charged both critics with using dirty rhetorical tricks and strawman arguments. *Literaturnaia gazeta*, they argued, had deliberately suppressed dialogue on the important issues Pomerantsev had raised.[56] Years later Mann remembered that the key role in publishing the letter had belonged to Aleksei Adzhubei, deputy editor of *Komsomol'skaia Pravda*, who, of course, wielded far greater power as Khrushchev's son-in-law. The open-minded Adzhubei, an old friend of Mann's from their student days, enthusiastically welcomed the letter, and soon it appeared in print.[57]

So, one major Soviet periodical ended up contradicting, indeed accusing another in regard to a highly sensitive political issue. The jab at his newspaper certainly fueled, if not directly prompted, Riurikov's article: in it he rewarded Mann et al. with a caustic paragraph. His subordinates at the paper also considered the letter a challenge.[58] Three months later, with the official attitude toward Pomerantsev finally apparent and the campaign against *Novyi mir* in full swing, *Komsomol'skaia Pravda* had to apologize for its "grave mistake" in publishing the letter.[59] Out of schadenfreude, a few members of the *Literaturnaia gazeta* team jeered their rivals, proud of having chosen the right stance themselves. Riurikov, however, promptly warned them against "resting on their laurels" and demanded they work incessantly to propagate the proper line of socialist realism, now that the line had become clear.[60]

But the line had not always been clear, and there was a moment in the winter and early spring of 1954 when officials did not quite know how to respond to "On Sincerity." The Central Committee Department of Science and Culture did treat it suspiciously, and it did take note of *Komsomol'skaia Pravda*'s "mistaken evaluation" of the letter supporting it as early as 24 March 1954 (*after* Riurikov's article), but this was only in an internal communication.[61] Even if we discount the publication of the letter as Adzhubei's royal prank, the Central Committee's reaction came late, the "mistaken evaluation" was not prevented from seeing print, and many propagandists were left guessing which attitude to Pomerantsev might be appropriate.

Not only did many writers and journalists share his criticism of the literary environment but they also felt the strong impact of the audience—and not just in Eastern Europe but at home as well. Soviet propagandists lived and functioned within a vast, literary-minded society that turned out to be highly receptive to the slogan of sincerity.[62] What fueled the controversy was that it unfolded not within a small circle of litterateurs and politicians but among thousands of fascinated readers, who besieged journals and newspapers, responding to every word in the polemic, influencing its course—and ultimately determining its significance.

Sincerity, Intimacy, Tradition

The journalists at *Literaturnaia gazeta* knew that they were being read. With hundreds of letters coming in weekly, they closely monitored readers' reactions to their articles. Thus it was all the more unpleasant for them when they discovered that their newspaper's position on Pomerantsev's article had met with universal disapproval. On 23 March 1954 Evgeniia Stashevskaia, head of the letters department, informed her colleagues that Vasilevskii's response to Pomerantsev had prompted thirty-six written responses from readers, all squarely in the negative column. Twenty of these responses, available to me in the newspaper's archive, were indeed uniformly supportive of Pomerantsev.[63] This was unusual. At the time, readers' reactions to a publication often were split, or perhaps even mostly negative, but such total rejection was rare. This spelled out a clear-cut propagandistic failure: the readers had independently formulated an opinion that directly challenged what the newspaper prescribed them to think.

Let us look at these responses. *Novyi mir*'s archive contains, on my count, 104 letters to Pomerantsev from more than 135 letter writers.[64] All except 2 were written in support of him and rebuffed his critics. The readers were defiant in stating their views: only 9 letters were anonymous, with the rest fully signed and including a return address. Although in their stances *Novyi mir* and *Literaturnaia gazeta* were exactly opposed on this issue, evidence from their archives is highly congruent. Perhaps, then, the preserved letters do fairly accurately reflect how Soviet readers reacted to "On Sincerity."

Just as Pomerantsev described it to Tvardovskii, the letters began to arrive almost immediately after the article was published. The earliest ones came in mid-December 1953, the last one as late as 11 November 1954.[65] With readers responding to it over the course of nearly a year, the article thus produced a major impact indeed. Interestingly, most letters arrived not in December or January but during the subsequent months—February (twenty-six letters), March (sixteen), and April (thirteen). In other words, most of the letter writers responded not as much to Pomerantsev's article itself as to the attacks on it in the press. Throughout the Thaw, this would be a common pattern in responses to literary publications: readers reacted not only to original texts but also, sometimes mostly, to media criticism of those texts. Aware of the political significance of letter writing, they rallied around their favorite authors and editors, using letters as both a form of individual self-expression and a tool for political action.

The letters about "On Sincerity" came from all over the USSR, but those from Russia, and from people in other republics who identified with Russian language and culture, prevailed. Moscow and Leningrad, although strongly represented, were in the minority: only twenty-eight letters (fewer than one-third) came from the two capitals. Relatively few came from small towns, and fewer still (only ten) were from readers in the countryside. It was from the large provincial cities—Kuibyshev, Odessa, Sevastopol, Khabarovsk—that most responses came (thirty-four letters, or 37.4 percent).[66] This pattern, too, would persist in responses to nearly all major *Novyi mir* publications during the Thaw. Contrary to Nekrasov's poetic dictum from the previous "thaw" of the 1850s and 1860s, a century later Russian provinces did not display "age-old silence" but played an important role in literature-centered political life.[67]

Young readers were prominent among the letter writers. No less than twenty letters came from college students, and eleven more were from junior-rank military servicemen. Apparently the military men applauded Pomerantsev without instigation from their superiors: all of their letters but one were individually signed and, more important, textually unique. Beyond students and the military, nearly all the letters came from members of the intelligentsia, in the Soviet understanding of this term, referring to educated professionals: three teachers, four librarians, two journalists, and so on. There were no workers or collective farmers, at least among those who identified their occupations. This was one major difference between readers who reacted to Pomerantsev's article and those who wrote about subsequent *Novyi mir* publications. Compared with the more socially mixed responses later, the 1953–1954 polemic on sincerity was almost exclusively an intelligentsia affair.

Pomerantsev was accurate when he stated that readers discussed his article everywhere. Entire offices would stop working while people argued about sincerity for hours at a time—obviously unafraid of repercussions. Sometime in January 1954 T. Permiakov, an instructor at the Khabarovsk Medical Institute, found the entire staff of an office at the city radio station engaged in a heated argument. When he asked why passions were running so high, the radio journalists responded that they were discussing Pomerantsev's article and were astonished to hear that he had not yet read it. "Do read it!" they urged. "This is astoundingly fresh and good!"[68] A few hours later he stopped by the editorial office of the regional newspaper *Tikhookeanskaia zvezda (Pacific Star)*, only to hear, again, journalists applauding Pomerantsev's article. A few days passed, and Permiakov (who was apparently involved in the world of letters), happened to be at the local branch of the Writers' Union. There, too, he heard ecstatic praise for the article. Intrigued, as he still had not read it, he finally went to a library and asked for the December issue of *Novyi mir.* The librarian gave him an understanding smile. With the words, "Of course, you came for Pomerantsev!" she produced a long list of readers who had signed up for that issue of the journal. Because he "did not have connections at the library," a full two months elapsed before Permiakov's turn came to read "On Sincerity." Throughout the months of anxious waiting, he kept hearing about the article everywhere, including at his department meetings at the medical institute. "And everywhere," he reported to *Novyi mir,* "the verdict was the same: 'Great! What a punch! What a knockout! That's where the truth is told!'"[69]

Clearly many of Pomerantsev's admirers in Khabarovsk were journalists. One might have thought that licensed agents of propaganda would be discrete if not utterly disparaging about the article, but on the contrary, many of them eulogized it with sheer delight. Riurikov's "magnifying glass" was at work here, as well. Their colleagues in Moscow were confused about how to react to the article—some praised it, while others kept a safe distance—but in the provinces Pomerantsev's success was multiplied several times over. He became the hero of the day, with people jubilantly greeting him in letters full of elated expressions and exclamation marks.

Although this was nothing like Nekrasov's "age-old silence," the nineteenth-century poet would have recognized a few aspects of this new letter writing. "*Vivat* Pomerantsev!" wrote an anonymous "Student" that winter. "The name of yours [*imia Vashe*] will forever live in the history of Soviet literature. Sneeze at the false and cowardly blasphemers of yours [*khulitelei Vashikh*]."[70] Except for the word "Soviet," the letter, with its laudatory Latin, elevated archaic prose, and epic inversions, read as if the writer had penned it a hundred years earlier. Allusions to classical literature were common in letters defending Pomerantsev and mocking his critics. Another student compared Vasilevskii's reliance on party guidelines to the anxieties of Famusov, a genteel character in Aleksandr Griboedov's 1823 *Woe from Wit* who measured his every step by the repercussions it might have in high society: "What will Princess Maria Aleksevna say?"[71] Yet another reader likened Skorino's article to the hollering of a boorish army sergeant straight out of Chekhov's stories.[72] Most radically, a letter writer from Petrozavodsk produced an entire literary composition in which he derided Pomerantsev's critics in the form of a long dialogue between Pushkin and the nineteenth-century satirical literary character Koz'ma Prutkov. Posing as "Prutkov Junior," he inserted in the dialogue nearly the entire text of Pushkin's 1830 article "The Society of Moscow Litterateurs," which, he thought, perfectly described the moeurs of the Writers' Union. The names of Soviet literary notables Aleksei Surkov, Vladimir Ermilov, and Nikolai Lesiuchevskii parenthetically accompanied those of Pushkin's characters. Given that Pushkin's text was itself a parody of editorial meetings at the conservative journal *Messenger of Europe*, the letter redoubled its satirical effect.[73]

With all parties, critics and readers, recruiting the authority of the classics and citing nineteenth-century analogies and quotations that everyone understood with the slightest hint, the sincerity polemic revealed an established culture whose insiders were deeply immersed in Russia's classical literary tradition. Pomerantsev himself was part of this culture. His article contains a passage in which he, a critic disappointed in modern literature, approaches a bookshelf to find inspiration in the old writers. What inspires him, though, are not just any authors but precisely the nineteenth-century classics, such as Fedor Tiutchev and Afanasii Fet. Modernist fin-de-siècle authors fail to impress him, as he finds in their writing nothing but verbose pretense and the emptiness of chasing after shallow commercial success.[74] In her diatribe against Pomerantsev, the critic Skorino chose to ignore this aspect of his article, as she accused him of dragging literature back to the modernist experimentation of the early 1900s. His ideas, she wrote, reminded her of the self-indulgent literary manifestos of the poet Igor Severyanin (1887–1941). The readers, though, made sure to call her on this. "If I were Pomerantsev," wrote a former editor, A. Zhernovkova, "I would sue Skorino for libel. Branding a Soviet person with the label 'Igor Severyanin' is an insult."[75] The year was 1954, and the Silver Age of Russian poetry was not yet revered or even known as such; its poetry was suppressed and dismissed as decadent. Only a few years later, the revival of interest in turn-of-the-century culture would make a comparison with Severyanin sound like a compliment, but at the time it still meant a political accusation and an insult. Ironically, all parties to the polemic—Pomerantsev, his critic, and the readers—agreed at least on one point in their perceptions of cultural tradition: they admired nineteenth-century classics and brushed the modernist legacy aside.[76]

Another traditional aspect of this literary-political culture was its striking intimacy. "My first New Year's toast," wrote N. K. Malina, a teacher of Ukrainian literature from Kiev, "will be for the creative success of Comrade Pomerantsev and the editorial board of *Novyi mir* in the New Year 1954. I believe that, after articles like this, not only will great works of literature emerge, but also many local governors [*gorodnichie*] will get what they deserve. Long live Soviet Belinskiis!"[77] Not only classical allusions, this time to Gogol and Belinskii, but also drinking to the writer's health at a family table, as if he were a relative or friend, were common in readers' letters of the 1950s (a bit less so in the 1960s). The readers presumed an atmosphere of intimate understanding and trust between themselves and the writer, in which hidden meanings of verbal expression would become transparent immediately, "with half-words." People often described themselves as the writer's friends, or "reader-friends" *(chitatel'-drug)*.[78] "When I finished reading Ovechkin's *District Routine*," a soldier Novitskii confided in Pomerantsev, ". . . I felt as if I had talked to a wonderful friend, intelligent and close, who shared his thoughts, impressions, and opinions with me just as a good pal would." "I just wanted to say a few warm words to you," explained another reader.[79] Few people shared full life stories with Pomerantsev, perhaps because his somewhat abstract topic of method did not particularly inspire autobiographical reflection. And yet they were always ready to indulge in personal revelations, to discuss how they felt while reading "On Sincerity" and how it matched their own experience.

Intimacy was not necessarily a benign quality: one could be intimate with opponents, too.[80] Sometime in the winter of 1954 an anonymous "Reader," incensed by Skorino's attack on Pomerantsev, responded to her with a crude but emphatically familiar versified diatribe, addressing the critic with the familiar form of "you" *(ty)*.[81] The writer's emotional, ad hominem attack stemmed partly from a similar satirical technique used in Soviet newspapers, and partly from the intelligentsia's tradition of bitter antistatism, a scourge of imperial Russian politics.[82] But perhaps more to the point, one may recall Pushkin's highly personal epigrams targeting his rivals. The letter writer's familiar "thou" and the practice of sarcastic versification dated back as early as the first decades of the nineteenth century, when literature was still the pursuit of noble connoisseurs familiar with one another. The "thou," the verses, and the shared laughter not only stressed the intensity of the polemic but also turned it into a humorous exchange among intimate acquaintances. Even one's opponents were presumed to be in the same close circle, bound together by a similar mindset and capable of appreciating all the nuances of the conversation.

To an extent, the familiarity in these letters may have also evolved from the myth of the "Great Family," which socialist realism promoted.[83] Yet the myth itself had more distant origins. The presumption of closeness among a literary-minded community suggests a continuity between the Soviet and prerevolutionary cultures: in this display of literary intimacy, readers of the early 1950s strikingly resembled their great-grandfathers and -grandmothers who had once shared their life stories with Tolstoy or Dostoevsky.[84] This traditional environment became the foundation for a surge of autobiographical, confessional writing with which thousands of people responded to the landmark publications of the Thaw.

The atmosphere of universal intimacy and familiarity goes a long way toward explaining the broad appeal of the term "sincerity" when it took center stage in Soviet culture in 1953 and 1954. Sincerity, if we interpret it as a candid expression of one's disposition—or, as Lionel Trilling put it, "congruence between avowal and actual feeling"—presupposes intimacy, and vice versa.[85] It is only with someone close that one can safely be sincere. Whereas the etymology of the English word from the Latin *sincerus* (clean, pure, unmixed) presumes the absence of hypocrisy or external influence, the Russian equivalent of sincere, *iskrennii,* primarily originates in the Old Slavonic *iskr* or *iskren,* meaning "close" or "proximate."[86] Russian dictionaries, old and new, frequently equate sincerity *(iskrennost')* and sincere *(iskrennii)* with intimacy and closeness. Vladimir Dal' in the 1860s listed "neighbor" in the Biblical sense *(blizhnii)* as a meaning for "sincere," while modern dictionaries also interpret sincere as "close" *(blizkii),* "warm" *(teplyi),* and "intimate" *(zadushevnyi)*—as in "sincere friend" *(iskrennii drug).*[87] Pomerantsev was fully aware of this connotation of sincerity. "I need more books that are serious *and warm,*" he wrote.[88] Literature was to be "warm," establishing not only truth but also an emotional bond between the author and readers, as well as among readers as a community.

This culture of literary-political intimacy explains why it was "sincerity" and not simply "truth" that Pomerantsev chose as his motto, and why the motto proved so successful. Truth was supremely important for him and his readers, but "sincerity" made truth feel personal, familiar, and universal, presuming everyone's longtime affiliation with it. Sincerity implied that this uniform truth was already in everyone's possession, and that all that was needed was for it to be publicly verbalized. The participants in the 1954 discussion spoke as if they perfectly understood this truth, instantly recognizing it with half-words, no further specification needed. "The sincerity of which Pomerantsev writes means honor, party conscience, and the artist's irreconcilability, his sense of life, of the new, devotion to his country's people, his demanding love of them," explained six female students of philology from Moscow University:

> Pomerantsev's sincerity includes the qualities of Mayakovskii's "tribune leader," Gorky's passionate love of the Human Being, Chekhov's refined soul tortured by life's monotony, Chernyshevskii's selflessness and persistence, Saltykov-Shchedrin's angry

> laughter, Nekrasov's "knout-flagellated Muse," and Lermontov's "iron verse awash with bitterness and anger." The sincerity of which Pomerantsev writes is a sense of the writer's responsibility before the people.[89]

Such categories were not meant to be subject to conventional analysis. It would be of little use to try to establish precisely how the letter writers meant to explain Pomerantsev's notion of sincerity as "Nekrasov's 'knout-flagellated Muse,'" other than by a very general reference to the poet's socially critical stance. Such arguments rested on emotive-associational reasoning, where the meaning of every characteristic was presumed universally clear. Except maybe for Mayakovskii, these were images long-internalized and associated with values of the literary-minded intelligentsia. Mentioning any of them, or even the writers' names alone, was like touching a button that immediately raised a variety of deep-seated meanings and associations, creating the necessary echo. The fact that the phrases and the images were clichés from Soviet textbooks underscores the twentieth-century symbiosis between state indoctrination and the old values of the intelligentsia.[90] Yet the values also possessed an independent power, and the classics' authority could one day be turned against the language and objectives of indoctrination. The sincerity debate of 1954 was an indication that this was beginning to happen.

Why, though, did the truth, whatever it was, need to be verbalized at all in this intimate circle, where everyone supposedly knew it already and had great success understanding each other in half-words? Pomerantsev's response, and that of his readers, was that at a certain point in the past (which none of them identified precisely) there had emerged a discrepancy between the shared values and the printed word. Intimate like-mindedness began to contradict verbal expression. Literature especially, traditionally the primary form of such expression, began to contradict its readers' experiences. The Thaw heralded a public discovery of this conflict, and it was "On Sincerity" that triggered a collective reformulation of values. Readers often mentioned that they had long felt what Pomerantsev wrote, but it was in response to his article that they began sharing similar ideas with him and with each other. "Your thoughts are the thoughts of many," the female students of Moscow University concluded their letter.[91] Indeed, there was a moment in the winter of 1953–54 when nearly everyone seemed to support Pomerantsev, or at least not oppose him.

This moment was doomed to be transitory—and not only because the authorities eventually came to their senses and clamped down on the rebellious author and journal. Pomerantsev's idea of sincerity was utopian from the start. He believed it was possible for writers and their audiences to hold a candid, open conversation about society's affairs while at the same time keeping the ranks intact and maintaining common ideals. His slogan of sincerity presupposed that this unrestrained conversation would merely remove a few artificial barriers, revealing what everyone already knew and thus rebuilding the intimate community of like-minded truth lovers. "And then," he declared, "your truth will merge with the truth of us all."[92] In this expectation of universal accord and eternal harmony, "On Sincerity in Literature" envisioned not just a literature but an entire society in which the lion would lie down with the lamb, everyone would be outspoken, and the world would return to conformity with the ideals that had long held this culture together.

Time would show that there was no "truth of us all." Discussions of the actual state of affairs in society, once literature launched them, would turn out to be intensely conflict-ridden. Literature became a battlefield on which fragments of the once-established culture clashed, destroying all appearances of uniformity, intimacy, and patriarchal harmony. Tradition, which the sincerity debate brought to the surface, would be instrumental in this destruction. Under the growing burden of the past, Russian culture became ever more unsettled. What awaited it in the next few decades was the shattering of ideals and illusions—sincerity among them.

Sincerity and Language

And yet it would be a mistake to consider Pomerantsev's theories entirely utopian. Illusory as his communitarian ideal was, the question remains: Why did so many readers identify with it? Traditional connotations of the ideal explain this only to a degree. They do not explain, for instance, why so many young people, presumably less immersed in tradition, enthusiastically responded to his call. Here we cannot escape discussing further the problem of language.

"On Sincerity in Literature" needs to be analyzed in the context of the widespread polemics of the 1950s and 1960s that stressed the abnormality of contemporary language and called for radical changes in verbal and artistic expression. Individual authors and emerging groups in literature, journalism, and the arts rejected the languages dominant in their respective fields as unfit for expressing human nature.[93] In particular, the Thaw was marked by a crisis of the printed word. Authors and audiences searched for new words, as the old ones seemed to have lost the power to reflect the emotional and experiential universe around them.

The language polemicists of the Thaw did not specifically address the question of when and how this linguistic crisis had emerged. In hindsight, one probable generator for it was World War II, which simultaneously heightened the people's sense of self-worth and authors' attention to human individuality.[94] However, although many agendas of the press and its audiences diverged already during the war, the idea that the entire language of the media was in crisis probably took shape later. Most likely this developed during the postwar years, when the common wartime effort was over but the hopes and expectations that victory had brought remained unfulfilled, and the regime forcefully sought to reimpose ideological orthodoxy—a combination that made the postwar media appear particularly unpersuasive.[95] A detailed chronology of these sociolinguistic perceptions would require a separate book, but whenever the crisis did originate, the notion that there was a glaring incongruity between human experience and its public verbalization, "between feeling and avowal," was clearly formulated around 1953 and 1954, mainly in *Novyi mir.*

Ultimately, the crisis of language meant a crisis of ethics. As the tireless language polemicist Kornei Chukovskii (1887–1969) observed in 1962, the issue of deficient words was an issue of presumably deficient moral values and behaviors—"philistinism," "emptiness of soul," "gaps in thought and conscience."[96] What drove the desire for words to regain power was a common perception that the failure of language revealed moral flaws in the body of contemporary society. Ethics translated into politics, too: the Thaw-era language polemicists often associated the linguistic-cum-ethical defects of a speaker or writer with government or literary bureaucracy. Much of the discussion revolved around purging "bureaucratese" *(kantseliarit)*—the office and newspaper lingo, full of clichés, that was now seen as an indicator of ethical inadequacy.[97]

None of this was particularly new: similar linguistic criticism of officialdom had marked the 1920s and 1930s, not to mention the nineteenth-century satires by Gogol, Herzen, and Saltykov-Shchedrin. Together with Mayakovskii, Zoshchenko, Il'f, and Petrov, Chukovskii had long worked to expose the evils of bureaucratese, continuing the tradition. However, the Thaw added a new page to the old story.[98] Chukovskii noted that, although passions about the insincerity of words had run high in early Soviet culture as well, in the 1950s and 1960s language-related polemics became especially widespread, commanding attention from mass audiences ostensibly unconnected to such esoteric issues.[99] Although the language anxieties of the Thaw reflected the chronic instability and ongoing reassessment of experience that characterized modern Russian culture, especially in the twentieth century, the year 1953 marked a particular unsettling of political and cultural balances—and hence, particular attention was paid to language. The uncertainty of the future, the nascent questioning of the "cult of personality" and thus of the legitimacy of the Stalin epoch, began to undermine all the norms this epoch had produced. In the next few years, revelations about Stalin's era would accelerate the demise of its verbal order.[100]

The language conundrum allowed for many possible solutions. One was to derive standards of speech from the past, returning to legacies and roots. In searching for new words, one could recall or recreate old ones, something Solzhenitsyn would practice a few years later. Tvardovskii's *Novyi mir* proved receptive to this retrospectivist trend. As early as June 1953 it published an article titled "On the Culture of Speech" by a known language purist, the writer Fedor Gladkov (1883–1958) who pontificated on "proper" ways of writing and speaking, "proper" stresses, spellings, or forms of address, deriving examples from his youth half a century earlier.[101] Tellingly, this antiquated advice brought many positive responses. One reader even proposed "an authoritative all-Union organ for the protection of the purity of our mother tongue."[102] In unsteady times, people sought stability premised on a static—in this case archaic—linguistic norm.

However, ideas about such a norm were becoming diverse. Purism and retrospectivism were not the only sources of linguistic inspiration. Contemporaries often chose other sources of new words: revolutionary romantics, lyrical poetry, irony, youth slang, Western borrowings, or any combination of the above. The polemic was not limited to literature and journalism. Each of the arts—painting, cinema, and so on—insisted on the specificity of its own language.[103] So far as words were concerned, efforts to replace the presumably ossified, compromised language with a "living word" became widespread. During the Thaw, much like in the

1920s, the spoken word from urban parlance, peasant dialects, and criminal or youth jargon invaded literature, unsettling not only bureaucratese but also the foundation of socialist realism: "cultured" speech.[104] Young people proved especially receptive to this trend. Inarticulate yet emotional, spontaneous talk also briefly became fashionable among them as a mark of authenticity.[105] The invasion of conversational speech horrified the purists and yet gradually habituated the audience to the idea of linguistic difference: legitimate publications sanctioned language novelty.[106] Overall, the Thaw greatly diversified the Russian linguistic landscape. Increasingly, people accepted the diversification and moved toward recognizing language as a dynamic, living system. From this point on, the notion of a linguistic norm would be on the decline, yielding ground to an ever more varied range of self-expression.[107]

Pomerantsev's article was an early manifestation of these tectonic shifts. Although he never formulated the language problem explicitly, he was highly sensitive to the multiple failures of the printed word to depict human nature. The clichés, the embellishment, the preposterous scenes in which a mechanic and his fiancée dreamt of jointly repairing collective-farm equipment, or a miner exclaimed, "I can't wait to use the elongated blast-holes! Wish the weekend were over sooner!"—all were, in his view, primarily failures of language. "Look how they [your characters] talk to each other!" he reproached the literary nemesis in his article, the Producer of Standard. "These are tirades borrowed straight from radio broadcasts. Does human conversation ever sound like this, does human speech flow like this. . . ?"[108]

His attention to language was not incidental. Pomerantsev had long been interested in verbalization, phraseology, vocal utterance, and their relationship to argument, as well as overall in the persuasive capacity of texts. This was not only because he was professionally involved in mass persuasion: the impact of language on an audience was a subject of genuine fascination for him. His World War II notebooks were full of observations about the efficiency of propaganda techniques.[109] As he wrote leaflets in German and broadcast radio messages on the Wehrmacht positions via loudspeakers, Captain Pomerantsev had had to make his words as persuasive as possible. With that aim, he had talked to prisoners and studied the diaries and letters of dead German soldiers, trying to understand how their minds worked, what made Nazi propaganda believable, and how it might best be counteracted.[110] He treated the enemy with respect. What made Goebbels's propaganda efficient, Pomerantsev believed, was that it sought the lowest common denominator, targeting soldiers not so much with grand patriotic slogans as with down-to-earth information about life at home. It was reassuring for the soldier to read in a local (not national) newspaper that the specific, named women and children in his hometown were safe, well fed, and that they cared about their fighting husbands, brothers, and sons in very practical ways: Martha had sewn (mended, laundered) this many soldiers' shirts (socks, mittens), while Britta had prepared that many gift parcels for the front. To persuade, the text had to strike close to the reader's daily concerns.[111]

For many years after the war, Pomerantsev retained an interest in techniques of language. One of his last works, an unfinished novel titled "Doctor Eschke," had a Nazi propagandist as its main character. The young philologist Hans Eschke, who advocates a theory of purifying the German language from foreign borrowings, is recruited to work in Goebbels's ministry of propaganda. There he learns valuable tools of textual persuasion—such as achieving maximum veracity based on selective manipulation of technically correct data, the importance of newspaper layout and fonts, and the advantages of tactical retreat for strategic gain.[112] The novel may have contained hidden autobiographical parallels and made allusions to contemporary Soviet affairs. During the war Pomerantsev, too, had recommended to his superiors the goals of factuality, specificity, authenticity, and timely counteraction of the enemy's propagandistic moves. He had advised against undue expectations, knowing that the impact of Soviet calls for surrender would be fairly modest. It would be best, he thought, if such calls could come from German prisoners, who knew the language and mindset of the target audience. He suggested recruiting prisoners of war to write letters to families or fellow soldiers, describing life in Soviet captivity as (reasonably) bearable. It was mandatory, he insisted, to avoid anything that might suggest that the letters were written under duress. "They should not contain expressions and words which the German soldier encounters in Russian leaflets and which are not characteristic of a prisoner of war. It is obligatory that nobody suspect these letters of *insincerity*."[113]

In this context of psychological warfare, sincerity was a language technique rather than something coming "from the heart." And so we run into the problem of two sincerities and two Pomerantsevs: one, of wartime vintage, a sober manipulator of words; the other, as of 1953, an ostensibly naive and idealistic truth seeker. Which of the two images is accurate, can they be reconciled, and what do they tell of the time and culture?

Early twenty-first-century studies suggest that sincerity, if not a language technique, is indeed best interpreted as a language effect, or a "media effect." Sincerity is framed by media rather than by subjectivity—it is a function of language rather than of a divide between one's outer and inner self, which analysts consider impossible to measure, least of all in a written text.[114] In the final tally, a demonstration of sincerity depends on "trust in a moment of grace," which makes sincerity a religious, confessional notion rather than an analytical one.[115] Yet it is precisely this religious capacity of sincerity that has determined its persistence in modern cultures, including such influential segments of society as law, politics, religion, and art. This resilient "unreflective presence" of sincerity has ultimately forced scholars to renounce postmodern irony and acknowledge that, because of its social prominence, sincerity cannot be thrown away. Moreover, although a media effect, sincerity cannot always be manipulated at will, nor does manipulation preclude belief in the authenticity of what is written or said. And even though sincerity may be a matter of performance, its students caution against taking a vulgarized approach to performance as mere play. "Sincerity cannot be dismissed because, while not an integrated consequence and qualification of subjectivity, it is an indispensable *affective* (hence, social) process between subjects."[116]

Pomerantsev and his article offer the best example here. Although aware of sincerity's intricacies, Pomerantsev was not a cynical manipulator of the concept but continued to value sincerity as an ideal. It was not the same to speak to German soldiers and to Soviet readers, to whom he was bound by a multitude of common experiences and values. The readers, on their part, reacted to his appeal with that very "trust in a moment of grace" necessary for sincerity to work, appreciating its confessional power. "Dry lessons and arguments," wrote a soldier named Smirnov in July 1954, "have always bored not only schoolchildren . . . but also mature people, for whom 'clear political formulae' remain but a 'common place.' . . . What is missing is a method that would make the 'common places' penetrate into souls. Only sincerity naturally constitutes such a method—a confession spontaneously growing into a sermon because it originates directly in the soul."[117]

When does the notion of sincerity become important in society, capturing the attention of people normally undisturbed by such arcane issues as authenticity of representation? Arguably, this happens in times of crisis—ethical, political, and thus also linguistic. The word "sincerity" entered the English language in the sixteenth century, a time of major upheavals during the Reformation and Counter-Reformation, accompanied by significant changes in secular representation, notably the emergence of theater.[118] These cataclysms might have commonalities with subsequent historic junctures when "religious and cultural conflicts take place at the same time that representational idioms and media undergo major transformations."[119] People begin talking about sincerity when they feel that the media language fails to convey experience, and that this failure portends moral and political issues threatening the social order itself. It is not incidental that talk of sincerity often begins, as did Pomerantsev's article, with a statement about its opposite, insincerity, manifesting a critical condition of public expression. Discussions of sincerity are the best indicators of a culture in crisis.

The early 1950s in the Soviet Union witnessed one such crisis, something Pomerantsev grasped with remarkable sensitivity. The main protagonist of his article was a character in linguistic-cum-ethical distress, heavily dependent on literature for his moral orientation, and fast losing that orientation because of the devaluation of the word. "Shabby structure, familiar plot, premeditated scheme, dullness and clogginess, all leave us indifferent to your book," Pomerantsev censured his Producer of Standard. "But what irritates us [the most] is the universality of your approach to any situation, which you resolve by false rhetoric. . . . One must be either frivolous or dishonest to clobber us readers with empty, dry phrases when we are defenseless, when anguish and bitterness have emerged within us. This is the cruelty of talentless people."[120]

His readers displayed the same sense of linguistic emergency, and so his use of first-person plural in speaking on their behalf was fully justified. Many of them complained about how literature, their most trusted intellectual companion, had ceased to speak to them in the recent years, how it failed to reflect their innermost concerns. A scholar of technical sciences, E. Sukhanova, protested against the "disrespect" writers' showed toward the reader, citing the latest novels by a classic of socialist realism, Fedor Panferov (1896–1960). "Everything insulted me in his texts: his calculated pursuit of cheap amusement, superficial analysis of very complex problems, and graphic naturalism. . . . [A]ll these details together produced an impression of a morally tainted man. Publishing such texts, comrade writers and editors, means disrespecting the reader."[121] A librarian, A. Zhernovkova, rushed to thank Pomerantsev, who evoked "such emotions . . . because the spot he touched had been sore for a long while."[122] Literature, she insisted, failed to depict human relationships, family life, youth, and love. Language was high on her list of literature's failures, too: "I would like to state my demands of the language of our books as well. We do not need Oscar Wilde's mannered beautification, but we do not need the language of office memos, either. Nor do we need crudity. . . . I would like to ask our writers: Friends, please write about living people, with all their pluses and minuses. Don't supply us with hagiographies, like Azhaev did in his book *Far from Moscow*."[123] Having stabbed the first-rank celebrity of socialist realism, she ended by quoting Ilya Ehrenburg: "A writer has to write well. If you cannot write, go get a job at a paper mill. Produce paper, so that Tolstoy may be printed on it."[124]

Even had he wanted to, Pomerantsev could not have formulated the problem of language explicitly and systematically. The topic was too dangerous, as it pointed to nothing less than a collapse of the apparatus of mass persuasion. So he indicated the problem as best he could: emotively and impressionistically. This proved more than enough for his readers, who responded with a surge of approbation. Together with readers' reactions to it, "On Sincerity in Literature" indicated that language in Russia had entered a widely perceived state of emergency. With its call for action, the article and its author became a barometer of the epoch.

The Hot Summer of 1954

Tvardovskii was excessively optimistic when he suggested to Pomerantsev in January that the discussion of "On Sincerity" would take the form of a free and open exchange of opinions. Openness was his favorite idea. Two days later he called for it again when speaking to other editors of literary periodicals: "You can hack me into pieces, but do that on a printed page, bearing full responsibility before the readers and society. If you disagree with what I say, let's talk it over on a printed page. But it is not good when we adopt statements furtively, applying labels, so that . . . something said behind closed doors assumes the importance of an evaluation and a directive. If we agreed on the above, we would have normal literary life."[125]

Normal literary life was not to be. By the summer of 1954, the Central Committee and the Writers' Union had finally overcome their confusion and begun to take coherent action. The massive attack on *Novyi mir* started with *Pravda*, which published articles by the top literary officials: Aleksei Surkov on May 25 and Vladimir Ermilov on June 3.[126] Pomerantsev always remained the chief villain, but the critics also targeted Lifshits, Abramov, and Shcheglov. These authors, and the journal that published them, were blamed for taking a "subjectivist" line slandering Soviet reality and undermining socialist realism. The charges grew increasingly ominous, until finally, on 24 June, Nikolai Lesiuchevskii (1907–1978), deputy head of the Sovetskii pisatel' publishing house, accused Pomerantsev of a "nihilist" attack on Marxist-Leninist theory itself, calling his idea of sincerity "anti-Marxist, anti-Leninist, and idealistic," akin to slogans put forward by "enemy forces."[127] These were grave accusations.

Tvardovskii had been forewarned of this by his old friend and former patron Aleksandr Fadeev, who, despite his declining power, was still the chairman of the board of the Writers' Union.[128] Although relations between them were quickly cooling, Fadeev called Tvardovskii by telephone on May 18 to share the impressions of his meeting with Petr Pospelov, the party's chief ideologist. Having summoned Fadeev and Simonov to his office, Pospelov had profusely criticized Pomerantsev, quoting many heretical excerpts from the article. Tvardovskii knew literary politics well enough to realize what this meant. "Probably he will summon me [too] . . . ," he surmised in his diary. "Most likely, I will have to leave the journal. No big trouble for me personally, just a pity that there won't be such a journal any more."[129]

Indeed, in early June he and his deputy editors—Aleksandr Dement'ev (1904–1986), Sergei Smirnov (1915–1976), and Sergei Sutotskii (1912–1974)—were invited to Pospelov's office. The conversation, if it may be called one, took place in the presence of several top members of the literary establishment—Surkov, Simonov, Nikolai Gribachev, and Boris Polevoi—and lasted an entire two days. Its tone was most unpleasant. Pospelov severely reproached the editors on two grounds. One was Tvardovskii's own lengthy poem *Tyorkin in the Other World*, completed that spring and yet unpublished, which Pospelov called "a slanderous piece" and "a libel of Soviet reality."[130] The other, more important issue was the literary criticism *Novyi mir* had published recently, Pomerantsev's article above all.

Pospelov accused the journal of promoting a separate line diverging from party strategy. This was a charge serious enough for Tvardovskii to write a letter to the Presidium of the Central Committee.[131] Although he assured the Presidium that his journal had no ideological differences with the party, the editor was not meek but defiant, showing his unmistakable irritation with Pospelov's attitude:

> I can say that what determined the low productivity of the conversation was its "scolding" nature. We faced formidable accusations for actions that I had expected to merit approval and support. Our objections and explanations (mine, principally) . . . were in vain. You refuse to plead guilty immediately, hence you behave not like a loyal party member, hence you will be punished. . . . Least of all, of course, did I expect the consideration of important literary issues to assume this nature within such a high organ of power.[132]

Pospelov, too, must have been incensed. Right after their meeting, on 5 June he approached the Presidium of the Central Committee with a long letter describing the conversation and proposing to dismiss Tvardovskii and Dement'ev from *Novyi mir*'s editorial board. He recommended the critic Vladimir Ermilov (1904–1965) as the new editor in chief.[133] This would have meant a radical reorientation of the journal's editorial policy. Ermilov had just spoken against *Novyi mir* in *Pravda* and suffered overall from an unsavory reputation, precisely because of his ready participation in campaigns against writers.[134] Tvardovskii had been among his targets more than once, the first time in 1947, when Ermilov attacked his book *Motherland and Other Land*.[135]

Pospelov also discussed readers' letters to Pomerantsev. Counting seventy of them, he accurately registered their support of "On Sincerity" but dismissed them on grounds of social marginality. They were written exclusively by members of the intelligentsia, he wrote, "without a single worker or collective farmer"—something that, in the Soviet class hierarchy, presumably made letters less significant. Moreover, they came from "unstable, philistine-minded people and the politically immature part of student youth." While dismissive, Pospelov's argument was awkward and could not hide his concern about such unequivocal dissent existing among the reading audience.[136]

The strengths were uneven. Initially the *Novyi mir* editors had contemplated publishing (in the June issue) a response to the media attacks, but it had to be taken out, on the Central Committee's order.[137] Tvardovskii then opted for tactical retreat. In mid-June he and Dement'ev attended a party meeting of Moscow writers, where the journal was again censured for its critical articles. In response, Dement'ev read a statement that acknowledged the editors' "mistakes," which consisted in publishing and then defending the articles. That, however, proved insufficient: on 1 July Riurikov's *Literaturnaia gazeta* published an editorial again bombarding the journal.[138] Then the heaviest ordnance joined the fray—or, at this point, the execution.

On 7 July 1954 the Secretariat of the Central Committee of the Communist Party held a meeting to discuss the work of *Novyi mir.* Khrushchev himself presided, with the top figures of the literary establishment—Fadeev, Konstantin Fedin, Valentin Kataev, Simonov, and Surkov—in attendance. The journal was represented by two of Tvardovskii's deputies, Dement'ev and Smirnov. Tvardovskii did not attend. The campaign must have finally taken its toll on him: later he remembered that the two-day showdown with Pospelov had led him to resort to alcohol, and the same might have happened this time.[139] The next day Fadeev unsuccessfully tried reaching him via his deputies and eventually sent a written report about the meeting to Tvardovskii's wife, Maria Illarionovna. Underscoring the gravity of the situation, the letter was delivered not by mail but privately.[140]

A stenographic record of the meeting has not yet been located, so this recently published letter is practically the only source on what was said there.[141] Apparently, Tvardovskii's absence produced a most unfavorable impression. When one of the CC secretaries inquired about the reason for his absence, Smirnov replied that the editor was ill. That did not satisfy the secretary, who insisted that the illness be identified. Khrushchev also remarked coldly: "He ought to seek treatment, then." Later the leader returned to Tvardovskii's absence, dotting the i's and crossing the t's. "He did not show up," Khrushchev triumphantly pronounced, "because the public criticism had led him to realize that he would have to either retreat or stand up against the opinion of such a power instance [the Central Committee], to which he has to submit."[142]

It was hard not to submit. Everyone present at the 7 July meeting (Fadeev included) unanimously condemned Tvardovskii's *Tyorkin in the*

Other World and the critical articles in his journal, Pomerantsev's among them. The censure was moderate, though: Tvardovskii's publishing decisions were characterized as "mistakes" rather than as deliberate political offenses ("mistakes" was also the term with which the journal's editors tried to defend themselves). The moderation stemmed from Khrushchev, who was fairly reserved, emphasizing his "desire to . . . give a chance to everyone who had erred." Generally, Fadeev concluded, "the meeting went under the rubric of criticizing Sasha [Tvardovskii], but doing so respectfully and with an understanding that he had a future." He advised Tvardovskii to acknowledge his "mistakes" by writing to Khrushchev personally and seeking a one-on-one conversation. That way, he predicted, the affair would result only in Tvardovskii's dismissal, without graver consequences. Should, however, "Sasha" decide to be obstinate and "struggle against the party," one could only imagine what might happen, and "no one, decidedly no one, would support him."[143]

Both Fadeev and Tvardovskii were children of their time. Both knew well that campaigns involving political forces of such magnitude had previously resulted in the physical destruction of the writers who became their targets. No one could be sure that this would not happen again.

On 16 July Tvardovskii followed Fadeev's advice and wrote to Khrushchev, asking for an appointment and proposing to discuss "not only my personal literary fate but also the general matters of principle concerning Soviet literature."[144] The first secretary received him on July 29. Their conversation lasted for an hour and fifteen minutes, and apparently Khrushchev was well disposed. He calmed Tvardovskii and assured him that the Central Committee's action against *Novyi mir* would not be publicized. Unlike with the infamous 1946 decree about the journals *Zvezda* and *Leningrad*, now everything was to happen via the Writers' Union.[145]

By the time of their conversation, *Novyi mir*'s fate had been sealed. A week earlier, on 23 July, the Central Committee Secretariat had held another meeting on this subject. In his concluding speech, Khrushchev had emphasized his commitment to the key political developments of the Thaw: curbing state repression and diversifying intellectual life. He recommended relieving Tvardovskii from his duties but indeed doing so through the Writers' Union. "It is necessary that, in all art-related matters, a general direction be set by the CC, whereas the struggle should be internal," Khrushchev insisted. He spoke against completely destroying the journal with the party's weight. "A decision by the Central Committee holds great power," the first secretary reminded his audience, "and we ought to exercise this power reasonably." He also objected to any further reprisals against the journal's staff, making a direct critical reference to Stalin's years: "Generally, we need to end the situation when, as was the case until recently, people subjected to official criticism [*prorabotka*] did not know where they would spend the following night, and whether that night they would not hear the knock on the door." The time of such reprisals had passed, Khrushchev stated, and the new times would be different.[146]

Following his message, on that same day the Secretariat adopted the decree titled "On the Mistakes of the Editorial Board of the Journal *Novyi mir.*" It confirmed all the previous criticism of the journal, removed Tvardovskii from his position as editor, and returned Konstantin Simonov to this post. As Khrushchev had promised, the decree was not published and all the formalities were to go through the Writers' Union. On 28 July, one day before Khrushchev's meeting with Tvardovskii, the Secretariat's decision was endorsed by the Presidium of the Central Committee, the highest ruling body in the Communist Party.[147]

The rest of the story was anticlimactic. On 3 August, Tvardovskii and Dement'ev were invited to the CC's Department of Science and Culture, where its deputy head, P. Tarasov, read the Secretariat's decree to them. He reiterated that it would not be publicized. "What remains," Tvardovskii wrote with visible relief in his diary, "is the [meeting of the] party group in the Board of the [Writers'] Union, the Presidium [of the Union], and the [ritual] 'handshake' in the editorial office."[148] On 10 August, following this scheme, the party group of the Writers' Union had its meeting. Facing the massive but, as he now knew, not lethal scolding by fellow writers, Tvardovskii even dared to be somewhat rebellious. While he acknowledged the "mistakes," he made it clear that he was doing so only as a matter of party discipline: "I cannot assure you that I have experienced an instant turnaround and understood everything, but I will try to understand everything and to draw [the] necessary conclusions." Concerning his poem *Tyorkin in the Other World,* he was even less pliable, stating in a calculatedly defiant way: "Because the CC says so, I am obliged to accept its evaluation of my work. . . . But you have to understand me. . . . My authorial attitude to this piece remains one of a parent to his child. Society may view it as a bastard, but the parent keeps a different, parental attitude." A CC official present at the meeting wrote a report on all this.

Khrushchev read it and made no comment.[149] Reflecting on the meeting the next morning, Tvardovskii noted that the criticism had been "padded" with complimentary rhetoric describing him as "great," "talented," and so on. "Could have been much worse," he summarized the outcome of the entire affair.[150]

With its decision of 11 August 1954, the Presidium of the Board of the Union of Soviet Writers formally relieved Aleksandr Tvardovskii of the editorship of *Novyi mir,* appointing Konstantin Simonov to the post. *Literaturnaia gazeta* reported the event.[151]

It was a hot summer. Meteorologists recorded more scorching days in Moscow during 1954 than in any other summer over nearly a quarter of a century. Politically, the season was just as hot. *Novyi mir*'s ordeal brought about major repercussions—not only in the top establishment but also among the journal's broad audience.

The Readers Respond

Readers reacted to the persecution of *Novyi mir* in ways that had long been unseen. The journal's archive contains at least twenty-one letters received in June through August 1954 and signed by more than fifty-seven individuals.[152] All, with the exception of one, unequivocally supported the journal, especially Pomerantsev. Many were addressed not only to *Novyi mir* but also, in a gesture of civic disobedience, to the agencies that attacked it: *Pravda, Literaturnaia gazeta,* the Central Committee, or even Pospelov personally.[153] Several letters were long exposés ostensibly intended for publication, although in practice their authors realized, and often stated, that publication was impossible: these letters were meant purely as expressions of opinion and support.

"At this time," wrote Nina Egorova from a village in the Krasnodar region, "you need to hear the voice of a reader-friend [*chitatelia-druga*]":

> I am not rushing to bury in panic all that is dear to me in *Novyi mir.* But I cannot hide from you my great fear of this avalanche of varnishers, who conceal with drum-beaten lofty words their far-from-lofty thoughts and intentions! Will you endure? Will they not crush the journal? . . . In sending my article to you, I do not deceive myself with the hope that it will see the light of day. But I want you to know HOW the reader evaluates the at-

> tacks against sincerity in literature. I want you not to forget, not for a single minute, that the readers are with you.[154]

Most people supported the journal overtly: just three letters were anonymous, while the rest were fully signed. In part, this openness rested on Soviet notions of political participation, the idea of common entitlement to have a say in matters of common importance. But given that it was only 1954, it is remarkable how promptly the letter writers adopted harsh language that explicitly contradicted the official view. This confrontational style was very different from reader responses written merely three or four years earlier. In the late Stalin years, when writing to Azhaev or Trifonov, readers would object to a detail in a book, but they hardly ever disagreed with its evaluation in the press in such radical terms.[155] The letters of 1954, in contrast, were fiercely argumentative, aggressively taking aim at opinions expressed in the media. This pattern of open disobedience developed with amazing speed and would persist throughout the next two decades. The Thaw quickly revived one of the most long-standing (and evidently not-too-deeply submerged) features of Russian political culture: the tension between the educated society and state power.

However, the verbal forms in which this tension revived had accumulated the experience of the first half of the century. The readers defended *Novyi mir* in the language of public self-expression that had become dominant during the Stalin years.

In June 1954 thirty-nine students from Moscow University signed a now well-known collective letter to *Pravda* defending Pomerantsev and *Novyi mir*.[156] An initiator and the first signatory to the letter was the future prominent human rights activist Kronid Liubarskii (1934–1996). According to his memoirs, he and three student coauthors had posted announcements all over the university, inviting everyone to a dormitory for a discussion of Pomerantsev's article and the letter. "To our surprise," Liubarskii remembered, "at the designated time the dormitory hall was literally packed to capacity. People sat very tightly: on chair armrests, in all kinds of ways. We had not expected [to have] such an effect."[157] The discussion itself did not actually take place, as it was stopped by a member of the university party committee. The students then gathered in a nearby garden, collectively signed the letter and decided to send it to several agencies, *Pravda* and *Novyi mir* among them. Initially there were forty-one signatories, but after pressure from "various people," two students removed their signatures.[158]

Then all hell broke loose. On 30 June (Liubarskii's chronology), an all-university meeting was convened in the campus student club. In attendance were the dean, Grigorii Vovchenko, and, amazingly, the top members of the Soviet literary establishment—Surkov, Simonov, Riurikov, and Polevoi. Obviously, the student letter had been deemed of major political importance. In a vitriolic speech, Surkov called the letter writers "Trotskyists," while Polevoi used the derogatory word "slime" *(plesen')*, common in contemporary characterizations of deviant youths. Liubarskii protested, but the meeting proceeded according to the script. The dean summed it up by reading aloud a resolution that condemned the letter writers on behalf of all students present in the room.[159]

According to both Liubarskii and the observers from the Central Committee who monitored this meeting, the audience reacted very intensely. Students loudly disagreed with the speakers and submitted written notes with challenging questions: "Do you consider it normal when our writers follow directives from above?" "Why are texts about the countryside created by writers who don't know, or deliberately conceal, the true situation on collective farms?" "Why didn't Pomerantsev have the right to criticize, while only Surkov is allowed to judge everyone?" "Why don't you publish Il'f and Petrov, Babel, Zoshchenko, Esenin, Akhmatova, Tynianov?" "What is the fate of Tvardovskii's poem *Tyorkin in the Other World?*" and so on. The students seconded Liubarskii's protest by shouting "Right!" Fortunately for him and his coauthors, the story did not have further administrative consequences: nobody was expelled or prosecuted.[160]

In his memoirs, Luibarskii claimed that this was "the first open letter of the post-Stalin years."[161] In reality, simultaneously or even earlier, similar acts that openly challenged the authorities took place in several locations across the Soviet Union. Readers, among them university students and professors, voiced their support for *Novyi mir*. They wrote individually and collectively, from Moscow and Kazan, Saratov and Novosibirsk.[162] In March 1954, well before Liubarskii's undertaking, students in the department of history and philology at Kazan University held a discussion of Pomerantsev's article and sent a "Brief Report" to *Novyi mir*.[163] According to the report, more than 200 students participated, including those from other colleges in Kazan. Fourteen people spoke, making this a more successful discussion than the abortive one Liubarskii and his friends would attempt in Moscow. As usual, the students enthusiastically supported Pomerantsev, booing his critics and deriding the classic authors of socialist realism: Babaevskii, Nikolaeva, Panferov, Nikolai Virta, Elizar Mal'tsev, and even Simonov. Their books, the students declared, were didactic and schematic, the characters one-sided, the language wooden and far from "the living conversational speech"—an echo of the contemporary debates on language.[164] Notably, all those authors, with the partial exception of Simonov, wrote about the countryside—a theme through which the press promoted social criticism. But this was neither the only nor the most striking example of the letter writers' incorporating media agendas and language in their criticism of the very same language and agendas.

Stalin, for one thing, was eminently present in the public statements of *Novyi mir*'s defenders in 1954—and not in any sense of "de-Stalinization." Pomerantsev's supporters mentioned Stalin's name favorably, hoping to increase their argumentative ammunition with its authority. "I. V. Stalin," proclaimed the future dissident Liubarskii and his coauthors, "has said that no branch of science (including, of course, literary scholarship) can develop without a struggle of opinions, without freedom of discussion. However, the criticism heaped on Pomerantsev creates an Arakcheevan regime in literature and does not allow for any struggle between different opinions."[165] Count Aleksei Andreevich Arakcheev (1769–1834), a strict disciplinarian and the creator of the infamous military land settlements, often figured in Soviet textbooks as a prime example of tsarist despotism. Most recently, "the Arakcheevan regime" had been targeted by Stalin himself, who in his 1950 article "Marxism and Problems of Linguistics" criticized the followers of the academician Nikolai Marr for creating such a regime in language studies.[166] In their defense of the agendas of the Thaw, Liubarskii and friends thus directly borrowed from Stalin.

Their counterparts at Kazan University acted very similarly. Among the speakers at the student meeting in March 1954 was Igor' Zolotusskii (b. 1930), the future literary scholar, critic, and prominent reformist intellectual during the Gorbachev perestroika. In his speech Zolotusskii, then a fifth-year student of philology, cast aspersions on the professors of his own department. According to him, they "forgot I. V. Stalin's dicta about the creative nature of Marxism." In particular, he said, one female associate professor, by the name of K. A. Nazaretskaia, "lacked a profound approach to studying the legacy of I. V. Stalin." Her teaching, Zolotusskii insisted, was "characterized by those mistakes to which our party has sternly drawn our attention: the theoretical foundations of socialist realism are taught scholastically, detached from the living practice of our Soviet literature. Almost ignored are . . . the latest comments in the party press about issues of ideological work."[167] Present at the meeting, Professor Nazaretskaia tried to defend her teaching approach, but the students dismissed her excuses as "trying to lead the discussion away into the field of general theoretical deliberations."[168] Returning to Pomerantsev and his critics, the letter reported: "The discussion came to the conclusion that Vasil'evskii and Sikrino [*sic* (both names misspelled)] had become theoretically confused and were sliding down to idealism via scholasticism [*teoreticheski zaputalis' i cherez skholastiku skatyvaiutsia k idealizmu*]."[169]

This was language borrowed directly from the Stalin-era newspapers, indeed often from Stalin himself. Professor Nazaretskaia might well have been an unpopular teacher and an unpleasant woman, but the student criticism of her evokes the identically phrased attacks on scholars during the darkest times of the Stalin purges.

It is relatively unproductive at this point to enter a discussion of whether such formulas reflected the speakers' and letter writers' actual state of mind or were skillful manipulations of political language. The one does not rule out the other: manipulation and belief are not mutually exclusive.[170] Rather than employing the notion of belief, it is more useful to interpret such statements as revealing the absence of a different public language.

In the 1950s and early 1960s, scholars and teachers of literature such as Boris Eikhenbaum (1886–1959) and Natalia Dolinina (1928–1979) noted that the humanities lacked a language for discussing literary texts or sociocultural phenomena, other than the clichés circulated in newspapers and textbooks. Dolinina once invited her class to analyze a work of literature without using any of the standard textbook formulations: "a typical representative," "image," "constitutes," and the like. The result was devastating. Even the best students proved literally unable to speak. At the blackboard they stumbled over words, trying hard but failing to come up with any other terminology for their analysis, eventually returning to their seats to the sound of everyone's laughter. With each new speaker, the situation repeated itself. "They *sincerely* [*iskrenne*] want to find words of their own, precise and strong," Dolinina commented, "but end up being completely incapable of doing so."[171] These observations have led subsequent scholars, notably Marietta Chudakova, to a broader conclusion about the destruction, by the early 1950s, of the Russian-language "vocabulary of philosophical, economic, or historical reflection . . . as well as literary scholarship and criticism, . . . swamped and replaced by the language of officious newspaper journalism."[172]

Reminiscences of participants in the 1954 debates about sincerity echo these observations. Liubarskii remembered his spontaneous reaction to the speeches of literary administrators at the university meeting, especially to the insulting description of the student letter writers as "slime" and "drunks":

> I did not expect accusations of this kind—as for "slime," I had never been known for anything like that. . . . I lost [my] presence of mind. First, I stormed out of the room into the hallway . . . and then dashed back into the room, jumped on the podium, and demanded the floor. Strangely, it was immediately given to me. I began yelling something out. . . . (Later I was told that this was something bold but completely unargumented [*nechto smeloe, no sovershenno ne argumentirovannoe*].) Then I sat down, and something broke in me.[173]

Liubarskii's emotional but inarticulate harangue appears to have been somewhat similar to the attempts by Dolinina's students to find words of their own, which they did not have. Possibly, had he been able to prepare his speech, it would have sounded clearer both to his fellow students and to the officials presiding at the meeting. Quite possibly too, it would have been phrased like his letter, duly employing quotations from Stalin. But his attempt to speak his mind spontaneously left him without words, because such words were not available for public speech. For someone who wanted to argue his opinion in a formal setting the alternatives were either to reproduce the ready-made newspaper phrases, something Zolotusskii and others did in Kazan, or to be left literally speechless. In a way, speechlessness was sincerity in its pure form, complete dispensation with the existing language—through which, however, verbal expression is by necessity mediated.[174]

Rather than rushing to conclusions about whether or not the student mentality remained effectively "Stalinist," it is helpful to think of these days and months in 1954 as a moment of intellectual evolution, when alternative ideas, including those of self-expression, were beginning to take shape, while the language was not yet ready to accommodate them. The words the students used resulted not only from tactics of rhetorical legitimization (although such tactics did play a role), but also from the underdeveloped argumentative apparatus, which still retained its ossified forms. Speakers and letter writers had little option but to voice their independent agenda in the same language against which they revolted.

Incorporating sanctioned media formulas in the articulation of agendas that would eventually undermine the formulas themselves was characteristic of the early Thaw. Later, in the 1960s, as authors and readers unsettled the media norms by producing or reviving a variety of modes of expression—classical, neo-archaic, conversational, peasant, Westernized, youth, and so on—the verbal options for sociocultural reflection would become increasingly diverse. For now, in 1954, public speech was still in a stable, rigid condition, its transformation only incipient. It was from within the established linguistic order that the destruction of this order began, with the sanctioned language employed, however deliberately, for the destructive purpose.

Despite these shifts in the making, on the surface the summer of 1954 looked very much like a triumph of the most callous conservatism. Even with firm support from their reading audience, Tvardovskii and his colleagues felt that it was dangerous to encourage this support any further. The editors began distancing themselves from their own views and telling the letter writers that the polemic, no matter how flattering to the journal, had to stop. In July the secretary of the editorial board, Aleksei Kondratovich, replied curtly to several readers who continued to defend "On Sincerity": "We cannot agree with your unconditional defense of V. Pomerantsev's article, since it contains flaws and mistakes. The discussion . . . has been dragging on excessively as it is."[175] The word "unconditional," though, suggested that on certain conditions *Novyi mir* might still agree with Pomerantsev. Equally unclear was the referent of "it," which could be either his article or the readers' defense thereof. Intelligent readers quickly recognized these tongue-in-cheek verbal tactics. One of them responded to Kondratovich with ironic understanding:

> I am satisfied with your reply. You are against an unconditional defense of the article—therefore, on conditions you still admit, even now, the correctness of its main idea—struggle against insincerity and standardization of party rhetoric, *quod erat demonstrandum.*

> It is quite clear that, given the current (unconditionally undeserved!) attacks on poor *Novyi mir*, it is untimely to begin a discussion in print defending Comrade Pomerantsev. To every thing there is a season. Still your reader-friend, . . . [etc.].[176]

To this Kondratovich could only reply, on 7 August, that this was not at all what he had meant, that Pomerantsev's article was indeed mistaken, that *Novyi mir*, too, had made a mistake by publishing it, and so on and so forth.[177]

Meanwhile, the time was up: only four days remained for Tvardovskii's editorial team at the journal. On 11 August, the "ritual handshake" he had foreseen did occur, and he yielded his chair to the new editor, Konstantin Simonov. Time would show, though, that this was only the beginning of the *Novyi mir* saga.

Setting the Agendas of the Thaw

Together with the responses to it, Vladimir Pomerantsev's article "On Sincerity in Literature" set the agenda—or rather, agendas—for major intellectual changes that were starting to develop in Russian culture and would continue throughout and beyond the years of the Thaw. Tvardovskii's anticipation of this may explain why he, with his keen eye for conceptual breakthroughs, promoted the article. The paradigm of sincerity heralded a crisis not only for the printed literary word but also for a multitude of ethical, political, and linguistic values established in this culture by the early 1950s. The intense reactions to the article indicated that the crisis had become apparent to numerous people, from rural schoolteachers and university students to powerful cultural magnates.

It was not incidental that the crisis came to be associated with the term "sincerity." Increased public use of this term has often accompanied such crises in different historical contexts. In Russian culture, moreover, "sincerity" had profound connotations, not only of a search for socially meaningful knowledge, but also of a community within which and for whose sake the search was supposed to take place. These connotations made the term particularly apt at the moment when the community found itself in a state of emergency.

The sense of this emergency was unmistakably present across the broad spectrum of political opinions. The campaign against *Novyi mir* that slowly unfolded in 1954 saw no united front against the journal. There was no coherent "they," no single dark force battling against the Thaw. Many journalists at various periodicals recognized the need for change, were receptive to *Novyi mir*'s ideas, and openly declared their views. Conceptually, there was less difference between the journal and its opponents than one might have expected.

Readers proved to be of key importance in determining the official attitudes to the journal. The negative reaction of powerful agencies to the texts by Pomerantsev and other *Novyi mir* critics resulted not so much from the content of those texts as from the turbulence they generated in society, both at home and abroad. The audience's enthusiasm for the reformist literary agenda was crucial in provoking the official backlash against that agenda. It was the readers who created much of the intellectual commotion now remembered as the early Thaw.

Indicative as they were of the broadly perceived need for a reformulation of society's ethical and linguistic premises, the readers' responses were expressed in conventional verbal forms. The imminent changes were still in an embryonic form. Pomerantsev's words fell on the fertile yet hard and dry soil of a firmly established culture and language. Shifting notions of socially meaningful truth preceded the actual shifts in the verbal order that would later give these notions new expression. Watering the soil enough for the new words to take root would be a decades-long process involving the mutual, dialogical effort of authors and their audiences. As of 1953 and 1954, the process was only starting.

Pomerantsev himself hardly succeeded in practicing what he preached. Although greatly respected in the literary community, he did not produce any other text of importance comparable to "On Sincerity." He continued to write and publish, but did so with great difficulty, in the aura (shadow?) of his article. On the one hand, what may have explained this difficulty was the utopianism of his idea of sincerity as a practical guide for writing. The union of the real and the ideal, the ethical and the political, the individual and the communal was hard if not impossible to realize in a written, let alone published text. On the other hand, literary administrators aware of his explosive potential now took extra caution in approaching his work. A highly sensitive and emotional person, Pomerantsev died of a heart attack in 1971, in the midst of a conflict with one such administrator over the unexpected rejection of the accepted, and even typeset, manuscript of his final book. The book did come out a few years later—unfortunately, too late for the author.[178]

And yet the impact of his 1953 article is hard to overestimate. The shifts in culture whose imminence he suggested did begin to take place. "Sincerity" as an emblematic term for a new relationship between experience and language became a code word for the entire epoch of the Thaw. Implanted in the readers' minds, it entered the vocabulary of the time and stayed there long after.[179]

3

NAMING THE SOCIAL EVIL

Dudintsev's Ethical Quest

PERHAPS THE GREATEST editorial accomplishment of Konstantin Simonov, who replaced Tvardovskii at the helm of *Novyi mir,* was the 1956 publication of the novel *Not by Bread Alone,* by Vladimir Dudintsev.[1] As of the early twenty-first century there remain fewer and fewer people who have read this book. Yet there was a time when its title was on everyone's lips in Russia.

When in September 1956 the reader L. G. Usychenko returned to Moscow from abroad, where he had worked for five years, he noticed something new going on in the city. "Everywhere," he exclaimed in a letter to *Novyi mir,* "—in the subway, in the streetcars, in the trolley buses—young people, adults, and seniors" were reading light-blue-covered issues of *Novyi mir* that contained Dudintsev's novel.[2] The same was happening in Leningrad, Gomel', Kishinev, Krasnoiarsk, Tashkent, Odessa, Riga, and many other places. Retail kiosks that sold the journal were emptied out in a few hours. Readers lined up in libraries for months waiting to get copies of the journal, and it was not uncommon for checked-out issues of *Novyi mir,* tattered and full of marginalia, to go missing.[3] The lucky subscribers were besieged by scores of friends, relatives, colleagues, and acquaintances who wished to borrow the journal, if only for a day or even one night.[4] Readers without such personal ties to someone who had a copy would turn to the market, buying the issues of *Novyi mir* that contained Dudintsev's novel at three times the state price.[5] People read the novel silently and aloud, on their own and in groups. Heated discussions broke out in homes, at workplaces, and at numerous readers' and writers' conferences—just as they had with Pomerantsev's article earlier, but this time on a much larger scale.[6] Gatherings of readers were sometimes monitored by mounted police, as happened at the Moscow Central House of Writers on 22 October 1956. Dudintsev himself was present there, together with many other authors and literary critics. It was there, in the second-floor Oak Hall jam-packed with hundreds of people, some of them apparently outside the building hanging on stepladders and drain-pipes, that the writer Konstantin Paustovskii (1892–1968) delivered his famous diatribe against the corrupt, ignorant, and parasitic state bureaucrats—the main target of *Not by Bread Alone*.[7]

Like most literary discussions of the time, Paustovskii's speech went far beyond pure literature, sending out an indisputably political message. So did the entire polemic around the book, which quickly developed into a collective examination of the economic and administrative problems, political challenges, past legacies, and ethical dilemmas that confronted the country at the time. *Not by Bread Alone* became a banner of the Thaw.

In their reactions to the novel, readers sought to explain the major issues Dudintsev raised—technological stagnation, bureaucratic sluggishness, corruption, and inefficiency. The debate gave people an opportunity to complain about a range of social injustices far beyond the themes of the book, manifesting new enthusiasm for political self-expression and the exchange of ideas inspired by the Twentieth Party Congress earlier that year. At the same time, as we shall see, the readers' reasoning was heavily influenced by the political culture that had taken shape during the earlier decades of Soviet history. Many people remained willing to lay blame for their own and the country's troubles on a variety of scapegoats, and to propose mechanistic and exclusionary recipes for social improvement. The attack against the so-called bureaucrats was often phrased in familiar witch-hunting terms, where "bureaucrats" recalled the erstwhile "wreckers" from the early Soviet years. As equivalents of fictional enemies were not easily identifiable in reality, readers often named them after Dudintsev's characters, which at the time became common nouns in the contemporary Russian vocabulary. The unprecedentedly large-scale polemic swirling around the novel made it an intellectual peak of the early Thaw, but it also highlighted all the ethical and linguistic ambivalence of those years, once again showing—as did the Pomerantsev affair shortly before—that the nascent new public language and ethos were inseparably fused with, and only gradually emerged from within, the rhetorical regime established during the Stalin epoch.[8]

Written, according to Dudintsev himself, in the late 1940s to early 1950s and finished in 1956, *Not by Bread Alone* tells the story of a thirty-year-old schoolteacher of physics, Dmitrii Lopatkin, who invents a machine for the centrifugal casting of pipes, thus streamlining a costly and labor-consuming industrial process. The novel, whose action takes place in the late Stalin years, is the saga of Lopatkin's attempts to put his invention into practice. Several years of persistent effort, punctuated by numerous rejections of the machine by corrupt and self-seeking bureaucrats at research institutes, design bureaus, and the responsible ministry in Moscow, lead him to poverty and the brink of starvation. Nonetheless, he doggedly persists in his battle against the system, aided by the a few close friends and a loving woman, Nadia, who ultimately joins him, leaving her husband and Lopatkin's main antagonist, a top industrial administrator named Drozdov. The adamant inventor even goes to prison at one point, when his rivals curtail his success in developing the machine. Eventually, in deus ex machina fashion, justice triumphs. After helpful intervention by friends, the court revises its decision in Lopatkin's case and he is released from prison. His long-time sympathizer, the thoughtful and influential Doctor Galitskii, steps in and assembles his machine at a Urals metallurgical plant, proving its practical efficiency to the authorities. The perpetrators of evil, however, escape largely unhurt and remain cynical about their defeat. The novel ends with Lopatkin facing his rival bureaucrats at a reception. Now empowered, he flings a declaration of war in their faces.[9]

Contemporary and subsequent observers alike noted that *Not by Bread Alone* retained many features of a socialist realist production novel (thus, the machine was essentially the novel's main protagonist) and that Lopatkin much resembled a traditional positive hero.[10] Yet the critics also pointed out that the book was unusual in Soviet literature. The party was barely mentioned, as if it did not exist. Lopatkin's victory was almost accidental, and his rivals got away unharmed. Unprecedentedly, Dudintsev created a powerful image of Soviet industrial management as a corrupt yet omnipotent bureaucratic machine that resisted improvement and innovation, a system in which capable administrators were exceptional, and against which the chances of a lonely inventor were practically nil.[11]

The novel came out at an apt moment. The years 1953 to 1956 were a moment when the country's leadership sought to improve the economy by encouraging local initiative and dismantling inefficient administrative mechanisms inherited from Stalin's time. In February 1956 the Twentieth Party Congress, in addition to Khrushchev's fateful attack on his predecessor's repressive policies and strategic blunders, also set the task of raising labor productivity. In particular, the congress called for technological innovation from below, promoting (not unlike the anti-"specialist" campaigns of the late 1920s and early 1930s) a grass-roots movement of inventors, innovators and "rationalizers."[12] Concerned perhaps not only with efficiency but also with factional struggles at the top (especially with Georgii Malenkov), Khrushchev contemplated reducing the power of ministries and shifting from the branch system to a territorial principle of economic administration.[13] This reform was endorsed at the February 1957 Central Committee plenum and became a law on 10 May, decentralizing industrial management, liquidating 141 union-level, union-republican, and republican ministries, and handing economic power over to the new regionally based "councils of the economy," *sovnarkhozy*.[14] Against the background of these transformations, at least two main themes of Dudintsev's *Not by Bread Alone*, the promotion of inventors and the attack on ministerial bureaucracy, sounded very up to date, perhaps explaining why *Novyi mir* decided to publish the novel.[15]

Inventors existed in reality, and so did inept economic administrators, but the press tried hard to lionize the former and denigrate the latter. Encouraged from above, technological innovation conflicts between noble innovators and scheming bureaucrats became a fashionable topic in literature and journalism in 1956. Newspapers published articles about inventors whose fortunes resembled Lopatkin's ordeal, often without a happy ending.[16] While many stories might have been true, the attacks on the bureaucracy of course misplaced the target, because the administrators, constrained by hierarchies of power and centralized planning, as well as deprived of market levers, usually had little incentive, time, or opportunity for promoting rationalization and innovation.

The press campaign for the "technical creative work of the masses" reached its peak in September–October 1956, at the very same time that *Novyi mir* published Dudintsev's novel. Simultaneously, it published several other pieces about technical innovators—notably, Daniil Granin's story "Independent Opinion," which appeared in the same issue with the first part of *Not by Bread Alone*.[17] A few months earlier, Simonov had published the monumental *Berezhkov's Life* by Aleksandr Bek (1903–1972), a novel whose main character was an aircraft engine designer.[18] With the simultaneous publication of these texts—and characteristically for this culture—the literary journal became a major center of discussion about industrial problems. Not surprisingly, when the "all-union conference of rationalizers, inventors, and innovators of production" was convened in Moscow on 17–19 October 1956, it was at *Novyi mir*'s editorial office that the inventors met with writers—Dudintsev among them.[19]

Vladimir Dmitrievich Dudintsev (1918–1998) was the right man to stand at the center of the campaign. A lawyer by training, like Pomerantsev he abandoned the law for journalism. His longtime theme was economic management. *Not by Bread Alone* was based on vast empirical data: Dudintsev claimed to have spoken to no fewer than six hundred individuals about issues of technological innovation.[20] Yet he never forgot that he was writing a novel: his characters were often vividly depicted, while his descriptions of human behavior were laconic and disarmingly precise. There was an explanation for this: Dudintsev was a disciple of none other than Isaac Babel (1894–1940), whom he had come to know closely in his youth. He was also an early admirer of Ernest Hemingway.[21] Inspired by these authors, his attention to language showed in the novel, and perhaps accounted for part of its triumph.

Readers' response to the book reached phenomenal proportions. At a time when an audience's intense reaction to a literary work rarely lasted longer than two or three months, *Novyi mir* kept receiving hundreds of letters about *Not by Bread Alone* for more than a year, in late 1956 and throughout 1957. In diminishing numbers, letters were also coming as late as 1958, 1959, and the early to mid-1960s.[22] Even for the literature-centered Soviet culture, and for a journal as important as *Novyi mir*, this was an outstanding public response. To date I have located 720 letters, from more than 820 readers, about *Not by Bread Alone*. Of these, 698 letters from more than 795 individuals were written specifically because of the novel, while others mentioned it in different contexts.[23] In *Novyi mir*'s archive, this is the single largest body of readers' responses to anything the journal published from the late 1940s through the late 1960s. In numbers of letters, if perhaps not in their significance, *Not by Bread Alone* may have surpassed Solzhenitsyn's *One Day in the Life of Ivan Denisovich*, for which the journal's archive thus far reveals 532 letters from more than 579 readers, dated from 1962 to 1969.

Most letter writers ecstatically welcomed *Not by Bread Alone.* Only 27 responses were unmistakably negative, while 51 more were unspecific or neutral, either asking questions or simply requesting Dudintsev's address. Seventeen others were mixed, with 4 more or less rejecting and 13 accepting the book. All the remaining 625 letters praised the novel, unconditionally or with small reservations. Massive support came from the military, engineers, teachers, college students, professors, researchers, and workers. Enthusiastic responses came even from such unexpected places as a local KGB branch in Latvia.[24] Newspaper propagandists opposed to the novel had a hard time persuading their colleagues who admired it, and, just as in Pomerantsev's case two years earlier, pitched rhetorical battles broke out at editorial board meetings of *Literaturnaia gazeta* and *Izvestiia.*[25]

Describing readers' responses as "positive" or "negative" may seem like a crude replication of the world of socialist realist literary characters.[26] Yet these categories may be helpful in discussing readers' reactions to Dudintsev. Just as the novel itself pitted upright champions of society against corrupt self-seeking bureaucrats, so was much of the audience's response to *Not by Bread Alone* formulated as either acceptance or, much more rarely, rejection of Dudintsev's socioethical blueprint. Some people suggested that his characters and problems transcended the divide between "positive" and "negative," but many more understood the central tension in the novel as a battle between mechanistically defined forces of social good and evil.

The Nightmares of Darkness

On 13 September 1956, a forty-five-year old teacher, B. Zherdina from Gomel', Belorussia, wrote to Dudintsev, after reading only the first part of his novel:

> For the first time in the forty-five years of my life I am writing a letter to an author. . . . At last, literature began talking about our painful problems, about something that hurts and has become, unfortunately, typical in our life! At last, a writer has appeared

> who saw predatory beasts enter our life, rally together, and stand like a wall in the way of everything honest, advanced, and beautiful!
>
> How numerously they have multiplied lately, these base people with a capitalist mentality, for whom the highest value in the world is their own status, their [fine] carpets, and their peace of mind. It is for the sake of the stability of their ideals that they suffocate everything that might unmask them, anything honest, noble, and advanced.[27]

Zherdina was afraid only that Dudintsev's powerful opponents would release "tigers" on him. "In your literary world, you know, there are no fewer . . . tigers, jackals, and chameleons than in any other one," she concluded.[28] The night before she had planned to mail her letter, someone brought her the second part of *Not by Bread Alone.* She immediately "gnawed into the novel with avidity and fear," afraid that somewhere along the way it would turn into regular bland socialist-realist produce. To her relief, the apprehension proved unfounded. When reading through such politically daring episodes as Lopatkin's conversation with the prosecutor, Zherdina grew so excited she would have to stop reading and put the book down for a while. She spent the night reading and returned to her letter at dawn, writing in haste and apologizing for the many blots:

> I had never thought that it would be so joyful, up to the nervous shivering, to read in the book those same ideas that had besieged me so painfully. "Their goal is to hold their offices and to keep enriching themselves!" How glad I am that Lopatkin's thoughts match mine! . . .
>
> I could not fall asleep, so excited I was. With your novel, you have just made me (and thousands of others) happy. The horizon becomes clearer, and the fresh breeze of a nascent morning blows when one reads your book.[29]

Morning came, but the nightmares of darkness had not yet released their grip on Zherdina. The world around her swarmed with predatory beasts—tigers, jackals, and chameleons—the evildoing bureaucrats who, just as in Dudintsev's novel, blocked the path to happiness for her and others.

"Bureaucrats" had long been traditional targets of Soviet literature and the press.[30] Yet perhaps never before *Not by Bread Alone* had they been represented not as individual exceptions to the rule of positive Soviet reality, but as a subversive class that entirely dominated the system. Whether or not Dudintsev had intended this message, many of his readers perceived his book as a battle cry against an entire caste of hidden enemies. Lopatkin's declaration of war on bureaucrats reached a very responsive audience.

The problem was, before combating villains in actual life one had to identify them. Equating the "bad" bureaucrats with the whole Soviet administrative cadre was clearly going too far, as that would challenge the system's very legitimacy, something most readers hardly wanted. Also, *Not by Bread Alone* did portray some "good" administrators, notably Lopatkin's benefactor, the intelligent Galitskii, who saved the dream machine. And so the nagging question for many enthusiasts of the book was how to define the forces of social evil, so vividly portrayed in the novel yet so elusive when it came to finding their real-life equivalents.

The names came in handy. In letter after letter, readers identified the bearers of evil in contemporary society by the last names of Dudintsev's characters. Those were Drozdov and his companions—the retrograde Professor Avdiev, the corrupt Deputy Minister Shutikov, the self-seeking experts Fundator and Tepikin, the cynical ministry gofer Nevraev, and the plagiarizing designers Uriupin and Maksiutenko. These names would surface in readers' letters again and again, describing real-life targets of the book as well as labeling the critics who attacked it. As a doctor from Leningrad, L. Grineva, wrote:

> Your book is not an assault on our state system, as your critics try to argue. On the contrary, your book calls for a defense of our system, our laws, and our way of life from the bark beetles that gnaw away at the main foundations of our life, precisely at what humanity dreamed of for centuries. The Drozdovs and Shutikovs, Avdievs and Fundators, Uriupins and Maksiutenkos play this system at will, to profit them at any given moment. . . .
>
> Your book has done its job: it awakened, with renewed vigor, the burning hatred against the Drozdovs, the Shutikovs, and other scum of all breeds and ranks. And as we know, anger helps to gain victory.[31]

Anger and hatred were common feelings among Dudintsev's readers. The disastrously malfunctioning economy, managed by well-positioned but inefficient administrators who, to make things worse, often displayed haughtiness and disregard toward the rank and file, produced understandable exasperation. In a gesture reminiscent of popular responses to the terror of 1937–1938, many readers of the mid-1950s readily recognized the press campaign against the bureaucracy as an opportunity to pour out their numerous grievances, blaming the bureaucrats for a range of society's misfortunes that went far beyond the themes of *Not by Bread Alone.*[32]

The readers were closely watching the language of the press, but it did not immediately dictate the language of their letters. The relationship between the two was based on experience, memory, and deeply internalized socioethical values. Just as newspaper journalists did, most letter writers declared basic acceptance of the existing order, presenting its problems as technical rather than systemic, and personifying responsibility for the numerous tensions and failures. Yet it was not the press that developed the "enemy" theme in 1956. The language of political violence was neither widespread nor very pronounced at the time: newspapers and journals rarely called for criminal prosecution of faulty administrators. As a rule, those were merely reproached, or, at worst, a removal from office would be suggested. The press also sent contradictory signals to readers, within the space of a few months attacking a minister and then reporting that he had received an award.[33] And obviously the country's leadership had no plans for a terror campaign against economic administrators. But what is obvious today was less than obvious in 1956. Given that in the recent past criticism in the media had often portended physical repression, few could be sure that the crusade against bureaucrats would not result in another purge. The letter writers kept reasoning in the same exclusionary terms to which they had become accustomed.

The language and logic of terror came not so much from the press as from the readers themselves. When labeling social evil-doers with the names of Dudintsev's characters, the readers of the early Thaw not only followed a Russian tradition that had produced such common nouns as "Mitrofan" from Fonvizin's *The Minor,* "Khlestakov" from Gogol's *The Inspector General,* and "Oblomov" from Goncharov's eponymous novel. They also followed the customary path of witch hunting, well trodden at least since the Civil War. An engineer-designer from the Moscow region, S. S. Kovalev, justified the struggle against "bureaucrats" in this way:

> Remember Gorky's . . . hatred of petty bourgeoisie—and he knew well whom to hate. Then remember Lenin's thesis that we will defeat capitalism only because we can—and will!—create a higher productivity of labor. And high productivity of labor means, first of all, the creative work of inventors and innovators freed from rascals and bureaucrats; it means science over which no rotten or cunning authorities preside. Consequently, anyone who, willingly or not, impedes technical progress, helps our enemies! This is the logic.[34]

Kovalev's hatred of the bureaucracy was understandable: he was an inventor, one of many Lopatkin-type innovators who praised the book after having had their own share of trouble with inefficient, corrupt, and haughty administrators. Engineers and technical specialists indeed were one of Dudintsev's largest constituencies—more than 110 letter writers (13.6 percent of the total and 21.7 percent of letter writers with identified occupations). In addition, at least 22 inventors (mostly unaffiliated) and 30 workers wrote to him. And yet the use of enemy imagery was not limited to exasperated engineers and inventors. Letter writers of various backgrounds kept reproducing the language redolent of the old witch hunts and purges. Victor Matveev from Moscow read the novel and attended three readers' conferences about it—at a district library, among inventors, and at Moscow University. Excited by Dudintsev's triumph, he produced a long eulogy of the book, combined with a furious tirade against "the Drozdovs":

> It is the author's principal accomplishment that he . . . brought complete clarity to our life. He unmasked the real enemies and shed bright light upon our true friends. In other words, in order for people not to confuse them, he marked, with his novel as if with a pencil, the Good apart from the Evil.
>
> Yes. It is true that, even before this book came into being, we had known the words "bureaucrat," "careerist," and "self-seeker." But V. Dudintsev . . . stopped the intermixing between the pure and the impure that had been so profitable for the Drozdovs. . . . In other words, he pulled out and showed to everyone the slime that had for decades hidden itself behind the backs of honest Soviet people. And it is well known that a discovered enemy is a step toward victory [*otkrytyi vrag—k pobede shag*]! . . .

> Like worms gnawing away at a tree, they do not think about the tree at all. . . . Our tragedy, and their strength, is that they are dispersed everywhere but at the same time coherent, bound together with mutual obligations and criminal patronage. They are omnipresent. They are few in numbers, but they are everywhere, they are in the pores of our life, and this is why they are exceptionally dangerous.
>
> The Drozdovs are double-faced people. Their legal activities are but a mask. Their illegal, criminal activities are their essence. . . .
>
> People, be vigilant![35]

It was as though Matveev had coauthored his letter with the teacher Zherdina, the doctor Grineva, and the engineer Kovalev. The metaphors they used to describe the vicious Drozdovs were very similar—only Grineva's "bark beetles" were replaced with Matveev's "worms gnawing away at a tree." Not only was the language identical but it was also disturbingly reminiscent of the newspaper campaigns against "enemies of the people" in the 1930s. Metaphors of social hygiene likened the hidden enemies to insects, rodents, reptiles, and beasts of prey, charging them with greed for self-enrichment—an "animal" trait that, many Russians had believed at least as far back as the turn of the twentieth century, befitted a petty bourgeois but not a human being in a model society.[36] And, as vigorously as ever, people insisted on demarcating Good from Evil—a problem that had long been pronounced in Russian culture but assumed rationalistic overtones in the twentieth century, especially after a practical attempt at separating the two was undertaken in 1937–1938.[37] The image of clandestine internal foes masked as friends, the likening of imaginary enemies to predators and vermin, the calls for vigilance, and the socioethical stratagems that many of Dudintsev's admirers reproduced in the mid-late 1950s, were identical to the formulas that had once heralded the terror.[38]

Although flesh of the flesh of this culture, the rhetoric of social conflict, explicitly turned against the entire class of state administrators, sent an alarming message to the political authorities. Ever watchful (as the Pomerantsev story had shown earlier) of developments in the socialist camp, during the fall of 1956 the Khrushchev leadership feared a replay of the Hungarian Revolution at home. In Hungary, the leaders believed, intellectual turbulence had been a crucial factor inspiring the armed uprising against Soviet power in late October to early November of that year.[39] Even before Hungary the Central Committee had harbored no warm feelings about Dudintsev's novel.[40] But after Hungary, the inflammatory book became the target of a massive and explicit political campaign. A Central Committee letter dated 19 December 1956, "On the Intensification of the Political Work of Party Organizations among the Masses," drew unambiguous parallels between the Hungarian events and the activities of "anti-Soviet elements" in Soviet literature, arts, humanities, and the media. The letter cited in particular Paustovskii's eulogy of Dudintsev's book at the Moscow Central House of Writers as an example of such dangerous intellectual tendencies.[41] After late November, the tone of the press coverage of the novel changed from qualified praise to censure or, increasingly, outright rejection.[42]

At this moment, however, an enormous reading audience rallied around *Not by Bread Alone.* Throughout 1957, even as the official castigation of the novel was in full swing, *Novyi mir* received hundreds of letters vigorously supporting Dudintsev and his book. Not only was the support as strong as before, but the talk of combating bureaucrats even intensified. The angry readers perceived the official criticism of the novel as a counterattack by those very bureaucrats whom Dudintsev had targeted. "Those who speak against you are the characters of your novel that still live and work at their old places. They are afraid to lose those warm places,"—a group of seven engineering students wrote in January 1957.[43] Even in the military, admiration for Dudintsev's novel did not cease in the wake of the administrative interference. Five young soldiers wrote to him on June 22:

> You are a great guy, thank you! . . . We were tired, our brains were depleted; we were entangled in terrible contradictions and only waited for something extraordinary, fresh, truly radiant and young, while knocking, like puppies, into the dark mildewed "corners" of dogmas, regulations, and other rubbish.
>
> But time began lifting the veil before our eyes, and your book, like a powerful fist, broke through that veil. . . .
>
> Shutikovs—go to hell!
>
> Avdievs—go to hell!
>
> Drozdovs—get out of our way![44]

The language and, judging by its intensity, self-perceptions of these and many other readers continued to be rooted in such fundamental values of modern Russian culture as the belief in human progress guided by literature and the worship of the writer as a standard-bearer of social ideals. Readers transformed literary characters into human beings and merged literary plots with reality.[45] Their widespread hunger for the writer's word and willingness to read literary texts as political manifestos made the early Thaw, together with the late Stalin years, a historical culmination of literature-centrism and a new peak of realism. However, the readers also displayed new qualities. In their letters of 1957, just as in reactions to Pomerantsev's article and the campaign against it three years earlier, there was now an eagerness to challenge the media when it launched a political attack against their trusted author. In Dudintsev's case, the readers' defiance of the media became bolder and more extensive than ever before. What was also noticeable in this defiance, and what must have troubled the authorities the most, was the visible crisis of state indoctrination—which the letter writers now dismissively referred to as "the dark, mildewed 'corners' of dogmas, regulations, and other rubbish." The search for alternative sources of inspiration had begun. Predictably, literature was the first place they looked.

This collapse of the old and the search for new intellectual authorities were important characteristics of the time that would persist and continue to develop long after, even beyond the Thaw.[46] And yet again, the new ethos and rhetoric developed *from within* the existing system of political, moral, and linguistic values, which would only gradually release their grip on the minds. What the 1954 polemic around "On Sincerity in Literature" had only suggested, the much larger public debate about *Not by Bread Alone* showed with full force. More than anywhere else, this was visible in the persistent imagery of "enemies" that the letter writers reproduced over and over again, as they raged against the "wrecking" bureaucrats and their presumable talking heads in the press. In 1958, Nikolai Agridkov, a newspaper editor from the Vinnitsa region in Ukraine, wrote that he resented the "feeble" end of the novel. "The Avdievs' gang should have been completely defeated and sent to the Urals or Siberia, to build bridges and mines," he insisted. Because "truth had not yet been completely resurrected, and the infiltrators [*lazutchiki*] were still around," the Vinnitsa editor proposed a sequel to the book that would show the triumph of justice and "the neat life of people building communist society."[47] A bricklayer named Iurii Babikov, from Tashkent, identified the struggle against "clear enemies yearning to slow down progress," as well as against "hidden enemies, the survivals of capitalism in the people's and our own mind," as a major element of his worldview.[48] "Aleksei Sapozhnikov"—a pseudonym that the letter writer defiantly acknowledged was a precaution against being "beaten up"—compared the notorious bureaucrats to "swarms of cockroaches" plaguing all institutions, from ministries to collective farms, "biting, and eating, eating, eating everywhere."[49]

The Terror in the Background

The persistence and even centrality of this enemy imagery in the letters raises the question of how their authors viewed the Stalin terror. Could it be that those who produced the abundant diatribes against bureaucrats belonged to the part of society that did not accept Khrushchev's denunciation of Stalin half a year before the publication of Dudintsev's novel?

The answer is apparently no. Only in a couple of radical cases did the book's defenders explicitly refer to the Stalin-era reprisals as a model and a useful social instrument. B. N. Analov from Leningrad suggested, in November 1956, a purge like the one of 1933 to rid the party of the wretched bureaucrats. And E. I. Bespomoshchnov from Voronezh wanted to "apply the Stalin line" to the Avdievs and Shutikovs.[50] Neither mentioned the Twentieth Party Congress. But many more of Dudintsev's admirers who did refer to the congress supported its decisions—passionately condemning "the cult of personality" and the repression, and at times even accusing the authorities of an attempt to bring it all back.[51] And yet the logic of scapegoating remained valid for many of these same letter writers.

The combination of an explicit rejection of terror with the implicit reproduction of the terror-associated language made some letters look grotesquely self-contradictory. Viktor Matveev, cited above, built his philippic against bureaucrats as follows:

> But it is not the year 1937 today! The 20th congress has particularly emphasized that the times are different now. The days of the Drozdovs' caste are numbered—but that is why they will, now as never before, dodge, slander, falsely philosophize, and invent more and more new theories of self-defense and attack based on Tartuffe-like hypocrisy. With the help of these pharisaical

> theories of "defending" socialism, they have long and successfully defended themselves, attacking the interests of the people like the sands of the desert slide down upon cities. Wherever they are, life dies out. These Jesuits are the main enemies of socialism, the main enemies of the Communist party. They are the fifth column.[52]

Here a passionate rejection of the Stalin terror was caught up in the replication of Stalin's own thesis about the enhancement of social strife along with the development of socialism. Having started with a renunciation of the terror—which he designated by the self-explanatory date "1937"—Matveev ended up, in the same paragraph, reinforcing one of the central arguments behind the terror, the presumption of a "fifth column," a hidden plot of subversive enemies operating within society. In a phantasmagorical mixture that characterized the early Thaw, the readers' condemnation of state violence and their overall support for the reform agenda coexisted with the language and logic of social cleansing. Rejection of "1937" was intertwined with those roots from which 1937 had grown.[53]

Responses to *Not by Bread Alone* indicate that the proponents of the Thaw in the mid-1950s did not possess a consistent, well-ordered worldview or a language diametrically opposed to a "Stalinist mentality" (by itself a very problematic term). The mindset of the early Thaw represented a mixture of contradictory values, recipes, and vocabularies; the new and the old stood shoulder to shoulder, with heavy borrowing from the political and linguistic culture of the earlier decades.

The logical question, then, is whether we can draw clear lines marking the supporters from opponents of the Thaw, in the way that some readers desired. The probable answer is that, just as the "friends" of the Thaw, its "enemies" would be an elusive group. To try to identify them socially and physically would be a futile and misleading exercise—akin to searching for the fictional Drozdovs, Avdievs, and Shutikovs in real life. In reality, the proponents and adversaries of change overlapped and could even turn into one another depending on the issue at stake, political circumstances, personal experiences, and perhaps even a momentary disposition. The front lines of the Thaw lay not so much between as *within* human subjects—within the mind and language of everyone who lived at the time and contemplated the country's past, its current situation, and the immense sociocultural transformation that was gradually taking place.

Stating the complexity of a phenomenon only partially explains it. The question is: Why, specifically, did so many people of the early Thaw abhor the terror and yet identify with its logic so readily? Why did so many letter writers ecstatically champion Dudintsev's critical message, opt for reforms, uphold the line of the Twentieth Party Congress, and condemn the purges, but still, for all that, keep reproducing the terror, consciously or not, as a viable social instrument?

The literary model the book suggested was partly responsible for this—but only partly. Although numerous readers construed Dudintsev's message in a clear-cut black-and-white fashion, he as a writer and thinker in fact recognized ambivalence. His long-term fascination was the problem of ethics—and particularly, with defining what, precisely, Good and Evil meant in human society. It was this theme that he sought to explore in *Not by Bread Alone*, rather than any issues of bureaucracy and rationalization, or social obstacles to them, per se—and the more he did so, the more sophisticated his answers became.[54] Even if the novel's plot and imagery might occasionally seem to suggest a "terror" solution, this was not so much what Dudintsev had proposed as how the readers interpreted his text.

Arguably, the explanation for the widespread persistence of the terror mentality among the reading audience was in the lack of open conversation about the problem of mass political violence in the contemporary media. For people to arrive at a systematic and introspective rejection of terror as a socioethical recipe, a discussion about the terror had to unfold in literature, the press, and the arts. During the mid-to late 1950s, despite some approaches to the theme, all these venues lagged far behind the numerous kitchen-table discussions in addressing the recent experiences of arrests, disappearances, and imprisonment in concentration camps—discussions that especially intensified with the return of Gulag survivors.[55] It was the gap between that smoldering subterranean polemic and its inadequate recognition in the media that explained, in particular, why so few letter writers of the late 1950s raised questions about their own part in the terror—either as victims or perpetrators, or through their own compliance, not to mention language and mindset.

Whether or not the readers asked themselves those questions, in letters they routinely distanced themselves from the terror, presenting it, usually in very restrained language, as an alien evil superimposed from above. Those who mentioned any abuses from Stalin's time did so vaguely and euphemistically. The elusive "cult of personality" was the most common description they used, probably because it became unmistakably legitimate after the 30 June 1956 Central Committee decree, "On the Overcoming of the Cult of Personality and Its Consequences."[56] More rarely, the letter writers ascribed the terror to Lavrenty Beria (the most publicly and unequivocally condemned of Stalin's lieutenants), or they used the self-explanatory date, "1937."[57] Among Dudintsev's correspondents of 1956–1959, those who admitted having been imprisoned were few and far between—only five, on my latest count.[58] Even those tended to write about the camps in reserved, reticent language. For example, former engineer Genrietta Rubinshtein, who had spent almost twenty years in the concentration camps and in exile and still resided in the settlement of Iagodnyi, Magadan region, wrote a detailed letter about her experiences of bureaucratic abuse in the Far East. However, in response to Dudintsev's agenda, she focused on the abuses *outside* the camps, bypassing the much more terrifying reality of the camps themselves.[59] Some of those who had suffered during the terror employed the fifth-column imagery of subversion, ascribing the terror itself to the "wrecking" activities of "enemies"—those Drozdovs again. "The Drozdovs, Shutikovs, and the like were able to establish themselves precisely because there was 1936–1938 [*sic*]; and on the other hand, so many people perished precisely because there were so many of those Drozdovs, Shutikovs, Nevraevs, and Abrosimovs," wrote Rita Bek, a Moscow librarian whose mother and father had perished during the 1930s.[60]

For readers to recognize the connection between the (precariously condemned) Stalinist terror and the witch-hunting impulses that Dudintsev's novel provoked in their own minds, discussions of the terror needed to become detailed and nuanced, thus prompting people to contemplate their own implicit participation in such purges through their deeds, words, and beliefs. To reach that stage, the polemic about camps, deportations, and executions had to be not only broad but also open and legitimate. The readers also needed to realize, through the help of literature and the press, the enormity and pervasiveness of the terror experience. Exceptions aside, and despite the revelations of the Twentieth Party Congress, by the late 1950s that realization was only dawning.

In the Long Run

Not all the readers of *Not by Bread Alone* looked for scapegoats. The novel did lead several letter writers to search for more profound origins of society's problems, rejecting the "bureaucratic" explanation as reductionist and simplistic. Thus, I. M. Smirnov from the Crimea wrote that it was "only in a society suffering from grave defects" that the bureaucrats portrayed in the novel could function.[61] An engineer from Moscow, N. I. Gerasimov, produced a forty-page critique of Dudintsev's novel, praising it but also arguing that it failed to analyze the nature of the socioeconomic crisis deeply enough. Gerasimov questioned the book's principal tension, the conflict between a progressive inventor and malicious bureaucrats. In his opinion, Dudintsev exaggerated "the role and significance of a single individual doing good or evil" by presenting social improvement as the work of a few discoverers hovering high above the rest of humanity. The other side of the coin, he wrote, was Dudintsev's overstatement of the power of a few corrupt bureaucrats to block the advancement of the entire society. As the engineer Gerasimov knew well, reality was more complex than a struggle between individual heroes and villains.[62]

Ivan Rogoshchenkov, a military serviceman, went further. Defending the novel in a letter of no less than fifty handwritten pages, he discussed the conditions that might have created the Drozdovs. Targeting and blaming scapegoats was not a sufficient explanation for society's misfortunes, he argued. The country had traditions that encouraged administrative abuse, inertia, and unrestrained bureaucratic blundering. Back in the early 1930s, the breathtaking tempo of industrialization imposed from above had produced a special type of ruthless manager who cared only about production and disregarded the people's basic needs. This type of administrator had survived into the present, Rogoshchenkov believed, and it was they whom the image of Drozdov embodied. He did not question the need for industrialization or the existence of enemies ("wreckers" and "kulaks") in the past. However, Rogoshchenkov insisted, enemies were no longer around. The struggle for socialism had been won, so administrative practices ought to move toward a greater appreciation of the people's needs. Given his attention to the past, and the fact that as early as 1956–1957 he sought more analytical explanations for social ills than mere scapegoating, one would like to know how Rogoshchenkov would read Solzhenitsyn's *One Day in the Life of Ivan Denisovich* a few years later.[63]

For some people the imaginary divide between the social good and evil, embodied in the struggle of positive literary heroes against a variety of literary villains, was becoming an increasingly unsatisfactory rationale for society's omnipresent flaws. As of the late 1950s, such letter writers were still few, compared with the many more who kept reproducing the old, familiar witch-hunting logic. And yet Dudintsev's book inspired a discussion of these issues, and a search for explanations. The answers were not there, but the questions remained and mounted over time.

Responses to *Not by Bread Alone* arrived throughout 1958 as well, but their numbers gradually diminished to a handful. Only seven came in in 1959, and just twenty-five more that mentioned the book would arrive over the next six years.[64] Practically all of them supported it, but the heated polemic had clearly subsided. In January 1965, a Moscow stenographer, A. Vasil'eva, remembered how enthusiastically readers had greeted the novel just eight years earlier. She complained that "*Not by Bread Alone* is now completely forgotten by many, and young people do not know it at all." It was clear to her that 'the Drozdovs and Agievs [*sic*, also a sign of forgetting]" had gained the upper hand and done "their best to finish off the novel."[65] Professor S. P. Khromov from Moscow University still admired the book eight years after its publication, not only for its social charge but also, he claimed, because of Dudintsev's "tense mastery and art of precise and fine exterior portraiture combined with psychological analysis."[66] Both Vasil'eva and Khromov suggested that the novel be republished, while Khromov even used the word "rehabilitate," arguing that Dudintsev had become "one of the last victims of the personality cult."[67]

Contrary to their expectations, *Novyi mir* reacted coldly to these two letter writers. Professor Khromov received a note from Tvardovskii himself (by then back in his editorial seat), which stated: "I do not share your apologetic evaluation of Dudintsev's novel *Not by Bread Alone*. Despite its many strong aspects, it strikes me as largely false and tendentious."[68] Tvardovskii's deputy, Aleksei Kondratovich, replied to Vasil'eva that the book "had done its job" and hardly needed republication—something which exasperated Vasil'eva so much that she wrote back asking whether "doing its job" was the sole purpose of a work of literature.[69] A similar response from Kondratovich urged Konstantin Gorpinich, a physics teacher from the Ukrainian town of Kriukov-on-the-Dnieper, to write back to *Novyi mir* that the intellectual process initiated by the novel was ongoing, and that regardless of official evaluations, no one could stop it.[70]

It could be this very intellectual process that undermined the readers' admiration for *Not by Bread Alone*. Certainly some readers kept praising the book as late as the mid-1960s, and others may have been even more strongly impressed—as late as 1981, Iurii Lotman quoted one of Dudintsev's characters in a letter to a colleague.[71] The difference, besides the diminishing numbers, was that back in 1956–1957 many of the favorable responses came from young people, mostly college students and soldiers. In the 1960s, every admirer of the novel who identified his or her age was fifty or older, perhaps confirming the stenographer Vasil'eva's comment that the country's youth no longer knew the book.[72] To some extent, the maturity of the letter writers in the 1960s may have also reflected the overall aging of *Novyi mir*'s active audience during Tvardovskii's second editorship (1958–1970), as his literary strategies emphasized remembrance and historical consciousness, themes to which older audiences were more receptive. Yet the fact that Dudintsev's younger readers of 1956–1957 mostly did not return to his novel a few years later does suggest that, in their eyes, the book became obsolete. The novel was reissued in 1968, 1979, and 1990, but it never again evoked a response comparable to that of the late 1950s.[73]

It was for good reasons that *Not by Bread Alone* lost the readers' attention. From the early 1960s onward, such publications as *One Day in the Life of Ivan Denisovich* and Ehrenburg's *People, Years, Life* provoked a truly widespread, open, and sophisticated discussion of the Stalin-era state violence, increasingly urging readers to recognize the country's troubles as structural and deep-seated. As society became ever more retrospective and introspective, people questioned the exclusionary social recipes that had once been so popular. The picture of noble innovators and callous bureaucrats painted by Dudintsev began to fade. In December 1962, engineer G. Levin from Karaganda, age fifty-two, who had spent ten years in the Gulag, remembered Dudintsev's book in a letter to Solzhenitsyn: "We still have fresh memories of the attacks on V. Dudintsev for his *Not by Bread Alone*—which, compared with your story [*One Day*], is merely a children's fairy tale."[74] Enemy images did not entirely disappear during the 1960s, of course, but blaming scapegoats became increasingly unacceptable as even a rhetorical solution for society's troubles. Discussions of the terror and the country's overall historical experience compromised the very idea and language of scapegoating. The debates of the Thaw, to which Dudintsev had so powerfully contributed, outgrew the agenda of his novel.

The readers' polemic about *Not by Bread Alone,* the book that became a symbol of its time, owed much of its language and imagery to the culture of political violence that had taken shape in Russian and Soviet society at least since the turn of the twentieth century and matured under

Stalin.[75] The dismantling of this culture was a lengthy process that only slowly, gradually—and yet steadily—unfolded during the Thaw. As of 1956 and 1957, most admirers of the novel still followed the old rhetorical recipes and paradigms of reasoning. However, *Not by Bread Alone* contributed to a massive intellectual fermentation that eventually transcended the book's conceptual framework. The discussions the novel provoked were, in scale and intensity, unprecedented in Soviet culture. It was these discussions that would ultimately transform readers' minds.

Aftermath

Vladimir Dudintsev survived his zenith of glory and continued to write and publish. However, for two decades after writing *Not by Bread Alone* he remained in relative obscurity and de facto ostracism, his work rarely appearing in print.[76] He focused instead on writing his second and last major book, a novel about Soviet geneticists of the late Stalin years. In his characteristically meticulous manner, he researched this previously unfamiliar subject for years and occasionally even took part in public discussions—such as in October 1965, when writers, scientists, and readers participated in an intense exchange between the journals *Novyi mir* and *Oktiabr'* about the period of Trofim Lysenko's domination in genetics.[77] Dudintsev spoke uncompromisingly against Lysenko's repressive treatment of opponents and posed acute problems in the ethics of science—the theme that became central to his new novel.[78] In the book, he returned to his principal theme of defining good and evil. However, he now approached it in a considerably more sophisticated and mature way, purposely eschewing easy answers and mechanistic formulas. Just as his readers had, Dudintsev had outgrown the ethical and linguistic agendas of *Not by Bread Alone*. Tvardovskii, who as we remember did not hold the first novel in great esteem, immediately recognized the value of the second one and wanted to publish it, in 1965, under the title "The Unknown Soldier."[79] The book, however, did not come out until twenty-two years later, in 1987, during Gorbachev's perestroika. When it finally saw the light of day, the novel had a new, now famous title. It was *The White Garments*—arguably Dudintsev's best work.

The saga of *Not by Bread Alone* cost Simonov his editorial job. On 1 January 1957, *Literaturnaia gazeta* published a large cartoon that portrayed several Soviet writers. The editors of thick journals were depicted as motorcyclists dashing forward, into the future. (Valentin Kataev, the editor of the youth journal *Iunost'*, was shown riding a children's scooter.) One exception was the motorcycle bearing a plaque that read "*Novyi mir.*" It stood idle, with Simonov beside it haplessly pumping a flat tire. The verses that accompanied the cartoon, and were meant to serve as New Year's wishes, poked fun at the editor:

> K. S.! When, crossing mounts and valleys,
> You lead the journal on its own,
> Make sure to load your trunk aplenty,
> Not, so to say, with bread alone![80]

As a result of the political campaign against *Novyi mir,* Simonov was gradually removed from the editorship. He spent most of 1957 and 1958 far away, in semivoluntary retirement in Tashkent, his functions at the journal performed by his deputy and the de facto editor in chief, Aleksandr Krivitskii. On 21 April 1958, via Secretary Ekaterina Furtseva (1910–1974), the Central Committee approached Aleksandr Tvardovskii with an offer to have him succeed Simonov and return to the helm of *Novyi mir.* On 5 May Tvardovskii accepted the offer, and on 19 June he received his official appointment.[81] Thus began the most famous period in the journal's history. The literary and political situation at that moment made it a turbulent beginning.

4

RECALLING THE REVOLUTION

The Pasternak Affair

ON 23 OCTOBER 1958, the Swedish Academy awarded Boris Pasternak the Nobel Prize in Literature. The news provoked a furious response from the Central Committee, even though the authorities in Moscow had long expected this outcome.[1] Despite the general language of the statement from the Nobel Committee, that the award was for "important achievement both in contemporary lyrical poetry and in the field of the great Russian epic tradition," Soviet officials associated the award with Pasternak's *Doctor Zhivago*, and it was that novel against which the brunt of the Central Committee's attack was directed.[2] The reaction had as much to do with the book's unsanctioned publication abroad and the acclaim it received in the West as with the novel's content. Written from 1946 to 1955, *Doctor Zhivago* offered a major ethical, historical, and philosophical reassessment of the Revolution and the Civil War, one of the best-remembered such reassessments to come from within Russia. The novel traced the origins of many evils that plagued the country in the first half of the century to the bloodshed of the Revolution, thus calling into question the foundations of Soviet society that even the Twentieth Party Congress had not attempted to disturb.

A campaign of media denunciation, background pressure, and blackmail forced Pasternak, despite his dignified resistance, to reject the prize on 29 October. By then, on 27 October, a joint meeting of the three highest administrative bodies in the country's literary establishment had expelled him from the Union of Soviet Writers.[3] He may have narrowly escaped expatriation, and on 14 March 1959 Procurator General of the USSR Roman Rudenko personally interrogated him, threatening criminal prosecution.[4] Fortunately the writer did not end up in the dock, but he came close to it, because his unsanctioned publishing of *Doctor Zhivago* in the West led him to face charges of anti-Soviet activity verging on treason.[5] Until his death on 30 May 1960, Pasternak remained persona non grata to the official establishment, a rejection at once provoked and checked by the massive support he received abroad, including a flood of letters from his Western sympathizers.[6] In the scope and intensity of the literary-political turmoil, and in the memories it generated, the crusade against Pasternak had few analogies in literary history.

The Pasternak affair was very much part of the *Novyi mir* story. It started in the journal and unfolded dangerously close to it, involving key figures in both of its editorial boards—Simonov's and Tvardovskii's. The readers understood this well—not incidentally, many responses to the affair were addressed directly to the journal. But this was a *Novyi mir* story from more than just a logistical viewpoint. The polemic around Pasternak's novel ultimately developed into a reexamination of the Revolution as the cornerstone of Soviet history and consciousness. The debate represented a crucial stage in the intellectual trajectory of the journal's audience—the gradual but comprehensive reassessment of the historical, moral, and linguistic foundations of the established order.

Very few in the Soviet Union had read *Doctor Zhivago* before the scandal broke out, although prior to his 1957 publication of the book in Italy, Pasternak had attempted to publish it in the USSR. In particular, he considered *Novyi mir* for this purpose as early as 1947, and a decade later he offered the completed manuscript to the journal. Besides *Novyi mir*, in 1956–1957 he offered the manuscript to other literary periodicals—*Znamia* and the short-lived *Literaturnaia Moskva*—as well as to the Goslitizdat publishing house. Several poems from *Doctor Zhivago* appeared in *Znamia*.[7] And so quite a few editors, not to mention party and KGB officials, were familiar with the book. Some of them even became its admirers, like the Goslitizdat director Anatolii Kotov (1909–1956), who apparently wanted to publish it but died in the middle of the pursuit.[8] For a number of years, starting probably in 1946, Pasternak had read excerpts from the novel and lent copies to friends and even distant acquaintances.[9] Rumors about the book circulated in Moscow, and so did a handful of samizdat copies.[10] Still, those who had actually read *Doctor Zhivago* were few and far between, and until October 1958 the novel had been largely unknown to the broad reading audience.

Despite that fact, many people reacted vigorously to the Pasternak affair. Their reactions were based on very limited information—for the most part, on what was available in the press. Responding, technically, not to the literary text but to its newspaper renditions, and often merely to journalistic portrayals of the accused author, the letters were best described by the contemporary Soviet cliché, *ne chital, no skazhu*—"I have not read, but I will say." This is, however, not a reason to disregard them. On the contrary, it is those letters precisely that reveal, perhaps better than others, the meanings that people were anxious to invest in a text, even, and especially, if it was unread. Such "readings" of unread texts are an excellent source for revealing which agendas of politics, history, and biography troubled the audience most. The "I have not read, but I will say" responses also show how those agendas shaped—and were shaped by—the letter writers' language and attitudes toward the printed word.

On 25 October 1958, shortly after the news of the Nobel Prize, *Literaturnaia gazeta* published several pieces denouncing Pasternak. Among them was an editorial titled "A Provocative Sortie by the International Reaction," and a very long letter to Pasternak from the editorial board of Simonov's *Novyi mir*, to which he had submitted the manuscript. Dated September 1956—and, as it is evident now, drafted in cooperation with the Central Committee's Department of Culture—the letter was signed by five editors of the journal: Boris Agapov, Boris Lavrenev, Konstantin Fedin, Simonov himself, and Aleksandr Krivitskii. With this letter, in which they vehemently and unequivocally rejected *Doctor Zhivago* because of its political philosophy, the editors returned the manuscript to the author.[11]

From the readers' contemporary viewpoint, the most important aspect of this letter lay not so much in the predictable rejection, but elsewhere. In their response to Pasternak, the editors extensively quoted the excerpts from *Doctor Zhivago* that they considered particularly inappropriate. By publishing the letter, the main literary newspaper of the Soviet Union thus inadvertently provided millions of its readers (it had a circulation of 880,000) with glimpses of the actual text of the heretical book.[12]

That same issue of *Literaturnaia gazeta* also contained another letter from *Novyi mir*, this time from the new editorial board headed by Tvardovskii. Dated 24 October 1958 (and thus prepared immediately upon receiving the news of the scandal), the letter was signed by Tvardovskii himself and his team—Evgenii Gerasimov, Sergei Golubov, Aleksandr Dement'ev, Boris Zaks, Boris Lavrenev, Valentin Ovechkin, and Konstantin Fedin. Unlike their predecessors, the new editors were brief. They simply confirmed Simonov's 1956 verdict and declared that Pasternak had been awarded the Nobel Prize for political rather than literary reasons, thanks to the anti-Soviet content of his novel. According to Vladimir Lakshin, Tvardovskii was from the outset uncomfortable with the anti-Pasternak campaign and later regretted his participation in it, claiming that Dmitrii Polikarpov, the head of the Department of Culture, had "cheated" him.[13] At the meeting that expelled Pasternak from the Writers' Union, Tvardovskii spoke against the expulsion and did not vote.[14]

On 26 October, *Pravda* published an article by David Zaslavskii titled "Reactionary Propaganda Uproar over a Literary Weed."[15] Then, on 28 October, *Literaturnaia gazeta* announced Pasternak's expulsion from the Union of Writers due to his "political and moral demise . . . , his treason against the Soviet people and the cause of socialism, peace, and progress, which was paid for by the Nobel Prize for the sake of kindling the Cold War."[16] In early November, *Pravda* published two apologetic but judiciously defensive letters that Pasternak had endorsed rather than written.[17] A few other reactions also appeared in print, the most notorious of them being the 29 October speech by the Komsomol general secretary Vladimir Semichastnyi (1924–2001) at the plenum of the Komsomol Central Committee, where he compared Pasternak to a pig.[18]

All of these publications—especially the letter from Simonov's *Novyi mir* to Pasternak—formed the basis for the readers' opinions of the affair. As was customary for the Soviet press, which often sought to legitimate an official motion with expressions of "popular support," the opinions also immediately became part of the campaign. On 1 November 1958 *Literaturnaia gazeta* published, in full or in part, twenty-two readers' letters under the heading, "Rage and Indignation: Soviet People Condemn B. Pasternak's Behavior." Some had their own titles: "The Right Decision," "The Word of a Worker," "Beautiful Is Our Reality," "A Frog in a Swamp," "Paid Calumny," "From Aestheticism to Moral Demise," "A Shameful Act," and "Slanderer."[19]

The published letters quickly became—and remain today—notorious among the intelligentsia for what is viewed as their offensive ignorance.

Upon reading them, Lidiia Chukovskaia (1907–1996) immediately concluded in her diary that they were a product of journalistic fabrication. "I clearly see before my eyes a wench [*devka*] from the editorial board," she wrote, "—I can hear how she dictated the text to them."[20] The words, "I have not read Pasternak, but I will say," which indeed figured in some of the letters, became a catchphrase that various commentators would cite as a supposedly perfect illustration of how the regime duped and manipulated the passive, ignorant, and unthinking Soviet audience. Perhaps for the same reasons, literary scholars have paid little attention to these responses, despite the fact that the pageant of letters in *Literaturnaia gazeta* was one of the three lengthiest contemporary Soviet publications on the affair.[21] It might have been a common assumption that, in a political campaign so intense, fabricating a semblance of loyal "popular opinion" went without saying; if so, the letters could be safely placed in that category.

The degree of administrative inspiration behind these 1958 letters is certainly worth checking, although fabrication is a problematic notion in a discussion of opinions. Even if someone else authored the letter's text, a signatory could nonetheless share its agenda and viewpoint. But a closer look at the letters—both the published ones, which I had a chance to compare with their originals, and the never-published epistles that have remained in editorial archives—reveals an even more complex story that goes beyond the technicalities of letter writing and leads us into the inner world of their authors.

Arguably, although there was some mobilization of support "from below" for the anti-Pasternak campaign, most of the letters were not products of such creative administrative pressure. Rather, they expressed the ideas and beliefs that originated in the letter writers' backgrounds and life experiences. What indicates this, above all, is their intensely autobiographical nature. Building their own life stories into their letters, readers expanded the Pasternak debate into a polemic on what the Revolution, the Civil War, the intelligentsia, and the fortunes of the existing order meant for them, personally.

The Pasternak Affair through Journalists' Eyes

Let us, however, begin with the administrative-journalistic side of the campaign. On 28 October 1958, shortly after *Literaturnaia gazeta* first published its reaction to Pasternak's Nobel Prize, its editors gathered to discuss how they had put together that issue of the newspaper. It turned out that everything had been done in great haste. The editorial had been written literally overnight. At 7:00 p.m. on 24 October, the instruction came from somewhere above to have the material on Pasternak ready for publication by the next morning. Journalist Boris Leont'ev, who told the story, did not specify which authority had commissioned the editorial but simply said that "the need for the article had emerged."[22] At the moment when it "emerged," the editors knew nothing about Pasternak's award except for the vaguest news of it: the authorities provided no information whatsoever, not even the Swedish Academy's statement about the award.

So, three journalists—Artur Sergeevich Terterian, Nikita Vladimirovich Razgovorov, and a certain Gavrilov—spent a sleepless night on 24–25 October hastily translating and working with articles from German, French, and American newspapers to get information for the editorial. By 7:30 the next morning the editorial and the two *Novyi mir* letters were ready for print.[23] Proud of their own efficiency under stress, at the 28 October meeting the journalists praised one another for their good work and professionalism. Vladimir Soloukhin (1924–1997), a rising star of retrospectivist Russophile prose who worked at the newspaper at that time, chaired the meeting and had actually been there when the urgent order for the article came in. At first, he said, he had doubted whether his colleagues would be up to the task, but when he opened the newspaper the following morning, he was "touched" by "how quickly and well this was done." Valerii Kosolapov (who would in 1970 replace Tvardovskii as *Novyi mir*'s editor in chief) remarked: "Here was shown good training in newspaper effectiveness and craftsmanship." Soloukhin agreed: "Yes, we can put it that way . . . this is really well done. Our newspaper came out of this deplorable event with honor."[24] Interestingly, unlike Riurikov in the Pomerantsev case four years earlier, the current editor in chief of *Literaturnaia gazeta*, Vsevolod Kochetov (1912–1973), who had headed the newspaper since 1955, does not seem to have taken part in these editorial deliberations.

At the next meeting, on 13 November, two weeks after publishing the readers' letters that condemned Pasternak, the editors discussed how those letters had been prepared for publication. This also seems to have taken place under severe time constraints. As the critic V. M. Litvinov described it:

> When writing in our comments about a stream of readers' letters, we sometimes exaggerate. But in this case it was not just a stream—it was a real flood, an avalanche of letters. We have hundreds and hundreds of such letters and telegrams. Our readers reacted to this event very unanimously. . . . On the page we used only the very first letters that arrived. Later others came that were far better, far more interesting, but the page had already been made. Here we wanted to show as many people as possible, so we selected somewhat brief letters.[25]

Despite all their efficiency, then, the editors of *Literaturnaia gazeta* had little opportunity to fabricate readers' letters. At the peak of the Pasternak affair, they had to act on the spot and appeared to be not so much a dark, manipulative force behind the scenes as a stressed-out institution pressured by higher authorities and constrained by extremely narrow time limits. More important, though, the editors did not really need to fabricate any letters. The readers' responses they wished to see kept coming in on their own, in overwhelming quantities, so there was no reason to contrive artificial ones. Pressed for time, the editors could not even afford the luxury of picking and choosing the best letters but used the very first ones available.

While it is impossible to measure the extent to which these letters represented the Soviet audience's reaction to the Pasternak affair, it is worth seeing how the letters chosen for publication compared with the entire pool of such correspondence. According to a summary report prepared in early December 1958 by the head of *Literaturnaia gazeta*'s department of letters, Evgeniia Leonidovna Stashevskaia, and her subordinate Vera Sergeevna Liubimova, from 25 October through 1 December 1958 the newspaper received 423 letters about Pasternak.[26] Of those, 338 letters expressed "*full* solidarity with all the materials that the newspaper had published with regard to the anti-patriotic acts of B. Pasternak." Most letter writers indeed viewed Pasternak's behavior as treasonable, seeing *Doctor Zhivago* as an act of calumny against the Soviet order, the Revolution, and "our achievements." They wrote they were astonished that Pasternak had failed to see the enormous transformative impact of the October Revolution and the people's post-1917 accomplishments. Some argued that Pasternak did not really know the life of his country. Many insisted that he had slandered the Soviet intelligentsia because, rather than standing aloof and apart from the rest of the people, as Yuri Zhivago did in the novel, the best part of the old intelligentsia had sided with "the people" in favor of Soviet power and engaged in building the new socialist society. Quite a few demanded more severe penalties for Pasternak, ranging from exile to criminal prosecution. The writer's own apologetic yet mildly defensive letters to Khrushchev and to *Pravda* did not assuage the readers' anger: many continued to view him as an enemy and demanded reprisals. Several readers, including at least one librarian, argued that Pasternak's writings had never been popular among "simple readers" and had caused nothing but "a sense of bewilderment, irritation, and chaos in the reader's mood" (a common point made about Pasternak since the 1920s).[27]

In the remaining minority of eighty-five letters, according to Stashevskaia, writers varied from expressing reservations about the anti-Pasternak campaign to voicing outright support for Pasternak. Seven of the letter writers said they believed the discussion should have started right away, in 1956, when Pasternak submitted *Doctor Zhivago* to *Novyi mir*, or at least right after the book had been published in the West (1957), when open criticism could have prevented the greater international scandal brought by the Nobel Prize. Twenty-two of the letters (nine of them anonymous) largely condemned Pasternak but argued that the novel should have been published in the USSR, because Soviet readers were mature and conscientious enough to form their own opinions about any book, even a counterrevolutionary one. Ten more responses (five of them anonymous) criticized the brutal tone of the campaign against Pasternak. For example, Komsomol members Vishnevskaia and Vakadaenko from Omsk wrote that a sixty-year-old man (Pasternak was actually sixty-eight) ought not be called a dog or a frog, regardless of what he has written. Finally, the newspaper received forty-two "anonymous letters of anti-Soviet content." Stashevskaia did not expand on this content, but since her report lists letters in the order of readers' decreasing enthusiasm for the campaign against Pasternak, those readers must have supported him.[28]

Stashevskaia wrote her report for internal consumption, and while this does not by itself guarantee its credibility, she had no apparent reason to distort the data. One conclusion that follows from her report is that the editors of *Literaturnaia gazeta* more or less accurately conveyed the general vector of readers' responses in the materials they published. Even though there was no absolute unanimity on the issue, most of those who wrote to the newspaper indeed sided with the official viewpoint and condemned Pasternak. A similar picture emerges from the letters received by *Novyi mir.*

How accurately did the editors reproduce the letters when publishing them? And, more important, who were the letter writers? How and why did they argue their particular viewpoints—either pro or contra Pasternak?

The Readers' Perspective

In the archives of *Novyi mir, Literaturnaia gazeta,* and the Pasternak family, I have located 154 letters that responded to the affair and were sent by or on behalf of more than 319 Soviet citizens.[29] Of these, 104 were dated 1958 and 1959 and 21 more, although undated, were probably penned in the fall of 1958. The different dates, recipients, and archival repositories allow for the groups of letters to check and complement each other. Their degree of congruence is fairly high. Among the letters written to the press, the proportions written in condemnation versus defense of Pasternak are roughly the same as in Stashevskaia's report.[30] *Literaturnaia gazeta*'s archive, moreover, contains seven originals from the group of letters Stashevskaia quoted in her report, and three originals of the letters the newspaper published in excerpts.[31] What they show is that the editors did accurately reproduce the letter writers' ideas, although sometimes edited them stylistically for publication—"making sense" of the letters, or in other words bringing them into linguistic conformity with the standards of newspaper verbal expression.[32] Very few of the condemnation letters (just about ten) carried such "birthmarks" of direct administrative interference as combinations of institutionalized letter writing, clichéd language, and depersonalized argument. Those most often came from army officers writing on behalf of their unit, factory managers claiming to represent their workers, or local writers' and composers' unions.[33] However, the majority of letters condemning Pasternak were not depersonalized but, on the contrary, intensely personal and autobiographical.

Let us take, for example, a letter by Maria Filipovich from Sverdlovsk, a brief excerpt of which appeared in *Literaturnaia gazeta* on 1 November 1958. The excerpt read as follows: "Doctor Zhivago—isn't he a spiritual son of Klim Samgin? Gorky unmasked Samgin. Pasternak, in Zhivago, ~~without wishing it,~~ has unmasked himself."[34] The crossed-out text was taken out by the editors, who removed any potential excuses and ambiguities that might speak in Pasternak's favor. But Filipovich's original letter of

26 October was much longer—six handwritten pages—more complex, and intensely autobiographical.[35]

It appears, first of all, that although she had not read *Doctor Zhivago*, Filipovich was not quite acting out of the "I have not read, but I will say" principle. She liked Pasternak's poetry and even called him "the master of verse." Furthermore, she had a connection to him, as she had once been a classmate and friend of Tatiana Ivinskaya, the sister of Olga Ivinskaia, Pasternak's mistress. Filipovich had visited Olga Ivinskaia at her home back in 1949 and had given her a photograph of herself as a gift, with the inscription, "To the happiest woman in the world, in memory of a wanderer. 15 April 1949." The "wanderer" must have referred to Filipovich's frequent traveling—she was a geologist—while "the happiest woman" apparently alluded to Ivinskaia's romantic relationship with Pasternak that had begun shortly before (in fact, they met in the editorial office of *Novyi mir*, where Ivinskaia then worked). Ivinskaia, by the way, remembered Filipovich's visit.[36]

Probably because of this connection, Filipovich was all the more astounded to learn of Pasternak's novel. Her words of condemnation were harsh:

> The author is not one of us. The author stuffed himself with food produced by collective farmers, used the language that, in its every word, embodies the people's genius, and in response the author spat in the people's faces. Well, such individuals are no big news: they are poisonous mushrooms in the wilderness of capitalism.
>
> But one thing is surprising: that it was Pasternak who did this.
>
> We did not expect this.
>
> Perhaps we should have expected.
>
> But we still did not expect.[37]

It was not Pasternak's publishing abroad that, in Filipovich's eyes, was his principal fault. What she abhorred the most was his individualistic rejection of the Revolution. In her eyes, Pasternak had violated the fundamental duty of the intelligentsia, particularly of a writer—to stay with the people rather than distance himself from them in times of great historic upheaval, to write and publish not for the sake of individual creative self-expression but out of a feeling of social responsibility.

Regardless of how accurately Filipovich interpreted Pasternak's artistic and political principles, she was apparently expressing her own beliefs, in which the traditional values of the intelligentsia and Soviet ideological maxims had merged to the point of seamlessness. What suggests this, above all, is her postscript:

> P. S. Of course, I do not hope that all this [the letter] will be published in your newspaper. I am sure that you will receive hundreds if not thousands of responses similar to mine. Nonetheless, I do not want to keep silent.
>
> M. F.
>
> Forgive me for my imperfect observation of decency. I wrote this in the heat of the moment [*Pisalos' pod goriachuiu ruku*].[38]

It would have taken a very clever letter writer to disguise a fabricated letter by including a postscript—an addendum that usually reveals spontaneous, hasty writing—and to conceal the letter's orchestration by adding that it was written on the spot. A fabricated letter would hardly have ended on a note of apology, either. Finally, had the letter been concocted as part of an organized campaign, Filipovich likely would have expected it to be published. Usually, remarks about writing on the spur of the moment, apologetic endings, and disbelief in the prospect of publication characterized letters from readers who challenged official viewpoints on important political issues rather than supported them, as in this case.

Above all, what points to the authenticity of this letter is its high degree of emotional intensity and the author's autobiographical investment in her writing. Maria Filipovich concluded her letter by saying: "I know Pasternak's poems by heart. I loved them. And this gives me the right to demand that not a single line of his ever appears in the Soviet press."[39] Her political disagreement with Pasternak was all the more bitter because it revealed a crisis of ideals: her favorite poet had not lived up to the same high standards in his political behavior. Her avowal of admiration for his poetry, although made in the past tense, as if stricken through by his political "misdeeds," was an unnecessary and even a potentially harmful gesture during the vicious campaign against Pasternak. All of these factors suggest that Filipovich wrote this letter of her own volition, to express her own deeply internalized ideas.

She was not alone. Nikolai Sokolov, a Muscovite in his late forties or early fifties who identified himself as "a Soviet *intelligent* originating from an old Russian intelligentsia family," considered the image of Yuri Zhivago an insult to himself and the entire intelligentsia. Such types as Zhivago, he wrote, had certainly existed but were by far in the minority and did not characterize the prerevolutionary intelligentsia.[40] As a child, Sokolov had witnessed the Civil War in the small Volga town of Vol'sk. In the letter, he described the day when the White Army took the city and paraded through the downtown. He inserted in his own recollection—in quotation marks and with much dark sarcasm—several passages from *Doctor Zhivago* (which he had taken from *Literaturnaia gazeta*), that contained Pasternak's own descriptions of the Whites:

> Along the street, neatly stepping and singing a frivolous song . . . marched the "boys and juveniles from the unmilitary strata of the capitals' (and local) society,["] as well as more senior people mobilized from the reserves. . . . From time to time, one or another boy or juvenile . . . would leave the ranks, dash into the crowd and stab some unsuspecting youngster in the curious crowd with a bayonet or a broadsword. This happened either because this latter youngster had not volunteered for the White Guard, or because of old rivalries over girls, or simply out of "sheer delighted youthful vigor" [*vostorzhennoe molodechestvo*].
>
> When passing by a two-story building, a group "with expressive, attractive faces" left the ranks, burst into a second-floor apartment and threw an old teacher, Vera Sergeevna Bogomolova whom everyone in town deeply respected, out of the window down on the bayonets of the likewise "sheerly delighted young men."[41]

What Sokolov described was apparently the July 1918 anti-Soviet revolt in Vol'sk, in which students from the local military gymnasium, seminary, and high school indeed had played a significant role and numerous atrocities were indeed committed.[42] In the unlikely event that any of the authorities had recruited Sokolov to write this letter, they chose the right man. Far from blindly identifying with propaganda, he based his condemnation of Pasternak on his own childhood memories. To him, the Civil War was not a paragraph in a newspaper or textbook: it was his own past, traumatic enough to have stayed with him for four decades. The published excerpts from *Doctor Zhivago* suggested to him that Pasternak wished to absolve the Whites of their atrocities and deny the Revolution—something Sokolov could not accept.

Many of the letter writers who defended the Revolution from Pasternak had seen it with their own eyes and had had a chance to compare the Soviet years with the tsarist past they remembered. Of the thirty-six letters that more or less precisely indicated their authors' ages, twenty came from people age sixty and older, and nineteen of those letters denounced Pasternak.[43] Not all of the letter writers were members of the intelligentsia. Konstantin Fedorovich Grigor'ev of the village of Pogost, Leningrad Oblast, a Civil War and World War II veteran, was exasperated by Pasternak's unsympathetic portrayal of the soldier Pamfil Palykh who, in the novel, "hated the intelligentsia, the nobles, and the officers, without slightest agitation, with ruthless, bestial hatred."[44] To this, Grigor'ev responded:

> Look, I am one of those Pamfil Palykhs. Here is how I would reply to him [Pasternak]. Dear friend, tell me please, would you have liked them had you been in my shoes? In the Shamovskaia district [*volost*], Mogilev province [*guberniia*], there was a mansion of Sochilovo. It belonged to a tsar's general. In this mansion, I was a junior shepherd [*podpasok*]. I was ten years old. During the summer, the general's sons, themselves children and cadets, used to come to the mansion. You know how they were brought up? When we were arguing about how birds and other [animals] could swim, they slapped me across the face and said that I had "black blood." I gave them both a due beating. And for that, the manager, himself of "black blood," lashed the whole of me [*ispolosoval vsiu shkuru*] with a knout. I long remembered that! So, why, exactly, are the Pamfil Palykhs supposed to like the nobles? What for are they supposed to like the intelligentsia? . . . Pasternak asks why it was necessary to make the revolution? Precisely so that there would be no nobles and no Pamfil Palykhs.[45]

Grigor'ev went on to remember and explain his own participation in the Revolution:

> I myself burned the mansion of Dobrosel'e, ravaged the mansion of Petropol'e and the mansion of Raevka. . . . And now

> there is a state farm of Dobrosel'e there, and there are women working at the state farm who are heroes of labor. And before, I was a seasonal laborer there, and when Pan Voronich with little *pannas* and *panichi* rode by, I used to take off my hat. And was it me alone? And think of how much dirt was poured into the people's souls. Think of how more or less good-looking girls and women were insulted, and what grief that was for the families of the offended. . . . The people did burn and ravage the mansions, even if those were already ours, for the people were so enraged by the nobles that they burned even what would have stayed with the people anyway. Pasternak asks, in Zhivago's words, why it was necessary to make the revolution. Look, at least in order to disperse all the scoundrels who, while enriching themselves and living at the expense of the peasant and the worker, for his very labor hated him and called him scum [*bydlo*].[46]

To Grigor'ev, the Revolution was a just and righteous cause, a beneficial historic upheaval that had removed the previously insurmountable and offensive caste barriers. He rejected what appeared to him as Pasternak's idealized view of the prerevolutionary past. Grigor'ev had no fond memories of a kind-hearted, enlightened nobility so dear to many among the intelligentsia: on the contrary, he remembered the nobles as arrogant and cruel to the peasants. And so he revolted against what he saw as Pasternak's apprehensive distancing from the people of lower social standing, those who had made the Revolution. There was, admittedly, a defensive note of insecurity in his letter, perhaps in part because he was attacking the unread novel for having questioned the legitimacy of the acts of violence he himself had committed. But Grigor'ev wrote a confident letter overall, not a frantic note of self-vindication. He had nothing against publishing *Doctor Zhivago* in the USSR and even reproached *Novyi mir*'s editors for refusing to do so. Its publication, he believed, would not have ruined anyone's support for Soviet power. "Having read it, every worker and peasant would say: right we were to have replaced 'God save the tsar, the powerful, the sovereign' with 'Arise, you prisoners of starvation.'"[47] Grigor'ev even approved of Pasternak's sending his novel to be published abroad, since that, he thought, could not really compromise the unquestionable superiority of the Soviet present over the tsarist past:

> And what about today? You cannot ignore the intelligence of the people that has produced a revolution in technology, in art, in literature—all this has been done by the people, and what people! The people free of nobles, landlords, and capitalists, and consisting of workers, peasants, and the intelligentsia that have come from the depths of the people. The entire world reads our writers, and you even have been awarded the Nobel Prize. What's bad about that?
>
> As for me, I am glad for you, but I know well that, had *Novyi mir* published your book, you would have received many letters from the people calling your Doctor Zhivago a puny little character [*melkaia dushonka*].[48]

The media's language certainly made its way into Grigor'ev's letter. He kept the hierarchies of terms as the press had them—"a revolution in technology, in art, in literature," "landlords and capitalists," "the workers, the peasants, and the intelligentsia"—and reproduced the characteristic self-perception of Soviet culture as appealing to the rest of the world. And yet the formulas quickly disappeared once he came to the main theme of his letter, the Revolution. There he wrote in his own words, clearly and forcefully arguing against the ideas of *Doctor Zhivago* as he saw them, and defending the Revolution on the basis of his own experience. His reproduction of propagandistic truisms did not mean that he had thoughtlessly copied them into his letter. Had Grigor'ev's letter been a fabrication, it would not have been so long, detailed, autobiographically contemplative, and vehemently defensive as it was. Had this and other similar letters about Pasternak been written by decree, had some girl from the editorial office dictated them, as Chukovskaia imagined, their confessional intensity of argument would have been simply not needed.

Many letter writers who remembered the country before and after 1917 neither shared Pasternak's view of the Revolution as a catastrophe nor idealized prerevolutionary Russia. In their eyes, the Revolution was just and necessary—and the Soviet cause was honorable—because, compared with the old regime, the Soviet power had indeed improved the fortunes of many people and extracted Russia from the historical dead end at which it had found itself by 1917. Pasternak's preoccupation with the value of human life did not rank highly with these letter writers, either. To them, the blame for the Civil War atrocities lay not with the supposedly "dark" people who had committed them, but primarily with the old regime and its dominant classes, which had kept the lower orders of society down at an ignominiously low level of material existence, education, and self-esteem. The atrocities of the Civil War came as retribution for the aloofness, arrogance, and disregard that the aristocracy (and even the intelligentsia) had so often displayed toward the lower castes. In the eyes of these people, the Revolution was beneficial, because it had brought about tangible improvements—in their daily lives, and primarily in their sense of self-worth.[49]

We do not know how those same letter writers would have reacted to Pasternak's ideas had they actually read *Doctor Zhivago*. Subsequent developments, especially the impact of Solzhenitsyn's *One Day in the Life of Ivan Denisovich*, suggest that a powerful literary text can radically alter readers' perspectives, even if initially it elicits protest. As of 1958, framed by the propaganda campaign and available to readers only in brief excerpts torn out of context, Pasternak's novel could not possibly have had the world-shattering influence on the readers' minds that Solzhenitsyn later would. What may also partly explain the extent of the negative reaction to Pasternak was the widespread anti-Western sentiment in Soviet society. Despite the opening to the West that came about during the Thaw, this was still the time of the Cold War, and its publication abroad did make the novel, intentionally or not, a weapon in the hands of Western media not exactly well-disposed toward the Soviet Union.

All in all, though, it would be unfair to regard the massive condemnation of Pasternak as solely the effect of "propaganda," however that is understood. Initiated by the letter writers themselves, the condemnations were a logical product of life experiences and worldviews. The Revolution remained central to these people's consciousness and socioethical order, the sacred foundation of a mental universe, and their reaction to the Pasternak affair was above all a defense against any attempt, real or imaginary, to undermine this intellectual cornerstone of their existence.

Defending Pasternak

Given that only five years had passed since Stalin's death, a remarkable number of letter writers—about 20 percent—openly criticized the campaign against Pasternak or even defended him. Fear did exist, judging by the fact that all of the forty-two letters of "anti-Soviet content," and quite a few others expressing reservations about the campaign, were written anonymously. The fear was justified, too. *Literaturnaia gazeta*'s archive has kept only one letter defending Pasternak, which suggests that the editors forwarded the others to higher authorities, possibly to the KGB. The fear factor also implies that the share of Pasternak supporters might have been greater than the share of those who actually wrote in his defense.

Who supported Pasternak, and why? An overview of the responses points first of all to younger readers. Among the twelve letters from people age thirty and under, five (four of them dated 1958–1959) supported the writer, three denounced him, and four were rather neutral. His defenders could be found among all age groups, but the young stood out for how often they did so, and for the language they used.[50]

Sometime in late October or November 1958, S. Udris, a female student at the Leningrad Pedagogical Institute, wrote to *Literaturnaia gazeta* demanding that *Doctor Zhivago* be published in the Soviet Union. "It seems to me," she wrote, "that you should not create an aura of obscurity around the book. Whenever I hear people talking about this book, their talk boils down to the following—the book's content matches reality [*sootvetstvuet deistvitel'nosti*]. As you see, the reaction is diametrically opposite to the one you probably would like to provoke. Once again! The less obscurity, the better: we want to know everything ourselves."[51]

The "we" that Udris mentioned, as well as the "people talking about this book," were likely her fellow students. Many young readers rejected, a priori, the newspaper interpretation of the affair, precisely because it came from a newspaper. "I have not read the book, but judging by the slanderous articles, I have formed a good impression of it," someone with an illegible signature communicated to Pasternak in January 1959.[52] Leonid Gonchar, twenty-eight, from an Altai village of Len'ki, packed his letter to the writer with bitter criticism of contemporary everyday life and the misadministration of local authorities—whom he repeatedly referred to as "they." Against this background of social ills, he praised and welcomed Pasternak's book. Gonchar and his friends had not read the novel, either, he wrote, but it must contain major criticism of the contemporary social conditions, he reasoned—otherwise why would the newspapers curse it so much? "In general, comrade writer," he reported in the fashion of Soviet public rallies, "many people are on your side, that is, they approve what you've written—which they certainly have not read, but they feel it, just because the Simibratovs have been up in arms. . . . [T]his is something like *Not by Bread Alone*, with which the entire reading Russia was down for a while."[53]

Just as Pasternak's opponents did, his defenders reacted not as much to *Doctor Zhivago* as to their own idea of what the novel must describe. In view of contemporary problems that troubled them, it was their notion of *a certain Doctor Zhivago* that they upheld—their wishful thought of a socially charged and critical book that would blast away the existing reality, just as Dudintsev's *Not by Bread Alone* had done two years before.[54] The defenders' radicalism was limited: whether out of conviction or habit, as a device of advocacy writing, or in a combination of these motives, they often stayed within politically acceptable language and logic.[55] Just like some accusers, who contemptuously styled Pasternak "Mister," Gonchar repeatedly called him "Comrade." A few other letter writers similarly tried redeeming the writer, perhaps for themselves as much as for the authorities, by claiming his immanent Sovietness.[56]

Such a defense of Pasternak was an "I have not read, but I will say" turned upside down. The press cursed the writer, so he must be a truth teller. As art historian Mikhail German, who was twenty-five in 1958, remembered it forty years later: "Of course, we scornfully laughed at the famous 'I have not read Pasternak, but I can say.' But we ourselves quite similarly, having not read *Doctor Zhivago* either, believed that the novel was a work of genius. With our miserable slavish negativism, were we any better than those who reviled the poet?"[57] While German's observation is incisive, the negativism revealed not only a continuing intellectual dependence on the media's language, but also a significant, and defiant, mistrust of it—an important sign of the times that had already revealed itself in readers' reactions to the media denunciation of Pomerantsev in 1954 and Dudintsev in 1956–1957. Over the next few years of the Thaw, this precarious equilibrium between reliance on media scripts and a growing search for other intellectual, ethical, and linguistic authorities would be increasingly imbalanced in the latter's favor.

Pasternak probably never received Gonchar's letter, because the editors of *Novyi mir* never forwarded it to him—in this case they apparently did not follow their usual practice of forwarding typed copies of readers' letters to the author. Anticipating similar obstruction, or possibly reprisals, a few young people sent him letters of support via Irina Emel'ianova, Ivinskaia's daughter and a student at the Literary Institute in Moscow.[58] She was probably not the only channel for such private communications. In Evgenii Pasternak's archive, at least one letter of admiration and praise for his father, written by a certain Kruglov on the day he learned of Pasternak's expulsion from the Writers' Union, is marked "received not by mail."[59] Many of Emel'ianova's classmates tried their best to avoid signing a collective letter denouncing Pasternak that the institute administration imposed on them: when a committee responsible for collecting signatures was going room by room around the dormitory, the students would lock their doors or escape to kitchens and bathrooms. In the end, only 110 out of about 300 students signed the letter.[60]

Among the intelligentsia, Pasternak had always had a special status, which greatly increased during the Thaw. Even before the affair, many writers and students developed the habit of making pilgrimages to his home in Peredelkino, sometimes just for a few minutes of conversation. With his literary fame, consistent remoteness from officialdom, and now the intense political discussions raised by his novel, he became an alternate moral authority, precisely what many people increasingly sought at the time—a person to whom they turned for guidance in questions not only of literature but also ethics.[61] Diarists and memoirists agree that youths were very visible at Pasternak's funeral on 2 June 1960: nearly everyone remembered a crowd of students reading his poetry at the grave until dusk on that day.[62]

Other characteristic forms of protest against the campaign also developed among young people. Memoirs relate that at the peak of the affair three students, including the poets Leonid Vinogradov and Vladimir Ufliand, painted "Long Live Pasternak!" in white on the granite Neva embankment near the Summer Garden in Leningrad.[63] Prior to that, Vinogradov, Ufliand, and their friend and fellow poet Mikhail Eremin, had mailed to *Pravda* a knockout response to a 26 October 1958 article written by its eldest journalist, David Zaslavskii (1880–1965), in which he called Pasternak a "literary weed."[64] The students' letter was made up of two quotations—the first, from a verse urging children to remember and study Lenin, and the second, from Lenin's own scornful remarks about Zaslavskii. *Pravda*'s most venerable columnist indeed was old enough (older than Pasternak himself, in fact) to have participated in Russian political life before the Revolution, and back then he had happened to be fervently anti-Bolshevik. In 1917 Lenin had repeatedly blasted Zaslavskii, fuming about "a dirty campaign of calumny by the dirty Messrs. Zaslavskii," "the rascals of blackmail—the Miliukovs, the Gessens, and the Zaslavskiis," and "the hired blackmailing pens (such as Zaslavskii and Co.)."[65] Lenin's words sounded quite topical for the Pasternak affair: "Mr.

Zaslavskii has acted only as a scandalmonger. We need to distinguish . . . a slanderer and scandalmonger from an unmasker [*razoblachitel'*], who demands the discovery of precisely identified facts."[66]

When quoting Lenin, the Leningrad students employed the common (and in this case, clearly sarcastic) device of legitimizing dissent by recruiting an indisputable ideological authority and, moreover, by pitting two such authorities against each other—*Pravda* of 1958 against Lenin of 1917. This must have been a fairly regular exercise among Pasternak's sympathizers. Ivinskaia, too, remembered the Lenin-versus-Zaslavskii ruse.[67] This tactic of playing on the internal contradictions of ideological messages should have sounded the alarm for Soviet propagandists. Here was an unmistakable sign that the dominant political language was losing its dynamism and flexibility and degenerating into a compendium of quotations, with its contenders using its ossified phrases to rhetorically outmaneuver it.[68] It was especially noteworthy that such tactics were being employed by young people, supposedly the new Soviet generation.

It would be an exaggeration to say that readers' reactions to the Pasternak affair revealed a clear-cut generation gap. Not all younger people defended Pasternak, and not all seniors condemned him. However, the young did react more flexibly and diversely, they did sound more politically defiant, and they did seem more readily fascinated with Pasternak. Whereas for many relatively senior letter writers the Revolution remained the foundation of their worldview, to the younger people it had become a distant past that was gradually losing its axiomatically heroic aura and the prophetic capacity for giving ready answers to all questions of politics and history.

Seeds of Doubt

The young people's fascination with Pasternak revealed, and originated in, the intellectual instability of the time, to which youth proved especially sensitive. With the established interpretation of the Stalin past having been officially undermined only two years earlier, Pasternak's ethical reassessment of the Revolution made the legitimacy of the Soviet order more questionable than ever. Some young people perceived, and acutely reacted to, this loss of historical and ethical landmarks. In his five-page handwritten letter dated 30–31 October 1958, a young physician's assistant, Bogomolov, from a village in Chernigov Oblast, Ukraine, produced no less than an outline of the intelligentsia's entire history under Soviet power.

Rejecting what he saw as Pasternak's apology for individualism (he went so far as to compare Yuri Zhivago to the Nazi doctors who had sacrificed human lives for the benefit of the chosen few) and the intelligentsia's elevated aloofness from the Revolution, Bogomolov concluded:

> All this chat [Pasternak's defense of the supreme value of individual human life] aims at disorienting the working people, distracting them from the fight for their rights, and at ruining their purposeful lives. No! You will not succeed, Mister Pasternak! One is born to live, and he lives. But he is also obliged to prepare a better life for future generations! . . . That way [if one follows Pasternak's reasoning] one can logically come to the end of the world [*do krusheniia mira*].[69]

What is most interesting in this passage is not Bogomolov's reproduction of propagandistic formulas but his fear that disorientation could lead "to the end of the world." This fear reveals his anxiety about the malfunctioning of those very formulas and their explanatory power. And it was this fear that compelled the young physician's assistant to spend two days in his village writing a "historical" rebuff to Pasternak. The writer's ideas, although Bogomolov received them in a processed and curtailed newspaper version, challenged everything that he, Bogomolov, had ever read and learned. His protest, for which he mobilized all his textbook knowledge of history, was so furious because it was a desperate defense of his own emotional and intellectual stability.

Perhaps Bogomolov was not alone. It might have been for the same reason that so many condemnations of Pasternak were so furious. It was a sudden unrest of thought and conscience—the fact that the controversy impelled people to think, shaking the previously unshakable cornerstone of their historical consciousness, disturbing the certainty of their beliefs and the ostensible quiet of their distant past—that explained the "rage and indignation" with which so many letter writers reacted to the Pasternak affair.

For a while, impressions of the affair proved fairly stable. Three years later, in 1961, Tvardovskii's *Novyi mir* published a chapter of Ilya Ehrenburg's memoir *People, Years, Life* in which, a year after the poet's death and for the first time in Soviet press, there appeared a sympathetic explanation of Pasternak's behavior. Ehrenburg tried to rehabilitate Pasternak in the customary Soviet way—the one Stalin reportedly had used when he decided not to obliterate Pasternak—that is, by suggesting his innocent otherworldliness.[70] To this, the readers reacted largely in the same way as before. Many senior people kept blaming Pasternak for treason—for publishing his book in the West, slandering the memory of the Revolution, and so on.[71] Younger readers, again, tended to be more accommodating.[72] Since in 1961 the authorities were no longer interested in organizing any campaign against the dead poet, no one would have forced the letter writers to express these views. The similarity between the letters of 1961 and those of 1958–1959 again indicates that the readers' immediate reactions to the Pasternak affair had had strong intellectual and autobiographical foundations.

And yet new overtones also appeared in readers' comments about Pasternak during the early 1960s. Lev Erleksov, sixty-nine, from the town of Novokuibyshevsk, thanked Ehrenburg for his depiction of Pasternak, whom he "respected and loved," despite his "egocentrism."[73] Boris Kultyshev from Novosibirsk, an admirer of Pasternak's poetry, thanked Ehrenburg for his discussion of the affair: "When this 'Zhivago' appeared, I was puzzled: what had happened there? Your explanation completely satisfied me. Casting away all rumors, I can now understand the tragedy of this talented man." One cannot know how the reader might have reacted had someone proved to him that Pasternak published his novel abroad not innocently, but in full realization of the political consequences of his act. But at the moment, perhaps, the pretext of naïveté was the wisest, safest strategy for stopping the attacks and the blaming. Kultyshev acknowledged that an author could write well even if his or her writings did not fit the official dogma, and argued for everyone's right to read a book without official guidance. He even brought up another literary name recently revived from oblivion—that of the poet Marina Tsvetaeva (1892–1941): "Or, take M. Tsvetaeva. Why can't we say that a poet is good without adding 'ideologically correct' [*ideinyi*]?"[74]

Overall, in the 1960s there was less anger, less "rage and indignation," and more reflection on what had happened—on how a writer could and was entitled to act. For some people, the brutal denunciation of Pasternak seems to have produced a lasting opposite result: a favorable interest in his writing. N. A. Nadeliaev, from the village of Barluk in Siberia, had known almost nothing about Pasternak before the 1958 campaign. However, he wrote, "they so laboriously and interestingly cursed him that I now want to read *Doctor Zhivago* and also something about the book's author."[75]

Evgenii Borisovich Pasternak remembers that in the 1960s and 1970s, his father's home in Peredelkino became destination not just for individual pilgrimages but for organized bus excursions. He himself lectured on Pasternak's poetry at several major plants and factories, where workers listened with great interest.[76] Perhaps, as political fumes cleared and time offered opportunities to think and read, Pasternak conquered some of his erstwhile accusers.

The 1958–1959 polemic around *Doctor Zhivago* was an embryonic historical and political debate that contributed to the growing anxiety about the sacred center of the Soviet world, the foundation of its legitimacy—the idea of the Revolution. The debate revealed generational differences in understanding Russia's past and present. Whereas for people of older ages the Revolution largely remained the foundation of intellectual and ethical stability, among youth the revolutionary ideal was waning, apparently with no comparable set of values capable of replacing it. In its stead there came an increasing sense of political, cultural, ethical, and linguistic insecurity. The defiantly negativistic disposition of many young people toward anything the press had to say in the campaign revealed a continuing intellectual dependence on the media and the lack of an autonomous language of self-expression. But it also indicated a profound and increasing crisis looming for the media's persuasive potential, suggesting that an elemental mistrust of propaganda could, in due course, become programmatic.

The Pasternak affair was a major step in that direction. During the affair, the central elements of Soviet historical consciousness became intensely and openly contested issues. Whether they attacked or supported Pasternak, readers shared a fundamental sense of disorientation, a shaken world no longer confident in the uprightness of its historical path and moral basis. This was already a much less stable culture than the one that had revealed itself in response to Pomerantsev four years earlier. Started in February 1956 at the Twentieth Party Congress, the reexamination of the past, and inevitably the present would continue for years, embracing new themes and producing long-term effects. In this sense, the Pasternak affair, which is often perceived as antithetical to the reformist line of the Twentieth Congress, had consequences similar to those of Khrushchev's "Secret Speech."

The journal *Novyi mir*, around which the affair unfolded, stood at the very center of these developments. It was precisely at this time, after the

Pasternak affair, that the classic *Novyi mir,* whose agendas we know today, began to emerge. It rose on the crest of the intellectual processes that had begun to unfold earlier in the 1950s, manifesting themselves in the polemics about Pomerantsev, Dudintsev, and Pasternak. But the main intellectual transformations of the Thaw were still ahead. They would be inseparably tied with *Novyi mir*'s publishing strategies, which took their ultimate form with Aleksandr Tvardovksii's return to the journal in 1958.

5

LITERATURE ABOVE LITERATURE

Tvardovskii's Memory

TVARDOVSKII RETURNED to *Novyi mir* on 20 June 1958, four summers after his departure. The years of his second editorship, from 1958 to 1970, became the journal's classical period, the peak of its glory, when *Novyi mir*'s strategic "line" took its ultimate shape. Much of this line came from the editor himself. Memoirists and historians are unanimous in arguing that *Novyi mir* became what it was largely owing to Tvardovskii, and documents confirm that his role at the journal was crucial. Tvardovskii had enormous authority as a poet and writer in his own right, and he combined this with the heavy political weight he wielded, far heavier than that of all the other members of his editorial team together. His name was a major factor behind the success and longevity of *Novyi mir* as a literary and cultural phenomenon. From the start he assembled a coherent, devoted editorial board (being able to hand-pick his board was a condition on which he had accepted the appointment), a group of people who worked closely with him but could also function independently.[1] He read all major incoming manuscripts, personally editing many of them for publication, and kept up an intense correspondence with authors and readers. He set a high standard for quality and a collegial, informal tone in editorial discussions.[2] His opinions about literature were strong, at times verging on the authoritarian, and his word in all publication issues was decisive. To a great extent (although not exclusively), *Novyi mir* was indeed Tvardovskii's own project.

This meant more than just his capacity as editor. Tvardovskii was the first and foremost reader of the journal—and indeed, the intellectual evolution of Soviet literary audiences during the Thaw in many ways followed his own intellectual evolution, which he had gone through earlier than many others and deliberately made into a strategy informing his editorial decisions. The strategy incorporated his own biography, Pomerantsev's notion of sincerity, Ovechkin's and Dudintsev's socioethical criticism, Pasternak's questioning of the Revolution, and, generally and above all, the problem of conceptualizing and verbally representing the tragedies of the country's recent past. The search for authenticity—historical, moral, and linguistic—was the essence of Tvardovskii's literary effort. At its heart lay the idea that historical experience transformed literature, and thereby life itself.

To understand this effort, one needs to look at Tvardovskii closely. From his papers, manuscripts, and diary, the editor in chief of *Novyi mir* emerges as both a literary figure and a historical thinker on a major scale—one of the most important intellectual figures in twentieth-century Russia.

Age

One impression immediately strikes a reader of Tvardovskii's diary—the author's perception of age. Although he lived a relatively short life (1910–1971), Tvardovskii quite early began to see himself as an old man. In October 1954, at the age of forty-four, he wrote in the diary:

> What year since and since what day,—
> I do not know that precisely,—
> A debt is burdening, oppressing me—
> For each occasion, torment is in storage.
>
> To life, to people, and to books I am indebted,—
> And all the harder is the payment pending,
> For all my good I have received from them,
> While of my own I had a meager handful.
>
> Sometimes it seems to me: I'll pay it all,
> Pay off without delay and with a surplus,

At other times, it seems that I cannot,
And every day I ask for a deferral.

And this becomes unbearable sometimes—
My strength is vanishing; old age is coming close,
And for a final tally time arrives,
And much remains unpaid on my account![3]

"Very poor" was Tvardovskii's strict judgment of these lines. He wrote them two months after his first dismissal from *Novyi mir* and would return to them several times later, polishing the verse.[4] Despite his self-criticism, the idea of the poem—an acute awareness of his own aging, imminent death, and debts unpaid—would be central to his life and work for years. It would often surface in his diary.

November 1954: "Something strange is happening to me. I have become so old spiritually that even the golden reserve of my soul—remembrances of childhood, dear nature, seasons of the year, dreams about 'the main book'—even all that has faded somehow and is no longer a safe haven from transient troubles."[5] October 1955: "I have little strength, my wishes are short-lived—could it really be old age? But—nonsense."[6] October 1956: "[My] strength and years are clearly not the same as before, and 'the threat of not managing on time' (T. Mann) becomes ever more vivid."[7] The same month, on a more optimistic note, quoting the famous diary of the censor Aleksandr Nikitenko (1804–1877): "There is a certain great consolation in that you feel, at the twilight of your days, still enough strength to go forward, rather than staying behind or at the same spot all the time. So, forward, forward, until we stumble over a grave—into which it is better to fall headlong than to crawl up to it like a worm."[8]

February 1957, on having found a quotation from his poem in a brochure: "This is also a sign of old age."[9] January 1958, at the age of forty-seven and the day before his wife's and daughter's birthday: "Masha is turning 50 tomorrow. Olia 17. I bought an 'album for verses'—in a velvet jacket, a product that even feels awkward to buy, as if it were something from a drugstore. . . . Wrote little senile verses [*starikovskie stishki*], saying that perchance we'll live to see our great-grandchildren."[10] September 1960, in the Crimea, after talking to a Czech composer who was scared of having grandchildren because he believed it was an ultimate sign of aging (Tvardovskii by then had a five-year-old grandson): "I laughed, although frankly, I am not getting along with my age that easily. . . . There remains a straw of hope, characteristic of human weakness, that this is not it yet. And to say: yes, this is it, but instead I have such and such achievements and spiritual accomplishments—no, I don't want this, although I may have nothing in fact besides that shaky spiritual compensation."[11]

In December 1959 and January 1960 he tried hard, and managed, to avoid going to the United States as the head of a Soviet writers' delegation—a reaction that was uncommon at this time of widespread fascination with the West, when foreign tourism beckoned scores of Soviet individuals.[12] Tvardovskii did not speak English, felt awkward about facing a new and unfamiliar country, and, above all, had much to do at home. He was about to turn fifty, a barrier that he perceived as "a threshold of old age," so two months of writing were more important for him than two months of cocktail-party conversations. A couple of days after his fiftieth birthday, he commented on Turgenev's words: "After fifty you live, in effect, in a besieged fortress, which will have to be surrendered, one way or another, in the not-too-distant future." Tvardovskii the war veteran developed Turgenev's military metaphor, working out a plan of defense for himself-as-fortress: fight as long as possible, do not limit yourself to defense but also undertake sorties, observe the regimen within the fortifications, expend ammunition sparingly, and maintain discipline and morale in the garrison. With age perceived so acutely, time for work became precious. Aging meant a multitude of tasks unaccomplished—texts unwritten, words unspoken, problems unsolved.[13]

However, Tvardovskii was not only uncomfortable about his advancing age, and his perception of aging was not always negative or apprehensive. He also seemed to take special pride and comfort in his idea of aging and in picturing himself as old. At forty-five, while at his dacha the poet was "enjoying my old man's [*starikovskii*] business of woodcutting, working about the house, and getting ready for the winter."[14] Five years later, when planning a visit to the countryside home of his friend, the writer Ivan Sokolov-Mikitov, he looked forward to "getting myself going to Karacharovo, to have some respite with Ivan Sergeevich, in an old men's fashion [*po-starikovski*]."[15] Sokolov-Mikitov (1892–1975) was eighteen years Tvardovskii's senior. A few months later, in the fall of 1960, Tvardovskii wrote at his dacha: "With an old man's pleasure [*so starikovskoi usladoi*], familiar to me since childhood, I gather a basket of last year's firewood from my clearings—boughs of aspen, walnut, apple-tree boughs from last year's pruning, stumps and twigs, and then stoke both of my stoves."[16]

His early perception of himself as an older man may have come not only from a sense of pressing and overdue responsibilities, but also from the idea that age brought its own advantages. It was not accidental that he mentioned childhood in this diary entry. Reverence for old age was a traditional peasant value, which he might have inherited from his early years in the countryside, together with the customary perception of a man of fifty as old. Attention, respect, and a special fondness for older people were Tvardovskii's distinct qualities. Thus, in the diary he would carefully record conversations between elderly men and women he overheard at a local store, gently sketching notes about their intonations, bearing, and appearance.[17]

By contrast, he felt much less comfortable when writing about youth. In January 1958, when he read his newly finished story, "The Oven-Makers," to his wife, Maria Illarionovna, her response was generally positive, except for one reservation: the young teacher in the story did not sound young at all. He sounded like an elderly man, and so it might be better to make him older, she thought. Tvardovskii kept the character as he was, but admitted that the teacher indeed seemed somewhat "old-fashioned."[18] Overall, creating images of young people was not exactly his cup of tea. Even when he wrote about the large construction and nature-conquest projects that the contemporary media and literature fashioned as grand exploits of youth, he differed from other writers—such as, for example, Vasilii Aksenov (1932–2009), who wrote at the same time and whose Far East was populated exclusively by twenty-year-olds.[19] Tvardovskii, on the other hand, having traveled to the construction site for the famous Bratsk hydroelectric power plant on the Angara River in Siberia in 1956, chose to write about an old carpenter, Paramon Paramonovich, the only elderly man he met at the construction site, which was packed with youthful workers. Asking himself why he preferred Paramon Paramonovich to the scores of youngsters, Tvardovskii reflected on the general popularity of elderly people's images in Soviet literature, a popularity to which he certainly subscribed:

> Why is it that our literature likes older people so much and cannot do without them? Be it a play, a novel, a poem, or a short story—one cannot do without older people. [That is] because they are broader, more picturesque, more distinctive, richer in

> language and popular wisdom—in a word, more interesting than the young, advanced, leading, and ideologically correct. In literature, older people are allowed more freedom than the young or simply mature. Older people are even allowed to criticize the government and remember the past as good old days. They have more memories, they stem from a thicker layer of years, traditions, and poetry. The past for them means not only need, privations, and hopelessness of fate, but also Easter, Christmas, Epiphany, team haymaking, the fair, the merry-go-round, the village gatherings, the fairy tales, and various other amusing little things. Here [with young people], on the contrary, the layer is thin.[20]

Amid the burgeoning literary and cinematic optimism of the Thaw that celebrated youth, novelty, and a reborn revolutionary romanticism, Tvardovskii's attention to elderly people sounded a dissonant chord. He revered age as a mark of precious life experience, a sign of the wisdom and profound knowledge of human nature that only the past could give. Important to him personally, these values also became central to his work.

Tvardovskii's biographers have shown how his early years were crucial in the formation of his personality. In 1930–1931 his peasant family was branded as kulaks, heavily taxed, and then exiled, in March 1931. Tvardovskii, then a young poet and journalist in nearby Smolensk, had to choose between his parents and his career. A beginning author whose poems about the countryside had already appeared in the local newspapers, he was expressly told by the party secretary of the Western Region (I. P. Rumiantsev, 1886–1937) to renounce his parents. There are times, the secretary told him, when one has to choose between mom and dad, on the one hand, and the Revolution, on the other. Six years later, the secretary would himself perish in a new wave of repression. But in January 1931, following Rumiantsev's advice, Tvardovskii made his choice and renounced his parents.[21] According to his brother, a few months later he again rejected his father, who had escaped from exile and come to him for help. In 1936 he did help his family move back to the Smolensk area, but—at least this is the impression his brother's memoirs create—never again became quite close to them.[22]

Renouncing his parents did not bring him safety. Even before his family's dekulakization, in June 1930 the twenty-year old Tvardovskii had been expelled from the Smolensk chapter of the Russian Association of Proletarian Writers (RAPP) for six months, for his alleged failure as a "proletarian poet."[23] Although in June 1934 he was admitted to the nascent Union of Soviet Writers, he remained under deadly suspicion all through the early 1930s, and his poetry was repeatedly accused of exhibiting kulak sympathies.[24] In July 1934 a local Smolensk newspaper branded him "a kulak yes-man" *(kulatskii podgolosok)*, and he had to go through a fierce two-day-long open debate, which looked more like a trial, defending himself and arguing that he had nothing to do with kulaks. His supporters were in the minority, and although he avoided severe reprisals (the deputy head of the culture and propaganda department of the Smolensk regional party committee eventually said Tvardovskii's "derangements" were not serious enough to warrant "wiping him off the face of the earth"), the danger nonetheless remained grave.[25] It was only his move to Moscow, enrollment since September 1936 at the newly opened and famous Moscow Institute of Philosophy, Literature, and History (MIFLI), and principally the approval of his poem *The Land of Muravia* (1934–1936) by an areopagus of celebrated writers and poets (Pasternak among them) that improved his situation—indeed saved him.[26]

On the night of 21 August 1937, when visiting his friend and fellow litterateur Adrian Makedonov (1909–1994) in Smolensk, Tvardovskii may have narrowly escaped arrest. He left his friend's home just half an hour before the NKVD officers came for Makedonov.[27] His attempts to defend his friend yielded no results. Tvardovskii's name was mentioned numerous times in Makedonov's investigation file, and a letter of denunciation duly recalled his connection to another "enemy of the people," the former regional party secretary Rumiantsev, who had once persuaded him to renounce his family. Fellow writers in Smolensk and Moscow began speaking of Tvardovskii as an enemy, and it looked more than likely that his arrest would soon follow.[28] What probably saved the young poet was the patronage of celebrities, among them Aleksandr Fadeev, and—infinitely more important—a benign attitude on the part of Stalin himself. In February 1939 Tvardovskii was awarded the Order of Lenin. In March 1941 *The Land of Muravia* received a second-degree Stalin Prize in Literature. Fadeev would long remain Tvardovskii's benefactor and friend; only in the last years before Fadeev's 1956 suicide would their relations deteriorate. Stalin, too, would remember the poet favorably.[29]

In July 1939 Tvardovskii graduated with distinction from the Institute of Philosophy, Literature, and History. Two months later he was drafted into the army: World War II had begun. It was the war—the 1939 Winter War with Finland and then the Great Patriotic War—that made him genuinely famous, first of all thanks to his verse epic about the common soldier, *Vasilii Tyorkin.* In 1946, on the height of his literary glory, Tvardovskii received his second Stalin Prize, for *Tyorkin,* and the next year he would receive a third one, for A *House by the Road,* his new major poem about the war. But even before the war Tvardovskii had already gone through many trials. His memories of collectivization, arrests of 1937, and years of living in mortal danger did not go away: on the contrary, they would grow on him. As time went on, the past increasingly pressed for explanations.

Thoughts on the Terror

Although Tvardovskii had certainly reflected on his experiences of state violence long before 1953, it was Stalin's death that prompted him to ponder the recent past with particular intensity. First of all, he turned to Stalin himself. In the winter of 1953–1954 he was working on a chapter of his long poem *Faraways,* which would become the first published literary attempt at critically evaluating Stalin's historic role.[30]

His attitude toward Stalin shows in his diary entry of 31 December 1953: "Yesterday, the chief physician [of the Barvikha health resort], Galenin Konstantin Alekseevich, told me that he had been to I. V. Stalin's 'museum cottage' and saw there Neprintsev's painting (reproduction?), the only one in the house. The guide who accompanies visitors . . . explains that this painting is there upon I. V. Stalin's personal request. I guess the Old Man [*Starik*] liked these laughing lads. If you think about it, this is touching, at once sad and pleasant: you know that this comes from me—this painting that brings him joy."[31]

The painting in question, Yurii Neprintsev's 1951 *Rest after Battle,* depicted happy Soviet soldiers at a moment of respite, and indeed it may have been inspired by Tvardovskii's *Vasilii Tyorkin.* But more important, these lines in the diary offer a glimpse of Tvardovskii's fascination with the image of the nation's supreme authority. He respectfully accompanied Stalin's name with two initials and called him "the Old Man," which—especially coming from Tvardovskii—was a tribute indicating warm reverence for the wisdom of the deceased leader. Moreover, it seems the leader was not quite yet deceased for Tvardovskii, because half a year after his death the poet was still writing about him in the present tense.

Traces of this reverence were to stay with Tvardovskii. His attitude toward Stalin never seemed to have come to a neat sense of closure, with all questions happily answered and all contradictions resolved. By faculty of reason, of course, he went through a reassessment of Stalin during the 1950s and 1960s, and few did more than he, and more consciously, to destroy the Stalin cult. And yet his fascination with Stalin never completely went away. Stalin's image remained important to Tvardovskii's poems, from *Faraways* to his final *By Right of Memory.* Up until his last years, from time to time he would write of Stalin in his diary—in words that sounded like a perpetual knocking down of the idol. It was as if he constantly needed to confirm for himself that the real Stalin and the reality of his time had been different from what they were passed for. Tvardovskii kept looking for and finding more and more confirmations.

17 October 1968: "Shinkuba told me, from the words of a female doctor . . . who was among the physicians tending to Stalin during his last days and hours, that she was surprised by what a little old man he was—lying in bed, narrow-chested, with shriveled small feet and a big hanging stomach." 20 October 1968: "I remember, again from what Shinkuba told me from the words of that female doctor, that Stalin had only a brim of hair above his forehead, and further up there was a bare skull, an earthy-colored bald spot."[32]

The Stalin of 1968 was no longer "the Old Man" that he had been for Tvardovskii fifteen years before. But what persisted from 1953 was a certain fascination with Stalin that prompted him again and again to revisit the image and even the physical appearance of the dead leader. Stalin still cast a certain spell that held Tvardovskii's eyes fixed on the dethroned monument, a spell he periodically had to shake off with a purposeful, demystifying effort. Until Tvardovskii's death, a portrait of Stalin remained on the wall of his dacha office in Krasnaya Pakhra.[33]

Stalin's time was Tvardovskii's time, the decades when he grew up and matured as a human being, a poet, a thinker. Influenced by collectivization and the great purges, he nonetheless shared a belief in the fundamental premises of the Soviet order, many of which had emerged in those decades. Reexamining the Stalin era meant, for him, reexamining himself, his deeds and beliefs. And yet, earlier than many of his contemporaries, he found the courage to begin this journey.

The past intruded constantly, sometimes at the most inconvenient junctures. In the spring of 1954, during a routine exchange of party cards, Tvardovskii learned that registration forms had him marked down as a son of a kulak. He appealed to the Krasnopresnenskii district party committee in Moscow, asking to change this categorization: first of all, his father had never used hired labor (the most common criterion for identifying a kulak, or supposedly "wealthy" peasant); second, the registration form contradicted many of his official biographies, which described him as "the son of a peasant blacksmith." The district party secretary replied that only the Central Committee could change the formulation and advised him to appeal to Khrushchev personally. On 15 April Tvardovskii did write to Khrushchev, who forwarded his letter to Ekaterina Furtseva, the future Soviet minister of culture and then first secretary of the Moscow city party committee.[34] Meanwhile, rumors about the case began spreading. At the meeting of the Moscow writers' party organization on the third of May, the literary critic Ivan Chicherov claimed that the head of the Writers' Union, Aleksei Surkov, had allegedly described Tvardovskii as refusing to accept a new party card until his "social origin" identifications were changed. This interpretation of Tvardovskii's behavior already sounded like a political *fronde.* Probably not by chance, the charges emerged precisely at the moment when the campaign against *Novyi mir* provoked by Pomerantsev's "On Sincerity in Literature" was gaining momentum.[35]

Tvardovskii protested right away, at the party meeting, and the next day he wrote to the Central Committee. On 6 May he met with Furtseva, who advised him to travel to Smolensk personally and inquire at the local party archive about his late father's official status. Eventually, with the intervention of Valentin Ovechkin, who then happened to be in Smolensk, the local party committee agreed that although Tvardovskii's father had owned a smithy and occasionally hired seasonal laborers, he did not do so on a permanent basis and therefore was a "middle peasant" *(seredniak)* rather than a kulak. Yet, even though in June 1954 the Smolensk regional party secretary duly informed Furtseva about this, no one took the responsibility to issue an official written document "vindicating" Tvardovskii.[36] The campaign against his journal was in full swing, and evidently the temptation to use this sensitive personal information against the rebellious editor was irresistible. Around this time, the chair of the Central Revision Committee, P. Moskatov, sent Khrushchev an informal note, again reminding him that Tvardovskii was the son of a kulak who had died in exile (which was factually incorrect: his father had survived the exile and died in Smolensk in 1949).[37] Finally, on 10 September Tvardovskii, by then dismissed from *Novyi mir*, was summoned to the bureau of his district party committee in Moscow. Creatively reversing the decision of their Smolensk counterparts, the committee concluded that his father's possession of a smithy and use of hired labor, although temporary, did qualify him as a kulak. Furthermore, the committee teleologically pronounced that the fact of his father's dekulakization and exile was by itself the best proof of his having been a kulak. And so Tvardovskii's petition to change the notation about his social origins was rejected. As behooved him, a dissenter ended up having an unclean past.[38]

The episode with the exchange of party cards clearly challenged him to rethink his youth and its historical background. For the next four years Tvardovskii held no official job and thus could focus on thinking and writing. It was shortly after these events, in the fall of 1954, that he wrote the poem about his indebtedness to the past.

He thought, among other things, about collectivization and the current deplorable state of the countryside. His conclusion was grim: "Half a century of this 'revolution from above' has passed, and up until today the business is not going smoothly. It needs various kinds of 'stimulation' from above and bears a mark of even officially acknowledged 'neglect.'" Authors writing about the countryside, he surmised, had to assume a position of fundamental doubt, as if questioning the very need for collectivization, "with full freedom given to sad observations." Any claim of normality that gave only passing recognition to unpleasant "difficulties" and "details" of collective-farm life was doomed to fail. Tvardovskii stayed firm in his political loyalties and still believed that the new writings about the countryside could ultimately endorse the validity of collectivized agriculture. Yet he insisted that the endorsement would require new, comprehensive proof. Of course, conducting such a severe test of collectivization via socioliterary criticism was not feasible at the time—not to mention the fact that the test would have likely resulted in a failure. With his ideas about literature as an uncompromising test of reality, Tvardovskii came remarkably close to Pomerantsev's contemporary ideas of sincerity. Yet Tvardovskii was mature enough to doubt the viability of his hypothesis. For the time being, he wrote, no author seemed capable of undertaking such a literary test of collectivization—not even Ovechkin.[39]

Collectivization was inseparable from the problem of terror. Thoughts about the massive violence of the Stalin years would surface ever more frequently in Tvardovskii's diary of the mid-1950s. In March 1955, he began working on a chapter of *Faraways* that was to be about the terror and the return of its survivors:

> I need to write a chapter about an encounter with a friend of my youth, a childhood friend who once wrote poems and dreamed with me about Moscow, etc. [In the chapter,] I recognize him but at first get scared: I know that he was repressed. In about [nineteen] thirty-seven. We talk, and later in my railway car I think it through and remember it all. This is real work [*Eto—delo*].[40]

His diary of April 1955 was full of searching for precise words for the "Childhood Friend" chapter. "It occurred to me only today," he wrote on 22 April, "that the theme of this chapter comes from my faraway youth—and this is a good sign—although I am walking upon the ice that is cracking down all across the river."[41] The now famous chapter had at least one prototype: Adrian Makedonov (1909–1994), Tvardovskii's friend from the Smolensk years, who had survived the camps and just returned after spending almost two decades there.[42] Tvardovskii had not personally gone through the Gulag, but in the spring of 1955, along with many recently released prisoners, he began an effort to verbalize the experiences of the arrests and concentration camps and to put them on paper. He was among those who elaborated the words in which the tale of the terror would, or would not, be written. By virtue of his status and the scale of his activities, Tvardovskii's efforts at coining this language would become central to the linguistic universe of late Soviet culture.

Meanwhile, as he confessed in a versified internal dialogue, the language did not yet exist:

> Even today I would not trouble
> Yesterday's angst without need.
> —Just say you were afraid.—If only.
> Then it would not have been so bad . . .
>
> No, I am yet unable
> To chisel that with common words.
> And my intelligence yet fears
> To title that, as they would say.[43]

As word about the purges began circulating privately in 1954–1955, Tvardovskii listened closely.[44] At different locations across the country, he scrutinized active or former prisons and camps, trying to picture what had happened behind their walls a few years earlier. In April 1955, while writing at a resort in Sukhanovo, near Moscow, he took a walk in the vicinity of a former monastery turned prison, which later had been shut down and remade into an archive. He walked around the monastery, peering into the de-crossed church tholobates, noting the barbed wire along the walls and outer fringes of rooftops, the searchlights, and the narrow windows of coal towers. He looked at the houses nearby, with flowers and curtains in the windows—the residences of prison "service personnel." And he closely looked at a chimney. "I very much did not like one square chimney there, deep inside the courtyard—devil knows what kind of smoke used to fly out of it."[45] Thus, in April 1955 Tvardovskii may have drawn parallels between Soviet and Nazi concentration camps, and he did not exclude the possibility that Soviet prisons had comprised a mass-extermination mechanism similar to that of Nazi death factories.

In August of that year he was still writing the "Childhood Friend" chapter. It was not going smoothly. Indeed, the task he imposed on himself was nothing less than charting, for the first time and for public use, a description of what had happened in 1937. Painstakingly he tried to formulate, as he put it, "for what sake I am writing all of this," remembering and dissecting his own behavior back in those years:

> It is important to say the main thing:
>
> By virtue of (someone's) external wisdom, I was relieved from the sorrowful errands of heart. The idea was that this had to happen, this was necessary, and there they knew. It was none of our business to judge. And had I thought otherwise, it would have been as if I myself was against everything good in the world. How can I best express this?—because this is the most important thing—a lock upon thoughts, "a sin"—an exemption from the need to think, to have your own human opinion and judgment. Someone up there sees more and knows better than I, even though I am a friend [of the arrested individual] and know this individual just as well as I know myself. It was a renunciation of any significance of my own belonging to the common cause.[46]

An equally vast problem was how to continue living, now that the arrests and executions were in the past and the surviving prisoners had returned. "I have taken up that same chapter," Tvardovskii wrote in the diary in late August 1955, "where I still cannot reach complete clarity: there is nothing to end it with. All right, he has served his term, they released him, his life is 'broken'—and so what? Or, otherwise: he has served his term, they released him, everything is fine, let's serve Motherland, our spirits are high."[47] Unclear to him were both the logic and the words that could be used to describe and rationalize the experiences of the terror. Realizing that the rubber-stamped vocabulary of current literature was no good for the task, Tvardovskii the writer dreaded the possibility of striking a false note with a cliché.

In September 1955, he read a draft of the "Childhood Friend" chapter to his old friend and would-be coeditor of *Novyi mir*, Igor Sats (1903–1980). An astute literary critic, Sats agreed with him that the discussion of the terror should begin with Tvardovskii's own confession of his personal guilt. He also advised Tvardovskii not to stop at that but to carry the discussion on to a more "general" level. Yet how was he to do that without sliding down into self-congratulatory, officious platitudes? "I do not know at present how to do this," Tvardovskii despaired, "so as to avoid the end result sounding like this: Okay, you were in the camps, and I was silent, and now you are free, and both of us aren't old yet, so let's go on living and working."[48] From whatever angle one approached it, the terror was an insurmountable obstruction to the existence of those who survived. It refused to fit any existing verbal formulas. The problem offered no easy solutions, and as time went on it was increasingly clear that verbalizing this experience would be a most formidable challenge:

> The theme is dreadful. Once you have taken it up, you cannot drop it. That would be the same as living in a room where, under the floor, the dead body of a family member is dug up, and we all have agreed not to talk about it, and to live well, and not to kill family members any more. The theme is multilayered, multipronged—wherever you go, it touches upon everything: modernity, the war, the countryside, the past—the revolution, and so on.[49]

While he struggled with this enormous task, Tvardovskii kept receiving news about the surviving ex-prisoners he once had known. In the same month, September 1955, Adrian Makedonov was reinstated as a member of the Writers' Union, while another old friend from Smolensk, the writer Efrem Mar'enkov (1898–1977), was summoned to the local branch of the KGB and plainly informed that he had served his term for nothing. "I wish they had told me that eighteen years earlier," Mar'enkov commented grimly to Tvardovskii. Dissatisfied with the progress of his chapter, Tvardovskii now thought of rewriting it in the form of a letter to Mar'enkov.[50]

In the fall and winter of 1955–1956, he almost reconciled himself to the idea that the chapter was "not working, and so be it." He kept remaking the draft and searching for the right words but found himself in "a certain stupor—at times the stanzas look okay, at other times you see that this is merely a stack of words."[51]

> And still, if only on that platform,
> In transit, meeting you (in haste) en route
> I could congratulate you, dear,
> On honor (freedom) given back to you.
>
> My tired friend, congratulations
> On freedom (truth) that, starting yesterday,
> Came late, by half of your existence,
> But still it found you, when calling
> For you to pack your things and go.[52]

Honor, freedom, freedom, truth. The words just did not sound right. "This 'and still' is bad and weak," Tvardovskii scolded himself. "It presupposes, after itself, something like: okay, already not so bad, already some 'rounding-up.'"[53] Any wording one could employ while staying within the limits of the acceptable print language was manifestly inadequate to describe the tragedy.

Then came the Twentieth Party Congress. It has become a commonplace to say that Khrushchev's February 1956 Secret Speech, which exposed the scale of the Stalin terror, was a revelation for many, but judging by his diary, Tvardovskii was indeed astounded by what he heard. "A terrible month after the speech about the cult," he wrote in the diary on 16 April 1956. "My head could not take it all at once."[54]

Why, one may ask, was he so shaken, if by then he had already heard so much about the arrests, camps, and executions—so much that he was prepared to equate the Stalin-era and Nazi repressive machines? The answer may be that the same information became much more significant when it went from being a rumor to an official political message delivered by the country's leader. Now the blame for the deaths and atrocities lay directly on Stalin, rather than on Beria or any other of the leader's lieutenants. Because political violence on an enormous scale now proved to have been at the very center of the country's existence, this information threatened to undermine nothing less than the country's legitimacy. Right after the lines about the Secret Speech, in his diary Tvardovskii contemplated the future of the socialist order. In trying to persuade himself, he wrote: "No, all is well, one has to live on and perform one's duties. The process of socialism is a natural historical process. It is like water, like grass—whatever you do with it, it will find its way, it will break through, grow through. Truth is necessary, because otherwise the world would cease to be manageable, at least to the miserable extent that people can manage it."[55]

In a twist of deadly irony, this self-admonition hinged on a quotation from his old friend and patron Aleksandr Fadeev, whose 1926 novel *The Rout* ended on that very sentence: "One had to live on and perform one's duties." Even more than Tvardovskii, Fadeev was a man of duty, for whom loyalty to the cause was a supreme value. A little more than a month prior to this entry in Tvardovskii's diary, and a few days after the Secret Speech, on 8 March 1956 Fadeev had sent Tvardovskii his last letter, decidedly breaking off all relations with him. It was "a terrible letter," in Tvardovskii's words, and no doubt there was a connection between it and what the two of them learned at the Twentieth Congress. Two months later, on 13 May, Fadeev committed suicide. In a deep personal crisis, the man who had long overseen Soviet literature under Stalin and been privy to the deaths and disappearances of numerous fellow writers and friends could no longer allow himself to live and perform his duties.[56]

Tvardovskii could, but it took him years of self-questioning to decide what his duties now were. One duty, for sure, was to write. Yet he had to decide on how to do that. The earth-shattering impact of the Twentieth Party Congress was a decisive factor in the collapse of the old and the formation of a new language of Russian literature—and more broadly, a new language of self-expression in Russian culture. To Tvardovskii, this became apparent earlier than it did to many of his contemporaries.

For a while after the Congress, he abandoned the "Childhood Friend" chapter. He reread another chapter he had written, about Stalin, and found everything to be "proper" there except for a few "traditional obligatory lines, words, and expressions," evidently words of reverence for Stalin, which now were unsuitable. Still, the chapter had to be redone: it was "dying off," its conception now manifestly "beyond the line."[57]

In the early summer of 1956, Tvardovskii traveled to Siberia. Aside from visiting the much-celebrated construction site of the Bratsk power plant, which became the subject of a chapter in *Faraways*, another place that made an impression on him was the old Alexander Prison or, as it was traditionally known, the Alexander Central *(Aleksandrovskii tsentral)*, as well as a (former?) concentration camp that he may have visited.[58] It must have been these impressions that dictated his diary entries of February 1957:

> They shot them in the interior courtyard of that sinister building, at night. They took them, two at a time, and led them to a fairly short alley by the gate laid up with bricks—a dead-end alley. People went through it differently. One lost consciousness and they dragged him to that alley, lit with a light bulb on a cord that was swinging from the shots. Another one yelled—beasts, what are you doing. Yet another one said: I am dying for the party of Lenin and Stalin. And this one stood, like everyone else, with hands tied up behind his back, and it looked as if he did not follow the operation at all. He was neither waiting nor bending. His head raised, he kept staring at the densely starry sky, without turning away, and it was as if that cold altitude had already drawn him in and carried him away from there, from this queue. And whatever was happening there—the commands, the feet shuffling on the stones, the shots—all of this was somehow below, far away and long past. And perhaps nothing of the kind ever happened at all, and it was only he who imagined this or remembered how it had been to someone else on earth.[59]

These lines must have been prompted by something he saw in Siberia—either at the prison or in a camp (the passage that follows them refers to some journey of his in the taiga). It is unclear whether Tvardovskii imagined the victims' behavior or someone had told him about it; the latter is more probable. But most interestingly, this description, although somewhat idealistic, was marked by indifference to the media standards for describing a Soviet victim's behavior during an execution. He did not contest such clichés as courage based on iron will and unflagging devotion to the party cause, but he did not sound excited about them, either. In the final tally, verbal intricacies and political appearances were irrelevant in the face of death.

Whatever Tvardovskii wrote in those months, the terror was always in the background of his mind. It broke out onto the pages of the diary in places expected and unexpected. In March 1957, amid deliberations on how best to portray the construction of the hydroelectric dam on the Angara River in Siberia, he inserted, suddenly and without comment, the well-known verse from prison-camp folklore:

> Ah Kolyma, hey Kolyma,
> You are a happy planet,
> Winter lasts for twelve months here,
> And the rest is summer.[60]

In June 1957, while reading a book by the nineteenth-century Russian historian Nikolai Kostomarov, Tvardovskii briefly marked a description of interrogations of heretics in medieval Rus': "pure 1937."[61]

In the winter of 1957–1958, at the Black Sea resort of Yalta he met Valentina Mikhailovna Mukhina-Petrinskaia (1909–1993), a writer who had spent eight years in the camps and nine years in exile. Mukhina-Petrinskaia, whom Tvardovskii laconically portrayed in the diary as "a happy little skeleton," eagerly talked about the camps in private yet refused to write about them. What she wrote, instead, were short stories about schoolgirls—by Tvardovskii's evaluation, "simplified, miserable, and helpless." When he asked her why she carried her burden of memory and did not want to "pour herself out" by putting it on paper, the answer was that no one would ever publish such an account. This left Tvardovskii upset:

> How could she write something so minuscule in content, compared with what she has been and lived through, what has filled up the main part of her life and can never be forgotten. If only she knew that without having settled accounts with this, she would never be able to do anything else in earnest. And how many people have I seen already who avoid the need to think this over, to express this, who wish to do without it, to forget and refuse. . . . [I]t is explained as follows: why do we need this? Why reopen old wounds? And so . . . society pretends that nothing ever happened,

> and whatever did happen has been corrected, and we should stay on our path. This is horrible, all the more so that the madness has been "corrected," that is, named madness.[62]

His words reflected a characteristic of Soviet conversations about the terror in the late 1950s, something that, for example, showed in readers' responses to Dudintsev's *Not by Bread Alone*—in fact, around the same time that Tvardovskii entered those lines in his diary. The evasiveness and near silence of the media produced a common impression that open discussion of the recent tragedy was not possible then, nor in the foreseeable future. The theme was driven deeper inside, into the realm of private conversations. As a result, there was effectively no public language for describing the terror. This elementary lack of words was visible in Tvardovskii's own poetry and diary entries: not incidentally, he would regularly refer to Mukhina-Petrinskaia's Gulag past with the vague demonstrative pronoun "this." Precise words, indeed, were not available, leaving even the best minds in the midst of a stark language gap.

Overcoming this gap became Tvardovskii's strategic goal, something that shaped the journal he soon came to lead again.

The Manuscripts

By the moment when, on 5 May 1958, Tvardovskii accepted Ekaterina Furtseva's formal offer to edit *Novyi mir* for the second time, he had realized that interpreting the phenomenon of mass political violence in Russia's recent past would be possible only within a comprehensive ethical reassessment of that past, as well as a linguistic reassessment of the verbal order it had engendered. This wide-ranging quest became a priority for *Novyi mir* during its "classical" years, the 1960s. The turn to the past was not limited to *Novyi mir* alone but paralleled the general vector of Soviet culture at the time. The growing, polyphonic discussion about the origins of the formidable problems that, decades after the Revolution, society faced in all walks of life, was also a sign of the aging of the dominant ideology and language and their increasing inability to account for what had happened—and was still happening—to the country and the people.

A major aspect of this historical turn was a boom in memoir writing and reading. From the mid-1950s, authors, generals, and scholars began putting their memories on paper, sometimes not even for publication purposes but principally as an outlet for expressing their experiences and thoughts. Readers eagerly consumed those texts that made it into print. Periodicals set aside special sections for memoirs, and so did *Novyi mir*, which under Simonov published dozens of memoirs by Civil War veterans—especially in 1957, on the occasion of the Revolution's fortieth anniversary. But what had been a one-time event in Simonov's days developed into a system under Tvardovskii. Memoirs became *Novyi mir*'s strategic literary project.

Tvardovskii approached memoirs with great discrimination and a set of strict criteria developed over years. In November 1958, he and his deputy editor, Aleksandr Dement'ev, responded to Konstantin Paustovskii, the famous writer who had spoken so conspicuously two years earlier in defense of Dudintsev. In 1958 Paustovskii submitted to *Novyi mir* the manuscript of his *Time of Great Expectations (Vremia bol'shikh ozhidanii)*, a memoir about Odessa during the Civil War. This was a resubmission; Paustovskii had already revised the manuscript. The editors' response was long, detailed, and scathingly critical:

> Your revisions do not change at all the general spirit, tone, and meaning of your piece. It still lacks the motives of labor, struggle, and politics; it still has the poetic solitude, the sea, assorted beauties of nature, and the self-value [*samotsennost'*] of art, which you interpret, we believe, in a very limited way; and . . . Odessa, which you approach from an aesthetically exotic viewpoint. . . .
>
> And the main thing—the entire [memoir] conveys, to say so, a pathos of irresponsible and essentially deeply egotistic "existentialism" [*sushchestvovatel'stvo*]—a philistine, excuse us, pride that spits at "world history" from the heights of its contemplative [*sozertsatel'skogo*], "above-the-stars" unity with eternity. Inadvertently, perhaps, you strive to establish, by literary means, an impoverished biography—a biography that does not bear an imprimatur of a greater time, of a greater fate of the people—in a word, of everything that has everlasting value.
>
> Therefore, Konstantin Georgievich, your "revisions" do not allow us to consider the manuscript suitable for publication in our journal. If we did that, we would invite heavy (and alas, justified!) critical attacks upon you, and the journal would also incur great losses.[63]

This criticism was followed by recommendations. Tvardovskii and Dement'ev advised Paustovskii to insert "a few good informal words about the people of labor"—that is, workers, whom he had purposely removed from the stage by saying that most of them had left to fight in the Civil War. His device did not escape the editors, who sarcastically compared it to a bad playwright's removing children from the action, "to a grandmother, an aunt, to the countryside, etc.," so that adults—in Paustovskii's case, the intelligentsia—could freely develop their relationships. The editors also asked him to reduce his apologetic descriptions of Isaac Babel'—"whom, please believe us, not everyone perceives as such a 'deity' as the literary circle of Odessans did."[64]

Tvardovskii and Dement'ev were not nice critics—and Paustovskii, in fact, never did publish this memoir in *Novyi mir* after that, although at the end of the letter both editors urged him to resubmit. To some extent their comments might have been dictated by political expediency: literally weeks after the Pasternak affair had exploded so closely to the journal, accepting for publication another text about the Civil War that could be interpreted as individualistic, and did not unequivocally accentuate the Revolution's beneficial role, could indeed have been dangerous for the journal. At the same time, Tvardovskii's censure of Paustovskii's memoir was based on a set of agendas that the editor in chief applied to all memoiristic writing. Central to his approach was the demand for "an imprimatur of a greater time."

Tvardovskii valued memoirists as political human beings—involved in the country's life, having an impact on and being impacted by society writ large, as well as conscious of this involvement and impact. His rejection of Paustovskii's "existentialism" was not so much a critique of a modern literary trend as a very specific requirement for the author writing about the past not to limit his focus to private life. The memoirist was to see his or her own fate as integrated in the fate of the people, with the memoir representing the author's own lifetime test of integrity against the background of the great historic trials of the land.

In the next few years, the number of memoirs on Tvardovskii's desk increased rapidly. At the Twenty-Second Party Congress in October 1961, Khrushchev renewed his attack on Stalin and the terror, this time making the attack much more explicit—and, importantly, public—than ever before. There was to be no new Secret Speech. Following the congress, Stalin's body was taken out of the Mausoleum in Moscow's Red Square, his numerous monuments were demolished, and the many cities named after him were renamed. Furthermore, relatively open discussion of Stalin-era repression was now allowed in the media. As a result, writing about arrests, prisons, and concentration camps became a mass pursuit, and there was an outpouring of literary, journalistic, and memoiristic efforts. Many Gulag survivors had started putting their life stories on paper even before these events, right after their release. Among them was the yet unknown Aleksandr Solzhenitsyn, who wrote his *One Day in the Life of Ivan Denisovich* in 1959. A few memoirists had tried submitting their writings to publishers as early as 1956, only to have them rejected.[65] But now, in the early 1960s, the unprecedentedly open media discussions brought on an avalanche of hundreds if not thousands of such memoirs, which camp survivors sent out to literary journals and to the Central Committee directly.[66] Khrushchev at some point may have claimed that the journals received ten thousand such manuscripts.[67]

Novyi mir was at the crest of this remembrance wave. Tvardovskii welcomed the camp memoirs, read hundreds of them, and was actively looking for something publishable. His approach to these manuscripts fully revealed his literary, aesthetic, and historical strategies.

For him, the writings of people who had gone through the Gulag were valuable as what he, following the well-developed French and Russian literary tradition that dated back to the late nineteenth century, called "human documents" *(chelovecheskie dokumenty)*.[68] The newly discovered underworld of human suffering was uncharted historical terrain, and the first step in exploring it was to chart it. Before anything else, Tvardovskii believed, it was necessary to obtain a factual picture—to learn what exactly had happened to the prisoners after their arrest. Archival research was still out of reach, so the only way to learn was through eyewitness accounts—as many and as detailed as possible.

Toward these goals, the literary merits of camp memoirs, such as plot, composition, and characterization, were of secondary concern for him. Veracity and authenticity mattered infinitely more. In fact, literariness could do more harm than good. Tvardovskii revolted against all traces of what he called belles lettres in these memoirs. Every device of fictionalization—intricacies of plot, flowery prose, development of "characters," descriptions of nature, cooked-up psychological conflicts between "personages"—all this had to go, or at least had to be minimized and subjugated to the main goal and purpose of the writing: producing an authentic, detailed account of human suffering. Tvardovskii had similar requirements for all memoirs, but when it came to remembering the terror, his insistence on veracity was particularly strong.

"Human documents" meant to him not only the eyewitnesses' capacity to convey information but also what he valued as the texts' testimonial quality. As he wrote after meeting with Mukhina-Petrinskaia in 1958, an experience like hers was a heavy burden, made even heavier by the official glossing-over and the lack of opportunity to share it openly. Oral reminiscences recounted among intimate circles were not enough. The camp survivors needed not only to share their experiences with others but also to secure and perpetuate the act of sharing, for both the memoirists' and the audience's sake. The way to do this was to put their recollections on paper. Since publication often remained a problem, this writing could hardly count as a truly broad and open sharing of experiences. But Tvardovskii never underestimated—and never failed to emphasize in his correspondence with memoirists—the therapeutic capacity of such writing. The very fact of putting reminiscences on paper was important for a camp survivor, purely as a form of speaking out. And in the end, he firmly believed, this writing would inevitably become public domain, indispensable for both the survivors and everyone else.

A demanding editor, Tvardovskii was no less demanding as a reader and correspondent—tough, exigent, at times authoritarian. He carefully read all memoirs about arrests and camps that *Novyi mir* received, and indeed may have read more of them than anyone else in Russia. As a rule, he replied to the authors personally. The length and tone of his responses varied from brief and curt to long and respectful, depending on what he thought of the manuscript and of the author's self-presentation.

In November 1961, he replied to Maria Sigizmundovna Klimovich, who inquired whether writing a novella *(povest')* about "the events of 1937" was "permissible and worth it at the present moment." Tvardovskii answered that the decision should ultimately depend on Klimovich's own disposition. He quoted his favorite Tolstoyan dictum, that one ought to write only if one could not but write. He also formulated his criteria for a camp memoir worth publishing: "Not knowing you as an author, and your potential for belles lettres, I still believe that the material of this kind would be of interest first and foremost as a veracious, factual rendition (memoirs, a personal testimony on the time and the events). The editorial board, let me tell you directly, has plenty of novels and novellas on this topic. Of course, the question is what kind of novel, what kind of novella, and what kind of memoir."[69]

Five days later, he repeated himself almost word for word when responding to Anna Emmanuilovna Patrunova-Kagan, a university graduate who had spent seventeen years in the Kazakhstan camps and subsequently took the last name of her husband, Patrunov, who had died in the camps. Telling the long story of her own and her husband's arrest and imprisonment, she argued that such tribulations were not to be forgotten. She also sent a copy of her letter to another writer she deeply respected, Mikhail Sholokhov.[70] The latter's response, if there ever was one, is not known. But Tvardovskii, deeply moved by her letter, responded at length. He wrote that the best way not to forget was to put her memories on paper. He urged Anna Emmanuilovna to write in detail about everything she had been through. He did not directly ask her to write for publication in *Novyi mir,* but he did imply the potential for publication, as he mentioned "literary help" with her memoir. He urged her to write back in about a month, and even suggested they meet in person, which was rare for Tvardovskii. His more specific advice to Patrunova-Kagan once again illustrated his approach to memoirs:

> Judging by your letter, you are a literarily well-educated person *(Vy chelovek literaturno-gramotnyi)*; however, "belles-lettristic" refinement is not only unnecessary but even directly contraindicated to any rendition of this material. Try telling everything you have outlined in your letter, in detail and substantially [*obstoiatel'no*], without striving toward any beautification of the form, but instead striving only toward the truth.
>
> You just need to try, and then, I think, you will feel that this work brings you the immense satisfaction of a duty fulfilled, to the memory and honor of the living and the dead, and with regard to your own path in life.
>
> Literary help will not be a problem. What is most important is to give as much factually veracious [*fakticheski-dostovernogo*] material (to the extent your memory has retained it)—details, episodes, and the like.[71]

Tvardovskii concluded his letter not with his standard "Wishing you all the best," but instead wrote, "With deep respect."

In the meantime, the legitimizing impact of the Twenty-Second Party Congress must have finally persuaded his old friend Mukhina-Petrinskaia to begin writing about her camp experiences. In 1962 she sent her memoirs to *Novyi mir.* However, despite their longtime acquaintance and the impression she had made on him in their private conversations, Tvardovskii was not satisfied with what she produced:

> I will not conceal from you that your memoirs appear to me less impressive than the stories you told me. Your memoirs are written "literarily" well [*literaturno*], but without that intensity of creative thought [*napriazhenie khudozhnicheskoi mysli*] that alone can make memoirs something greater than reminiscences of what I, so-and-so, have been through.[72]

His responses to all these memoirists read much like what he and Dement'ev had written to Paustovskii four years earlier. Memoirs about historic events such as the Revolution and the terror were to write human biography into larger history, focusing on details of individual lives only to the extent that those bore an "imprimatur of a greater time." Reminiscences of a great epoch were valuable only insofar as they managed to be history.

The publication of *One Day in the Life of Ivan Denisovich* in November 1962 greatly increased the influx of memoirs to the journal. "After Solzhenitsyn's novella, we have mountains of camp manuscripts," Tvardovskii wrote to another memoirist and potential author, Tat'iana Aleksandrovna Aksakova from the town of Viatskie Poliany. Even under the most favorable political circumstances it would have been impossible to publish them all. Tvardovskii, therefore, organized a special archive at the offices of his journal where these memoirs were to be kept—in their capacity as eyewitness accounts valuable as historical evidence. Only a handful from these "mountains" of manuscripts has survived, however, and the fate of the rest is thus far unclear.

After *One Day* had been published, Tvardovskii often expressly compared similar works with Solzhenitsyn's novella. None seemed to match. *One Day* set a standard below which the editor did not want to descend. There was always something wrong with the other manuscripts: either the picture was not authentic enough, muddled by fictionalization and clichéd literariness, or the author's vision was not sufficiently broad and the text did not live up to the demand of being history. After Solzhenitsyn, "we cannot address this material at a different creative level," he wrote to

Aksakova.[73] But "the Solzhenitsyn standard" was, in many ways, something that *Novyi mir*'s editor had set long before he read Solzhenitsyn—and it was indeed that standard itself that led him to publish the novella. After *One Day*, Tvardovskii continued to approach memoirs of the terror with the same criteria he had applied before. His demands for authenticity and aversion to belles lettres persisted in nearly every one of his responses to the memoirists. So did his insistence on the act of writing itself, and his encouragement of the Gulag survivors to produce "a document of their time, pages for a tragic chapter in the history of our society."[74]

In October 1963, he rejected the camp memoirs of the Leningrad ethnographer Nina Ivanovna Gagen-Torn (1900–1986). Tvardovskii read them with great interest and discovered many new aspects of the terror he had not known before, despite having read, by then, "a whole library" of such accounts. Nonetheless, he refused to publish Gagen-Torn's work. Like many others, in his view, she had written something between memoir and fiction. Her notes were "not factual enough, as the veracity of personal testimony is largely obscured in them by claiming, so to say, a belles-lettrism of the account." He agreed that, thanks to fictionalization, many episodes and portraits in the text became quite vivid—but again, he believed that in this case fiction and authenticity did not go together: "As they say, here it must be one way or the other."

> You do not fulfill your own authorial pledge: "I am taking down these notes as a historical document for the future generations. They contain neither embellishment nor distortion. This is not a propaganda piece and not belles lettres—this is an account of a lived experience, an observer's attempt to fix precisely what she has seen, as we ethnographers are used to during fieldwork." . . . Alas, you often violate this "ethnographic principle." Thus, your exceptionally witty and winning replies to the investigators cannot but raise, forgive me, doubts about their authenticity. These are, more probably, responses "from the staircase," that is, those which came with time, after the fact. There are also a bit too many quotations and your own verses—by themselves not bad verses, it is just a pity that their literary origins at times overpower the real-life material on which they are built.[75]

Despite Gagen-Torn's mixing of genres, Tvardovskii still requested her permission to keep her text in *Novyi mir*'s memoir archive as a human document. Hers is one of the few manuscripts that survived there. It surfaces in other archives, too: in addition to Tvardovskii, she sent it to other writers, among them Anna Akhmatova. Only after three decades, and after Gagen-Torn's death, would the memoir finally see the light of day. It is now a well-known and respected account of the terror. So is her poetry.[76]

Veracity had its limits, too, as it needed to be played against the rules of acceptability. An unrestrictedly veracious account of the full detail of suffering in prisons and camps would not be allowed into print—perhaps ever. In December 1962 Tvardovskii read one such memoir "of the year 38," written by Aleksandr Nikanorovich Zuev. The memoirist informed the editor that he had not shown his notes to anyone else, unsure as to whether the time was appropriate for publishing them. He had lived through everything he described and did not allow room for any flight of imagination, having even included the original last names of all who figured in his account. He cautiously inquired about the possibility of publication, and, in case that it was not possible, asked Tvardovskii to return the manuscript without sending it to "the instances"—the repressive ones. However, Zuev mentioned that he was also going to send a copy of his memoir to the Central Committee. In a telling glimpse of where the memoirist placed his trust, *Novyi mir* and the highest party organ were the only listeners to whom he chose to tell his life story.[77]

Tvardovskii replied at length, clearly touched by Zuev's "truthfulness and modesty," qualities he always appreciated. He liked the author's "sincere and authentic testimony about the terrible times of lawlessness [*bezzakonie*] and voicelessness [*bezglasie*]." But this was also why he told the memoirist upfront that his testimony was not publishable: its unmitigated veracity precluded publication. As always, though, he mentioned that the act of writing was "the right and necessary thing to do." "I am shaking your hand," the editor concluded with an additional sign of respect.[78]

At times it is hard to accept Tvardovskii's logic and one feels the urge to argue with him, futile as the exercise would be. Not only did he apply rigorous textual demands to the manuscripts, but he also approached their authors with stringent ethical criteria. His response could depend on the tone in which an author presented him or herself. Tvardovskii valued modesty, as in Zuev's case, and intensely disliked aggressiveness, big and bold authorial claims, and any trace of what he saw as marketing and self-promotion. In such cases he was ruthless. A slightest suspicion that an author was seeking publication because the subject of the terror had become "a spicy topic" and could earn the author a "name" meant a death sentence for the manuscript.

In late December 1962 he received a letter from Evgeniia Ginzburg (1904–1977), the author of the now famous *Journey into the Whirlwind.* Having been released in 1955 after eighteen years of imprisonment, Ginzburg lived in L'viv and worked as a journalist for the newspaper *L'vovskaia Pravda.* Tvardovskii knew her son, the writer Vasilii Aksenov, who was a *Novyi mir* author. According to her letter, Ginzburg had initially wanted to approach the editor via Aksenov, but, she wrote, since her son was going on a trip abroad, she decided to write to Tvardovskii on her own.

She began her letter with a deep bow of gratitude to Tvardovskii for having published Solzhenitsyn's *One Day.* Then she informed the editor that she had written her own memoir about the camps and wanted to offer them to his journal for publication. After Solzhenitsyn had been published, "all our rehabilitated people"—her acquaintances among the ex-prisoners who had read her manuscript—became anxious and began urging her to offer it to Tvardovskii. So Ginzburg inquired whether the publication of another piece on the same topic would be possible. "If for some reason another turn to the same subject were not possible now," she would not come back to working on the text, she wrote, explaining, "You know, working on it is painful every time." But if "the principled possibility of its publication" existed, she was willing to get back to the manuscript and even offered to bring it to Moscow personally.[79]

Tvardovskii responded briefly and coldly. His letter informed Ginzburg that there could be no preliminary guarantee that *Novyi mir* would publish her memoir. "Solzhenitsyn's novella has set quite a high standard of <u>creative</u> demands for works devoted to similar themes—a standard from which the journal will not be able to retreat. The 'principled possibility' for publishing your manuscript is this [standard] only. Send me the manuscript."[80]

Ginzburg did send him the manuscript, and he read it. His review of it bears no date, but the file is dated 1964. Judging by the extensive length and language of his review, Tvardovskii was impressed—and yet he rejected this memoir, too. It was not that he denied the merits of Ginzburg's text. Among all the recent writings on "the theme of the year 37," he wrote, hers distinguished itself "by its great impressibility [*vpechatliaemost'*] as a human document, deeply suffered through [*gluboko vystradannoe*], of the tragic fate of the party intelligentsia, in which the author's individual experience stands within a coherent and consistent historical picture." Thus, Ginzburg met the highest and toughest of Tvardovskii's criteria for writing about the terror: first, testimonial capacity based on authentic experience, and second, the "imprimatur of a greater time," through depiction of an individual life within the broader history. The text was also a fine work of literature, he recognized: "The rendition of facts of an individual fate is, from a properly literary standpoint, almost impeccable—this is a free and confident account by a person sophisticated enough in literary writing."[81]

But then came his criticism. Often, Tvardovskii argued, Ginzburg's literary sophistication worked against her. It imposed on the memoir "a shadow of belles lettres"—that curse again. In some instances, he wrote, she ruined the authenticity of her "confession" by revealing "a certain literary coquetry, juggling, wishing to look all-too-heroic, and self-admiration [*samoliubovanie*]." For example, she gave this impression in the author-hero's caustic responses to her investigators and judges and in her numerous witticisms, obviously thought up after the fact, "on the staircase"—the expression Tvardovskii often used.[82]

His response to Ginzburg was phrased almost in the same words as his 1963 answer to Nina Gagen-Torn. In both cases, he resented elements of fictionalization that undermined the power of the eyewitness account. But with Ginzburg he went further; in addition to the superfluous literariness of her text, Tvardovskii attacked her conceptual approach. He read her memoir as an attempt to present the life of her social stratum, the privileged party elite prior to arrest, as a happy, carefree existence that, he felt, she treated nostalgically. "Nor can one accept," he wrote, "the author's overall conception, which evaluates everything that happened 'before' from the viewpoint of [the] material and moral well-being of the 'leading strata' of a certain scale ('oh how well we lived before all that, how happy we were, how clear and beautiful everything was')."[83]

This point should not be underestimated. "Before" 1937, there had been collectivization, which Ginzburg, glaringly for Tvardovskii with his life experience, had all but missed. For her, the terror began in 1936 and 1937, or at the earliest with the Kirov murder on 1 December 1934. Indeed, the opening sentences of her book read: "The year thirty-seven began, essentially, at the end of the year 1934. More precisely, on 1 December 1934."[84] The repression that had taken place prior to that date did not receive enough of her thought and attention. It is not known, of course, which version of her manuscript Ginzburg sent to Tvardovskii, and what she did or did not say in it about collectivization. But regardless of how fair his evaluation was, this was a major factor that disposed him against her memoir.

All this criticism, he then suddenly added, was secondary to his main objection, one that must have sounded rather unpersuasive to Ginzburg. *Novyi mir*'s portfolio was packed with camp memoirs, and the editorial board simply could not turn "a journal of contemporary Soviet life in all its variety" into a version of the journal "Penal Labor and Exile" *(Katorga i ssylka)*. Tvardovskii's verdict was to refrain, "at least presently," from publishing Ginzburg's manuscript.[85]

His letter makes the reader wonder if the last reason was indeed his main one for rejecting her memoir. Tvardovskii's skepticism of Ginzburg's work transpired by the end of his letter, when he mentioned that those other manuscripts about the camps in the journal's portfolio deserved publication "in essence" [*po sushchestvu*] much more pressingly than hers. Showing good memory, he also recalled that he had responded to her earlier, "in a reserved manner but approximately in the same vein as here."[86] His decision to reject might have been made a priori.

Both of Tvardovskii's responses to Ginzburg were not transparent, and the rejection may have had other motives besides those he listed. In addition to textual and conceptual disagreement, what may have repelled him was that she began by mentioning her connections, through Aksenov, to the literary world and to Tvardovskii in particular. He was not fond of authors who warmed up their submissions with name-dropping. Unfair as he might have been, Ginzburg's introduction probably predisposed him against her manuscript from the start. As for considerations of politics, which might not have favored a battle for her text similar to the one he had fought earlier for Solzhenitsyn's *One Day*, those were likely of secondary importance. Judging by his letters, even under the most favorable political circumstances he would have never fought such a battle for Ginzburg's memoir.

And yet, considering how he responded to other memoirists, Tvardovskii fully meant everything he wrote to Ginzburg. Concerning the theme of terror, he was ever on guard against literary professionalism, against writing that showed expert sophistication but also suggested the author's familiarity with literary clichés, against the very milieu that associated publication with career. Literary professionalism, to him, meant a compromise between human experience and conventions of verbal self-expression that inhibited the essence of a writer's effort: his Tolstoyan credo of writing only because one could not but write. Conventional literariness inhibited authenticity. The terror, in the meantime, required a new verbal and ethical approach as well as a new author—new wine that was not to be poured into old wineskins.

This was why he so actively looked for amateur authors, continuing another nineteenth-century tradition of Russian literature, that of searching for literary talent "from the people."[87] Tvardovskii himself had come to literature "from the people" and was perhaps the most famous living embodiment of that phenomenon. For the terror, his hope was to find a masterful writer possessing extensive life experience yet unengaged with the literary profession, someone who would take the pen on Tolstoyan grounds only. This seemed utopian, but occasionally Tvardovskii did find—or thought that he found—such authors. Solzhenitsyn was the prime example. Ginzburg, on the other hand, had too much in her from literature, and from the intelligentsia, to tell the tale as he wanted it told.[88]

So did, apparently, Lidiia Chukovskaia, who submitted the manuscript of her now famous novella *Sofia Petrovna* to *Novyi mir* in 1961, even before the publication of Solzhenitsyn's *One Day*. Chukovskaia's text was not a memoir but a work of fiction, and a remarkable one. She argued that this was the only fictional representation of the repression of 1937–1938 written not after the fact but *during* the events or in their immediate aftermath—in 1939, when the peak of the purges had just passed but arrests and executions still continued. In this sense, her book, too, claimed the authenticity of a document based on a lived experience.[89]

Sofia Petrovna received at least two internal reviews in *Novyi mir* and was squarely rejected. The first brief response came in December 1961 from Dement'ev:

> The novella is about "the events of 1937." Written precisely. Even minutely. But we should not publish it. In the novella, the author's attitude to the Soviet order is not clear. And without this, I believe, it is impossible to approach such a complex theme.[90]

The second, lengthier and decisive rejection came from Tvardovskii himself:

> The reader knows and thinks of everything related to this "material" [terror] much more extensively, sharply, and broadly. He will be bored reading this "literary" composition on a "spicy" topic, because composing is worth nothing here. The reader pities no one and fears nothing in the novella, since all those who suffer—the director, the party administrator, the female protagonist's son, the son's friend, et al.—are not living people who have become dear and close to us, but mere literary signs [*oboznacheniia*], "personages."[91]

Tvardovskii's insistence that an author of fiction must induce the reader to feel for her literary characters by making them into "living people," "dear and close to us," cannot be explained simply as a manifestation of his allegiance to realism. His messages to authors of memoirs and fictional prose had much in common, and this commonality needs to be explained with regard to his intellectual strategies, particularly his supreme criterion of authenticity—be it factual or, as in Chukovskaia's case, emotional. A work of fiction had to be no less authentic than a memoir. Central to *Novyi mir*'s philosophy, this idea of authenticity also revealed the broader zeitgeist of intellectual concerns paramount to the Thaw, as well as to the entire late Soviet culture. One needs to remember the emphasis on authenticity in Pomerantsev's "On Sincerity in Literature," which Tvardovskii had published seven years earlier. His demands in 1961 sounded remarkably similar to Pomerantsev's insistence on "books serious and warm," and he measured the literary profession by the same Tolstoyan standard that Pomerantsev once had. These were manifestations of a literary strategy, a programmatic quest for a new literature.

There was also another problem with Chukovskaia's text. It was, "of course, not that 'in the novella, the author's attitude to the Soviet order is not clear,'" Tvardovskii added, refuting Dement'ev's argument. The problem was that Chukovskaia failed to handle "the events of 1937" from a broad, historical point of view:

> These "events" are presented through the eyes of an *intelligentnaia* female typist "from the former people" [*iz byvshikh*]. She does not care about what is really going on and why. Her view of "the events" is naive, they do not force her for a single minute to pause and think of something that lies outside her little philistine

world, deprived of any background of the entire people's [*obshchenarodnoi*] life.[92]

This was very similar to how Tvardovskii and Dement'ev had evaluated Paustovskii's memoir three years earlier, and indeed any memoir. Just as both literature and memoirs had to be authentic, both had to place individual fate within a broader historical narrative. However, while it sufficed a memoirist simply to incorporate an authentic account of her life into that narrative, a writer had a more challenging mission—one that, in Tvardovskii's opinion, Chukovskaia did not accomplish. The writer needed to create a major canvas of life, portraying both human lives and the country's existence with equal breadth and "intensity of creative thought." Where memoirs had to be history, literature was to be metahistory.

In Search of a New Literature

The situation seemed paradoxical: the editor in chief of the country's foremost literary journal insisted that literature needed to be as unliterary as possible. Understanding this paradox may be feasible if we take into account two factors.

First, Tvardovskii's insistence on unliterariness was itself premised on a literary agenda—the problem of language. For many years, *Novyi mir*'s editor had searched for new words with which to depict the ordeal of the terror, finding the rubber-stamped Soviet phraseology unfit for the task. The existing print language killed all possibility of either authenticity or productive reflection. His own search for a new vocabulary did not strike him as particularly successful, and it was Solzhenitsyn who gave him the first example of such a language. That was one reason why Tvardovskii held the author of *One Day* in such high esteem.

It is not obvious whether the editor of *Novyi mir* ultimately resolved all aspects of this language-and-terror conundrum, for here the second major factor comes into play: his idea of literature as metahistory. The question of language, taken broadly, was a question of values. Tvardovskii was one of the classics of Soviet literature, and in his case that was not a ceremonial title. He was among those who, in the 1930s and 1940s, had cast and coined the verbal regime for this literature—the regime he now had to reject. Moreover, he not only propagated but also professed his faith in the fundamental principles of the Soviet order. The inadequacy of the existing verbal formulas, their inability to explain or even describe the historical realities of the terror, suggested to him the inadequacy of the political and cultural values of the established order he had treasured. Those values, and the language itself, were now on trial.

The trial proved formidable. It turned out to be impossible to write the terror into any existing system of ideological, ethical, or linguistic coordinates. Tvardovskii's work on his own poetry shows how long and how painstakingly he sought, in himself and in others, those words that would both fully depict the tragedy of an individual placed in extreme conditions against the background of "a greater time" and would also accommodate the major principles of the established order, giving them license to further life. In the end, he seems to have been left with at least as many questions as answers.

And yet there was one moment—before he even heard about Solzhenitsyn—when Tvardovskii did find a book that came close to his ideal of great literature. The book was Vasilii Grossman's (1905–1964) *Life and Fate.*

Grossman offered his manuscript to Tvardovskii in the fall of 1960—but not really for publication purposes. Despite Grossman's desire (ultimately fatal) to publish the book, both men were experienced enough to realize that publication was out of the question. Rather, he valued Tvardovskii's expert opinion as coming from one of the most perceptive readers of his time.

Tvardovskii read the manuscript in October—three folders containing more than one thousand typed pages. For him, this novel became, as he stated in his diary, "the strongest literary impression, perhaps in many years":

> This work is so significant that it transcends, by far and decisively, the boundaries of literature. And its "unliterariness" may be its principal literary value. . . . This is one of those books, upon reading which you feel, day after day, that something serious has happened to you and within you, that this is a milestone in the development of your consciousness, that you will never be able to think apart from it . . . about anything else, including your own life.
>
> It is a joyful and liberating impression, which reveals to you a new (and not quite new but rather concealed, conventionally

> forbidden) vision of the most important matters in life—the impression that instantly removes, reduces to zero, the oppressing uniformity and conventionality of contemporary novels and other writings, with their ephemeral "correctness" and lifelessness.[93]

Tvardovskii, as it must be clear by now, was an exceptionally demanding reader. For him, such an elated confession of admiration was extremely rare—aside from Solzhenitsyn's book, this might be the only time he so praised a contemporary work of literature. His diary entry this time sounded like a reader's letter. And indeed, in this case he saw himself as a simple reader, "not as an editor, who needs to decide, from the very first pages, whether this fits or not, . . . but rather, just as a certain Tvardovskii." This was how Grossman had asked him to evaluate the manuscript, and Tvardovskii's evaluation was the highest conceivable.[94]

It was not that he found Grossman's book impeccable. He thought the title was ridiculous, the author's epic claims pretentious, the scientific-philosophical digressions muddled, and the descriptions of physical labor at once condescending and helpless. Conceptually, as well, Tvardovskii had issues. He was impressed but also appalled by the vivid parallels Grossman drew between the Soviet Union and Nazi Germany—in the very structure of the book, with action taking place alternately in the Soviet and Nazi headquarters, in the concentration camps of Magadan and Buchenwald, in the Soviet and German trenches. He saw the culmination of this parallel in the Battle of Stalingrad episode, when two soldiers, one Soviet the other German, jump into the same crater to escape the artillery fire, sit there side by side waiting for a break in the bombardment, and then climb out and part ways without ever attempting to hurt each other. Tvardovskii did not try to refute Grossman's Nazi-Soviet comparisons, as he realized their power. The most he could do, in a last-ditch effort of intellectual defense, was to note that Grossman had emphasized the parallels on purpose. But, just like Grossman, Tvardovskii had gone through this war. He had come out of it with a very different, much more conservative perception of "us versus them": the people of his country defending it from the deadly threat of a merciless enemy. Persuasive as they were logically, Grossman's Nazi-Soviet parallels were something he just could not accept.[95]

All his criticisms, however, dwindled in comparison with Tvardovskii's admiration and respect for Grossman's accomplishment. He concluded his diary entry by placing *Life and Fate* high above the two most famous books of the Thaw thus far—Pasternak's *Doctor Zhivago* and Dudintsev's *Not by Bread Alone.* "Compared with it [*Life and Fate*], *Zhivago* and *Bread Alone* are kids' stuff. . . . To publish this work (if one could imagine removing its manifestly incorrect motifs) would mean a milestone in literature, would mean returning to literature its authentic significance as a truthful testimony about life. This would mean a tremendous turn for our entire literature, which has lost its way in who knows how vast an entanglement of mendacity, conventionality, and blockheaded premeditation."[96]

Had Tvardovskii published it, *Life and Fate* would have become the greatest literary landmark of the Thaw, probably eclipsing even Solzhenitsyn's *One Day.* But publication did not happen, and it could not have happened, as Tvardovskii himself realized. "The entire book," he wrote in the diary, "resembles a conversation, sincere to the utmost, with a person dear to you, that kind of conversation that once in a great while breaks out, in which you are completely outspoken, and you speak under the great influence of the moment, forgiving nothing to the times and making no allowances—a delightful conversation. And yet the day after, you feel somewhat awkward. You need to keep living your life, and so you live, and you act not at all according to the program of this conversation—which, in real life, is completely unfeasible."[97]

The question of how to go on after reading *Life and Fate* would have inevitably come to the readers' minds. And if Tvardovskii himself found Grossman's book too formidable in its statement, then perhaps the book was indeed too big for the Soviet audiences of the 1960s to digest. His evaluation, in fact, sounded not too far from the well-known words of the Central Committee secretary Mikhail Suslov, who reputedly told Grossman that his book would not see the light of day for two or three hundred years.[98] Had it been published in 1960, when Tvardovskii read it, Grossman's *Life and Fate* would have become the first major work of literature to analyze the phenomenon of state violence in modern Russian history against the broader background of twentieth-century Europe. But this was not to be. The next year, in 1961, the KGB confiscated several copies of the manuscript from the editorial offices of both *Novyi mir* and *Znamia*, where Grossman had also submitted it, as well as from the writer himself. Aside from a few excerpts in the newspapers, he never managed to publish it. The book would not be published until 1988, twenty-four years after Grossman's death.[99]

Life and Fate came closest of all contemporary texts to Tvardovskii's literary ideal. His diary and responses to other literary works of the time reveal what he meant when he said that this book could return to literature its "authentic significance as a truthful testimony about life." Crucial here was what he called the "unliterariness" of Grossman's text—or, to be more accurate, its supraliterariness: the fact that the book "transcended the boundaries of literature." Indeed, the literature Tvardovskii desired was to transcend literature itself. It was to offer a comprehensive depiction of human existence in historic times—an empire of human knowledge that would combine qualities of fiction, memoir, political reflection, journalism, legal discourse, psychology, philosophy, history, and many other fields. In a way, this was the literature that Vladimir Pomerantsev once dreamed of when he imagined a writer's truth merging "with the truth of us all." This would no longer be literature as a guide to life, but literature as life itself.

The heights that the editor of *Novyi mir* set out to conquer were impressive indeed, and whether they were conquerable remains a question. Apparently none of the journal's publications, not even Solzhenitsyn's *One Day,* met his criteria for epic, metahistorical, supraliterary writing. It also may have been that, by setting such high standards, Tvardovskii missed as much as he found in the literature of his time. Ginzburg and Chukovskaia were just two examples. However, the strategies of his second editorship embodied at least a striving toward this programmatic ideal. And while the ideal was unattainable, the striving, and the rigorously chosen texts the journal did publish, contributed to seismic shifts in Russian culture. In that sense, Tvardovskii's effort succeeded. He was aware of this—and that was his best reward.

6

REASSESSING THE MORAL ORDER

Ehrenburg and the Memory of the Terror

IN THE EARLY 1960S, Tvardovskii's *Novyi mir* initiated a massive and widespread polemic on twentieth-century political violence and its peak phase in the Soviet Union under Stalin. Among the journal's publications on this theme, two became especially significant. One, of course, was Solzhenitsyn's *One Day in the Life of Ivan Denisovich*, which came out in November 1962. But a full year before Solzhenitsyn, thousands of readers responded to another publication that engaged the problem of state violence. It was Ilya Ehrenburg's memoir *People, Years, Life.*

These two books were neither the first nor the only publications that referred to the arrests, concentration camps, and executions of the Stalin era. With varying degrees of subtlety, such references surfaced in many literary texts during the Thaw, Ehrenburg's own eponymous 1954 novella *Thaw* (*Ottepel'*) being an early example.[1] Overt and detailed discussions, however, did not see print until around 1961, following or shortly preceding the Twenty-Second Party Congress and its renewed attack on Stalin.[2] And it was these two authors, Ehrenburg and Solzhenitsyn, who touched the audience's nerve.

Soviet letter writers of the 1960s rarely used the word "terror" to describe the mass violence of the Stalin epoch. Most often they did not give the phenomenon any overarching name. Decades later, such a name is still missing from the Russian language. Despite the collapse of the Soviet

Union, despite the long, intense conversations about the destruction of human lives under Stalin, the language still lacks a definitive term with which to describe what happened. The words currently in use—"the terror," "Stalin Terror," "Great Terror," "Great Purges," "(mass) repression"—are calques, or translations from Western languages and Western authors. Some of these words, such as "repression," became operational early in the history of Soviet bureaucratese, while others did not enter broad circulation until years after Stalin.[3] It was a Western historian, Robert Conquest, who coined the term "the Great Terror" at the end of the 1960s, drawing a parallel with revolutionary France. About two decades later, during the explosive historical debates of the Gorbachev perestroika, the term entered the Russian vocabulary.[4] However, while established among academics, writers, journalists, and other members of the intelligentsia, "the terror" is hardly in common use among the Russians today. When invoking the tragedy of the Stalin years, people most often use a different word, exactly the one they or their parents and grandparents used back in the 1960s. They call it by the date when the arrests and executions reached their peak—"the year thirty-seven." No one needs an explanation. In the Russian popular memory and media, "the year thirty-seven" has come to symbolize the Stalin-era state violence in its entirety.

Although death sentences indeed skyrocketed to unprecedented heights in 1937, the designation of this particular year as the epitome of all repression takes the emphasis away from the earlier chronology of state violence. The collectivization of the late 1920s and early 1930s, when the death toll was also very large but less well recorded, usually stands under its own name in the media, *kollektivizatsiia,* and therefore heuristically apart from "the year thirty-seven." Arguably, the linguistic distinction is rooted in the nature of the educated society that produced this country's culture of written expression—an urban domain shaped in the tradition of the intelligentsia and long accustomed to viewing the peasantry as an object and a tool rather than as an independent actor in history (or as human beings for their own sake). Even though many among the intelligentsia originated in the peasantry, and some later came to speak on its behalf, for others it still felt qualitatively different when repression hit the "silent" class, as opposed to history's presumed agents, the pride and flower of Russian culture. It was from this point of view that much of the educated society has come to describe the political violence of the Stalin era. The story of repression, specifically in 1937–1938, also has received a decided emphasis on the intelligentsia, with the educated strata viewing themselves as the repression's principal victims.[5]

To a large extent, this tradition of representing the year thirty-seven took shape during the Thaw. *Novyi mir* played a role here, although Tvardovskii resisted the trend as much as he could: witness his rejection of Ginzburg's and Chukovskaia's manuscripts and his promotion of Solzhenitsyn. But inevitably, as he certainly realized, most of his authors were the intelligentsia—including Solzhenitsyn and, against his innermost wishes, Tvardovskii himself. It was the intelligentsia who, by virtue of being best equipped for the task, would chronicle the year thirty-seven—or would at least begin telling its tale.

To this day, the tale is not completely told. The persistent language gap in reference to one of the central phenomena in Russia's modern history indicates, better than anything else, that the process of accounting for the unprecedented extermination of human lives in that country is far from over. In this book I also use the word "terror"—in awareness of the terminological problem, yet for lack of a better word.

That said, a considerable part of the tale *has* been told. During the decades that passed since Stalin's death, the knowledge and interpretation of the year thirty-seven have evolved, and it is not an exaggeration to say that the theme has become central to Russian historical and political consciousness. The legacy of twentieth-century mass violence has come to define the relationship between the state and the individual in this part of the world. As often the case in modern Russia, this fundamental self-perception originated in literature—and first of all in the texts published by Tvardovskii's *Novyi mir.* One of them was Ehrenburg's memoir.

The Art of Remembrance and Its Critics

It took *Novyi mir* nearly five years, from August 1960 to April 1965, to publish *People, Years, Life*—a 1,400-page book that a biographer of Ehrenburg has aptly called "nothing less than an attempt to restore the country's cultural history."[6] The book meant even more than that. For the readers, it became an eye-opening rediscovery of Europe's twentieth century, where Russia and the Soviet Union were for the first time written into an international, primarily European historical and cultural context. And Ilya Grigor'evich Ehrenburg (1891–1967) was probably in a better position than anyone else to write such a book.

A thinker who had witnessed the entire span of the century thus far, a prolific writer, and a journalist, Ehrenburg was an undisputed authority among both readers and the literary establishment. Although he had published widely in the interwar decades, it was during World War II that a broader audience came to know him. Over the four years of the war, Ehrenburg produced literally thousands of newspaper articles. Always using vivid human examples, he explained to his readers what they were fighting for, what kind of enemy they were facing, and why victory over Nazi Germany was the only option, not just for the Soviet Union but for humanity in general, for world culture. He was a truly cosmopolitan intellectual who had spent much of his life in Western Europe, notably France, in communication with some of the best contemporary minds. No one was better equipped for the memoiristic effort that Ehrenburg undertook during the Thaw—the epoch whose name he himself had coined a few years before.[7]

One of his many accomplishments in *People, Years, Life* was to return or introduce to public circulation the names of hundreds of individuals—writers, scholars, actors, painters—who had shaped the modern history of Russia and the West but later had been rhetorically, and often surgically, removed from Russia's cultural memory. By portraying the similarly tragic fate of artists and authors in the USSR, France, Germany, and Spain, Ehrenburg presented his country as part of the larger world in this century of ordeals. Soberly and laconically, he commented on the epoch when they had lived and died. He described the Soviet-Nazi reconciliation in 1939 as shameful, remembering the German occupation of Paris in 1940 and the pro-German sentiment that the Soviet press, diplomats, and quite a few among the intelligentsia had then displayed. He talked at length about Soviet anti-Semitism—its pre–World War II manifestations, wartime growth, and postwar culmination. He was the first one after 1958 to write a few good words about Pasternak.

And he also described the arrests and disappearances of 1937–1938. It was Ehrenburg who mentioned by name, for the first time in many years, the numerous people who had been killed during those years. Indeed, one integrating theme of his memoir was life in terrible times—human survival under a constant, decades-long threat of physical extermination. Ehrenburg discussed the Stalin phenomenon and proposed a collective responsibility for it, not only blaming Stalin and his retinue but also arguing that what had happened became possible via the compliance, and indeed willingness, of a great many people. Among them, he listed himself.

Tvardovskii and Ehrenburg disliked each other. They were just too different—one conservative, patriarchal, and traditional, the other dynamically versatile, cosmopolitan, and urbane. Yet strategically they became allies. *People, Years, Life* was exactly what Tvardovskii imagined as the ideal memoir. It was a text that bore the "imprimatur of a greater time" he so desired—the author's life written into a larger historical context in order to make sense of the epoch. As far apart as they were, Tvardovskii and Ehrenburg both realized that the recent past required such an explanation, and they shared much the same view of that past. When preparing the memoir for publication, both knew how much this text would mean for its readers. On 17 August 1961 Tvardovskii wrote to Ehrenburg:

> This book of yours is probably destined to have a far longer life than some "broad canvases of the epoch" performed in a "purely artistic" genre. The first sign of a truly great book is the reader's perception of its absolute necessity. . . . This is a book of duty, a book of conscience, of courageous understanding of one's own misconceptions, of willingness (perhaps even excessive, it seems to me) to forgo literary prestige for the sake of more precious things in life.
>
> In a word, thus far you are the only writer of your generation who has overstepped a certain forbidden boundary. . . . For all the possible, thinkable and real, deficiencies of your tale of lived years, you have accomplished what others have not even dared try.[8]

Despite this praise, the correspondence between Tvardovskii and Ehrenburg revealed their intense arguments over what was and was not to be published. At work was the ultimate incarnation of censorship at three overlapping levels—state, editorial, and authorial—a sparring between two literary master swordsmen over a text's political acceptability as well as their conflicting worldviews. *Novyi mir* was publishing *People, Years, Life* in installments, each right after Ehrenburg had finished the new batch of chapters. As he received them, Tvardovskii, with his colleagues Dement'ev and Boris Zaks, would send comments on the chapters to the author. Realizing the memoir's significance, the editor in chief vowed to be maximally noninterfering. "I consider my editorial role in this work of yours very limited—that is, I am not going to ask you to recall what you do not remember and to omit what you cannot forget. But it is my duty to ask you about something else. When looking through these proofs, keep in mind the reality of our days and, wherever possible, make it easier for the proof to go through certain agencies."[9]

In actuality, Tvardovskii did interfere a lot—and not only in cases where, as he transparently hinted, state censorship could present an obstacle to publication. With his usual keen eye for detail, he picked out every name and characteristic in the manuscript that he found questionable, whether in anticipation of a censor's reading or in view of his own strong opinions. This was especially true when Ehrenburg made attempts at broad historical interpretation. "Here we no longer talk about your assessment of this or that artistic phenomenon," the editor wrote, ". . . but about an entire period in the country's historical and political life in all its complexity. Here every word counts. I repeat my longtime promise not to 'edit' or teach you. . . . I merely point out the opinions that are not only at odds with *Novyi mir*'s editorial view but also are such that we cannot convey them to readers."[10]

Thus, Ehrenburg's parallels between Soviet and Western anti-Semitism raised Tvardovskii's protest, reminiscent of his objections to similar parallels in Grossman's *Life and Fate.* "It is possible, I believe, to send a historic bill to Soviet power, too, for a variety of items, but one has to do that on a separate sheet," he wrote.[11] Ehrenburg's idea that the Nazi-Soviet pact of August 1939 had led to the war rather than helped to postpone it also met with Tvardovskii's rejection.[12] Just as unacceptable to him were Ehrenburg's descriptions of the macabre atmosphere of Nazi-Soviet friendship that had followed the pact. In a letter of 5 April 1962, he wrote: "Soviet embassy staff greeting Hitlerites in Paris. 'L'vov' sending caviar to Abetz. It is unpleasant for me, Ilya Grigor'evich, to have to convey to you the self-evident tactlessness and inadmissibility of this 'historical detail.'" And in the same letter: "A 'wedding mood' in Moscow in 1940? This is, forgive me, not true. This was already after the little bloody war in Finland, at the time of an alarming nationwide premonition. You really cannot take the tone of contemporary newspapers and radio broadcasts for some 'wedding mood' in society."[13]

Tvardovskii's personal predilections also came out—such as when he rejected Ehrenburg's unsympathetic portrayal of Aleksandr Fadeev: "What you say about Fadeev . . . is so incompatible with my idea of Fadeev that I simply cannot allow this to appear on the pages of our journal. This is purely personal, of course, but the editor is a human being, too." "In general," Tvardovskii concluded adamantly: "these are suggestions [stricken out: 'demands'] of whose obligatory nature we are convinced, not out of editorial arbitrariness or caprice but out of direct necessity."[14]

Ehrenburg fought back with equal doggedness. "Some of your comments surprise me," he replied to Tvardovskii on 10 April 1962. "I know your good disposition toward me and value the fact that you are publishing my book, even though you disagree with much in the text. I also know about your difficult situation. Therefore, despite what you wrote about 'suggestions of whose obligatory nature we are convinced,' I still do not consider these suggestions as an ultimatum, and am trying to find a solution mutually acceptable for you and me."[15] In the end, though, Ehrenburg had to accept many of Tvardovskii's demands. Fadeev's characterization had to be modified, while the descriptions of a "wedding mood" in 1940 in Moscow, as well as of Soviet diplomats entertaining their Nazi counterparts in Paris, had to go. Ehrenburg did retain his negative assessment of the Nazi-Soviet pact but had to shroud it in (fairly transparent) ambiguity: "The end of chapter," he wrote, "will look like this: 'On September 1 Molotov declared that this pact served the interests of universal peace. However, two days later [*sic*] Hitler started World War II.'"[16] Among many other omissions and circumventions, Ehrenburg was forced (despite his personal appeal to Khrushchev) to take out the chapter about his friends from youth, the future Bolshevik leaders Grigorii Sokol'nikov (1888–1939) and Nikolai Bukharin (1888–1938), both of whom had perished in the purges.[17] He allowed himself the small satisfaction of coding his message—and so, an undisclosed "Nikolai Ivanovich" appeared in the text, pleasing those few readers who understood.[18]

Self-censorship and the author's discretion also played a role in which memories saw print. Intentionally selective in what he remembered, Ehrenburg defended his right of choice. Several times in the memoir he turned to the theme of keeping silent. He argued that silence and selectivity were dictated not only by politics but also by his personal preferences and ethical concerns. First, he wrote only about the people he liked. Second, the times he remembered were fairly recent, so he had to be careful not to hurt those who were still alive.[19] Finally, there were issues in the past he preferred not to disclose. Thus, in just a half-sentence he mentioned a certain letter that he had refused to sign in 1952 (1953?). He did not explain what the letter was about, noting that the time had not yet come to tell.[20] Some argue today that he was referring to an orchestrated collective petition that was circulated supposedly on behalf of the Jewish intelligentsia, urging the government to deport Soviet Jews to Siberia during the Doctors' Plot, and thus to "protect" them from "the people's wrath."[21] Others deny that the deportation project ever existed, while pointing out that Ehrenburg did sign a (never published) collective letter to *Pravda* in January 1953 that expressed the Jewish people's loyalty to the Soviet cause and demanded punishment for the arrested doctors. (Separately, though, Ehrenburg wrote to Stalin to try to convince him that the massive media attention to the Jews was inexpedient).[22] However the actual events had developed, recounting them required extreme caution, and had Ehrenburg even wanted to tell the whole story, he would never have been able to publish it. The only option was to allude to the events in this disturbingly vague fashion.

The result of this multilevel war of words and wits came out as a memoir of great significance but also singular ambiguity. Right away *People, Years, Life* became as famous for what Ehrenburg said as for what he did not. The point of highest controversy was his laconically understated description of the events of 1937–1938. For his information-hungry audience in the 1960s, his references to the arrests and disappearances were brief, elusive, and achingly incomplete—a maze of elaborately disguised expressions and half-sentences. As heartrending as they were, his descriptions of the arrests and deaths of Vsevolod Meyerhold and Isaac Babel' took only one brief paragraph each.[23] A short section described Soviet writers vilifying "enemies of the people" at a literary congress in Paris in July 1937.[24] Another section, equally brief, described Ehrenburg calling Moscow by telephone from Republican Spain, where he worked as a Soviet war correspondent in the spring of 1937, and asking about the strange disappearance of his fellow journalist Mirova—only to be told by his daughter Irina that the weather in Moscow was remarkably good.[25]

Only once did he talk about the arrests at length—when describing his half-year-long stay in Moscow from December 1937 through May 1938, between trips to Spain.[26] Published in May 1962, even today these seven pages remain an interesting account of the Moscow intelligentsia's life at the peak of repression—with details like an announcement posted in an elevator forbidding residents from flushing books down the toilet, and name slots on the doors at the *Izvestiia* editorial office staying perpetually empty due to revolving-door appointments. Ehrenburg also recalled the journalist Mikhail Kol'tsov (1898–1940), who would himself soon perish, taking him to the bathroom to tell him a fresh joke—"They took Teruel. And his wife too?"—revealing an emotional palimpsest of fear that shined through the politically acceptable conversation about the Spanish Civil War.[27]

Overall, the account of the year thirty-seven in *People, Years, Life* was quite ambiguous. Yet it was this account that produced much of the readers' fascination with Ehrenburg's memoir—perhaps more than his portraits of Western intellectuals. Many people did not mind the ambiguity. For older readers who had experienced repression firsthand, the book still meant a long-overdue victory for justice. Although Ehrenburg only briefly mentioned the suicide of Paolo Iashvili, the arrests and deaths of Osip Mandel'shtam, Perets Markish, Titsian Tabidze, Meyerhold, Babel', and other intellectuals, this was the first time in more than twenty years that good words about them appeared in print. Readers took this as a sign of the delegitimization of repression and the exoneration of its victims. Evgeniia Ginzburg was among the first to thank Ehrenburg for bringing the victims' names back from oblivion.[28] Vladimir Chlenov, a former Gulag inmate, wrote that he was grateful to the memoirist for mentioning his brother, Semen Chlenov (1890–1938?), a lawyer and diplomat who had disappeared in the purges.[29] Those who had not suffered directly were still moved by the writer's remembrance of those who had—as in his description of how, twenty years after Meyerhold's death, both the prosecutor and Ehrenburg himself rose when reading aloud his last letter.[30] A. M. Kliachkin in Leningrad, who had admired Meyerhold's theater since his youth in the 1920s, confessed to reading these lines with tears in his eyes.[31] And just as Ehrenburg and the prosecutor had, V. G. Iakovenko from Novorossiisk rose after reading Meyerhold's last words.[32]

Whereas for senior readers Ehrenburg brought back—rehabilitated, to use the Thaw language—the past they had known, for his younger audience he revealed an altogether new history of their country, not to mention the outside world. In letters from young and middle-aged people, gratitude for restored justice fused with an even stronger motif of new knowledge—their discovery of the terra incognita of the historical and cultural universe that Ehrenburg opened and populated for them.[33] A thirty-nine-year-old reader, T. S. Gorbshtein from Tashkent, thus described the impact *People, Years, Life* had on her:

> Your book is great and thrilling. It offers much to those of my age and to me, who have received a one-sided education, because it opens our eyes. . . . Effectively, we do not know the history of literature and art in this century, be it Western or our own. . . . I am most grateful to you for Babel', Tsvetaeva, Mandel'shtam, and others. It is a shame to confess, but until recently I knew nothing about them. Babel's stories have stunned me—but those my age and I did not even know his name. I repeat: yours is a great book.[34]

Many other letter writers—such as the young military doctor German Dolgii from Kazakhstan, the librarian E. V. Botova from Gatchina, or Iu. M. Suvorov from Minsk—confessed similar gaps in their education when it came to the names of the murdered writers, artists, and poets.[35] Isaac Babel' and Osip Mandel'shtam figured especially frequently in the letters. Quite a few people complained that these names had been "carefully concealed" from them by their educators.[36] Twenty-three-year-old Botova wrote in April 1961 that even a couple years earlier her professors at the Leningrad Library Institute had passed over in silence the lives and works of repressed authors. Some young people began seeing Ehrenburg as an encyclopedic oracle on all aspects of life, similarly to how others had recently viewed Pasternak. Twenty-three-year-old Rudol'f Bakhvalov, a college graduate from Tambov, sent him a list of eleven questions on topics ranging from Ehrenburg's favorite opera to the media's silence on the current food shortages to the chances that color photography would replace landscape painting. Notably, though, he also asked why Fadeev had committed suicide, what Ehrenburg thought of Vano Muradeli's censured opera *The Great Friendship* back in 1947 and today, and how he regarded the saying, "Russian people cannot live without a tsar." Clearly, the young reader was fascinated by what the contemporary press obscurely termed "the cult of personality."[37]

In the early 1960s, extracting information about the state violence of the Stalin epoch from Soviet publications was an exercise in comparative Aesopianism. The alternative to Ehrenburg's hazy descriptions was to read the dried-up, filtered, and processed formulas of newspaper editorials. Most readers clearly preferred Ehrenburg, as he at least began telling about the human experiences of repression, something the media almost completely bypassed. "We have understood all your hints," the young physicist Leonid Rinenglaz confided in a letter in October 1961. For him, Ehrenburg's obituary for his friends became a preciously rare personal account of "the terrible days of the year '37."[38] Compared with anyone else, the memoirist was hiding less and telling more of what his readers desired to know.[39]

Yet they wanted to know still more. Many were upset by the incomplete and fragmentary reminiscences, the excessive caution, and justly suspected a censor's hand. They complained that Ehrenburg wrote "with half-strokes and half-hints" or "with hands tied up."[40] Some reproached him for writing too much about Western artists and writers and too little about the Soviet victims of repression. This attitude revealed not so much xenophobia as the readers' priorities. Their need to learn about their own compatriots who had been killed and forcibly consigned to oblivion was more pressing than their interest, however strong, in foreign luminaries. Samuil Isaakovich L'vov wrote to Ehrenburg:

> Could there be doubt that the lives of such people as Lozovskii and Smushkevich interest readers much more than the lives of the Spanish poet Antonio Machado or the French painter Albert Marqué? We do justice to these two outstanding figures in world culture, but we cannot agree when you make but a hasty, cursory reference to Raskol'nikov, a hero of October, and yet spend entire pages discussing these two. I assure you, Ilya Grigor'evich, that most readers will skip your pages about Machado and Marqué or will at best skim through them. But the readers will keep asking themselves with sadness why you wrote nothing about Army General Pavlov, whom you had known in Spain, and nothing about such an outstanding individual as Berzin, whom you also had met there.[41]

Wholesale rejection by readers was fairly rare: only 31 out of 336 letters to *Novyi mir* rejected Ehrenburg's memoir, and there was a similar share of negative responses in the writer's personal archive. Yet his elegant but elusive writing, combined with the privileged status he had long enjoyed under Stalin, alienated some readers who saw his evasiveness, then and now in the 1960s, as a sign of complicity. What especially annoyed them was his extensive and relatively uninhibited travel abroad—voyages back and forth between Western Europe and the USSR, long sojourns in France and Spain—in the 1930s, when such traveling was unthinkable for nearly anyone else in the Soviet Union (and largely remained so in the 1960s). Irritated by this sign of elite exclusivity, some readers accused Ehrenburg of having traded his writerly obligation to share the people's tribulations for a comfortable life in the West.

They also accused him of escaping repression by the same route. Ehrenburg described his desperate efforts, at the height of the purges, to leave the USSR and go back to Spain—which he accomplished in May 1938 only by playing the deadly game of twice appealing to Stalin: first refused, the second time he was successful. On reading this, a certain Koloiartseva acrimoniously slammed the memoirist:

> At the time when the best people of our country, "the Lenin Guard" and your own friends, were perishing, you rushed headlong, overcame all obstacles, obtained a travel passport, and fled to Spain. . . . This is your essence, and right was F. F. Raskol'nikov who reproached you for half-heartedness and vacillation back in the twenties. . . . "A house in Banyuls. There I took rest from air bombardment. Savich and other friends came to visit me." Yes, that was more serene than in Russia during those years.[42]

The fact that Ehrenburg had not exactly taken a vacation in Spain but had worked there as a war correspondent made no impression whatsoever on this reader. Compared with the Soviet year 1937, the Spanish year 1937 seemed to her nothing but a comfortable retreat. Her bitterness had an explanation, though: in the 1930s her husband, a Leningrad academic, had been branded "a notable SR [member of the Socialist Revolutionary Party]" in a newspaper article. Unlike Ehrenburg, he did not manage to escape abroad. Why, indeed, was he to die and Ehrenburg to survive?[43]

Accusations of self-seeking and privilege, to which Russian culture was traditionally hostile, blended with equally conventional charges of double-dealing and servility. Like any Soviet journalist, Ehrenburg had—and had to—put his brick in the edifice of the Stalin cult. Now some readers, recalling this, branded him an opportunist and a turncoat. Few as they were, those philippics did convey a characteristic disposition created by a grotesque mixture of cultural tradition and Soviet media indoctrination. On the one hand, the intelligentsia's long-established code of honor proclaimed a chasm between state authority and human decency. A writer, in particular, was to stay away from the state machine, "suffer with the people," and serve as a moral beacon in times of hardship. By so conspicuously benefiting from the establishment, Ehrenburg had violated the code and deserted his post, becoming part of the much-distrusted authority. Could he be trusted now? On the other hand, the readers' militant moralizing was a by-product of the Soviet media ethos. Having long heard and read the many uncompromising calls for public displays of heroism, they had learned to be harsh and unforgiving in their own ethical judgments. It was thus conceivable to reproach someone for "lack of heroism," while an escape abroad, even from a danger as ominous as the purges, could be seen as a moral desertion.[44]

Again, relatively few letter writers pressed those charges against Ehrenburg. At the same time, the charges revealed the readers' state of mind, an ethical dimension that was to play a key role in the reassessment of the year thirty-seven. Before proceeding to generalizations about history and politics, people had to reevaluate individual human choices made in the past. The tragedy was recent, and any interpreter needed to begin with the issue of his or her own accountability. This ethical dimension became central to the polemic about Ehrenburg's memoir, especially about his depiction of the events of 1937–1938. Key to this debate was the question of silence.

The Question of Silence

The question was raised long before the publication of *People, Years, Life.* As early as 1956 it resounded at numerous conferences and meetings following Khrushchev's Secret Speech. Among the first to raise the question were men of letters. Thus, on 29–30 March 1956, at a party meeting at the newspaper *Izvestiia,* several journalists admitted their guilt in having kept silent in times of repression. One senior journalist, Grigorii Ryklin (1894–1975; editor in chief of the satirical journal *Krokodil* in 1938–1948), argued: "Many of us began hesitating in 1937. We saw that something was going wrong. We were appalled, and yet we kept silent." Another newspaper veteran, Konstantin Sevrikov (1907–1985), agreed: "We, Communists, saw a lot, and we sensed even more that something was going wrong about the reprisals and arrests. . . . We also felt that Stalin was being deified, and yet we kept silent, we were afraid of speaking up." "Comrade Syrtsov" added:

"We newspapermen did a lot for the creation of the cult of personality. . . . We sang many praises while frequently passing over major flaws in silence."[45] Other journalists at the meeting, however, objected to such statements, and a passionate debate broke out on fear versus belief, on whether compliance had resulted from delusion or mere slavish obedience. Someone invoked a moral imperative and quoted Chekhov's famous confession about his lifelong effort to squeeze the slave out of himself, drop by drop. Others protested. "I was not a slave, and the people were not slaves either," retorted one M. G. Semenov. "Comrade Raspevin" seconded: "I absolutely disagree with Comrade Sevrikov's allegation that we 'stood on our knees,' that we were cowards. This is not true. Stalin acted on Lenin's behalf . . . and swore on Lenin's name. At first we believed him, but as the reprisals unfolded we began having doubts and grumbling. And yet, every time when a high government official collapsed in another surge of reprisals, we thought that Stalin had finally taken care of the problem. So it repeated many times."[46]

Again and again at this meeting in March 1956 agitated people rose and spoke, trying to explain their silence during the annihilation of their friends, colleagues, relatives. Silence was obviously a most sensitive issue for them—the question of whether compliance equaled complicity, whether it was possible to maintain dignity in terrible times, to act politically rather than to be blind prisoners of the circumstances.

To a certain extent, the agenda of silence came from the media, too—from the much-propagated ethos of consciousness, the same idea of mandatory civic bravery that urged people to condemn Ehrenburg's "escape" to Spain. It was hard to fathom that comprehending the phenomenon of mass violence required a revision of the entire system of values underlying such publicized notions of human behavior. And a political interpretation was especially difficult. The regime had continued to exist after Stalin's death and never failed to stress this continuity—even though in 1961 it would programmatically reject mass violence as a tenet of its doctrine, transitioning from the "dictatorship of the proletariat" to an "all-people's state."[47] In view of this official continuity, awkwardly combined with the attack on Stalin, how could one explain one's past behavior using the customary political language? The familiar notions of boundaries between good and evil, "us and them," victims and perpetrators, the guilty and the innocent, were quickly becoming blurred, while more and more disturbing questions emerged. Civic activity for the sake of what? Freedom from what? Courage in front of what? Bravery against whom?[48]

Ethics was the core issue. The question of silence in the year thirty-seven was one of the more disturbing questions of the Thaw, because it posed the problem of personal responsibility for the extermination of fellow human beings. It was an ethical question, because it involved intense moral self-assessment, where the answerer not only had to judge him- or herself on the scale of good and evil but also had to revisit those fundamental notions themselves. It was a political question, because defining individual responsibility could not proceed without evaluating the sociopolitical order on the same ethical scale.

Who asked the question of silence during the Thaw? To whom was the question addressed? And exactly how was it formulated?

In the famous 1979 film by Vladimir Men'shov, *Moscow Does Not Believe in Tears,* the question comes up at a private get-together at a Moscow apartment in 1958. The party guests are an interesting mixture of young and somewhat older, more established people. One of them, an eminent gentleman in his fifties played by the actor Vladimir Basov (1923–1987), raises the issue of *that* silence. He presents it as if contemporary youth were demanding an answer to this very question—"Why did you keep silent?"—from their seniors. A note of resentment sounds in his complaint about the young holding their fathers responsible for acquiescing in murder, and thus misrepresenting the complexity of the Stalin epoch. Basov plays a prosperous administrator whose elevated status detracts from his credulity. In the film, he receives no answer: the discussion does not follow through with the question, and the entire episode ends up easily overlooked by an uninitiated viewer—one of many fine Aesopian allusions at which late Soviet culture excelled. Significantly though, *Moscow Does Not Believe in Tears,* which was seen by 85 million people and became a cultural icon, presented silence during the purges as a generational issue. The film—a nostalgic memorial to the Thaw, in which half of the action takes place in the 1950s and the other half in the 1970s—depicts the awareness of the past as driving a wedge between the younger and the older, a conflict of generations that supposedly demarcated the cultural territory of the Thaw.[49] Yet during the Thaw itself, was the question of silence limited to this bifurcation between "fathers" and "sons"? Was it simply that younger people demanded answers from their fathers and grandfathers as to why *they*, the older ones, had kept silent? Was the question of silence—in other words, of the origins of, responsibilities for, and effects of the mass bloodshed—a generational issue?

The issue was more complex than that. The question of silence did exist, and it was indeed addressed to eyewitnesses of the tragedy. However, "Why did *you* keep silent?" was rarely asked.[50] It was not necessarily younger people who raised the question: often the fathers would speak on their own initiative. At the 1956 meeting of *Izvestiia* journalists, there was no "you" in the question. For the journalists, many of whom had seen the 1930s themselves, it was, rather, "Why did *we* keep silent?"

In addition, although younger people did actively discuss the purges, they usually refrained from generational interrogations. Instead, they often presumed that they also belonged to, if not exactly were accountable for, the tragic historical reality. In October 1961 the young physicist Leonid Rinenglaz wrote to Ehrenburg on behalf of people of his age—twenty-five to thirty, born around 1931–1936. He called them "the silent generation." In their teenage years, he wrote, during "that period which has already received the modest label, 'the cult of personality,'" they too had learned lessons of survival:

> We were taught not to believe in people, to suspect a scoundrel in every one of us, and to fear brassy phrases, because behind them was self-interest.
>
> We wanted to fight. We understood that it was not worth it to make a revolution, suffer for so many decades, and bear through the war, only to be afraid of doorbells ringing at night, afraid of saying openly what you thought. Many of us were moving toward "nihilism." I myself did not believe at the age of 18 in Marx's theory and began studying it only to disprove it. . . . And since we could not fight, the only option for us was to keep silent.[51]

I will return to this polysemantic "we," which was overwhelmingly present in letters to Ehrenburg from readers old and young. For now, it is worth stressing one of the several meanings this word assumed—collective belonging. Although Rinenglaz spoke a generational language and created an image of youth rebelling against the moral flaws of contemporaneity (a common image for a *shestidesiatnik*, a self-admitted "person of the sixties"), he did not hurl accusations at "fathers." Instead, he viewed people his age as also morally deformed by the Stalin epoch. As of 1961, only the very youngest people could say they did not remember the Stalin years. The majority, of all ages, did remember—if not 1937 then 1949, and if not 1949 then the winter of 1952–53.[52] The past was fresh in everyone's memory. That was one reason why, in the debate on silence, "we" prevailed over "you."

The distinction between "you" and "we" is crucial. The first-person pronoun suggested that the letter writers of the early 1960s, regardless of age, perceived their lives as integrally connected to the Stalin past, with even the youngest viewing themselves as its eyewitnesses and products. There certainly was a note of passivity in such statements, a perception of being acted upon, rather than acting. And yet the sense of belonging to the system of values formed during the Stalin past prepared people to acknowledge a measure of their own accountability for this past. Rather than blaming someone else, they sought explanations and reevaluated their own lives. In this respect, the letter writers displayed a remarkably high degree of intellectual maturity when addressing one of the most formidable questions of their time.

Readers and the Campaign against Ehrenburg

Although most readers did not stop admiring Ehrenburg's memoir because of its understatements, and if charges of duplicity, servility, and "lack of heroism" were relatively few in their letters, these charges nonetheless became central to the media campaign against the memoirist. On 30 January 1963 *Izvestiia* published an article by the well-known literary critic Vladimir Ermilov, titled "The Need to Argue: Reading I. Ehrenburg's Memoir *People, Years, Life*." It was the same Ermilov who, back in 1954, had already jabbed at Tvardovskii's *Novyi mir*—by way of slamming Pomerantsev's "On Sincerity." His 1963 article was another attack not just on a specific publication but on the entire journal. The article brought the discussions around Ehrenburg's memoir to their highest intensity. It also came out soon after *One Day in the Life of Ivan Denisovich*, and many people responded to the Ermilov-Ehrenburg controversy freshly affected by reading and discussing Solzhenitsyn.[53]

Important political developments were taking shape that winter. Shortly after Solzhenitsyn was published, Khrushchev undertook his well-known visit to the contemporary art exposition at the Manège, the central exhibition hall in Moscow, on 1 December 1962. This visit led to an ideological freeze. The Central Committee secretary Leonid Il'ichev delivered two speeches in an attempt to reimpose orthodoxy in literature and the arts—one at the meeting between party leaders and "the creative intelligentsia" on 17 December, the other at the session of the CC Ideological Committee on 26 December, in the presence of 140 young writers and artists.[54] On 7–8 March 1963, at the second meeting between party leaders and the intelligentsia, Khrushchev and Il'ichev delivered more speeches, with Khrushchev specifically targeting Ehrenburg's notion of silence.[55] According to Aleksei Adzhubei, then *Izvestiia*'s editor in chief, it was none other than future General Secretary Leonid Brezhnev who commissioned Ermilov's article.[56] Against this background, and with the simultaneous discussion of Ehrenburg's and Solzhenitsyn's texts in society, the winter of 1962–1963 became the peak of the literary polemic on the Stalin past during the Thaw.[57]

The brunt of Ermilov's attack, like Khrushchev's, was directed against Ehrenburg's ostensible credo of informed silence. Quoting several passages from the memoir in which Ehrenburg described silence as a survival skill he had learned from Soviet reality—what he called "the need to live with my teeth clenched"—Ermilov denied that this fairly portrayed the mood of the 1930s. "Living with your teeth clenched" meant understanding that things were going wrong and yet continuing to accept them. For Ermilov, this separated Ehrenburg from the majority of Soviet people because, unlike Ehrenburg, most of them had not realized back in 1937–1938 that the state's reprisals were wrongful and criminal. "The tragedy," Ermilov wrote, "was precisely in the prevailing confidence that Stalin was right and that everything done in his name was spotless. . . . Had there indeed been a deliberate decision to 'clench teeth' and silently turn the 'bitter pages' of history, this would have meant that already in 1937–38 it was completely clear that such phenomena as mass reprisals were unfounded. But if this was already clear then, the ethical principle of 'living with your teeth clenched' cannot withstand moral criticism. I. Ehrenburg simplifies the tragedy."[58]

Ermilov also proposed that, although most people had supported the purges back in the 1930s, they somehow also frequently protested against those instances of repression they did find unjust. "Many of them," he wrote, "defended justice regarding this or that individual who they were sure was not an enemy. They struggled, and they struggled not by means of silence. . . . There were also many statements at public rallies and in print, which, although protesting against an individual fact or a particular phenomenon, actually referred to the essence of Stalin's personality cult." Ermilov was remarkably unspecific, neither naming any protesters nor mentioning concrete instances of protest, but instead speaking of "a certain action," "this or that individual," "an individual fact," or "a particular phenomenon."[59]

He did not have to be specific, though, because ascertaining historical realities was not his subject. The subject was Ehrenburg's political persona. Protest or no protest, Ermilov's theme was loyalty to the cause, which in his article seamlessly translated to loyalty to the leadership. His argument favored belief above rationality and selflessness above self-interest: in all situations, a transparent, predictable devotee was preferable to a tongue-in-cheek skeptic. Within the media ethos of self-sacrificing devotion to the cause, the lack of protest against evil looked better as a product of earnest delusion than informed calculation. "We kept silent because we did not know the purges were wrong" was better than "We kept silent because we knew and yet minded our best interests." Calculated nonresistance meant hidden opposition, and Ermilov portrayed Ehrenburg exactly as such a calculating skeptic, whose silence was redolent of disloyalty.

"The Need to Argue" was one of the more sophisticated propaganda pieces of its time, not only because Ermilov praised Solzhenitsyn (he did) and condemned the purges, and not even because, in writing "I. Ehrenburg simplifies the tragedy," he played with the title of another, Stalin-era article in *Pravda*—"Comrade Ehrenburg Simplifies," which in 1945 had made Ehrenburg a temporary political outcast by accusing him of indiscriminate Germanophobia.[60] Ermilov's originality lay in the fact that he engaged the unexplored set of socioethical issues implicated in the recent mass violence in order to exonerate the same regime that had produced the violence. Skillfully, he disguised his redemption of the regime behind the redemption of individual citizens, covering his political agenda with an ostensibly ethical argument.

However, the argument did not work. The readers' reactions to Ermilov exposed the vulnerability of any attempt to make the story of the year thirty-seven serve an ideological purpose by writing it into an established propagandistic narrative.

Ehrenburg himself reacted promptly. He wrote, among other things, that he had never heard of any open protest against repression in 1937–1938—no speeches at rallies, no publications. The only objections that then could be heard were voiced in private conversations.[61] Ermilov responded, with *Izvestiia* effectively taking his side. A scholar specializing in Leo Tolstoy's oeuvre, this time he declared that Ehrenburg's informed silence and calculated behavior in the past contradicted nothing less than Tolstoy's moral principle, "I cannot keep silent."[62]

It was at this point that the argument began drawing massive response from the reading audience. More than a third of the letters about *People, Years, Life* in *Novyi mir*'s archive (117 out of 336) are dated February and March 1963, the two months following the Ermilov-Ehrenburg exchange. This was the peak of readers' letter writing in reaction to the memoir.

Very few letter writers agreed with Ermilov.[63] Some pointed to the logical inconsistency of his argument: as architect Sila Dagniia from Riga succinctly put it, he presented the situation as if during the purges "ordinary people" had not known about the evil and yet somehow struggled against it.[64] But above all the readers challenged him precisely on the ethical grounds he himself had chosen.

First, they argued, Ermilov was a poor candidate to don Tolstoyan garb and appeal to the Russian tradition of writers' protesting against social ills. Under Stalin, Ermilov himself had acted very differently. Two students from Sverdlovsk found a 1949 issue of *Literaturnaia gazeta* that featured his article praising Stalin on the occasion of his seventieth birthday, titled "The Great Friend of Soviet Literature." "The title," they caustically remarked, "conveys all the content of this well-rounded narrative."[65] Sixty-one-year-old Vasilii Kolokolov from Donetsk remembered more recent times, when Ermilov had participated in the 1954 campaign against *Novyi mir* and Pomerantsev. In his letter he concluded: "We readers are used to the fact that, if Ermilov's article appears in the newspapers, that means a signal for a Massacre of the Innocents—a slaying of some luckless author only for showing a spark of independent thought—take Pomerantsev, Dudintsev, Iashin, and others. In such cases Ermilov is always nearby. Like a scavenger, he dashes forward and tears up his victim."[66] Generally, the readers agreed that Ermilov was the least qualified to play arbiter in questions of ethics and to press moral charges against those who had kept silent, because charges far worse could be pressed against him. People often referred to his servility, and the frequent "Comrade Ermilov" and "dear Comrade Ermilov" in the letters were thickly sarcastic, framing the rebukes in acceptable official language while also stressing that Ermilov himself had mastered that language like no one else.

But the main basis on which the readers challenged Ermilov was their own personal experience of repression. Among those who indicated their age in these responses, two-thirds (thirty out of forty-four letters in *Novyi mir*'s archive) were people who remembered the year thirty-seven first-hand. The time had come for them to speak.

Why They Kept Silent

Without exception, every one of the letter writers who had lived through 1937 at a mature age disagreed with Ermilov on the issue of protest. Open protest had been impossible, they argued, first of all because it would have been suicidal. E. Briantseva from Novosibirsk denied any guilt of those who, like Ehrenburg, had kept silent:

> Ermilov writes about certain statements of protest at rallies and even in print (?!). What nonsense! Where did they take place, those rallies?! Who heard of them, and when? Any public statements of protest were out of the question then! Of course, there must have been select brave people who tried protesting or stepping in for someone. . . . But others knew nothing of that, and the brave ones either paid the high price or fell under suspicion and had to shut up. And millions and millions of Soviet people continued, like Ehrenburg, to live in silence "with their teeth clenched." Why then pick Ehrenburg and blame him for keeping silent? Could that be because he openly said the truth about the silence and the clenched teeth? I wonder what Ermilov himself did at that time—probably sat as quietly as a mouse. Or, perhaps, he "spoke up" at his mythical public rallies?[67]

Many people argued that keeping silent had been dictated not necessarily by an acceptance of the reprisals or by blind trust in Stalin, which Ermilov proposed, but by the need for self-preservation.[68] An "authoritative" opinion to that effect came from a former relatively senior NKVD officer, S. V. Levshin from Moscow, who himself had been arrested back then, although he was quickly released. In 1937–1938, he stated, the NKVD had not known of any open protest against its activities.[69] Other letter writers, of course, did not have police data on those years, but their individual impressions uniformly matched one another.

Boris Pavlovich Vishnevskii, an elderly man from a village in the Orenburg region, did not indicate his profession, but the good prose of his long, typed letter suggests that he could have been a schoolteacher, doctor, or librarian.[70] Besides *Novyi mir,* he mailed a copy of his letter to *Pravda,* attaching a defiant statement of mistrust in the country's principal newspaper: "Throw it [the letter] in a trash bin if it proves of no use. I think the *Pravda* editors will eagerly fulfill my request—that is so easy to do, ~~far easier than struggling to understand how and why people think~~ . . ."[71] While seeing his letter as a tool of political action, he had no illusions about its different audiences.

Reciprocating for the title of Ermilov's article, Vishnevskii titled his "If Arguing, Argue for Real!" ("*Sporit'—tak sporit'!*"). Apparently not too familiar with the literary world, he did not know whether Ermilov was old enough to have experienced the 1930s firsthand. But Vishnevskii had been "already a man of mature age during those years." He remembered them well, and he defended those who had knowingly kept silent. Rejecting Ermilov's moralizing stance, he did not view the silence as reprehensible. The generational language he used underscored his sense of the importance of both the phenomena he described and his very act of writing:[72]

> I belong to that generation. I do not consider the people of that generation worse or less intelligent than their fathers or children. I know that the people of that generation may be reproached for faint-heartedness, because they kept silent on what was forbidden from discussion, and yet should have been discussed. . . . But how was one supposed to speak up, if [even] members of the Central Committee . . . lost their heads when they began talking. . . . On what could an ordinary individual count? Only on being promptly and quietly taken away and for having a case concocted against him. . . . And no one might survive who knew how and why this person died, since those who knew were usually taken along.
>
> This is why Soviet people kept silent, dear Comrade Ermilov, and there was nothing shameful in their silence.[73]

Five readers from Leningrad, including a college student and a pensioner, wrote jointly that silence in the year thirty-seven could even be a sign of integrity—such as, for example, when someone refused to renounce a repressed relative. Those who did not loudly castigate "enemies of the people" risked falling under suspicion and having their own careers or lives terminated. "'I cannot keep silent!' is a beautiful concept," the readers concluded. "The only problem is that it hardly applies to the issue and the epoch." Newspaper heroism and after-the-fact moralizing had nothing to do with the choices real people had faced.[74]

The five letter writers employed a common tactic for legitimizing their argument. It was worth remembering, they wrote, that today's party leaders had also witnessed the purges but kept silent.[75] Similarly, Yulia Samarina from Cherepovets retrieved a 1949 issue of *Pravda* celebrating Stalin's seventieth birthday (the lavish celebration must have impressed people, as quite a few mentioned it). In her letter to Ehrenburg, she noted Khrushchev's praise of Stalin in that newspaper issue and then compared it with Khrushchev's subsequent attacks on Ehrenburg's alleged cynicism and duplicity: "Having read all this, Ilya Grigor'evich, I am disgusted by accusations against you, leveled by people who stood at the helm . . . and knew much more than you did."[76] Recruiting Khrushchev's name was a win-win rhetorical move, a surefire appeal to the authority of the current leadership. The letter writer thus wrenched the weapon of authoritative speech from her media opponents and turned it against them. Nothing could better disarm the charge of culpability in informed silence. No Ermilov could object if Khrushchev himself had known but did not dare speak.[77]

Such devices had a long lineage in the Soviet culture of public speaking, and their use shows again that the letters were meant as tools of political action. In fact, similar though less confrontational tactics had been in use in 1937–1938 itself. While only a handful of exceptionally brave or desperate individuals had dared to protest openly, usually with catastrophic results, people did cautiously try to recruit propagandistic formulas or motifs (such as "the honest but wronged worker") in order to stem and redirect the reprisals.[78] Those indeed might have been the voices of disagreement Ermilov meant. Yet, importantly, a quarter of a century later such efforts failed to register in popular memory as acts of protest.[79] This may have been because the notion of protest, for the readers, presupposed a conscious rejection of the opponent's values, a confrontation of principles. There had been no such confrontation in 1937, no conscious rejection. At least in public conversation, all parties shared similar political values and a similar ethos.[80]

As some readers began to realize in the early 1960s, it was this ethos that had made the year thirty-seven possible. Fear had been a powerful and often sufficient explanation for why people had not protested, but the letter writers did not attribute their silence to fear alone. Many of them conveyed extensive deliberations about their own past behavior, the behavior in which fear torturously overlapped with belief.

Unlike in Ermilov's article, belief was never a vague homogeneous category for the readers of *Novyi mir.* They took great pains to clarify exactly what and whom they had or had not believed back in 1937. For example, few if any admitted ever disbelieving the principles of socialism. What people did admit was their past questioning of select elements of belief within the Soviet worldview—such as the existence of "enemies," the justification of reprisals, or Stalin's political persona. Rarely did the readers argue that their rejection of the purges had grown into systemic disagreement with the regime: disintegration of loyalty appeared in their letters as only partial. Someone might confess disenchantment with Stalin but would usually reconfirm his or her continuing identification with the socialist ideal.

The question of whether people in 1937 had believed Stalin and justified the repression was one of the most aching for the letter writers, and to this they produced the longest and most nuanced answers. Boris Pavlovich Vishnevskii, whose remembrance was among the most detailed, argued that views of Stalin in the 1930s had varied. To begin with, many people held two different sets of ideas simultaneously—one expressed in public, the other reserved for the trusted few, whispered "in someone's ear, while cautiously glancing back." Fear devalued public pronouncements, so everyone's unspoken question in 1937–1938 was: What are you going to say in the privacy of your own circle?[81] The opinions reserved for intimate consumption also varied. Vishnevskii remembered that some people in the 1930s had described Stalin as "a party cane," a tool of repression created by the party itself—Trotsky's idea from the 1920s, as the letter writer proposed. Others had thought that Stalin was simply a boorish, uncouth man, dictatorial by nature. "If I am not mistaken," Vishnevskii wrote, "this evaluation of Stalin was associated . . . with a certain letter by Lenin to the CC VKP/b/." Thus, vague rumors about Lenin's letter to the Twelfth Party Congress continued to circulate in the 1930s. Apparently detached from the latest developments in the capitals, Boris Pavlovich did not know that the letter actually existed and, moreover, that it had been published as early as 1956.[82]

Yet another opinion in the 1930s, Vishnevskii wrote, had been that Stalin was "smart but rough"—a straightforward politician who "went ahead regardless of obstacles, breaking the people's bones." Finally, he acknowledged, utter disloyalty had existed as well. He recalled some people arguing that it was from Stalin that Hitler learned his lessons of dictatorial rule. In this light, the letter writer surmised, the attribute "Stalin's"—as in "Yezhov, Stalin's people's commissar"—had not necessarily meant praise.[83]

Things were not simple with silence, either. Even in 1937 people had criticized Stalin and his repressive policies, although certainly not at rallies. Vishnevskii remembered jokes about Stalin that had circulated in the late 1930s—"about the dog and the mustard," "about the donkey and the camel," "about Lenin's shoes and Stalin's boots"—jokes whose meaning is lost for today's reader, but which once must have been proverbial, if mortally dangerous, for those who told and laughed at them. Also in the 1930s, Vishnevskii wrote, a friend of his refused—privately—to read Mikhail Isakovskii's poetry after Isakovskii had publicly asked Stalin for permission to bow to him for his "greatest care about the people." Many did bow to Stalin, but Vishnevskii surmised that they had done so following another popular saying: "Your head won't fall off if you bow."[84]

Did people in the year thirty-seven believe in the existence of "enemies"? Here too, according to the letter writer, opinions differed. There were skeptics who thought that all or most of the trials were "provocational," nothing but scapegoating. "I used to hear the following bitter statement: 'Had there been no enemies of the people, they should have been invented.'" What bred further skepticism was that many trials went on behind closed doors, not even reported in the press. The concealment could not have been intended to keep state secrets from "our ill-wishers abroad," the skeptics reasoned, because if the accused had indeed been foreign spies, enemy intelligence would already have known whatever the trials could divulge. Therefore, the accused must have been innocent. There also had been those, Vishnevskii remembered, who thought that real enemies existed yet were few in number, while many more people suffered in reprisals innocently, from overkill. Finally, there were those who blindly trusted anything the press had to say. He did not discuss what kinds of individuals had held those opinions, or how widespread each opinion had been: "Whoever of those comprised the majority is not for us to judge." But overall Vishnevskii, and many other readers, recreated a complex panorama of views, showing that, contrary to Ermilov, not everyone in 1937–1938 had unquestionably believed the media.[85] Many of these readers' memories are confirmed by the picture of the time that is emerging today from other documents of the 1930s.[86]

Frequently, letter writers told of the gradual evaporation of belief. They recalled hierarchies and downward trajectories of support for the purges, where the degree of proximity to a victim had determined one's attitude toward repression. The better one knew the victim, the less one tended to justify his or her arrest: belief dissolved as the axe moved closer.[87] Predictably, hierarchies of belief overlapped with hierarchies of status. I. O. Kal'veit, a veteran of the Civil War and World War II and a graduate of the Moscow Military Engineering Academy, recalled that in 1937 cadets at the academy initially did not question the arrests of top military commanders and politicians. "We all" believed that Marshal Tukhachevskii was "a careerist and a Bonapartist"—"although we were greatly surprised."[88] However, when the arrests began hitting closer to home, attitudes started to change. "It was when they began arresting as enemies of the people those we knew well, when our nearest, whose innocence we did not doubt, began disappearing, that we realized that savage arbitrariness was taking place."[89] Soon enough, Kal'veit's trust in the purges dropped to zero as his proximity to them became immediate. His own brother, a Civil War commissar and a party member since 1917, was arrested. During the war, the letter writer himself followed his brother to the camps. He was ethnically German, and even being a career army officer did not help. Straight from the front, Kal'veit was sent to the Gulag for twelve years, from 1942 to 1954. "And after all that," he grimly commented on Ermilov's allegations, "someone shows up stating that people believed in the fairness of reprisals and did not keep silent with teeth clenched. What nonsense."[90]

Translated into historians' language, this may suggest that many people in 1936–1938 did not mind the first two stages of repression: "the purge of the dispossessed" (those on the society's margins), which they barely noticed, and "the purge of the powerful" (political and military elites), which they did notice but treated distantly, if with astonishment. It was at the third stage, the mass operations that directly affected millions of families, that belief in the justice of the repression began crumbling. Kal'veit observed, as well, that it was only at that stage that people around him had begun treating the purges as a dangerous topic of conversation, and only then had they "started talking about the arrests in whispers."[91]

Similarly, mining engineer V. A. Semenov, from a small town in the Far East, squarely denied Ermilov's assertion that people had blindly believed the leaders in 1937. That year, Semenov was a student at the Irkutsk Mining Institute and lived together with four other students in a dormitory room. His parents were arrested and later killed. Never admitting that they could be enemies, he began to doubt the overall justice of the unfolding repression. His roommates, though, acted as if they genuinely supported it: they hung up a portrait of the NKVD head, Nikolai Yezhov, in the room and praised him daily. "Only later did it become clear that these Komsomols had instructions to watch even the director of the institute," Semenov wrote. He did not articulate how that became clear, whose instructions those were, and whether praising Yezhov was part of the instructions, but the tone of his letter suggested that the portrait drill had been deliberately aimed at provoking him, the son of "enemies of the people." A word of objection to this daily exercise would have meant his expulsion from the institute, or worse. Thus, he quoted Ehrenburg, "Using your words, it was necessary 'to live with teeth clenched, to learn the hardest of disciplines—silence.'"[92]

The macabre ritual with the portrait ceased when arrests began in the families of the other four students. Once each of them had a relative imprisoned, Semenov noted, "the students became quieter: they no longer praised 'Yezhov's mitten.'" Yet "none of us even thought about protesting. We knew how this would end." And so, his roommates became like him: they, too, fell silent.[93]

Semenov's letter depicted an Arendtian environment of atomization, in which the massively promoted facade of popular support was an effective psychological weapon that, added to fear and conviction, was instrumental in suppressing doubt. The aura of universal approval made it exceptionally hard to develop, let alone voice, any disbelief. The community of believers, genuine or imagined, outweighed the lone dissenter. Even if belief was undermined within a small group, as it was among the five students in the dormitory, they nonetheless felt part of the larger world that precluded protest through a combination of fear, persuasion, and conformity.[94] Yet, like other letter writers, Semenov outlined the same downward, proximity-based trajectory of belief. The students' praise for Yezhov might have contained genuine feeling: had they been completely cynical they would have kept praising him even after their relatives' arrest. But once repression hit those they knew, the praise dissolved and so, presumably, did at least part of the feeling.

To reverse the logic of proximity, however, denying the guilt of one's nearest did not necessarily lead to disbelief in the existence of distant enemies. The closer the axe got, the less one trusted its justice, but the opposite could also be true. It was possible to retain one's belief in Stalin this way, too. Some letter writers remembered exactly that, although here opinions differed. Kal'veit, for example, wrote: "Where the critic [Ermilov] is right is that we believed Stalin and thought he had nothing to do with those reprisals." Some people, he remembered, had considered the purges the work of Yezhov and his lieutenants. After Yezhov's removal from office in November 1938, which was also the end of the peak phase of repression, rumors began circulating that the removal took place because Stalin had finally learned about the unjustified purges. "Most people trusted Stalin," Kal'veit insisted, and "learned the truth only from the materials of the 20th Congress."[95]

Others made the opposite argument. Boris Vishnevskii denied ever having had warm feelings for the leader: "I did not like Stalin when he was alive, and I did not start liking him after he died."[96] E. Briantseva insisted that it was precisely after Yezhov's removal that any belief in Stalin's lack of awareness disappeared. Beria's appointment as Yezhov's successor brought only limited improvement. Mass executions did cease, some inmates were released, and families could send letters and a handful of necessities to their imprisoned relatives. But the releases were few, and such extrajudicial bodies as the Special Conference continued to operate, not to mention the continued use of physical torture. Briantseva did not indicate whether people had known about torture at the time, but she insisted that after Yezhov's removal the ongoing repression could not but be associated with Stalin's name.[97]

Carrying the disbelief beyond Stalin to a systemic level apparently had been still more difficult in the 1930s, and this is likely why such statements are practically absent from the readers' letters. Fear of mentioning disbelief in the socialist system explains this absence only to a small degree. Many letter writers of the 1960s were extremely forward and fearless in their self-expression, sometimes not sparing even Khrushchev.[98] More plausible is the explanation that, to transform individual qualms into systemic doubt, people in the 1930s would have to have seen the scale of the repression—to have realized that what was happening to them was not an exception but a nationwide rule. Even a quarter of a century later, the big picture was only beginning to emerge. Not incidentally did Khrushchev's revelations at the Twentieth Congress shake even Tvardovskii. Also, the idea of systemic abnormality worked against what many people *wanted* to believe, both in the 1930s and in the 1960s: the general normalcy of the world they inhabited.[99] Recognizing that the opposite was true was hard. This is partly why the letter writers explored the issue of belief in such agonizing detail and with such contradictory results. Still, many did indicate the arrests of their relatives and friends in 1937–1938 as the starting point for their disbelief, if only in the justice of the purges themselves.[100] Silence could also shroud the origins of doubt.

There was an aspect of this discussion that may have helped the readers continue on their downward trajectory of belief now, in the 1960s. Letter writers such as Vishnevskii and Semenov openly challenged the media ethos embodied in Ermilov's article. The notion of belief as unlimited selfless devotion to the cause may or may not have been valid for them even in 1937, since belief is always limited by self-interest and self-preservation, but by 1963 it had become possible to acknowledge these limitations out loud. The letters asserted the normalcy of self-interest, the ethical acceptability of calculation in times of mortal danger. This open assertion of pragmatism was vastly different from the media-imposed standards for selfless political behavior. As to whether the letter writers had always espoused different standards and were merely verbalizing them now, or were reformulating the standards themselves now, in 1963, the answer may be that verbalization meant reformulation. The act of fixing norms of human action in writing for public consumption denoted the crystallization of those norms into a new, dominant status.

There were people who, back in the 1930s, had taken the official standards of loyalty seriously, but for whom since then belief had come to mean something different. The sixty-three-year-old Iurii Aleksandrovich Fridman, who had spent fifteen years in the Gulag and identified himself as a "rehabilitated communist" (as well as a "personal pensioner," a designation that carried special retirement benefits for a distinguished service record), expressed this most eloquently. Like others, Fridman was outraged by Ermilov's cavalier moralizing. "You play an innocent child ignorant of the horrible practice of those years," he censured Ermilov. "You cannot but know that right after a party member or a nonmember was arrested, immediately and without even waiting for his official sentence, all his friends and comrades were required to renounce him and to repent 'overlooking' an enemy of the people. Penitence often did not help either, because relatives (first priority) were still expelled from the party and arrested." This is exactly what had happened to Fridman himself. Back in 1938, he dutifully informed his party organization about his brother's arrest, confident that the case would be quickly pronounced a mistake. Instead the organization immediately expelled him from the party, and soon he was arrested.[101]

Still, even though no one had the right to accuse those who had been silent, the origins of the silence troubled Fridman. It was understandable, he wrote, that an average individual had not dared protest. But how was it possible that Old Bolsheviks, the guard of the Revolution, veteran fighters who had risked their lives and had once been ready to go to tsarist prisons or even to the gallows—how was it possible that they did not fight back? The answer, for Fridman, would be the key to the silence of the year thirty-seven.

His answer was that the Old Bolsheviks viewed protest against Stalin as discrediting the common cause. Although they did not necessarily have warm feelings for the leader and his policies, they dreaded unleashing factional struggles and disputation. "To speak against Stalin and the system of arbitrariness was tantamount to speaking against the party and Soviet power, and no true Communist would do that. 'Better if I died,' they reasoned, 'but let the party and Soviet power be well and prosper, because sooner or later everything will become clear and mistakes will be corrected.' "[102] At the root of the silence of veteran communists in 1937 was a characteristic understanding of higher loyalty—a concern for the unity of the ranks, an apprehension that dissent would undermine this unity and endanger the cause. Regardless of whether such unity existed, people in the 1930s considered the idea of it a blessing. On top of that, unity was a necessity in view of the impending and inevitable battle against Nazi Germany.[103] Here was another dimension of the tragedy of silence in the year thirty-seven. Many people who recognized the injustice or repression refrained from protesting—not even because they feared for their lives, but because they feared the very idea of disagreement.[104]

This preoccupation with maintaining the appearance of unity, Fridman reflected, was what distinguished the Soviet mind from its imperial-era forebears. When Leo Tolstoy protested against the Stolypin executions of peasants in 1908, he proclaimed "I cannot keep silent!" in the Russia of the tsars, where the democratic intelligentsia took a split between state and society for granted. Presuming it an issue of honor to oppose the monarchical authority, it was in these traditionally confrontational terms that educated Russians received Tolstoy's call for above-party clemency and forgiveness.[105] But in the Soviet Union of the 1930s, where opposition between state and society was declared nonexistent, and where indeed many presumed those two concepts to be one and the same, the Tolstoyan stance was not just physically deadly—it did not make sense.[106]

And here, too, was something that distinguished the people of the 1960s from those of the 1930s. In 1963, Fridman did not fear disagreement any more: in fact, he disagreed as intensely as he could. What previously had not made sense now received a new meaning. The traditional state-society fractures that had marked Russian political culture before the Revolution and remained latent in the early Soviet years resurfaced during the Thaw.[107] The idea of difference, the principle of remonstrance to authority as a moral duty of an educated person, became an ethical norm again—along with a new level of appreciation for the value of individual human life. In the winter of 1962–63, the massive protest against the media's attempt to employ the theme of mass violence for the regime's self-congratulatory reaffirmation showed that, even for those who had built the Soviet order, socialism no longer meant automatic acceptance of any government policy or message. Silence was to be no more.

Belief and Accountability

The fact that the eyewitnesses to the purges rejected the ostensibly convenient journalistic theory on open protest was remarkable. One might imagine that at least some of those who had lived through 1937 would be tempted to embellish their past by grabbing onto Ermilov's thesis and arguing that they had in fact protested. Yet practically none of the letter writers assumed this heroic posture. Instead, they sought an explanation for what had made the purges, and the silence that accompanied them, possible. Finding out the truth was more valuable to them than achieving peace of mind through a quick fix of mythmaking. This aversion to myths was generally symptomatic of the intellectual culture of the Thaw, which was premised on a quest for authenticity—historical above all.

Mythmaking was hard to avoid, though, and it became a stumbling block when discussions of the year thirty-seven approached the issue of personal accountability. In various incarnations, the problem of social ethics was of central importance for literary audiences during the Thaw. Historical accountability was part of this context. Moral responsibility for the past was the other side of the problem of belief: this was indeed why the letter writers examined belief so persistently and in such detail. However, the letters suggest that in the 1960s the discussion of accountability for the recent tragedy reached only an embryonic, if important, stage—the one at which memories of fear and belief mostly served the purpose of self-absolution.

Absolving oneself was one of the most common themes in the accounts of those who had seen the repression firsthand. This motif came out even in the best-argued and cogent letters. Some people tried absolving themselves radically: thus, E. Briantseva of Novosibirsk, whom we have already met, argued that the executioners had been few, while "the overwhelming majority of our wonderful, cordial Soviet people" had sympathized with the victims and, when possible, quietly helped them or their families. And when people refused to help, she insisted, they did so while "turning their faces away in embarrassment."[108]

Such statements, usually coming from fairly elderly letter writers, were meant to persuade their authors that despite all the cost they had built something of lasting value—a fair and upright society. Identifying with this society, they sought to justify it in its new trial of moral legitimacy—and also to justify themselves, to step away from the chasm that had suddenly opened so nearby. The crux of Briantseva's letter, the reason she summoned images of "our wonderful, cordial Soviet people" silently helping the victims, was self-vindication, and her use of generational language emphasized, as such language always does, the importance she attached to this polemical effort. "Even if we talk about everything that the victims' relatives went through," she wrote, ". . . would such a summation be <u>an indictment for the entire generation?</u> Would such a summation be <u>an offense</u> to this generation? No, and once again, no!"[109] With similar emotional investment, Boris Vishnevskii wrote:

> We, ordinary Soviet people, have nothing to blush for. Let those blush, if they are alive and capable of feeling shame, let those be responsible before history who created Stalin's cult of personality, who glorified Stalin in all their public statements. . . . Let them blush, and let shame fall upon their heads, not the heads of those who became victims of Stalin's cult of personality against their will.[110]

It was the emotionality of such statements that revealed their authors' distress—and perhaps their lack of confidence in what they so passionately proclaimed. What also revealed it was that same generational rhetoric, the frequent "we" that the letter writers used instead of the lonely, disconcerting "I." The "we" came not from the Soviet habit of speaking on behalf of a collective: if need be, the letter writers were perfectly capable of making individual statements. In this case, though, it was *safer* to feel part of a group, a cohort, to be not alone when facing the ocean of blood spilled for reasons increasingly obscure.

But then, inevitably, came the time when one had to face it alone. And here people became far more reflective and less assertive. Even the authors of the most upbeat statements about their innocence did not seem to find their own words very uplifting. Despite proclaiming that his generation had nothing to blush for, Vishnevskii did blush. He was not pleased with how he had acted during the 1930s. "This was a strange and difficult time," he wrote. "You remember it—and deep inside you feel something unpleasant: so much waste has accumulated there. . . . At my advanced age, I finally should not lie. The time comes when I need to tell the truth."[111]

Because this discussion of accountability went hand in hand with reflection on belief, it may be appropriate to use religious terminology when analyzing it. The striving toward self-absolution was an initial step, and a promising one, not a definitive conclusion in the increasingly introspective remembrance of the year thirty-seven. Self-absolution was not yet repentance. But it surely was a step above the "zero" stage of (non-)remembering—denial. None of those who wrote to Ehrenburg, and indeed none of the thousands of people who wrote to *Novyi mir* throughout the Thaw, ever denied that massive violence had taken place and was a tragedy of universal scale.[112] Many letter writers were victims of that violence in a very direct, physical sense, while others had suffered less directly. But all had been affected. It was the recognition of this universal impact of the tragedy that brought the letter writers together and kept them thinking, regardless of their actual proximity to it in the past. Self-absolution, also, was not too far from repentance. Christian theology, whether Orthodox, Catholic, or Lutheran, views absolution and repentance as inseparable—provided, of course, that the repentant does not absolve herself but seeks the higher authority for that sake.

An additional problem was that the letter writers did not know a higher ethical authority. The time when they wrote witnessed the collapse of such authorities, especially those considered stable only a few years before. During the Thaw, thousands of people began looking for other moral criteria and values—new, old, ancient—to give meaning to their past and present lives. Given the literature-centric tradition, this was another reason why writers became such moral authorities at the time. The quest was to take many years, but what was reassuring was the visible and growing discomfort with which people remembered their past, the dozens of troubled hours and pages they spent remembering it. Better than anything else, this showed that their reflection on historical accountability was beginning.

"*I Am Afraid This Past May Come Back*"

The year thirty-seven had a powerful grip on the mind. Whoever once looked into this massive, inexplicable extermination of human beings could not walk away from it. One after another, the letter writers insisted that the arrests, disappearances, and executions, together with years of enforced silence about them, had irreparably damaged society's moral fiber.[113] The growing awareness of the multitude of lives, destroyed for no apparent reason and long banned from mentioning, undermined people's confidence in their world's legitimacy, as well as in their own integrity.

A world replete with ethical disorientation, a sense of lost markers between the very basic ethical categories framing human existence, opened up in a letter by the thirty-nine-year-old V. Grigor'eva from Moscow. "Your book," she wrote to Ehrenburg in early 1961, ". . . is good because white is called white in it and black is called black. Many have long stopped understanding what is white and what is black." Ehrenburg in fact did not differentiate between white and black so clearly—he preferred shades to polarized colorations of human behavior. Yet this was what the reader carried away from his book: a clearer identification of basic ethical values that, she believed, society had forsaken.[114] About the same age as Grigor'eva, A. Vorob'ev, a history teacher from Siberia in his early thirties, had been five or six years old in 1937–1938. He remembered how his elder sister would come home from school and tell him that Marshal Vasilii Bliukher (1889–1938) was an enemy of the people. "She would sit down at the table, take the book, and blot out the portrait of a man whom everyone had mentioned with respect just the day before. It is only now that one realizes how people's souls were mutilated."[115] Anatolii Popov, a journalist in his forties from Ukraine, remembered how *Pravda* had praised Bruno Jasieński's (1901–1938) novel *Man Changes His Skin* but then, after the author was arrested (and later shot), took the novel apart. He also remembered the name of the journalist who had attacked Jasieński: it was David Zaslavskii, the same Zaslavskii who would twenty years later call Pasternak a literary weed. Popov did not refer to the Pasternak story—but likely in 1958 he had not given much credit to its newspaper rendition, knowing who was writing.[116]

To many letter writers, the moral crisis that originated in the past suggested that this past was not safely gone. They feared that, with the people's minds distorted by decades of living in a repressive environment, the repression could return any time. In these parts of their letters, 1937 began to stand for the entire Stalin epoch, and its repercussions for the future. "The period from 1937 to 1953 is the most shameful in the history of Russia. Every Soviet person who was eighteen to twenty years old in 1937 should be ashamed for all his subsequent life," wrote G. Neverov, an economist from Kiev. "Today there is no guarantee that a cult of personality or personalities will not repeat."[117] Samuil Mirkin, in his fifties, from Omsk, who once had to answer his children's question, "Dad, why was so-and-so shot?" was concerned with persistent anti-Semitism and did not exclude the possibility of another Stalin-style "anticosmopolitan" campaign.[118] "A group of indignant readers, friends of Ilya Grigor'evich Ehrenburg," numbering no fewer than eighty-seven people ("students, office employees, workers, and housewives"), urged Tvardovskii to defend Ehrenburg from the campaign whose style reminded them of the purges. "You were the first one," they wrote to Tvardovskii, "who began talking about those terrible years. And this entire situation is reminiscent of them."[119]

"Damn it, we are building the most equitable, the most upright state [*sic*], and yet we lie!" exclaimed the thirty-four-year-old electrician and war veteran Iurii Boglovskii from Leningrad. "We have raised an entire generation of people who negotiate, in minor things, their own conscience. . . . Things have become quite lively today, but time and again comes a harsh administrative bellow suggestive of the recent past! And frankly, I am afraid this past may come back."[120] In Boglovskii's opinion, the past had bestowed a persistent moral deficiency on society, a deficiency that he chose to identify with the concept proposed nine years earlier by Pomerantsev—insincerity. Thus, for the sake of career advancement some of his friends were ready to pretend that the purges had never happened. One newly minted low-level manager and party member, he wrote, believed that "the thousands of most honorable people who had perished were nothing but fantasy." "I tell him," Boglovskii despaired, "'Look, you are negotiating with your conscience, this is insincere!' He replies: 'I act in full accordance with the [party] regulations and program.'"[121]

Perhaps the one who best formulated the idea of the permanent ethical damage the Stalin epoch had inflicted by dragging everyone in, either as victims or hangmen but with no bystanders, was Eva Vil'gel'movna Miuntser, the sixty-year-old widow of a Polish communist murdered in 1937.[122] Back then, she had a ten-year-old son and was pregnant. After her husband's arrest, everyone turned their back on her. She was fired, her apartment was taken away, and her son was deprived of library privileges—because, the librarian told him, the son of a foreign spy had no reason to read in a library together with Soviet children. In April 1938 Eva Vil'gel'movna was in labor. She came to the hospital at the last moment because she needed to leave some food for her son: friends, neighbors, and teachers refused to help. At the hospital, she was in labor for fourteen hours. Reluctant to deal with an enemy's wife, none of the medical personnel approached her. Only one nurse, whose husband had also been arrested, finally called for a doctor when the patient lost consciousness. In the end, the child suffocated and died.

> Why, of everything I have been through, does this haunt me the most? It seems to me that the birth of a child brings forth something fair, humane, and compassionate even in the worst kind of people. And here is some fascist savagery. This is incomprehensible, and it is scary that something like that could exist inside humans. But why only "could"? Several generations have been trained in the "Stalinist" spirit—the spirit of suspicion and mistrust of the individual. All these "trainees" now occupy leading administrative positions.[123]

Miuntser's memories were very different from the ones we find, say, in the reader Briantseva's letter quoted above. According to Briantseva, the hangmen of the year thirty-seven were few, while "the overwhelming majority of our wonderful, cordial Soviet people" quietly helped those who were arrested or their families.[124] For Miuntser, there were no wonderful, cordial people. No one sympathized, and no one helped. The hangmen's names were legion, and they were still around, alive and well.[125]

What emerged from all such accounts was the idea of a moral catastrophe, a black abyss directly beneath the present, everyday existence—the Terror, indeed. Eva Vil'gel'movna Miuntser did not hesitate to bring charges against her people—charges of complicity in murder. This was why she made the analogy between 1937 and fascism—an analogy that had not escaped Ehrenburg, either. This was also why she subscribed to his words, which he made the leitmotif, subtly and incisively unnerving, of his writing about the terror: "It was not the idea that received a blow. It was the people."[126] Ehrenburg, in fact, had put it slightly differently. He wrote "a fatal blow."[127]

In Search of New Values

The readers' polemic around *People, Years, Life* revealed a host of problems in remembering and explaining the terror. A major one among them was that, unlike in many post–World War II European societies, where regimes of mass extermination were crushed in 1944 and 1945, and the new governments, at least in general terms, dissociated themselves from their predecessors, the Soviet regime staked its legitimacy on continuity with its immediate past.[128] More than elsewhere, in the Soviet Union remembrance of state violence worked against the state's vital interests. Logically, the media followed the initial earth-shattering revelations about the Stalin epoch with an effort to present this epoch as an integral, overwhelmingly positive historical stage. Ermilov's 1963 attack on Ehrenburg was an early attempt at writing the terror into the established, noncontroversial, and sanitized historical narrative, where neither the system nor the people bore responsibility for the tragedy. The violence thus appeared to be a momentary aberration, an accidental, unfortunate sidetrack from the country's predominantly normal, progressive path.

The attempt failed spectacularly. It revealed all the vulnerability of journalistic efforts to "normalize" the terror, to inscribe it neatly into history by employing ready-made newspaper rhetoric. Rather than lending itself to such uses, the terror proved inexplicable and unusable for any kind of didactic or propagandistic purposes. Instead the terror itself turned out to have shaped and "used," and to continue to use, those who tried to interpret it—or, unsuccessfully, to cover it up. The terror proved a formidable entanglement that implicated everyone, impinging on everyone's memories and lives.

The discussions of Ehrenburg's memoir demonstrated that the language and ethos of the Soviet media were decidedly unfit for conveying and comprehending one of the central experiences of the twentieth century. What Tvardovskii had discovered a few years earlier now received public confirmation. When it came to explaining the terror, the Thaw rapidly melted the ice of existing ideological constructs, moral notions, and verbal formulas, right beneath the interpreters' feet. The ice was becoming dangerously thin, and the option was either to risk drowning or look urgently for new, firmer intellectual ground. Explaining the terror required a new system of values, and describing it required new words. Both were manifestly absent.

With his memoir, Ehrenburg took an initial, but important, step toward addressing the ethical dimension of the problem. By emphasizing the centrality to history of individual human experience, he gave his audience an ethical criterion with which the past could be approached differently from familiar textbook or newspaper recipes. Facing the terror with this new criterion proved a challenge: many readers reported a sense of moral disorientation that plagued them in their new reflections.

The other part of the problem, language, remained unsolved and largely untouched in discussions of Ehrenburg's memoir. However, simultaneously with him another author began to approach the same set of issues, trying to merge the ethical and the linguistic dimensions of accounting for the past. The impact of his effort was emblematic—as his name would become. That name, of course, was Aleksandr Solzhenitsyn.

FIGURE 1. Aleksandr Tvardovskii, editor in chief of *Novyi mir*, 11 July 1961. (ITAR-TASS)

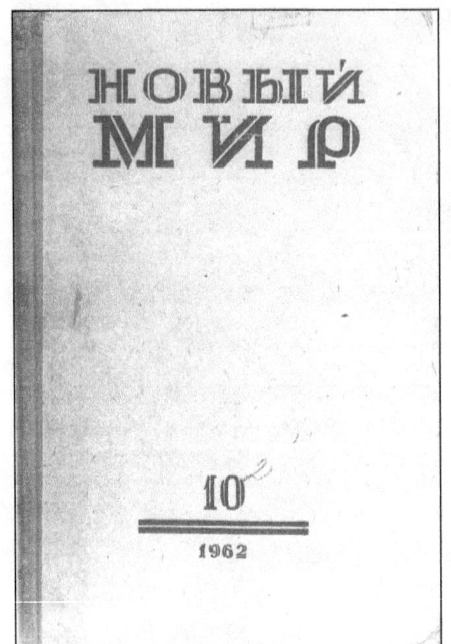

FIGURES 2 AND 3. The front covers of the October (left) and November 1962 issues of *Novyi mir*, from the collection of the State Public History Library in Moscow. The November issue contained Solzhenitsyn's *One Day in the Life of Ivan Denisovich*. Compare its worn cover, a visible sign of the issue's popularity, with the cleaner cover of the preceding issue. (Courtesy of *Novyi mir*)

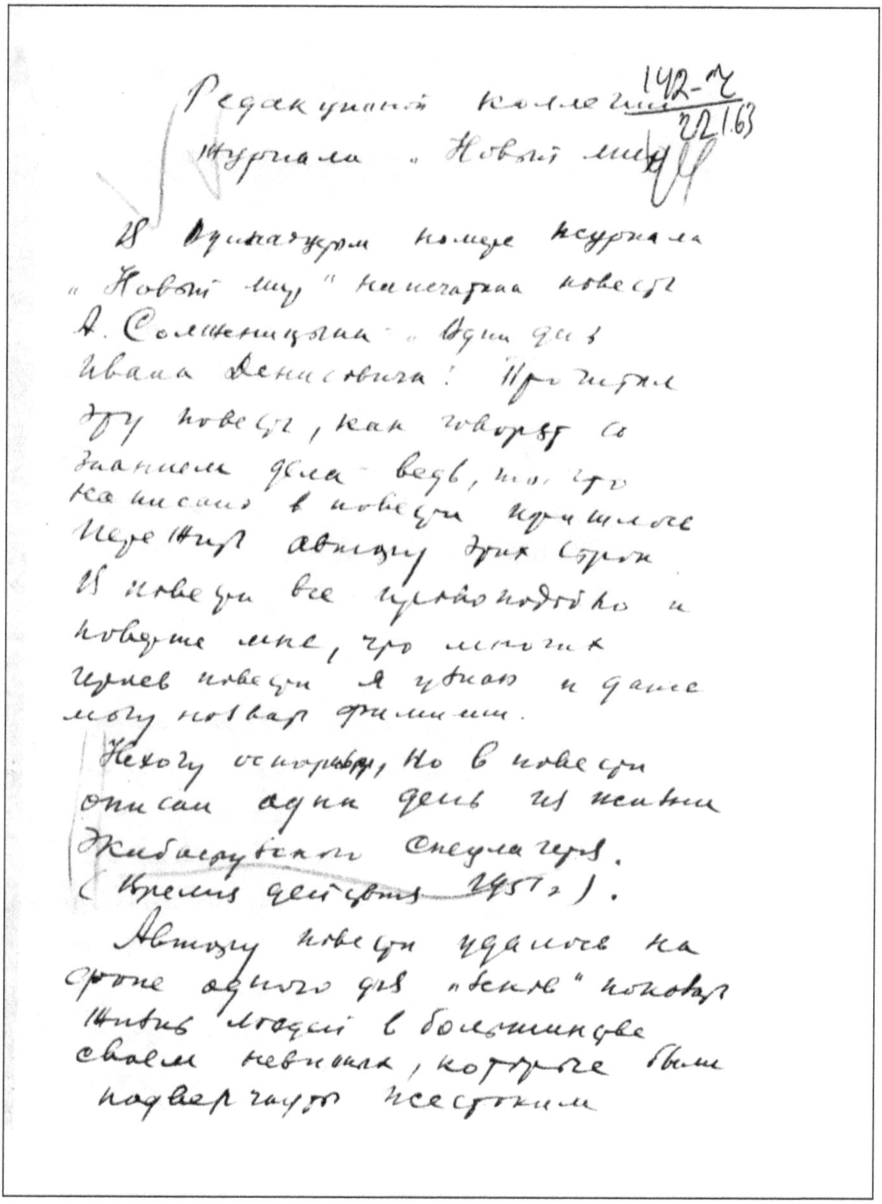

Редакционной коллегии журнала «Новый мир»

142-Ч
22.1.63

В одиннадцатом номере журнала «Новый мир» напечатана повесть А. Солженицына «Один день Ивана Денисовича». Прочитал эту повесть, как говорят со знанием дела — ведь, то, что написано в повести пришлось пережить автору этих строк. В повести все правдоподобно и поверьте мне, что многих героев повести я узнаю и даже могу назвать фамилии.

Нечего оспаривать, но в повести описан один день из жизни Экибастузского Спецлагеря. (Время действия 1951 г.).

Автору повести удалось на фоне одного дня «жизни» показать жизнь людей в большинстве своем невинных, которые были подвергнуты жестоким

FIGURE 4. The opening page of a letter to the editorial board of *Novyi mir,* dated 15 January 1963 and written by Vasilii Chubar' of Kokhchetav, Kazakhstan, in response to Solzhenitsyn's *One Day in the Life of Ivan Denisovich.* The letter writer recognizes the place Solzhenitsyn describes in the novella. This part of the letter has been marked, possibly by Tvardovskii. (RGALI, f. 1702, op. 10, d. 76, l. 44)

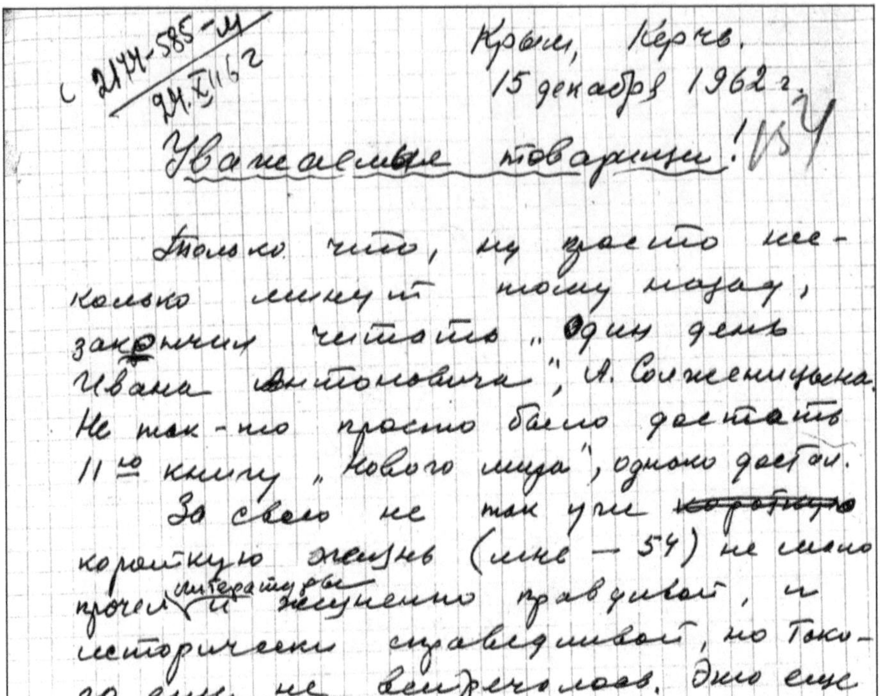

С 2174-585-м
24.XII 62 г

Крым, Керчь.
15 декабря 1962 г.

154

Уважаемые товарищи!

Только что, ну просто несколько минут тому назад, закончил читать „Один день Ивана Антоновича“, А. Солженицына. Не так-то просто было достать 11-ю книгу „Нового мира“, однако достал.

За свою не так уж ~~коротую~~ короткую жизнь (мне — 54) не много прочел литературы и жизненно правдивой, и исторически справедливой, но такого еще не встречалось. Это еще не совсем определенное, до конца пока не осознанное, но совершенно новое направление в литературе. И хорошее! То самое, которое следует расширять и углублять во-всю. Это ничем не подкрашенная Правда, выраженная великолепными художественными формами и яркими образами. Наконец-то!..

В самом деле.

FIGURE 5. The opening page of a letter dated 15 December 1962 from Daniil Markelov of Kerch, Ukraine, responding to Solzhenitsyn's *One Day.* (RGALI, f. 1702, op. 10, d. 2, l. 154)

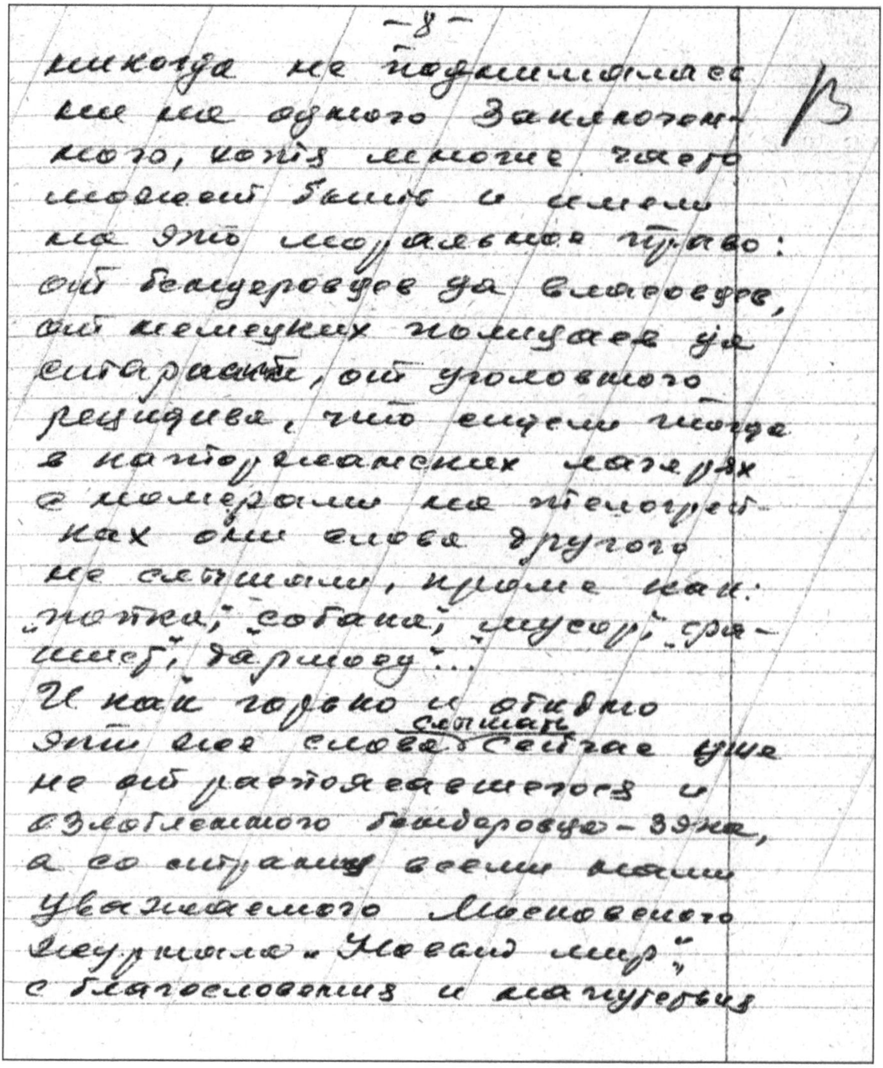

-8-

никогда не поднимались
ни на одного заключен-
ного, хотя многие часто
может быть и имели
на это моральное право:
от бандеровцев да власовцев,
от немецких полицаев из
старосты, от уголовного
рецидива, что сидели тогда
в каторжанских лагерях
с номерами на телогрей-
ках они слова другого
не слышали, кроме как:
„попка", „собака", „мусор", „[illegible]",
„дармоед"...
И как горько и обидно
эти все слова слышать сейчас уже
не от настоящего и
озлобленного бандеровца-зэка,
а со страниц всеми нами
уважаемого Московского
журнала „Новый мир",
с благословения и напутствия

В

FIGURE 6. A page from the letter dated 7 December 1962 by the former Gulag camp guard Vasilii Zagorodskii, responding to Solzhenitsyn's *One Day.* While denying that the guards ever beat the prisoners, Zagorodskii claims they had the "moral right" to do so. (RGALI, f. 1702, op. 10, d. 2, l. 13)

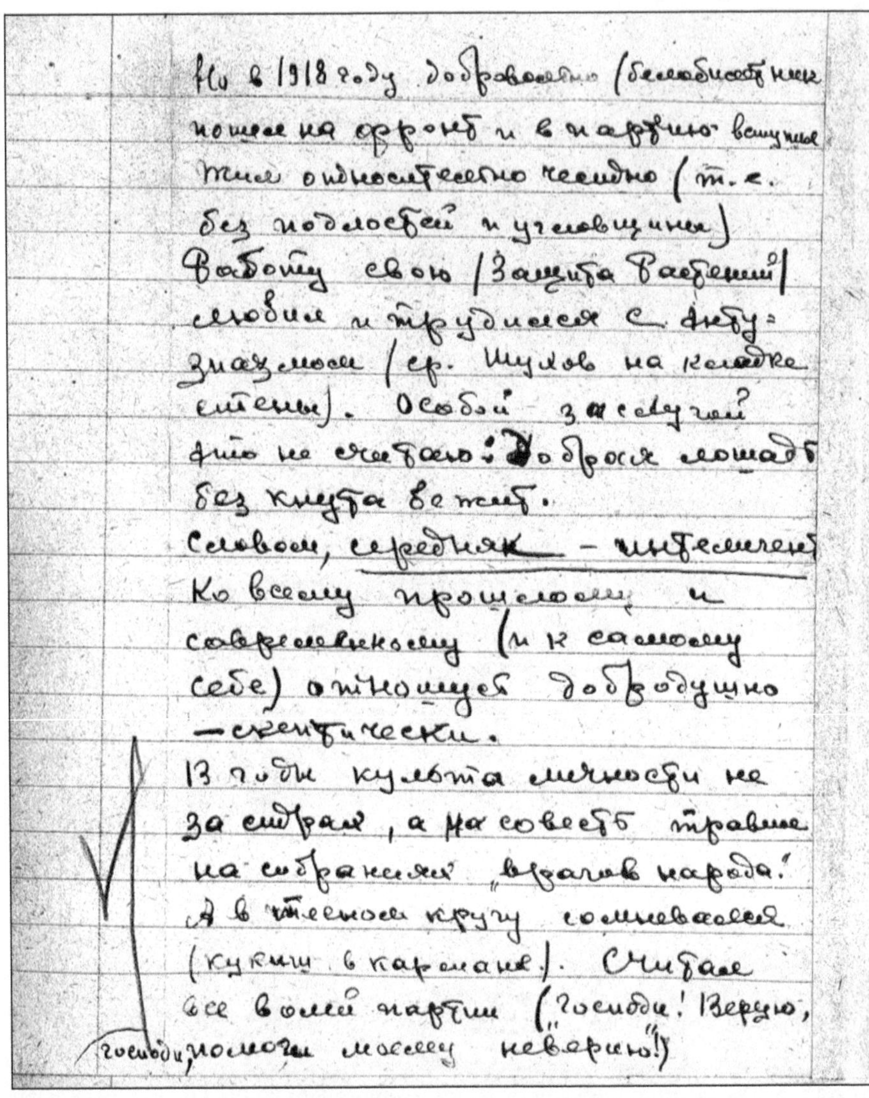

Но в 1918 году добровольно (бессребреник
пошел на фронт и в партию вступил
Жил относительно честно (т.е.
без подлостей и уголовщины)
Работу свою (Защита растений)
любил и трудился с энту-
зиазмом (ср. Шухов на кладке
стены). Особой заслугой?
этого не считаю: добрая лошадь
без кнута везет.
Словом, середняк — интеллигент
Ко всему прошлому и
современному (и к самому
себе) отношусь добродушно
—скептически.
13 годы культа личности не
за страх, а на совесть травил
на собраниях „врагов народа."
А в тесном кругу сомневался
(кукиш в кармане). Считаю
все волей партии („господи! Верую,
господи, помоги моему неверию!")

FIGURE 7. A page of a letter dated 24 December 1962 from D. A. Vakhrameev of Karaganda Oblast, Kazakhstan, responding to Solzhenitsyn's *One Day*. Vakhrameev describes his own participation in the bashing of "enemies of the people" during the years of the "cult of personality." (RGALI, f. 1702, op. 10, d. 73, l. 83ob)

FIGURE 8. The Second All-Union Conference of Founding Organizations of the Press Agency "Novosti," 1 June 1967. Left to right: secretary of the USSR Union of Writers Konstantin Simonov, editor in chief of the journal *Inostrannaia literatura* Boris Riurikov, chairman of the USSR State Committee on Cinematography A. V. Romanov. Photograph by Mikhail Ozerskii. (Courtesy of RIA Novosti)

FIGURE 9. Vladimir Dudintsev, author of *Not by Bread Alone*, 1 January 1958. (Courtesy of RIA Novosti)

FIGURE 10. Ilya Ehrenburg, 1 February 1959. (Courtesy of RIA Novosti)

FIGURE 11. Aleksandr Solzhenitsyn at work, 14 December 1962. (Courtesy of RIA Novosti)

FIGURE 12. Aleksandr Krivitskii, the author of the myth of twenty-eight Panfilovites, during World War II. (From Aleksandr Krivitskii, *Ne zabudu vovek: Zapiski voennogo korrespondenta* [Moscow: Voenizdat, 1964])

FIGURE 13. Boris Burkovskii, the prototype of a central character in *One Day in the Life of Ivan Denisovich* (right), with the actor Kirill Lavrov. Photograph probably taken in 1965 during the production of the feature film *Zalp Avrory* (The *Aurora*'s Salvo). (Courtesy of the Burkovskii family archive)

FIGURE 14. Lathe operator and Hero of Socialist Labor Mikhail Egorovich Zakharov (center) during a party committee session at the Podol'sk Machine-Building Plant, 1 January 1971. (Courtesy of RIA Novosti)

FIGURE 15. Konstantin Simonov (right, in black) at Tvardovskii's funeral, 21 December 1971. Also pictured are the secretary of the board of the USSR Union of Writers, Aleksei Surkov (left, in spectacles), the writer Sergei Mikhalkov (taller man in spectacles directly behind Simonov), and (far right, background) Aleksandr Solzhenitsyn. (Courtesy of RIA Novosti)

FIGURE 16. Aleksandr Tvardovskii, 20 June 1967. (ITAR-TASS)

7

FINDING NEW WORDS

Solzhenitsyn and the Experience of Terror

SOLZHENITSYN'S *One Day in the Life of Ivan Denisovich* is the best-remembered work of literature that appeared in Tvardovskii's *Novyi mir*, and it is widely considered the most famous literary product of the Thaw.[1] If the numbers of readers' reactions at least partly reflect the societal impact of a literary text, then indeed this book was one of the most influential publications to appear in the journal from the late 1940s through the late 1960s. *Novyi mir*'s archive for 1962 through 1969 has so far yielded 532 letters about *One Day* from more than 579 readers, a number bested only by Dudintsev's 1956 *Not by Bread Alone* (720 letters from more than 820 readers).

Solzhenitsyn by no means initiated the literary polemic on the terror. However, with his work the polemic received a clear voice, tone, and direction. Just as Ehrenburg, he set the ethical framework for verbalizing the human experiences of the twentieth century's mass violence. He also suggested new linguistic means for reaching this objective. Together, these became the criteria of ethical and stylistic authenticity that would structure and measure the numerous subsequent discussions of the central phenomenon in Russia's modern history.

A longtime champion of Solzhenitsyn's novella who must be credited with the success of its publication (particularly for obtaining Khrushchev's personal sanction to publish it), Tvardovskii correctly anticipated the surge of readers' reactions.[2] He also predicted that they would vary. On the eve of publication, in the atmosphere of growing suspense and fast-accumulating rumors in Moscow's literary circles about the forthcoming sensation, he wrote to Solzhenitsyn: "There will be good press, there will be enormous mail, and I am sure this mail will be *diverse*."[3] When *One Day* came out and the responses began flooding in, the jubilant Tvardovskii wrote again: "The torrent of letters in my name and in yours keeps coming to the editorial office, and the responses, take courage, are diverse—this is how it should be. But the bad ones, of course, comprise only a small part, and as a rule they are anonymous, which sufficiently characterizes their authors. . . . In a word, all is going well, dear A.[leksandr] I.[saevich], and hopefully will go the same way in the future."[4]

I will return to the question of anonymity in the responses, but let us first look at their diversity, which Tvardovskii repeatedly mentioned. Reactions to *One Day* indeed varied, more so than responses to Ehrenburg's memoir or in fact to any other major publication in *Novyi mir* in the two and a half postwar decades. From the total of 532 letters, the vast majority, 422 (79.3 percent, from 478 letter writers), approved of the novella overall, while another 100 (18.8 percent, 109 letter writers) evaluated it largely negatively. Ten more were fairly neutral or unspecific. Whether because of an editorial preference for keeping positive responses, the readers' inclination to send mostly approvals, or, perchance, the actual distribution of opinions, in the journal's archive one-fifth was a high proportion for negative reactions to a publication.

Just as in other cases, of course, these reactions cannot be divided unequivocally into negative and positive. Many letters combined elements of both attitudes and, moreover, different attitudes did not manifest incompatible worldviews. Whether positive or negative, most letters were written in a similar language that reflected a fairly coherent, if dynamic, order of perceptions and reasoning. It is this order of reasoning that is the main theme of my analysis.

Words, Ages, Truth

There is something that makes us read these letters—long, convoluted texts, often twenty, thirty, or even forty handwritten pages of awkward prose. As always, but perhaps especially in the responses to Solzhenitsyn, the question is: Why would somebody write several dozen pages that would go essentially nowhere, into the void, bringing the letter writer no recognition and no credit? There was practically no chance of their publication, and the readers realized that: only 5 out of more than 500 expressly mentioned that they desired to see their responses published.[5] Many more knew, and often directly predicted, that this would never happen. In fact, many people specifically declared that their letters were not for publication, that they were mere statements of opinion for the information of the addressee. Who was this addressee? Who were the letter writers? What did they write, and what for?

It is useful to begin with some general characteristics. Apparently, such categories as ethnicity, gender, place of residence, and party or Komsomol membership neither stood out as determining factors in readers' attitudes toward the novella nor made their responses to *One Day* a special case. Age, on the other hand, was a distinct characteristic among Solzhenitsyn's correspondents. Middle-aged and older readers had always been prominent in *Novyi mir*'s active audience, but in reaction to *One Day* the journal received more letters from older people and fewer from the young than at any other point in the previous two decades.[6] Age by itself did not determine a reader's acceptance or rejection of Solzhenitsyn's text, though. Among those who identified their ages, the young particularly seemed to welcome it: 40 out of 42 younger readers did so. But most of the middle-aged (99 out of 121) and older letter writers (28 out of 38) also reacted to the book positively. Just as in Ehrenburg's case, the many disagreements over *One Day* did not split neatly along the lines of age but instead cut *within* age groups—and often within the mind of the same readers, who accepted some of Solzhenitsyn's agendas yet rejected others. The ultimate force underlying these reactions was not merely age but experience.

Former Gulag prisoners wrote at least 159 of the 532 letters to Solzhenitsyn in *Novyi mir*'s archive. A further 15 letters came from ex-camp guards or those who had worked in the camps as hired personnel *(vol'nonaemnye)*. Overall, no less than a third of the responses to *One Day* came from people who knew the camps inside out. Considering that these were self-identified former prisoners (guards, free hires), and that some letter writers probably did not disclose their Gulag background, the share of ex-inmates or camp personnel, not to mention those who had relatives and acquaintances repressed, may be even larger.

By responding to *One Day*, these people wanted to share their own experiences with a sympathetic and understanding listener, envisioning in this capacity Solzhenitsyn or Tvardovskii, their most frequent addressees.

According to the theory of testimony (based predominantly on studies of the Holocaust), the presence of a listener is crucial to the testimonial process.[7] Solzhenitsyn, in this case, was a particularly good listener because he himself had gone through the camps. As he and Tvardovskii were at a substantial physical distance from the readers, their accounts had to take a written form: letter writing instead of telling. This was the kind of therapeutic writing that Tvardovskii recommended to authors and other correspondents who had been through the Gulag. While he could not publish their letters, he still urged people to write, assuring them that the very process of putting memories on paper would help them come to terms with the past. He also promised that the writings would not be lost, that he would store them in the journal's archive for the use of future authors and historians. This he did—and the degree of trust that the letter writers had in him and in Solzhenitsyn was remarkable.[8]

The initial premise of their writing was actually not far from Tvardovskii's own vision of memoirs. As always with the Soviet reading audience, the letters were not simply testimonies of individual traumatic experiences. Many blended eyewitness accounts, political statements, and attempts at historical interpretation of the recent mass violence, all strengthened by a desire to leave a lasting record of the phenomenon. Like Tvardovskii, those who shared their Gulag experiences with him often viewed themselves as political subjects, eager not only to tell their life stories but also to place them in a broader historical context in an effort to explain the origins and implications of the terror.[9] And just as Tvardovskii himself did, many letter writers continued to identify with the very political order that had generated this repressive machine. Despite parallels with Nazi Germany that some readers occasionally drew, this political identification was an important difference between accounts of Soviet camp experiences and those of the Holocaust. Soviet eyewitnesses usually did not, could not, and did not wish to distance themselves from the regime that had brought the terror into being. Instead, many of them wrote in a desperate and tragic attempt to rescue this regime and its history, inseparably tied to their own lives and ideas.

Their predicament was more than a political and historical problem. It concerned the very groundwork of the culture in which they functioned—its moral order and its language. Indeed, it was language that became a major point of controversy around Solzhenitsyn's novella and one of the most frequent targets of attacks against it. No less than 73 out of the 532 letters about *One Day* contained critical comments about its language. Here age did come to matter. Thirty-one out of these 73 letters indicated their authors' ages—and most, 24 out of 31, came from people age fifty-five and older.[10] Advanced age, in other words, was highly relevant in determining why readers criticized Solzhenitsyn's prose.

The prose was indeed unusual. *One Day* was the first published Russian literary text in decades in which the author used swearwords. Those appeared in print nearly openly, with only one letter changed—an *f* instead of *kh*, for example, masking an obscenity like a fig leaf. Those "fig leaves" were the work of Tvardovskii and other editors at the journal who, after some struggle, persuaded Solzhenitsyn that otherwise the censors would not allow the text to be published. In his famous preface to *One Day*, anticipating the readers' reaction, Tvardovskii defended Solzhenitsyn's use of obscenities, arguing that the horror of the camps called for a special vocabulary to describe it. Therefore, he wrote euphemistically, "the moderate and expedient use of words and expressions from that environment where the hero spends his workday" was justified, even though "it might bring objections from those of a particularly fastidious taste."[11] He foresaw the problem accurately. *Fuiaslitse, fuimetsia, smefuëchki,* and so on—by the standards of today's Russian prose these disguised swearwords seem timid, but in 1962 and 1963 they drew close attention and received intense criticism from the reading audience.

Readers also attacked Solzhenitsyn for the many neologisms or, rather, neo-archaisms he used in *One Day*, and which later became his trademark. To verbalize human thoughts and feelings in an environment of brutal repression, especially those of uneducated people outside the customary literary-minded circle of the intelligentsia, the writer introduced words imitating "simple," popular speech. Some of these words he borrowed from Vladimir Dal's nineteenth-century dictionary, while others he invented. Generally, at least from the mid-1960s on, neo-archaic linguistic experimentation became part of Solzhenitsyn's deliberate effort to revive the impoverished, that is, Sovietized, Russian literary language.[12] His plan was to replenish the prose "by a judicious use . . . of such words which, although they do not exist in the modern spoken language . . . are used so clearly by the author that they may meet the approval of speakers, attract the speakers, and in this way return to the language."[13]

Solzhenitsyn's linguistic efforts were part of the broader diversification of language that began in the early 1950s and was in many ways central to the Thaw as well as to all post-Stalin culture. Numerous authors and artists at the time—among them Pomerantsev, in 1953—increasingly perceived the established forms of verbal or visual articulation as inadequate for conveying human experiences. They began experimenting with other approaches to self-expression. Solzhenitsyn was not the only author in the early 1960s who introduced jargon to literature: another example, although very different in form and spirit, was Vasilii Aksenov, whose short story "Halfway to the Moon," full of "youthful" slang, appeared in *Novyi mir* in the same year, 1962.[14]

The audiences' reactions to such experiments were by no means benign—in fact they were often furious.[15] In responses sent to *Novyi mir*, people criticized both Aksenov's and Solzhenitsyn's linguistic innovations, sometimes in the same breath.[16] Vigilance against jargonization and the allegedly impending subversion of the Russian language had also long preceded the polemics of 1962. At least since the early Thaw, linguistic conservatism had shown in numerous media discussions about the "proper" ways of writing and speaking, "proper" stresses, spellings, forms of polite address, and so on. Such discussions were abundant in print, and *Novyi mir* actively participated in them. They were yet another manifestation of a general crisis of the spoken and printed word, a widespread perception of the abnormality of the contemporary verbal order, and a search for alternatives. The perceptions of an ethical and a linguistic emergency during the postwar decades were two sides of the same coin, indicating that Russian culture had entered a stage of profound transformation. The intensity of readers' reactions to language novelties only emphasized the scale and significance of the transformation. In a cultural environment increasingly perceived as unsettled and flawed, many people were desperately looking for firm ground: a single standard of self-expression.

Classical Russian literature readily offered itself as one such standard, an anchor of stability, especially because it had long been legitimized by the socialist realist doctrine, itself deeply classicist.[17] Now that socialist realism had entered a crisis, many readers distanced themselves from its didactic straightforwardness by resorting to the presumably more refined, ethically and emotionally complex literature of the preceding century. At this time, when language norms were fast collapsing, many people sought precisely such a norm by loudly appealing to the standards set by Tolstoy, Pushkin, and Gogol'. At the core of their revulsion for Solzhenitsyn's verbal experimentation was an anxious cultural conservatism premised on, among other aspects, the notion of a static language once carved in stone and never changing.[18]

It was not incidental that so many of those who attacked Solzhenitsyn's prose were of an advanced age. People long accustomed to measuring texts (and often lives, as well) by the classical literary standards could not easily part with their ideal. This was the case not only with Soviet readers. One letter criticizing Solzhenitsyn's use of swearwords came from an old Russian émigré who resided far from the shores of socialist realism—in Florida.[19] Another émigré, Vera Carpovich, who later compiled a glossary of Solzhenitsyn's language, would note in 1976 that "many Western readers, including native Russians, find his books 'difficult'; some are actually discouraged from reading them."[20] Coming from people who had not for a long time, or ever, set foot on Soviet soil, such attitudes were repercussions of the more distant, prerevolutionary era, possibly including fin-de-siècle reactions to the advent of modernism. The debate over authenticity in verbal expression had had a long history in Russia. The continuum of crisis that the country had entered at the turn of the century had a linguistic dimension that extended for decades, ultimately surfacing in the cultural polemics of the Thaw.[21]

That said, the readers' frequent rejection of Solzhenitsyn's prose did not necessarily mean they rejected his ethical and political agendas. Nor did it equate to a rejection of the actual Gulag returnees. Many of those who attacked his style were themselves Gulag returnees, and probably a few more chose not to declare their concentration camp background.[22] Just as in responses to Ehrenburg's memoir, all letter writers saw the terror as a formidable problem with which they personally felt obligated to deal, and even if they resented the author's prose, most still welcomed his book, recognizing its importance.[23] Ultimately, this recognition overrode their qualms about Solzhenitsyn's language. And in the end, quite a few readers realized that the language itself contributed to, rather than subtracted from, the novella's main significance—its truth value.

One Day was a book about them—and repeatedly they would stress that everything Solzhenitsyn wrote was pure truth. Vsevolod Petrovich Golitsyn, a fifty-five-year-old engineer who had spent ten years in the camps and was then sentenced to Siberian exile for life, even specified the year when the action of the novella took place, 1951.[24] Several other readers recognized not only the time but also the location: the Ekibastuz special camp in Kazakhstan, where Solzhenitsyn indeed had served part of his term. They also claimed to have met the author in the camp.[25] Some identified real-life prototypes for various characters in the book.[26] Interestingly, while these letter writers placed the action in Kazakhstan, others made different geographical attributions. "Dear Editors," wrote a navy officer, O. A. Bliuman, from Liepaia,

> In 1950–51, I lived in the area where the action of this novella takes place. My father worked in the settlement of Ust-Omchug in the Kolyma region. I studied at a night school and worked at the CMRW (Central Mechanical Repair Workshop), in the technical design bureau, if you could apply that name to a small wooden hut with an iron stove and four tables inside. There were five of us: four prisoners and one free hire, myself. . . . We were friends. I learned a lot from them about life in the camps, and [Solzhenitsyn's] novella strikes me precisely with its deep truthfulness. . . . It would be interesting to learn about the fate of my comrades at work, although that is hardly possible.[27]

That was indeed hardly possible: Solzhenitsyn had never been either to Ust-Omchug or to the Kolyma region. *Novyi mir*'s deputy editor Aleksei Kondratovich had to disappoint Bliuman, informing him that Solzhenitsyn had served his term in a different area and therefore could not know anything about Bliuman's campmates.[28]

One may certainly interpret Bliuman's response as a culmination of socialist realism—the ultimate satisfaction of the demand for life-likeness, verisimilitude, and "total realism" that had originally stood at the source of the new creative method.[29] But perhaps it makes better sense to reject this condescending approach and instead listen to Kondratovich, who explained Bliuman's mistaken recognition by the fact that Solzhenitsyn had managed to capture the universal Gulag reality—which, Kondratovich supposed, had been very similar for many camps, in Kolyma and elsewhere.[30] Solzhenitsyn himself emphasized authenticity as one of his strongest creative facets, and Bliuman's letter testified to the success of the writer's project.[31]

Notably, the Far Eastern camp settlement of Ust-Omchug, which was founded in 1939 and from 1949 to 1956 accommodated the Ten'kinsky Correctional Labor Camp, or Ten'lag, left its record in literary history more than once. Back at the time when Bliuman was working at the "Central Mechanical Repair Workshop," no fewer than 180 readers from

Ust-Omchug sent a telegram to the writer Vasilii Azhaev, praising his novel *Far from Moscow*—"a highly ideological and patriotic book that brings up Soviet readers in the spirit of communism."[32] It could well be that Bliuman, together with his father and the four prisoners in the workshop, were among those 180 signatories. We do not know if another letter writer, Ivan Sergeevich Korolev from Tadzhikistan, had ever happened to go through Ust-Omchug at any point during the thirteen years (1937–1950) he spent in the camps. But he, too, had read Azhaev's book, and now had a chance to compare it with *One Day*:

> I have read the novel *Far from Moscow* by the author Azhuev [*sic*], who took it from construction site no. 115 Sofiisk [illegible] Komsomol'sk, where there was a dense network of prison camps and arbitrariness exclusively 70–80% article 58 and the rest was the criminal [*blatnoi*] world, and following the bosses' directions they exterminated beat honest Soviet people, but the author V. Azhuev placed there improbable [*nepravdopodobnykh*] heroes, I think [two words illegible]. Solzhenitsyn's novella that you published is truthful, and it opened Soviet people's eyes, because such a cult of personality and the victims of its arbitrariness are innumerable. I have spent more than 4,000 such days. I am an eyewitness to how thousands of honest Soviet people perished.[33]

Transfigured into a picture of model socialist labor, Azhaev's own Gulag experiences were buried too deeply in *Far from Moscow* for the reader Korolev to recognize them. But now, in 1962, the two worlds, Azhaev's socialist realist "montage of life" and the world of prisoners who had populated the actual construction sites of the Far East, came face to face with each other. Thanks to *One Day in the Life of Ivan Denisovich*, the prison camp underworld of Azhaev's images rose to the surface. The second layer of text in his literary-historical palimpsest exposed itself to the readers' eyes. More precisely, there were not two but three worlds clashing here: Azhaev's "montage of life," Solzhenitsyn's novella (which was, after all, a literary text, and thus also a "montage"), and the reality of the camps. Or, still more precisely, perhaps the palimpsest had not three but four layers, as the readers' memories were also in a sense a montage, a construct put on paper after the fact and phrased in the acceptable language of public self-expression. The layers, the worlds that clashed when people read *One Day,* were probably innumerable. There were as many memories of the past as there were those who remembered it.[34]

The clash of the worlds did not produce an immediate revolution of the mind. The reader Korolev continued to speak the language of the "Big Other" (for example, "victims of arbitrariness," "opened Soviet people's eyes"), remained loyal to the standards of realism, and stayed within the limits of the acceptable in his self-expression.[35] But the limits themselves were becoming far wider than those he had known a decade earlier. Azhaev's *Far from Moscow* probably had never persuaded him, but now, having read Solzhenitsyn in a legitimately published journal, Korolev could openly explain why that was so. Realism remained in place, but now it could address new themes previously forbidden from circulation. The legitimacy of publication, something on which Tvardovskii had always insisted, was crucial for the impact of Solzhenitsyn's prose. The importance of the fact that his novella appeared in print openly and officially—with the highest sanction, as many knew at the time—was that readers received an opportunity for a *public* conversation about the part of their lives they previously had been able to share only with a chosen few.

They also received new words for this conversation—and, as unhappy as many people were about it, quite a few did recognize the value of the new vocabulary. Boris Stepanovich Khokhlov, a "personal pensioner" who had spent ten years in the prison camps, wrote to Solzhenitsyn:

> A few days ago, I read your novella, One Day in the Life of Ivan Denisovich.
>
> I read it THREE TIMES, in order to relive, again and again (in my heart, my soul, my thoughts, and somehow even in my body, physically) the TRUTH—I repeat, the TRUTH of my past, from 1936 to 1946. . . .
>
> And you know what? I relived again everything I had been through in 1936–46 and even later, up to the rehabilitation.
>
> Time has taken the edge off a few things and sharpened others. Yet still, impressed by your truthful novella, I lived through everything again.
>
> Everything, everything, and everything, WHAT and HOW you describe in your novella—everything, everything is authentic, everything is truthful to the utmost and is also rendered in a simple, human way.[36]

Accustomed to academic skepticism toward the notion of truth, a scholar is tempted to brand such statements as manifestations of realism, socialist or otherwise, and to hurry on, looking for some "thesis" in what the reader argued, for a certain "substantive" point that could provide grist for analyzing political opinions, cultural viewpoints, and so on. Yet perhaps it is best to slow down. Excited commentaries about Solzhenitsyn's truth were legion among the readers' responses to *One Day.*[37] Some resented his jargon, but many more conveyed a clear sense of liberation by truth, a delight in both "what" and "how" Solzhenitsyn described. It was not incidental that Khokhlov wrote all three words—TRUTH, WHAT, and HOW—in capital letters. In his and many other readers' responses, all the three categories were inseparable from one another. The truth that so many readers found in Solzhenitsyn's novella was in both the authentic detail of the camps he brought to light and in the words he found to portray this reality. And some of those who admired his truth also explicitly praised his language—not despite but specifically thanks to the swearwords and the neologisms he employed.[38] Both "What" and "How" mattered equally for these letter writers—"What," because a wealth of genuine detail about the camps was now unearthed, and "How," because a terminology for making these details known had finally entered the public domain. The truth of *One Day* was in its detail and its language, fused together and indivisible.

Combined, all the three factors—the legitimacy of depicting life in the Gulag, the authenticity of this depiction, and the new verbal means the writer adopted for the task—produced the impact of *One Day in the Life of Ivan Denisovich.* Solzhenitsyn coined the terms and categories in which a discussion of the terror could now proceed.

The Terror as People's History

The need to share memories, to speak out, without any underlying self-interest or possibility of gain, was a common reason readers gave for their letter writing. But they had a more practical reason as well. They wrote for the information of the author, whose judgment and mastery they trusted—and who, they believed, should use their letters in creating an unwritten chapter of the country's history, a comprehensive tale of the terror. "Please bear in mind that my letter is <u>by no means intended for publication</u>. This is just my need to express my opinion and feelings," wrote the fifty-four-year-old Daniil Il'ich Markelov from Kerch'. His biography was remarkable. During World War II Markelov, a POW, escaped from German captivity to Switzerland and then organized a guerrilla detachment in France to fight against the Germans. After the war he returned home and was first greeted as a hero, with the newspaper *Izvestiia* even publishing an article about his wartime courage. Then he was arrested and spent the next ten years in the camps.[39]

"This is truth, without any extra additives," Markelov wrote in his twelve-page letter about *One Day*, "truth expressed in magnificent artistic forms and vivid images. At last!"[40] And yet, he argued, for all its authenticity and literary quality, *One Day* did not tell the whole story of the political violence in this country. A former prisoner of war, Markelov admired not only Solzhenitsyn's *One Day* but also Mikhail Sholokhov's *The Fate of a Man* (1956)—one of the first publications in Soviet literature to create a positive image of a former Soviet POW (named Sokolov).[41] What Markelov wanted was that someone integrate the messages of these two stories, Solzhenitsyn's and Sholokhov's, add any similar stories, and finally give meaning to the so far unnamed, unexplained, and yet somehow coherent historical phenomenon they all described:

> This is what I want.
>
> While I am still alive, I would like to read and learn about this:
>
> Sokolov + Shukhov + X = . . .
>
> What does it equal? This is what I would like to know.
>
> Who will solve this difficult equation, and how?
>
> And it has to be solved. Life demands this and will demand [it] ever more pressingly.[42]

The aim of solving this equation, with its two unknowns, was to answer why, in this country, innocent people had been proclaimed enemies, for what reason innumerable lives had been destroyed and mutilated. Remarkably, in the view of Markelov and many other readers, generating such a comprehensive explanation was the task not of a historian but of a writer—the most trusted intellectual figure of all.

On the other side of the Gulag spectrum, Vadim Viktorovich Kasatskii, a doctor who had worked in the Kolyma camps as a free hire and must have compared himself with the doctors portrayed in *One Day*, also praised Solzhenitsyn's novella. Kasatskii noted its "absolute photographic accuracy. Accuracy—but not more. Isn't that too little? Isn't it time to move toward generalizations? Let us presume that political generalizations have been made. But artistic generalizations are also necessary, in order to bring [about] in people an aversion toward what happened, bring that [about] by emotional means, by imagery."[43]

Generalizations would be possible only on the basis of a detailed and comprehensive description. Many letter writers who had experienced repression firsthand suggested exactly what aspects of it Solzhenitsyn had missed and would have to cover in the future. I. Lilenkov, a former prisoner, proposed such themes as society's attitudes to the repressed, the fate of the wives who stayed behind, exile, and the experiences of rehabilitation.[44] Zhanna Blinova, a war veteran who had spent eleven years in the camps (1945–1956), insisted that Solzhenitsyn had failed to tell about the prisoners' intellectual and spiritual life: the numerous conversations, the reciting of poetry, the writing of letters home—all that had indeed taken place and was indispensable to them.[45] S. Prokofieva, an Old Bolshevik who spent seventeen years in the camps, would agree with Blinova, as she reproached Solzhenitsyn for his sarcastic and skeptical portrayal of the intelligentsia (such as in the image of the filmmaker Tsezar Markovich), with their egghead conversations about literature and film amid the horror of the camps. No, argued Prokofieva, such conversations had been vital for saving the prisoner's mind and body. She enclosed her own poetry written in the Gulag.[46] Nikolai Adamovich Vilenchik, a party member since 1931 who had spent sixteen years in the camps, added that Solzhenitsyn disregarded the intense political reflection that had incessantly taken place in many prisoners' minds. And Mikhail Alekseevich Poliakov, a former technician at the Simferopol telephone station who had been in the Gulag for eighteen years, 1941–1959 [*sic*], argued that *One Day* painted too mild and beautified a picture of the camps.[47] Some (not many) former prisoners even rejected the novella altogether because it was still a far cry from a full account of the atrocities they had seen.[48]

Such responses were not meant only to share the burden of the readers' untold experiences. By filling the gaps in Solzhenitsyn's story, they were intended to help him develop that story into an all-encompassing history of the not-yet-described human tragedy. The driving force behind these letters, and the reason why they were so long and detailed, was both personal and public at once. Readers' letters about *One Day in the Life of Ivan Denisovich* were part of an immense, dispersed, and yet somehow coherent collective effort at creating a polyphonic history of the terror—a common text that would give meaning to these people's lives.

Let us return to the January 1963 letter by Boris Stepanovich Khokhlov. As much as he admired *One Day*, he saw it as only the first step in creating a full account of the terror—a task that, he argued, Solzhenitsyn was to accomplish:

> You were courageous enough to step forward with a novella that sheds light only on one day of an innocent prisoner in the late [19]40s and early 50s. But who will dare—precisely, dare—tell, just as publicly [*tak zhe vsenarodno*], the truth about those innocent people who perished at the time of the Ezhov-Beriia arbitrariness, or about the people who, although they survived, had suffered through all the horrors of the NKVD torture chambers of [19]36–46, be that a cellar, a prison, a Stolypin railway car, or a camp for the prisoners who were at the time called "enemies of the people"! And it is necessary to tell about all that, it is necessary, as N. S. Khrushchev put it, "while we are alive, to tell the truth about that to the party and the people."
>
> If we do not do this, then our children or grandchildren will—but they will do it, all the same!
>
> And it seems to me that this is your direct duty, your sacred obligation as a writer who has created, with amazing talent, with human truthfulness, and with Bolshevik honesty, a novella about one day of an innocent prisoner. I would like to know whether you have plans for such a work.[49]

Solzhenitsyn did have plans for such a work—it was *The Gulag Archipelago*. Written from 1958 to 1968 and based on at least 227 oral and written testimonies he had collected, that book would come as close as possible to what Khokhlov and many other letter writers envisioned as a polyphonic, collectively authored history of the terror, told through stories of human lives.[50] In part, this immense project grew out of readers' responses to *One Day*. Solzhenitsyn could not reply to all of the readers' letters, but he did read and use them, occasionally seeking out and interviewing his correspondents.[51] A special chapter in *Archipelago* contained excerpts from readers' letters about *One Day*. As the chapter did not seem to fit into the main text of the new book, Solzhenitsyn circulated it via samizdat. Soon, even before the *Archipelago* itself, the chapter was published in the West as part of a documentary collection.[52] It contains excerpts from sixty-three readers' letters about *One Day*, accompanied by Solzhenitsyn's (rather moralistic) comments. I have the full texts of twenty-one of those letters. Among them are those by Golitsyn, Markelov, Lilenkov, Vilenchik, and a few others cited here.[53]

A step toward a history of the terror, *One Day* was, however, a work of literature—and as all good literature, it steered clear of providing ready answers. Solzhenitsyn left the job of explaining and generalizing to the readers. And so they desperately tried to explain, often exasperated and overwhelmed by the formidable task. For the time being, Markelov's equation remained unsolved.

The Many Lives of Terror

One of the many powerful messages of *One Day in the Life of Ivan Denisovich* was that Solzhenitsyn treated all prisoners alike, making no distinction between the guilty and the innocent, right or wrong, be they political prisoners or common felons, Red Army veterans or Vlasovites, Banderovites or even, possibly, actual spies. In his picture of the camps, the notions of friend and foe meant little, as the incessant struggle for survival could at any moment drive human beings together as well as pit them against each other, reversing the roles of enemy and friend several times a day. The magnitude of suffering and humiliation in the camps made every prisoner a victim, a tormented human being fighting for his life, and dwarfed to a trifling insignificance all paper definitions, categorizations, and accusations. This was a strong statement, quite unlike what the readers were accustomed to seeing in print. Many rebelled against it. Quite a few letter writers argued that somewhere, whether at the helm of power or right there in the camps, there had been real enemies and real criminals, not just innocently imprisoned victims, and that treating every prisoner as innocent was simply not right.

What should we make of these voices? Shall we conclude that in the 1960s, despite a slight modification of the rhetoric, the fundamental militant creeds usually attributed to the Stalin era—the existence of enemies, the need to purify society, to cast out and exterminate infidels—still stood, effectively undamaged? Reaching this conclusion would imply that the Thaw had not changed the fundamental aspects of a Soviet weltanschauung, that people's ideas had remained effectively the same as they had been in Stalin's time.

Such a pronouncement, arguably, would be premature. Despite the density of "enemy" images, letters to Solzhenitsyn do not reveal an established, static worldview among his readers. In fact, they reveal just the contrary.

I have located variously formulated images of "enemies" in at least 59 out of 532 letters, that is, in approximately 11 percent of letters about *One Day*. Although not overwhelming, it is a substantial number, and it is not to be disregarded. Yet it is also necessary is to ascertain who the letter writers were.

Just as with the issue of language, these letters point to age as an important factor in the tendency to seek and find enemies. Twenty-four of the 59 letters indicate the exact or approximate age of their authors, and 19 of the 24 came from people who described themselves as either "pensioners" or age fifty-five and above.[54] In other words, just as in the case of the critics of Solzhenitsyn's language, most letter writers who argued that the camps had contained some "real" enemies were of fairly advanced age.

In their youth these people had gone through the Revolution, the Civil War, and the subsequent decades when the military mentality reigned supreme.[55] Formed by this past, in their letters they continued to stand by it. Remarkably, no less than fifteen of them had been camp prisoners, too. A few were Old Bolsheviks who had retained their creed in the camps, viewing the guards or fellow inmates as real enemies, while regarding themselves as the torchbearers of a pure, untarnished idea. The Gulag did not ruin their willingness to divide humankind into the pure and impure.[56] Others who advocated the "enemy" interpretation of the camps were younger, but whenever they began describing their lives, it became clear that what they had gone through had by its nature fostered a vision of the world as sharply divided between good and evil. It was experience, and not simply age, that defined readers' reactions against Solzhenitsyn's agenda.

One such experience was the Second World War. A significant difference between *One Day* and other texts about the political violence of the Stalin years—for example, Ehrenburg's memoir (at least as of the winter of 1962–63, when only the first parts of it had been published)—was that these texts described different stages of the violence and different categories of victims. While Ehrenburg depicted the atmosphere of arrests in 1937 and 1938, Solzhenitsyn portrayed the prison camps of the early 1950s, the postwar years. Secondary as this may seem today, the distinction was important to readers in the 1960s. While they nearly unanimously viewed the victims of the 1930s, the classical "stream of 1937," as innocent, the letter writers were far more ambivalent about admitting the innocence of those who had ended up in the camps because of the war.[57] Among the prisoners in *One Day* are former Ukrainian, Estonian, and Latvian "nationalists," and even Ivan Denisovich himself is shown, indirectly but rather transparently, as a former soldier in the Second Shock Army of General Vlasov.[58] None of these details escaped the readers' attention. If we look at what kinds of "enemies" the letter writers identified in *One Day*, it becomes clear that the legacy of World War II was crucial for those identifications. Many correspondents of Solzhenitsyn were war veterans or, in any case, had lived through the war. Some had gone through it all—the fighting, the German captivity, and then the Gulag. It was hard for them to agree with Solzhenitsyn, who treated all prisoners alike. Someone identified as a militant Ukrainian nationalist ("Banderovite") or a former German-occupation police officer *(Polizei)* was definitely an enemy to the veterans, because they had faced those as real enemies during the war, in battle and in captivity.

Even Soviet prisoners of war subsequently transferred from German to Soviet camps were not necessarily innocent in the readers' eyes. An aging veteran and former POW, S. Zhuravlev from Orenburg, was not sure that Ivan Denisovich was above suspicion. "There were different prisoners of war: martyrs and fighters, self-seekers [*shkurniki*] and traitors," he wrote. "I myself was a prisoner of war, I know the sufferings of our people and the beastly triumph of the *Polizei* and traitors of the Motherland who tormented us not less and often even more than the most bestial Fascists did, because they were serving their masters. And so, I do not see that Ivan Denisovich feels himself like a Soviet man."[59] "The author," argued another war veteran, A. Stoliarov from Vinnytsia, "did not take the trouble to distinguish between real criminals, who had fed the Banderovites, and honest people; [in the text] they all look the same. This is not true either. Barbed wire does not make brothers of people who treat their Motherland so differently."[60] "I do not feel pity for the dark individuals of the Patriotic War," snapped a female reader, E. A. Ignatovich, who had faced the camp prisoners while working as a transport forewoman in Karaganda in 1954. In his chapter on the readers of *One Day*, Solzhenitsyn somewhat rashly grouped her with the "practical workers" (of the regime), although Ignatovich herself had suffered from repression: her father had been killed in 1937.[61] "Vlasovites," "Banderovites," and "traitors" figured prominently in a letter by Lev Arkad'evich Meerson, sixty-seven, who had spent six years in the camps in 1949–1955 and now wrote about those prisoners without much sympathy.[62]

These responses did not originate simply in a paranoid witch-hunting impulse or an abstract, Manichean search for the social good and evil. The Second World War drew not only imaginary but also very real front lines across the territory of the Soviet Union. For millions of people, the fighting forces of their wartime adversaries were not imaginary but very real enemies. After the unparalleled bloodshed and atrocities of that war, it was only natural for those who had witnessed it to continue viewing yesterday's opponents on the same wartime terms.

The war had yet another effect on the people's minds. In letters to Solzhenitsyn, readers often spoke unaffectedly and even condescendingly about the suffering he described. Such responses did not necessarily come from former camp inmates; some could also be written by war veterans, or actually by anyone who had seen wartime or postwar life, in the army or in the rear. "I have never been imprisoned," wrote P. S. Petrov from Moscow, "but when I served in the army, I saw all of this, and much more. We used to cut bread with a saw because it was frozen, and for a few months we ate nothing but wheat, for both the first and second course. People got dystrophy—and mind you, we were getting ready for the front."[63] Another World War II veteran, A. Tambovtsev from Groznyi, argued that life had not been much easier outside the Gulag after the war, and that had the camps had decent living conditions, everyone would have flocked there.[64] In 1943, a Red Army unit where Viktor Sorokin served was stationed in an abandoned prison camp:

> We soldiers lived in the very same barracks and dugouts where the "zeks" had lived before us. Bunk beds and single-pane windows coated with ice, mattresses (we, by the way, did not have them at all for a while)—this is much like what Solzhenitsyn describes. So, what do you suggest, should we have built solid structures for prisoners in 1946–50? How, then, would prisoners have been different from us, from a nation that had been through a severe disaster and was living in pits and dugouts, on the ashes of our homes?[65]

Daily life during and immediately after World War II was such that Solzhenitsyn's text easily paled in comparison to reality. Many readers had been through trials much worse than those of Ivan Denisovich. Their wartime and postwar experiences had habituated these people to privation, violence, and death, creating in them a hardened insensitivity to human suffering.[66]

The impact of the war overlapped with the experiences of the camps themselves, which many letter writers had seen on one side of the barbed wire or the other. In an outburst of chilling mockery, forty-one-year-old Vasilii Sergeevich Zagorodskii from Kotlas, a war veteran who, according to his letter, had served at the front as a private throughout the war, wrote: "How can we not feel pity over this poor, poor prisoner, that is, a Banderovite and a Vlasovite, subjected to such inhuman treatment by the Chekist hangmen! But what about the fact that during the war this very Banderovite and Vlasovite, like a cruel beast, committed horrible atrocities against little children and old women in the villages of Belorussia, Ukraine, and the Baltics, and, together with German soldiers, 'organized' the ditch graves of Katynshchina, where thousands and thousands of people, innocently shot and buried half-alive by you, Banderovite, are asleep and will never wake up? Well, that's a thing of the past!"[67]

The grim irony of Zagorodskii's letter was that Katyn, a place near Smolensk, was the site of mass executions of Polish army officers, not by Banderovites, Vlasovites, or German troops, but by the NKVD in 1940, a fact that the Soviet government at the time denied, ascribing the execution to the Germans.[68] Vasilii Sergeevich may or may not have known the Katyn story, but he was not only a war veteran. In 1950, he wrote, the local party organs had "directed" him to serve in the Gulag, doing "educational work among the prisoners, including the category of political prisoners." He served in the camps from 1950 to 1957, then spent a couple of years working "in the apparatus of the district party committee and the Executive Committee of the Council of People's Deputies" (local administration). Then "the party again directed" him to carry out "political education work among the prisoners," something he did from 1959 on.[69]

Zagorodskii's letter was a twenty-page-long handwritten attack on Solzhenitsyn that accused the writer of badly and intentionally misrepresenting the camp guards. Wrote Zagorodskii on behalf of the guards, "We never allowed anything of the kind that Solzhenitsyn describes to happen."[70] Nobody ever beat the prisoners, he repeated again and again. So did other former police officers, such as Aleksei Mikhailovich Egorov from Cherepovets, who argued that a guard beating a prisoner would have gone straight to jail.[71] Many of the prisoners were guilty, too, Zagorodskii insisted—take those Banderovites and Vlasovites, for example. And even if some were not guilty, he wrote, how were the guards supposed to distinguish between the guilty and the innocent?[72]

There were quite a few such letters in Solzhenitsyn's mail, from people who had been on the other side of the camp spectrum or somewhere in the middle. No fewer than 10 of the 59 letters that advanced the "enemy" argument and attacked Solzhenitsyn on those grounds came from the former camp guards, career police officers, and former free-hire personnel at the camps.[73] Some of the former free hires accepted Solzhenitsyn's viewpoint, but most of them—and all the officers and guards—vehemently rejected it.[74]

We should not, of course, necessarily believe what they wrote about the camps, such as the statements that prisoners were never beaten. What exposes such statements is, for example, Zagorodskii's claim that, although they never beat the prisoners, the guards did have "a moral right" to do so—because the prisoners were, again, nothing more than Banderovites, Vlasovites, *Polizei*, German-appointed village elders, or common criminals.[75] What we should do, rather, is to try to understand why these officers and guards wrote long autobiographical letters attacking Solzhenitsyn—letters that would most likely get no response whatsoever and end up with a laconic editorial verdict, "To the archive."

Zagorodskii continued his letter. "During all these years, I have been twice awarded the medal 'For Distinguished Service in the Organs of the MVD [Ministry of Internal Affairs],' received a Letter of Commendation many times, and have had a number of honorable citations."[76] After *One Day in the Life of Ivan Denisovich*, the letter of commendation was a useless piece of paper, and the medal for distinguished service in the organs of the MVD, just as the word "honorable," looked like a bad joke. And so they protested, poorly prepared to argue but furious about what they had read. It was certainly a reaction premised on the criteria of realism, a guild response to the writer's negative portrayal of their trade. But it was also something else. *One Day* gnawed at the very foundation, the core, of these people's lives, exposing it and suggesting that the core was, and had always been, black and hollow. This was impossible for them to acknowledge, and that was why they wrote.

Again, the importance of the fact that *One Day* was published openly and legitimately cannot be overstated. Its publication in the country's principal literary journal suggested to readers that Solzhenitsyn's interpretation of the camps was now the official interpretation, automatically relegating the ex-guards and police officers to the unfortunate role of social pariahs. The roles were being reversed, and the former guardians of the existing order found themselves in the position of its implicit rhetorical enemies. In their letters against Solzhenitsyn, these people not only desperately defended their own past and self-esteem but also struggled to maintain their social membership and status.

Apparently, *One Day*'s idea that what they had done in the camps was cruel came as big news to the former guards. Thus, Aleksei Grigor'evich Panchuk, from a village in the Moscow region, a party member since 1940 and World War II veteran who had been an MVD officer for sixteen years and retired in 1962, wrote:

> Well, what did you expect? Perhaps you thought, Solzhenitsyn, that a prison camp is a health resort or something of the kind? Having committed a heaviest crime against the state, you would like to stay warm, to be well fed and decently clothed, not to work, and to serve your term in that fashion? There are no such camps in the Soviet state, and they cannot exist. . . .
>
> Solzhenitsyn's Shukhov sleeps for 7–8 hours, has felt boots, wadded pants, a padded jacket and a pea-jacket, an ear-flap hat, and mittens. He went to work in the temperature of [minus] 27 degrees and complains that it is cold. Solzhenitsyn had better visit a construction site today and see how construction workers function in the same or even worse cold, and what they wear. A man who works is not afraid of cold, while a sloth will freeze even in a sheepskin coat. Shukhov gets three hot meals a day, for breakfast he gets even three courses, and 900 grams of bread. . . .
>
> It is unclear what facts of cruelty, arbitrariness, and what violations of socialist legality Tvardovskii sees in this novella. That prisoners were kept in intense custody, that they had to work, that they were clothed to the season and fed according to the norms, that they were required to observe the regimen, and that malicious violators were locked up? These are legitimate limitations to certain rights of a Soviet citizen who has committed a crime against the Soviet state.[77]

Declarations like this were not frequent in Solzhenitsyn's mail, and yet the justification of reprisals, the failure to recognize cruelty, spoke volumes about the time and the culture. Such statements had to do not simply with the readers' overall insensitivity to suffering as a result of war and privations, not just with their background of service in the camps, and not only with their desire to justify the past and validate their social membership. The letter writers' confidence that such opinions could and ought to be expressed was *uninhibited.* Justification of violence came from an underdeveloped state of public discussion, and hence consciousness, of the terror.[78]

During the Thaw it was becoming ever harder to defend mass violence openly by quoting clichés from history textbooks and newspaper editorials, because the textbooks and the editorials themselves were being increasingly discredited. Yet such a defense remained possible—certainly more so than, say, during the late 1980s and early 1990s, when the terror again came into the public spotlight and a much more resolute verdict on it was pronounced. In the early 1960s, not only were the regime's ideologues unwilling to push the analysis of the violence any further than it had gone at the Twenty-Second Party Congress in 1961, but also the ethical condemnation of the camps and executions had not yet reached the finality and decisiveness that it would reach three decades later. Until the early 1960s, discussions of this theme had been relegated largely to kitchen-table talks, leaving the public forums of political conversation silent on the issue.[79] The situation did change with the Twenty-Second Congress, but by 1962–1963 too little had yet been published, too timid a discussion had been openly held. It was this void in the media, the absence of a narrative of the terror, the lack of detailed information and of a decisive, comprehensive rejection of state violence that allowed the defenders of the camps to go public when, with the publication of *One Day,* Ehrenburg's memoir, and several other texts, the discussion finally started. The forging of common ethical attitudes to the terror was at only an embryonic stage. While thirty years later people like Panchuk would be more likely to refrain from an open defense of the Gulag, in 1963 they still thought it acceptable. With time, however, arguments in favor of state violence would be progressively compromised. Much credit for this goes to the writers, as they were the ones who cast the terms and formulated the main principle of approaching the problem—asserting the supreme value of an individual human life.

Although most letter writers did not advance "enemy" arguments when either criticizing or praising Solzhenitsyn, the enemy theme did resound loudly in quite a few of the letters. The theme originated in the experiences of the letter writers, many of whom were older people who had since their youth imbibed the socially divisive, militant ethos characteristic of the early stages of the Soviet order. They had also gone through World War II, carrying from it an acute sense that real threats existed to the survival of their country, an apprehension that did not easily go away. Finally, a number of these individuals had been directly involved in the functioning of the Gulag system. Their attack on Solzhenitsyn was an attempt to justify their past to others and perhaps also themselves, a desperate effort to maintain a public face and status that, after *One Day*, they were destined to lose.

The terror had many faces, and behind each face there was a person and a life.

The Power of One Day

Something new was in the air after *One Day* came out. In his letter of December 1962, as we will recall, Tvardovskii informed Solzhenitsyn that most of the negative responses to the novella were anonymous.[80] In the archive, most such responses are signed, so technically speaking he may have been wrong. But a few negative letters were indeed anonymous—either not signed at all or signed contractedly, illegibly, and missing a return address.[81] As few as they were, they are not to be ignored. Even more than the former police officers, these letter writers must have felt strongly that, with the publication of *One Day*, the tide had turned—that the prisoners' view of the terror had become the new official line and the opposite view, previously in the mainstream, was now considered alien and seditious. Although they expressed orthodox and callous opinions with no trace of dissent whatsoever, these letter writers opted to be on the safe side and remain incognito. Perhaps their intuition did not fail them. What started as the Thaw indeed portended a change of intellectual climate.

Negative or even furious as they were, the letters from Solzhenitsyn's critics nonetheless betrayed that their authors were deeply impressed by *One Day*. Even if they wanted to, people could not ignore the force of Solzhenitsyn's prose. Pavel Ivanovich Kol'tsov, a veteran of three wars (the Civil, the Finnish, and the Great Patriotic) and a Gulag prisoner for seven years (1949–1956), spent several pages arguing that Solzhenitsyn did not show all the complexity of the terror, that he had missed important distinctions between various categories of prisoners, and that his language, too, was inappropriate. Yet Kol'tsov felt compelled to add: "I cannot but sense the power of this work." Tvardovskii (it was to him that Kol'tsov wrote) underlined these words.[82]

The inability to withstand the power of Solzhenitsyn's prose was disturbing. At times a letter writer would lose his nerve, and his argument would slide into a frustrated, hysterical outcry. "The author simply does not know Soviet people, they are not like that at all, they are not cannibals," exploded A. Stoliarov, a party worker and war veteran.[83] "Who is this book going to bring up, what does the author want to express in this book, when he so much vilifies the Soviet countryside and thousands of Soviet people, the workers of the MVD and MGB, who are not like that, they are better, more humane, they are Soviet people, not self-seekers and bribe-takers, not hunters after a slice of lard, he vilifies not just the cult of personality but everything," almost shrieked in his letter Mikhail Sykchin, a collective-farm party organizer from the Novosibirsk region.[84]

It was the detail that killed, the minute record of human existence in a camp. Yuliia Pilipchuk from L'viv argued that, despite the numerous general words the press had used before to describe the violence, the readers were "caught unawares" and shocked by Solzhenitsyn's precise description of what the camps—and, more broadly, all the repression—were about. "Soviet [literary] criticism," she wrote, "had more than sufficiently employed the words 'lawlessness,' 'arbitrariness,' 'flagrant,' 'the cult,' and 'despotism.' But after reading the novella, many well-educated and highly positioned people looked as if they were publicly exposed as having participated in anti-Soviet activities."[85] Readers spoke about the "horrible truth" of *One Day.* Some even felt that discussing the terror in the way Solzhenitsyn proposed could be dangerous, if not lethal, for the regime. Fifty-nine-year-old Andrei Ivanovich Fedin, from a village in Tatarstan, had spent six years in the camps (1936–1942) and five years in exile. He admired *One Day* but suggested taking the book out of circulation because, he said, Solzhenitsyn's truth was too dangerous for the minds of "our sons and grandsons."[86] Aleksei Kondratovich, deputy editor of *Novyi mir,* felt it necessary to respond to Fedin, insisting that "such formidable truth as the truth about the year 1937" could not be concealed from the people, and that open and full discussion of this violence was the best guarantee against its return.[87]

"Oh no, I do not want this novella!"—exclaimed Liudmila Sosnina, a middle-aged woman whose father had been expelled from the party in the 1930s. Her brother and sister had been sent to the Gulag, and eight years later, after the brother was apparently transferred to exile, Sosnina received permission to join him. She spent the next fifteen years in the north, working in the camps as a free hire. Never imprisoned, she technically stayed on the other side of the barbed wire but had obviously suffered from the repression. Still, in her remarkably long letter—forty handwritten pages—she protested against *One Day*.[88]

Why did she write those forty pages, replete with grammar mistakes, exclamation points, and question marks? "It was hard for Solzhenitsyn to write this novella, but it was even harder for me to read it," she wrote. Sosnina admired her father—a Bolshevik, a self-made man, and an altruistic enthusiast of industrialization who had struggled, in the 1930s, to manage a large industrial plant while teaching himself engineering in the process. The main part of her letter was actually not about the camps or exile—it was about her father and family in the 1930s. Solzhenitsyn's book had invaded and threatened the world of her childhood, which she portrayed as a time of family unity and happiness. Her letter was very much a defense of the 1930s. She defended the spirit of selfless devotion to the cause, which, she argued, had reigned in their family, and in which her father had raised her. And yes, he did believe in the existence of wreckers and enemies—foreign specialists, old tsarist engineers, and the like. Associated with her father, these images also became part of her fond remembrances. The purges had destroyed her family, but the notions that stood behind the purges had made their way into a nostalgic idyll that she had created out of the 1930s. Probably this helped her survive her fifteen years in the Far North.[89]

At the same time, her letter was more than just a piece of nostalgic writing. Sosnina wanted to explain what had actually happened in the 1930s, how the ideals of her childhood could match the grim reality of the terror. "The cult of personality deeply and powerfully touches me personally, and it makes me endlessly think," she wrote. How was the industry created, she wondered—was it enthusiasm or, "perhaps, it was the iron will of the cult that built the country's industry, or helped to build it?" Why did her father, the enthusiast, get expelled from the party, why were her brother and sister arrested? "I am not looking for consolation, at all. I bear neither grudge nor malice. It's only thoughts, endless thoughts. This is some gigantic nonsense!"[90]

Solzhenitsyn provoked protest from many readers in part because, by showing the survival-oriented, primeval underside of human nature that left no room for political beliefs, high sentiments, and noble pursuits of the mind, he violated the conventions of socialist realism. But he also did much more than that. *One Day* threatened to erase people's lives, in which they claimed to have seen, or been, heroes, martyrs, intellectuals, and high-spirited enthusiasts—everything he failed to portray. Not unlike Ehrenburg's opponent Ermilov, critics such as Sosnina wanted to write the terror into mainstream Soviet history and imagery, to explain the violence while keeping their worldview intact, to reassure themselves that, despite the camps, their country and they themselves were, and had always been, on the right track.

However, unlike Ermilov, the reader Sosnina eventually acknowledged the impossibility of such a papering-over project. After Solzhenitsyn, it was not feasible to limit oneself to cosmetic intellectual revisions while otherwise maintaining the status quo. The power of *One Day* was that, no matter whether readers agreed with its interpretation of the terror, this book, more than any other text during the Thaw, compelled them to reconsider and question their entire past.

Such reconsideration was a prominent theme in a letter from D. A. Vakhrameev, a seventy-year-old agronomist from the Karaganda region who was also a Civil War volunteer, a veteran, and a party member since 1918. Imprisoned in 1939 "for praising Trotsky," he spent the next seven years in the camps. His wife renounced him, and his daughter, who attempted to maintain ties with him, was driven to suicide. Inspired by Solzhenitsyn's *One Day,* which he described as "a truthful work written in good language," Vakhrameev's twenty-six-page handwritten letter to the editors of *Novyi mir* was a detailed story of his imprisonment.[91] Like many others, he did not intend the letter for publication but instead offered his life story to Solzhenitsyn, who would be able to use it in a future history of the terror. Also like many other readers, Vakhrameev insisted that creating such a history was the job not of historians but of writers: "One must issue a call for all the participants of those events to send their memoirs and thoughts to the writers, so that the latter could rework this 'raw material' into a literary form. . . . I am not going to join the literary circles, with my simple mug. But I would be happy if I got a note [saying] that someone used what I've written."[92] We cannot send him such a note, but we can include and interpret his letter, and many other similar letters, as part of the history he so much desired to see.

Vakhrameev was one of the few letter writers who admitted their willful contribution to the terror. After suffering through many days worse than the one of Ivan Denisovich, he came out of the camps with a sense of his own share of responsibility for the country's tragedy. Unlike many other former prisoners, he did not see himself as a victim and refused to dissociate himself from the hangmen. "During the years of the personality cult, I conscientiously badgered 'enemies of the people' at rallies. And in a private circle, I doubted (useless protest that no one could see).[93] I thought there was the party's will for everything ('God! I believe! God, help my disbelief!'). And so, I do not want to spit in my own face, and I consider myself just as guilty as Stalin."[94] After his release from the camps, the Old Bolshevik and Civil War veteran Vakhrameev did not apply for reinstatement in the party. "You and I are the two shores of one river," he wrote, quoting a popular song while addressing Stalin's portrait that was still hanging on his wall—just as it was still hanging in Tvardovskii's office. He added, "One cannot throw a word out of a song. And I do not want to be reinstated in the party, because of my guilt. . . . As for the 'father with moustache,' I do not hold it against him. I treat him as one treats a natural disaster. The entire people together have created this nightmare."[95]

Not many letter writers admitted their responsibility for the terror as directly as Vakhrameev did. More common were confessions to having believed in the existence of "enemies of the people"—but then readers added that they had stopped believing that after their own arrest or the arrests of relatives and friends. This was a common motif in letters to Ehrenburg, and it was often repeated in responses to Solzhenitsyn.

Also much like those who responded to Ehrenburg, many people bitterly described contemporary society.[96] They wrote about "the epidemic of universal suspiciousness" that had seized the country in Stalin's time, and to which they did not want to succumb again.[97] When he finally got hold of a library copy of *Novyi mir* containing *One Day,* tattered and greasy from hundreds of readers' hands, seventy-one-year-old S. A. Kolendovskii from Kharkov, who had spent fifteen years in the Gulag, noticed a question that someone had penciled in in the margins: "Why do camps and starvation constantly accompany socialism?" He agreed: the camps, and their persistence even after Stalin, were the country's shame. Why do we need them, he asked? "For disinfection? By what political and social means? Should there be a new bloody revolution? Against whom now? Revolution has absolutely and forever become repulsive to the people, because it cruelly deceived all the 'Christian folk,' making them die many times over, of starvation and typhoid lice." Like others, Kolendovskii proposed that writers create a history of the terror, "in order for this nationwide camp tragedy never to repeat with honest working people in Russia."[98]

The emerging sense of responsibility for the terror, and the desire to prevent its return, drove readers to reflect on the terror's origins. Ivan Alekseevich Pupyshev, a sixty-six-year-old retired schoolteacher from the village of Rozhdestveno in the Moscow region, had spent six years (1949–1955) in the camps. He responded to *One Day* with two letters, one in 1962, the other in 1964. In his second letter he concluded that the origins of the recent violence lay in an "exclusivity complex." By this he meant one person's claim to the undivided, undisputed possession of society's truth. Widespread in the revolutionary era, as well as later, this claim no longer seemed convincing to him. Having read *One Day*, Ivan Alekseevich thought back to his young years, to the revolutionary origins of the social order in which he had spent nearly all his life. He now rejected messianic ideas that monopolized the truth and projects to bring light and happiness to humanity regardless of the cost. Such projects, as he had had ample opportunity to observe, brought nothing but suffering.[99]

A reconceptualization as profound as this was not very common in *Novyi mir*'s mail. However, such letters did exist, and they were significant. Readers like Vakhrameev, Pupyshev, or Kolendovskii belonged to the generation that had brought the Revolution to victory, defended it against enemies real and imaginary, and long seen it as an indispensable, vital development in Russia's history. Only four years earlier, their peers had chastised Pasternak for his assault on the Revolution as a historical blessing. After *One Day*, that blessing was far less obvious. In the early 1960s, the explosion of printed information and the debate about the terror at once enabled and urged members of this cohort, perhaps more than their children and grandchildren, to rethink the past. Many of them kept defending it, but there were others who came to judge their past and themselves soberly. They had seen it all and no longer had anything to fear. For the most part, they did not regret what they had built. And yet now they asked themselves whether the cost had not been too high.

Everyone's Living Past

Inspired to a great extent by Solzhenitsyn's *One Day in the Life of Ivan Denisovich,* the polemic about the nature and origins of mass political violence in modern Russian history stood at the center of intellectual life during the Thaw. While revealing the power of long-held conservative and residual tendencies in Soviet culture, the polemic at the same time suggested that those tendencies were on the decline, and that important new ideas were developing in the people's minds. Perhaps, looking just at a few years means holding the interpretive lens too close to be able to see long-term intellectual change. However, it may also be that holding the lens closely enables us to notice the very moment when intellectual change begins to take place. I would argue that the early 1960s were precisely such a moment. It was then that, with the legitimate publication of literary texts about the terror and their widespread and open discussion, the language and mentality shaped under Stalin received the ultimately mortal blow.

The readers' debate around *One Day* confirmed once again what had become clear in the simultaneous discussions of Ehrenburg's *People, Years, Life.* The language and ethical order upheld in the Soviet media were categorically unsuitable for interpreting or even describing the tragedies of the twentieth century. In the meantime, readers' letters revealed that people badly needed such an interpretation and, even before that, a description. These objectives required a new system of values and a new verbal order.

Thus, the readers of *Novyi mir* came to face the same issue over which Tvardovskii had agonized several years before, and which he finally recognized as unresolvable within the existing framework of ideas, ethical models, and literary conventions. That was why he was so jubilant when he found Solzhenitsyn—his greatest literary discovery of the Thaw. The power and significance of *One Day* was that it not only urged the readers to rethink their past but also offered them the ethical and linguistic terms for doing so. Whereas Ehrenburg's memoir for the first time highlighted the centrality of individual human experience to history, Solzhenitsyn brought the theme to its logical perfection and also offered new verbal approaches to it, giving readers the means with which to describe a previously indescribable historical reality.

The readers ultimately recognized this, if sometimes against their will. Their anxious concern for the legitimacy and stability of the existing sociopolitical and linguistic order was rooted in the crisis of biography that they faced at the time. In their new roles as amateur historians, social psychologists, and political analysts, numerous people were driven by a genuine desire to preserve the system, to salvage it in the face of its new predicament, and thereby to justify their own lives. Many of those who had matured during the Revolution, the Civil War, and especially World War II, retained and defended the ethos of social militancy in which they had been raised. Their persistent, at times desperate defense of those values had a strong impact on how they represented the terror in their letters.

And yet, under the impact of books they read, first of all those by Solzhenitsyn and Ehrenburg, at least some of them began to reassess the social and moral order that they and their fathers had brought to life. When putting their own thoughts and memories on paper and sharing them with trusted authors and editors, the letter writers made an intense interpretive effort, coming to a reassessment of their own values and deeds—which, as they increasingly realized, had been integral to the tragedy. Several letter writers, though not many, began to suspect that the roots and effects of the terror lay within themselves. Perhaps most important, in the early 1960s a number of people began to arrive at the idea that their society was, to a large extent, formed by the terror. Their dialogue with literature provoked the recognition that practically everyone had been privy to—indeed complicit in—the violence of the past. On the one hand, this realization suggested that a society formed by the terror could not interpret the terror at will. On the other hand, here was the root and the first growth of departing from the terror: recognizing its impact and resolving to gain distance from it.

8

DISCOVERING HUMAN RIGHTS

The Siniavskii-Daniel' Trial

WITH KHRUSHCHEV'S REMOVAL from power in October 1964, a new stage opened in Soviet history. The Thaw was not over yet: its lasting effects would continue to affect society and culture throughout the second half of the 1960s and indeed long after. Also, the new leadership under Leonid Brezhnev was famously slow to reimpose ideological orthodoxy, at least until the Soviet invasion of Czechoslovakia in 1968. And yet, although there was no clear-cut chronological break that marked the end of the Thaw, the situation did begin to change. *Novyi mir*, as the institution visibly embodying the spirit of this epoch, perceived the changes most acutely. During the last five years of Tvardovskii's editorship, from 1965 to 1970, the journal increasingly felt the pressure of censorship and mounting resistance to its line from both the political authorities and the literary establishment.

The second half of the 1960s was also the time of *Novyi mir*'s highest intellectual maturity—its golden autumn, when the journal's strategies became the clearest, as did those of its rising opponents. In this uphill and uneven battle, Tvardovskii defended his line expertly. During his last years at the helm, *Novyi mir* made its priorities explicit in several major publications of great impact. At the same time, the editor and his team closely followed new developments in Soviet political life, sensitive to the climatic changes they portended. One such development was the Siniavskii-Daniel' affair of 1965–1966.

In September 1965, a philologist and research fellow at the Moscow Institute of World Literature, Andrei Donatovich Siniavskii (1925–1997), and a translator, Iulii Markovich Daniel' (1925–1988), were arrested for publishing their literary writings in the West. They had been doing this since 1959 under the pseudonyms of, respectively, Abram Tertz and Nikolai Arzhak.[1] At the time of their arrest, both were established literary professionals whose work, although hardly familiar to the general audience, had won the approval of their guild. On 10–14 February 1966 the Supreme Court of the Russian Federation tried the two authors and sentenced them to lengthy terms of imprisonment: seven years for Siniavskii and five for Daniel'. Iulii Daniel' served his term in full, was released in September 1970, and spent about three years in exile in Kaluga before being allowed to move back to Moscow. After his return, only occasionally and with difficulty did he obtain translation jobs, publishing under the KGB-imposed pseudonym Iu. Petrov, and only at the very end of his life, during the perestroika, did the press turn a favorable eye to him.[2] Andrei Siniavskii was released ahead of time in June 1971 and soon thereafter (in 1973) emigrated from the Soviet Union to France, where he spent the rest of his life writing and teaching Russian literature at the Sorbonne.

Due to its extensive repercussions, especially in the West, the trial of Siniavskii and Daniel' became one of the most famous literary-political scandals in Soviet history. The affair received exceptionally broad nationwide and foreign media coverage. For many observers, Western and Russian alike, the trial heralded the advent of the regime's new repressive policies in intellectual life, as well as the beginnings of the dissident movement.[3] What did not escape contemporaries and subsequent scholars, either, was the analogy between this affair and the 1958 crusade against Pasternak. The two campaigns were similarly forceful, originated in comparable circumstances, and produced major ripple effects at home and abroad. Although he did not end up in the dock, publishing in the West did lead Pasternak, like Siniavskii and Daniel', to face charges of anti-Soviet activities that were dangerously close to treason. Among the many ties between the two affairs, there was also the fact that Siniavskii had been one of the first scholars of Pasternak's poetry, earning the ultimate recognition in this capacity in 1957, when he received compliments from Pasternak himself.[4] Both Siniavskii and Daniel' were present at Pasternak's funeral in 1960, and a contemporary photo captured them carrying the lid of the poet's coffin, an image for which a witty caption was later suggested: "Siniavskii and Daniel' carry the bench for their dock."[5]

Both literary affairs unfolded in the close vicinity of *Novyi mir.* Tvardovskii had often published Siniavskii's writings and repeatedly praised his literary analysis and style. "Written, as always, well, in your own way, with elegance and affection," he commented on Siniavskii's 1960 essay "The Poetry and Prose of Olga Berggol'ts."[6] Unsurprisingly, when the scandal broke out various domestic and foreign audiences noted its *Novyi mir* connection. Some Western observers even supposed that the entire affair was only a pretext for a forthcoming assault on *Novyi mir.* As his winter 1966 diary suggests, Tvardovskii feared the same thing and initially expected those to be the last days of his editorship. Well enough versed in politics, he realized that although his journal was not directly involved, the lightning had struck dangerously close: time and again he would note the media's attempts to identify Siniavskii with *Novyi mir.*[7] Yet despite the increasing pressure, he was determined to preserve the journal. His strategy was to take a defensive stance, keeping to *Novyi mir*'s principles but avoiding any publications that might be perceived as openly defiant. In early March he wrote in the diary: "To preserve the journal in its current principal quality, even if without sensations, without any dashes into 'the unknown,' is [my] great task and duty. But not at the cost of abandoning the main position. Every issue [of the journal] means holding on to that position, one more month of standing our ground and perhaps even partially advancing."[8]

In practice, this calculated defense strategy did not quite work, as precisely in the same year, 1966, *Novyi mir* published some quite sensational materials that brought about major political repercussions for the journal. But in a high-profile court case such as that of Siniavskii and Daniel', the editor in chief had no option but to be extra careful. Tvardovskii could not escape being asked for his opinion about the case, and any imprudent comment would subject his journal to lethal risks. In early March he wrote draft letters on the affair to the Secretariat of the Writers' Union and the Presidium of the Central Committee. On 5 March, in the presence of several top figures in the literary establishment—Aleksei Surkov, Konstantin Voronkov, and Georgii Markov—he discussed the affair with the Central Committee secretary Petr Demichev. Everywhere, he diligently began by censuring Siniavskii and Daniel'.[9] On 13 April, in a conversation with the secretary of the European Community of Writers (COMES),

Giancarlo Vigorelli, Tvardovskii, together with Surkov, "harshly condemned" the acts of the two dissenters.[10]

His actual opinion of them was more complex, a question to which I will return. But whatever his motivation, Tvardovskii found himself between a rock and a hard place. *Novyi mir*'s "liberal" reputation encouraged those who sympathized with Siniavskii and Daniel' to seek the editor's help, although he was unable to render it. To complicate things further, the Western media became involved as well. It was Tvardovskii to whom Daniel's wife, human rights activist Larisa Bogoraz, wrote a letter in May 1967, after visiting her husband in a prison camp. Bogoraz did not ask for relief, and her fifteen-page letter, describing in detail the harsh conditions in the camp, was a manifestation of remonstrance and noncompliance as much as a plea for help.[11] Like the other eminent writers to whom she sent copies of her letter, Tvardovskii failed to respond. Bogoraz then forwarded the letter abroad, and a West German radio station broadcast it back to Soviet audiences. In August the letter reached Tvardovskii again, this time via a reader of his journal. Having heard its text in a "radio broadcast from the FRG [Federal Republic of Germany]," one Ivan Lysenko from the village of Sargamys in Kazakhstan was appalled by the fact that Daniel', a man of weak health, had to spend weeks in a damp prison cell. Lysenko was indignant about the writers' failure—Tvardovskii's, above all—to respond to Bogoraz and help the prisoner. That was "not gentlemanly," he wrote, adding that *Novyi mir*'s editor had thereby lost his "personal respect, the respect of an admirer of his work." Tvardovskii did not respond to him, either. What could he say?[12]

This letter raises a more general question about how Soviet audiences reacted to the Siniavskii-Daniel' affair. Also, the analogy frequently drawn between this and the Pasternak affair calls for a comparison of readers' reactions to them. Just as with *Doctor Zhivago* in 1958, few common readers had seen the texts for which Siniavskii and Daniel' were blamed. In fact, people knew even less in 1966, because unlike in Pasternak's case, this time the Soviet press wisely refrained from publishing excerpts from the writings of the two culprits and thus from offering them any semblance of a public voice. Responses to both affairs largely followed the same principle, "I have not read, but I will say." The question is whether anything had changed between 1958 and 1966 in what people would say without reading—in their a priori assumptions about literature, politics, and history.

Arguably, one significant change was the new prominence of the language of legality, democracy, and human rights. In the 1960s many people began to see these values as guarantees against a return of the recent violent past. In this regard, perhaps, Soviet culture paralleled the contemporary developments in countries west of the Iron Curtain. During the post–World War II decades, in West Germany and France as well, a new attention to legal procedure originated in a widespread perception that distortions of law had been a major cause of twentieth-century mass violence.[13]

The emphasis on legality during the Thaw years became visible at various levels of the Soviet state and educated society. The doctrine of the presumption of innocence would not enter Soviet law expressly until 1989, but during the Thaw it was no longer rejected as a bourgeois leftover, as it often had been in the early Soviet years. Discussions among legal experts on this issue had already started in the late Stalin period and they intensified in the 1950s and 1960s, with advocates of the presumption of innocence slowly gaining the upper hand. (Their victory would be ultimately secured by a 1978 ruling of the USSR Supreme Court).[14] In 1960, the new Code of Criminal Procedure of the Russian Federation rejected the use of confession as decisive proof of guilt, thus refuting Andrei Vyshinskii's arguments in the 1930s about establishing guilt in political "conspiracy" cases.[15] A number of legal theorists in the 1960s and 1970s launched a fairly successful attack on Vyshinskii's ideas.[16] The new 1961 Criminal Code prevented, at least on paper, the repression of individuals who had committed no formal crime, as well as the repression of their family members. The code ruled out repression by extrajudicial bodies such as the *troikas* and *dvoikas* of the Stalin years, by requiring that criminal punishment be meted out only by courts.[17] These shifts proved lasting and undermined many foundations of Stalin-era justice.[18] Significantly, legality became important not only to experts in the law but also to a broad, nonspecialist educated audience. It was in the 1960s that the Soviet human rights movement was born—largely out of widespread concern for preventing the return of mass repression. Many people came to believe that a new terror could be prevented by means of observing proper legal procedures, such as open trials and the presumption of innocence, as well as by maintaining the basic norms of a democratic society, notably the acceptability of open disagreement with an official ideological line. As was often the case in Russia, it was through the impact of literature, and in the literary realm, that the concerns for legality found an outlet. The occasion was the Siniavskii-Daniel' affair.

Words of Prosecution, Words of Defense

Let us highlight some of the intellectual shifts that the Thaw brought about, and let us do that by comparing readers' letters about the 1966 affair and about the campaign against Pasternak eight years before. The sources, it must be said right away, hardly allow for a clear-cut comparison. Most letters about Pasternak were addressed to literary periodicals and remained in their archives, held for unknown purposes but likely without much selection. By contrast, most letters about Siniavskii and Daniel' come from the archive of the Komsomol Central Committee and from investigation files, and they were probably selected from a larger variety of responses. The differences in provenance, as well as in record keeping, prevent an accurate correlation. Nonetheless, the forms and tactics of writing, the ideas and language the letter writers used in each case, are telling.[19]

There were many letters that condemned Siniavskii and Daniel'. Unlike in the Pasternak affair, though, many of the condemnations were not only collectively signed (by workers in a particular factory, or college students in an academic group), but were also textually almost identical.[20] Interesting variations did occur: thus, a letter from Workshop no. 1 of the Minsk Machine-Building Plant, signed by "E. Krakov," was plain and standard, but in Workshop no. 3 of the same plant a certain V. Ronin showed unusual familiarity with Siniavskii's work—and with *Novyi mir*, blemished by extension. According to Ronin, someone had brought old issues of *Novyi mir* with Siniavskii's articles to the workshop, and for a while the workers "could not calm down" as they compared his smooth and ideologically correct pieces, written for domestic consumption, with his anti-Soviet writings published abroad. Whether or not the events had developed the way Ronin described, at least his letter was distinct and original. Yet it had the same layout as its drab counterpart from Workshop no. 1: the same address captions located identically on the page, as well as similarly capitalized and underlined titles.[21]

Above all, the declared authors were absent from these condemnations. We do not know who V. Ronin and E. Krakov were, we know nothing of their past, childhood, parents, education, or any remarkable experiences in their lives. Compared with the 1958 condemnations of Pasternak, those of Siniavskii and Daniel' more frequently seemed depersonalized, offering the reader nothing but a more or less inventively edited pack of catchphrases. The anti-Pasternak campaign had also included some administratively endorsed letters crammed with clichés, but in 1966 the clichés became too thick and too common. When people wrote letters blaming Pasternak for treason and his renunciation of the revolutionary ideal, they often told stories of their own lives, citing their memories of the Revolution or the Civil War and turning their criticisms into long autobiographies. This confessional writing was not entirely absent in the case of Siniavskii and Daniel', but it came into view much less frequently. I have seen it in only four responses—such as, for example, in letters from two middle-aged women, Galina Filippova from Saratov and M. S. Litvinova, both of whom remembered the war years when they had toiled selflessly to help save their country. Both demanded severe punishment for the literary "traitors."[22] But the balance of emotional investment in the responses had shifted. Whereas in 1958 clichéd letters of condemnation were drowned out in a torrent of highly personal, autobiographical confessions bitterly accusing Pasternak, in 1966 such life stories were much less visible, while the charges against Siniavskii and Daniel' were rather standard and colorless. The letters were also remarkably brief now, usually no longer than one and a half to two typed pages. Unlike in Pasternak's case, many accusers of Siniavskii and Daniel' appeared to be simply going through the motions.

Chronology also raised some red flags. The trial took place in February (10–14 February 1966), but many of the collectively submitted condemnations in the Komsomol file were dated late March or early April—a month and a half or even two months later. The press and postal services could hardly be blamed for such delays: newspapers covered the trial promptly, and some people did respond immediately.[23] The explanation is, rather, that most of these condemnations were provoked not so much by the trial itself as by the post-trial Western media campaign in support of the two writers. Another reason the letters mentioned (in nearly identical expressions) was the few loud protests from the Soviet intelligentsia against the 1966 trial.[24] Unlike with the Pasternak affair, which had struck like lightning, with the news from the West urging everyone to improvise, in the case of Siniavskii and Daniel' the literary-political establishment had ample time for coordination.

The affair was monitored by the country's highest authorities: the Central Committee Secretariat, the Politburo, and First (since April 1966

General) Secretary Brezhnev himself.[25] Informing the Central Committee on popular responses to the affair, the KGB summary reports *(svodki)* drew a picture of unanimity, loyalty, and overwhelming support from "the public" for the court sentence.[26] Yet the format, declared authorship, language, and timing of many such expressions of support indicate that the condemnations rarely went beyond the media script prescribed by the mobilization campaign. Some evidence of this campaign has survived in the archives, too. On 18 January 1966 the writer and journalist Marietta Shaginian (1888–1982) proposed the idea of exiling Siniavskii and Daniel', advising the editors of *Izvestiia* to present this idea as a suggestion coming from "readers," a word she put in quotation marks. When forwarding her letter to the Central Committee, *Izvestiia*'s editor in chief, Lev Tolkunov (1919–1989), commented that, in his opinion, Shaginian "raised important issues." Attached to this document is a resolution instructing the receiver "to inform the secretaries of the CC CPSU." Judging by their signatures, at least two powerful secretaries, Mikhail Suslov and Iurii Andropov, were indeed informed and read Shaginian's suggestions.[27]

If the mobilization campaign was indeed so prominent, then how did people actually respond to the 1966 trial? Incomplete as the evidence is, it indicates first of all that opinions were divided and complex, and that there was certainly no unanimity that the KGB sought to represent.[28] This, parenthetically, questions the reliability of those KGB reports. Unlike in Pasternak's case, when official documents and readers' letters were in great congruence, in 1966 the *svodki* and the surviving letters contradicted each other. Unity and loyalty were just a façade.

Technically, the letters available to me are arrayed as follows. Among those written at the time of the trial, whose immediacy suggests the authors' emotional involvement, at least half defended Siniavskii and Daniel'.[29] Many letters in their defense in the Komsomol archive and in the investigation file were anonymous, while in the *Novyi mir* archive most were fully signed. The letter writers appeared to have greater trust in Tvardovskii's journal than in any institution of power. Geographically, the capital cities looked more "unreliable": there were quite a few letters written in defense of Siniavskii and Daniel' coming from Moscow and Leningrad.[30] Ages of letter writers varied: while most defenders in the Komsomol and investigation files were relatively young, *Novyi mir*'s correspondents appeared to be mostly middle-aged.[31]

Given the fragmentary nature of the evidence, a technical assessment of these responses, just as of those to the Pasternak affair, is unlikely to take us far. Intended for different audiences and collected (selected?) by different record keepers for different purposes, these batches of mail do not withstand systematic analysis by social categories. It is more fruitful, instead, to look at the ideas formulated in the letters and at the language their writers used, and to see if something new appeared in 1966 compared with 1958.

One principal difference, again, was that in 1966 the emotional investment of the letter writers was present more often in the defense letters than in the condemnations. Many years later, a famous playwright of the Thaw, Leonid Zorin (born in 1924), remembered signing a collective letter in defense of Siniavskii and Daniel' and then having to answer to his institutional party organization for doing so. As he recalled, the obligation to censure him aroused little enthusiasm among his colleagues. "This was a rather cheerless performance. Except for a couple of rascals, no one rushed to stigmatize the apostates. . . . Everyone was dourly going through the motions. I think my responses were much more aggressive than the questions addressed to me. My hot-headedness was, perhaps, not quite appropriate or justified. . . . But I was expected to say that I had made a serious mistake, while I kept repeating that I had done the right thing, and that the future would show that." Zorin was not expelled from the party, and the committee limited itself to mildly reprimanding his behavior.[32]

Not only were the defenders of Siniavskii and Daniel' commonly bolder and more aggressive than the accusers (the reverse of the 1958 situation), but the defenders' arguments were also quite different than those in 1958. One letter of defense, predictably anonymous, was written in the first-person plural and entitled "Petersburgers Speak" *(Pitertsy govoriat)*, at once revealing the authors' geographical origin and enriching their message with a flavor of historical *fronde*. Declaring that they were appalled by "the sheer idiocy of the authorities with regard to this trial," the letter writer(s)—"non-Komsomols" age "20 and above"—squarely rejected Soviet power, including its theoretical foundations, which the trial presumably compromised beyond repair. Their conclusions were radical indeed: "We are writing this to let you [no addressee indicated] know that there are people in Russia who are capable, at their age, of consciously taking up arms and killing Communists. But this is not enough: it is necessary to slaughter the bosses in the Central Committee, the Supreme Soviet . . . for all the Soviet power has done over the 50 years of its existence."[33]

Even more interesting than this vituperative and avowedly anti-Soviet rhetoric (which, after all, might have been in use in 1958, too—remember the letters of "anti-Soviet content" missing from the *Literaturnaia gazeta* files) was what prompted the young people's outrage. It was the parallels they drew between the 1966 trial and the terror of the Stalin years. They accused the authorities of putting Siniavskii and Daniel' in a "Stalinist camp" and argued that the press described the two writers "like enemies of the people from the times of Iagoda and Ezhov." This, the letter writers explained, meant there were "no specific charges on which a normal criminal trial is built—only senseless, foolish phrases of empty accusation." In fact, "there was no trial as such—only a well-acted theatrical play." "Enough," the young people protested, "Stalin has trained [*podressiroval*] us well—so much for that." Just as in the campaign against Ehrenburg three years earlier, the press entourage of the Siniavskii-Daniel' affair reminded readers of the machinery of the show trials from the 1930s, raising apprehensions that the terror was coming back.[34]

Stalin's ghost unfailingly rose from the pages of letters that responded to the 1966 trial. "First of all, I am becoming concerned about the future of our Motherland," wrote an anonymous "worker" from the Donetsk region. "One thing is clear: Stalin's belated followers are yearning for power. How otherwise can we explain the beginning of the persecution of our writers, which we are witnessing now[?]"[35] To yet another "Worker" the trial suggested that nothing had changed since Stalin's times. This affected his pessimistic view of the country's entire history after Lenin (whom he still treated respectfully, perhaps responding to the post-1953 "back to Lenin" propagandistic euphoria) as an unbroken chain of distortions, abuses, and pointless sacrifice:

> The people have shed a sea of blood, but what have they achieved? They have only strengthened the dictatorship, which is by now sophisticated with subterfuge, lying, and cruelty. "What about achievements?" you will ask. There could have been more of those, but for you. . . .
>
> [The authorities' current reasoning is:] free the dead (Tukhachevskii and others) but arrest the living (Pasternak, Siniavskii,

> Esenin, Daniel', and thousands more). The authorities' name has changed, but their crimes remain the same.[36]

Like many of his contemporaries, this Worker saw parallels between the Siniavskii-Daniel' and the Pasternak affairs. And, emblematically, writers occupied a prominent place in his view of the social hierarchy: they stood right next to Marshal Tukhachevskii on his list of terror victims.[37] But perhaps even more significantly, the terror went hand in hand with another major theme of this letter—democracy. The Worker called *Komsomol'skaia Pravda*'s coverage of the trial an "anti-democratic concoction" *(antidemokraticheskaia striapnia).*[38] By staging the trial, he argued, the authorities violated their recent promises to the people: "What is the worth of your Third [Party] Program, in which you guarantee the freedoms of speech, press, assembly, and the like? It's useful only for appropriating the people's labor and ascribing our achievements to the degenerating party. . . . I am telling you as a worker and on behalf of all the workers: take your bloodstained hands off our freedom!"[39]

The Worker's ideals were "freedom" and "democracy," in the way of which stood some abstract evildoers, the never-deciphered "you" that, once put in the third person, would become "them." In a rhetorical mixture characteristic of the Thaw years, his letter reproduced the traditional "us and them" logic while in the same breath rebelling against it. The mixture was symptomatic: the defenders of Siniavskii and Daniel' who deduced the wish for democracy from the experiences of terror had also been formed by those experiences. Many of those who tried chasing out the terror with new ideals were torn between revulsion for the reality of their existence and the inability—perhaps unwillingness—to formulate a conceptual alternative to that reality. The result was a hodgepodge utopia, an eccentric assortment of political ideals that combined "democracy" with an unspoiled organic Leninism, and occasionally (but not too frequently yet) added Russian patriotism to the mix as well.[40]

However, "democracy" was a significant ingredient in this mix—a notion that the letter writers commonly regarded as a bulwark against the return of mass repression. One after another, they recited the list of Soviet constitutional freedoms, most often freedom of speech and freedom of the press, presenting them as antithetical to Stalinist methods of governance. "True democracy and freedom of speech" were something that the country had not had since Lenin's time, one person argued, ending the letter with a slogan: "Long live true democratism! [*sic*]."[41] One Kravchenko from Mari ASSR rejected the "futile attempts to pass off beating dissenters as a democratic act."[42]

Democracy above all meant legality. An economist, V. Dmitriev from Moscow, noted that Soviet newspapers habitually described Siniavskii and Daniel' as guilty, when the court had not yet pronounced a verdict. This, Dmitriev argued, violated the basic presumption of innocence, producing the impression that the verdict was prearranged and the trial was a mere formality. As officials must have been aware of (although outwardly oblivious to) the legal issues he described, his letter was not an attempt to enlighten those in power about the basics of law. It was a caustic declaration of the letter writer's own intellectual and civic maturity. Refusing to accept the press accounts that presumed him uninformed and unthinking, he vowed not to pass over in silence the authorities' disregard for the laws of their own making and to hold them to their own promises.[43]

Drawing attention to legal norms did not exhaust Dmitriev's agenda, however, as he proceeded to make a bigger statement. Personally, he said, he had no sympathy for Siniavskii and Daniel'. To him they were "quite pessimistic personalities" and even "disgusting individuals."[44] But personal disaffection was beside his point. What he wished to defend was anyone's right to express his or her political opinion freely, regardless of convictions. Even if one were anti-Soviet, in a democratic society one ought to be able to express those ideas publicly:

> It is not Siniavskii and Daniel' who are on trial, on trial is the rejection of a social order, the rejection of a social doctrine; on trial is a worldview. There is no doubt that the defendants are guilty under article 70 [of the Penal Code]. And it is in vain that they deny their engagement in anti-Soviet propaganda. But why are the citizens of our country deprived of the right to reject the existing order and the dominant ideology? The only thing that may be punishable is a call for or an attempt at a violent overthrow of power.[45]

Dmitriev cited examples of capitalist countries where a substantial degree of agitation against the existing government was tolerated, such as with the communist parties in Italy and France. Why, he asked sarcastically, was "dying, rotten" capitalism not afraid of dissent, while "healthy and young" socialism brutally suppressed every dissenting voice? This was a dead end from which society needed to extricate itself as soon as possible:

> The main thing is: people do not have to believe in this or that ideology. They have the right to hold their own opinions, including wrong ones, and to propagate those opinions. A society that suppresses criticism and acts by constraint rather than persuasion in ideological affairs cannot develop successfully. It is doomed to rot. This is why Article 70 is unconstitutional, let alone inhumane, in a broad sense of the word. We are cutting the branch on which we are sitting.[46]

"It is awful to think about this," he concluded, "but the country of socialism deprives its citizens of the very basic civic rights! How long will Stalin's shadow hang over us?"[47]

In the clarity with which he articulated the ideas of civic rights and freedoms, Dmitriev was unusual even among the defenders of Siniavskii and Daniel', and it is safe to presume that few people at the time were capable of formulating these ideas so clearly and openly. Yet his statements marked a symptomatic development, common among many contemporary letter writers. The key element in the letters defending Siniavskii and Daniel' was the high frequency with which references to democracy and legality overlapped with references to the Stalin terror. No fewer than 40 percent of the letters written in the defense of these two authors referred to the legacy of mass repression, and just as many, often written by the same individuals, mentioned legality. The overlap was not accidental. It was his contemplation of the Stalinist past that made Dmitriev so concerned with constitutionality and law. For him and for many others, democracy and legality, no matter how vaguely defined, became safeguards against a new surge of uninhibited destruction of human lives.[48]

This was very different from how people had defended Pasternak back in 1958. Although they protested against the persecution of the writer on ethical grounds, his defenders had not paid much attention to civic freedoms or legal formalities. The fact that Pasternak was not formally prosecuted does not sufficiently explain this: the 1958 campaign against him had much in common with those of the Stalin years, and few could be sure that physical reprisals against the writer would not follow. Furthermore, despite their criticism of the campaign, the defenders of Pasternak did not reject all such campaigns in principle and did not link them so boldly with Stalin's name and the terror.

Yet another difference was that in 1966, unlike 1958, the letter writers themselves set the rhetorical and analytical agenda of the conversation. Their concern about the terror was not a reaction against any contemporary media script. Whereas in 1958 it was the press that, by rendering the content of *Doctor Zhivago*, suggested the Revolution as the theme for discussion, in 1966 the media did not at all raise the issue of the terror. Nor did it provide a synopsis of Siniavskii's and Daniel's texts (which, in fact, dealt intensely with the terror's legacy).[49] Generally, by 1966 mentions of the tragedy of the Stalin years had almost completely vanished from the press, and any that remained were becoming increasingly rare and thickly disguised.[50] Yet without any journalistic prompting, on their own initiative the letter writers made the terror the principal subject of their reactions to the affair.

Something must have changed between 1958 and 1966 that now compelled people to write about democracy and legality so strongly and in such direct conjunction with the issue of mass repression. Arguably, the change was "the Solzhenitsyn factor," although the phenomenon I describe with this term reached beyond Solzhenitsyn alone to encompass the broad and fairly open polemic about the terror that had taken place in literature and the press in the early 1960s, between the Pasternak and Siniavskii-Daniel' affairs. During the Pasternak debate, in spite of the recent Secret Speech and the widespread knowledge of the repression, open discussions of the camps and executions had lagged far behind kitchen-table conversations.[51] Also, relatively few letter writers of the mid- to late 1950s would explicitly identify themselves as victims of repression. But after more candid writing about the experiences of that repression became acceptable, readers' interactions with the published texts produced a broad and far-reaching reinterpretation of reality.

The details of twentieth-century mass violence, newly available in works of literature, had an impact on the entire order of the readers' historical and political reasoning. At the time of the Pasternak affair, the battle cries that had once pitted Russians against each other still appealed to many people, whether or not they remembered the Revolution and the Civil War. In 1958, the Revolution still remained a criterion against which numerous individuals continued to measure their own and others' political integrity. A principal question of the Pasternak affair, debated by both parties, the poet's accusers *and* his defenders, was whether his writings were Soviet or anti-Soviet, whether they matched certain uniform criteria of loyalty to the pervasive image of the Revolution-as-blessing. By the mid-1960s, however, it was the terror that came to the forefront in many people's thinking. The Revolution was not altogether gone from the stage, as some continued to idealize Lenin's time. But the idealization of the Revolution during the Thaw, and the "back to Lenin" slogan, were themselves derived from, and secondary to, the new awareness of the scale of the terror. "Back to Lenin" was only a temporary antidote against the ever more unsettling and disenchanting revelations about the state violence that had followed Lenin's rise to power.[52] In 1958, what explained the letter writers' nervous defense of the Revolution were not only personal experiences of 1917 but also the post–Secret Speech fears of a further historical unsettling and disenchantment. By 1966 the situation had become even more precarious. The readers' ideas about the historical foundations of their society had now been informed—and transformed—by the recent literary and media discussions of the terror. As a result, unlike in the 1950s, the people of the 1960s explicitly began to draw the lineage of the Soviet order from 1937 as much as, if not more than, from 1917. Reading about the increasingly inexplicable phenomena of human suffering in their own country made people question the legitimacy of the country itself.

The awareness of the past violence drove numerous letter writers to watch for signs that the violence might be returning, and to seek safeguards against its return. Their letters displayed such revulsion toward the campaign against Siniavskii and Daniel' (and earlier, the campaign against Ehrenburg) because of the common perception that similar campaigns had once served as instruments of terror. And the heightened attention to legality and courtroom procedure, as well, came from the realization that without those "technicalities," unrestrained bloodshed would be easily unleashed, as it had been in the past.

The new presence of the terror's legacy in this culture also led to a gradual redefinition of social membership. Uniform standards for inclusion and exclusion, such as loyalty to the Revolution, which had previously been in use, now became increasingly muddled. Loyalty to the Revolution could hardly serve as a rallying point anymore because it had not prevented those loyal to it from plunging into the bloodbath and killing others who were just as loyal. Loyalty to the Revolution ceased to serve as an intellectual panacea: on its own, it could no longer ensure even a semblance of peace of mind or social agreement.

Perhaps another rallying standard that could have worked was the Great Patriotic War. Individual records of participation in the war were certainly a powerful factor defining social consciousness during the postwar decades.[53] It was not incidentally that the letter writers Galina Filippova and M. S. Litvinova cited their wartime remembrances when branding Siniavskii and Daniel' as traitors.[54] But again, victory in the war had not ended the repression. Victory had not stopped Soviet people from continuing to stigmatize and kill each other once the war was over.[55] Mediawise, too, in the mid-1960s the war was only beginning to garner the public attention that it would claim a few years later. The first major Soviet celebration of victory in World War II did not come until its twentieth anniversary, in 1965. By the time of the Siniavskii-Daniel' affair the next year, a new emphasis on the war was only beginning to gain strength. By contrast, the literary discussions of the camps and purges were still fresh in readers' minds. Furthermore, the problem of the terror seemed much less resolved and less clear-cut than questions about the war. In 1963, when arguing with her editor about the comparative significance of the Great Patriotic War and the Stalin-era repression, Lidiia Chukovskaia maintained that, while the death toll of the war had probably been much higher, the repression lasted longer and presented more conundrums, because its origins and significance were far less obvious than those of the war.[56] The early to mid-1960s thus might have been a moment in Soviet history when the terror overshadowed even World War II as the people's primary historical concern.

Once the enormity and pervasiveness of the recent violence entered open discussions via the printed word, no uniform criteria for social membership could provide reassurance to those who read about it. The 1960s may have been the point at which many people began abandoning the search for such criteria. It was then that the voices in at least some letters changed, not so much in *what* but in *how* the letter writers argued. There were those who became militantly defensive about the established social order and their own past—defensive to the point of desperation. But, as in Solzhenitsyn's case, there were other, new voices that sounded more reflective. Importantly, those voices often belonged to people who remembered the early Soviet years firsthand.

"Let us take the past," a woman in her sixties wrote to the Supreme Court of the Russian Federation in 1966:

> Look how many innocent people have perished in our country. You cannot read about this without tears. And perhaps they were tried in the same room as Siniavskii and Daniel'. . . . And so I am asking that Siniavskii and Daniel' receive a simple reprimand, but not 5 and 7 years. . . . Look, dear Judges, how is it that in our Soviet days so many people have been killed and later found not guilty? Where is the just Soviet Law? . . . I am over 60 years old, and I so much do not want to hear or read about show trials any more. I have grown sick and tired of trials during this nearly half a century.[57]

Instead of exclusionary rallying points and unifying battle cries, more and more letters of the 1960s conveyed an aversion to political violence, a desire to avoid it in the future. After decades of bloodshed, and praising bloodshed, they argued that the country at last had to find peaceful ways of resolving its domestic issues. It would be premature to say that this desire for peace reflected a conceptual rejection of political violence—and yet these might be the first signs that people had begun to distance themselves from it.

In this sense, the 1960s could be the moment when, under the growing weight of knowledge about the past, an influential part of the Soviet audience took its first steps toward national reconciliation. In the historic case of Russia, what the notion of national reconciliation presumed, above all, was a rejection of the long-standing imagery of endemic social strife, inbuilt hostilities, and internal "enemies."[58] Dispelling the phantoms was a slow process, and many letter writers continued to resort to them. But in doing so, they were arguably fighting a rearguard action. By 1966 it had become possible to say openly, as the economist Dmitriev did, that one could hold a dissenting opinion and still be a loyal member of society, or that a writer could publish abroad and nonetheless remain accepted at home. And more: that one could be anti-Soviet and still be welcome in Soviet society, unless one was violently hostile to the existing order. Nonviolent anti-Sovietness was nothing more than an exercise of civic freedom. The idea of using physical repression against dissenters, although not gone, had been significantly compromised. Ever more aware of, and concerned about, the tragic past, at least some people began evaluating society by the success with which it protected human dignity and life.[59]

It was also in the 1960s that the critically minded readers began paying attention to the textbook definitions of socialism. They discovered that the definitions included the word "democracy," as well as a long list of civic freedoms. Newspapers and textbooks presumed—on paper, but that was enough—that democracy was a primary attribute not of bourgeois societies but of the Soviet state, where democratic freedoms were to be fully realized. Now a common desire arose to test the validity of this presumption. The letter writers of 1966 held the authorities accountable for what they had long promised. The trial of Siniavskii and Daniel' presented the perfect and timely target, because under the guise of legality it violated the democratic principles in which many people now vested their hopes. This notion of unfulfilled promises was yet another reason why in 1966, unlike 1958, the writers' defenders proved more vigorous and aggressive than their accusers. Originating in the literary discussions of the terror, it was this notion that made the polemic around Siniavskii and Daniel' crucial in generating the Soviet human rights movement.[60]

The evidence is, and always will be, insufficient for measuring how widespread these ideas became in the 1960s. Impressionistically, it appears that such ideas characterized mostly the intelligentsia, and not all of it. Among the defenders of Siniavskii and Daniel' who identified their occupations, we find mostly intelligentsia types: an economist, a lawyer, a schoolteacher, an associate professor *(dotsent)*, two lower-ranking researchers, and two engineers, but only two soldiers and three workers. However, the intelligentsia of the 1960s should not be thought of as a tight circle of savants or a conspiracy of revolutionaries. It was a large and fast-growing class of educated professionals, inseparable from the rest of society.[61] And more importantly, as this book repeatedly argues, what matters are not so much fixed numbers as tendencies and long-term impact. From this viewpoint, the new intellectual phenomena were symptomatic. Initially characteristic of the intelligentsia, in the long run the changing notions of social membership and normalcy would affect a great many Soviet people.

The Verdict

To end on this note would make a beautiful cadence, but we risk not doing justice to the demands of accuracy. It may appear that the condemnations of Siniavskii and Daniel' were mostly orchestrated, while "true" opinions were unequivocally on the writers' side, and that sensibilities had entirely changed between 1958 and 1966, with most people earnestly condemning Pasternak before, and just as earnestly supporting Siniavskii and Daniel' now. This is only partly accurate. Compared with 1958, the letter writers of 1966 did, overall, sound more reflective and less susceptible to the media's impact, more eager to look for explanations and less willing to rush to the site of execution. However, this did not mean that those who supported Siniavskii and Daniel' did so wholeheartedly and unreservedly.

For all his defense of the two authors' right to speak freely, the economist Dmitriev, as we remember, did not personally sympathize with them. Many other letter writers, too, advocated the authors' entitlement to publish abroad, but aside from a few antiregime orators, no one particularly celebrated what Siniavskii and Daniel' had done. Telling in this sense were the readers' letters written in reaction to other literary-political events of the same years. There, people would often briefly refer to the Siniavskii-Daniel' affair, summarizing their attitude in just a few words. In the same months of 1966, for example, many letter writers rose to the defense of another *Novyi mir* author, the journalist Emil' Kardin, whose iconoclastic article appeared in print at the same time as the trial, provoking the authorities' wrath. The Kardin story, discussed in the next chapter, is worth mentioning here because letter writers often referred to both affairs in one breath. And, while generally favorable toward Kardin, they were far more ambiguous about Siniavskii and Daniel'.[62] "One cannot write in the same tone about Siniavskii and Daniel' and about Kardin and the editors of *Novyi mir*," wrote one D. Smirnova.[63] In attacking the journalist who was the main target of Kardin's article, one reader argued that this journalist "brought no less harm than the activities of Siniavskiis and Daniel's who transported their creations abroad."[64]

These letters conveyed not much "rage and indignation" about the two literary dissenters, but they contained no applause either. Instead, there was detachment verging on dislike. Three years later, in 1969, the situation would repeat itself when authors of the well-known "Letter of the Eleven Writers" attacked Tvardovskii's *Novyi mir* for having published Siniavskii (presented as an early sign of the journal's depravity). In response, readers defended the journal by arguing that it had published Siniavskii long before his "treason" was disclosed. "It is not that easy to guess traitors," wrote D. Ivanov from Khabarovsk, drawing a parallel between Siniavskii and another *Novyi mir* author, Anatolii Kuznetsov (1929–1979), who had recently found asylum in Britain.[65] Six young Georgian workers from Batumi likened "the former writer," "scoundrel," and "traitor of the Motherland" Kuznetsov to "the political criminal A. Siniavskii," yet defended *Novyi mir* by arguing that its editors were not to blame for unknowingly publishing either of these future turncoats.[66] Of course, such peripheral condemnations of dissident writers might have been a diversionary tactic: the letters were often intended for agencies not as receptive to unconventional opinions as *Novyi mir* was. Praising Siniavskii in a letter meant to defend *Novyi mir* would have been not only unsafe but also unwise, as this would have defeated the letter's main purpose. Yet it is doubtful whether the letter writers were that calculating. Also, for mere subterfuge their language was unnecessarily strong: to defend *Novyi mir*, one did not have to call Siniavskii and Kuznetsov traitors and scoundrels. It might be that this was what the letter writers thought.

Be they defenders or accusers of literary dissent, the readers of *Novyi mir* remained flesh of the flesh of Soviet culture. Some even urged the authorities to be less protective, less afraid of the audience's subversion by anti-Soviet propaganda, because they believed such subversion was improbable.[67] Even the angry anti-Soviet diatribes revealed not so much their authors' disengagement from Soviet values as, on the contrary, a strong sense of belonging to the agendas of home culture. One of those agendas was the traditional apprehension about things Western. Numerous letter writers continued to display elements of the old "besieged fortress" mentality, maintaining an alienation from foreigners and perceiving contacts with them as subversive or, at best, extraordinary.[68] Even those who accepted the idea of interaction with the West theoretically were not always comfortable about it in practice. Unsanctioned publishing abroad still seemed awkward, even if, hypothetically, it ought to be normal. Especially uncomfortable was the fact that, technically speaking and whether one liked it or not, the West remained a hostile political camp. The letter writers often identified publishing in the West with sharing or promoting Western political interests, and while they admitted that the author might have had no such agenda, they nonetheless presumed that the opposing camp would exploit his text to its own advantage.

The charge of anti-Soviet agitation that the court pressed against Siniavskii and Daniel' had as much to do with their ideas as with the venue that the two writers chose for expressing them. The prosecution argued that the very act of unsanctioned publishing in the hostile camp had turned the works of Abram Tertz and Nikolai Arzhak into weapons that

Western propaganda could and did use against the Soviet Union. It was this, and not only the alleged meanings of their texts that, in the eyes of the court, made their acts anti-Soviet.[69] Apparently quite a few readers believed that the prosecution had a point. While in principle few denied that an author ought to be free to publish wherever he or she wanted, in practice that would work only if one were oblivious to the existence of a world torn apart by the Cold War. In this world, the real world, publishing in the West placed the Soviet writer, perhaps against his will, in the camp of his country's strategic rivals—an awkward position for someone who did not necessarily wish to sever all ties with his homeland. During the investigation and at the trial, Andrei Siniavskii and Iulii Daniel' effectively disproved all charges based on identifying their fictional characters' political views with their own, but they were noticeably less adamant in defending the very act of publishing in the West.[70] In his concluding statement, Daniel' said: "We are guilty—not of what we have written but of the fact that we sent our works abroad."[71] In the first letter he wrote to his family from the camp, he returned to that statement: "Again: I recognized myself (us) as guilty only of not foreseeing the possibility that these writings could be exploited to harm Russia (if there was such harm)."[72] Unease about cooperating with foreigners remained a powerful attitude in the 1960s. Images of foes abroad dissipated more slowly than specters of enemies at home.[73]

This lack of personal sympathy for Siniavskii and Daniel' in the letters offers a correction to some descriptions of the reformist intelligentsia during the Thaw, in which "reformism" unproblematically accompanies "Westernization."[74] The desire for change at home did indeed frequently go hand in hand with an urge for closer ties with the West. And yet the flawlessly consistent image of a reformist *and* Western-oriented *shestidesiatnik* might be little but an ideal type, as mythical and ephemeral as its antithesis, the inveterate Stalinist, nativist, and counter-reformist. The reality of the 1960s was complex. One could praise *Novyi mir*'s critical realism, admire Ehrenburg and Solzhenitsyn, opt for change, and speak for democracy, but also maintain etatist patriotism and a sense of the country's profound distinctness.

Still, however, in the final tally aversion to a potential return of the terror overshadowed antipathy toward Siniavskii and Daniel' and their dealings with the West. A good example of this was Tvardovskii himself. Highly placed and well informed, the editor in chief reacted to the affair not unlike many readers of his journal. While respecting Siniavskii as a literary scholar, he held a low ethical opinion of his and Daniel's enterprise. Tvardovskii thought this not because he believed their Western publications to be particularly criminal; nor was he impressed intellectually or literarily by their texts, although he did read some of them. "I have read [Siniavskii's] *Liubimov*—utter rubbish," he noted in his diary of November 1965.[75] Rather, he was disposed against the two writers because, in his opinion, once published abroad their texts could be turned into weapons of propaganda against the USSR. And so, until mid-February 1966, in his diary he would refer to Siniavskii and Daniel' as "these rogues" *(eti mazuriki)*.[76]

What changed Tvardovskii's attitude was the court verdict on 14 February, in which Siniavskii was sentenced to seven and Daniel' to five years of imprisonment. This produced a devastating impact on him. The day after, he wrote in the diary:

> Seven and five years of strict regime. . . . Result: my usual words . . . that S[iniavskii] and D[aniel'] not only inspire no sympathy but, on the contrary, deserve contempt, etc.,—these words have somehow been extinguished within me. 7 and 5 of intense custody. Now . . . the question is directly about our internal existence. Now there is already something not to be discussed in a more or less broad circle, something from that horrible memory . . . , something cold and dismal that burdens the soul of every one of us. . . . I could say that I do not even want to live—[because] if this is a turn to "that," then the only thing which remains is to drag out existence. But of course, this is hardly a real "turn"—just an abyss of blindness and stupidity of ignoramuses (However, is that not it, precisely?).[77]

By "a turn to 'that,'" Tvardovskii meant the return of repression. It was one thing to condemn Siniavskii and Daniel' morally, but it was quite something else to send two human beings to a concentration camp, one thing to imagine distant "enemies" abroad but something else to resume physically imprisoning people at home. After the verdict, he wrote several appeals to the Secretariat of the Writers' Union, to the Presidium of the Central Committee, and to other agencies, warning about the danger of sliding back into terror.[78] He did not change his mind about publishing in the West and kept condemning Siniavskii and Daniel' in public. But his diary remarks about them became milder, and he followed their fates with great anxiety.[79] His disapproval of them paled in comparison with a much more important moral and political concern. Images of enemies might not be gone, but, like many readers of his journal, Tvardovskii was anxious never to see those images materialize in another purge.

A number of literary scholars have observed that the trial of Siniavskii and Daniel' was premised on a straightforward, linear identification of a literary text with its author's political views. Perceiving as anti-Soviet the language that the two authors ascribed to their fictional characters, the court projected that language directly onto the writers and presented the words of their protagonists as conveying the authors' own political ideas. In criticizing the court for this exclusionary and simplistic reading, scholars have referred to the Soviet and traditional Russian identification between fiction and life, word and deed, language and authority. They have argued instead for "limitless possibilities of interpretation," where the author neither prescribes nor even knows the meanings of his text, and as many meanings exist as there are readers.[80]

The possibilities for interpretation are indeed limitless, but this is precisely why the Soviet interpretations of texts by Siniavskii and Daniel' deserve as much attention as any others. Moreover, the reactions of those who had no access to the texts and read only the newspaper coverage of the trial are not to be disregarded, either. By ostracizing those opinions, one risks mirroring the approach of a Soviet court. The affair was certainly a product of traditional Russian views of literature, but it also revealed many people's perceptions of their time, politics, and history. The letter writers who followed the proverbial path of "I have not read, but I will say" exposed those perceptions perhaps best of all. Just as the Pasternak affair did eight years earlier, the case of Siniavskii and Daniel' transcended the framework of literature, because in 1966, as in 1958, most people who participated in these affairs or read about them in the press cared little about literature for its own sake.[81] For the courts, the journalists, and scores of ordinary readers, the main concern in every such literary polemic was its relevance to the country's past, contemporary situation, and future, and, ultimately, to their own, increasingly unstable, self-perceptions and beliefs.

But there were also major differences from the Pasternak story. Reactions to the Siniavskii-Daniel' affair revealed profound shifts in the readers' consciousness that had taken place in the 1960s—first and foremost under the impact of literature. In this sense, the affair was a logical sequel, the next chapter in the literary polemics that began with the discussions about books by Ehrenburg and Solzhenitsyn. Their growing awareness of the past prompted a shift in how readers perceived the norms of individual and societal existence. Thanks to literature, what began to replace the system of aggressively exclusive ideological affirmation was a greater propensity for reflection, self-questioning, and political as well as intellectual tolerance. Perhaps, once the terror became the domain of critically minded readers, its physical return was ever less probable.

9

IN SEARCH OF AUTHENTICITY

The "Legends and Facts" Controversy

TVARDOVSKII'S PLAN to keep a reasonably low profile for *Novyi mir*, maintaining the editorial strategy but avoiding provocative publications that might cost the journal dearly, did not work. And it probably could not have worked, as his strategy was increasingly at odds with the ideological project on which the country's new leadership embarked during the second half of the 1960s. The journal and the political establishment were on a collision course. Nowhere did this become clearer than in the controversy around "Legends and Facts."

Written by the literary critic Emil' Vladimirovich Kardin (1921–2008), an article under this title appeared in *Novyi mir* in February 1966. The article challenged several foundational myths from Soviet history textbooks. One was "the salvo of the *Aurora* cruiser," which had presumably given the revolutionary forces the signal to storm the Winter Palace in Petrograd on 25 October 1917. Another myth involved "the battles of Pskov and Narva," in which the Red Guards had allegedly stopped the advancing German troops on 23 February 1918—the day that later became the Soviet Army Day. The third myth told of "the twenty-eight Panfilovites"—a 1941 battle near Moscow, in which a handful of soldiers from the division under General Panfilov had supposedly delayed a superior German force but fallen in the uneven combat. Kardin argued that there had been no salvo, that the battles of Pskov and Narva had never taken place, and that there was no documentary evidence for the battle of the twenty-eight Panfilovites.[1]

The article brought a harsh response in the media—first of all from Aleksandr Krivitskii, a journalist whom Kardin exposed as the self-serving author of the Panfilovite story. According to Kardin, Krivitskii had invented this battle and fully capitalized on publicizing it. In response, Krivitskii effectively accused Kardin of political and ideological treason.[2] *Krasnaia zvezda (Red Star)*, the main newspaper of the armed forces, published a letter signed by the top brass of the military (including Marshal of the Soviet Union Konstantin Rokossovskii), who blamed Kardin and *Novyi mir* for dishonoring the World War II past.[3]

Kardin hit the right target at the right time. The years between 1965 and 1970 could be called the Time of Anniversaries—when the new Brezhnev leadership launched a series of large-scale festivities commemorating the milestones of the Soviet past. Among those were the twentieth anniversary of Victory (1965), the fiftieth anniversary of the Revolution (1967), the fiftieth anniversary of the Soviet army (1968), and the one hundredth anniversary of Lenin's birth (1970), to name just a few. The Soviet system of cultural management often operated on an anniversary principle: cultural initiatives were legitimized by building a logical connection between them and a certain forthcoming anniversary, commemorated with an appropriate contemporary emphasis.[4] The celebrations of the late 1960s were important in that regard. Reversing the recent denunciations of the Stalin past, they were meant to reaffirm the regime's historical legitimacy. History was to be celebrated as a succession of victories rather than revisited as a source of disturbing collective memories. Accordingly, around 1966, mentions of the state violence under Stalin nearly disappeared from the media.[5] Against this background, *Novyi mir*'s critical stance became especially unwelcome. Kardin's article was noted disapprovingly by Brezhnev himself and simultaneously triggered a ban on subscriptions to *Novyi mir* in the military.[6]

"Legends and Facts" was indeed very much a *Novyi mir* text, written in the vein of Tvardovskii's quest for factual authenticity—a rediscovery of dark and previously closed corners of history, the new knowledge presumably guiding the reader in settling unpaid accounts with the past. Along this line, too, Kardin exposed the three textbook stories as products of Stalin-era propaganda. They indeed originated in the Stalin years—at least this was when they were perpetuated in verbal formulas and visual images, becoming firmly entrenched in popular memory. One of the myths, the Panfilovites, is especially emblematic both of the making of Soviet mass persuasion under Stalin and its unmaking during the Thaw.

Soviet Thermopylae

The story of the twenty-eight Panfilovites began in November 1941, during the critical days of the Battle of Moscow, when the 316th Rifle Division of Major General Ivan Panfilov (1893–1941) resisted the German advance on the capital. On 18 November Panfilov was killed in battle, whereupon the division was given his name—hence the Panfilovites.[7]

On 27 November, *Red Star* published an article by its frontline correspondent, Vasilii Koroteev. Praising the division's contribution to the defense of the capital, he described a battle in which a few dozen soldiers from this division held off the Germans for four hours, destroying eighteen tanks and 800 troops. Although all the Soviet soldiers fell, they managed to delay the enemy until the arrival of reinforcements. Koroteev mentioned neither the date nor the place of the engagement, nor the number of soldiers. Meant to be inspiring, his prose was rich with exclamation marks and high-flowing, antiquated phrases.[8] Yet his description paled in comparison to the one *Red Star* published the following day—an editorial titled "The Bequest of the 28 Fallen Heroes," written by Aleksandr Krivitskii. For the first time, the number of soldiers—twenty-eight—appeared in print, so far without names. Another new detail was that originally there had been twenty-nine soldiers. One turned out to be a traitor, who tried surrendering but was shot dead at once by his comrades. The date and location of the battle were still not specified.[9]

Krivitskii certainly outdid Koroteev in lofty, clichéd rhetoric. He described German tanks as "armored monsters" *(bronirovannye chudovishcha)*; in describing the Red Army soldiers he used such expressions as "without tremor" *(ne drognuv)*, "clenching teeth" *(stisnuv zuby)*, "brave hearts" *(otvazhnye)*, "will forever shine" *(naveki ozarit)*, and so on. The clichés overlapped with other signs of the time. His representation of surrender as treason and premeditated enemy activity reflected the contemporary Soviet mistrust of POWs. The article followed the wartime turn to historical examples of Russian military prowess—in particular, the revival of the imperial tradition of elite guard units.[10] Panfilov's division was among the first to receive this status, of which Krivitskii made much.[11] "Our people," he wrote, "fought remembering the old motto: 'the Guards die but do not surrender.'"

Unlike Koroteev, who pioneered the story but then shied away from it, Krivitskii became an avid propagandist for the Panfilovites. In January 1942, *Krasnaia zvezda* published his second article about them, significantly developing the story. He named the date and place of the battle—16 November 1941, near the railway stop at Dubosekovo, a few miles west of Moscow—and listed all the twenty-eight soldiers and their commanding officer, political commissar Klochkov, by name.[12]

The story received wide currency and was reprinted several times during the war.[13] The dramatic statement, "Russia is vast, but there is nowhere to retreat. Behind us is Moscow," which Krivitskii ascribed to Klochkov, became legendary. Poets wrote verses about the Panfilovites.[14] In 1942, a poem about Moscow that mentioned the twenty-eight heroes was put to music by the composer Isaak Dunaevskii and gained nationwide popularity, which it retains today.[15] On 21 July 1942, the Presidium of the Supreme Soviet of the USSR posthumously awarded each of the twenty-eight soldiers the country's highest military decoration—the title "Hero of the Soviet Union."

Despite all the rhetorical beautification, Krivitskii's account was personal and poignant—a vivid example of wartime journalistic prose. Historians would question the origins of the direct speech, literary aesthetes would frown on the cheap phraseology, and military experts would doubt whether so few soldiers could destroy so many tanks. But this was not an entry in an essay contest or a scholarly paper. This was propaganda, and as propaganda it was timely, lively, and imaginative—in other words, it worked. The story also had respectable literary and mythological origins. The noble tale of a handful of warriors standing in the way of an enormous enemy horde and falling in battle while defending their land dates back to Thermopylae and *The Song of Roland*—a classical plot, universally successful and invariably appealing.[16] As for the veterans of real battles, who could have cast doubt on the technical side of Krivitskii's account, they refrained from open criticism—not necessarily out of fear but also because they perceived the article as a necessary propagandistic message.[17] The text was written with a mobilizing purpose, and at the time, it achieved its goal.

However, the story was also a newspaper creation, to be analyzed with reference to the principles of Soviet journalism. One of those principles, declared in numerous manuals, was truthfulness. Newspaper materials were to be based on authentic evidence, never to deceive the reader. The demand for truthfulness, of course, coexisted with selectivity and expediency, offering rich opportunities for skepticism and cynicism.[18] Still, the cynical inflection of evidence was never overtly recognized in the journalistic profession, and the discovery of such episodes was a serious embarrassment. Time and again, experienced professionals instructed their junior colleagues about the need for meticulous "verification of facts." Entire newspaper departments were busy verifying the facts—names, dates, and places—in every article before it could see the light of day.[19]

Given the ubiquitous importance of authenticity, it was embarrassing for the authorities to discover, almost immediately, that the saga of the twenty-eight Panfilovites had little or no factual background. Soon after Krivitskii publicized the heroes' names, the military command began hearing from their families, former colleagues, and local administrators that some of the soldiers pronounced dead might be alive, as they had been sending letters and pictures of themselves to their families, and even showing up in person.[20]

Soon after the war, not only the casualty list but also the authenticity of the battle itself was challenged. In November 1947, the military prosecutor's office of the Kharkov garrison in Ukraine opened a criminal investigation against the former sergeant Ivan Dobrobabin, whom Krivitskii had listed among the fallen Panfilovites. Not only had Dobrobabin survived, but he also had apparently "surrendered" to the Germans in 1941 and, to make things worse, entered German service as a member of the Polizei, the occupation police. When interrogated, he confessed that he had never participated in the battle of the twenty-eight Panfilovites. A further investigation established that at least four other soldiers of the twenty-eight were alive. Moreover, no military documents mentioned the engagement, and no one remembered even hearing about it.[21]

The investigators summoned Koroteev and Krivitskii, together with the commander of the regiment in which the twenty-eight soldiers had served, as well as the *Red Star*'s former editor, David Ortenberg (1904–1998). It quickly became clear that the entire story was their invention, particularly Ortenberg's and Krivitskii's. Although there had been heavy fighting in the area in November 1941, the battle of the twenty-eight never took place. It also turned out that Krivitskii had obtained the soldiers' names from an officer who gave them to him "from memory."[22]

It was, of course, not publicized that one of the most famous wartime feats was an invention. The information was of considerable state importance—from the initial level of a garrison judiciary it reached the country's top leadership, possibly including Stalin himself. Ortenberg remembered Lev Mekhlis, the chief of the Army Political Directorate, telling him that Stalin had liked Krivitskii's editorial.[23] This may explain why the story had so much currency and continued to circulate for decades. In most textbooks, moreover, this was the *only* episode that mentioned any World War II defenders of Moscow by name.

Crucial to the perpetuation of the Panfilovite story was its author, Aleksandr Krivitskii (1910–1986). As he came to play an important role in the history of post–World War II Soviet literature, and notably *Novyi mir*, it is worth taking a closer look at him.

The Gray Cardinal of Simonov's Novyi mir

A professional journalist, Krivitskii had a passion for history, especially military history. Not incidentally did he put so much emphasis on the Panfilovites' belonging to a guards' unit, and on the Russian guards' historical bravery.[24] When the war began, his passion received a powerful boost. Resurrecting the past glory of the Russian military and emphasizing a continuity of traditions between the imperial Russian and the Soviet armies became an important propagandistic strategy, and here Krivitskii came to the forefront.[25] During the war he produced several brochures about military traditions—for example, removing the stigma from shoulder boards, once emblematic of the tsarist military uniform, which were restored by the Red Army in early 1943. On commission from the Central Committee and the military command he also wrote a book, *Traditions of Russian Officers*.[26]

His creation of a Soviet Thermopylae—the story of the twenty-eight Panfilovites—originated in an auspicious combination of the moment's exigencies and his own predilections. The merger of personal passion and state interest created a memorable, powerful story that became a legend lasting for decades. In a letter dated 1955, Konstantin Simonov, with his aristocratic-military background and lifetime penchant for the army, addressed Krivitskii as, "Dear author of the traditions of Russian officers!"—as if Krivitskii had authored not only the book but also the traditions themselves.[27]

Simonov adored Krivitskii, just as Krivitskii admired Simonov. Almost since their first meeting in 1939 and for the next forty years, up until Simonov's death, the two men were bound by a close friendship that developed during the war, when both worked as correspondents for *Red Star*.[28]

After the war, during both terms of Simonov's editorship in *Novyi mir* (1946–1950 and 1954–1958), Krivitskii was his right hand at the journal—the "responsible secretary" of the editorial board. Because of Simonov's frequent absences, Krivitskii effectively governed *Novyi mir.* People who then worked at the journal remembered him always present in Simonov's office, always conferring with Simonov about every single editorial affair. The two were an editorial board within an editorial board. No major publication was accepted without a conversation between them, no significant editing of a manuscript bypassed Krivitskii's eye, no decision was made without Krivitskii's input.[29] Simonov trusted him with everything, from editing manuscripts to verifying quotations to preparing important papers for the Central Committee.[30]

The tone of many notes they exchanged was humorous and warm, revealing Simonov's full confidence in and longtime affection for his friend. Krivitskii was often "Sasha" for him—and sometimes also "dear" *(golubchik)*, "kiddie" (*detka*, although Krivitskii was five years older), and the like. Krivitskii responded in kind, although he always showed his awareness of their unequal standing in the literary ranks. He was an old friend, but also a subordinate addressing the boss. Both, however, took this seniority with a dose of humor, often making fun of bureaucracy and bureaucratese.[31] The wartime origins of this friendship appeared in their correspondence: sometimes Simonov would half-jokingly sign a letter with his former military rank: "Lieutenant Colonel Simonov."[32] Perhaps the ultimate recognition of how important Krivitskii was for him came when he made Krivitskii the prototype of Boris Gurskii, a central character in several of Simonov's novels about the war.[33]

The friendship between these two men offers us a window on the time and the zeitgeist. It was also of major significance for literature. Both—Simonov, obviously, but Krivitskii as well—occupied positions of key importance in the literary establishment. It is not an exaggeration to say that, in the late 1940s and 1950s, the two of them not only decided the strategy of *Novyi mir* but also had a great impact on the overall course of Soviet literature. Besides editorial matters, Krivitskii also had Simonov's trust in regard to literature as such, being his most incisive reader, critic, and perhaps even ghost writer.[34] On several occasions the two discussed Simonov's writing in the presence of a stenographer, so that no word would be lost.[35]

These conversations became especially important in the late 1940s when all literature, including Simonov's work, was subject to particularly ominous political supervision. On 8 August 1947 he and Krivitskii got together to discuss Simonov's forthcoming novella *Dym otechestva (The Smoke of the Fatherland)*. This was a book Simonov particularly cherished: some scholars go so far as to suggest that it was programmatic for him.[36] Written in the wake of his 1946 trip to the United States, it portrays a Soviet officer and war veteran, Petr Basargin, returning from a military-diplomatic mission in the United States to a hometown devastated by the war. The book is full of reflection on postwar America and Russia, the meaning of patriotism (not by chance is its title a quotation from Griboedov's *Woe from Wit*, whose main protagonist also returns home from the West), and the complexity of postwar life.[37] For today's reader, Simonov's characters are fairly wooden: they speak in didactic monologues about patriotism, morality, and self-interest versus selflessness, their individual lives governed by the greater cause of societal duty.[38] Yet arguably both Simonov and Krivitskii took this greater cause seriously.

Their ideas rested on fundamental premises about the meaning of artistic and social truth. When the two discussed the novella in 1947, they talked not about verbal precision or psychological finesse for their own sake, but rather about the text's political charge and correspondence with social reality. Thus, they took extra care to make sure that the image of one "negative" character in the book, a self-seeking dealer who was a homegrown replica of American capitalists—a "neo-kulak," as Simonov put it—would be realistic and historically accurate, while at the same time not excessively disheartening for the readers. "I seek the truth," Simonov remarked at this point. "The truth is dear to me because, among other things, no one would be able to spit in my face and say that I am a varnisher [of reality]." "No one will say that," Krivitskii reassured him.[39]

Rather than dismissing this dialogue as a standard discussion of socialist realism by two experienced practitioners, it may be fruitful to pay close attention to these words. Not incidentally, Simonov's most informed commentators—in the 1980s, Aleksandr Karaganov and Lazar' Lazarev, and back in 1947 none other than Ilya Ehrenburg—did not at all dismiss *The Smoke of the Fatherland* as hackwork. On the contrary, they thought of it highly and devoted long, approving commentaries to its various twists of plot and character.[40] Simonov also was fond of this book. What did they all see in it?

The notion of truth is central here. Contemporaries believed that Simonov, like no one else at the time, had candidly and accurately depicted the harsh reality of postwar daily existence in Russia—hunger, poverty, homelessness, the lack of most elementary comforts.[41] For them, the book's achievement was its truth value. And because Simonov also insisted that he sought the truth, it is worth asking what he meant by this. How did he—and Krivitskii—understand truth?

In her analysis of socialist realism, Katerina Clark has recorded several phases in attitudes toward truth in Soviet literature. During the years of the First Five-Year Plan (1928–1932), positivist values prevailed, as writers desired to record concrete economic achievements measured with unquestionable statistics and facts. From about 1931, however, the literary environment began to distance itself from the positivist "pseudo-objectivism," which came to be then seen as pedestrian. Instead, writers sought to convey what Clark terms "higher-order truth," inherently accessible to the top leadership and handed down to the people as a matter of revelation. The 1930s were depicted as the age of the extraordinary, a time of heroes transcending reality and nature: in this world everything was possible if willed. The late 1940s and early 1950s witnessed a return to a somewhat more prosaic understanding of truth, with debates on the "glossing over" or "varnishing" of reality, and the problem of what was "false" (and, by extension, true) in literature. From that phase, in Clark's view, there was a direct link to the literature of the early Thaw, which combined a revolt against the values of "High Stalinism" with "a return to a milder version of the First Five-Year Plan ethos"—efficiency, rationality, scientific and technological achievement (Dudintsev's *Not by Bread Alone* is an example). One may add, then, that during the early Thaw truth made a return in its positivistic rather than "higher-order" incarnation. But then, according to Clark, around 1956 the discussion of truth as rationality reached a dead end when those modern values proved irreconcilable with the intelligentsia's traditional ideal of transcending human limitations. The literary answer to this dilemma in the 1960s was to recognize that "truth is complex" and to pay increasing attention to the individual, acknowledging that no "epic wholeness," no integral uncontroversial representation of human nature, was possible.[42]

While accepting this trajectory of Soviet literary representations of truth, I would suggest that, just like "higher-order truth," concern for the depiction of real life was always on the agenda of socialist realist writers and their readers.[43] Socialist realism, for them, was about the coexistence of these two truths—factual and higher-order. Simonov is an important case in point. In his understanding in 1947, literature was to depict not only "life as it should be" but also life as it was. Truth lay in finding a non-controversial combination, a proper balance between the two. Literature, then, was to combine, in a manner ethically acceptable for the writer and persuasive for the reader, a candid depiction of complex, problematic social reality with a response to the commandments of state necessity.

A problem, of course, was that the final judgment on how successfully this balance of truths was maintained belonged to the ultimate possessor of the higher truth, the top leadership. In the case of *The Smoke of the Fatherland,* the balance proved unsuccessful—if not for Simonov then certainly for Stalin. Despite Simonov's and Krivitskii's careful reading for potential problems, Stalin strongly disliked the book. Immediately the press attacked it in what was the severest campaign against Simonov ever.[44] He would not publish the book again until 1956. And yet, after that he did regularly republish it.[45] For many years Simonov would maintain the ideas about truth and its literary incarnation that he expressed in this novella and in his 1947 conversation with Krivitskii.

These ideas also became instrumental during his editorship of *Novyi mir.* In 1957, for example, he would praise a submission of poetry by Grigol Abashidze (1914–1994), but with one reservation: while writing about his native Georgia, the poet had completely missed the forty years of its Soviet history. "Meanwhile," wrote Simonov, "during these forty years Georgia, out of a tsarist colony, has become a free state, a unified socialist republic. . . . What is it that prevents the poet from saying this—the poet who said this many times before. . . ?" Simonov continued:

> Generally, I have noticed that the word "socialism" suddenly has ceased fitting the rhythm of poetry. This happens too often now, whereas earlier even Pasternak found ways to rhyme it. To some extent, this is understandable—as a reaction to the earlier drumbeating. . . . However, just because it was drum-beaten out of all proportion, socialism has not ceased to be a proud and poetic word. Of course, I am talking not about the word itself but about the heart of the matter.[46]

As late as 1957, for Simonov, the poetic, evidential, and any other qualities of a literary text were inseparable from its ideological component. Literature could convey no truth outside the framework of "higher-order truth." His right hand and expert counsel in literary writing, Krivitskii shared these ideas. It is, then, with attention to this paradigm of higher-order truth and its relationship to evidential truth that one needs to approach the making—and the unmaking—of the Panfilovite story.

That story and his friendship with Simonov earned Krivitskii a place in the literary guild. Having entered the war as an unknown young journalist, he came out of it as a recognized professional who had built a reputation in a highly demanded theme, military patriotism. For years he would continue to write and publish about the Panfilovites, continuing to build a name and a career on them and apparently encouraged by the fact that the investigation of 1947–1948 had no impact on the story's circulation.[47]

Many of his fellow journalists were obviously irritated by his self-promotion, especially since rumors did circulate about how the story had been created.[48] Critics, Kardin among them, accused Krivitskii of capitalizing on the soldiers' blood, of shameless careerism and cynicism. It did not help Krivitskii that colleagues generally hated him. From diaries and memoirs, it appears that Simonov's fondness for him was rather exceptional: many others remember him as perennially rude, quarrelsome, and tyrannical. Perhaps they also hated him because for years this man was so close to one of the most powerful people in the literary world, the two of them deciding the outcome of thousands of manuscripts, making or breaking literary careers and lives. Simonov was too important to criticize, but Krivitskii was the perfect target.[49]

Cynicism and aggressive self-promotion indeed may have been Krivitskii's prominent qualities. But personal dislikes, career considerations, and other ad hominem arguments alone do not explain the storm that broke in the 1960s around his creation, the twenty-eight Panfilovites. At stake was a broader evolution of ideas about socially meaningful knowledge, the language of public self-expression, and the mission of a writer as a politically engaged intellectual—in other words, the evolving set of notions that contemporaries loosely described as "truth."

Although he knew better than anyone else how he had created the Panfilovite story, for years Krivitskii himself also tried to meet the demands of factual precision, on which Soviet journalism insisted. In multiple editions of the story, he attempted to reach if not truth then verisimilitude, to reconcile invention and reality by adding or subtracting details or names and thereby produce a maximally credible, evidentially correct account. For example, Sergeant Ivan Dobrobabin, who later turned out to be a member of the Polizei, had initially played a major role in the text.

Krivitskii even put him in temporary command of the Panfilovites, up until the arrival of the political commissar Klochkov.[50] After 1948, he minimized the account of Dobrobabin's participation, taking him out everywhere except in the main list of the twenty-eight soldiers, which was sealed by the official decree. This diminution could, of course, be explained by political rather than informational concerns. But when it turned out that another soldier, Grigorii Shemiakin, had also survived the fighting, in 1950 Krivitskii took him out as well.[51] In the early 1960s he revised the text once again, taking out yet another soldier, Ivan Shadrin, also proven to have survived.[52]

For decades Krivitskii kept gathering information on the Panfilovites and updating the story.[53] His lifelong revision of his invention was an effort to legitimize self-conscious mythmaking through the authenticity of detail. The result was a merging—all but seamless, to the point of the author's own persuasion—of the two truths, factual and higher-order. Perhaps this was the ideal of socialist realism to which he and Simonov had aspired in 1947.

But Krivitskii was not Simonov, and the 1960s were not 1947. The intellectual climate of the Thaw was different from the late Stalin years in that, among other aspects, one of the two crucial components in representing reality, higher-order truth, was undermined. After the official revelations about the recent past compromised Stalin's legacy, the "higher order" began to look rather low, and finding evidence of its correspondence with actual life became increasingly hard. What remained was the other component of the erstwhile equation for intellectual harmony—the truth of fact—which now stood on its own.

The Soviet Positivist Renaissance

The Thaw was a great era of facts—a renaissance of aspirations to positive, certain, scientific knowledge. Young people turned to the hard sciences, viewing them as the emblem of contemporaneity and a hedge against the uncertainty of the rambling, fledgling humanities, with their tendency to succumb to fluctuating political demands. For a while, the humanities appeared out of fashion, especially against the background of Soviet scientists' breakthroughs in nuclear technology in 1949 and space exploration in 1957–1961.[54] In September 1959, a widespread and heated polemic broke out between "physicists" and "lyricists." As usual in Russia, it was started by writers. Ilya Ehrenburg once again proved to be a key figure of the

Thaw by publishing the first article in this debate, and a few weeks later the poet Boris Slutskii (1919–1986) coined the phrase "physicists and lyricists."[55] Yet, although launched by writers, the argument did not necessarily go in their favor. Passions ran high, readers fervently wrote to newspapers debating the relative advantages of science and art., and many were on the side of science.

Soviet audiences were not alone in holding such debates. The post–World War II advances in nuclear and space technology created a universal fascination (if not exactly unbridled optimism) with science, leading to very similar discussions in many modern societies. The year 1959 saw the literally simultaneous birth, in the USSR and in the West, of lasting polemics about the comparative societal impact of science and the humanities. Initiated in Britain by C. P. Snow (1905–1980) in his famous Rede Lecture at Cambridge in May 1959, the Western debate became known by the title of this lecture, "The Two Cultures." Suggesting a mutual antagonism between the scientific and humanistic cultures of cognition, Snow resolved it in favor of science. Recent discoveries, he argued, especially in physics, and the scientists' commonly active political stance, made science the leading force of the modern age. The humanities, on the other hand, which he characterized as the archaic domain of asocial snobs, were doomed to lose their impact, although humanistic knowledge might still serve to broaden the scientists' narrow horizons. Snow's ideas became familiar to Soviet audiences: he frequently visited the USSR, and later (in 1973) his book *The Two Cultures* was translated into Russian. He also met with Tvardovskii and was one of the few Westerners whom the editor of *Novyi mir* genuinely liked. So it is possible that, when Ehrenburg started the polemic in the newspaper in September 1959, he knew about Snow's hypothesis. But even if he did know, the hundreds of readers who responded to his article certainly did not.

Here was a principal difference between this discussion in the Soviet context and similar contemporary polemics in the West.[56] While in the West it remained the domain of highbrow intellectuals, in Soviet culture the polemic between "physicists" and "lyricists" became truly widespread.[57] Its popularity stemmed not just from such traditional Russian phenomena as the writer's authority, the merger of literature and journalism in a mission of enlightenment, or the idea of readership as an active contributor to cultural and political processes. The key reason why the "physicists-lyricists" debate grew so massive in the Soviet Union was the Thaw-era political-epistemological conjuncture—the moment when the compromised nature of humanistic teaching reinforced the already pervasive Russian reverence for science.[58] In the context of the Thaw, the term "physicists" assumed a political meaning, delineating not so much the representatives of that particular profession as, rather, all adepts of scientific precision and truthfulness, which seemed to offer a way out of the societywide crisis of values. The authority of scientists rested on their presumed allegiance to an untarnished, unbiased truth—often expressed in the word "fact."[59]

To save physicists from potential charges of technical narrow-mindedness and undereducated senses, writers and filmmakers endowed them with emotional richness, aesthetic finesse, and a good sense of humor.[60] And indeed, a considerable degree of intellectual independence, wide-ranging interests, and relative freedom of conversation on subjects far from pure science (literature, film, theater, music, art, and the ubiquitous history and politics), as well as a cult of humorous amateurish theatricality—all of this characterized the habitat of Soviet physicists, and scientists in general.[61]

In other words, contrary to the fashionable distinction, physicists were often "lyricists," too. A fringe benefit of the privileged status of science in society, the intellectual, cultural, and emotional vibrancy of the scientific environment bred uninhibited thinkers of broad erudition, making them avid participants in polemics about the humanities and at times translating into claims for global cultural and political authority.[62] Here was another difference between the debates in the USSR and the West: Russian scientists were part of not only a culture of scholarly cognition but also of the traditional culture of the intelligentsia.[63]

But just as physicists were to some extent "lyricists," the lyricists were, in a way, physicists. The clout of science in modern Russia blurred the boundaries between sciences and humanities, suggesting "the scientific method" as a general approach for all walks of life, a cure for social evils and ethical ills. At least since the times of Chernyshevsky, the humanities had traditionally shared the reverence for scientific knowledge.[64] Positivism had been a banner of the nineteenth-century intelligentsia, and despite the fin-de-siècle challenges, positivistic attitudes survived both Russia's Silver Age and the Revolution. Although Marxists since Plekhanov and Lenin had frowned at the antiphilosophical, "mechanistic" nature of positivism, during the Soviet years the scientific ideal in its positivistic forms became central to the officially endorsed culture of enlightenment.[65]

"Fact" was a much-celebrated word in this culture—not only in the hard sciences but in the humanities as well. Indeed, there was no such distinction in the Soviet taxonomy of academic disciplines. All scholarly domains were called "sciences," with added specifications: "exact sciences," "natural sciences," and "human sciences" *(gumanitarnye nauki)*. History, for example, was classified as a human science and was thus presumably another domain of facts.[66] The legitimacy of the notion of scientific fact was not widely disputed, although scholars were, of course, mindful of its limitations.[67] And outside academia, all parties to any polemic, whether in a specialized or lay audience, presumed fact to be a valid, useful category of inquiry.[68]

The cult of facts had political implications. The universal reverence for factual knowledge created potential difficulties for a sanctioned representation of reality. Hard evidence is a double-edged sword, and an ideology professing loyalty to facts is especially vulnerable if its own tenets are criticized on an evidential basis. Such criticism has the strength of coming from within the accepted ethos and thus retains all the attributes of political and rhetorical legitimacy.

Positivism gained a new life during the Soviet years—and, we may say, a double life. The legitimate use of evidence assumed qualities of sarcasm and ethical *fronde*. Revisionist attitudes grew from within the system, gradually undermining it. The capacity of evidential argumentation to undermine empty theoretical pronouncements allowed the practitioners of this method a convenient, unobtrusive niche for their intellectual pursuits, and for exercising doubt. This may explain why positivistic approaches in Russia have done so well for so long, indeed until today.[69]

History is a case in point. The fact-oriented intellectual culture heavily influenced Soviet historical studies and lay conversations about the past. Dating back to the imperial period, the ideals of scientific objectivity and factual certainty were not destroyed by the Revolution but, on the contrary, experienced a revival during the Soviet decades.[70] This was especially so after Stalin, when prerevolutionary legacies enjoyed a powerful comeback.[71] In the field of historical learning, one example was *istochnikovedenie*—the discipline of primary-source study, whose origins dated back to the nineteenth century. Although taught since the 1930s, the discipline gained pride of place in the humanities after 1953, gaining both official recognition and countercultural significance. Since the Thaw, the insistence on "facts taking precedence over schemas" had become almost a motto among historians.[72]

But then, historians were part of a broader cultural-intellectual landscape. For any Soviet audience at the time, evidence was never just evidence. People were prepared to take new data on sensitive topics as a challenge to the sanctioned interpretation. The most sensitive topics, of course, were the upheavals and calamities of the recent past—the Revolution, the Civil War, collectivization, the terror of 1937–1938, and World War II. Here the evidence was most lacking, and the hunger for information most acute. As new data became available, it immediately entered the fray of political discussions.

Despite its positivistic outlook, then, the chasing of facts during the 1960s was not entirely positivist. The desire for facts was not innocent of interpretation—above all, political interpretation—as the audience, in any camp, was predisposed to a *critical* rereading, a refutation of the established version of history. Revisiting sensitive historical issues first of all meant revising the textbook stories, increasingly seen as compromised a priori, by the very fact of having been created in Stalin's time.

With his "Legends and Facts," Emil' Kardin spearheaded this revisionist movement of the Thaw. He had a personal interest in it. For Kardin the World War II veteran, who (unlike Krivitskii) had seen real combat, the origins of military defeats at the start of the war and the enormous cost of life at which this war had been won became the most acute historical problem. Like many in the 1960s, he tended to explain the military tragedies of the war by referring to another black hole of the recent past—the repression of the late 1930s. In his concentration on the problem of terror, and in his perception of the ultimate, autonomous power of historical evidence to help solve the problem, Kardin stood very close to the ideas of the editor of *Novyi mir,* Aleksandr Tvardovskii.[73]

The actual facts about which Kardin wrote—such as all the details of actual events behind the Panfilovite legend—remained unknown to most of his readers, and largely to himself. As of 1966, broadly available evidence about World War II was very limited. But this was beside the point. His article was not so much about facts as about legends. What Kardin and his readers extolled was the Legend of Facts—or, we may say, the Myth of Facts, because its disseminators, despite their sarcastic and multilayered use of evidence, still associated themselves with its ideal quality, still "lived the myth as a story at once true and unreal."[74] Stripping the textbook stories of their mythical nature, the worshippers of fact perpetuated another myth instead—that of objective knowledge supposedly sweeping away the incorrect, flawed, biased, corrupt, compromised, and morally wrong language of the Stalin past. A genuine language of facts was to lead to a genuine understanding of reality—the so-far hidden, yet certainly existing, truth.

A *Mythmaker's Downfall*

Krivitskii's predicament, if the word applies, was that he missed, or chose to ignore, these tectonic shifts in culture. He clung—conspicuously—to maintaining the old harmony of two truths, evidential and ideological, betting his name on it at a time when contemporaries began to view it as intellectually unacceptable and ethically unsavory. This increasingly turned him into a pariah in his guild and logically drove him to committing acts that sealed his reputation once and for all.

In 1960, he no longer worked at *Novyi mir.* Rumor had it that he had offered his services to Tvardovskii when the new editor in chief took the helm again in 1958, but that Tvardovskii had rejected the offer.[75] Krivitskii then moved to another thick journal, *Znamia.* It was there that he read the manuscript of a novel by his old wartime colleague from *Krasnaia zvezda*—Vasilii Grossman's *Life and Fate.* Krivitskii wrote a long internal review of Grossman's manuscript, completely destroying the book. *Life and Fate,* he argued, was the darkest possible calumny against the Soviet order and easily the most politically dangerous literary text ever written about the Soviet past. Grossman, he wrote, was equating the Soviet Union and Nazi Germany by saying that both states were "police-totalitarian," with the one no better than the other. It was not clear from the book why the Soviet people had fought in the war. Where would we all have been, asked Krivitskii, had the Soviet army and its leaders not perfected military art, "and, principally, had they not been able to bring together ideologically the soldiers who . . . produced not 28 but dozens of thousands of Panfilovites?" "*Doctor Zhivago,*" Krivitskii concluded, "is just a stinking little thing compared to the harmful effect that V. Grossman's novel could produce."[76]

This was a political denunciation of the first order, and a death sentence for Grossman's *Life and Fate.* A few years earlier it also could have meant a death sentence for the book's author. In a way, it did contribute to Grossman's death. The review likely was instrumental in the misfortunes of his novel—its confiscation by the KGB the next year and its disappearance for the subsequent two decades. Grossman died in 1964.[77]

But his scathing review was also a death sentence for Krivitskii's reputation. Documents like this do not remain secret for long, and his colleagues probably knew or at least suspected what role he had played regarding Grossman's *Life and Fate.*[78] During the 1960s, when an association with the perpetrators of state violence began to spell the end to one's good name, Krivitskii earned himself precisely such an association. He was now seen as one of the perpetrators. His literary and journalistic masterpiece, the story of the twenty-eight Panfilovites, also became associated with the perpetrators' position, because of the timing and the linguistic conventions within which the story had been created, and because of its author's notoriety. A memoirist thus wrote, in connection with this story: "I would not call Aleksandr Krivitskii a talented person. Rather, he was a capable person, or—to be completely precise—capable of just about anything."[79]

The role he played in Grossman's fate in 1960 was probably relevant to the attack that his colleagues—by far not Kardin alone—launched against Krivitskii and his Panfilovite creation several years later.[80] In the culture of his time, where political differences easily translated into moral verdicts and vice versa, he became "unhandshakeable," as the Russian term nicely puts it. In a personal interview in 2002, Elena Vladimirovna Pasternak said to me about Krivitskii: "You do know—do you?—that he was a *horrible* man."[81]

The Readers

As with other similar campaigns before, the Krivitskii-led campaign against *Novyi mir* in 1966 only served to draw yet more appreciative attention to the journal and its agenda. Undeterred, readers openly sided with the journal: nearly all their letters were fully signed. Also as before, people defiantly sent copies of their letters to the periodicals that attacked *Novyi mir.* The patterns of public behavior set during the Thaw persisted afterward.[82]

Veracity and authenticity proved high on the list of the readers' priorities. A twenty-six-year-old letter writer summarized his reasons for supporting Tvardovskii's journal in this way: "*Novyi mir* for me is a journal of facts, progress, and truth [*zhurnal faktov, progressa i istiny*]."[83] The letters often described hard historical evidence as having an independent value, being intellectually superior to politically charged interpretations. In the spirit of the time, people drew parallels between history and the exact sciences, insisting that these realms of knowledge had the same epistemological toolbox. A historian, Iurii Iakovlev from Kazan, wrote: "I only want to say that history is precisely as much of an exact science as mathematics."[84] "History," concurred Aleksandr Maiorov from Ivanovo, "stops being a science then and there, when and where the desired is substituted for the actual, where events are embellished, and where facts are given only a subsidiary role."[85]

Some readers turned into amateur historians, carrying out independent historical and textological research in pursuit of veracity. A land surveyor from Kazakhstan, the birthplace of the Panfilov Division, meticulously compared Krivitskii's different publications about the Panfilovites and found that the story had gone through many alterations in adding or subtracting the soldiers' names.[86] *Novyi mir* also received a letter from a military lawyer who had participated in the official investigation of the Panfilovite story and revealed some details about it. He was aware of Krivitskii's interrogation by the military prosecutors and confirmed the essence of the deposition: "Krivitskii confessed that his book was total fiction [*sploshnoi vymysel*]."[87]

Crucial to these letters was the connection between insistence on factual knowledge and the legacy of terror. People often argued that their predilection for raw data over politicized textual constructions stemmed from the past violence, which for them was firmly synonymous with the Stalin period. The letters lay blame for the textbooks' distortions of history on Stalin, under whose tutelage the textbooks had been produced. And, just as with publications by Ehrenburg and Solzhenitsyn, the readers yearned for new evidence on what they saw as the main historical problem: the human cost of the Soviet experience.[88] Frequently people would describe a departure from the flawed propagandistic narratives as the "restoration of the historical truth" *(vosstanovlenie istoricheskoi pravdy)* or the "return of forgotten heroes" *(vozvrashchenie zabytykh geroev)*.[89] The implication was that it was in the Stalin era that the truth had been forsaken and the heroes forgotten.[90] Historical evidence played the supreme role in the restorative impulse: the previously unmentionable events were to receive a full description, with the names of heroes-cum-victims brought back from oblivion. Heroes of World War II, in this logic, were commonly represented as victims of the terror, and readers' letters emphasized not so much the victory as its darker side—the human cost of this war. The command's wartime disregard for individual life now came out as another tragedy of the Stalin time.

The desire to "rehabilitate" the repressed past was not coterminous with the positivistic "truth of fact." The "facts," to which so many referred, were not random facts. The letter writers used the term to refer to unorthodox data that would shine a light onto the hidden corners of the twentieth-century past and thereby undermine the established version of history. Although proclaiming purity and distance from politicized interpretations, the call for historical factuality in the 1960s was a call for a politically charged reassessment. The new emphasis on "facts" was thus not very far from the earlier preference for a "higher-order truth."

Still, the two versions of truth were increasingly parting ways. What distinguished the new approach was its rejection of the idea of state necessity in favor of a skeptical approach to information handed down from the state ideologues and the media. There was also a growing emphasis on the human dimension of history—an understanding of history as made by individual human beings. In these ideas, the letter writers of 1966 were on the same page with the authors—Ehrenburg, Solzhenitsyn, and Kardin among them—who embodied the line of Tvardovskii's *Novyi mir*.[91]

Reconceptualizing the truth also meant rejecting the media language, which was compromised as a product of Stalin's time. Just as the Ehrenburg-Ermilov polemic and the Siniavskii-Daniel' affair, the campaign against Kardin and *Novyi mir* reminded readers of the verbal mudslinging that had accompanied physical repression in the 1930s and 1940s. A full 40 percent of the letters associated the campaign's sweeping accusations with the methods of terror. "Krivitskii completely distorts Kardin's thoughts, resorting to utterly unacceptable methods once used by the Chekists of the Stalin cult epoch," wrote N. Z. Konzhukova. "He speaks in 'that' same language, investing suspicion, accusation, and the desire to 'unmask' and if possible drown [his opponent]."[92] "I firmly believe," wrote Nina Mikhailovna Sobinova from Leningrad, "that we will never come back to the times when people suddenly became 'enemies' and their names were forbidden. From the pages of *Literaturnaia gazeta,* I sensed the cold breath of those years, and this is why I wrote this letter."[93] "I am not sure how to define the genre of this piece, but a dense and heavy odor of the past is coming from it," reflected the journalist Raisa Lert. "It even seemed to me, for a minute, that the dates have somehow [been] mixed up. . . . Is it really 1966 now? I used to read such articles in 1937, 1949, and 1952."[94] And the engineer V. M. Savchenko from Kiev noted a specific journalistic device that originated in 1937: "The critic is mentioned neither as 'V. Kardin,' nor as

'Com.[rade] Kardin,' but rather, simply as 'Kardin.' As if he is no longer free." Someone in *Novyi mir*'s editorial office put a checkmark near this last comment.[95]

Marshal Konstantin Rokossovskii (1896–1968), whose signature appeared on the letter from the military top brass censuring Kardin, received a good share of the readers' outrage. The illustrious commander was not only widely perceived as one of the top architects of Soviet victory in World War II, but he was also a former Gulag inmate. In the eyes of many letter writers, by joining the attack on *Novyi mir* he committed an act of double treason, betraying the memory of his soldiers and also his fellow camp prisoners. Nina Gagen-Torn, who had earlier tried publishing her own Gulag memoir in *Novyi mir,* wrote "An Open Letter to Marshal Rokossovskii," which she sent to *Novyi mir, Literaturnaia gazeta,* and to the marshal himself:

> It is to you, Marshal and camp prisoner [*marshal i lagernik*] Rokossovskii, that I want to respond. . . .
>
> Tell me: Where is Iakir? Where is Tukhachevskii? Where are your comrades, the talented and honorable commanders murdered on the war's eve?
>
> They were murdered in the name of the legend about the existence of an internal enemy, whom one had to fight. . . .
>
> How dare you, then, demand to preserve "legends" and to hide, conceal facts in the name of traditions? How dare you forget about the suffering of millions murdered in the name of the legend about a paradise-come-true?
>
> Lie, falsehood, and torture hidden from human eyes created this "legend" about justice and prosperity. Are you not the one to know this, camp prisoner Rokossovskii? . . . Shame on you for signing such letters![96]

It must be added that Rokossovskii might have had little to do with his signature on the letter. Shortly before his death in 1968, the marshal got in touch with Kardin, confessed that he had never read "Legends and Facts," and apologized.[97]

The letter writers often presumed that everyone who participated in the 1966 campaign formed a united front in championing the restoration of the linguistic, ethical, and epistemological order associated with repression—and perhaps also the return of repression itself. Yet was there such a united front? Did all the participants in media attacks on Kardin champion such an ancien régime, and were they prepared to restore and perpetuate that regime, to the point of celebrating and even retrieving the terror?

Smile, Commander!

When *Literaturnaia gazeta* published Krivitskii's response to Kardin, this produced a veritable explosion on the editorial board. On 22 March 1966, three days after Krivitskii's article came out and during a regular discussion of the newspaper's recent issues, a young journalist, Irina Ianskaia, made a passionate statement attacking Krivitskii and defending Kardin.[98] Her direct challenge of her newspaper's policy was supported by other journalists. One of them, Z. A. Rumer, said: "I am a bit older than Ira Ianskaia, but I must say that it's been a long time since I read . . . such a rude article, unacceptable in its tone and inexplicable for us, as Krivitskii's article is. . . . This is an emergency. . . . It has been long since I encountered in our or any other newspaper anything of the kind. Strange things are happening."[99] Rumer also mentioned the readers' responses to Krivitskii—which he knew well because he headed the letters department at the newspaper. According to him, only a couple of days after Krivitskii's publication as many as eight letters about it arrived at the paper, seven of them supporting Kardin. "I know from experience," Rumer added, "that if eight letters arrive one or two days after an article is published, you should expect many letters indeed."[100]

Zalman Afroimovich Rumer (1907–1981) had indeed had a lifetime of experience. Twenty-seven years earlier, on the night of 31 December 1938, he was arrested—right in the editorial office of *Komsomol'skaia Pravda*, where he had just finished working on the New Year's issue of the newspaper and was about to celebrate with his colleagues. He came back seventeen years later.[101] Colleagues knew his life story well, since Rumer had told it to them on many occasions and had proudly written in his autobiography for the department of cadre (human resources) that he had been arrested "on a personal order of the enemy of the people, Beria."[102] Proudly is the right word. Rumer was among those former prisoners whom their Gulag experience propelled toward taking an active political stance—ever suspicious of the repressive state machine, ever in favor of confronting the violent past, and ever on guard against its return. Fellow journalists remembered that in 1961, when Stalin's body was about to be removed from the Mausoleum,

Rumer quietly went to Red Square every night, determined not to miss the occasion. One morning, tired but satisfied, he came to the office and reported, contentedly, "They took him out."[103]

He also wrote a memoir in which he rendered his Gulag experiences in graphic detail. In the Gulag he once had to bury a friend, a fellow inmate. Standing over the grave, he swore that one day he would write about this man:

> I was whispering. In that base, hateful whisper. All my life I had whispered obediently. But now, among the hills, I felt the irrepressible urge to scream out loud. To shriek, to howl. So I screamed. I was swearing loudly. And it seemed to me that the taiga would pick up my oath and carry it all over the gullies, along the Kolyma River, that it would have repercussions very far away. I stopped and listened for a moment. . . . There was deathly silence. No repercussions, not even an echo responded to my call. . . . And then I felt bitter and afraid. And I cried—of despair, injury, and helplessness. . . . And I despaired of getting an answer from people—why it was that, simply for nothing, such a great multitude of innocent lives had been butchered, why so many souls had been ruined, extinguished, killed with bullets and hunger, why a sea of blood had been shed, why an entire generation had been crippled and dishonored—and all that was done not by some foreign enemy, but by people of our own kind.[104]

The dead prisoners did not disappear: the permafrost preserves them well. The day would come, Rumer trusted, when the truth would surface:

> Years will boil away, and one day . . . people will dig up these giant graves, these largest-in-the-world cemeteries of the largest-in-the-world penal exile. And, stunned, people will bow their heads. And they will ask—in the name of those innocently executed, those buried alive and shot during the murderous interrogations, those tortured in prison punishment cells, those dead of beatings, those whom the Lubianka investigators finished off with butts of heavy Nagant revolvers, those smothered and beaten to death by thieves at train stations; in the name of those who went insane in solitary cells, those who suffocated in prison

> railway cars and steamboat holds, those stripped bare and eaten by mosquitoes and midges, those starved to death, those dead of thirst and scurvy; in the name of those who were herded into camps and disappeared without trace at remote outposts, those frozen to death in mines, those thrown away to be shamed and torn apart by felons. . . . In the name of boys and girls—our children, our orphans taken away right from their school desks and put in prisons, exiled to the tundra, to the Far North, and lost in special-purpose orphanages. In the name of the hungry village kids, who, on Stalin's order, were sentenced to five years of Kolyma for taking a few bunches of rye; in the name of all the mothers whose sons and daughters were rotten in the camps. . . . People will ask: who are their hangmen? The day will come, and even in the Kremlin Wall, in the dark alleys of the Novodevichii Monastery, people will find those who took away their lives . . . and will call them by name, each and every one. The decay of the grave will not help their dishonor. People will find them and will put their ashes to the wind.
>
> And let it be that somewhere . . . beyond the mountain crests, in the wilderness of the taiga, let one prison camp be preserved intact, just as it was. . . . Let it be preserved for centuries, let it stand, so that people remember, so that they bring their children to this place and tell them:
>
> —Bow to the memory of the dead. Watch, think, and do not forget. Sense, at least for a brief moment, the pain of your fathers and grandfathers.[105]

Zalman Afroimovich wrote those lines in his sixties—not long after the polemic around Kardin's article. He died before his memoir could be published, but he had never made secret of his ideas. And so his colleagues knew what he meant when, in that heated exchange in the editorial office on 22 March 1966, he mentioned his age and described the resurfacing of the language of the bygone era as an emergency. For him, the time of whispering was over.[106]

So was it for many others. What followed Rumer's statement was extraordinary. One after another, journalists present at the meeting began speaking up and stating their revulsion for Krivitskii's article.[107] Striking details of the publication process emerged. Apparently, before the article came out, many in the editorial office had had no idea of its content. When it was being discussed, senior members of the editorial board had asked everyone else to leave, and when some journalists asked for permission to stay, their request was denied. At the 22 March meeting, the journalist Ata Bel'skaia openly protested against this to her superiors: "I believe that this is unacceptable practice, and there is something undemocratic in it. . . . You had better not do so, comrade bosses: this produces a very strange impression. . . . What kind of mistrust of your own colleagues is this?" Another journalist, Boris Galanov, had been charged with preparing Krivitskii's piece for publication. A soft-tempered man with the reputation of "our most delicate comrade," Galanov was to "edit out all the rough parts" in the text, a job he obviously did insufficiently. Delicate as he was, at the meeting Galanov suddenly defended Kardin and attacked Krivitskii, calling his polemical devices "dishonorable."[108]

Faced with this barrage of criticism, the senior editors of *Literaturnaia gazeta* tried to reimpose order, but in vain.[109] This was a mutiny. The media professionals directly responsible for implementing the anti–*Novyi mir* campaign proved to be neither willing participants nor complacent executors. Charged with maintaining the old media toolbox of propagandistic devices, they rebelled, seeing it as a compromising legacy of the past. And so, the journalists proved to stand not far from Kardin and *Novyi mir.* Their mutiny had the same root as the readers' protests against the Siniavskii-Daniel' trial in this same year, 1966: personal experiences of repression articulated by the recent literary polemic. Back in 1958, the journalists at *Literaturnaia gazeta* had displayed a certain pride in staging a similar campaign against Pasternak. By 1966 the pride was gone, having yielded to moral aversion.

The opaque language of hints with which Rumer and other journalists at the meeting referred to the Stalin-era origins of Krivitskii's rhetoric deserves a mention. The opacity portended not only caution but also a common awareness of the terror that no longer needed to be identified at length. At times, no words were needed at all. Let us consider another participant in the campaign whose name appeared as "B. Burkovskii" in March 1966 under a short article in the journal *Ogonek* that attacked Kardin and *Novyi mir.*[110] Titled "An Unworthy Task," the article did not go unnoticed by readers, and when condemning it they also invoked the specter of "the cult."[111]

Boris Vasil'evich Burkovskii (1912–1985) had also lived a long life. A navy commander (*kapitan vtorogo ranga*, or *kavtorang*), he spent seven years in the Gulag. There he met a fellow inmate, Aleksandr Solzhenitsyn, who would later use him as a prototype for a central character in *One Day in the Life of Ivan Denisovich*—Kavtorang (commander) Buinovskii, an appealing character who stoically defends his ideas of justice in the camp environment, where they have no currency.

The offspring of a noble family whose traditions of military service dated back to the prerevolutionary era, Burkovskii graduated from two naval academies, served in the Black Sea Fleet, and fought in World War II. His wartime experiences included service as lead navigator in a torpedo boat division and, at least once, hand-to-hand combat, in which he received a bayonet wound.[112] In 1945, thanks to his good command of English, he was appointed liaison officer for the U.S. Navy ships that were visiting the Crimea during the Yalta Conference. This became the source of his future trouble, which Solzhenitsyn fairly accurately depicts in *One Day*. Four years later, in 1949, Burkovskii was imprisoned for contacts with foreigners. He was rehabilitated in 1956, reinstated in his rank and party membership, and came back to his home in Leningrad. Yet he was denied a return to active service and found a compromise job as a guide on the cruiser *Aurora*—that symbol of the October Revolution whose mythical "salvo" Kardin would later expose in his 1966 article. Shortly before, the cruiser had been turned into a museum. The outgoing and knowledgeable commander quickly won his colleagues' good opinion, despite (or thanks to) his prison camp past. Soon, he became the museum's director.[113]

The publication of *One Day* briefly made him famous. Solzhenitsyn visited him on the *Aurora*, and the two men sat for a long time, talking and drinking in the old officers' mess.[114] One can picture this surreal episode: the writer and his character, both Gulag ex-prisoners, celebrating their reunion in the heart of a symbol of that regime whose myths the character was entrusted to keep up, while the writer used his image to bring them down. *Izvestiia* published an article about Burkovskii, an upbeat report on how he had gone through his ordeal while keeping his trust in the party and a "Leninist truth"—that truth, again.[115] He received many letters of admiration from readers, and responded to some.[116]

He also briefly became part of *Novyi mir*'s environment. Tvardovskii was impressed by the commander's story and, ever sensitive to literary politics, took the *Izvestiia* article as an endorsement of Solzhenitsyn's (ultimately unsuccessful) nomination for the Lenin Prize.[117] In March 1964 Tvardovskii and his deputy editors Dement'ev, Lakshin, and Aleksandr Brainin visited

Leningrad. Burkovskii was invited to their readers' conference. When the chair announced that the prototype of the *kavtorang* in *One Day* was present in the room, the entire audience rose and burst into applause. If the stenographic record captured this correctly, people began rising and applauding right after they heard Burkovskii's name and even before the chair had a chance to announce his credentials. They knew who he was.[118]

The commander gave a short speech complimenting the "brave" journal and telling how, for four and a half years, he had been in the same camp with Solzhenitsyn. He described the writer as an honest man who had enjoyed respect among the prisoners, never cringed before anyone, and always tried to settle disputes and quarrels. Boris Vasil'evich praised *One Day* as a truthful depiction of prison camp life:

> When reading this novella, I clearly imagined our *zona,* our camp, the main characters, because they are so vividly depicted in the novella. I named them right away—here is this one, and there is that one. . . . I may be partial, but as a human being I can tell that this is an exceptionally talented novella. It is written truthfully, . . . and it is certainly very urgent. My great thanks to Aleksandr Trifonovich Tvardovskii, who has invested much effort so that the novella could see the light of day. *(Stormy applause.)*
>
> I would like to wish this wonderful group, the editorial board of the journal *Novyi mir,* great success in their activities for the benefit of our nation, so that the journal would always raise urgent, vital questions bravely. *(Stormy applause.)*[119]

The man whose name would two years later appear under "An Unworthy Task," the article attacking *Novyi mir,* was not only the keeper of a symbol of the Revolution. He was himself a living symbol—of the Thaw as the end of terror, of the terror's legacy, of the striving toward a new evidential truth as a method of engaging that legacy, and of the fusion between literature and society that made those efforts the order of the day. The clash and coexistence of all these symbols in one person, the collision of the past as glory and the past as tragedy, was itself symbolic of those years. The efforts of the regime to reestablish the higher-order truth, including the attack on *Novyi mir* and "Legends and Facts," were not only received but also implemented by people aware of, and reflecting about, the phenomenon of mass violence on the basis of their own lives.

A contemporary photograph captured the atmosphere of the time. Burkovskii is depicted side by side with the famous actor Kirill Lavrov, the star of numerous Soviet movies about the Revolution. The photograph was likely taken in the fall of 1965, during the production of a feature film titled, of all things, *Zalp Avrory* (The *Aurora*'s Salvo), for which Burkovskii worked as a historical consultant. Lavrov played the role of Aleksandr Belyshev, the commissar of the revolutionary cruiser in 1917 who would also be a signer, with Burkovskii, of "An Unworthy Task" in 1966. Lavrov is wearing sailor's garb, with the *Aurora*'s insignia on his hat. The commander is in his usual naval uniform and a raincoat: the weather is cold and wet. Both are smiling. And something in Burkovskii's smile immediately captures our attention. It is his teeth. None of them are his own. He smiles at us with a perfectly even, dimly shining set of metal dentures.

It is not clear whether Burkovskii actually wrote "An Unworthy Task," signed it, or was even aware of its preparation.[120] But if he did sign it, there are some clues to why this could happen. In March 1955, while still in the camp, Boris Vasil'evich had written a letter to his family—his wife's sister and her husband:

> Good day, Sasha and Tatka! . . .
>
> I live as usual, without any significant changes. I am very involved in social work [*obshchestvennaia rabota*]. . . : we teach [fellow prisoners] various professions, liquidate illiteracy, and get ready to merge into the Soviet family [*gotovimsia vlit'sia v sovetskuiu sem'iu*]. During all this time, and it has been about six years, I have made it all the way up from a digger, bricklayer, and cement-layer to an assembly lathe operator and rate-setter. It was a very hard path, but there is also something instructive and edifying about it. A human being gets used to work—and work is the foundation of life. . . .
>
> During all these years, I have thought a lot and have come to understand a lot in life, something that I had not understood before; and I learned to treasure life. . . . Spring has started here, the snow has all but melted down, and the warm season is about to begin. The winter is over. What this year will bring—we shall see.[121]

Boris Vasil'evich knew that the letter would be subject to inspection, and his writing was circumscribed—all the more so because he was expecting a reply to his appeal for rehabilitation. He did not include any negative details of camp life and made sure to mention his reeducation through labor as well as his involvement in reeducating others, the "social work" that supposedly prepared prisoners for rejoining "the Soviet family." But perhaps more important are his other words—that he had learned to treasure life.

Life was to be treasured, and so was freedom, because both could be taken away at any moment—even though the winter was over and spring began. In the late 1960s, as Solzhenitsyn was falling out of favor with the authorities, Burkovskii became alarmed. He broke ties with the writer and safely hid his copy of *One Day* with the author's signature.[122] No one could guarantee that reprisals would not follow, and that they would not touch the *kavtorang* and his family. *The Gulag Archipelago* was not yet out (it would be published in 1973 and 1974), but had Burkovskii seen it he would have had even more reason for alarm: in that book he is mentioned by his real name.[123]

He was a naval officer, trained to respect discipline, and that helped. Former prisoners who knew him remembered this character trait, at times with certain aggravation.[124] Order was to be maintained, orders were to be followed, and emotions were not to be displayed. Burkovskii's involvement in the literary-political life of the Thaw—the newspaper article, his brief speech at the readers' conference—appears to have been momentary. Unlike the politically engaged Gulag returnees, he did not write memoirs or letters to the editor and seldom told stories about his camp experiences, even to his family.[125] His former colleagues at the Naval Museum remember him as an upright, urbane gentleman who liked good company, told funny jokes, played the piano, and waltzed with female colleagues at holiday parties. They also remember him as a completely closed person—someone who never told anyone about his past.[126]

Burkovskii's stance was probably common. While many former prisoners spoke and wrote about their camp experiences, not everyone did. Remembrance was painful, and the therapeutic nature of testimony not always obvious. By the late 1960s, with the suppression of the terror theme, remembering also began to look unsafe. References to arrests and camps in readers' letters, even those addressed to the uniquely receptive *Novyi mir*, became less frequent and direct than in 1961 to 1964. The share of anonymous letters among those received on politically controversial literary subjects increased from 3.5 percent in Kardin's case to 14.5 percent three years later—not an overwhelming change, but one indication of the growing apprehension.

Still, references to the repression did not disappear. And although Burkovskii did hide his copy of *One Day* signed by Solzhenitsyn, he did not destroy it or throw it away: the book is kept in the family.

The Time of Anniversaries in the late 1960s witnessed a major clash between state-affirming and reflectively critical interpretations of the Soviet past. This was a clash of two views of societally meaningful truth—as a state necessity for upholding the legitimacy of the established order versus information leading to fundamental reassessments of the past and present. The problem of terror was crucial to both views. By the end of the decade, backed by state authority, the version of the past as glory had seemingly prevailed, the new media silence about the terror signaling the ostensible victory of the one party over the other.

However, a closer look suggests that dividing lines between the parties were blurred, their members were often the same individuals, and the victory thus hardly took place. By the late 1960s, literary and journalistic professionals on all sides of the political spectrum, as well as their audiences, had become one community, informed and profoundly affected by both the experience of repression and the recent discussions of that experience. Those years, then, were neither the end nor even an interruption in the contemplation of the past terror. Instead, the polemic went underground and lay beneath other, legitimate agendas of conversation. Outwardly suppressed, the problem of twentieth-century mass violence became a subtext of other, open conversations on cultural and historical themes. With Kardin's "Legends and Facts," this problem underlay all three points of controversy—the Revolution, the Civil War, and World War II. The argument in such controversies was about verbal formulas and logical or intonational emphases, which either upheld the rendition of history formed during, and now associated with, the terror, or, to the contrary, questioned and subverted that rendition. All parties to any such controversy operated within a system of universally and easily recognizable codes of sign, speech, and writing, wherein the slightest hint worked as a reference to the terror experience—for any audience and regardless of creed.

Burkovskii's colleagues at the Naval Museum were aware of his past. He did not like to remember it. But he liked to smile.

Unsettling the Balance of Truths

How does intellectual change take place in society? How, in particular, does it emerge and affect a large mass of people in a relatively closed society, such as the Soviet Union remained during and after the Thaw? Broadly conceived, the story of "Legends and Facts" suggests that, to succeed, the change must assume the terms familiar to the culture in which it occurs. The preoccupation with factual authenticity, which was prominent in Soviet culture during the Thaw, and which Tvardovskii's *Novyi mir* exemplified, was rooted in the positivistic intellectual tradition of modern Russia. Originating in the nineteenth century, this tradition became important for the regime and characterized at once the official ethos and the intellectual *fronde* that challenged it, on its own terms.

The notion of authenticity was crucial to socialist realism, where truth combined two major components—the higher-order truth of state necessity and the positivistic, evidentiary truth of fact. The success of any literary or propagandistic project was measured by the success with which its authors achieved a seamless combination of the two components. The entire enterprise relied on ethics—on the moral authority that higher-order truth was able to command, and the conviction that demands of state necessity were morally justified to guide individuals in their efforts. To the extent that authors succeeded in merging the two truths into a noncontroversial, convincing account, and to the extent that they themselves remained convinced of the need for such a merger, the system remained intellectually stable.

The Thaw drastically unsettled this balance of truths. With the official acknowledgment of the enormity of state violence at the foundation of the Soviet order, the means of mass persuasion shaped during the founding years came to be associated with state violence as well, and thereby lost ethical authority. Higher-order truth began to collapse. What remained from the erstwhile balance was its other component, a survivor from prerevolutionary times and heir apparent to the golden age of positivism—the truth of fact. It was to this old-fashioned but surefire interpretation of truth as evidentiary veracity that many people increasingly gravitated in search of intellectual stability. The new positivistic impulse was not entirely positivist in nature: at its heart was a desire for a critical reevaluation of the existing set of ideological, ethical, and linguistic values.

The ethos of *Novyi mir* exemplified and articulated this turn to factuality. Between the 1940s and the late 1960s, the journal did not have one uniform line, but instead went through an intellectual evolution. In its aesthetic-epistemological program, Tvardovskii's *Novyi mir* was very different from the *Novyi mir* of Simonov's editorship. The 1966 conflict between Kardin and Krivitskii was the ultimate clash of the two different lines these authors represented, each being a proxy for his literary patron—Tvardovskii and Simonov, respectively—a confrontation between two understandings of truth as literature's societal mission.

The two approaches, Tvardovskii's truth of fact and Simonov's higher-order truth, were not unrelated to each other, in that both set didactically rigid criteria for what was historically important. Neither was free of monopolistic claims to the "proper" political and aesthetic interpretation of texts and social phenomena. Nonetheless, the shift of emphases is hard to disregard. Whereas for Simonov and Krivitskii in the 1940s the significance of texts was largely decided by their correspondence to the state's demands, for Tvardovskii and Kardin state necessity became far less important, with authenticity taking front and center. In the 1960s, under Tvardovskii's auspices, the strategy of evidentiary criticism focusing on the individual increasingly took precedence over the line of state necessity—in his journal as well as in the broader panorama of Soviet intellectual life.

The problem of political violence in the country's recent past was the prime mover of the evolution of ideas about truth during the Thaw. The open formulation of the problem destabilized old certainties and compelled people to look for new epistemological and ethical authorities. Ousted from public circulation by the end of the 1960s, the issue of the terror remained present beneath the surface of practically all major cultural polemics. The history of the late Soviet decades cannot be understood outside this context.

10

LAST BATTLES

The End of Tvardovskii's *Novyi mir*

THE DAYS OF Tvardovskii's *Novyi mir* were numbered. The final three years of his editorship, between 1967 and early 1970, became the last stand for the journal, as the administrative pressure increased slowly yet steadily, softly yet inexorably. The editor himself realized what was happening better than anyone else. After the turbulence of 1966, which brought both the Siniavskii-Daniel' trial and the massive campaign around "Legends and Facts," Tvardovskii anticipated having to resign virtually at any moment.

The concluding days of 1966 firmly convinced him that the end was near. In December two of his closest colleagues, Aleksandr Dement'ev and the responsible secretary of the editorial board, Boris Zaks (1908–1998), were forcibly removed from their jobs. To effect their ouster, Tvardovskii was summoned by Vasilii Shauro (1912–2007), since 1965 the head of the Central Committee Department of Culture. At first he resisted Shauro's pressure to remove the two editors, but eventually had to accept the inevitable, under the guise of voluntary resignation. The incident prompted him to submit his own resignation, but at that point his departure was not yet desired. Reportedly, Mikhail Suslov, the party's chief ideological officer, refused to consider Tvardovskii's resignation and even resorted to the argument of party discipline to ensure that the editor would stay.[1]

The other members of his team—Vladimir Lakshin, Aleksei Kondratovich, Igor' Sats, Igor' Vinogradov, and Aleksandr Mariamov—still retained their positions. Yet Tvardovskii feared that he would be forced to accept new members, just as he had been forced to dismiss Dement'ev and Zaks. If that happened, the key functions at the journal would inevitably go to new appointees tasked with overseeing its ideological purity, while the editor in chief would play a merely ceremonial role. This was precisely the scenario under which Tvardovskii would have to resign three years later, and his diary shows that he foresaw such an outcome. So far he had managed to avoid this, thanks to the hesitation of his Central Committee overseers, but he failed to bring Dement'ev and Zaks back. Both men remained part of his circle of trusted comrades-in-arms, however—Dement'ev especially: just as before, Tvardovskii made few major decisions at the journal without getting his opinion. Both Dement'ev and Zaks would be present in the only group photograph of Tvardovskii's editorial board, taken during its last days.[2]

Thus, the year 1967 opened inauspiciously. Misfortunes continued: in January *Pravda* published an editorial that slammed *Novyi mir* for "lagging behind the [historic] time." Kardin's article was duly mentioned as an example.[3] On 15 March, the Secretariat of the Board of the Writers' Union held a discussion about the journal. For five long hours, Tvardovskii and his colleagues listened to the criticisms of the top literary bosses—Aleksandr Chakovskii, Nikolai Tikhonov, Nikolai Gribachev, Leonid Sobolev, Aleksei Surkov, Georgii Markov, and others. Tvardovskii spoke several times, vigorously defending his line. As he noted the next day, the criticism was still fairly mild at this point, and thickly layered with compliments. The Secretariat also accepted his nominations for the new editorial board, including three new members—the eminent writers Chingiz Aitmatov and Efim Dorosh, as well as the young literary critic Mikhail Khitrov. And yet, despite the conciliatory tone of the discussion, its punitive bottom line was clear. In the eyes of the literary-political establishment, *Novyi mir* had become undesirable.[4]

The subsequent months were a bit quieter, but things would not stay quiet for long, as the editors realized. The journal was subjected to increasing pressure from state censors—by itself nothing new, but the growing frequency and intensity of the pestering was alarming. Under the Central Committee's supervision, the main censoring agency, Glavlit, repeatedly turned down manuscripts, insisted on innumerable cuts, often at the last minute, or simply delayed its consideration of texts for weeks and even months. Readers and subscribers, just like the editors, were left guessing whether the journal's next issue would bear Tvardovskii's name—and indeed whether there would be a next issue at all.

The political background of these years also looked increasingly grim. Despite the proliferation of ominous symptoms, the cultural policies of the early Brezhnev period, between 1964 and 1968, remained relatively mild. But the Warsaw Pact invasion of Czechoslovakia in August 1968 altered the situation dramatically. From then on, ideological affairs took a much more rigid outlook. Literature was the first area to suffer, with administrative interference becoming ever more visible. The invasion of Czechoslovakia also led to an ethical and political polarization among the intelligentsia. Some began distancing themselves from the regime, which in their eyes had compromised itself beyond repair. Others adopted an increasingly conservative and statist position, entrenching themselves in a variety of nationalistic theories. The question of "where one stood" was becoming increasingly pertinent to everyone who read and thought.[5]

Tvardovskii took the events in Czechoslovakia to heart. In his diary notes of 1968 there was little of the statist, patrimonial logic he had often exhibited before. A communist and a firm believer in the Soviet socialist cause, as he remained until his last days, he was nonetheless sympathetic to the Prague Spring. In his opinion, the Czech and Slovak reformists proposed an up-to-date, honest discussion of the most urgent issues that socialism was facing at the moment: freedom and the legacy of terror, above all. In many ways, as he confided in the diary during the summer of 1968, he agreed with the programs of the Czechoslovak reformers, such as the *Two Thousand Words* manifesto. Tvardovskii took quiet satisfaction in watching the utter bewilderment of the Brezhnev leadership in its negotiations with recent allies. "I would have never believed that I would be so happy to see the confusion of my country in the eyes of the entire world," he wrote on 5 August. "However, it is certainly not the confusion of the country but only that of its leadership, who tried to give yesterday's answers to today's questions."[6]

The military invasion two weeks later, on 21 August, became his country's shame for him, a moral collapse of irreparable proportions. "Horrible ten days," Tvardovskii wrote in the diary on 29 August—and even, uniquely for him, admitted crying.[7] Like any Soviet institution, *Novyi mir* was obligated to hold a meeting of its party cell to support the invasion and condemn the Czechoslovak apostates. Not to do so would be unthinkable: it was the only way for the journal to survive. Shattered by all the news,

Tvardovskii was out of the office, and so on the day of the proposed meeting the junior editors had to decide on their own what to do. Only one of them, Igor' Vinogradov, refused to participate, while the others decided to proceed with the meeting, quickly and quietly adopting a resolution in support of the invasion. No formal vote was taken, as no one wanted to aggravate the situation. A few days later Tvardovskii took a three-month leave from his duties in the Writers' Union. When approached with a request to sign a collective letter from Soviet writers to their Czech and Slovak colleagues, he refused. "I decidedly cannot sign the letter to the writers of Czechoslovakia, because I see its content as rather unbecoming to the honor and conscience of a Soviet writer," he wrote in a personal note to Konstantin Voronkov (1911–1984), the secretary of the Writer's Union board.[8]

Following August 1968, *Novyi mir* continued to fight for one monthly issue after another. This became an increasingly uphill battle in which, while eventual defeat was inevitable, every small success counted, and called for celebration as a feat of brinkmanship. Every piece of writing that carried the journal's line further was a publishing struggle—and even if the editors did manage to shepherd a text through multiple hurdles into print, it was then likely to become a target of vicious press attacks, which now closely followed one another. According to the memoirs of Al'bert Beliaev (b. 1928), then the head of the literature sector in the Central Committee Department of Culture and thus the top literary officer in the country, it was in 1968 that the Central Committee secretaries agreed not to respond to letters from Tvardovskii and not to meet with him personally. Simultaneously they decided, in principle, to "strengthen the journal's editorial board"—which meant Tvardovskii's impending removal.[9]

In its November and December issues—which actually came out in early 1969 because of the censorship delays—*Novyi mir* published *Youth in Zheleznodol'sk*, an autobiographical novel by Nikolai Voronov. Zheleznodol'sk, an imagined city whose name translates literally as "the City of Iron Fate," stood in the novel for Magnitogorsk, where the author, born in 1926, had spent his childhood and adolescence during the 1930s and 1940s. Voronov wrote the novel, very much a work of memory, in crisp and clear prose, describing with unusual candor and in uncommonly dark detail the workers' horrific living conditions during industrialization and World War II. The cramped barracks, the overnight wait and early morning battles among hundreds of men, women, and children standing in bread lines, the defective equipment, the polluted air and water, the drinking, the fighting, and the looming fear of imprisonment—for wrecking, stealing, infractions of labor discipline, or just about anything else—all these and many other hallmarks of the time figured richly in the book. Not everything could be said, let alone published—for example, Voronov only briefly mentioned the terror—but what he did say was enough. The novel was a work of psychological prose that carefully analyzed human behavior, transcribed conversations in local dialects, and depicted the complex retrospection of a mature man looking back at the time when, as a child, he had looked up at the world of adults. *Youth in Zheleznodol'sk* depicted the Soviet past as a tragedy, only partly redeemed by the author's belief in the capacity of human nature to overcome its own dark side and survive life's tribulations. The novel's end brought few rewards to its main protagonists and left the reader at a crossroads of mixed feelings and unanswered questions about the meaning of sacrifice for a greater cause. In its historical retrospection, scarcity of propagandistic rattle, and open-ended conclusions, Voronov's book very much followed the Tvardovskii line.[10]

The 500-page novel—which the editor in chief, displaying his usual penchant for doing more with less and for avoiding grand claims of genre, restyled a "novella"—was not the first but certainly the most important piece that Voronov published in *Novyi mir.* As he always did when he liked a manuscript, Tvardovskii delivered a long emotional speech before the editorial board, praising the writer's uncompromising realism, psychological finesse, and linguistic precision. Voronov, with his working-class background, was for him somewhat akin to Solzhenitsyn—another talent "from the people" whose power could presumably revive Russian literature. That said, Voronov's authenticity was sometimes too much even for Tvardovskii. Earlier in their relationship there had been cases when the editor had to take out some particularly dark detail in the author's writing—such as, in 1961, the episode in a wartime short story titled "Train Horns" in which an entire train crew responsible for a railroad disaster was shot without trial, right in front of their locomotive. This, Tvardovskii had realized, stood no chance of passing any censor's eye. But seven years later he decided to fight for Voronov's book to the bitter end.[11] What followed was a several-months-long battle with the Central Committee Department of Culture that took all of his influence and ingenuity—plus, sometimes, direct confrontation. The last act of the struggle happened literally in the eleventh hour—at 10:30 one night in 1968, when Voronov returned to *Novyi mir*'s editorial office after a long conversation at the Central Committee with Beliaev. Tvardovskii was waiting for him, despite the late hour. When Voronov had barely entered the office, Beliaev telephoned the editor and nonchalantly reported that the writer had just agreed to "rework" the ending of his book and thus postpone its publication indefinitely. In fact, Voronov had expressly refused to do so, and he had managed to tell this to Tvardovskii just moments before the call. A dramatic telephone conversation between Tvardovskii and Beliaev ensued—and, Voronov remembered: "I heard swearing of such power that only a great poet of a great people, completely exhausted by infinite patience, was capable of producing." Hanging up the phone, Tvardovskii said to him: "The time of the end is coming."[12]

It was coming, indeed. When *Youth in Zheleznodol'sk* finally saw the light of day in the early months of 1969, the book provoked the last and deadliest series of attacks against *Novyi mir.* On 5 March *Literaturnaia gazeta* published an article by Mikhail Sinel'nikov entitled "Contrary to the Truth."[13] In the same issue there was an open letter by six highly positioned former Komsomols who had participated in the construction of Magnitogorsk back in the 1930s. All of them charged the journal with blackening Soviet reality and distorting the image of the Soviet worker. Voronov's book, they insisted, showed workers as living hard and grim lives devoid of either hope for a better future or "the cheerful pathos of creative labor."[14]

By this time, *Novyi mir* had excelled at repelling such attacks. Tvardovskii, for one thing, immediately noted that this was not the first letter in which the old Komsomols spoke against Voronov's book. They had already written another, unpublished letter to the Komsomol Central Committee, which forwarded it to the Writers' Union and thence to *Novyi mir.* The problem was that this first letter was dated 30 December 1968, and the first part of Voronov's book appeared in the journal only ten days later, on 10 January 1969. Thus, the letter writers had protested against an unpublished novel. They themselves stated this clearly in the letter, saying that their aim was "not to allow the publication of this work," which mysteriously "had come to their attention" as being prepared for publication in the journal. As Tvardovskii noted in his response, this pointed to the fact that both letters were orchestrated—"a verdict pronounced before hearing the parties and the witnesses' depositions."[15] Its orchestration, to be sure, did not preclude the signatories from sharing the views expressed in the letter. A few months later, one of them wrote again, this time individually and directly to *Novyi mir*, defending the collective statement he had signed. This was apparently the only point on which he disagreed with the journal, while otherwise he claimed to be its supporter. Tvardovskii did not reply.[16]

None of this was, by then, very new. But what complicated the situation in 1969 was that *Novyi mir* now had to fight not only against its usual rivals with their familiar devices. Another force had arrived on the literary-political stage, joining ranks with the journal's customary opponents. The newcomers were writers and journalists who professed the ideas of Russian nationalism.

The mid- to late 1960s witnessed the resurgence of multiple nationalistic trends of thought in the Soviet Union. Their rise dated back at least to 1953, if not before, and like many other cultural phenomena of the time, had much to do with the growing attention to the past as a source of alternative intellectual and moral legitimacy during the post-Stalin decades. That one could foresee the end of the Thaw in the second half of the 1960s boosted this historical transition, for at this point the inflexibility of the regime's ideological and rhetorical strategies was apparent to educated audiences. The inability of the media to update its obsolete and morally compromised rhetorical weaponry, and the failure to adjust to the changing intellectual and ethical realities provoked massive frustration. By itself, scrutiny of the past was not necessarily nationalistic: among the proponents and practitioners of this view were many broad-minded cosmopolitans, such as the poet Bulat Okudzhava (1924–1997). The sense of a flawed present compensated through historical inquiry transcended ethno-ideological borders and did not originate in a nationalistic impulse—rather, nationalistic images came as only one of many remedies for the disturbed consciousness of the increasingly diverse, pluralistic, and intellectually complex late Soviet audience. And yet the popularity of these images rose quickly, proving that nationalism was never too deeply submerged. The logic of the historical turn was politically divisive, bringing nationalist sentiment to the surface of cultural polemics.[17] Russian nationalism, in particular, had the advantage of finding many sympathizers among the party leadership, who saw it as the perfect means of rejuvenating the stale ideology. The result was a merger of nationalistic intellectuals and party politicians, a phenomenon that one historian would fortuitously term "the Russian Party."[18]

Novyi mir watched these tendencies with a great degree of skepticism and, one must add, undue condescension. The journal's ethos had been traditionally internationalist, in the vein of the Soviet intelligentsia's ideals, and at least in this aspect it was in accordance with the tenets of the established ideology. With their high level of literary sophistication, the editors on Tvardovskii's team were also annoyed by the many intellectual gaps and stylistic flaws in the writings of the nationalists. To the *Novyi mir* group, the newcomers seemed like undereducated upstarts playing with fire. These were the lines along which the journal attacked the nationalists in its April 1969 issue.

The attack came from a rather unexpected author—Aleksandr Grigor'evich Dement'ev, who had been recently removed from the editorial board. His previous career, one might suppose, hardly made him the likeliest candidate for speaking against the Russian nationalistic writers. Before joining *Novyi mir* in 1950, Dement'ev had taught at Leningrad University for many years, prior to and after World War II. In the late Stalin years, he headed the university's department of history of Russian Soviet literature. The ideologically charged position inevitably involved him in the "anticosmopolitan" campaigns of the time—something his opponents would later remember. This administrative experience also taught him extreme caution. Dement'ev was a careful, skillful politician who had mastered the art of maneuvering texts to publication across the Soviet literary minefields. One of Tvardovskii's oldest and most loyal colleagues, he was also one of the most prudent; always able to foretell the reaction of *Novyi mir*'s political overseers, he acted at the journal as a voice of bureaucratic reason. His internal reviews of manuscripts erred on the side of caution, too, as he evaluated texts from the viewpoint of Soviet-style political correctness. It was he who advised, back in 1961, against the publication of Lidiia Chukovskaia's *Sofia Petrovna*, arguing that it would be impossible to discuss the theme of the terror without clarifying "the author's attitude to the Soviet order."[19]

In January 1966, during the Siniavskii-Daniel' affair, Dement'ev might have overplayed the caution card. One day he returned from Moscow's city party committee with the news that he had agreed to speak against Siniavskii at the trial. His reason, allegedly, was to avoid being used by the court as a literary expert in the shameful investigation. But Tvardovskii was appalled and did not accept that excuse. The next day he angrily wrote in his diary that the Dement'ev of 1966 did not differ from the

Dement'ev of the late 1940s, the one who had participated in the bashing of "cosmopolitans." "He turned out to be a sly man and a coward," Tvardovskii fumed, "although many said lately that under the influence of different factors, first of all *N[ovyi] mir*'s successes, . . . he had decidedly changed for the better." Politically too, Dement'ev's participation in the trial would not have been advantageous, as it would have merely emphasized *Novyi mir*'s connection to Siniavskii and thus compromised the journal. Tvardovskii decided then to fire Dement'ev. "If he does not submit his resignation," the editor added, "I myself will have to make a certain decision." Eventually the conflict was somehow resolved: Dement'ev did not speak at the trial, and he did not resign at that point. The two men restored their friendly relations, and when Dement'ev did have to leave a few months later, under the Central Committee's pressure, Tvardovskii defended him. Still, the 1966 episode was telling.[20]

Dement'ev thus appeared an unlikely candidate to take up the fight against the Russian nationalists. And yet that is what he did. Perhaps it was his scholarly background that did not allow him to tolerate what they were doing to literature. For Dement'ev, a literary historian of great erudition, the founding editor (1957–1959) of the prestigious scholarly journal *Problems of Literature (Voprosy literatury)*, and the author of several monographs and textbooks, it was utterly offensive to read what the nationalistically minded authors were publishing at the time.

He targeted several publications by young Russophile literary critics that had appeared in 1968 in the journal *Molodaia gvardiia (Young Guard)*—the articles "Great Explorations" and "Inevitability" by Viktor Chalmaev (b. 1932), as well as "Enlightened Philistinism" by Mikhail Lobanov (b. 1925). Their arguments included calls for reviving what they viewed as the Russian tradition, idealized portrayals of the countryside, hatred of modernist art, anticommercialism, anti-Americanism, and an overall protest against the spread of Westernized mass culture, with its materialism, consumerism, "cult of the dollar," and dictatorship of common taste. Much of the above for them was embodied in the popular melodies people listened to on portable transistor radios, objects these critics for some reason particularly seemed to hate.

They also undertook a retrospective view of Russian cultural history in search of the roots of its immanent opposition to things Western. Chalmaev, for instance, rejected fin-de-siècle modernist artistic experimentation, such as futurism and constructivism. In literary history he displayed a vehemently statist worldview, denying even such staple commodities of Soviet literary criticism as admiration for the democratic thought of the 1860s—for the intelligentsia of the Great Reforms era that had grouped around the old thick journals, such as *Sovremennik* and *Otechestvennye zapiski*. Instead, he extolled the Nicholaevan 1830s, with their widely circulated images of strong national authority and the emerging Slavophile thought. Chalmaev went so far as to call the 1830s "our spiritual Hellas" *(nasha 'dukhovnaia Ellada')*. As for the more distant seventeenth and eighteenth centuries, he saw there a certain Russian "civilization of the spirit," fundamentally opposite to Western "other-devilishness" *(chuzhebesie)*.[21]

All of this vastly annoyed Dement'ev. Published in the April 1969 issue of *Novyi mir*, his article "On Traditions and Nationality" was a sarcastic response to Chalmaev-style nationalistic writing. Dement'ev fully employed the contemporary tactic of evidential criticism in exposing his opponent's factual errors—which were many. Indeed, Chalmaev had ascribed Blok's poetry to Bunin, described Konstantin Leont'ev as Leo Tolstoy's friend, and come up with a new historical personage—a certain "Nil of Sarov," whom, Dement'ev assumed, Chalmaev had evidently "montaged" from two real characters of Russian ecclesiastical history, the sanctified monks and religious thinkers Nil Sorsky (1433–1508) and Seraphim of Sarov (1754–1833). "The author's 'erudition' is stupefying," Dement'ev summarized acrimoniously.[22]

He minded the nationalists' aggressive xenophobia, anti-Westernism, and populism (which he called neo-Slavophile), as well as their exaggerated fear of urban consumerism. Politically, he did not fail to notice their rampant statism embodied in the tacit reglorification of Stalin. Neither Dement'ev nor his opponents named the dictator outright, instead resorting to transparent euphemisms. Thus, Dement'ev attacked a poem by Feliks Chuev (1941–1999), in which victory in the Great Patriotic War was ascribed to "the generalissimo and his great marshals." By now, Dement'ev noted in response, "the very military rank of generalissimo has been somewhat forgotten, and it has become clear that marshals of the Soviet Union are the marshals of our country and people—not 'his.'" This was the most he could say in 1969. Yet the Stalin subtext was transparent, and everyone saw it clearly.[23]

It did not help that the nationalists' prose was frustratingly crude. Archaic vocabulary, appropriate to a degree in Solzhenitsyn's language (which Dement'ev did not mention), reached an absurd density in their writings.

As for their depictions of the village, Dement'ev noted incisively that the nationalists extolled not real life in the countryside, full of privations and hard labor, but rather a romanticized "poetry of rest" and communion with nature—milk drinking, mushroom picking, sunbathing, strolling in the woods and fields, and so on. All of that was nice and true for a Moscow writer taking a pleasant countryside vacation, but it was infinitely far from how the peasants actually lived. Born in a village, Dement'ev knew what he was talking about—as did Tvardovskii. The countryside that *Novyi mir* sought to show in its publications was very different from the Russophiles' idealized woodcuts. Also, as Dement'ev observed, despite their eulogizing of village life and denigration of urban creature comforts, the nationalistically minded "villagers" quite enjoyed life in big cities and were not in any hurry to return to the actual countryside for good.[24]

All of these sarcastic points were well taken. And yet at the same time, one cannot but think that Dement'ev might have missed the main point. Crude as it often was, the Russian neo-nationalistic literature and thought of the late 1960s portended the revival of nothing less than an ideology. Powerful and aggressive, as well as broadly accessible, this ideology had the potential to become a dominant political force and supplant the aging Soviet dogmata. The humanistic, internationalist philosophy of the broad-minded, well-educated intelligentsia, with which Dement'ev opposed this new and formidable rival, was certainly more refined and tolerant than the primeval, earthy logic of the nationalists. Yet perhaps it was too refined to have a mass appeal. What Dement'ev and his colleagues in *Novyi mir* were facing was the rise of a secular religion, and it is not entirely obvious whether they fully realized the significance of this process. The new Russian nationalism occupied little if any place in the diaries of Tvardovskii, Kondratovich, or Lakshin in those years. Hostile as they were to this nascent political and intellectual force, they may have made a mistake by underestimating its potential.

That said, even had they noticed the scope of the new phenomenon, there was little Dement'ev and his colleagues could have done beyond what they actually did. Just like their nationalistic opponents, and probably more so, they had to operate within the framework of established Soviet reasoning—much of which they also shared. Thus, Dement'ev grounded his conceptual rejection of nationalism in Lenin's writings, such as the 1914 article "On the National Pride of the Great Russians." Chalmaev may have disliked fin-de-siècle artistic experimentation and created embellished images of Stolypin-era prosperity, but Dement'ev's assessment of those years was also far from sophisticated. To show the rottenness of the tsarist regime, he cited the rise of the revolutionary movement and the "Stolypin reaction"—perhaps well-founded but also distinctly Soviet arguments verbalized in the very same ossified textbook phraseology that *Novyi mir* was undermining at the time. Similarly, Dement'ev's counter to Chalmaev's criticism of Western cultural influences was that, unlike tsarist Russia, the new, infinitely stronger and more modern Soviet order had nothing to fear from the West. Much of this argumentation, to be sure, was tongue-in-cheek and skillfully based on rich layers of subtext. And yet one wonders whether the same Aesopian tactics that worked so well against the Soviet media discourse could be equally effective against the nationalists. *Novyi mir* could be fighting a new enemy with an old, rusty weapon. Not incidentally, Dement'ev's criticism of the Russophile writers was not far, logically and phraseologically, from other contemporary criticisms of their work advanced in print by authors completely unaffiliated with *Novyi mir*.[25]

Be it as it may, in response to his article the old and the new opponents of the journal eagerly joined forces. In 1969 *Novyi mir* came under attack simultaneously for its critical stance toward the Soviet past (as in the case of Voronov's novel) and its skepticism toward the reviving Russian national idea. On 26 July the journal *Ogonek*, edited by the conservative writer Anatolii Sofronov (1911–1990), published the "Letter of the Eleven," as it became informally known. It was an open letter, officially titled "What *Novyi mir* Speaks Against" and signed by eleven writers of rather secondary acclaim.[26] Years later it turned out that they had been mere signatories, while the real authors of the letter were those very critics Dement'ev had ridiculed—Chalmaev and Lobanov, along with their colleagues Oleg Mikhailov (b. 1933), Viktor Petelin (b. 1929), and Nikolai Sergovantsev (b. 1934).[27] The brunt of their attack was, of course, directed against Dement'ev, whom they accused of poorly concealed neglect of patriotic values, both Russian and Soviet. Characteristically, just as Dement'ev himself did, his opponents employed the officially acceptable rhetoric, arguing, for example, that Chalmaev's writing was "saturated with the pathos of struggle for the ideal of a man of the future, for the ideas of the program of the Communist Party of the Soviet Union."[28]

They also remembered Dement'ev's own Stalin-era past. In particular, they cited his erstwhile anticosmopolitan statements and publications of the late 1940s, which were ostensibly in sharp contradiction to his present criticism of the nationalists.[29] Interestingly, the only reader's response to Dement'ev that survives in the archive of *Novyi mir*'s rival, the journal *Molodaia gvardiia*, also expressed skepticism of Dement'ev's article because its tone reminded the letter writer of the "now faraway and forgotten time"—a common euphemism for the Stalin years.[30] By the late 1960s, not only *Novyi mir*'s proponents but also its critics had started to use the method of compromising their literary adversaries by associating them with the Stalin past.[31]

However, unlike the *Novyi mir* group, its conservative opponents combined these outwardly anti-Stalinist rhetorical tactics with deliberately reviving the Stalin-era media language. The authors of the "Letter of the Eleven" discussed Dement'ev's contemptuous description of the Russophile writers as *muzhikovstvuiushchie* (glorifying the presumably crude peasant man), a term whose origins they ascribed to Trotsky. The implicit association with Trotskyism brought back one of the gravest political accusations from the Stalin years. The writers also characterized *Novyi mir*'s ideas as "cosmopolitan," using the term pejoratively and thus reproducing another device from Stalin-era media rhetoric.[32]

Strategically, of course, the "Letter of the Eleven" was an attack not against Dement'ev alone but against *Novyi mir*—where, according to the writers, "the tendency of skepticism toward the socio-ethical values of Soviet society, its ideals and hard-won gains, was methodically and purposefully cultivated." The authors duly cited the journal's other heretical publications. Here, again, was Kardin's "Legends and Facts," which had cast doubt on "the heroic past of our people and the Soviet Army," especially by denying the historical existence of "the *Aurora*'s round" (but not "salvo" anymore). Here, too, was Voronov's *Youth in Zheleznodol'sk*, which "made fun of the Soviet society's growth pangs" and "blackened" Soviet reality. Those were heavy charges.[33]

The issue of *Ogonek* in which the letter appeared was quickly snapped up and immediately became a rarity—despite its circulation of 2.125 million, sixteen times more than that of *Novyi mir*. Even Tvardovskii himself had difficulty obtaining a copy and had to borrow one from his friend and editorial board member, the poet Rasul Gamzatov. The battle-hardened editor in chief was amused rather than frightened. "Truly, nothing like this has ever happened before—in stupidity, impertinence, deception, etc.," he wrote in his diary. Tvardovskii correctly suspected that the letter might have been written by someone other than the signatories. He noted, too, that each of the eleven signatories had previously been sharply criticized in the pages of *Novyi mir* for the low quality of their writing, and thus had personal grudges against the journal. It was in this vein that *Novyi mir* briefly responded to the "Letter of the Eleven," although the next issue of the journal, which contained the response, was much delayed and did not come out until September. But Tvardovskii's main conclusion was unequivocal: the letter represented the peak of ideological "reaction" in literature and portended the nearing end of his editorial board. By then he and his colleagues had long expected it. They were ready.[34]

The next barrage of criticism came only five days later. Just as the first one, it appeared in the form of a letter, this time by a reader. On 31 July 1969 the newspaper *Sotsialisticheskaia industriia (Socialist Industry)* published an open letter to Tvardovskii signed by Mikhail Egorovich Zakharov, a lathe operator at a machine-building works in Podol'sk, near Moscow. The letter mentioned Dement'ev, but its main target was Voronov's *Youth in Zheleznodol'sk*—which, according to Zakharov, had portrayed the working class as "primitive," "bogged down in everyday life routine," and "devoid of ideals."[35] Apt at deciphering campaign tactics, Tvardovskii wrote to the newspaper with a transparent expression of doubt that Zakharov had indeed penned this letter, and he asked for the letter writer's address as well as the original of his epistle. A week later, *Sotsialisticheskaia industriia* published a response by the offended Zakharov and a facsimile of one page of his letter, with an editorial comment. It turned out that, although a worker, Zakharov enjoyed a fairly high social status. He was a Hero of Socialist Labor, a delegate to the Twenty-Second and Twenty-Third Party Congresses as well as the RSFSR Supreme Soviet, plus a candidate member of the party's Central Committee. Both he and the newspaper editors fumed over Tvardovskii's mistrust. "You have become completely detached from our brother Soviet worker," Zakharov wrote. "Whoever does not believe in the working class will be refused trust by the workers themselves." The editors added: "It is surprising that Aleksandr Trifonovich Tvardovskii and the staff of *Novyi mir* know so little about the best representatives of the working class."[36]

However, the published facsimile of Zakharov's handwritten text differed greatly from the one that had initially appeared in *Sotsialisticheskaia industriia*. First of all, the letter was originally addressed not to Tvardovskii but to the newspaper. And then, even if Zakharov had been the real author, the differences between his original letter and its published version betrayed heavy editing. For example, he initially stated: "What prompted me to write was a discussion that took place recently." In the published version, the editors added: "in our factory workshop." Zakharov wrote: "A friend of mine asked me about the journal *Novyi mir.*" After "a friend of mine," the editors inserted "our worker," and used inversion—*rabochii nash,* instead of *nash rabochii*—thereby emulating colloquial speech and intimate familiarity. Zakharov reported: "Workers made critical remarks about the editorial board [of *Novyi mir*]." The editors replaced "workers" with "our brother worker," *nash brat rabochii,* thus again imitating blue-collar parlance.[37]

Although *Sotsialisticheskaia industriia* had come into being only in July 1969, four weeks prior to the publication of Zakharov's letter, in their molding of this letter its editors followed an old journalistic blueprint for representing the working class. Inherited from the early Soviet decades, the blueprint relied on the image of the simple-minded yet loyal and conscientious worker. The use of inversion and pseudo-archaic expressions imitated the "simple" colloquialisms allegedly in use among workers, while exaggerated "producerist" phraseology conveyed a sense of the centrality of the workplace in their lives. Even literary conversations could take place nowhere else but in a factory workshop. Originating as far back as the 1920s and 1930s, these clichés had been applied in Soviet newspapers ever since. The game was old, and all the players knew its every move.[38]

Readers and the Last Campaign

So did the watchful audience. The 1969 press campaign against *Novyi mir* brought in one of the most intense responses from readers: no less than 145 letters from over 140 people, written mostly during August and September (in addition to the 32 responses to Voronov's *Youth in Zheleznodol'sk* shortly before).[39] As always, the full dimensions of the response are impossible to fathom, because *Novyi mir*'s rival periodicals and institutions have kept only a handful of letters in their archives—3 in this case—suggesting an intense selection process.[40] But in the *Novyi mir* archive, all but 10 responses to the campaign defended the journal. The share of anonymous letters increased somewhat compared with their usual minuscule proportion. Apparently, by 1969 readers had noted the escalating ideological pressure on *Novyi mir* and the growing risk of expressing support for the ostracized journal. Yet the fear should not be overestimated: even at this late hour, the vast majority of readers' letters, 85.5 percent, were fully signed and contained a return address.

Many people forwarded copies or wrote separately to *Ogonek* or *Sotsialisticheskaia industriia*. As usual, responses from the intelligentsia prevailed, but over a quarter of the letters—the highest proportion since World War II—came from workers. And not a single worker sided with Zakharov. Some were so outraged by his letter that they wrote more than one response—as did Gennadii Kucherenko from the town of Borispol' in Ukraine, a worker with fifty-five years of experience.[41] "What particularly surprised me," he wrote, "were the lines in which Zakharov claimed [to be] representing the entire working class in his own persona. This cannot be characterized otherwise than conceit, arrogance, and a threat on top of that." The reader added: "Knowing well the industrial production, the people, the everyday life and culture of factories, I recognize with pain that drunkenness, lack of culture [*beskul'tur'e*], and self-seeking flourish nowadays among the workers. . . . Why do you, dear author, think it unnecessary to discuss all of that, why are you driving the evil deeper inside, why do you reconcile with it?"[42] In a gesture common for the readers of the Thaw, Kucherenko declared his doubt about his letter's prospects for publication and stated his low opinion of the media. In doing so, he sarcastically converted the media language to serve his own rhetorical purposes, also, like Zakharov, claiming the status of a "simple worker" whose opinions, by virtue of this simplicity as well as his labor experience, were presumably true. "Of course, this letter of mine will never see light in the press, because I am not a hero [of labor] but a simple worker who has toiled for 55 years among the rank-and-file, and because I am telling the truth, without making up and embellishing anything."[43]

Quite a few workers read the facsimile of Zakharov's letter with a magnifying glass. To do so, Anatolii Shishkov, a pensioner and a former mining timekeeper from a village in Tula Oblast, traveled all the way to the city of Tula, where he finally obtained a copy of the newspaper. Reading it left him intensely skeptical of Zakharov's letter, and he accused the newspaper of fabrication: "I believe that the author of the "Open Letter" is just a figurehead. . . . The original is published in an edited form, which gives us grounds to consider the published version mostly a product of the editors following orders from their masters."[44] Readers routinely noted that

Zakharov's letter had undergone heavy editing. Natalia Vasil'eva and Bella Magid from Leningrad divided a page into two columns and copied Zakharov's facsimile and the published letter, one beside the other. The comparison made it obvious to them that the letter, "in its stylistic incoherence, rather resembled the product of a second-rate journalist." They were offended by what they saw as the newspaper's cynical confidence in the readers' blindness and naïveté.[45]

Many readers also derided the artificial "simple folk" language of Zakharov's letter. Some noted the contradiction between his claim that he routinely read periodicals and his purportedly semiliterate speech. Mikhail Tomshin from Sverdlovsk, who had spent many years as a worker before becoming an engineer, argued that real workers did not speak and behave like that, and that the letter therefore was a cheap journalistic fabrication:

> I have shown his "Open Letter" to many people, and nobody (I emphasize—nobody) said that a worker had written it. Everyone said that it was the work of an experienced journalist posing as a worker, and that Zakharov only signed it. People even suggested that Zakharov might not exist at all. . . . Under his "We haven't graduated from academies" style one senses a very experienced hand.[46]

As always during these years, the dark side of the Soviet past continued to preoccupy the letter writers, who readily brought up personal experiences to disprove the agendas of the campaign against *Novyi mir.* As many of them were former workers who had seen industrialization firsthand, the readers almost uniformly defended Voronov's *Youth in Zheleznodol'sk.* I. P. Kopysov from the Voronezh region, who had spent his childhood and adolescence in a Urals industrial town similar to Magnitogorsk, confirmed everything Voronov wrote about the workers' desperate struggle for physical survival during the 1930s and the war. Kopysov also pointed out some omissions in Voronov's book: it had only a few vague sentences on the arrests of the 1930s, although those, he argued, had been a constant subject of conversation at the time.[47] Iurii Shur, who also had spent his childhood and adolescence in a Urals factory town—before, during, and immediately after World War II—wrote that Voronov did not at all "blacken" the workers' lives. On the contrary, he said, he had accurately portrayed and perhaps even smoothed over the harsh reality of the prewar and war years.[48] Engineer Tomshin also thought, on the basis of his childhood memories, that Voronov had somewhat "brushed up" the picture of the workers' everyday existence, which in actuality had been even "more severe, more ruthless, and more disgusting—so that I would not like to see all that again." Still, he welcomed *Youth in Zheleznodol'sk*—because, even if brushed up, Voronov's representation of the past was far more accurate than those available in newspapers and radio or TV broadcasts.[49]

Reflecting another common feature of Thaw-era readers' letters, many of their authors continued to trace the lineage of the attacks on *Novyi mir* to the press campaigns of Stalin's time and, once again, to perceive the crackdown on the journal as a sign of a potential return of the terror. Zakharov's letter produced "an unpleasant impression" on the worker Sidorov from Kalinin, for whom "in its tone as well as content, [the letter] looked like the 'criticism' of 1937–39, as a result of which one could at best lose his literary job, and at worst end up in the dock."[50] First brought into the open in the early 1960s, the awareness of the past terror had not at all faded by the end of the decade, even though open discussions of the subject had been curtailed.

As to Russian nationalism, a remarkable number of the letter writers—nearly all—rendered support for Dement'ev's skeptical stance on the issue. Their responses were full of sarcastic and deprecating comments about the crudity of the new Russophile prose and neo-Slavophile aspirations. The more sophisticated letter writers even cited Petr Chaadaev's (1794–1856) dictum that love of truth was superior to love of one's motherland.[51] However, some did reproach Dement'ev for not taking the nationalist threat seriously enough or explaining its origins, which they discerned in the flaws of the modern reality. This skeptical view of Russian nationalism in the late 1960s is noteworthy, as it offers a caveat to ideas about the contemporary rise of this phenomenon. The rise was slow, and nationalism had serious checks in its way, with both Soviet internationalism and the humanistic intelligentsia mentality acting as counterweights.[52]

Overall, in reaction to the campaign many readers proved perfectly capable of discerning and counteracting an (admittedly crude) orchestrated attack against *Novyi mir*. In so doing, they employed the entire arsenal of intellectual weaponry with which the journal and the literary environment had armed them over the decade. By the end of the 1960s, much unlike earlier, the readers had come to display a sharply critical stance toward anything emanating from the established authority. They expressed this criticism in their own words, which were noticeably if not entirely different from the parlance of newspapers. They were ready to bring up the dark details of the past, including personal backgrounds, to discredit authoritative pronouncements about Soviet history. And they showed intimate knowledge of a broad repertoire of media devices, which in their eyes were now decidedly compromised. What marked the literary audience of 1969 were experience, disillusionment, and considerable intellectual maturity. For much of this the readers could, and often did, thank *Novyi mir.*

Such was the level of affinity and tacit understanding between the readers and the journal that, now just as earlier, not all sought an answer to their letter. Some added lines like this: "Feel free not to answer this letter. I think you have enough work."[53] And yet this time the readers' support was vital to the journal—so vital that Tvardovskii himself took the time to respond to nearly every letter. This was a unique situation even for *Novyi mir,* where usually much of the correspondence would be handled by Tvardovskii's deputies, with the editor in chief only selectively involved. Thus, in August 1969 he personally replied to a long letter by three college students from Gor'kii who defended the journal, traced the campaign's origins to the Stalin years, and compared *Novyi mir*'s role in society to that of *Sovremennik* and *Otechestvennye zapiski* in the nineteenth century. Obviously moved, Tvardovskii wrote in response:

> Dear friends,
>
> Your letter of 11.08.69 is one of those letters dear to us, in which we see the good-hearted attention of our distant friends, the readers, to *Novyi mir.* We are deeply grateful for your kind words about the journal.
>
> Yours,
>
> (A. Tvardovskii)[54]

The authors of a few negative letters, who condemned *Novyi mir* and Dement'ev's article, also received replies. To demonstrate his journal's impartiality, Tvardovskii even considered publishing one such letter, but then apparently changed his mind.[55]

Better than anything else, his direct and extensive involvement in correspondence with the readers showed his sense of the gravity of the situation. It also showed that the readers were *Novyi mir*'s principal allies, their reaction being the best reward for all the years of the editors' work. It was at this point that Tvardovskii and his colleagues ultimately realized what role their journal had played in Russian culture. In mid-September 1969, the editor wrote in his diary:

> Even the people of the *Novyi mir* generation do not imagine the reality of these letters as a phenomenon of the readers' activity. . . . Half a year or a year ago, even we ourselves did not imagine this powerful support behind us. As Dement'ev says, it was worth having suffered and not collapsed under the burden of humiliation, invective, threats, and the sheer hopelessness of the entire situation—[all worthwhile] because of this reward.[56]

How Journals Die

Valuable as it was, the readers' backing could not save the journal from what was coming. Dispersed intellectual communities like this are rarely capable of direct political action: they tend to have a different modus operandi and significance. Meanwhile, the pressure on *Novyi mir* was mounting, to what increasingly looked like a siege.

It was a slow siege, with the top political leadership reluctant to get overly involved in reprisals against the journal. These were no longer the Stalin years, and not even the early Thaw of the 1950s, when literature had still felt the breath of the high authority immediately above. Stalin had in many respects tried to manage Soviet literature personally. Khrushchev, already more remote, had yet to some extent inherited the idea of the leadership's direct participation in literary politics: not incidentally, he had personally presided over the 1954 crushing of *Novyi mir.* But Brezhnev's time was different. Intellectual life had grown much more diverse and complex by the late 1960s, while political action became less direct or conspicuous. Eye-catching involvement of the top echelons of power in literary affairs was no longer in vogue: everything had to be done by the hands of literary officials and with the least possible disturbance of the peace. It was the Writers' Union that applied quiet but growing pressure on Tvardovskii—so much so that the editor seriously contemplated resigning as early as May and June 1969.[57] The Central Committee, in contrast, took a position above the fray. Indeed, the top leadership was rather displeased with both parties—*Novyi mir* as well as its opponents, *Ogonek, Molodaia gvardiia, Sotsialisticheskaia industriia,* and others—precisely because they had made internecine literary struggles way too conspicuous.

It did not help in this respect that Western observers were commenting extensively on all the nuances of the conflict. The frequent involvement of the Western media was an additional irritant to the party leaders (although possibly also a check on their repressive action). On 27 July 1969 the *New York Times* published an article by its Moscow bureau chief, Bernard Gwertzman, describing the latest Soviet literary struggle.[58] Tvardovskii's opponents immediately noted the article, and whatever Gwertzman's intentions might have been, he thus in fact supplied ammunition for even heavier pressure on *Novyi mir.* On 3 August, the newspaper *Sovetskaia Rossiia* drew transparent parallels between the journal and Western "ideologues," commenting on "the protracted flirt between *Novyi mir* and the bourgeois press."[59]

This put Tvardovskii in an awkward position. Generally, he kept an eye on reactions abroad to his journal's publications and had a fairly good idea of how *Novyi mir* was perceived in the West. He was a frequent listener to Western radio broadcasts, especially those of the BBC, and he did not necessarily disagree with the foreign commentaries on Soviet political and literary life.[60] At the same time, these commentaries never guided him in his work—and, moreover, they frequently created unpleasant situations for him. Tvardovskii was a Soviet citizen and a communist by persuasion. He always viewed his journal as a distinctly Soviet publication that worked in the existing political-cultural framework, trying its best to change and improve the established order from within, by legitimate methods. Sympathetic as he was to many dissidents, a direct association with them contradicted his beliefs. So did an association with any Western opinions and positions, convincing though he might have found them. Such associations threatened to delegitimize *Novyi mir,* to make it look oppositional—and nothing could more easily spell the journal's end. In its final days, caught between the fires of the Cold War, *Novyi mir* found its legitimate platform increasingly unstable.

The entire polemic of 1969 was becoming more and more scandalous. That, as well as the uncontrolled rise of nationalistic ideas in the literary community, alarmed the moderates in the Central Committee. Among them was Aleksandr Iakovlev (1923–2005), the future architect of perestroika and Gorbachev's closest ally, and as of 1969 deputy head of the Central Committee's Department of Propaganda and Agitation. On 12–13 August 1969, the editors of the periodicals involved in the polemic were summoned to the Central Committee compound, where Iakovlev reproached them for the inadmissible tone of the discussion. In the opinion of the Central Committee, he said, the style of the polemic compromised the Soviet press and the party's general image. Iakovlev did not spare anyone:

> It seems to us that both parties are starting to incline toward prejudice. All of this goes beyond the limits of party ethics and provides food for foreign propaganda. . . . We are not against discussion, but we are against such a tone, against such clamor, and against applying labels. We would not like this entire polemic to be used abroad as an indicator of our attitudes to problems of literature and art. I would also urge comrades that, leaving this discussion, they should not think that it is their neighbor who got reproached. Both parties are to blame.[61]

Iakovlev's criticism was intentionally balanced and might have reflected his own apprehensions about the rise of Russian nationalism. Three years later, in 1972, he would speak publicly against it—an act that would cost him his position in the Central Committee.[62] But in 1969 he also conveyed the views of his superiors, and probably their uncertainty about the new and unfamiliar intellectual developments taking place. For the time being, as a preventive measure, not only *Novyi mir* but also its opponent *Molodaia gvardiia* was censured. In 1970, for advancing rampantly nationalistic ideas and showing disrespect toward the accepted ideological pronouncements, its editor in chief, Anatolii Nikonov (1923–1983), was removed from his post together with two colleagues. However, their dismissals did not radically alter the journal's line. Most members of the editorial board remained, and the new editors, Feliks Ovcharenko and then Anatolii Ivanov, espoused, if more cautiously, the same nationalistic principles.[63]

With *Novyi mir* things were very different. Although its battle with the nationalists ended in a formal draw, the official criticism only added to long-accumulating resentment against the journal at the top. On 12 September 1969 an editorial in *Pravda* once again, however ambiguously, censured *Novyi mir* for "abstract humanism" and "exposurism" *(oblichitel'stvo)*, that is, a propensity toward criticism for its own sake.[64] Later in the fall, plans for a radical reshuffling of the journal's editorial board—something Tvardovskii and his team had long expected—finally began to materialize.[65]

This time it went rather quickly. On 5 November 1969 Solzhenitsyn was expelled from the Union of Writers. Tvardovskii had hardly approved of his protégé's increasing civic activity during the years that had followed the publication of *One Day in the Life of Ivan Denisovich*, nor had their personal relations remained exactly stellar.[66] But the editor in chief understood only too well that the association between Solzhenitsyn and his journal was immediate and permanent. An assault on Solzhenitsyn meant an assault on *Novyi mir.* It was also an assault against Tvardovskii's entire literary and intellectual strategy. "The last bastion of literature as such has fallen," he commented in the diary. "He was the only one of us with his disobedience, and when we yielded him, we yielded everything. They never forgave him for returning from there and telling, for the first time, what was there." Tvardovskii's closest confidant in editorial affairs, Dement'ev, confirmed the gravity of the situation. "This is a catastrophe," he said.[67]

Two days later, Tvardovskii informed the secretary of the board of the Writers' Union, Konstantin Voronkov, of his intention to leave the journal. Voronkov was probably relieved to hear it, as for many months he had pushed the editor toward this decision. As soon as Tvardovskii returned to his office from the meeting with Voronkov, he received a piece of confidential information from his colleagues. Three members of the editorial board—Vladimir Lakshin, Aleksei Kondratovich, and Igor' Vinogradov—had just been slated for removal. In their place, new board members, the long-dreaded ideological "commissars," would be appointed. The editors thus learned for sure what they had suspected earlier. The decision that the Central Committee had made a full year before was now being put into practice.[68]

At this point, even had Tvardovskii wanted to stay at the helm, this would have been impossible. Solzhenitsyn's expulsion meant that the *Novyi mir* line was being officially terminated. The reshuffling of the editorial board would ensure this by turning the editor in chief into a mere figurehead, one who would reign but not rule. Never would Tvardovskii agree to that. This time, unlike during his first dismissal from the journal fifteen years earlier, he did not intend to confess, repent, or ask for forgiveness. "We are ready to defend," he wrote in the diary, ". . . and ready to leave. We will not shame ourselves with confessions. Come whatever may."[69]

In December 1969, his new poem *By Right of Memory* was published by the Italian magazine *Espresso.* Quickly republished by several other

Western periodicals, including the journal *Possev,* which the Soviets somehow considered particularly notorious, the poem created an emergency in the literary establishment. It is unclear who sent the text abroad, and Tvardovskii himself might have felt awkward about this. But now he had ended up in a situation very similar to that in which many literary dissenters, including Pasternak, Siniavskii, and Daniel', had found themselves before. Perhaps for him this was a logical outcome.

Written from 1966 to 1969, *By Right of Memory* was Tvardovskii's last major work and the summation of his literary oeuvre. In the poem, he returned to the most tragic moment of his past—his renunciation of his parents during collectivization. The central section of the poem, "Son Does Not Answer for His Father," owed its title to Stalin's 1935 dictum, in which the leader had ostensibly exculpated the children of "kulaks" from responsibility for their parents' alleged crimes.[70] Tvardovskii revisited and analyzed this statement, asking what it meant to be a father and a son in the tragic upheavals of Russia's twentieth century. The poet's ultimate verdict contradicted that of Stalin. Children were morally answerable for the fathers—not only for what the fathers had done but also for what they, the children, had done to the fathers and their memory. And then there was a different "father"—Stalin, who once claimed the status of "the father of nations," to the admiration of millions who accepted the role of "children." As clearly as no one before in Russian literature, Tvardovskii posited the idea of nationwide complicity and responsibility for the tragedy of the past, and the universal obligation to face this legacy. Inherently connected to the present, indeed forming the present and the future, the past was to be remembered, with everyone held accountable for their own deeds and for those of their ancestors:

> Sons have long grown to be fathers,
> But for the universal father
> We all turned out to be answerable.
> The trial of decades is ongoing,
> And there is no end in sight.[71]

Interestingly, it was Konstantin Simonov who suggested the title of the poem to Tvardovskii.[72] In this final hour, the two great editors of the journal, one former, the other current, became closer than ever before. More and more, the last years of Simonov's life compelled him to reevaluate his own past, especially as he reassessed the World War II experience that had been formative for him. Increasingly reflective, he gravitated further and further away from his earlier statist ideas about "higher-order truth," moving toward a new understanding of truth embodied in a human being. He thought about the human cost of this war, about history as it had, rather than should have, been. Ultimately, it was this that drove him closer to Tvardovskii. In 1966 Simonov had intended to publish the manuscript of his book *100 Days of War* in *Novyi mir.* Based on his wartime diaries and notebooks, this new work described the first and most tragic several weeks of the war, and the text was accompanied by Simonov's ex post facto reflective commentary. Tvardovskii was eager to publish it, but the censors stood in the way. In the end the volume did not come out until the 1990s—long after both Tvardovskii and Simonov had died.[73]

But in the late 1960s this experience brought them closer together. They increasingly talked with each other, exchanged manuscripts, and Tvardovskii even spent some time in Simonov's dacha on the Black Sea, taking a rest from the mayhem of Moscow literary politics. He always had been, and still remained, rather skeptical about Simonov's prose, but he did value Simonov's growing sense of historical and memoiristic accountability. Simonov, on his part, increasingly supported Tvardovskii, using all of his influence—which, alas, was not enough—to help *Novyi mir* in its predicament. Perhaps the ultimate sign of their growing alliance, and Simonov's decisive recognition of Tvardovskii's literary and intellectual strategy, was when, in March 1969, the two of them considered Simonov's rejoining *Novyi mir*'s editorial board—this time under Tvardovskii's command. But this was not to be.[74]

The publication of *By Right of Memory* sped up the bureaucratic machine. No shaming campaign, let alone prosecution, was intended against Tvardovskii, and yet the uproar surely added to the long list of grudges the establishment had accumulated against him and the journal. Everyone involved realized what this portended for *Novyi mir.* The Russian nationalists were particularly jubilant, looking forward to the downfall of their powerful opponent. In Rostov-on-Don, gatherings of nationalistic writers celebrated the latest developments by openly singing a wartime song that included the famous line, "When Comrade Stalin sends us into battle."[75]

Plans to remove Tvardovskii had long been in existence, but the literary officials entrusted with finding replacements for him and his team ran into many difficulties and delays. Few writers would agree to become the executioners of Russia's most important literary journal of the twentieth century, a status by then clear to practically everyone.[76] Yet eventually the replacements were found. On 3 February 1970, the Board Secretariat Bureau of the Writers' Union, in the presence of Al'bert Beliaev, the party's chief literary officer, officially decreed to "strengthen the editorial board and apparatus of *Novyi mir.*" In particular, the bureau appointed D. G. Bol'shov, an administrator on the Committee on Radio and Television, as Tvardovskii's first deputy. In three days, other candidates for "strengthening" the editorial board were to be submitted.[77]

Tvardovskii was informed of the decree on the same day. He had never met Bol'shov, although their paths had crossed earlier: in 1966 Bol'shov, then the editor of the newspaper *Sovetskaia kul'tura,* had vehemently criticized a theatrical version of Tvardovskii's poem *Tyorkin in the Other World.* As unpleasant as that association was, it was not the main issue. More important was the fact that the appointment was made forcibly, in flagrant violation of the editor in chief's right to select the members of his team. The next day, Tvardovskii protested to the Secretariat, stating that the appointment would directly induce him to resign. He knew that his protest would have no effect.[78]

On 6 February, at the Union of Writers, Voronkov informed Tvardovskii of the entire scope of the impending changes to the editorial board. Five members of Tvardovskii's team—Igor' Sats, Aleksei Kondratovich, Vladimir Lakshin, Igor' Vinogradov, and Aleksandr Mariamov—were to leave the journal. Instead, besides Bol'shov, the new board was to include the writers Oleg Smirnov, Aleksandr Rekemchuk, and Sergei Narovchatov (who eventually declined the appointment), as well as Valerii Alekseevich Kosolapov, the former editor in chief of *Literaturnaia gazeta* and currently editor in chief of the major literary press Khudozhestvennaia literatura. The long-anticipated "commissars" were at the door. On 7 February Tvardovskii wrote to the highest power—Brezhnev himself—again explaining that in this situation the only option for him would be to resign. As he half-expected, the letter was ignored. "I have a hard time imagining how I could stay now," he wrote in the diary on 8 February.[79] He was right. The day after, on 9 February 1970, in his presence the Board Secretariat Bureau of the Writers' Union approved the previously suggested changes to the editorial board of *Novyi mir.* The only addition to the new team was the literary critic Aleksandr Ovcharenko, a staunch opponent of the Tvardovskii line. This time no one from the Central Committee was present: everything was done strictly within the literary guild. On February 11, the press informed the readers about the new board.[80]

There was no way out now. The next day, 12 February 1970, Tvardovskii officially resigned:

> To the Secretariat of the Board of the Union of Writers of the USSR
>
> Bearing in mind the fact that, despite my numerous oral and written protests, the appointment, contrary to my will, of a new editorial board of the journal *Novyi mir* [took place]—the appointment of a nature offensive to me—I am forced to submit my resignation from the post of the journal's editor in chief.
>
> I request that the journal be accepted from me, and that my signature be removed from the last page of its latest (February) issue.
>
> A. Tvardovskii[81]

After this, only a few days remained. On 20 February, he walked around the offices of his journal one last time, stopping by every room and saying good-bye to every worker—including librarians, correctors, typists, and all others whom he had rarely spoken with before. Many people cried. On 2 March, he met with Kosolapov, the newly appointed editor in chief, and gave the journal over to him. The "ritual handshake"—the second and last one in his life—took place. Tvardovskii's *Novyi mir* was no more.[82]

Again, this was no longer the Stalin era. The dissolution of his editorial board did not lead to violent reprisals against either Tvardovskii or his colleagues. There were no reprisals against relatives, either. Some of Tvardovskii's deputies, like Vinogradov, did spend a long time looking for new employment, while others stayed on at *Novyi mir* under the new editors, at least for a while.[83] Politics or no politics, people needed to provide for their families. But his closest colleagues, Kondratovich and Lakshin, received jobs immediately—Kondratovich at the journal *Soviet Literature in Foreign Languages*, and Lakshin at the journal *Foreign Literature*. Tvardovskii himself was offered a rather generous retirement package: a new edition of his collected works to be published by his upcoming sixtieth birthday, access to a special "Kremlin" food supply, access to privileged medical facilities, and a sinecure position in the Secretariat of the Writers'

Union with a salary of 500 rubles a month (several times above the national average)—regardless of whether he would actually work there or not. Being of sufficiently independent means, he accepted the benefits but declined the salary. Less than two years of life remained for him, and only a few months of active life. The advent of cancer and the prolonged treatment for it took much of his remaining time.[84]

On 2 June 1970 Tvardovskii made the last entry in his diary. It ended with a poem he had written three decades earlier, in 1938:

Father, father, where, where
Are you journeying in the world?
What roof covers you at midnight?
Are you alive, and are you well?
. . .
Maybe you are dreaming now
How they'd give it back to you—
What you dreamed of, not the real
Home you had a while ago:

Hillside garden, spacious house,
Well-fed cattle in the stables,
Richly growing fields of clover,
Light warm honey in the combs . . . [85]

Aleksandr Tvardovskii died in his country house in Krasnaia Pakhra near Moscow on 18 December 1971, at the age of sixty-one.

EPILOGUE

Tradition, Change, Legacies

A FEW WEEKS after leaving *Novyi mir,* Tvardovskii wrote to his brother: "My resignation has been accepted. The press has not reported it, so few people know in Moscow. I do not regret my decision. I could not have acted differently. My honor did not suffer, nor did I suffer in a material sense. But of course, it was hard to leave the work that meant so much in my life."[1]

Already then it was clear that this work had meant much to other people's lives as well. Initially, there were fewer reactions to the dissolution of his editorial board than one could have expected—possibly indeed because Tvardovskii's resignation was not widely announced. But rumors did circulate, and letters began to arrive. The readers got an idea of what was happening "from half-words," a skill their experience had taught them well.

"Dear comrades and friends," wrote Ada Aleksandrovna Shkodina from Moscow on 11 February 1970, "upon the instruction from a group of readers":

> Having read in today's *Literaturnaia gazeta* the information about the changes in *Novyi mir*'s editorial board, we understood everything. We are rushing—in those few days while you are all still together—to express our indescribable and overwhelming

> gratitude for everything you have done. . . . We are grateful for the talents you have discovered and revived, for your honesty, steadfastness, and principled stance, for your loyalty to the cause of our literature. We trust that we are parting with you only for some time: everything evil goes away, while everything good remains forever. We, your readers, are always with you—you should know and remember this. We are ever grateful to you and proud of you. Thank you for everything you have managed to do while you could.[2]

Tvardovskii knew that such farewell letters revealed only the earliest recognition of what *Novyi mir* meant in the country's history. With time and distance, he predicted, the journal's legacy would grow more and more apparent.[3] Decades have passed, and today it is possible to see the full scale of this legacy and the place *Novyi mir* occupies in the Russian culture of the twentieth century.

The intellectual, ethical, and linguistic shifts of the 1950s and 1960s to a great extent originated in literature. Thanks to reading literature, the people who came out of the Thaw were vastly different from the people who had entered it a decade and a half earlier. They knew more and feared less. They were more aware of their past and less confident about their present. They had fewer illusions and treated even the highest authoritative pronouncements with skepticism. They spoke and wrote in their own words, and even if they borrowed someone else's, they now had a variety of vocabularies to choose from. They had greater respect for the value of individual human life, dignity, and opinion. And they—at least many—were prepared to speak about all of this openly. Perhaps most important, there was no longer a single "they," not even in appearances. Out of a semblance of moral, political, behavioral, and linguistic uniformity and homogeneity there had emerged myriad individuals willing to think on their own and express themselves with a great variety of ideas and words.

Literature, of course, was not the only venue for these transformations. People socialized, took care of their material needs, watched movies and television, listened to the radio, attended concerts, theaters, and museums. Many acted very differently in 1969 than in 1949 in the ways they dressed and talked, in the music, songs, and dances they enjoyed, art exhibits they visited, homes they inhabited, and furniture they had inside those homes. And yet reading occupied a special place in their lives. Traditionally the central mechanism for coining and exchanging ideas in Russia, literature retained this role during and after the Thaw. This would continue to be the case in the 1970s and early 1980s, years that are beyond the scope of this book but that, as it becomes increasingly clear, hardly deserve to be labeled as a time of stagnation. This concerns the country's overall history, including literature and, specifically, *Novyi mir.* After Tvardovskii, the journal no longer had the same glory, but it retained considerable cultural prominence, in part capitalizing on the renown it had achieved during the Thaw. Indeed, many of the works it published in the early 1970s originally had been part of Tvardovskii's editorial portfolio. Even later in the Brezhnev years, *Novyi mir* would occasionally fascinate readers by publishing texts of high literary value and major social importance.

But it was after the mid-1980s that the lasting impact of the Thaw and the continuing significance of literature in this intellectual culture became clearer than ever. Mikhail Gorbachev's policy of perestroika reclaimed the Thaw heritage. Many proponents of change, including Gorbachev himself, were members of what one historian has termed the "Thaw generation," even if they did not necessarily speak this generational language.[4] Having matured in the 1950s and 1960s, they viewed the Thaw as unfinished business and Gorbachev's reforms as its logical continuation. The literary, scientific, and artistic intelligentsia, in particular, claimed victory during perestroika, remembering their youth and carrying its ideals into modern cultural and political practice. In the late 1980s, the agendas of the Thaw were revived, often by the same people who had forged them two decades earlier.

This revival once again took the forms established in modern Russian culture. Just as it had during the Thaw, literature again came to the forefront of Russian politics as a crucial (although this time by far not the only) setting for socially meaningful conversation. The late 1980s and the very early 1990s became the golden age—or, as one observer later put it, "the golden moment"—of thick journals.[5] Not only literary texts, but also hundreds of important articles by economists, historians, and political commentators appeared in those journals, captivating readers' minds. The numbers of readers, too, increased dramatically in comparison with the Thaw and even the Brezhnev years. The circulation of thick journals skyrocketed, reaching hundreds of thousands and sometimes millions.

The journal *Zvezda* attained a circulation of 344,000 in 1990, compared with 95,000 in 1967 and 115,000 in the mid-1980s. *Oktiabr'* circulated 380,000 copies in 1989, as opposed to 130,000 in 1967 and 175,000 in 1986. *Neva* reached 600,000 copies in 1990, while *Znamia* boasted 1,000,000—compared, respectively, with the 250,000 and 170,000 they had had back in 1967.[6] *Druzhba narodov* reached an even more impressive circulation of 1,100,000 in 1989. And, crowning this impressive list, was *Novyi mir.* At its peak in 1990, the journal circulated a stunning 2,710,000 copies—more than any other thick journal ever, and sixteen times more than Tvardovskii's *Novyi mir* in the best of its days.[7]

To a great extent, *Novyi mir* of the perestroika years capitalized on its old glory, reviving the Tvardovskii tradition of social criticism, factuality, and reevaluation of the past. Its editor in chief in 1986–1998, Sergei Zalygin (1913–2000), was one of many writers whose literary agendas had taken shape under Tvardovskii's tutelage. And in fact, most of the books and authors that would capture the readers' minds during the late 1980s and early 1990s had their origins in the Thaw. Many of the literary texts that produced a significant impact on society during perestroika had been written two to three decades earlier, in the 1950s and 1960s. Often they had even passed through Tvardovskii's hands—and their authors' names appear in the pages of this book.

Here was Vladimir Dudintsev, who lived to see the new times. His last and perhaps his best book, *The White Garments*, a novel about geneticists of the late Stalin years, came out in 1987 in the journal *Neva.* Dudintsev had started writing the book in the 1960s, with the intention of submitting it to *Novyi mir.* Tvardovskii even announced it as forthcoming—but in the end the publication had to wait for twenty years.

Here was Boris Pasternak, whose *Doctor Zhivago* came out in 1988 in Zalygin's *Novyi mir.* The writer had died long before his novel saw the light of day in his country. Yet it would have pleased him to know that when the book did come out there was no mudslinging, no yelling, and no proverbial "I have not read, but I will say." This time people did read—with intense discussion, but with much admiration as well.

Here was Vasilii Grossman, who had also died long before his *Life and Fate* was published. Written between 1950 and 1959, the novel finally saw print in 1988 in the journal *Oktiabr'* and became one of the most significant literary publications of the perestroika years.

Here was Ilya Ehrenburg, whose *People, Years, Life* was republished twenty-three years after his death. This time, in 1990, the book was restored to its original version, free from the intrusion of the censor's hand.

Here was Lidiia Chukovskaia, whose novella *Sofia Petrovna* finally came out in Russia in 1988, published in the journal *Neva.* Lidiia Korneevna did live to see the publication of this book of hers, and many others.

Here was Aleksandr Solzhenitsyn, whose previously forbidden books finally reached Russian audiences during the late 1980s and early 1990s. Among them was his magnum opus, *The Gulag Archipelago,* several chapters of which Zalygin's *Novyi mir* published in 1989. Reportedly, it was subscription to the issues that contained Solzhenitsyn's works, including the *Archipelago,* that brought *Novyi mir* to its record circulation in 1990. A few years later, in 1994, Solzhenitsyn returned to Russia from exile to claim his broadly recognized, if just as broadly contested, position as literary patriarch and social oracle in his home country.

Here was Emil' Kardin, who not only lived to see perestroika but also became one of its energetic publicists. Formulated in the 1960s, his ideas about historical truth, authenticity, and factuality now enjoyed wide-ranging success, which he had many chances to observe.

The list of authors and titles that had originated in the Thaw and came to prominence during perestroika is long. As one last example, let us mention a writer who has not figured in this book: Anatolii Rybakov (1911–1998). His novel *The Children of the Arbat* came out in 1987 in the journal *Druzhba narodov* and became one of the most influential literary texts about the Stalin period published during the last Soviet years. Rybakov had written the book in the mid-1960s and also, like many other authors, submitted it to Tvardovskii's *Novyi mir.* There it was announced as forthcoming in 1967. Again, the publication had to wait for two decades.

The overarching theme of all these books was twentieth-century mass political violence, and in particular the peak phase that it had reached in the Soviet Union under Stalin. Suppressed for twenty years, the theme of the past as tragedy burst into the public conversation with far greater force than ever, shaking the political system to its foundation. The literary texts written during the 1950s and 1960s set the standards and provided the framework for this societywide philosophical, political, and moral reevaluation of the established order.

The Thaw and its literature were thus at the root of the ultimate crisis of legitimacy the Soviet Union experienced during its last years. Many aspects of the crisis would continue long after the country's collapse in 1991. The texts that were published in the 1950s and 1960s, and the dialogue between literature and its readers that they generated, set the agenda for the future. Starting with the Thaw, the tragedies of the twentieth century became, and remain to this day, the defining theme of Russian political consciousness.

Much controversy surrounds the question of whether late Soviet and post-Soviet society succeeded in holding a meaningful conversation on this theme. The story of *Novyi mir* and its readers proves that the discussion did take place—perhaps not on a universal scale, but within a very significant, influential segment of society. This discussion, however, took place in the forms intrinsic to modern Russian culture. Literature and letter writing, the long-established mechanisms of political self-expression, played a crucial role in both initiating and accommodating the conversation. Just as later, during perestroika, the country's intellectual life of the Thaw developed within the framework of Russian cultural tradition.

The continuing eminence of literature as the prime mover of ideas in late Soviet society raises the question of interaction between tradition and intellectual change, of mechanisms by which the minds of a great number of people become different over a span of time. How does intellectual change occur in a relatively closed and restrictive society, which the Soviet Union remained during and after the Thaw—despite the end of mass violence, the cultural and linguistic diversification, and the new emphasis on the individual? The case of *Novyi mir* and its readers suggests that, for large groups of people to begin thinking differently in such a society, new ideas need to work from within the established culture, to take forms acceptable and familiar to the environment in which they spread. One reason why *Novyi mir* succeeded as a long-term intellectual project, and had such an impact, was that Tvardovskii and his colleagues worked from within the existing order rather than attempting to negate it. The journal inherited, but also deliberately reclaimed and revived, the traditions that had characterized the Russian intellectual habitat of the pre-revolutionary era and had survived throughout the Soviet years. The focus on individual experience, attention to the language that formulated it, the belief that literature was the primary means for conveying that experience and making it politically significant, as well as the conviction that society would receive those literary messages and would change under their impact, were important aspects of this tradition.

One cannot unilaterally ascribe the initiative in these intellectual shifts to the writers or to their audiences. It is true that Soviet readers reacted to published texts and thus to agendas formulated by writers and by their critics in the media. Yet arguably the agendas themselves originated in larger processes within society, of which the written and published literary texts were only one product. The readiness with which the readers responded to those texts suggests that the agendas indeed had been ripening long before the writers formulated them. The relationship between literature and its audience was mutual and dialogical. And then the precedent of legitimate publication raised the texts and the agendas to a new, higher plane of societal prominence. Following publication, literary writings took on their own life in society, generating a long-term and widespread impact that neither the writers nor the political administrators of literature nor even the readers could entirely foresee.

In the early twenty-first century, *Novyi mir* still exists. It remains a highly respected literary journal in Russia, one of the most prestigious in the literary community and among educated audiences. And yet it is nowhere near the level of influence it once enjoyed. In 2011 the journal's nationwide circulation was slightly higher than 4,000 copies. The circulation of other thick journals, practically all of which also still exist, was about the same or even lower. Their decline began around 1991, shortly before the collapse of the Soviet Union. The golden age indeed proved to be a golden moment: in a matter of a few years during the 1990s the circulation rates of literary journals plummeted even more drastically than they had risen in the late 1980s. Their impact on society also fell precipitously. Very few people read thick journals in post-Soviet Russia, and still fewer are moved by them to any kind of political action. From its erstwhile status as the master of minds, sophisticated literature in Russia has turned into something like what it is in the contemporary West—the domain of highbrow connoisseurs and enthusiasts, plus a handful of those who still remain loyal to the old values of the intelligentsia. In today's Russia, intellectual change, not to mention political change, operates by different rules than in the bygone Soviet years.

But that is to a large extent because Russia itself has become different. Despite remaining far from the ideals of political democracy, Russian society has evolved from a very closed, regimented, and restrictive system into a much more open, diverse, and pluralistic environment. Today Russian culture is dominated by market mechanisms, largely (although not entirely) devoid of censorship, and well connected to the outside world by nearly unrestricted travel, social networks, and the flow of information via the Internet and other modern media. People have numerous venues for self-expression besides reading literature and writing letters in response to it.

That said, however, many Russians still read. Hundreds of people pack large bookstores in Moscow and Saint Petersburg in the evenings, browsing through the volumes, and thus suggesting that reverence for literature has survived into the early twenty-first century, even if it has taken new forms. The selection has vastly expanded, the tastes have been dramatically liberated, and the relative pluralism and modern communication mechanisms have diminished the impact of books on politics. And yet writers continue to be prominent in the media, drawing sizable audiences by their literary texts as well as by their televised, radio, and Internet appearances, even if their public presence is not nearly as loud or explosive as it was half a century ago. In 2008, Solzhenitsyn's death produced an outburst of polemics about the historic role of his oeuvre, and not only among connoisseurs. Hundreds and hundreds of his readers—the country's president among them—came to the writer's funeral to bid him farewell.[8]

Literature continues to enjoy considerable moral authority in Russia—not least because the vast opening and diversification of Russian culture during the second half of the past century, and the ideas that are dominant in this culture today, largely originated in literature. They especially date back to the Thaw years, and to the light-blue-covered journal that once conquered so many minds. *Novyi mir* and its readers transformed the ways in which people in this country thought, spoke and wrote about the world around them, as well as about themselves. As a result, there emerged a new climate of opinions and a new public. So significant was this transformation that not even the post-Soviet advent of statism and "longing for order" destroyed its effects. Even the political authority has adopted some of the ideas originally forged by this literature. The distancing of the country's top leaders from Stalin, and the homage they paid to Solzhenitsyn, are just two examples. Nor is the polemic on the legacy of the terror over in Russia, by any means. In the early twenty-first century it is one of the most vividly present themes in all of the media, and in society. The values established during the Thaw continue to dominate intellectual life.

Despite many challenges, the ideas, linguistic practices, and conversations that literature launched into broad public circulation more than half a century ago are still a strong presence in Russia. And so, had Aleksandr Tvardovskii lived to see the new epoch, he might have lamented the decline of literary journals, to which he devoted so much of his life. But perhaps he also would have been glad to discover that the seeds he and his colleagues once planted in fertile soil have matured into the rich forest of a new Russian culture. The forest still grows.

ARCHIVES CONSULTED

RGALI (Rossiiskii gosudarstvennyi arkhiv literatury i iskusstva)—Russian State Archive of Literature and Art, Moscow

Fond 1702	Redaktsiia zhurnala *Novyi mir*
Fond 634	Redaktsiia *Literaturnaia gazeta*
Fond 1204	Ehrenburg, Ilya Grigor'evich
Fond 3126	Krivitskii, Aleksandr Iur'evich
Fond 1710	Grossman, Vasilii Semenovich
Fond 1816	Tvardovskii, Aleksandr Trifonovich
Fond 619	Redaktsiia zhurnala *Oktiabr'*
Fond 2843	Dymshits, Aleksandr L'vovich
Fond 3133	Mar'iamov, Aleksandr Moiseevich
Fond 2846	Zaslavskii, David Iosifovich

ORF GLM (Otdel rukopisei, Gosudartsvennyi literaturnyi muzei)—Manuscript Division, State Museum of Literature, Moscow

Fond 168	Simonov, Konstantin Mikhailovich
Fond 468	Krivitskii, Aleksandr Iur'evich

RGAE (Rossiiskii gosudarstvennyi arkhiv ekonomiki)—Russian State Archive of the Economy, Moscow

Fond 3527	Ministerstvo sviazi SSSR

RGANI (Rossiiskii gosudarstvennyi arkhiv noveishei istorii)—Russian State Archive of Contemporary History, Moscow

Fond 5	Tsentral'nyi Komitet KPSS

RGASPI (Rossiiskii gosudarstvennyi arkhiv sotsial'no-politicheskoi istorii)—Russian State Archive of Socio-Political History, Moscow

Fond 17	Tsentral'nyi Komitet KPSS (VKP[b])
Fond 560	Spetsial'nyi fond rukopisnykh materialov o narushenii zakonnosti v gody kul'ta lichnosti Stalina
Fond 638	Redaktsiia gazety *Sotsialisticheskaia industriia*
Fond M-1	Tsentral'nyi Komitet VLKSM
Fond M-73	Redaktsiia zhurnala *Molodaia gvardiia*

Archives Consulted

GARF (Gosudarstvennyi arkhiv Rossiiskoi Federatsii)—State Archive of the Russian Federation, Moscow

Fond 1244 Redaktsiia gazety *Izvestiia*

Fond 9425 Glavnoe upravlenie po okhrane gosudarstvennykh tain v pechati (Glavlit)

TsAOPIM (Tsentral'nyi arkhiv obshchestvenno-politicheskoi istorii Moskvy)—Central Archive of Socio-Political History of Moscow

Fond 453 Partiinaia organizatsiia gazety *Izvestiia*

Fond 534 Partiinaia organizatsiia apparata pravleniia Soiuza pisatelei SSSR

Fond 1957 Partiinaia organizatsiia redaktsii zhurnala *Molodaia gvardiia*

Fond 3079 Partiinaia organizatsiia pravleniia Soiuza pisatelei RSFSR

Fond 3226 Partiinaia organizatsiia redaktsii gazety *Pravda*

Fond 3243 Partiinaia organizatsiia redaktsii zhurnala *Ogonek*

Fond 8131 Partiinaia organizatsiia Soiuza Sovetskikh pisatelei SSSR

Fond 8132 Partiinaia organizatsiia Moskovskogo otdeleniia Soiuza pisatelei SSSR

TsGALI SPb (Tsentral'nyi gosudarstvennyi arkhiv literatury i iskusstva Sankt-Peterburga)—Central State Archive of Literature and Art, Saint Petersburg

Fond 97 Gosudarstvennaia publichnaia biblioteka im. M. E. Saltykova-Shchedrina

Fond 107 Granin, Daniil Aleksandrovich

FKhRD TsVMM (Fond khraneniia rukopisei i dokumentov, Tsentral'nyi voenno-morskoi muzei)—Manuscript Collections, Central Naval Museum, Saint Petersburg

Hoover Institution Archives, Stanford University, Stanford, California

Andrei Siniavskii Papers

Archive of Evgenii Borisovich Pasternak

Archive of Yulia Borisovna Zaks

Burkovskii family archive

NOTES

Unless otherwise indicated, English translations of Russian texts in this book are my own.

Abbreviations

AEP	Archive of Evgenii Borisovich Pasternak
ASP	Andrei Siniavskii Papers
FKhRD TsVMM	Manuscript Collections, Central Naval Museum (Fond khraneniia rukopisei i dokumentov, Tsentral'nyi voenno-morskoi muzei)
GARF	State Archive of the Russian Federation (Gosudarstvennyi arkhiv Rossiiskoi Federatsii)
KP	*Komsomol'skaia pravda*
KZ	*Krasnaia zvezda*
LG	*Literaturnaia gazeta*
LGZh	*Liudi, gody, zhizn'*
ND	*Novomirskii dnevnik*
NM	*Novyi mir*
ORF GLM	Department of Manuscript Collections, State Museum of Literature (Otdel rukopisnykh fondov, Gosudarstvennyi literaturnyi muzei)
RGAE	Russian State Archive of the Economy (Rossiiskii gosudarstvennyi arkhiv ekonomiki)
RGALI	Russian State Archive of Literature and Art (Rossiiskii gosudartsvennyi arkhiv literatury i iskusstva)
RGANI	Russian State Archive of Contemporary History (Rossiiskii gosudartsvennyi arkhiv noveishei istorii)
RGASPI	Russian State Archive of Socio-Political History (Rossiiskii gosudartsvennyi arkhiv sotsial'no-politicheskoi istorii)
RT	"Iz rabochikh tetradei (1953–1960)"
RT-60	"Rabochie tetradi 60-kh godov"

TsAOPIM Central Archive of Socio-Political History of Moscow (Tsentral'nyi arkhiv obshchestvenno-politicheskoi istorii Moskvy)

TsGALI SPb Central State Archive of Literature and Art, Saint Petersburg (Tsentral'nyi gosudarstvennyi arkhiv literatury i iskusstva Sankt-Peterburga)

Introduction

For a detailed statistical picture of the *Novyi mir* reading audience, analyzed by geographical distribution, gender, age, ethnicity, occupation, party membership, and several other categories, see Denis Kozlov, "The Readers of *Novyi mir*, 1948–1969: A Social Portrait," at http://www.nceeer.org/papers.html.

1. Vladimir Nabokov, "Speak, Memory: An Autobiography Revisited," in Nabokov, *Novels and Memoirs, 1941–1951* (New York: Library of America, 1996), 585.
2. Ibid., 584–585.
3. For this, and for other uses of Nabokov's metaphor, see Cristina Vatulescu, *Police Aesthetics: Literature, Film, and the Secret Police in Soviet Times* (Stanford: Stanford University Press, 2010), esp. 1–26. While I open with the same metaphor, my book is, of course, a very different project.
4. See, e.g., Andrei Zorin, *Kormia dvuglavogo orla: Literatura i gosudarstvennaia ideologiia v Rossii v poslednei treti XVIII—pervoi treti XIX veka* (Moscow: Novoe literaturnoe obozrenie, 2001); Mark Al'tshuller, *Beseda liubitelei russkogo slova: U istokov russkogo slavianofil'stva* (Moscow: Novoe literaturnoe obozrenie, 2007); Maria Maiofis, *Vozzvanie k Evrope: Literaturnoe obshchestvo "Arzamas" i rossiiskii modernizatsionnyi proekt 1815–1818 godov* (Moscow: Novoe literaturnoe obozrenie, 2008); Mikhail Berg, *Literaturokratiia: Problema prisvoeniia i pereraspredeleniia vlasti v literature* (Moscow: Novoe literaturnoe obozrenie, 2000), 183–205.
5. Irina Paperno, *Chernyshevsky and the Age of Realism: A Study in the Semiotics of Behavior* (Stanford: Stanford University Press, 1988), 9–12, 27, 38, 51, 221. See also Jeffrey Brooks, "Readers and Reading at the End of the Tsarist Era," in *Literature and Society in Imperial Russia, 1800–1914*, ed. William Mills Todd III (Stanford: Stanford University Press, 1978), 97–150; Brooks, *When Russia Learned to Read: Literacy and Popular Literature, 1861–1917* (Princeton: Princeton University Press, 1985), 295–352; Klaus Mehnert, *The Russians and Their Favorite Books* (Stanford: Hoover Institution Press, 1983), 15; Catriona Kelly and David Shepherd, "Introduction: Literature, History, and Culture," in *Constructing Russian Culture in the Age of Revolutions*, ed. Kelly and Shepherd (Oxford: Oxford University Press, 1998), 1–7, esp. 1–2; Louise McReynolds and Cathy Popkin, "The Objective Eye

and the Common Good," in Kelly and Shepherd, *Constructing Russian Culture*, 57–98, esp. 89, 93–98; Petr Vail' and Aleksandr Genis, "Rodnaia rech'," in Vail' and Genis, *Sobranie sochinenii v dvukh tomakh*, vol. 1 (Ekaterinburg: U-Faktoriia, 2003), 5–271; Kathleen Parthé, *Russia's Dangerous Texts: Politics between the Lines* (New Haven: Yale University Press, 2004), esp. 1–50.

6. Vera Dunham, *In Stalin's Time: Middleclass Values in Soviet Fiction* (Cambridge: Cambridge University Press, 1976), esp. 24–38; Katerina Clark, *The Soviet Novel: History as Ritual* (Chicago: University of Chicago Press, 1981); Régine Robin, *Socialist Realism: An Impossible Aesthetic* (Stanford: Stanford University Press, 1992); Thomas Lahusen, *How Life Writes the Book: Real Socialism and Socialist Realism in Stalin's Russia* (Ithaca: Cornell University Press, 1997); Berg, *Literaturokratiia*, 61–75, 220–221.
7. Matthew Lenoe, *Closer to the Masses: Stalinist Culture, Social Revolution, and Soviet Newspapers* (Cambridge, Mass.: Harvard University Press, 2004), 212–254, esp. 239.
8. Sheila Fitzpatrick, "Cultural Orthodoxies under Stalin," in Fitzpatrick, *The Cultural Front: Power and Culture in Revolutionary Russia* (Ithaca: Cornell University Press, 1992), 238–256, esp. 248; Fitzpatrick, "Becoming Cultured: Socialist Realism and the Representations of Privilege and Taste," ibid., 216–237, esp. 224–225; Evgeny Dobrenko, *Formovka sovetskogo chitatelia: Sotsial'nye i esteticheskie predposylki retseptsii sovetskoi literatury* (Saint Petersburg: Akademicheskii proekt, 1997); Stephen Lovell, *The Russian Reading Revolution: Print Culture in the Soviet and Post-Soviet Eras* (New York: St. Martin's Press, in association with the School of Slavonic and East European Studies, University of London, 2000), esp. 10–44; Catriona Kelly and Vadim Volkov, "Direct Desires: *Kul'turnost'* and Consumption," in Kelly and Shepherd, *Constructing Russian Culture*, 291–313, esp. 300–304; Volkov, "The Concept of *Kul'turnost'*: Notes on the Stalinist Civilizing Process," in *Stalinism: New Directions*, ed. Sheila Fitzpatrick (New York: Routledge, 2000), 210–230, esp. 223–225.
9. Abram Reitblat, "Chitatel'skaia auditoriia v nachale XX veka," in Reitblat, *Ot Bovy k Bal'montu i drugie raboty po istoricheskoi sotsiologii russkoi literatury* (Moscow: Novoe literaturnoe obozrenie, 2009), 278–280.
10. I borrow the term "reading revolution" from the title of Lovell's book, *The Russian Reading Revolution.*
11. Boris Raymond, *Krupskaia and Soviet Russian Librarianship, 1917–1939* (Metuchen, N.J.: Scarecrow Press, 1979); Dobrenko, *Formovka;* B. V. Biriukov, "'Tsel' vpolne prakticheskaia. Tol'ko i vsego.' Repressirovannaia kniga: Istoki iavleniia," in *Chelovek chitaiushchii. Homo legens-2*, ed. Biriukov and I. A. Butenko (Moscow: Rossiiskii institut kul'turologii, 2000), 87–121.

12. Lovell, *The Russian Reading Revolution.*
13. See, e.g., Valerii Prozorov, *Chitatel' i literaturnyi protsess* (Saratov: Izdatel'stvo Saratovskogo universiteta, 1975), 118–132; Brooks, *When Russia Learned to Read,* 295–352.
14. Not incidentally, one of the most influential studies of late-Stalin and post-Stalin society adopts precisely this method, relying on literary sources to measure changes in mass political consciousness: Elena Zubkova, *Obshchestvo i reformy: 1945–1964* (Moscow: Rossiia molodaia, 1993), published in English as *Russia after the War: Hopes, Illusions, and Disappointments, 1945–1957* (Armonk, N.Y.: M. E. Sharpe, 1998); see also Zubkova, *Poslevoennoe sovetskoe obshchestvo: Politika i povsednevnost'. 1945–1953* (Moscow: ROSSPEN, 2000).
15. Robert A. Maguire, *Red Virgin Soil: Soviet Literature in the 1920s* (Princeton: Princeton University Press, 1968), xi; Deborah Martinsen, ed., *Literary Journals in Imperial Russia* (Cambridge: Cambridge University Press, 1997).
16. Maguire, *Red Virgin Soil,* 37–38, 42–43, 60, 69–70, 415.
17. Ibid., 42–43, 414–415. This paradigm applies predominantly to the times when censorship existed and literature remained a concern for Russia's political authorities. The post-Soviet decades belong to a different literary landscape, in which the thick journal has largely lost its place. See the Epilogue to this volume.
18. Abram Reitblat, "Tolstyi literaturnyi zhurnal i ego publika," in Reitblat, *Ot Bovy k Bal'montu,* 38–53, esp. 40, 42–45; see also Robert Belknap, "Survey of Russian Journals, 1840–1880," in Martinsen, *Literary Journals,* 91–116; Victor Terras, "Belinsky the Journalist and Russian Literature," in ibid., 117–128; Alexis Pogorelskin, "The Messenger of Europe," in ibid., 129–149.
19. Vsevolod Troitskii, *Kniga pokolenii: O romane I. S. Turgeneva "Ottsy i deti"* (Moscow: Kniga, 1979); S. E. Shatalov, "Roman Turgeneva 'Ottsy i deti' v literaturno-obshchestvennom dvizhenii," in *Literaturnye proizvedeniia v dvizhenii epoch,* ed. N. V. Os'makov (Moscow: Nauka, 1979), 75–131.
20. Brooks, *When Russia Learned to Read;* Reitblat, *Ot Bovy k Bal'montu;* Louise McReynolds, *The News under Russia's Old Regime: The Development of a Mass-Circulation Press* (Princeton: Princeton University Press, 1991); Joan Delaney Grossman, "Rise and Decline of the 'Literary' Journal: 1880–1917," in Martinsen, *Literary Journals,* 171–196.
21. Maguire, *Red Virgin Soil,* 68–71; Katerina Clark, "The 'Quiet Revolution' in Intellectual Life," in *Russia in the Era of NEP: Explorations in Soviet Society and Culture,* ed. Sheila Fitzpatrick, Alexander Rabinowitch, and Richard Stites (Bloomington: Indiana University Press, 1991), 210–227.

22. On this guidance, see Reitblat, "Tolstyi literaturnyi zhurnal," esp. 42–46.
23. See Mariia Zezina, *Sovetskaia khudozhestvennaia intelligentsiia i vlast' v 1950e–60e gody* (Moscow: Dialog MGU, 1999).
24. Quoted in Lidiia Chukovskaia, *Zapiski ob Anne Akhmatovoi* (Paris: YMCA Press, 1980), vol. 2, 137.
25. Among the literature on the Thaw, see, e.g., Vladislav Zubok, *Zhivago's Children: The Last Russian Intelligentsia* (Cambridge, Mass.: Harvard University Press, 2009); Stephen V. Bittner, *The Many Lives of Khrushchev's Thaw: Experience and Memory in Moscow's Arbat* (Ithaca: Cornell University Press, 2008); Aleksandr Pyzhikov, *Khrushchevskaia ottepel', 1953–1964* (Moscow: Olma-Press, 2002); Pyzhikov, *Opyt modernizatsii sovetskogo obshchestva v 1953–1964 godakh: Obshchestvenno-politicheskii aspekt* (Moscow: Gamma, 1998); Vladimir Kozlov, *Massovye besporiadki v SSSR pri Khrushcheve i Brezhneve* (Novosibirsk: Sibirskii khronograf, 1999); Natalia Lebina and Aleksandr Chistikov, *Obyvatel' i reformy: Kartiny povsednevnoi zhizni gorozhan v gody NEPa i khrushchevskogo desiatiletiia* (Saint Petersburg: Dmitrii Bulanin, 2003); Zubkova, *Obschestvo i reformy*; Donald Filtzer, *The Khrushchev Era: De-Stalinisation and the Limits of Reform in the USSR, 1953–1964* (London: Macmillan, 1993); Filtzer, *Soviet Workers and De-Stalinization: The Consolidation of the Modern System of Soviet Production Relations, 1953–1964* (Cambridge: Cambridge University Press, 1992); Thomas C. Wolfe, *Governing Soviet Journalism: The Press and the Socialist Person after Stalin* (Bloomington: Indiana University Press, 2005); Mariia Zezina, "Shokovaia terapiia: Ot 1953-go k 1956 godu," *Otechestvennaia istoriia* 2 (1995): 121–135; Zezina, *Sovetskaia khudozhestvennaia intelligentsia i vlast'*; Oleg Leibovich, *Reforma i modernizatsiia v 1953–1964 gg.* (Perm': Istoriia otechestva XX vek, 1993); Liubov' Sidorova, *Ottepel' v istoricheskoi nauke: Sovetskaia istoriografiia pervogo poslestalinskogo desiatiletiia* (Moscow: Pamiatniki istoricheskoi mysli, 1997); Iurii Aksiutin, *Khrushchevskaia ottepel' i obshchestvennye nastroeniia v SSSR v 1953–1964 gg.* (Moscow: ROSSPEN, 2004); N. I. Barsukov, "XX s"ezd v retrospective Khrushcheva," *Otechestvennaia istoriia* 6 (1996): 169–177; V. V. Zhuravlev, ed., *XX s"ezd KPSS i ego istoricheskie real'nosti* (Moscow: Izdatel'stvo politicheskoi literatury, 1991), 169–177; Roger Markwick, *Rewriting History in Soviet Russia: The Politics of Revisionist Historiography, 1956–1974* (New York: Palgrave, 2001).
26. Miriam Dobson, *Khrushchev's Cold Summer: Gulag Returnees, Crime, and the Fate of Reform after Stalin* (Ithaca: Cornell University Press, 2009); Polly Jones, "Strategies of De-mythologization in Post-Stalinism and Post-Communism: A Comparison of De-Stalinisation and De-Leninisation," D.Phil. thesis, Oxford University, 2003.

27. Anne Applebaum, *Gulag: A History* (New York: Doubleday, 2003), esp. 564–586; Catherine Merridale, *Night of Stone: Death and Memory in Twentieth-Century Russia* (New York: Viking, 2001); Nanci Adler, *The Gulag Survivor: Beyond the Soviet System* (New Brunswick, N.J.: Transaction Publishers, 2001). For a contrary argument, see Kathleen E. Smith, *Remembering Stalin's Victims: Popular Memory and the End of the USSR* (Ithaca: Cornell University Press, 1996, repr. 2009).
28. Orlando Figes, *The Whisperers: Private Life in Stalin's Russia* (New York: Metropolitan Books, 2007), esp. 597–656; Figes, "Private Life in Stalin's Russia: Family Narratives, Memory and Oral History," *History Workshop Journal* 65 (Spring 2008): 117–135.
29. On the rise of the discourse on legality and rights during the late Soviet decades, see Benjamin Nathans, "The Dictatorship of Reason: Aleksandr Vol'pin and the Idea of Rights under 'Developed Socialism,'" *Slavic Review* 66, no. 4 (2007): 630–663; Nathans, "Soviet Rights-Talk in the Post-Stalin Era," in *Human Rights in the Twentieth Century*, ed. Stefan-Ludwig Hoffmann (Cambridge: Cambridge University Press, 2011): 166–190.
30. Henry Rousso, *The Vichy Syndrome: History and Memory in France since 1944* (Cambridge, Mass.: Harvard University Press, 1991), 99; Tony Judt, *Postwar: A History of Europe since 1945* (New York: Penguin Press, 2005), 300–301, 416–418, 810; Herbert Marcuse, *Legacies of Dachau: The Uses and Abuses of a Concentration Camp, 1933–2001* (Cambridge: Cambridge University Press, 2001), 199–220; Rebecca Wittmann, *Beyond Justice: The Auschwitz Trial* (Cambridge, Mass.: Harvard University Press, 2005), 13, 246–247.
31. For analyses of this issue in Western Europe, see, e.g., Luisa Passerini, *Fascism in Popular Memory: The Cultural Experiences of the Turin Working Class* (Cambridge: Cambridge University Press, 1987); Rousso, *The Vichy Syndrome*; Jeffrey Herf, *Divided Memory: The Nazi Past in the Two Germanys* (Cambridge, Mass.: Harvard University Press, 1997), 6–7, 274–275; Konrad Jarausch, "Critical Memory and Civil Society: The Impact of the 1960s on German Debates about the Past," in *Coping with the Past: West German Debates on Nazism and Generational Conflict, 1955–1975*, ed. Philipp Gassert and Alan E. Steinweis (New York: Berghahn Books, 2006), 11–30, esp. 19; for the memories recorded after 1990, see Eric A. Johnson and Karl-Heinz Reuband, *What We Knew: Terror, Mass Murder and Everyday Life in Nazi Germany: An Oral History* (Cambridge, Mass.: Basic Books, 2005), esp. xvi, xxii, 387–398.
32. For Western Europe, see, e.g., Herf, *Divided Memory*, 6–7, 11, 212, 236–37, 243–46, 274–275, 334–342; Jan-Werner Müller, *A Dangerous Mind: Carl Schmitt in Post-War European Thought* (New Haven: Yale University Press, 2003), 63–68; Wittmann, *Beyond Justice*, 48–53; Sarah Farmer, *Martyred Village: Commemorating the 1944 Massacre at Oradour-sur-Glane* (Berkeley:

University of California Press, 1999), 135–170; Rousso, *The Vichy Syndrome*, 96–97; Samuel Moyn, *A Holocaust Controversy: The Treblinka Affair in Postwar France* (Waltham: Brandeis University Press, 2005), 142–149. For the Soviet Union, see, e.g., Denis Kozlov, "'I Have Not Read, but I Will Say': Soviet Literary Audiences and Changing Ideas of Social Membership, 1958–1966," *Kritika: Explorations in Russian and Eurasian History* 7, no. 3 (2006): 557–597. On the late Soviet ideas of rights, see Nathans, "The Dictatorship of Reason."

33. Marcuse, *Legacies of Dachau*, 200–201; Jarausch, "Critical Memory," 20; Wittmann, *Beyond Justice*, 247, 269–271.
34. For comparable dilemmas in other contexts, such as post–World War II Europe and postrevolutionary France, see, e.g., Herf, *Divided Memory*. See also Luc Huyse, "The Criminal Justice System as a Political Actor in Regime Transitions: The Case of Belgium, 1944–50"; Peter Romijn, "'Restoration of Confidence': The Purge of Local Government in the Netherlands as a Problem of Postwar Reconstruction"; Sarah Farmer, "Postwar Justice in France: Bordeaux 1953"; and Tony Judt, "The Past Is Another Country: Myth and Memory in Postwar Europe," in *The Politics of Retribution in Europe: World War II and Its Aftermath*, ed. István Deák, Jan T. Gross, and Tony Judt (Princeton: Princeton University Press, 2000; Bronislaw Baczko, *Ending the Terror: The French Revolution after Robespierre* (Cambridge: Cambridge University Press, 1989).
35. Jochen Hellbeck, *Revolution on My Mind: Writing a Diary under Stalin* (Cambridge, Mass.: Harvard University Press, 2006); Hellbeck, "Working, Struggling, Becoming: Stalin-Era Autobiographical Texts," *Russian Review* 60, no. 3 (2001): 340–359; Hellbeck, "Fashioning the Stalinist Soul: The Diary of Stepan Podlubnyi (1931–1939)," *Jahrbücher für Geschichte Osteuropas* 44, no. 3 (1996): 344–373; Igal Halfin and Jochen Hellbeck, "Rethinking the Stalinist Subject: Stephen Kotkin's *Magnetic Mountain* and the State of Soviet Historical Studies," *Jahrbücher für Geschichte Osteuropas* 44, no. 3 (1996): 456–463; Igal Halfin, *From Darkness to Light: Class, Consciousness, and Salvation in Revolutionary Russia* (Pittsburgh: University of Pittsburgh Press, 2000); Halfin, *Terror in My Soul: Communist Autobiographies on Trial* (Cambridge, Mass.: Harvard University Press, 2003); Halfin, *Stalinist Confessions: Messianism and Terror at the Leningrad Communist University* (Pittsburgh: University of Pittsburgh Press, 2009).
36. Hellbeck, *Revolution on My Mind*, 9; for the term "purificatory zeal," see 96.
37. A different model of the disintegration of the Soviet language, proposed by Alexei Yurchak, suggests that late Soviet individuals increasingly wanted to be outside the media language altogether, perceiving it, together with the entire panoply of political rituals that it accompanied, as meaningless and void.

Yurchak argues that the language became ossified following Stalin's death in March 1953, largely because there was no longer a single undisputed linguistic authority that could give it a dynamic interpretation, i.e., Stalin himself. The endless repetition of the same verbal formulas drained them of meaning. See Alexei Yurchak, *Everything Was Forever, Until It Was No More: the Last Soviet Generation* (Princeton: Princeton University Press, 2006), 36–76. While not denying this interpretation, I also see other reasons why the Soviet language lost credence—first of all being its inability to describe, let alone explain, the phenomenon of mass violence, central to the country's twentieth-century history. Also, not every late Soviet person practiced political absenteeism. While the desire to "be outside" politics well describes many young people of the 1970s, numerous other individuals did take contemporary issues and political conversations seriously. Close involvement in political life characterized not only dissidents but also a great many other citizens.

38. Dina Spechler, *Permitted Dissent in the USSR:* Novyi mir *and the Soviet Regime* (New York: Praeger, 1982); Grigorii Svirskii, *A History of Post-War Soviet Writing: The Literature of Moral Opposition* (Ann Arbor: Ardis, 1981), in Russian as Svirskii, *Na lobnom meste: Literatura nravstvennogo soprotivleniia, 1946–1986* (Moscow: Kruk, 1998); Edith Rogovin Frankel, Novyi mir: *A Case Study in the Politics of Literature, 1952–1958* (Cambridge: Cambridge University Press, 1981); Zezina, *Sovetskaia khudozhestvennaia intelligentsiia*; Wolfram Eggeling, *Politika i kul'tura pri Khrushcheve i Brezhneve. 1953–1970 gg.* (Moscow: AIRO-XX, 1999).

39. Nelly Bioul-Zedginidze, *Literaturnaia kritika zhurnala "Novyi mir"* (Moscow: Pervopechatnik, 1996); Marina Askol'dova-Lund, "Siuzhet proryva: Kak nachinalsia "Novyi mir" Tvardovskogo," *Svobodnaia mysl'*, no. 1 (2002): 72–82, and no. 2 (2002): 70–80.

40. Among hundreds of publications on Solzhenitsyn, there are at least two major biographies, with a quarter of a century understandably separating the American from the Russian one: Michael Scammel, *Solzhenitsyn: A Biography* (New York: Norton, 1984), and Liudmila Saraskina, *Aleksandr Solzhenitsyn* (Moscow: Molodaia gvardiia, 2008). Tvardovskii has been the subject of extensive research in Soviet and post-Soviet Russia (but so far not in the West)—as a poet and lately also as an editor and thinker. For the early studies of his poetry, see, e.g., Elena Liubareva, *Aleksandr Tvardovskii: Kritiko-biograficheskii ocherk* (Moscow: Sovetskii pisatel', 1957); Liubareva, *Epos A. T. Tvardovskogo* (Moscow: Vysshaia shkola, 1982); Andrei Turkov, *Aleksandr Tvardovskii* (Moscow: Gosudarstvennoe izdatel'stvo khudozhestvennoi literatury, 1960); Turkov, *Aleksandr Tvardovskii* (Moscow: Molodaia gvardiia, 2010); Petr Roshchin, *Aleksandr Tvardovskii* (Moscow: Prosveshchenie, 1966); Aleksandr Muraviev, *Tvorchestvo A. T. Tvardovskogo: Posobie dlia uchitelei*

(Moscow: Prosveshchenie, 1981); Andrei Kulinich, *Aleksandr Tvardovskii: Ocherk zhizni i tvorchestva* (Kiev: Vyshcha shkola, 1988); *Tvorchestvo Aleksandra Tvardovskogo: Issledovaniia i materialy*, ed. P. S. Vykhodtsev and N. A. Groznova (Leningrad: Nauka, 1989); Iurii Ivanov, *Aleksandr Tvardovskii: Ocherk tvorchestva* (Saint Petersburg: RGPU im. A. I. Gertsena, 1999). For archival studies integrating Tvardovskii's poetic, editorial, and reflective themes, see Tat'iana Snigireva, *A. T. Tvardovskii: Poet i ego epokha* (Ekaterinburg: Izdatel'stvo Ural'skogo universiteta, 1997); Turkov, *Aleksandr Tvardovskii* (Moscow: Molodaia gvardiia, 2010). For a thorough chronicle of Tvardovskii's life, see Regina Romanova, *Aleksandr Tvardovskii: Trudy i dni* (Moscow: Vodolei, 2006). For discussions enriched by personal familiarity, see, especially, Aleksei Kondratovich, *Aleksandr Tvardovskii: Poeziia i lichnost'* (Moscow: Khudozhestvennaia literatura, 1978); Adrian Makedonov, *Tvorcheskii put' Tvardovskogo: Doma i dorogi* (Moscow: Khudozhestvennaia literatura, 1981); Svirskii, *Na lobnom meste*.

41. Lazar' Lazarev, *Konstantin Simonov: Ocherk zhizni i tvorchestva* (Moscow: Khudozhestvennaia literatura, 1985); Aleksandr Karaganov, *Konstantin Simonov vblizi i na rasstoianii* (Moscow: Sovetskii pisatel', 1987); Boris Pankin, *Chetyre Ia Konstantina Simonova* (Moscow: Voskresen'e, 1999); Figes, *The Whisperers*.
42. Nelly Bioul-Zedginidze's work, for example, is based on extensive interviews with former editors and writers from Tvardovskii's *Novyi mir*. The number of published memoirs and diaries that touch on *Novyi mir* is enormous: e.g., Aleksandr Solzhenitsyn, *Bodalsia telenok s dubom: Ocherki literaturnoi zhizni* (Paris: YMCA-Press, 1975); Vladimir Lakshin, *Solzhenitsyn, Tvardovsky, and Novy mir* (Cambridge, Mass.: MIT Press, 1980); Lakshin, *Novyi mir vo vremena Khrushcheva: Dnevnik i poputnoe (1953–64)* (Moscow: Knizhnaia palata, 1991); Lakshin, *Golosa i litsa* (Moscow: Geleos, 2001); Lakshin, *Solzhenitsyn i koleso istorii* (Moscow: Veche, 2008); Aleksei Kondratovich, *Novomirskii dnevnik (1967–1970)* (Moscow: Sovetskii pisatel', 1991); Natalia Bianki, *K. Simonov, A. Tvardovskii v "Novom mire": Vospominaniia* (Moscow: Violanta, 1999); Yuri Trifonov, "Zapiski soseda" [1972], in *Rasskazy. Povesti. Roman. Vospominaniia. Esse* (Ekaterinburg: U-Faktoriia, 1999), 658–739; Boris Zaks, "Interviews" (typed transcript), Archive of Yulia Borisovna Zaks; Boris Zaks, "Censorship at the Editorial Desk," in *The Red Pencil: Artists, Scholars, and Censors in the USSR*, ed. Marianna Tax Choldin and Maurice Friedberg (Boston: Unwin Hyman, 1989), 155–161.
43. Interview with Sof'ia Grigor'evna Karaganova, 24 February 2002. Karaganova, who for many years headed the poetry section of *Novyi mir* under Simonov and Tvardovskii, remembers that it was a general rule of the editorial board to preserve all readers' letters. For Tvardovskii's own statement of this policy, see his "Po sluchaiu iubileia," *Novyi mir* (hereafter *NM*) 1 (January 1965): 15.
44. RGALI, f. 1702, op. 9, d. 70, ll. 43–46 (November 1962).

45. For example, I found far fewer responses to Vasilii Grossman's 1952 *Za pravoe delo (For the Just Cause)* than would be expected, judging by the fame of that book. RGALI, f. 1702, op. 6, d. 55, ll. 1–88; see also Semen Lipkin, "Zhizn' i sud'ba Vasiliia Grossmana," in Lipkin, *Kvadriga* (Moscow: Agraf, Knizhnyi sad, 1997), 536–537. For responses to Grossman's sequel, *Life and Fate,* see RGALI, f. 1710, op. 2, d. 14, ll. 7–7ob, 10–14ob, 15–15ob, 17–18ob. I have also located surprisingly few responses to Valentin Ovechkin's important sketch *Raionnye budni (District Routine)* and its four sequels, published in 1952–1956. RGALI, f. 1702, op. 6, d. 54, ll. 35–55; op. 6, d. 80, ll. 13–13ob; op. 8, d. 9, ll. 8, 20–22; op. 8, d. 145, ll. 8–12, 14–15. There must have been many more letters about Ovechkin's sketches: see Ovechkin's letters to his son, Valentin Valentinovich Ovechkin, of 20 March and 17 April 1954, in Ovechkin, *Stat'i, dnevniki, pis'ma* (Moscow: Sovetskii pisatel', 1979), 315–316. Unexpectedly few responses have also surfaced for General Aleksandr Gorbatov's 1964 memoir *Gody i voiny (Years and Wars)* and Yurii Dombrovskii's 1964 novella *Khranitel' drevnostei (The Keeper of Antiquities).*
46. Nikolai Mitrokhin, *Russkaia partiia: Dvizhenie russkikh natsionalistov v 1953–1985 gg.* (Moscow: Novoe literaturnoe obozrenie, 2003), 31–32; Figes, *The Whisperers,* xxxii–xxxvii. Doubting the validity of Soviet written sources, these historians choose instead to rely on oral history. Without indulging in a debate about the relative value of written documents versus interviews, I treat both groups of sources as useful and mutually complementary.
47. Compare a similar idea implied in Raul Hilberg, *Perpetrators, Victims, Bystanders: The Jewish Catastrophe 1933–1945* (New York: Harper Collins, 1992), 195–268.
48. Alla Verkhovskaia, *Pis'mo v redaktsiiu i chitatel'* (Moscow: Izdatel'stvo Moskovskogo universiteta, 1972), 28. What this study did establish was that authors of letters to the press had a higher overall level of social activity. More often than others, they spoke at public gatherings, participated in local self-government, contributed to factory and so-called wall newspapers (handmade large-format postings produced in a single copy by amateur teams and displayed in common areas), and so on. They also, apparently, had a higher-than-average level of education. Ibid., 149–162, 164–166, 168, 177. If this is so, then the letter writers appear to have belonged to a part of society that was both best informed about and most responsive to political developments. Interesting as they are, these findings are of relatively little use for intellectual history: concerned with patterns of public behavior rather than individual biography, this study did not undertake a close reading of the letters' most important part, their texts.
49. E. M. Sakharova, "Glazami chitatelei," in *Chekhov i ego vremia,* ed. L. D. Opul'skaia et al. (Moscow: Nauka, 1977), 332–347, here 343, 345.

50. T. G. Morozova, "Tvorchestvo Korolenko v vospriiatii chitatelei," in *Istoriko-funktsional'noe izuchenie russkoi literatury: Mezhvuzovskii sbornik nauchnykh trudov*, ed. N. V. Os'makov (Moscow: MGPI im. V. I. Lenina, 1984), 120–133.
51. T. V. Romanova, "Otkliki pervykh russkikh chitatelei 'Voskreseniia' (Po materialam Otdela rukopisei Gosudarstvennogo muzeia L. N. Tolstogo)," in *Roman L. N. Tolstogo "Voskresenie": Istoriko-funktsional'noe issledovanie*, ed. K. N. Lomunov (Moscow: Nauka, 1991): 72–81, here 78.
52. "Vospominaniia o Turgeneve N. A. Ostrovskoi (neizvestnye stranitsy)," in *Turgenev i ego sovremenniki*, ed. M. P. Alekseev (Leningrad: Nauka, 1977), 196.
53. E.g., V. A. Zhdanov, "Iz pisem k Tolstomu (Po materialam tolstovskogo arkhiva)," *L. N. Tolstoy: V 2-kh knigakh.* Literaturnoe nasledstvo, vol. 37/38 (Moscow: Izdatel'stvo Akademii nauk SSSR, 1939), book 2, 369–396; Boris Meilakh, *Ukhod i smert' L'va Tolstogo* (Moscow: Khudozhestvennaia literatura, 1979), 155–196; Romanova, "Otkliki"; V. M. Rodionova, "L. N. Tolstoi i A. P. Chekhov i ikh chitateli iz naroda," in *Istoriko-funktsional'noe izuchenie russkoi literatury*, ed. N. V. Os'makov, 147–164; Sakharova, "Glazami chitatelei."
54. Zhdanov, "Iz pisem k Tolstomu"; Meilakh, *Ukhod i smert'*, 155–196; Romanova, "Otkliki"; see also Gennadii Ishchuk, *Lev Tolstoy: Dialog s chitatelem* (Moscow: Kniga, 1984).
55. Igor' Volgin, "Pis'ma chitatelei k F. M. Dostoevskomu," *Voprosy literatury* 9 (September 1971): 173–196; Volgin, *Dostoevskii—zhurnalist ("Dnevnik pisatelia" i russkaia obshchetsvennost')* (Moscow: MGU, 1982), 41–65; Volgin, *Vozvrashchenie bileta: Paradoksy natsional'nogo samosozmnaniia* (Moscow: Grant, 2004), 56–93; Deborah Martinsen, "Dostoevsky's *Diary of a Writer:* Journal of the 1870s," in Martinsen, *Literary Journals*, 150–168.
56. E.g., Maurice Friedberg, *Russian Classics in Soviet Jackets* (New York: Columbia University Press, 1962).
57. Vladimir Lakshin, "Pisatel' chitatel', kritik. Stat'ia pervaia," *NM*, no. 4 (1965): 222–240; Lakshin, "Pisatel' chitatel', kritik. Stat'ia vtoraia," *NM*, no. 8 (1966): 216–256.
58. Lenoe, *Closer to the Masses*, 83.
59. Ibid., 70–100, 158–159; Sheila Fitzpatrick, "Supplicants and Citizens: Public Letter-Writing in Soviet Russia in the 1930s," *Slavic Review* 55, no. 1 (Spring 1996): 78–105.
60. RGALI, f. 634, op. 4, d. 684, ll. 13, 20–24, 29–30 (*Literaturnaia gazeta*, 1954); GARF, f. 1244, op. 1, d. 157, ll. 135–173 (*Izvestiia*, 1955); TsAOPIM, f. 3226, op. 1, d. 37, ll. 49–51 (*Pravda*, 1952); ibid., d. 56, ll. 29–51 (*Pravda*, 1956); ibid., d. 60, ll. 4–5 (*Pravda*, 1958); ibid., d. 71, ll. 23–24 (*Pravda*, 1963); ibid., d. 72, ll. 69–112 (*Pravda*, 1964); ibid., d. 78, ll. 49, 57–58, 135–151 (*Pravda*, 1967).

61. RGASPI, f. M-1, op. 32, d. 764, ll. 7, 38.
62. E.g., Vladislav Matusevich, *Zapiski sovetskogo redaktora* (Moscow: Novoe literaturnoe obozrenie, 2000), 18–19. Compare Karin Wahl-Jorgensen, *Journalists and the Public: Newsroom Culture, Letters to the Editor, and Democracy* (Cresskill, N.J.: Hampton Press, 2007).
63. RGALI, f. 634, op. 4, d. 676, l. 27 (2 February 1954).
64. Fitzpatrick, "Supplicants and Citizens"; see 79 for her definition of public letter writing.
65. There is an interesting difference between the letters written to *Novyi mir* in the 1950s and 1960s and the citizens' letters of the 1930s that Fitzpatrick has analyzed. While many of the letter writers of the 1930s desired to have their letters published, that does not seem to have been the case for *Novyi mir*'s readers during the Thaw. This may have to do with the different nature of the press organs with which the readers were corresponding: a newspaper versus a renowned literary journal. Fitzpatrick, "Supplicants and Citizens," 93–94, 104.
66. On this see, e.g., Anna Krylova, "The Tenacious Liberal Subject in Soviet Studies," *Kritika: Explorations in Russian and Eurasian History* 1, no. 1 (Winter 2000): 119–146.
67. Wahl-Jorgensen, *Journalists and the Public*, 20–28. See also Seyla Benhabib, "Toward a Deliberative Model of Democratic Legitimacy," in *Democracy and Difference: Contesting the Boundaries of the Political*, ed. Benhabib (Princeton: Princeton University Press, 1996), 67–95; T. Christiano, "The Significance of Public Deliberation," in *Deliberative Democracy: Essays on Reason and Politics*, ed. James Bohman and William Rehg (Cambridge, Mass.: MIT Press, 1997); M. Warren, "Deliberative Democracy," in *Democratic Theory Today: Challenges for the 21st Century*, ed. April Carter and Geoffrey Stokes (Malden, Mass.: Blackwell Publishers, 2002), 173–202; Tanni Haas and Linda Steiner, "Public Journalism as a Journalism of Publics: Implications of the Habermas-Fraser Debate for Public Journalism," in *Journalism* 2, no. 2 (2001): 123–147; James S. Fishkin, *When the People Speak: Deliberative Democracy and Public Consultation* (Oxford: Oxford University Press, 2009).
68. See, e.g., Dobrenko, *Formovka sovetskogo chitatelia*. For a critique of Dobrenko's concept of the Soviet library as a primarily propagandistic, totalitarian institution, see Efim Dinershtein, "Kniga v sovetskom obshchestve" [1997], in Dinershtein, *Rossiiskoe knigoizdanie (konets XVIII–XX v.): Izbrannye stat'i* (Moscow: Nauka, 2004), 442–457, esp. 443–445, 449.
69. Thomas Lahusen's study of the production and reception of Vasilii Azhaev's novel *Far from Moscow* in the late Stalin years suggests that readers did not necessarily conform to all the standards and language that writers projected on them. Lahusen, *How Life Writes the Book*, 151–178.

70. Stanley Fish, "Literature in the Reader: Affective Stylistics," in *Reader-Response Criticism: From Formalism to Post-Structuralism,* ed. Jane P. Tompkins (Baltimore: Johns Hopkins University Press, 1980), 70–100.
71. Joan W. Scott, "The Evidence of Experience," *Critical Inquiry* 17 (Summer 1991): 773–797, esp. 797 (quotation; emphasis in the original). For a discussion of Scott's concept and the scholarly criticism it faced, see Martin Jay, *Songs of Experience: Modern American and European Variations on a Universal Theme* (Berkeley: University of California Press, 2005), 249–255; John Zammito, "Reading 'Experience': The Debate in Intellectual History among Scott, Toews and LaCapra," in *Reclaiming Identity: Realist Theory and the Predicament of Postmodernism,* ed. Paula M. L. Moya and Michael R. Hames-Garcia (Berkeley: University of California Press, 2000), 302–303.
72. Pierre Nora, "Between Memory and History: *Les Lieux de Mémoire,*" *Representations* 26 (Spring 1989): 7–24; Maurice Halbwachs, "Historical Memory and Collective Memory," in Halbwachs, *The Collective Memory* (New York: Harper and Row, 1980), 50–87; Halbwachs, *On Collective Memory* (Chicago: University of Chicago Press, 1992).
73. To some observers, early twenty-first-century Germany appears to be a culture in which public memory has performed its edifying functions and is now on a decline, at least in academia. Gavriel Rosenfeld, "A Looming Crash or a Soft Landing? Forecasting the Future of the Memory 'Industry,'" *Journal of Modern History* 81 (March 2009): 122–158. While this may or may not be true, in the early twenty-first century in Russia such functions were still taking shape.
74. Susan A. Crane, "Writing the Individual Back into Collective Memory," *American Historical Review* 102, no. 4 (December 1997): 1372–1385, esp. 1382 (quotation), 1383; see also Crane, *Collecting and Historical Consciousness in Early Nineteenth-Century Germany* (Ithaca: Cornell University Press, 2000).
75. For an intelligent application of "memory" and "historical consciousness" to the case of Soviet Ukraine (mostly for the late Stalin years), see Serhy Yekelchyk, *Stalin's Empire of Memory: Russian-Ukrainian Relations in the Soviet Historical Imagination* (Toronto: University of Toronto Press, 2004). On historical consciousness in late Soviet and post-Soviet Russia, see also Irina Paperno, *Stories of the Soviet Experience: Memoirs, Diaries, and Dreams* (Ithaca: Cornell University Press, 2009).
76. The citizenship paradigm comes from Fitzpatrick, "Supplicants and Citizens." See also her (untitled) review of literature on imperial and Soviet "ego-documents" in *Kritika: Explorations in Russian and Eurasian History* 10, no. 2 (Spring 2009): 398–405.

1. A Passion for the Printed Word

1. The 1939 all-union census recorded a literacy rate of 81.2 percent among the Soviet population over age nine, and 89.1 percent among people age nine to forty-nine. For analyses of early Soviet literacy campaigns, see Sheila Fitzpatrick, *Education and Social Mobility in the Soviet Union, 1921–1934* (Cambridge: Cambridge University Press, 1979), 168–176; Benjamin Eklof, "Russian Literacy Campaigns, 1861–1939," in *National Literacy Campaigns: Historical and Comparative Perspectives*, ed. Robert F. Arnove and Harvey J. Graff (New York: Plenum Press, 1987), 123–145, here 141; Charles E. Clark, *Uprooting Otherness: The Literacy Campaign in NEP-Era Russia* (Selinsgrove, Pa.: Susquehanna University Press, 2000).
2. RGALI, f. 1702, op. 6, d. 27, ll. 50, 55–55ob; d. 40, ll. 8–99ob; d. 41, ll. 146–146ob, 166–170, 174–175, 275, 276–277; d. 54, l. 148. Iurii Trifonov, "Studenty," *NM*, no. 10 (1950): 56–175;*NM*, no. 11 (1950): 49–182.
3. Yuri Trifonov, "Zapiski soseda" [1972], in *Rasskazy. Povesti. Roman. Vospominaniia. Esse* (Ekaterinburg: U-Faktoriia, 1999), 672.
4. RGASPI, f. M-1, op. 32, d. 732, l. 18. The only department that received more letters than the literature department was the newspaper's special department of letters, which received 19,600, all apparently less thematically specific correspondence.
5. Ibid., d. 764, ll. 7–9, 39–40; d. 732, ll. 16–17. In December 1953 the department of literature received 1,626 letters, compared with 284 letters in the workers' department, 711 in the studying youth department, 520 in the peasant youth department, and so on.
6. Ibid., d. 732, l. 18; d. 764, ll. 7, 38.
7. Svetlana Boym, *Common Places: Mythologies of Everyday Life in Literary Russia* (Cambridge, Mass.: Harvard University Press, 1994), 168–214.
8. For the first six documents, see Denis L. Babichenko, ed., *"Literaturnyi front": Istoriia politicheskoi tsenzury, 1932–1946 gg.* (Moscow: Entsiklopediia rossiiskikh dereven', 1994), 40, 43–44, 88–90, 144, 221–225. For the last three documents, see Andrei Artizov and Oleg Naumov, eds., *Vlast' i khudozhestvennaia intelligentsiia: Dokumenty TsK RKP(b)-VKP(b), VChK-OGPU-NKVD o kul'turnoi politike, 1917–1953 gg.* (Moscow: Mezhdunarodnyi fond "Demokratiia," 1999), 641–642, 643–646, 662–663.
9. Katerina Clark et al., eds., *Soviet Culture and Power: A History in Documents, 1917–1953* (New Haven: Yale University Press, 2007), 351.
10. Denis L. Babichenko, *Pisateli i tsenzory: Sovetskaia literatura 1940-kh godov pod politicheskim kontrolem TsK* (Moscow: Rossiia molodaia, 1994), 142–143, 150.
11. Clark et al., *Soviet Culture and Power*, 140–141; Robert Service, *Stalin: A Biography* (Cambridge, Mass.: Harvard University Press, 2005), 560–570.

12. Konstantin Simonov, "Glazami cheloveka moego pokoleniia," in *Stikhotvoreniia i poemy. Povesti raznykh let. Posledniaia rabota* (Moscow: OLMA-PRESS, 2004).
13. RGASPI, f. 17, op. 132, d. 78, ll. 46–48, 50.
14. See, e.g., ibid., op. 133, d. 322, ll. 223, 225.
15. "Postanovlenie Orgbiuro TsK VKP(b) 'O zhurnalakh 'Zvezda' i 'Leningrad'," 14 August 1946, *Pravda*, 21 August 1946.
16. *Vtoroi vsesoiuznyi s"ezd sovetskikh pisatelei,15–26 dekabria 1954 goda. Stenograficheskii otchet* (Moscow: Sovetskii pisatel', 1956), 36; [N. N. Dikushina,] "Zhurnalistika i kritika 40-kh—nachala 50-kh godov," *Istoriia russkoi sovetskoi literatury v chetyrekh tomakh*, vol. 3 (Moscow: Nauka, 1968), 448–471, here 449; *Apparat TsK KPSS i kul'tura. 1953–1957: Dokumenty* (Moscow: ROSSPEN, 2001), 344.
17. Among the best-known regional Russian-language literary journals were *Sibirskie ogni* (Novosibirsk, launched in 1922), *Don* (Rostov-na-Donu, 1925), *Zvezda Vostoka* (Tashkent, established in 1932 and published under this title since 1946), *Ural* (Sverdlovsk, established in 1958), and *Volga* (Saratov, established in 1966).
18. RGAE, f. 3527, op. 27, d. 122, ll. 16, 21.
19. Ibid., ll. 16, 17ob. For Ukrainian population statistics in 1945, see Lubomyr Luciuk, "Ukraine," in *The Oxford Companion to World War II*, ed. Ian Dear and Michael Foot (Oxford: Oxford University Press, 2001), 909.
20. In 1945, 800 annual subscriptions to *Oktiabr'* went to Moscow, 300 to Leningrad, 1,650 to Ukraine, and 700 to Belarus. RGAE, f. 3527, op. 27, d. 122, ll. 18ob, 19ob, 20, 21.
21. Ibid., d. 152, l. 116.
22. Ibid., d. 216, l. 18. Belarus also received 1,200 sets of *Oktiabr'*, 1,100 of *Znamia*, and 400 of *Zvezda* in 1947. In 1950, the republic's population was 7,709,000: "Chislennost' naseleniia Respubliki Belarus'," http://belstat.gov.by/homep/ru/publications/population/tables.php (accessed 24 November 2010); David Marples, *Belarus: A Denationalized Nation* (Amsterdam: Harwood Academic, 1999), 16.
23. ORF GLM, f. 168, op. 1, d. 40, l. 4; RGAE, f. 3527, op. 27, d. 122, ll. 16ob, 17ob; "Demograficheskie pokazateli po 15 novym nezavisimym gosudarstvam," *Demoskop Weekly* 457–458 (7–20 March 2011), http://demoscope.ru/weekly/ssp/sng_pop.php (accessed 24 November 2010).
24. RGASPI, f. 17, op. 132, d. 226, ll. 26–27. The circulation stated on the back page of *Novyi mir*'s August 1949 issue was 66,300.
25. Ibid.; RGAE, f. 3527, op. 27, d. 171, l. 138; d. 176, ll. 45, 47.
26. RGAE, f. 3527, op. 27, d. 203, ll. 9–11. Soiuzpechat' operated under the purview of the People's Commissariat of Posts and Telegraphs, in 1932 transformed into the People's Commissariat of Communications.

27. Ivan Kuznetsov, *Istoriia otechestvennoi zhurnalistiki (1917–2000)* (Moscow: Flinta, 2002), ch. 4, http://evartist.narod.ru/text8/09.htm (accessed 5 August 2010).
28. RGAE, f. 3527, op. 27, d, 123, l. 33; see also ibid., d. 191, l. 43.
29. RGASPI, f. 17, op. 132, d. 226, ll. 26–27. RGAE, f. 3527, op. 27, d. 171, ll. 137–138; d. 123, ll. 30–31, 123; d. 124, ll. 91–91ob, 142–144; d. 191, l. 45a.
30. RGAE, f. 3527, op. 27, d. 152, ll. 103–116; d. 159, ll. 16–18.
31. Ibid., d. 159, ll. 16–21, 26–27, 55–56; d. 1423, l. 173.
32. Ibid., d. 1423, ll. 18, 56.
33. Ibid., d. 176, ll. 45, 13.
34. Ibid., d. 213, l. 33 (January 1955).
35. Ibid., d. 1416, l. 44.
36. Ibid., d. 123, l. 30ob; "U gazetnogo stenda," http://visualrian.ru/images/item/718003 (a 1970 photo, accessed 26 November 2010).
37. RGAE, f. 3527, op. 27, d. 176, ll. 16–17, 19 (1950); d. 204, ll. 15–16 (1954); d. 213, ll. 24–26 (1955); d. 733, l. 75 (1958).
38. Ibid., d. 204, l. 16.
39. Ibid., d. 830, ll. 21–21a, 112–114.
40. Ibid., l. 115 (14 February 1961).
41. Ibid., d. 834, l. 138. For the Pskov population statistics as per the 1959 USSR census, see http://demoscope.ru/weekly/ssp/rus_mar_59.php?reg=53&gor=3&Submit=OK (accessed 25 November 2010).
42. RGAE, f. 3527, op. 27, d. 844, ll. 19ob, 82ob, 114ob, 180ob, 212ob, 309ob.
43. Ibid., d. 733, ll. 59–62; d. 760, ll. 1–2; d. 830, l. 184.
44. Ibid., d. 1416, l. 109; d. 1423, ll. 5, 8–10.
45. Ibid., d. 687, ll. 16–17; for reminiscences by readers, see, for example, http://pda.sxnarod.com/index.php?showtopic=156806&st=0; http://www.liveinternet.ru/users/wolfleo/post136943880/ (accessed 25 November 2010).
46. RGAE, f. 3527, op. 27, d. 687, l. 11.
47. Ibid., d. 1423, ll. 174, 177–179.
48. RGALI, f. 619, op. 4, d. 88, l. 4.
49. Cited from *Novyi mir*'s issues for those months.
50. *Apparat TsK KPSS i kul'tura, 1953–1957*, 439, 445 (October 1955).
51. RGAE, f. 3527, op. 27, d. 789, l. 6; d. 830, l. 124.
52. Ibid., d. 830, l. 5; d. 708, l. 87; d. 896, l. 4; d. 1189, l. 12; d. 1274, l. 27.
53. For 1966, 1968, and 1970, see, respectively: RGAE, d. 1416, l. 44; d. 1619, l. 17ob; d. 1822, l. 177ob.
54. *NM*, no. 12 (December 1945), see back cover; ibid., no. 12 (December 1946), back cover.
55. *NM*, no. 2 (February 1948), back cover.

56. One could subscribe to *Novyi mir* for three, six, or twelve months. For the terms and prices of subscription, see *NM*, no. 12 (December 1951): 320.
57. *NM*, no. 11 (November 1953): 288; no. 12 (December 1958): 288; no. 12 (November 1964): 288; no. 8 (August 1969): 286 (subscription advertisement for 1970). *Apparat TsK KPSS i kul'tura, 1953–1957*, 440.
58. *Narodnoe khoziaistvo SSSR v 1965 g.: Statisticheskii ezhegodnik* (Moscow: Statistika, 1966), 567; Alec Nove, *An Economic History of the USSR* (Penguin Books, 1969), 309. The official (State Bank of the USSR) exchange rate was 5.3 U.S. dollars to 1 ruble in January through March 1950, and 4 U.S. dollars to 1 ruble from April 1950. Thus, officially 7,668 rubles in 1950 converted to anywhere between $1,447 and $1,917 in contemporary U.S. currency. See the statistics published by the Central Bank of Russia: http://www.cbr.ru/currency_base/OldVal.aspx.
59. RGAE, f. 3527, op. 27, d. 687, l. 13; Nove, *Economic History of the USSR*, 345; salary data for 1955.
60. *Narodnoe khoziaistvo SSSR v 1970 g.: Statisticheskii ezhegodnik* (Moscow: Statistika, 1971), 519. Wages for 1970 are in post-1961 rubles revalued at one-tenth of their previous worth. The State Bank of the USSR exchange rate in 1969 was 0.9 U.S. dollars to 1 ruble. Thus, officially 1,402.8 rubles converted to 1,558.6 contemporary U.S. dollars. See the statistics published by the Central Bank of Russia: http://www.cbr.ru/currency_base/OldVal.aspx.
61. Collective farmers began receiving salaries in 1966. The average yearly wage of a state farm worker in 1969 was 1,089.6 rubles. *Narodnoe khoziaistvo SSSR v 1970 g.*, 519.
62. Aleksandr Solzhenitsyn, "Odin den' Ivana Denisovicha," *NM*, no. 11 (1962): 8–74; Solzhenitsyn, "Odin den' Ivana Denisovicha," *Roman-gazeta* (Moscow: Goslitizdat, 1963); Solzhenitsyn, *Odin den' Ivana Denisovicha* (Moscow: Sovetskii pisatel', 1963; Vilnius: Goslitizdat, 1963; Tallinn: Gazetno-zhurnal'noe izdatel'stvo, 1963; Moscow: Uchpedgiz, 1963); Tatiana Goriaeva, ed., *Istoriia sovetskoi politicheskoi tsenzury: Dokumenty i kommentarii* (Moscow: ROSSPEN, 1997), 587–588 (Glavlit [Glavnoe upravlenie po okhrane gosudarstvennykh tain v pechati pri Sovete Ministrov SSSR, Main Directorate for the Protection of State Secrets in the Press under the Council of Ministers of the USSR] order to remove all copies of *One Day* from libraries and bookstores, 14 February 1974).
63. For more on the thick journals during perestroika, see the Epilogue.
64. Vladislav E. Evgen'ev-Maksimov, *Poslednie gody "Sovremennika." 1863–1866* (Leningrad: Khudozhestvennaia literatura, 1939), 113; Robert Maguire, *Red Virgin Soil: Soviet Literature in the 1920s* (Princeton: Princeton University Press, 1968), 36, 368, 382; Jeffrey Brooks, "Readers and Reading at the End of

the Tsarist Era," in *Literature and Society in Imperial Russia, 1800–1914*, ed. William Mills Todd III (Stanford: Stanford University Press, 1978), 97–150, here 102. In the 1880s and 1890s, according to Brooks, the circulation of the most successful thick journals usually did not exceed 15,000. In the 1920s *Novyi mir* had a circulation above 10,000 (28,000 in 1927, then a record among thick journals). The circulation for *Oktiabr'* was 4,000 to 5,000 copies after 1924; 2,500 in 1928; and 10,000 in 1929. Maguire, *Red Virgin Soil*, 368–370; Vladimir Lakshin, "Pisatel', chitatel', kritik: Stat'ia pervaia [1965]," in *Literaturno-kriticheskie stat'i* (Moscow: Geleos, 2004), 92.

65. Vladimir Lakshin, the journal's most famous literary critic of the Tvardovskii years, was the first to note the dramatic growth of its audience. Lakshin, "Pisatel'," 86, 92–93.
66. Maguire, *Red Virgin Soil*, 369–370.
67. Babichenko, "*Literaturnyi front*," 89–90, 93–104.
68. Ibid., 102.
69. Artizov and Naumov, *Vlast' i khudozhestvennaia intelligentsia*, 549. For another such criticism of *Novyi mir*, see Iu[rii] Lukin, "Zhurnal, otstaiushchii ot zhizni," *Kul'tura i zhizn'*, 28 June 1946.
70. Clark et al., *Soviet Culture and Power*, 401.
71. Ibid., 549–550.
72. RGASPI, f. 17, op. 132, d. 78, l. 21; Simonov, "Glazami," 505; Oleg Khlevniuk et al., eds., *Politbiuro TsK VKP(b) i Sovet Ministrov SSSR, 1945–1953* (Moscow: ROSSPEN: 2002), 247.
73. ORF GLM, f. 168, op. 1, d. 38, ll. 1–9; d. 40, ll. 1–4; d. 41, ll. 1–6. RGASPI, f. 17, op. 132, d. 78, ll. 22–23.
74. ORF GLM, f. 168, op. 1, d. 38, l. 4.
75. Ibid., d. 41, l. 1.
76. Simonov, "Glazami," 506.
77. Ibid., 494–95, 507; Mikhail Zoshchenko, "Nikogda ne zabudem: rasskazy" *Novyi mir*, no. 9 (1947): 148.
78. Konstantin Simonov, "Dym otechestva," *Novyi mir*, no. 11 (1947): 1–123.
79. "O povesti K. Simonova 'Dym otechestva'," *Literaturnaia gazeta*, 7 December 1947; Simonov, "Glazami," 500–502, 511–518.
80. Vasilii Azhaev, "Daleko ot Moskvy," *Novyi mir*, nos. 7–9 (1948); Thomas Lahusen, *How Life Writes the Book: Real Socialism and Socialist Realism in Stalin's Russia* (Ithaca: Cornell University Press, 1997), 142–146.
81. Simonov, "Glazami," 541–542.
82. Valentin Ovechkin, "Raionnye budni," *Novyi mir*, no. 9 (1952): 204–221.
83. Georgii Malenkov, "Otchetnyi doklad Tsentral'nogo Komiteta VKP(b) XIX s"ezdu partii," *Pravda*, 6 October 1952.

84. RGALI, f. 1702, op. 6, d. 55, ll. 1–90; Semen Lipkin, *Zhizn' i sud'ba Vasiliia Grossmana*, and Anna Berzer, *Proshchanie* (Moscow: Kniga, 1990).
85. See, e.g., Juliane Fürst's excellent analysis of Soviet youths reading Fadeev's *The Young Guard*, in Fürst, *Stalin's Last Generation: Soviet Post-War Youth and the Emergence of Mature Socialism* (Oxford: Oxford University Press, 2010), esp. 159.
86. This discussion is based on RGALI, f. 1710, op. 2, d. 14, ll. 1–31 (Grossman); RGALI, f. 1702, op. 6, d. 7 (Azhaev); ibid., d. 27, ll. 50, 55–55ob; d. 40, ll. 8–99ob; d. 41, ll. 146–146ob, 166–170, 174–175, 275, 276–277; d. 54, l. 148 (Trifonov); d. 54, ll. 35–55 (Ovechkin).
87. Elena Zubkova, *Obshchestvo i reformy: 1945–1964* (Moscow: Rossiia molodaia, 1993); Mark Edele, *Soviet Veterans of the Second World War: A Popular Movement in an Authoritarian Society 1941–1991* (Oxford: Oxford University Press, 2008); Fürst, *Stalin's Last Generation.*

2. *Barometer of the Epoch*

1. Olga Berggolts, "Razgovor o lirike," *Literaturnaia* gazeta, 16 April 1953; Ilya Ehrenburg, "Ottepel'," *Znamia*, no. 5 (May 1954): 14–87.
2. Mikhail Lifshits, "Dnevnik Marietty Shaginian," *NM*, no. 2 (February 1954): 206–231.
3. Fedor Abramov, "Liudi kolkhoznoi derevni v poslevoennoi proze (Literaturnye zametki)," *NM*, no. 4 (April 1954): 210–231; Mark Shcheglov, "'Russkii les' Leonida Leonova," *NM*, no. 5 (1954): 220–241.
4. Vladimir Pomerantsev, "Ob iskrennosti v literature," *NM*, no. 12 (December 1953): 218–245.
5. Vladimir Pomerantsev, *Dom siuzhetov: Rasskazy, dnevniki* (Moscow: Sovetskii pisatel', 1978), 85, 197.
6. Vladimir Pomerantsev, "'Vnimanie! Slushaite nas! Chitaite nashi listovki!' Frontovye zapisi," in *Na voine i posle nee* (Moscow: Sovetskii pisatel', 1977), 205, 277.
7. Pomerantsev, *Dom siuzhetov*, 203.
8. Vladimir Pomerantsev, *Doch' bukinista* (Moscow: Sovetskii pisatel', 1951).
9. RGALI, f. 1702, op. 6, d. 88, l. 60ob; "Knigi i ikh obsuzhdenie: V sektsii prozy Soiuza pisatelei," *Literaturnaia gazeta* (hereafter *LG*), 15 January 1953; Karl Loewenstein, "The Thaw: Writers and the Public Sphere in the Soviet Union 1951–57," Ph.D. diss., Duke University, 1999, 72.
10. Pomerantsev, "Ob iskrennosti," 218–219.
11. Ibid., 219.
12. Edward J. Brown, *The Proletarian Episode in Russian Literature, 1928–1932* (1953; New York: Octagon Books, 1971), 141–142; Herman Ermolaev, *Soviet Literary Theories, 1917–1934: The Genesis of Socialist Realism* (1963; New York:

Octagon Books, 1977), 68, 196; Katerina Clark, "Germanophone Contributions to Stalinist Literary Theory: The Case of Georgy Lukacs and Mikhail Lifšic, and Their Roles in *Literaturnyi Kritik* and IFLI," *Russian Literature* 63, no. 2–4 (February–May 2008): 513–532, here 525, 527.

13. Pomerantsev, "Ob iskrennosti," 220.
14. Ibid.
15. Ibid., 220–221.
16. Ibid.
17. Katerina Clark, "'Wait for Me and I Shall Return': The Early Thaw as a Reprise of Late Thirties Culture?" in Denis Kozlov and Eleonory Gilburd, eds., *The Thaw: Soviet Society and Culture during the 1950s and 1960s* (Toronto: University of Toronto Press, 2013), 85–108, here 90. Analyzing Berggol'ts's case, Clark does not insist on this "cover-up" interpretation, asking rhetorically: "Casuistry or conviction? Who can say?"
18. Pomerantsev, "Ob iskrennosti," 221–228.
19. Ibid., 228.
20. Ibid., 231.
21. At its September 1953 plenum, just three months before Pomerantsev's article came out, the Central Committee not only formally elected Khrushchev first secretary but also released some of the tax pressure on collective farms. Shortly afterward, in March 1954, it launched the Virgin Lands campaign. See Michaela Pohl, "From White Grave to Tselinograd to Astana: The Virgin Lands Opening, Khrushchev's Forgotten First Reform," in Kozlov and Gilburd, *The Thaw*, 269–307; Anatolii Strelianyi, "Khrushchev and the Countryside," in *Nikita Khrushchev*, ed. William Taubman, Sergei Khrushchev, and Abbott Gleason (New Haven: Yale University Press, 2000), 113–137; William Taubman, *Khrushchev: The Man and His Era* (New York: W. W. Norton, 2003), 262–267.
22. Pohl, "From White Grave to Tselinograd to Astana."
23. Valentin Ovechkin, "Raionnye budni," *NM*, no. 9 (1952): 204–221.
24. Edith Rogovin Frankel, *Novy Mir: A Case Study in the Politics of Literature, 1952–1958* (Cambridge: Cambridge University Press, 1981), 15–17; Kathleen Parthé, *Russian Village Prose: The Radiant Past* (Princeton: Princeton University Press, 1992).
25. Semen Babaevskii, *Kavaler Zolotoi Zvezdy* (Moscow: Molodaia gvardiia, 1947); Galina Nikolaeva, *Zhatva* (Moscow: Gosudarstvennoe izdatel'stvo khudozhestvenoi literatury, 1952).
26. Pomerantsev, "Ob iskrennosti," 234–235.
27. Ibid., 238–239.
28. Pomerantsev, "Ob iskrennosti," 242–244, 245 (quotation).
29. Clark, "'Wait for Me.'"

30. E.g., George Gibian, *Interval of Freedom: Soviet Literature during the Thaw, 1954–1957* (Minneapolis: University of Minnesota Press, 1960), 7; Robert Stacy, *Russian Literary Criticism, a Short History* (Syracuse: Syracuse University Press, 1975), 223; Geoffrey Hosking, "The Twentieth Century, 1953–1980: In Search of New Ways," in *The Cambridge History of Russian Literature*, ed. Charles Moser (Cambridge: Cambridge University Press, 1992), 527.
31. Elena Zubkova, *Russia after the War: Hopes, Illusions, and Disappointments* (Armonk, N.Y.: M. E. Sharpe, 1998), 156–158, here 156. Zubkova's analysis of Pomerantsev's article and its impact is one of the most insightful to date. Interestingly, though, the English-language translation of her book renders the Russian word *iskrennost'* not as "sincerity" but as "truthfulness": the article's title is translated as "On Truthfulness in Literature." The translation thus sets the terms of analysis in a somewhat simplified way, highlighting literature's rendition of reality but omitting Pomerantsev's emphasis on the writer's self-expression and interaction with the larger society.
32. RGALI, f. 1702, op. 9, d. 8, l. 6 (Pomerantsev to Tvardovskii, no date, but no earlier than 23 January 1954). A shortened version of the letter was published in An. Petrov and Iu. Burtin, eds., "'Edva raskrylis' pervye tsvety': 'Novyi mir' i obshchestvennye umonastroeniia v 1954 godu," *Druzhba narodov*, no. 11 (1993): 208–239, here 211–212.
33. RGALI, f. 1702, op. 9, d. 8, l. 6.
34. Ibid., ll. 6–6ob.
35. RGALI, f. 634, op. 4, d. 708, l. 13.
36. RGALI, f. 1702, op. 9, d. 8, ll. 6–6ob.
37. Ibid., l. 6.
38. Ibid.
39. RGALI, f. 1702, op. 9, d. 8, l. 5 (Tvardovskii to Pomerantsev, 23 January 1954).
40. Vladimir I. Lenin, "Statistics and Sociology," in Lenin, *Collected Works* (Moscow: Progress Publishers, 1964), vol. 23, 271–277.
41. Vitalii Vasilevskii, "S nevernykh pozitsii," *Literaturnaia gazeta*, 30 January 1954.
42. Liudmila Skorino, "Razgovor nachistotu (Po povodu stat'i V. Pomerantseva 'Ob iskrennosti')," *Znamia*, no. 2 (February 1954): 165–174, esp. 166, 172 (quotation). Skorino is often portrayed as a dark figure in the history of Soviet literature, usually by literary memoirists who hold grudges against her for rejecting many manuscripts during her long service at *Znamia*. Yet she may not deserve being painted uniformly black: Varlam Shalamov, for example, said Skorino was "twice his godmother," as it was she who had arranged for his first publications in the 1930s. Decades later, when he returned from the concentration camps, it was Skorino again who helped him. Varlam Shalamov, "Moia zhizn'—Neskol'ko moikh zhiznei" (1964), http://shalamov.ru/library/27/#t17 (accessed 9 August 2010).

43. Boris Riurikov, "O bogatstve iskusstva," *LG*, 20 March 1954. On the genesis of the term "cult of personality" in Soviet political culture, see David Fel'dman, *Terminologiia vlasti: Sovetskie politicheskie terminy v istoriko-kul'turnom kontekste* (Moscow: RGGU, 2006), 17–64.
44. *Apparat TsK KPSS i kul'tura. 1953–1957: Dokumenty*, ed. V. Iu. Afiani et al. (Moscow: ROSSPEN, 2001), 200–201.
45. Ibid., 206–207.
46. Ibid., 206–210.
47. RGALI, f. 634, op. 4, d. 703, l. 22 (15 June 1954).
48. Ibid., ll. 22–23. On the impact of the Soviet Thaw on Polish literature, and on the Warsaw meeting in particular, see Anthony Kemp-Welch, *Poland under Communism: A Cold War History* (Cambridge: Cambridge University Press, 2008), 66–67.
49. On this, see Amir Weiner, "The Empires Pay a Visit: Gulag Returnees, East European Rebellions, and Soviet Frontier Politics," *Journal of Modern History* 78, no. 2 (June 2006): 333–376; Benjamin Tromly, "Re-Imagining the Soviet Intelligentsia: Student Politics and University Life, 1948–1964," Ph.D. diss., Harvard University, 2007, 258–309.
50. RGALI, f. 634, op. 4, d. 703, l. 23.
51. Ibid., d. 702, ll. 17–18 (the journalist was Konstantin Lapin; editorial board meeting, 8 June 1954).
52. Ibid., d. 684, l. 20.
53. Ibid., d. 676, ll. 22, 25 (editorial board meeting, 2 February 1954); d. 684, l. 31 (23 March 1954); d. 687, l. 24; d. 702, ll. 25–27 (Tamara Trifonova, 8 June 1954).
54. Ibid., d. 687, l. 32 (V. M. Ozerov, 6 April 1954).
55. Ibid., d. 684, ll. 13–14 (M. Karpovich, 23 March 1954); d. 687, ll. 15–18, 27–28 (6 April 1954)—see statements by K. Lapin, M. Karpovich, V. Sokolov. The latter argument occurred between Sokolov and Boris Agapov, mainly about Agapov's response to Lifshits's *Novyi mir* article: Agapov, "Protiv snobizma v kritike," *LG*, 6 April 1954.
56. S. Bocharov, V. Zaitsev, V. Panov, Iu. Mann, and A. Askol'dov, "Zamalchivaia ostrye voprosy. Pis'mo v redaktsiiu," *Komsomol'skaia pravda*, 17 March 1954. One of the letter's authors, Aleksandr Iakovlevich Askol'dov (b. 1932) later became a film director, famous for his banned film *Commissar* (1967).
57. Iurii Mann, "V piatidesiatye gody i pozzhe (epizody)," *Voprosy literatury*, no. 2 (2001): 288–304, here 297–298.
58. RGALI, f. 634, op. 4, d. 684, ll. 4, 13 (A. P. Petrashik, M. D. Karpovich [quotation], 23 March 1954 editorial board meeting); Riurikov, "O bogatstve iskusstva."
59. "V zhizneutverzhdenii—sila nashei literatury," *Komsomol'skaia pravda*, 6 June 1954.

60. RGALI, f. 634, op. 4, d. 702, l. 35; d. 703, ll. 24, 27.
61. *Apparat TsK KPSS i kul'tura. 1953–1957*, 211.
62. In the past, scholars explained the confusion and delay in attacking *Novyi mir* as stemming from the power struggle between Malenkov and Khrushchev. Presumably, the more liberally inclined Malenkov would ensure the relative safety of *Novyi mir* and other Thaw-oriented cultural forces. In the early months of 1954 the outcome of their struggle was unclear, but by the summer Khrushchev had secured his victory and proceeded to clamp down on *Novyi mir.* See Frankel, *Novy Mir*, 67; Dina R. Spechler, *Permitted Dissent in the USSR:* Novy mir *and the Soviet Regime* (New York: Praeger, 1982), 26–27. While this interpretation may be accurate, so far I have not seen evidence supporting it.
63. RGALI, f. 634, op. 4, d. 684, l. 20; d. 747, ll. 1–97 (twenty readers' letters dated January 31 through March 6, 1954).
64. RGALI, f. 1702, op. 6, d. 72, ll. 1–148ob; d. 80, ll. 1–2; d. 85, ll. 86–88ob; d. 88, ll. 1–144; d. 89, ll. 1–154ob; d. 90, ll. 78–84; d. 91, ll. 1–133; d. 92, ll. 1–152; d. 93, ll. 1–88.
65. Ibid., d. 93, ll. 87–88.
66. The percentage is based on the number of letters from identified locations (ninety-one letters).
67. The quoted phrase appears in the following lines of verse: "The capitals are rocked with thunder / Of orators and wordy feuds. / But in the depths of Russia, yonder / An age-old awful silence broods." Nikolai Nekrasov, "The capitals are rocked with thunder," trans. B. Deutsch and A. Yarmolinsky, in *Russian Poets*, ed. Peter Washington (New York: Alfred A. Knopf, 2009), 92.
68. RGALI, f. 1702, op. 6, d. 89, l. 127 (23 March 1954).
69. Ibid. For similar reactions, see RGALI, f. 1702, op. 6, d. 72, ll. 49–56 (Valentina Klimova, engineer and leading technical designer, Leningrad, 27 January 1954).
70. Ibid., d. 72, l. 128 (no date, registered 15 February 1954).
71. Ibid., d. 89, l. 100 (Al. Reshetov, student of philology, Kharkov University, 15 March 1954).
72. Ibid., l. 65 (I. Viakhirev, Moscow, March 1954). See also ibid., d. 88, ll. 19, 94; d. 89, l. 127.
73. Ibid., d. 93, ll. 1–5 (A. Sinditskii, 6 July 1954, no occupation stated); Aleksandr Pushkin, "Obshchestvo moskovskikh literatorov" (1830), in *Polnoe sobranie sochinenii* (Moscow and Leningrad, 1937–1959), vol. 11, 85–86.
74. Pomerantsev, "Ob iskrennosti," 236–237.
75. RGALI, f. 1702, op. 6, d. 91, l. 86 (no address, registered 5 April 1954); d. 88, ll. 45–46.
76. Skorino, "Razgovor nachistotu," 166, 172. On the concept of the Silver Age and its revival in the 1950s and 1960s, see Omry Ronen, *The Fallacy of the Silver*

Age in Twentieth-Century Russian Literature (Amsterdam: Harwood, 1997); Galina Rylkova, *The Archaeology of Anxiety: The Russian Silver Age and Its Legacy* (Pittsburgh: University of Pittsburgh Press, 2007), esp. 8–9, 19, 129.

77. RGALI, f. 1702, op. 6, d. 72, l. 25 (24 December 1953). *Gorodnichii*, an archaic term for city governor, most likely came from Gogol's 1835 *The Inspector General*, obligatory reading in the Soviet school curriculum.

78. RGALI, f. 1702, op. 6, d. 92, l. 106 (Nina Fedorovna Egorova, 1 June 1954); ibid., ll. 137–137 ob. (anonymous, registered 29 June 1954); d. 93, l. 70 (N. Podgug, Moscow, 31 July 1954); d. 93, l. 88 (anonymous, registered 11 November 1954).

79. First quotation: ibid., d. 72, l. 34 (21 December 1953); second quotation: ibid., d. 92, ll. 137–137ob. (anonymous, registered 29 June 1954).

80. On this, see also Igal Halfin, *Intimate Enemies: Demonizing the Bolshevik Opposition, 1918–1928* (Pittsburgh: Pittsburgh University Press, 2008).

81. RGALI, f. 1702, op. 6, d. 88, l. 73: "Skazhi mne, kritik Skorino, / Ty on, ona ili ono? / Akh, vprochem, chto ia . . . Netu roda / U pugala bez ogoroda. / V lakeiakh net (chto znachit shkola!) / Ni chuvstv, ni sovesti, ni pola." (Tell me, critic Skorino, / Art thou a he, a she, or an it? / But what is wrong with me— / A scarecrow is neutral. / Lackeys possess (that's proper training!) no conscience, sentiments, or gender.) Because of the neutral appearance of her last name, accompanied in the publication by only her first initial, many readers did not know whether Skorino was a man or a woman.

82. Marc Raeff, *Understanding Imperial Russia: State and Society under the Old Regime* (Chicago: The University of Chicago Press, 1984).

83. Katerina Clark, *Soviet Novel: History as Ritual* (Bloomington: Indiana University Press, 2000), 114–135; Hans Günther, "Wise Father Stalin and His Family in Soviet Cinema," in *Socialist Realism without Shores*, ed. Thomas Lahusen and Evgeny Dobrenko (Durham: Duke University Press, 1997), 178–190.

84. See the introduction to this volume. Also, see Rufus Mathewson, *The Positive Hero in Russian Literature* (1958; Evanston, Ill.: Northwestern University Press, 2000).

85. Lionel Trilling, *Sincerity and Authenticity* (Cambridge, Mass.: Harvard University Press, 1972), 2.

86. Maks Fasmer [Max Vasmer], *Etimologicheskii slovar' russkogo iazyka*, ed. O. N. Trubachev (Moscow: Progress, 1986), vol. 2, 140–141.

87. *Tolkovyi slovar' zhivogo velikorusskogo iazyka V. I. Dalia*, http://www.slovopedia.com/1/200/735185.html (accessed 20 August 2010); S. A. Kuznetsov, ed., *Bol'shoi tolkovyi slovar' russkogo iazyka* (Saint Petersburg: Norint, 1998), http://www.gramota.ru/slovari/dic/?word=%C8%D1%CA%D0%C5%CD%CD%C8%C9&all=x&bts=x (accessed 20 August 2010); A. Abramov, *Slovar' russkikh sinonimov i skhodnykh po smyslu vyrazhenii* (Moscow: Russkie slovari, 1999),

http://www.gramota.ru/slovari/dic/?word=%C8%D1%CA%D0%C5%CD%CD%C8%C9&all=x&bts=x (accessed 20 August 2010).

88. Pomerantsev, "Ob iskrennosti," 233, emphasis added.
89. RGALI, f. 1702, op. 6, d. 88, ll. 18–19 (Gal'perina, Davydova, Kalenova, Karpova, Levshina, Moldaver, Moscow, 16 February 1954). See also RGALI, f. 634, op. 4, d. 747, ll. 13–20.
90. On this, see Boris Groys, *The Total Art of Stalinism: Avant-Garde, Aesthetic Dictatorship, and Beyond* (Princeton: Princeton University Press, 1992); Katerina Clark, *Petersburg, Crucible of Cultural Revolution* (Cambridge, Mass.: Harvard University Press, 1995); Igal Halfin, *From Darkness to Light: Class, Consciousness, and Salvation in Revolutionary Russia* (Pittsburgh: University of Pittsburgh Press, 2000).
91. RGALI, f. 1702, op. 6, d. 88, l. 24; see also d. 92, l. 1 (N. Chernykh, teacher of literature, Kurgannaia, Krasnodar Krai, registered 20 April 1954).
92. Pomerantsev, "Ob iskrennosti," 228.
93. Alexei Yurchak explains the late Soviet language crisis largely by the fact that Stalin's death left the country without an undisputed linguistic authority. What ensued were innumerable automatic repetitions of the same verbal formulas, which drained them of meaning and thus led to the ossification of the old language. Yurchak, *Everything Was Forever, until It Was No More: The Last Soviet Generation* (Princeton: Princeton University Press, 2005), 36–76. While Stalin's death was an important factor, the linguistic controversy reached a peak as early as 1953 and 1954, presumably a bit soon for the language to have become ossified. The perception of linguistic abnormality had likely already started to spread in the Stalin years.
94. See Jeffrey Brooks, *Thank You, Comrade Stalin! Soviet Public Culture from Revolution to Cold War* (Princeton: Princeton University Press, 2000), 161–184.
95. See Zubkova, *Russia after the War.*
96. Kornei Chukovskii, *Zhivoi kak zhizn'* (Moscow, 1962), ch. 2, http://vivovoco.rsl.ru/VV/BOOKS/LANG/LANG_2.HTM#20 (accessed 21 August 2010); Chukovskii, *Za zhivoe, obraznoe slovo* (Moscow, 1967).
97. Denis Kozlov and Eleonory Gilburd, "The Thaw as an Event in Russian History," in Kozlov and Gilburd, *The Thaw,* 18–81, here 51–52; Aleksandr Morozov, "Zametki o iazyke," *Zvezda,* no. 11 (1954): here 143; Vit.[alii] Bianki, "Mysli vslukh," *Zvezda,* no. 7 (1955): here 138; Pavel Nilin, "Opasnost' ne tam. . . ," *NM,* no. 4 (1958): 276–277; S. Radin, "Iazyk i slovar'. Pis'mo v redaktsiiu," *Zvezda,* no. 1 (1959): 218–219.
98. Chukovskii, *Ot dvukh do piati* (Leningrad, 1933); Irina Lukianova, *Kornei Chukovskii* (Moscow, 2006), 589, 617–619, 621.
99. Chukovskii, *Zhivoi kak zhizn',* esp. ch. 2.

100. On linguistic anxieties and reassessment that characterized twentieth-century Russian culture, as well as on the formation of its language, see Clark, *Petersburg*. See also Michael S. Gorham, *Speaking in Soviet Tongues: Language Culture and the Politics of Voice in Revolutionary Russia* (DeKalb: Northern Illinois University Press, 2003); Matthew E. Lenoe, *Closer to the Masses: Stalinist Culture, Social Revolution, and Soviet Newspapers* (Cambridge, Mass.: Harvard University Press, 2004); Marietta Chudakova, "Iazyk raspavsheisia tsivilizatsii: Materialy k teme," in *Novye raboty: 2003–2006* (Moscow: Vremia, 2007), 234–348.
101. Fedor Gladkov, "O kul'ture rechi," *NM*, no. 6 (June 1953): 231–238.
102. RGALI, f. 1702, op. 6, d. 85, l. 61 (Nikolai Alekseev, journalist, Leningrad, 1954). For the letters, see ibid., ll. 1–93. A few were published: "Tribuna chitatelia. O kul'ture rechi," *NM*, no. 4 (April 1954).
103. See, e.g., Eleonory Gilburd, "Picasso in Thaw Culture," *Cahiers du monde russe* 47, no. 1–2 (2006): 65–108; Peter Schmelz, *Such Freedom, If Only Musical: Unofficial Soviet Music during the Thaw* (Oxford: Oxford University Press, 2009); Susan Reid, "Modernizing Socialist Realism in the Khrushchev Thaw: The Struggle for a 'Contemporary Style' in Soviet Art," in *The Dilemmas of De-Stalinization: Negotiating Cultural and Social Change in the Khrushchev Era*, ed. Polly Jones (London: Routledge, 2006), 209–230; Reid, "In the Name of the People: The Manège Affair Revisited," *Kritika: Explorations in Russian and Eurasian History* 6, no. 4 (Fall 2005): 673–716; Oksana Bulgakowa, "Cine-Weathers: Soviet Thaw Cinema in the International Context," in Kozlov and Gilburd, *The Thaw*, 436–481.
104. Kozlov and Gilburd, "The Thaw as an Event," 52. On the 1920s, see Gorham, *Speaking in Soviet Tongues*, 7–15, 39–42, 59–70, 134–136; Clark, *Petersburg*, 224–241, 284–288; M. Golubkov, *Utrachennye al'ternativy: Formirovanie monicheskoi kontseptsii sovetskoi literatury, 20–30-e gody* (Moscow, 1992), 56–64; N. Primochkina, *Pisatel' i vlast': M. Gor'kii v literaturnom dvizhenii 20-kh godov* (Moscow, 1996), 138–145.
105. E.g., I. Dukhovnyi, "Ne govorit' gotovymi formulami," *Komsomol'skaia pravda*, 31 October 1954. Also S. Volodina, "Sila dushevnogo slova: O chem govorit'?"; P. Konoplev, "Sila dushevnogo slova: bez bumazhek"; A. Lukin, "Sila dushevnogo slova: Shpargalka vredna'"; and V. Ermolin, "Sila dushevnogo slova: Glavnoe—zainteresovat' molodezh'"; all in *Komsomol'skaia pravda*, 18 November 1954.
106. See Kozlov and Gilburd, "The Thaw as an Event," 52–53; Anatolii Gladilin, "Khronika vremen Viktora Podgurskogo," *Iunost'*, no. 9 (1956): 5–35; Vasilii Aksenov, "Na polputi k lune," *NM*, no. 7 (1962): 86–98. For the language debates of the Thaw, see, e.g., Aleksei Iugov, *Sud'by rodnogo slova* (Moscow, 1962); Iugov, "Tak chto zhe nam delat'?" *Literatura i zhizn'*, 30 March 1962;

V. G. Kostomarov, *Kul'tura rechi i stil'* (Moscow, 1960); S. Tsalanchuk, "Prav li A. Iugov?" and L. Barlas, "Spornaia pozitsiia," *LG*, 28 April 1959; "Berech' russkii iazyk," *LG*, 3 March 1959; L. I. Skvortsov, "Ob otsenkakh iazyka molodezhi," *Voprosy kul'tury rechi*, no. 5 (1964): 45–70; N. A. Leonova, "O proiznoshenii sovremennoi molodezhi," *Uchenye zapiski Kurskogo gosudarstvennogo pedagogicheskogo instituta* 25, no. 2 (1966): 106–113.

107. Kozlov and Gilburd, "The Thaw as an Event," 52–53.
108. Pomerantsev, "Ob iskrennosti," 229.
109. Pomerantsev, *Dom siuzhetov*, 123–175; Pomerantsev, "'Vnimanie! Slushaite nas! Chitaite nashi listovki!' Frontovye zapisi," in *Na voine i posle nee*, 202–430.
110. Pomerantsev, "'Vnimanie! Slushaite nas!'" 246–251, 286–295, 336–338, 364–366, 385–399.
111. Pomerantsev, *Dom siuzhetov*, 136–137; Pomerantsev, "'Vnimanie! Slushaite nas!'" 266–267. On Soviet World War II propagandists' close attention to German culture, see Jochen Hellbeck, "'The Diaries of Fritzes and the Letters of Gretchens': Personal Writings from the German-Soviet War and Their Readers," *Kritika: Explorations in Russian and Eurasian History* 10, no. 3 (Summer 2009): 571–606.
112. Pomerantsev, "Doktor Eshke," in *Na voine i posle nee* (Moscow: Sovetskii pisatel', 1977), 4–199, esp. 21–24, 34–36, 42–43, 46–48, 50–52.
113. Pomerantsev, "'Vnimanie! Slushaite nas!'" 295–296 (quotation, emphasis added), also 282–286, 298, 336–338, 364–366.
114. Ernst van Alphen and Mieke Bal, "Introduction," in *The Rhetoric of Sincerity*, ed. van Alphen, Bal, and Carel Smith (Stanford: Stanford University Press, 2009), 1–16, here 4–5. Jill Bennett, "A Feeling of Insincerity: Politics, Ventriloquy, and the Dialectics of Gesture," in *Rhetoric of Sincerity*, ed. van Alphen, Bal, and Smith, 195–213.
115. Yasco Horsman, "Like a Dog: Narrative and Confession in J. M. Coetzee's 'Disgrace' and 'The Lives of Animals,'" *Rhetoric of Sincerity*, ed. van Alphen, Bal, and Smith, 144–156, here 154–155; David McNeill, "Putting Sincerity to Work: Acquiescence and Refusal in Post-Fordist Art," in *Rhetoric of Sincerity*, ed. van Alphen, Bal, and Smith, 157–173, here 163.
116. This discussion is based on van Alphen and Bal, "Introduction" 1–16, esp. 3, 5 (quotation; original emphasis) as well as McNeill, "Putting Sincerity to Work," 161.
117. RGALI, f. 1702, op. 6, d. 92, ll. 146–147 (A. V. Smirnov, Dmitrov, registered 9 July 1954).
118. Jane Taylor, "'Why Do You Tear Me from Myself?' Torture, Truth, and the Arts of the Counter-Reformation," in *Rhetoric of Sincerity*, ed. van Alphen, Bal, and Smith, 19–43.
119. Van Alphen and Bal, "Introduction," 2.

120. Pomerantsev, "Ob iskrennosti," 230–231.
121. RGALI, f. 1702, op. 6, d. 93, l. 60 (Moscow, registered 12 July 1954).
122. Ibid., d. 91, ll. 85–92, here 85 (registered 9 April 1954).
123. Ibid., ll. 88–90, 92 (quotation).
124. Ibid., l. 92. For expressions of similar ideas, see RGALI, f. 1702, op. 6, d. 89, l. 154ob (E. Roldugin, Seredinskaia MTS, Moscow region, 27 March 1954); d. 92, ll. 94–97ob (K. S. Fedorovich, Moscow, 26 May 1954); d. 88, l. 46 (Postnov, registered 19 February 1954).
125. Tvardovskii speaking at the conference of editorial board representatives in the Union of Writers, 25 January 1954. Central Archive of the Union of Soviet Writers of the USSR, op. 28 p/kh, d. 49, cited in Regina Romanova, *Aleksandr Tvardovskii: Trudy i dni* (Moscow: Vodolei, 2006), 412.
126. A.[leksei] Surkov, "Pod znamenem sotsialisticheskogo realizma," *Pravda*, 25 May 1954; V.[ladimir] Ermilov, "Za sotsialisticheskii realizm," *Pravda*, 3 June 1954; also T.[amara] Trifonova, "O shtopanykh rukavichkakh i literaturnykh skhemakh," *LG*, 25 May 1954; "Za glubokuiu ideinost' i vysokoe masterstvo v tvorchestve pisatelei, *Leningradskaia pravda*, 28 May 1954.
127. N.[ikolai] Lesiuchevskii, "Za chistotu marksistsko-leninskikh printsipov v literature," *LG*, 24 June 1954.
128. Fadeev had been de facto head the Union of Soviet Writers since 1934, and was officially its head in 1938–1944 and 1946–1954.
129. Aleksandr Tvardovskii, "Iz rabochikh tetradei (1953–1960)," *Znamia*, no. 7 (July 1989): 137 (entry of 19 May 1954); cited hereafter as *RT*.
130. Romanova, *Aleksandr Tvardovskii*, 417. Read by the author to fellow editors of *Novyi mir* on 2–3 May 1954, *Tyorkin in the Other World* was scheduled for publication in the journal's July 1954 issue. It came out, heavily edited, only in 1963: see *Izvestiia*, 18 August 1963; *NM*, no. 8 (August 1963): 3–42.
131. Tvardovskii to the Central Committee Presidium, 10 June 1954, in *Apparat TsK KPSS i kul'tura, 1953–1957*, 225–227. In his diary, the draft of the letter is dated 7 June 1954: *RT*, 138.
132. *Apparat TsK KPSS i kul'tura, 1953–1957*, 226–227.
133. Petrov and Burtin, "'Edva' raskrylis'," 216–221.
134. Starting with Mayakovskii in the late 1920s, when Ermilov was a secretary of the Russian Association of Proletarian Writers (RAPP), from 1928 to 1932.
135. Vladimir Ermilov, "Fal'shivaia proza," *LG*, 20 December 1947; Tvardovskii, *Rodina i chuzhbina* (Smolensk: Smolgiz, 1947).
136. Petrov and Burtin, "'Edva raskrylis'," 217.
137. Tvardovskii, *RT*, 137 (29 May 1954); Petrov and Burtin, "'Edva raskrylis'," 214.
138. "Uluchshit' ideino-politicheskuiu rabotu sredi pisatelei," *LG*, 15 June 1954; Romanova, *Aleksandr Tvardovskii*, 423; RGALI, f. 634, op. 4, d. 703, ll. 23–24, 27 (15 June 1954); "O kriticheskom otdele zhurnala 'Novyi mir'," *LG*, 1 July 1954.

139. Tvardovskii, *RT*, 170 (entry of 7 July 1955).
140. Fadeev to Maria Illarionovna Tvardovskaia, 8 July 1954, in *Aleksandr Fadeev. Pis'ma i dokumenty*, ed. N. I. Dikushina (Moscow: Izdatel'stvo Literaturnogo instituta im. A. I. Gor'kogo, 2001), 331–333.
141. The 7 July 1954 meeting is referred to in the brief decision of the Central Committee Secretariat from the same day, which obliged Pospelov and the two top officers of the Department of Science and Culture, A. Rumiantsev and V. Kruzhkov, to prepare a draft committee resolution on *Novyi mir:* Petrov and Burtin, "'Edva raskrylis'," 225. The meeting is also mentioned in the 21 November 1954 from by the department: "O podgotovke ko vtoromu Vsesoiuznomu s"ezdu pisatelei," in T. Domracheva, ed., "'S"ezd dolzhen mobilizovat' pisatelei'," *Voprosy literatury*, no. 3 (1993): 260–301, here 268–292 (note), esp. 281.
142. Fadeev to Tvardovskaia, 331; N. I. Dikushina, "'Budem govorit' o literature i o zhizni.' Iz perepiski Aleksandra Tvardovskogo i Aleksandra Fadeeva," *Druzhba narodov*, no. 5 (2000): 186–205. In Fadeev's letter all participants of the meeting, save for Khrushchev, were unnamed: confidentiality was part of his idea of party discipline.
143. Fadeev to Tvardovskaia, 331–332, esp. 332 (quotations).
144. Tvardovskii to Khrushchev, 16 July 1954, in *Apparat TsK KPSS i kul'tura, 1953–1957*, 284. In his diary the letter is dated 17 July: Tvardovskii, *RT*, 141.
145. Tvardovskii, *RT*, 141–142 (entry of 5 August 1954). See also Mariia Zezina, *Sovetskaia khudozhestvennaia intelligentsiia i vlast' v 1950e–60-e gody* (Moscow: Dialog MGU, 1999), 141.
146. Khrushchev's speech at the 23 July 1954 meeting of the CC Secretariat, recorded by P. Tarasov, in Petrov and Burtin, "'Edva raskrylis'," 227–229, here 228 (also quotations).
147. Ibid., 232.
148. Tvardovskii, *RT*, 141.
149. P. Tarasov, memo on the 10 August 1954 meeting of the party group of the Writers' Union Board, 12 August 1954, in *Apparat TsK KPSS i kul'tura, 1953–1957*, 292–293, 295.
150. Tvardovskii, *RT*, 142 (11 August 1954).
151. "Ob oshibkakh zhurnala 'Novyi mir.' Rezoliutsiia prezidiuma pravleniia Soiuza sovetskikh pisatelei," *LG*, 17 August 1954. For Tvardovskii's speech at the 11 August session of the Writers' Union board (where he repeatedly protected his deputies Dement'ev and Smirnov and claimed full responsibility for the journal's strategy), see Central Archive of the Union of Soviet Writers of the USSR, op. 28 p/kh, d. 89, published in Romanova, *Aleksandr Tvardovskii*, 427–429, here 428.
152. RGALI, f. 1702, op. 6, d. 92, ll. 94–152; d. 93, ll. 1–85ob. A few letters were written on behalf of an indentified number of people, such as "a group of students"; see, e.g., ibid., d. 92, ll. 113–119.

153. Ibid., d. 93, ll. 37–41 (Iu. Vardashkin, Kamensk, Buriatiia, June 1954); d. 92, ll. 131–135ob; ll. 113–119.
154. Ibid., d. 92, ll. 106–107 (Novo-Kubanskoe, 1 June 1954), original emphasis.
155. Azhaev: ibid., d. 7; Trifonov: ibid., d. 27, ll. 50, 55–55ob; d. 40, ll. 8–99ob; d. 41, ll. 146–146ob, 166–170, 174–175, 275, 276–277; d. 54, l. 148.
156. Ibid., d. 92, ll. 131–135ob (registered 23 June 1954). The students were mostly mathematicians, joined by three philologists, an economist, a geologist, and a journalist.
157. Kronid Liubarskii, *Kronid: Izbrannye stat'i K. Liubarskogo* (Moscow: Rossiiskii gosudarstvennyi gumanitarnyi universitet, 2001), 33; see also Tromly, "Re-Imagining the Soviet Intelligentsia," 216–217.
158. Liubarskii, *Kronid,* 33.
159. Liubarskii, *Kronid,* 35; Petrov and Burtin, "'Edva raskrylis'," 221–223 (CC Department of Science and Culture note, 17 July 1954). On party monitoring see also Tromly, "Re-Imagining the Soviet Intelligentsia," 217.
160. Petrov and Burtin, "'Edva raskrylis'," 222; Tromly, "Re-Imagining the Soviet Intelligentsia," 217.
161. Liubarskii, *Kronid,* 33. He remembered writing this collective letter "in the spring of 1954." *Novyi mir* received the letter on 23 June, so it could have been written later than the Liubarskii suggested. RGALI, d. 1702, op. 6, d. 92, l. 131.
162. RGALI, d. 1702, op. 6, d. 88, ll. 37–58 (Postnov, instructor of literature, Novosibirsk Pedagogical Institute, registered 19 February 1954); d. 89, ll. 24–30 (Postnov again, 2 March 1954); d. 92, ll. 112–119 (registered 17 June 1954); d. 93, l. 86 ("a group of students from Saratov," 14 October 1954).
163. Ibid., d. 91, ll. 118–122 (30 March 1954, registered 13 April 1954). The author, one Vladimir Chebaev, who introduced himself as "a historian and mechanical engineer," had already written to *Novyi mir* before in support of Pomerantsev, on behalf of history students at Kazan University. Ibid., d. 89, ll. 7–8ob (registered 2 March 1954).
164. Ibid., d. 91, ll. 119–120.
165. Ibid., d. 92, l. 133.
166. Iosif Stalin, "Marksizm i voprosy iazykoznaniia," *Pravda,* 20 June 1950.
167. RGALI, d. 1702, op. 6, d. 91, ll. 121–122.
168. Ibid., ll. 120–121.
169. Ibid., l. 122.
170. This topic has been the subject of extensive and sophisticated scholarly discussions. For insightful analyses, see Stephen Kotkin, *Magnetic Mountain: Stalinism as a Civilization* (Berkeley: University of California Press, 1995); Jochen Hellbeck, *Revolution on My Mind: Writing a Diary under Stalin* (Cambridge, Mass.: Harvard University Press, 2006).

171. Natalia Dolinina, "Maskarad slov," *Izvestiia*, 29 November 1960, emphasis added; Boris Eikhenbaum, diary entries of 9 December 1949 and 13 March 1953, cited in Marietta Chudakova and Evgenii Toddes, "Nasledie i put' B. Eikhenbauma," in Boris Eikhenbaum, *O literature: Raboty raznykh let* (Moscow: Sovetskii pisatel', 1987), 29.
172. Chudakova, "Iazyk raspavsheisia tsivilizatsii," here 285, see also 286–287.
173. Liubarskii, *Kronid*, 34.
174. Clark, "'Wait for Me.'"
175. RGALI, f. 1702, op. 6, d. 93, l. 36 (Kondratovich to Iurii Vardashkin, 26 July 1954); ibid., l. 7 (Kondratovich to A. Sinditskii, no date).
176. Ibid., l. 70 (N. Podgug, Moscow, 31 July 1954), original emphasis.
177. Ibid., l. 69.
178. For a vivid description of Pomerantsev's character (based on personal acquaintance), see Grigorii Svirskii, *Na lobnom meste: Literatura nravstvennogo soprotivleniia, 1946–1986* (Moscow: Kruk, 1998), http://lit.lib.ru/s/swirskij_g/text_0010.shtml (accessed 15 May 2010); Pomerantsev, *Dom siuzhetov*.
179. See, e.g., TsGALI SPb, f. 97, op. 4, d. 758, ll. 9–9ob, 12–12ob.

3. *Naming the Social Evil*

1. Vladimir Dudintsev, "Ne khlebom edinym," *NM*, no. 8 (August 1956): 31–118, no. 9 (September 1956): 37–118, and no. 10 (October 1956): 21–98.
2. RGALI, f. 1702, op. 6, d. 242, l. 111.
3. Ibid., d. 240, l. 37 (Novosibirsk), 85 (Tashkent); d. 241, l. 67 (Lviv oblast'), 117 (Kostroma); d. 243, l. 25 (Yalta); d. 245, l. 57 (Leningrad); ibid., op. 8, d. 127, l. 222 (Velikie Luki); d. 134, l. 14 (Minsk); d. 136, l. 18 (Kazan'); d. 268, l. 15 (Odessa); ibid., op. 8, d. 133, l. 132 (Baku).
4. Ibid., op. 6, d. 240, l. 15; d. 241, l. 16.
5. Ibid., d. 242, ll. 22–23; d. 243, l. 121 (Magnitogorsk).
6. Ibid., d. 241, l. 16 (Gomel'), l. 76 (Molotov region); d. 242, l. 128 (Kiev). RGALI, f. 1702, op. 8, d. 131, l. 4 (Leningrad).
7. Vladimir Dudintsev, *Mezhdu dvumia romanami* (Saint Petersburg: Zhurnal "Neva," 2000), 9–14; Hugh McLean and Walter N. Vickery, eds., *The Year of Protest, 1956: An Anthology of Soviet Literary Materials* (New York: Vintage Books, 1961), 155–159. For eyewitness accounts, see Natalia Bianki, *K. Simonov, A. Tvardovskii v "Novom mire": Vospominaniia* (Moscow: Violanta, 1999), 186; Evgenii Dolmatovskii, "I Didn't Sleep All Night Because of You," *Russian Studies in History* 38, no. 4 (Spring 2000): 7–20. See also Karl Loewenstein, "The Thaw: Writers and the Public Sphere in the Soviet Union 1951–57," Ph.D. diss., Duke University, 1999, 299–311.
8. For a persuasive discussion of continuity between Stalin-era and early post-Stalin (1950s) fiction, including Dudintsev's novel, see Katerina Clark, *The*

Soviet Novel: History as Ritual (Chicago: The University of Chicago Press, 1981), 216–220; Clark, "The Changing Image of Science and Technology in Soviet Literature," in *Science and Soviet Social Order*, ed. Loren R. Graham (Cambridge, Mass.: Harvard University Press, 1990), 259–298, esp. 280–284. Compared with the 1950s, Clark observes, more significant departures from socialist realist clichés were made during the 1960s.

9. Dudintsev, "Ne khlebom edinym," *NM*, no. 10 (october 1956): 97.
10. B. Platonov, "Real'nye geroi i literaturnye skhemy," *LG*, 24 November 1956; Clark, *Soviet Novel*, 218–220; Clark, "The Changing Image," 282.
11. Clark, *Soviet Novel*, 217; Richard Chapple, "Vladimir Dudintsev as Innovator and Barometer of His Time," *Australian Slavonic and East European Studies* 6, no. 2 (1992): 1–19, esp. 1–8.
12. "Direktivy XX s"ezda KPSS po shestomu piatiletnemu planu razvitiia narodnogo khoziaistva SSSR na 1956–1960 gody," *Pravda*, 26 February 1956.
13. William J. Tompson, "Industrial Management and Economic Reform under Khrushchev," in *Nikita Khrushchev*, ed. William Taubman, Sergei Khrushchev, and Abbott Gleason (New Haven: Yale University Press, 2000), 138–159, esp. 141–144.
14. Aleksandr Pyzhikov, *Khrushchevskaia "ottepel'"* (Moscow: OLMA-Press, 2002), 156–157; Tat'iana Korzhikhina, *Sovetskoe gosudarstvo i ego uchrezhdeniia: Noiabr' 1917g.–dekabr' 1991g.* (Moscow: RGGU, 1994), 231–233.
15. On these themes, see also Susanne Schattenberg, "'Democracy' or 'Despotism'? How the Secret Speech Was Translated into Everyday Life," in *The Dilemmas of De-Stalinization: Negotiating Cultural and Social Change in the Khrushchev Era*, ed. Polly Jones (London: Routledge, 2006), 64–79.
16. E.g., "Vnimaniiu ministra A. Zvereva," *Trud*, 8 June 1956; "Biurokratov i chinush—na chistuiu vodu!" *Trud*, 15 June 1956; "Chem ob"iasnit' molchanie ministra tov. Sheremet'eva?" *Stroitel'naia gazeta*, 29 July 1956; "Novomu—bol'shuiu dorogu!" *Trud*, 16 September 1956; "Pytlivyi um—zolotye ruki," *Trud*, 26 September 1956; "Ratsionalizator—borets za novoe, peredovoe," *Komsomol'skaia pravda*, 29 September 1956; "Tvorchestvu izobretatelei i ratsionalizatorov—shirokuiu dorogu!" *Pravda*, 6 October 1956; "Izobretateliam i ratsionalizatoram—vsemernuiu podderzhku," *Izvestiia*, 13 October 1956; "Pogovorim o brizakh," *Trud*, 13 October 1956; "Za dal'neishii pod"em massovogo tekhnicheskogo tvorchestva," *Pravda*, 18 October 1956; "K novomu pod"emu tekhnicheskogo tvorchestva mass," *Izvestiia*, 27 October 1956.
17. Daniil Granin, "Sobstvennoe mnenie," *NM*, no. 8 (August 1956): 129–136.
18. Aleksandr Bek, "Zhizn' Berezhkova," *NM*, nos. 1–5 (1956).
19. "Vsesoiuznoe soveshchanie ratsionalizatorov, izobretatelei i novatorov proizvodstva," *Pravda*, 18–20 October 1956; TsGALI SPb, f. 107, op. 3, d. 41, ll. 1–64 (19 October 1956).

20. TsGALI SPb, f. 107, op. 3, d. 41, l. 45.
21. Dudintsev, *Mezhdu dvumia romanami*, 37–42.
22. The last responses on record are dated May 1965. RGALI, f. 1702, op. 9, d. 178, l. 52 (stenographer A. Vasil'eva, Moscow, 13 May 1965); ibid., op. 10, d. 250, ll. 64–67 (Pavel Suprunenko, Zaporozh'e, registered 14 May 1965).
23. RGALI, f. 1702, op. 6, dd. 240, 241, 242, 243, 244, 245 (entire); ibid., op. 8, dd. 10, 11, 127, 128, 129, 130, 131, 132, 133, 134, 135, 136, 137, 267, 268, 279, 404, 405 (entire); d. 735, ll. 63–64; ibid., op. 9, d. 82, ll. 32–33ob, 144–145; d. 167, ll. 13–18ob, 27–30; d. 176, ll. 19–20; d. 178, ll. 7–16ob, 52, 79–79ob; ibid., op. 10, d. 1, l. 70; d. 2, ll. 49–50; d. 3, ll. 4–7, 18; d. 74, ll. 14–14ob, 44–53; d. 75, ll. 7–14ob, 69–70ob; d. 76, ll. 43–43ob, 67–67ob; d. 78, ll. 94–113ob; d. 79, ll. 76–77, 85–86ob; d. 83, l. 55, 191–192; d. 173, ll. 136–136ob; d. 250, ll. 64–67. A letter sometimes had several authors; conversely, one reader may have written several letters.
24. RGALI, f. 1702, op. 6, d. 243 (Lt. Col. M. A. Ershov, "commissioned by the staff of the Latvian SSR Council of Ministers KGB Plenipotentiary office in the town of Rezekene," 27 November 1956).
25. RGALI, f. 634, op. 4, d. 1271, ll. 1–53, esp. 14a–17, 42–47 (*Lieraturnaia gazeta* editorial board meeting of 18 October 1956); GARF, f. 1244, op. 1, d. 178, ll. 7–33, 132–140 (*Izvestiia*, meetings of 3 December and 11 December 1956). On December 13 and 27–28, 1956, *Izvestiia*'s party organization reprimanded those editors who spoke in favor of Dudintsev's novel. TsAOPIM, f. 453, op. 2, d. 27, ll. 87–88, 104–106, 133, 159, 220–231, 233, 235.
26. Katerina Clark, "Socialist Realism *with* Shores: The Conventions for the Positive Hero," in *Socialist Realism without Shores*, ed. Thomas Lahusen and Evgeny Dobrenko (Durham: Duke University Press, 1997), 27–50.
27. RGALI, f. 1702, op. 6, d. 241, l. 15.
28. Ibid.
29. Ibid., l. 16.
30. Clark, *Soviet Novel*, 75–79, 203; Sheila Fitzpatrick, "Cultural Revolution as Class War," in *The Cultural Front: Power and Culture in Revolutionary Russia* (Ithaca: Cornell University Press, 1992), 115–148, esp. 118, 125, 128, 129, 132–136.
31. RGALI, f. 1702, op. 6, d. 245, ll. 91–92 (original emphasis).
32. Sheila Fitzpatrick, "How the Mice Buried the Cat: Scenes from the Great Purges of 1937 in the Russian Provinces," *Russian Review* 52 (July 1993): 299–320.
33. See, e.g., M. Ures, "Dozhdetsia li tokar' N. Smirnov otveta ot ministra A. Kostousova?" *Promyshlenno-ekonomicheskaia gazeta*, 13 May 1956; "Ukaz Prezidiuma Verkhovnogo Soveta SSSR O nagrazhdenii tov. Kostousova A. I. ordenom Lenina," *Pravda*, 6 October 1956.
34. RGALI, f. 1702, op. 6, d. 241, l. 53 (registered 12 October 1956).

35. RGALI, f. 1702, op. 6, d. 244, ll. 63, 67–68 (registered 12 December 1956). Matveev did not indicate his occupation.

36. On the rhetoric of social hygiene and cleansing, see Amir Weiner, *Making Sense of War: The Second World War and the Fate of the Bolshevik Revolution* (Princeton: Princeton University Press, 2001), 34–37; Jeffrey Brooks, *Thank You, Comrade Stalin: Soviet Public Culture from Revolution to Cold War* (Princeton: Princeton University Press, 2000), 51, 128–146. On "romantic anticapitalism" as fundamental to Russian revolutionary culture of the 1910s to the early 1930s, see Katerina Clark, *Petersburg: Crucible of Cultural Revolution* (Cambridge, Mass.: Harvard University Press, 1995), 16–23, 66.

37. On the ethical and, in Igal Halfin's argument, eschatological dimension of the terror of 1934–1938, see Brooks, *Thank You, Comrade Stalin*, 139–148; Igal Halfin, *Terror in My Soul: Communist Autobiographies on Trial* (Cambridge, Mass.: Harvard University Press, 2003), esp. 7–42.

38. Sheila Fitzpatrick, *Stalin's Peasants: Resistance and Survival in the Russian Village after Collectivization* (New York: Oxford University Press, 1994), 239; Fitzpatrick, "Making a Self for the Times: Impersonation and Imposture in 20th-Century Russia," *Kritika: Explorations in Russian and Eurasian History* 2, no. 3 (Summer 2001) 469–487, esp. 477–480; on the rhetoric of enemies' elusiveness developed around 1937, see Weiner, *Making Sense of War*, 35.

39. Johanna Granville, *The First Domino: International Decision-Making during the Hungarian Crisis of 1956* (College Station: Texas A&M University Press, 2004), 19, 42–43.

40. *Apparat TsK KPSS i kul'tura. 1953–1957: Dokumenty* (Moscow: ROSSPEN, 2001), 537 (a note by the Central Committee's Department of Science, School, and Culture, 26 September 1956). The note called Dudintsev's book and several other recent *Novyi mir* publications "unprincipled and apolitical."

41. *Reabilitatsiia: Kak eto bylo. Dokumenty Prezidiuma TsK KPSS i drugie materially*, vol. 2 (Moscow: Mezhdunarodnyi fond "Demokratiia," 2003), 208–214, esp. 210.

42. See, e.g., "Obsuzhdaem novye knigi," *LG*, 27 October 1956; Platonov, "Real'nye"; N. Kriuchkova, "O romane 'Ne khlebom edinym," *Izvestiia*, 2 December 1956; Dmitrii Eremin, "Chem zhiv chelovek?" *Oktiabr'*, no. 12 (December 1956): 166–173; "Literatura sluzhit narodu," *LG*, 15 December 1956; "Pod znamenem kommunisticheskoi ideinosti i sotsialisticheskogo realizma," ibid., 15 January 1957; "Sozdavat' proizvedeniia, dostoinye nashego naroda," ibid., 26 January 1957; Tamara Trifonova, "Ne khlebom edinym," *Kul'tura i zhizn'*, no. 1 (1957), 18–19 (a milder reaction, perhaps because the journal targeted foreign audiences); V. Nazarenko, "Kryl'ia literatury," *Zvezda*, no. 3 (1957): 192–204; Nikolai Shamota, "Chelovek v kollektive," *Kommunist* no. 5 (1957): 75–87; Iakov El'sberg, "Neopravdannoe vysokomerie," *LG*, 13 June 1957.

43. RGALI, f. 1702, op. 6, d. 240, l. 41.
44. Ibid., op. 8, d. 134, l. 81.
45. Thomas Lahusen, *How Life Writes the Book: Real Socialism and Socialist Realism in Stalin's Russia* (Ithaca: Cornell University Press, 1997); Evgeny Dobrenko, "The Disaster of Middlebrow Taste, Or, Who Invented Socialist Realism?" in *Socialist Realism without Shores*, 135–164; Dobrenko, *Formovka sovetskogo chitatelia: Sotsial'nye i esteticheskie predposylki retseptsii sovetskoi literatury* (Saint Petersburg: Akademicheskii proekt, 1997), 263–264.
46. See also Alexei Yurchak, *Everything Was Forever, Until It Was No More: the Last Soviet Generation* (Princeton: Princeton University Press, 2006).
47. RGALI, f. 1702, op. 8, d. 267, l. 8.
48. Ibid., d. 279, l. 25; see also ibid., d. 268, ll. 78, 75ob–76 (A. Nezvanov, Crimea).
49. Ibid., d. 268, l. 60.
50. Ibid., d. 240, l. 43 (registered 11 January 1957).
51. RGANI, f. 5, op. 30, d. 236, ll. 5–6 (anonymous, mid-late December 1956).
52. RGALI, f. 1702, op. 6, d. 244, l. 68.
53. On the fifth column argument as central to the terror of 1937, see Oleg Khlevniuk, *1937-i: Stalin, NKVD i sovetskoe obshchestvo* (Moscow: Respublika, 1992), 82–85. Cf. RGALI, f. 1702, op. 8, d. 133, ll. 103, 106, 107 (Chirchik, Uzbekistan); d. 130, l. 111 (Sokol, Vologda region).
54. Interview with Natalia Fedorovna Dudintseva, recorded 15 July 2006; Dudintsev, *Mezhdu dvumia romanami.*
55. Stephen F. Cohen, *The Victims Return: Survivors of the Gulag after Stalin* (London: I. B. Tauris, 2011); Raisa Orlova and Lev Kopelev, *My zhili v Moskve: 1956–1980gg.* (Ann Arbor: Ardis, 1988), 27–29, 43, 46, 56–60; Ludmilla Alexeyeva and Paul Goldberg, *The Thaw Generation: Coming of Age in the Post-Stalin Era* (Pittsburgh: University of Pittsburgh Press, 1990), 68–71, 76–77, 83–84.
56. RGALI, f. 1702, op. 6, d. 240, ll. 16, 18, 38, 98; d. 241, ll. 5, 7, 30, 130; d. 243, l. 2; d. 244, ll. 59, 108, 117; d. 245, ll. 24, 33, 43–44, 68, 132–134; ibid., op. 8, d. 127, ll. 32, 42–45, 195–203, 225–228; d. 128, l. 21ob; d. 129, ll. 19–21; d. 132, ll. 124–124ob; d. 133, ll. 19–20; d. 136, ll. 70–92; d. 145, ll. 8–12; d. 268, ll. 1–1ob, 75–79. For the decree, see *Pravda*, 2 July 1956.
57. RGALI, f. 1702, op. 8, d. 130, l. 118; d. 268, ll. 1–1ob; ibid., d. 127, l. 37; d. 244, l. 136.
58. Ibid., op. 6, d. 242, ll. 22–23 (instructor, Novocherkassk Automobile and Roads Technical School); d. 245, l. 81 (associate professor, Krasnodar State Pedagogical Institute); op. 8, d. 127, ll. 148–149 (Iagodnyi, Magadan region), 216–217 (former senior employee at the Ministry of Transportation, rehabilitated but still living in Magadan); d. 134, ll. 23–24 (refrigeration specialist, Kiev).
59. Ibid., op. 8, d. 127, ll. 148–149 (registered 21 January 1957).

60. Ibid., op. 6, d. 242, l. 120 (registered 26 September 1956).
61. Ibid., op. 8, d. 127, l. 160–161 (15 January 1957).
62. Ibid., d. 132, ll. 62–102 (21 April 1957), here 95, 99–101.
63. Ibid., d. 127, ll. 61–73, 74–124, esp. 65–66 (no date).
64. Ibid., d. 404, ll. 3–7, 9, 11, 13–16ob; d. 405, ll. 1, 2, 6; d. 735, ll. 63–64; op. 9, d. 82, ll. 32–33ob, 144–145; d. 167, ll. 13–18ob, 27–30; d. 176, ll. 19–20; d. 178, ll. 7–16, 52, 79–79ob; op. 10, d. 1, l. 70; d. 2, ll. 49–50; d. 3, ll. 4–7, 18; d. 74, ll. 14–14ob; d. 75, ll. 7–14ob, 69–70ob; d. 76, ll. 43–43ob, 67–67ob; d. 78, ll. 94–113ob; d. 79, ll. 76–77, 85–86ob; d. 83, ll. 55, 191–192; d. 173, ll. 136–136ob; d. 250, ll. 64–67.
65. Ibid., op. 9, d. 176, ll. 19–20.
66. Ibid., d. 178, l. 79 (1 April 1965).
67. Ibid., l. 79ob.
68. Ibid., l. 77.
69. Ibid., d. 176, l. 18 (23 March 1965); d. 178, l. 52 (13 May 1965).
70. Ibid., d. 82, ll. 32–33ob (4 January 1962).
71. Lotman to Boris Andreevich Uspenskii, 18 May 1981, in Lotman, *Pis'ma* (Moscow: Shkola "Iazyki russkoi kul'tury," 1997), 619.
72. E.g., RGALI, f. 1702, op. 10, d. 75, ll. 69–70ob (Gorshunov, age sixty-six); d. 78, ll. 94–113 (Meerson, seventy); ibid., op. 9, d. 178, ll. 7–16ob (Pantiukhin, fifty-two), 79–79ob (Khromov, sixty); d. 167, ll. 13–18ob (Borisov, fifty-nine).
73. Dudintsev, *Ne khlebom edinym* (Moscow: Khudozhestvennaia literatura, 1968; Moscow: Sovremennik 1979; Moscow: Sovetskii pisatel', 1990).
74. RGALI, f. 1702, op. 10, d. 2, ll. 49–50.
75. Weiner, *Making Sense of War*, 21–39; Peter Holquist, *Making War, Forging Revolution: Russia's Continuum of Crisis, 1914–1921* (Cambridge, Mass.: Harvard University Press, 2002), 202–205.
76. Dudintsev, *Mezhdu dvumia romanami*; Dudintsev, "Novogodniaia skazka," *NM*, no. 1 (January 1960).
77. B. M. Kedrov, "Puti poznaniia istiny," *NM*, no. 1 (January 1965): 213–235; G. V. Platonov, "Dogmy starye i novye," *Oktiabr'*, no. 8 (August 1965): 149–162.
78. RGALI, f. 619, op. 4, d. 87, ll. 75–84.
79. "Ot redaktsii," *NM*, no. 10 (October 1964), 287.
80. *LG*, 1 January 1957.
81. Aleksandr Tvardovskii, "Iz rabochikh tetradei (1953–1960)," *Znamia*, no. 8 (August 1989): 174 (21 April 1958), 176 (6 May 1958), 177–178 (13 May and 8 June 1958).

4. *Recalling the Revolution*

1. Vitalii Afiani and Natal'ia Tomilina, eds., "*A za mnoiu shum pogoni . . .*": *Boris Pasternak i vlast'. 1956–1972: Dokumenty* (Moscow: ROSSPEN, 2001), 133–143. For evidence of backstage political manipulations around *Doctor Zhivago*,

including pressure on Pasternak, see ibid., 63–94. For additional details of the affair and its aftermath, see Evgenii Pasternak, "V osade," ibid., 10–60.

2. Nobel Committee quoted in Christopher Barnes, *Boris Pasternak: A Literary Biography*, vol. 2: 1928–1960 (Cambridge: Cambridge University Press, 1998), 340.
3. The meeting gathered the board presidium of the Union of Soviet Writers, the board presidium of its Moscow branch, and the organizing committee bureau of the Writers' Union of the Russian Federation (the union itself came into existence in December 1958). *LG*, 8 December 1958.
4. Afiani and Tomilina, "A *za mnoiu shum pogoni* . . . ," 187–193.
5. An incomplete list of works on the Pasternak affair and its aftermath includes: Gerd Ruge, *Pasternak: A Pictorial Biography* (New York: McGraw-Hill, 1959), 91–124; Robert Conquest, *The Pasternak Affair: Courage of Genius* (Philadelphia: J. B. Lippincott Company, 1962); Guy de Mallac, *Boris Pasternak: His Life and Art* (Norman: University of Oklahoma Press, 1981), 208–271; Ronald Hingley, *Pasternak: A Biography* (London: Weidenfeld and Nicholson, 1983), 231–272; Lazar Fleishman, *Boris Pasternak: The Poet and His Politics* (Cambridge, Mass.: Harvard University Press, 1990), 273–314; Peter Levi, *Boris Pasternak* (London: Hutchinson, 1990), 236–283; Jacqueline de Proyart, preface to *Le dossier de l'affaire Pasternak: Archives du Comité Central et du Politburo* (Paris: Gallimard, 1994), i–liv (the French translation of documents published in 2001 as "A *za mnoiu shum pogoni* . . ."); Evgenii Pasternak, *Boris Pasternak: Biografiia* (Moscow: Tsitadel', 1997), 615–720; Barnes, *Pasternak: A Literary Biography*, 300–372; Evgenii Pasternak, "V osade."
6. Afiani and Tomilina, "A *za mnoiu shum pogoni*," 101–127, 201–278; Barnes, *Pasternak: A Literary Biography*, 350–351.
7. Evgenii Pasternak, *Boris Pasternak*, 676; Barnes, 245, 314–318; Boris Pasternak, "Stikhi iz romana v proze 'Doktor Zhivago,'" *Znamia*, no. 4 (April 1954), 92–95.
8. Zinaida Pasternak, "Vospominaniia," in *Boris Pasternak. Vtoroe rozhdenie. Pis'ma k Z. N. Pasternak. Z. N. Pasternak. Vospominaniia* (Moscow: GRIT, 1993), 362; Evgenii Pasternak, *Boris Pasternak*, 687; E. Pasternak, "V osade," 18; Barnes, *Pasternak: A Literary Biography*, 314, 324.
9. ORF GLM, f. 143, op. 1, d. 33, ll. 1–6 (written notes by P. A. Kuz'ko from one such reading by Pasternak in Kuz'ko's apartment, 5 April 1947).
10. See, e.g., Boris Pasternak to Sergei Spasskii, 12 July 1948, in *Boris Pasternak: Biografiia v pis'makh*, ed. Elena Pasternak and Evgenii Pasternak (Moscow: ART-FLEKS, 2000), 328; Pasternak to Nina Tabidze, 3 June 1952, ibid., 344–346; Pasternak to Simon Chikovani, 14 July 1952, ibid., 348; Pasternak to Tat'iana Nekrasova, 9 November 1954, ibid., 377; Pasternak to Nikolai Smirnov, 2 April 1955, ibid., 377–381; Ol'ga Freidenberg to Boris Pasternak, 29

November 1948, in *Boris Pasternak: Perepiska s Ol'goi Freidenberg*, ed. Elliott Mossman (New York: Harcourt Brace Jovanovich, 1981), 273–274; Pasternak to Freidenberg, 30 November 1948, ibid., 274–275; Aleksandr Gladkov, *Vstrechi s Borisom Pasternakom* (Moscow: ART-FLEKS, 2002), 212, 225–226; Zoia Maslenikova, *Boris Pasternak* (Moscow: Zakharov, 2002), 35, 40, 58; E. B. Pasternak and A. M. Kuznetsov, eds., "'Vysokii stoikii dukh': Perepiska Borisa Pasternaka i Marii Iudinoi" *Novyi mir*, no. 2 (February 1990): 168; Lev Losev, "29 ianvaria 1956 goda," in *Norwich Symposia on Russian Literature and Culture*, vol. 1: *Boris Pasternak, 1890–1990* (Northfield, Vt.: Russian School of Norwich University, 1991), 278; Evgenii Pasternak, *Boris Pasternak*, 618–623, 650–651; Barnes, *Pasternak: A Literary Biography*, 240–243.

11. Simonov to the Central Committee, 7 December 1957, in Afiani and Tomilina, "*A za mnoiu shum pogoni . . .* ," 89–90.
12. RGAE, f. 3527, op. 27, d. 708, l. 19; *LG*, 25 October 1958.
13. *LG*, 25 October 1958; Vladimir Lakshin, *Novyi mir: Dnevnik i poputnoe (1953–1964)* (Moscow: Knizhnaia palata, 1991), 29–30 (what Tvardovskii meant by "cheated" is unclear, and his published diary does not elucidate it).
14. Konstantin Vanshenkin, "Kak iskliuchali Pasternaka," *Voprosy literatury*, no. 2 (1990): 161, 163.
15. David Zaslavskii, "Shumikha reaktsionnoi propagandy vokrug literaturnogo sorniaka," *Pravda*, 26 October 1958.
16. *LG*, 28 October 1958.
17. *Pravda*, 2 and 6 November 1958. On the writing of these two letters, see Olga Ivinskaia, *Gody s Borisom Pasternakom: V plenu vremeni* (Moscow: Libris, 1992), 283–284, 326–327; Viacheslav Ivanov, "Kak bylo napisano pis'mo B. Pasternaka: Segodniashnii kommentarii," in *S raznykh tochek zreniia: "Doktor Zhivago" Borisa Pasternaka*, ed. Leonid Bakhnov and Leonid Voronin (Moscow: Sovetskii pisatel', 1990), 111–112; Irina Emel'ianova, *Legendy Potapovskogo pereulka. B. Pasternak. A. Efron. V. Shalamov. Vospominaniia i pis'ma* (Moscow: Ellis Lak, 1997), 130–135.
18. *Komsomol'skaia pravda*, 30 October 1958. In 1989 Semichastnyi claimed that it was Khrushchev who, before the plenum, had dictated the paragraphs on Pasternak to him. Leonid Bakhnov and Leonid Voronin, eds., *S raznykh tochek zreniia: "Doktor Zhivago" Borisa Pasternaka* (Moscow: Sovetskii pisatel', 1990), 116–117.
19. *LG*, 1 November 1958.
20. Lidiia Chukovskaia, *Zapiski ob Anne Akhmatovoi*, vol. 2 (Paris: YMCA-Press, 1980), 267.
21. E.g., Conquest, *Pasternak Affair.*
22. The authority might have been the Central Committee's Department of Culture via the Secretariat of the Writers' Union Board. It was the Secretariat

that instructed *Literaturnaia gazeta* to publish information on Pasternak's expulsion from the Writers' Union on 27 October 1958. RGALI f. 634, op. 4, d. 1841, l. 1.

23. RGALI f. 634, op. 4, d. 1883, ll. 17–18.
24. Ibid., ll. 27–28.
25. Ibid, d. 1884, ll. 11–12.
26. Ibid., d. 1903, ll. 1–7.
27. Ibid., ll. 1–4; Evgeny Dobrenko, *Formovka sovetskogo chitatelia: Sotsial'nye i esteticheskie predposylki retseptsii sovetskoi literatury* (Saint Petersburg: Akademicheskii proekt, 1997), 121–122.
28. RGALI f. 634, op. 4, d. 1903, ll. 4–7. Interestingly, the letters described by Stashevskaia add up to only eighty-one, not eighty-five. Some data might be missing from her report, or entered in error.
29. Ibid., dd. 2117, 2118, 2119 (seventy-five letters); RGALI f. 1702, op. 8, d. 269 (twenty letters, eighteen of them from Soviet letter writers); the family archive of Evgenii Pasternak, hereafter AEP (evidence of thirty-four letters). In addition, ten letter writers responded to Ilya Ehrenburg's cautious defense of Pasternak in his memoir *People, Years, Life* in 1961–1963. RGALI f. 1702, op. 8, d. 631, ll. 4–5, 8, 14; d. 632, ll. 5ob, 9, 41, 79; d. 735, ll. 63–64, 143–144; ibid., op. 10, d. 82, l. 6. A further seventeen letters to *Novyi mir* in the 1960s mentioned Pasternak and the Nobel Prize affair in other contexts. RGALI f. 1702, op. 9, d. 82, ll. 79–82, 118–119ob; d. 167, ll. 4, 79–79ob, 95–96, 110–111ob; d. 176, ll. 4–5; d. 255, ll. 5–6; ibid., op. 10, d. 1, ll. 106–110; d. 2, ll. 4–5; d. 166, ll. 83–85, 234–234ob; d. 178, ll. 7–16ob; d. 251, l. 45; d. 252, ll. 10–14, 65, 66. Nineteen of these letters were collectively signed or written on behalf of a group, which is why my count has more letter writers than letters. Ol'ga Ivinskaia reproduced some letters and mentioned many more letters from Soviet readers that Pasternak had received during the campaign, but their originals were unavailable to me. Ivinskaia, *Gody s Borisom Pasternakom*, 321–323.
30. Of seventy-five letters to *Literaturnaia gazeta* dated 1958 and 1959, one was mildly supportive of Pasternak, three were neutral or unspecific, and the remaining seventy-one condemned him. Of the eighteen letters to *Novyi mir* in 1958–1959, five supported Pasternak, twelve condemned him, and one was undetermined. Evgenii Pasternak's archive reveals almost exclusively letters supporting Pasternak.
31. RGALI, f. 634, op. 4, d. 2117, ll. 46–47; ll. 74a–78; d. 2119, ll. 77–82: letters by Tat'iana Rozing, village schoolteacher, Kaluga Oblast; A. I. Ianushevich, biology professor, the Kirgizian Academy of Sciences; Maria Filipovich, geologist, the Urals Industry Construction Design Institute, Sverdlovsk.
32. On the editors' "making sense" of readers' letters, see Thomas Lahusen, *How Life Writes the Book: Real Socialism and Socialist Realism in Stalin's Russia* (Ithaca: Cornell University Press, 1997), 162–163.

33. RGALI f. 634, op. 4, d. 2118, ll. 1–3, 5–7, 8, 10–12, 15–16, 18, 19; d. 2119, ll. 55–56ob, 75–76ob; d. 2117, ll. 52–53ob.
34. *LG*, 1 November 1958.
35. RGALI, f. 634, op. 4, d. 2119, ll. 77–82.
36. Ibid., l. 77; Ivinskaia, *Gody s Borisom Pasternakom*, 318.
37. RGALI, f. 634, op. 4, d. 2119, l. 78.
38. Ibid., l. 82.
39. Ibid., l. 81.
40. Ibid., d. 2117, l. 23 (26 October 1958). Sokolov was a Candidate of Sciences in geology and mineralogy and a senior research fellow in the Laboratory of Hydrogeology Problems at the USSR Academy of Sciences in Moscow.
41. RGALI f. 634, op. 4, d. 2117, ll. 24–25.
42. His description closely matches the one given by Donald Raleigh in *Experiencing Russia's Civil War: Politics, Society, and Revolutionary Culture in Saratov, 1917–1922* (Princeton: Princeton University Press, 2002), 62–64.
43. Stashevskaia also noted that an especially large number of letters came from pensioners, quite a few of whom were Civil War veterans. RGALI f. 634, op. 4, d. 1903, l. 1.
44. Pasternak, *Doctor Zhivago*, quoted in *LG*, 25 October 1958.
45. RGALI f. 1702, op. 8, d. 269, ll. 63–63ob (26 October 1958).
46. Ibid., ll. 63ob–64.
47. Ibid., l. 64ob. The first quotation comes from *God Save the Tsar*, the anthem of imperial Russia; the second one from *The Internationale*.
48. Ibid., l. 64ob.
49. See also RGALI, f. 634, op. 4, d. 2117, ll. 114–121 (Romanova, Sverdlovsk, 31 October 1958).
50. By young, I mean letter writers with declared ages under thirty and college students, normally seventeen to twenty-two. Art historian Mikhail German remembers that in 1958 skeptical thoughts about the campaign occurred to a "few young and not-so-young." Mikhail German, *Slozhnoe proshedshee* (Saint Petersburg: Iskusstvo-SPB, 2000), 349.
51. RGALI f. 634, op. 4, d. 2117, l. 79ob.
52. AEP, 28 January 1959.
53. RGALI f. 1702, op. 8, d. 269, l. 44–44a-ob (17–18 November 1958).
54. See also ibid., l. 81 (Lebedev, age twenty, Lesogorskii settlement, Leningrad Oblast, 2 November 1958).
55. That said, I have not seen the "letters of anti-Soviet content" that Stashevskaia mentioned in her report.
56. RGALI f. 634, op. 4, d. 2117, ll. 39, 107; RGALI f. 1702, op. 8, d. 269, l. 93.
57. German, *Slozhnoe proshedshee*, 349.
58. Emel'ianova, *Legendy Potapovskogo pereulka*, 106–107, 109–110.

59. AEP.
60. Emel'ianova, *Legendy Potapovskogo pereulka,* 106–107. An excerpt from the letter appeared in *LG,* 1 November 1958.
61. RGALI f. 1702, op. 8, d. 269, l. 81 (2 November 1958); Leonid Vinogradov, "Da zdravstvuet Pasternak!"; Vladimir Ufliand, "Liubov' prostranstva"; Lev Losev, "29 ianvaria 1956 goda"; and Aleksandr Zholkovskii, "21 avgusta 1959 goda (Vos'moe avgusta po-staromu)," in *Norwich Symposia,* 286–289, 291–295, 276–283, 297–298.
62. Interview with Elena Vladimirovna Pasternak and Evgenii Borisovich Pasternak, 2 June 2002. See also Afiani and Tomilina, "A *za mnoiu shum pogoni,*" 287–288; Chukovskaia, *Zapiski ob Anne Akhmatovoi,* 2:331–332; Emel'ianova, *Legendy Potapovskogo pereulka,* 201–202; Ivinskaia, *Gody s Borisom Pasternakom,* 381–382; Tamara Ivanova, "Boris Leonidovich Pasternak," in *Vospominaniia o Borise Pasternake,* ed. Elena Pasternak and Mael' Feinberg (Moscow: Slovo, 1993), 261; Gladkov, *Vstrechi s Borisom Pasternakom,* 238, 246.
63. Vinogradov, "Da zdravstvuet Pasternak!" 284–289; Ufliand, "Liubov' prostranstva," 290–295. Vinogradov and Ufliand differ on the students' names. See also Ufliand, "Piatidesiatnyi shestidesiatnik," in *"Esli Bog poshlet mne chitatelei . . ."* (Saint Petersburg: BLITs, 1999), 199.
64. David Zaslavskii, "Shumikha reaktsionnoi propagandy vokrug literaturnogo sorniaka," *Pravda,* 26 October 1958.
65. Vinogradov, "Da zdravstvuet Pasternak!" 289; Vinogradov appears to have aggregated several comments by Lenin about Zaslavskii. See Vladimir Lenin, "Raskhliabannaia revoliutsiia," in *Sochineniia,* 4th ed., vol. 25 (Moscow: Gospolitizdat, 1950), 108; Lenin, "Politicheskii shantazh," ibid., 238; Lenin, "Pis'mo k tovarishcham," in *Polnoe sobranie sochinenii,* vol. 34 (Moscow: Gospolitizdat, 1962), 414.
66. Vladimir Lenin, "V iuridicheskuiu komissiiu," in *Polnoe sobranie,* vol. 49 (Moscow: Politizdat, 1964), 441.
67. Ivinskaia, *Gody s Borisom Pasternakom,* 266.
68. On the post-Stalin ossification of the Soviet political language, see Alexei Yurchak, *Everything Was Forever, until It Was No More: The Last Soviet Generation* (Princeton: Princeton University Press, 2005).
69. RGALI f. 634, op. 4, d. 2117, l. 108, 108ob (the village of Petrashchi, Chernigov Oblast).
70. Ilya Ehrenburg, "Liudi, gody, zhizn'," *Novyi mir,* no. 2 (February 1961): 91.
71. RGALI f. 1702, op. 8, d. 631, ll. 4–5; d. 632, l. 41 (Kosharnivskii, sixty, retired village schoolteacher, May 1961; T. N. Aksel'rud, retired schoolteacher, Frunze, November 1961).
72. Ibid., d. 632, ll. 79–80.

73. Ibid., l. 9 (october 1961).
74. Ibid., ll. 79–80.
75. RGALI f. 1702, op. 8, d. 632, l. 4.
76. Interview with E. V. and E. B. Pasternak, 2 June 2002. See also Evgenii Pasternak, "V osade," 59.

5. *Literature above Literature*

1. Aleksandr Tvardovskii, "Iz rabochikh tetradei (1953–1960)" (hereafter *RT*), *Znamia*, no. 8 (August 1989): 174 (21 April 1958); Regina Romanova, *Aleksandr Tvardovskii: Trudy i dni* (Moscow: Vodolei, 2006), 484. The other members of *Novyi mir's* editorial board, as of 25 June 1958, were Boris Lavrenev, Sergei Golubov, Valentin Ovechkin, Boris Zaks, and Evgenii Gerasimov. Tvardovskii's editorial board also included Konstantin Fedin (1892–1977), the only member who stayed on from Simonov's time. Fedin's political weight as first secretary of the Writers' Union (since 1959) was considerable. However, his participation in the journal's editorial work was nominal, so he was never part of Tvardovskii's "team."
2. In 1959 he may have written no less than 1,000 pages of letters to authors and readers. In 1962 his correspondence with only with the leading authors in the journal comprised about 500 pages, while in 1967 his correspondence with readers alone totaled about 400 pages. Tat'iana Snigireva, A. T. *Tvardovskii: Poet i ego epokha* (Ekaterinburg: Izdatel'stvo Ural'skogo universiteta, 1997), 186–187. My estimates suggest a somewhat more modest volume for his correspondence but do confirm that he devoted considerable time and effort to editorial work.
3. Tvardovskii, *RT*, *Znamia*, no. 7 (July 1989): 144–145 (5 October 1954).
4. Ibid., 145 (17 October 1954): 169 (20 March 1955).
5. Ibid., 146 (19 November 1954).
6. Ibid., 177 (12 October 1955).
7. Ibid., 185 (8 October 1956).
8. Ibid., 188 (26 October 1956).
9. Ibid., *Znamia*, no. 8 (August 1989): 124 (26 February 1957).
10. Ibid., 168 (27 January 1958).
11. Ibid., *Znamia*, no. 9 (September 1989): 197 (20 September 1960).
12. Eleonory Gilburd, "Books and Borders: Sergei Obraztsov and Soviet Travels to London in the 1950s," in *Turizm: The Russian and East European Tourist under Capitalism and Socialism*, ed. Anne E. Gorsuch and Diane Koenker (Ithaca: Cornell University Press, 2006), 227–247; Anne E. Gorsuch, *All This Is Your World: Soviet Tourism at Home and Abroad after Stalin* (Oxford: Oxford University Press, 2011).
13. Tvardovskii, *RT*, *Znamia*, no. 9 (September 1989): 185 (23 June 1960); 186 (23 June 1960); 165 (18 December 1959).

14. Ibid., *Znamia*, no. 7 (July 1989): 176 (16 September 1955).
15. Ibid., no. 9 (September 1989): 186 (3 July 1960).
16. Ibid., 200 (5 October 1960).
17. Ibid., *Znamia*, no. 7 (July 1989): 181 (7–8 May 1956).
18. Ibid., no. 8 (August 1989): 158 (11 January 1958).
19. See, e.g., Vasilii Aksenov, *Apel'siny iz Marokko* (1962; Moscow: Izograf, 2000).
20. Tvardovskii, *RT*, *Znamia*, no. 8 (August 1989): 122–123 (17 February 1957).
21. Tvardovskii to Anatolii Kuz'mich Tarasenkov, 31 January 1931, in "Nesgorevshie pis'ma (A. T. Tvardovskii i M. I. Tvardovskaia pishut A. K. Tarasenkovu v 1930–1935 gg.)," ed. M. Belkina, V. A. Tvardovskaia, and O. A. Tvardovskaia, *Znamia*, no. 10 (October 1997): 153–154; Tvardovskii, "U menia kak by dve biografii," ed. Regina Romanova, *Literaturnaia gazeta*, 16 December 1992.
22. Ivan Tvardovskii, *Rodina i chuzhbina* (Smolensk: Posokh, 1996), 108.
23. Belkina, Tvardovskaia, and Tvardovskaia, "Nesgorevshie pis'ma," 167; Regina Romanova, ed., "Materialy k tvorcheskoi biografii A. T. Tvardovskogo. Smolenskii period. 1925–1936," *Literaturnoe nasledstvo* 93 (1983): 399–420, esp. 406; Adrian Makedonov, "Epokhi Tvardovskogo," in Makedonov, *Epokhi Tvardovskogo*; Vadim Baevskii, *Smolenskii Sokrat*; Nikolai Il'kevich, *"Delo" Makedonova* (Smolensk: TRAST-IMAKOM, 1996), 24; Romanova, *Aleksandr Tvardovskii*, 62–67.
24. Makedonov, "Epokhi Tvardovskogo," 24–28.
25. Mariia Tvardovskaia to Anatolii Tarasenkov, 17, 22, and 27 July, and 3 and 22 August 1934; Tvardovskii to Tarasenkov, 20 July and 2 August 1934, Belkina, Tvardovskaia, and Tvardovskaia, "Nesgorevshie pis'ma," 159–163. Romanova, "Materialy k tvorcheskoi biografii A. T. Tvardovskogo," 416; Makedonov, "Epokhi Tvardovskogo," 35.
26. For details, see Andrei Turkov, *Aleksandr Tvardovskii* (Moscow: Molodaia gvardiia, 2010), 9–80.
27. Romanova, *Aleksandr Tvardovskii*, 131.
28. For Makedonov's published NKVD file, see Il'kevich, *"Delo" Makedonova*; for mentions of Tvardovskii's name in the file, see 230–231, 235–236, 239, 249–251, 262, 271, 278, 279, 281, 283, 301–303. See Romanova, *Aleksandr Tvardovskii*, 131–143, for a most detailed documentary record of Tvardovskii's life in 1937.
29. N. I. Dikushina, ed., *Aleksandr Fadeev: Pis'ma i dokumenty* (Moscow: Izdatel'stvo Literaturnogo instituta im. A. M. Gor'kogo, 2001), 303–338. Notably missing from this publication is Fadeev's last and intensely confrontational letter to Tvardovskii of 8 March 1956; Turkov, *Aleksandr Tvardovskii*, 66–68.
30. Tvardovskii, *RT*, *Znamia*, no. 7 (July 1989): 127 (22 January 1954). For this chapter, see *Novyi mir*, no. 3 (March 1954).
31. Tvardovskii, *RT*, *Znamia*, no. 7 (July 1989): 127.

32. Tvardovskii, "Rabochie tetradi 60-kh godov," *Znamia*, no. 10 (October 2003): 154 (17 October 1968); 156 (20 October 1968). Bagrat Shinkuba (1917–2004), an Abkhazian writer, was a friend of Tvardovskii's who hosted him several times in Abkhazia.
33. "Valentina Tvardovskaia, doch' poeta: Ego glavnoi knigoi byli dnevniki" (interview), *Izvestiia*, 18 June 2010, http://www.izvestia.ru/culture/article 3143038/ (accessed 10 December 2010).
34. Tvardovskii to Khrushchev, 15 April 1954, in Romanova, *Aleksandr Tvardovskii*, 415–416; Tvardovskii, *RT*, *Znamia*, no. 7 (July 1989): 134.
35. TsAOPIM, f. 8131, op. 1, d. 86, ll. 81–82.
36. RGANI, f. 5, op. 30, ll. 6–7 (P. Doronin to Furtseva, 9 June 1954); Tvardovskii, *RT*, *Znamia*, no. 7 (July 1989): 131–133, 135–136, 138 (4, 7–8, and 29 May 1954).
37. P. Moskatov to Khrushchev, undated, in An. Petrov and Iu. Burtin, eds., "'Edva raskrylis' pervye tsvety': 'Novyi mir' i obshchestvennye umonastroeniia v 1954 godu," *Druzhba narodov*, no. 11 (1993): 208–239, here 226.
38. RGANI, f. 5, op. 30, d. 84, l. 10.
39. Tvardovskii, *RT*, *Znamia*, no. 7 (July 1989): 144 (8 October 1954).
40. Ibid., 162 (29 March 1955).
41. Ibid., 168 (22 April 1955).
42. Ibid., 177 n. 1. This interpretation comes from Mariia Illarionovna Tvardovskaia.
43. Ibid., 167 (draft of the "Childhood Friend" chapter, 22 April 1955).
44. On contemporary private conversations about the purges, see, e.g., Raisa Orlova and Lev Kopelev, *My zhili v Moskve: 1956–1980 gg.* (Ann Arbor: Ardis, 1988), 27–29, 43, 46, 56–60; Ludmilla Alexeyeva and Paul Goldberg, *The Thaw Generation: Coming of Age in the Post-Stalin Era* (Pittsburgh: University of Pittsburgh Press, 1990), 68–71, 76–77, 83–84.
45. Tvardovskii, *RT*, *Znamia*, no. 7 (July 1989): 167 (18 April 1955).
46. Ibid., 172 (20 August 1955), original emphasis.
47. Ibid., 173 (26 August 1955).
48. Ibid., 175 (13 September 1955).
49. Ibid.
50. Ibid., 175–176 (15 September 1955).
51. Ibid., 176 (16 September 1955), 177 (19 September 1955).
52. Ibid., 178 (6 January 1956).
53. Ibid.
54. Ibid., 178 (in the diary, incorrectly dated 16 February). The entry is published with lacunae.
55. Ibid.
56. Aleksandr Fadeev, "Razgrom," in *Sobranie sochinenii*, vol. 1 (Moscow: Sovetskii pisatel', 1969), 275; N. I. Dikushina, "'Budem govorit' o literature i o

zhizni.' Iz perepiski Aleksandra Tvardovskogo i Aleksandra Fadeeva," *Druzhba narodov*, no. 5 (2000): 186–205, esp. 203; Tvardovskii, *RT*, *Znamia*, no. 7 (July 1989): 178 (16 April 1956?).

57. Tvardovskii, *RT*, *Znamia*, no. 7 (July 1989): 180 (27 April 1956).
58. Ibid., 183 (14 September 1956).
59. Ibid., no. 8 (August 1989): 123 (18 February 1957).
60. Ibid., 125 (2 March 1957).
61. Ibid., 129 (6 June 1957).
62. Ibid., 156 (3 January 1958), 151 (26 December 1957) ("skeleton" quotation).
63. RGALI, f. 1702, op. 9, d. 13, ll. 16–17 (26 November 1958).
64. Ibid., ll. 15–17.
65. E.g., RGALI, f. 1702, op. 6, d. 189, ll. 18–24, 63 (August–November 1956).
66. RGASPI, f. 560, op. 1, dd. 1–50. No less than twenty-two of the fifty manuscripts in this Central Committee collection were completed during the Khrushchev years.
67. Ludmilla Alexeyeva, *Istoriia inakomysliia v SSSR. Noveishii period* (Moscow: Vest', 1992), http://memo.ru/history/diss/books/ALEXEEWA/index.htm (accessed 17 December 2010).
68. The origins of the term *human documents* are French. The term *documents humains* was first used by Edmond de Goncourt in 1878 (or possibly 1876) in the preface to his novel *A Few Creations of Our Times (Quelques créatures de ce temps)*. In 1880, Émile Zola developed the concept into an entire novel of his, *Le Roman experimental*. The popularity of Zola in Russia at the turn of the century may in part explain why the concept became so common among Russian authors.
69. RGALI, f. 1702, op. 9, d. 60, l. 97 (9 November 1961).
70. Ibid., ll. 123–128.
71. Ibid., ll. 109–110 (14 November 1961).
72. Ibid., d. 81, ll. 54–55 (26 December 1962).
73. Ibid., l. 1 (24 December 1962).
74. Ibid., l. 49 (Tvardovskii to Ol'ga Mikhailovna Kuchumova, Moscow, 24 December 1962); d. 102, l. 52 (Tvardovskii to Raisa Semenovna Levina, Khar'kov, 4 May 1963).
75. Ibid., d. 103, ll. 8–9 (28 October 1963).
76. Ibid., d. 145; Nina Gagen-Torn, *Memoria* (Moscow: Vozvrashchenie, 1994); http://www.prison.org/nravy/art/art001_4.htm (accessed 18 December 2010). Several other memoirs that Tvardovskii's *Novyi mir* did not publish also came out during and after perestroika.
77. RGALI, f. 1702, op. 9, d. 81, l. 32 (6 December 1962).
78. Ibid., l. 30.
79. Ibid., ll. 5–6 (evidently 3 December 1962). The letter is dated "3/1/62"—apparently by mistake, since Ginzburg cited Solzhenitsyn's *One Day*

published in November. It could not be 3 January 1963, either, since Tvardovskii's response is dated 26 December 1962.

80. Ibid., l. 3 (26 December 1962, original emphasis).
81. Ibid., d. 141, l. 4.
82. Ibid.
83. Ibid., ll. 4–5.
84. Evgeniia Ginzburg, *Krutoi marshrut: Khronika vremen kul'ta lichnosti,* 2 vols. (Riga: Kursiv, 1989), 1:7.
85. RGALI, f. 1702, op. 9, d. 141, l. 5.
86. Ibid.
87. Evgenii Dobrenko, *Formovka sovetskogo pisatelia: Sotsial'nye i esteticheskie istoki sovetskoi literaturnoi kul'tury* (Saint Petersburg: Akademicheskii proekt, 1999), 134–175.
88. RGALI, f. 1702, op. 9, d. 141, l. 4.
89. Several memoirs by fugitive camp prisoners that appeared in the West in the 1930s were not fictionalized. For an analysis, see Leona Toker, *Return from the Archipelago: Narratives of Gulag Survivors* (Bloomington: Indiana University Press, 2000).
90. RGALI, f. 1702, op. 9, d. 86, l. 17 (8 December 1961).
91. Ibid., l. 18 (3 January 1962).
92. Ibid.
93. Tvardovskii, *RT, Znamia,* no. 9 (September 1989): 201 (6 October 1960). Also RGALI, f. 1710, op. 2. d. 14, ll. 7–7ob: readers' responses to a published excerpt (*Vecherniaia Moskva,* 14 September 1960.)
94. Ibid.
95. Ibid., 201–202.
96. Ibid., 202.
97. Ibid., 201.
98. Robert Chandler, "Introduction: 'Speaking for Those Who Lie in the Earth': The Life and Work of Vasily Grossman," in Vasily Grossman, *Life and Fate,* trans. Robert Chandler (New York: New York Review of Books, 2006).
99. For details, see John Garrard and Carol Garrard, *The Bones of Berdichev: The Life and Fate of Vasily Grossman* (New York: Free Press, 1996), 260–262.

6. *Reassessing the Moral Order*

1. Ilya Ehrenburg, "Ottepel'," *Znamia,* no. 5 (1954): 14–87.
2. Among the publications that came out before the congress (October 1961), was Viktor Nekrasov's *Kira Georgievna* in *Novyi mir,* no. 6 (June 1961). For an analysis, see Polly Jones, "Memories of Terror or Terrorizing Memories? Terror, Trauma, and Survival in Soviet Culture of the Thaw," *Slavonic and*

East European Review 86, no. 2 (2008): 346–371, here 355–357. Among readers, however, Nekrasov's novella did not generate a large-scale polemic comparable to that surrounding Ehrenburg's or Solzhenitsyn's texts.

3. On the Soviet etymology of "repression," see David Fel'dman, *Terminologiia vlasti: Sovetskie politicheskie terminy v istoriko-kul'turnom kontekste* (Moscow: RGGU, 2006), 118–261.
4. Robert Conquest, *The Great Terror: Stalin's Purge of the Thirties* (New York: Macmillan, 1968), in Russian as Robert Konkvest, *Bol'shoi terror* (Riga: Rakstnieks, 1991).
5. On the perceptions of the terror, see also Cathy Frierson, "An Open Call to Focus on Russia's Young Adults," *Problems of Post-Communism* 54, no. 5 (2007): 3–18; Irina Paperno, *Stories of the Soviet Experience: Memoirs, Diaries, Dreams* (Ithaca: Cornell University Press, 2009). On the social composition of the victims in 1937–1938, see, e.g., Paul Gregory, *Terror by Quota: State Security from Lenin to Stalin: An Archival Study* (New Haven: Yale University Press, 2009); David Shearer, *Policing Stalin's Socialism: Repression and Social Order in the Soviet Union, 1924–1953* (New Haven: Yale University Press, 2009); Paul Hagenloh, *Stalin's Police: Public Order and Mass Repression in the USSR, 1926–1941* (Washington, D.C.: Woodrow Wilson Center Press; Baltimore: Johns Hopkins University Press, 2009); Denis Kozlov, "The Leningrad Martyrology: A Statistical Note on the 1937 Executions in Leningrad City and Region," *Canadian Slavonic Papers* 44, no. 3–4 (September–December 2002): 175–208; Melanie Ilic, "The Great Terror in Leningrad: A Quantitative Analysis," *Europe-Asia Studies* 52, no. 8 (2000): 1515–1534.
6. Ilya Ehrenburg, "Liudi, gody, zhizn'," (hereafter LGZh), *NM*, no. 8 (August 1960): 24–60; no. 9 (September 1960): 87–136; no. 10 (October 1960): 7–51; no. 1 (January 1961): 91–152; no. 2 (February 1961): 75–121; no. 9 (September 1961): 88–153; no. 10 (October 1961): 124–157; no. 11 (November 1961): 126–162; no. 4 (April 1962): 9–63; no. 5 (May 1962): 96–154; no. 6 (June 1962): 106–152; no. 1 (January 1963): 67–112; no. 2 (February 1963): 107–143; no. 3 (March 1963): 116–139; no. 1 (January 1965): 103–125; no. 2 (February 1965): 7–65; no. 3 (March 1965): 77–129; no. 4 (April 1965): 29–83. Quotation is from Joshua Rubenstein, *Tangled Loyalties: The Life and Times of Ilya Ehrenburg* (New York: Basic Books, 1996), 339.
7. On Ehrenburg in World War II, see Jeffrey Brooks, *Thank You, Comrade Stalin! Soviet Public Culture from Revolution to Cold War* (Princeton: Princeton University Press, 2000), 167–173, 181–182; Katerina Clark, "Ehrenburg and Grossman: Two Cosmopolitan Jewish Writers Reflect on Nazi Germany at War," *Kritika: Explorations in Russian and Eurasian History* 10, no. 3 (2009): 607–628.
8. RGALI, f. 1702, op. 9, d. 58, l. 56 (Tvardovskii to Ehrenburg, 17 August 1961).

9. Ibid., l. 57.
10. Ibid. d. 79, l. 122; d. 78, l. 101 (Tvardovskii to Ehrenburg, 5 April 1962).
11. Ibid., d. 58, l. 58.
12. Ibid., d. 78, l. 103; d. 79, l. 122.
13. Ibid., d. 79, l. 123. SS Brigadeführer Otto Abetz (1903–1958) served as Nazi Germany's ambassador to Vichy France in 1940–1944. 'L'vov' was the pseudonym Ehrenburg gave to a Soviet diplomatic officer, whose real name could not be disclosed.
14. Ibid.; compare ibid., d. 78, ll. 103–104. See also RGALI, f. 1204, op. 2, d. 2625, ll. 7–8ob (2 March 1961, illegible signature, ten years younger than Ehrenburg)—a reader who had known Fadeev and, just as Tvardovskii, disagreed with Ehrenburg's (mollified) characterization of him.
15. Ehrenburg to Tvardovskii, 10 April 1962, in E. Berar, ed., "Vokrug memuarov Il'i Erenburga," *Minuvshee: Istoricheskii al'manakh* 8 (1992): 387–406, http://vivovoco.rsl.ru/VV/THEME/STOP/ERENBURG.HTM (accessed 12 December 2010).
16. Ibid.
17. Ibid.; see Boris Frezinskii's commentary in Ehrenburg, *Liudi, gody, zhizn'* (hereafter *LGZh*), 3 vols. (Moscow, 1990), 1:569.
18. RGALI, f. 1204, op. 2, d. 2619, ll. 25–29 (L'vov, pensioner, Moscow, 24 August 1960); *LGZh*, 3:233.
19. *LGZh*, 1:48, 127, 250.
20. *LGZh*, 3:228.
21. Benedikt Sarnov, "U vremeni v plenu," in *LGZh*, 1:34–37; Sarnov, *Sluchai Erenburga* (Moscow: Tekst, 2004), 172–185, 234–277; Iakov Etinger, *Eto nevozmozhno zabyt' . . . : Vospominaniia* (Moscow: Ves' Mir, 2001), 105–125; and see Frezinskii's commentary in *LGZh*, 3:396.
22. Gennadii Kostyrchenko, "Deportatsiia—mistifikatsiia (proshchanie s mifom stalinskoi epokhi)," *Otechestvennai istoriia*, no. 1 (2003): 92–113, esp. 96.
23. LGZh, *NM*, no. 9 (1961), 152; no. 4 (1962), 62.
24. Ibid., no. 5 (1962), 143.
25. Ibid., 134.
26. Ibid., 148–154.
27. Ibid. The Spanish town of Teruel changed hands several times in 1937–1938 during the Spanish Civil War.
28. RGALI, f. 1702, op. 8, d. 631, l. 44 (20 March 1961).
29. Ibid., d. 735, l. 119 (Osinki, Kemerovo region, 20 June 1962).
30. LGZh, *NM*, no. 2 (February 1961), 84.
31. RGALI, f. 1702, op. 8, d. 631, l. 49 (Leningrad, 16 March 1961); see also RGALI, f. 1204, op. 2, d. 2625, l. 15 (L. Liubashevskii, Leningrad, 3 March 1961).
32. RGALI, f. 1702, op. 8, d. 631, ll. 8–10 (23 May 1961).

33. RGALI, f. 1204, op. 2, d. 2661, ll. 46–46ob (Margarita Pisareva, student, Leningrad, 27 February 1965).
34. RGALI, f. 1702, op. 8, d. 632, l. 1 (Tashkent, 26 November 1961); also RGALI, f. 1204, op. 2, d. 2617, ll. 39–41; d. 2620, l. 115; d. 2626, l. 89.
35. RGALI, f. 1204, op. 2, d. 2615, l. 33ob; d. 2625, l. 80.
36. RGALI, f. 1702, op. 8, d. 632, l. 25 (registered 15 December 1961), l. 42 (registered 10 April 1961), ll. 74–74ob (3 October 1961).
37. Ibid., d. 632, ll. 19–20 (registered 28 December 1961). *The Great Friendship*, an opera composed by Vano Muradeli (1908–1970), was censured by the Central Committee in 1948.
38. Ibid., l. 38 (Sukhumi).
39. See also ibid., d. 735, l. 130 (Airat Ibragimov, soldier, Far East, registered 31 July 1962).
40. Ibid., l. 143 (Aleksandr Dunaev, Dushanbe, registered 10 August 1962), l. 121 (registered 23 July 1962); ibid., op. 10. d. 250, ll. 13–14 (L. Ia., engineer, 23 April 1965); ibid., op. 8, d. 735, ll. 20–22 (Vsevolod Vibelius, actor, Irkutsk, 30 January 1962), l. 113 (Skhodnev, technician, Ivanovo region, 16 June 1962).
41. Ibid., op. 8, d. 735, ll. 107–108 (age unspecified, 1 July 1962); also his letter in RGALI, f. 1204, op. 2, d. 2619, ll. 25–29. Solomon Lozovskii (1878–1952), an Old Bolshevik and head of the Soviet Information Bureau, was executed together with other members of the Jewish Anti-Fascist Committee. General Iakov Smushkevich (1902–1941), commander of the Soviet air force, was executed at the beginning of the Great Patriotic War on charges of conspiracy. Fedor Raskol'nikov (1892–1939), a revolutionary and later diplomat, refused to return to the USSR and published an open letter to Stalin accusing him of unwarranted extermination of the Bolshevik cadre. A few weeks later, he died under suspicious circumstances. General Dmitrii Pavlov (1897–1941), a Spanish Civil War veteran, commanded the Soviet Western Front at the start of the German invasion in June 1941. He was made a scapegoat for the defeat and executed in October 1941. Ian Berzin (1889–1938), another victim of repression, headed the Intelligence Directorate of the Red Army and was the principal Soviet military advisor in Spain.
42. RGALI, f. 1702, op. 8, d. 735, ll. 135–135ob, 136ob (14 August 1962), original emphasis. Ovadii Gertsovich Savich (1897–1967), a writer and translator, was Ehrenburg's closest friend. Banyuls-sur-Mer is a small French seaside resort near the Spanish border, where Ehrenburg and his wife rented a cottage in the summer of 1938. Ehrenburg to Valentina Aronovna Mil'man, 3 July 1938, in Ilya Ehrenburg, *Pis'ma 1908–1967*, vol. 2 (Moscow: Agraf, 2004), 262.
43. RGALI, f. 1702, op. 8, d. 735, l. 137ob.
44. Ibid., d. 632, ll. 26–27 (Abram Veisbrod, age unknown, Moscow, 11 December 1961), l. 52 (anonymous, registered 17 March 1961).

45. TsAOPIM f. 453, op. 2, d. 27, ll. 16–17, 19. On Ryklin: Dmitrii Mamleev, "My vse zhivem pod gos . . . strakhom," *Izvestiia*, 23 November 2006. On Sevrikov: Grigorii Vodolazov, "Shkafy knig proglatyval. . . ," *Izvestiia*, 4 December 2007.
46. TsAOPIM f. 453, op. 2, d. 27, ll. 22, 27, 33–34.
47. *Programma Kommunisticheskoi partii Sovetskogo Soiuza: Priniata XXII s"ezdom KPSS* (Moscow, 1961), 100–101 (section III, preamble); Aleksandr Pyzhikov, *Khrushchevskaia "ottepel'"* (Moscow, 2002), 31–32, 115–151.
48. On this, see Wendy Goldman, *Terror and Democracy in the Age of Stalin: The Social Dynamics of Repression* (New York: Cambridge University Press, 2007), 8, 163–201, esp. 194, 200.
49. On the film, see Birgit Beumers, "Soviet and Russian Blockbusters: A Question of Genre?" *Slavic Review* 62, no. 3 (Fall 2003): 441–454, esp. 452; David Gillespie, "The Sounds of Music: Soundtrack and Song in Soviet Film," ibid., 473–490, esp. 478–481.
50. RGALI, f. 1702, op. 10, d. 82, ll. 1–3 (S. D. Serebrianyi, young age, Moscow, registered 1 March 1963); this letter presents a rare exception.
51. Ibid., op. 8, d. 632, ll. 37–38 (16 October 1961).
52. RGALI, f. 1204, op. 2, d. 2641, l. 111 (Oleg Sidel'nikov, writer, b. 1923, Tashkent, 31 January 1963), l. 116ob (Roman Amirov, worker, thirty-three, Niazepetrovsk, Cheliabinsk Oblast, January 1963).
53. Vladimir Ermilov, "Neobkhodimost' spora: Chitaia memuary I. Erenburga "Liudi, gody, zhizn'," *Izvestiia*, 30 January 1963.
54. Leonid Il'ichev, "Tvorit' dlia naroda, vo imia kommunizma: Rech' sekretaria TsK KPSS na vstreche rukovoditelei partii i pravitel'stva s deiateliami literatury i iskusstva 17 dekabria 1962 goda," *Pravda*, 22 December 1962; Il'ichev, "Sily tvorcheskoi molodezhi—na sluzhbu velikim idealam," *Literaturnaia gazeta*, 10 January 1963; *Sovetskaia kul'tura*, 10 January 1963. For the stenographic record of the session (24–26 December 1962), see *Ideologicheskie komissii TsK KPSS. 1958–1964: Dokumenty* (Moscow: ROSSPEN, 2000), 293–381.
55. Nikita Khrushchev, "Vysokaia ideinost' i khudozhestvennoe masterstvo—velikaia sila sovetskoi literatury i iskusstva," *Pravda*, 10 March 1963; Leonid Il'ichev, "Ob otvetstvennosti khudozhnika pered narodom," *Pravda*, 9 March 1963.
56. M. Levin, "Ia veriu v propoved'," interview with Aleksei Adzhubei, *Molodezh' Estonii*, 6 May 1988.
57. Priscilla Johnson, "The Politics of Soviet Culture, 1962–1964," in *Khrushchev and the Arts*, ed. Johnson and Leopold Labedz (Cambridge, Mass.: MIT Press, 1965), 1–89, esp. 84–89; Patricia Blake, "Freedom and Control in Literature, 1962–63," in *Politics in the Soviet Union: 7 Cases*, ed. Alexander Dallin and Alan F. Westin (New York: Harcourt, Brace, and World, 1966), 165–205. On the Manège affair, see Susan Reid, "In the Name of the People: The Manège

Affair Revisited," *Kritika: Explorations in Russian and Eurasian History* 6, no. 4 (2005): 673–716.

58. Ermilov, "Neobkhodimost' spora"; see also Ehrenburg, *LGZh* 1:250.
59. Ermilov, "Neobkhodimost' spora."
60. G. Aleksandrov, "Tovarishch Erenburg uproshchaet," *Pravda*, 14 April 1945.
61. Ilya Ehrenburg, "Ne nado zamalchivat' sushchestvo spora," *Izvestiia*, 6 February 1963.
62. Vladimir Ermilov, "Otvet avtoru pis'ma," *Izvestiia*, 6 February 1963.
63. For a rare exception, see RGALI f. 1702, op. 10, d. 82, ll. 1–3.
64. RGALI, f. 1204, op. 2, d. 2646, l. 158–159 (4 February 1963); also RGALI, f. 1702, op. 10, d. 82, l. 19; ibid., d. 83, l. 192 (Yulia Samarina, Cherepovets [9 March 1963]).
65. RGALI, f. 1702, op. 10, d. 82, ll. 73–74 (Emlin and Chervonyi, 19 February 1963); Vladimir Ermilov, "Velikii drug sovetskoi literatury," *Literaturnaia gazeta*, 21 December 1949.
66. RGALI, f. 1702, op. 10, d. 83, l. 242 (registered 11 February 1963).
67. Ibid., ll. 92–92ob (February 1963; registered 6 March 1963).
68. E.g., RGALI, f. 1204, op. 2, d. 2641, ll. 89ob–90 (Lilia Karpych, b. 1928, 19 February 1963), l. 110ob (Tatiana Bushinskaia, Tbilisi, 31 January 1963).
69. RGALI, f. 1204, op. 2, d. 2642, ll. 1–4 (Moscow, 30 January 1963)
70. RGALI, f. 1702, op. 10, d. 83, ll. 211–222 (Ivanovka Bazarnaia, registered 5 March 1963).
71. Ibid., l. 211 (original strike-through).
72. On generational discourse and historical consciousness in twentieth-century Europe, see Stephen Lovell, "Introduction," in *Generations in Twentieth-Century Europe*, ed. Lovell (Houndmills: Palgrave Macmillan, 2007), 1–18, esp. 8–12; Bernd Weisbrod, "Cultures of Change: Generations in the Politics and Memory of Modern Germany," ibid., 19–35, esp. 20–21; Richard Vinen, "Orphaned by History: French Youth in the Shadow of World War II," ibid., 36–56; Hodger Nehring, "'Generation' as a Political Argument in West European Protest Movements during the 1960s," ibid., 57–78, esp. 58–60; Anna Krylova, "Identity, Agency, and the 'First Soviet Generation,'" ibid., 101–121.
73. RGALI, f. 1702, op. 10, d. 83, ll. 217–218.
74. Ibid., l. 41, quotation (engineer Medova, economist N. Lysenko, agronomist G. Tolokonskii, college student E. Ramanovskaia, and personal pensioner B. G. Tolokonskaia, 25 February 1963); ibid., l. 19 (Fridman, 9 February 1963); RGALI, f. 1204, op. 2, d. 2641, l. 14 (Nikolai Engver, young engineer, Arsen'ev, 6 January 1963); ibid., d. 2643, l. 89 (Ia. Zviagin, Kalinin, 7 February 1963).
75. RGALI, f. 1702, op. 10, d. 82, l. 41.
76. Ibid., d. 83, l. 192 (9 March 1963).

77. RGALI, f. 1204, op. 2, d. 2642, ll. 27–52ob, here 52–52ob (Irina Alekseeva, Mochishche-na-Obi, 11 February 1963).
78. Goldman, *Terror and Democracy*, 197–198.
79. So, apparently, did the numerous acts of peasant resistance to collectivization in the 1930s. On the resistance, see Lynne Viola, *Peasant Rebels under Stalin: Collectivization and the Culture of Peasant Resistance* (New York: Oxford University Press, 1996).
80. On this, see Jochen Hellbeck, *Revolution on My Mind: Writing a Diary under Stalin* (Cambridge, Mass.: Harvard University Press, 2006); Igal Halfin, *From Darkness to Light: Class, Consciousness, and Salvation in Revolutionary Russia* (Pittsburgh: University of Pittsburgh Press, 2000); Halfin, *Terror in My Soul: Communist Autobiographies on Trial* (Cambridge, Mass.: Harvard University Press, 2003); Halfin, *Stalinist Confessions: Messianism and Terror at the Leningrad Communist University* (Pittsburgh: University of Pittsburgh Press, 2009).
81. RGALI, f. 1702, op. 10, d. 83, ll. 214–216, 219.
82. Lenin's letter appeared in 1956 in the journal *Kommunist* and in 1957 in the complementary volumes to the fourth edition of his works: "Neopublikovannye dokumenty V. I. Lenina," *Kommunist*, no. 9 (June 1956): 15–26, esp. 16–18; Vladimir Lenin, *Sochineniia*, 4th ed., vol. 36 (Moscow: Gosudarstvennoe izdatel'stvo politicheskoi literatury, 1957), 541–547. In Lenin's *Complete Works*, the letter did not appear until 1964. Lenin, *Polnoe sobranie sochinenii*, vol. 45 (Moscow: Izdatel'stvo politicheskoi literatury, 1964), 343–348. See also Valentin Sakharov, *"Politicheskoe zaveshchanie" Lenina: Real'nosti istorii i mify politiki* (Moscow: Izdatel'stvo Moskovskogo universiteta, 2003), 313.
83. RGALI, f. 1702, op. 10, d. 83, ll. 214–215.
84. Ibid., l. 219.
85. Ibid., ll. 215–216, 219; also ibid., d. 82, l. 84 (Konstantin Boltenko, geologist, fifty-one, Nizhnii Domanik, Komi Republic, registered 15 February 1963); RGALI, f. 1204, op. 2, d. 2642, ll. 1–4 (Moscow, 30 January 1963)—a statement by a former NKVD officer, who argued that back in 1937–1938 even most of his fellow officers in the NKVD did not believe in the guilt of those whom they interrogated.
86. Sarah Davies, *Popular Opinion in Stalin's Russia: Terror, Propaganda, and Dissent, 1934–1941* (Cambridge: Cambridge University Press, 1997), 170–175, 180–187.
87. See also Hellbeck, *Revolution on My Mind*, 95–96. Other reactions apparently could include total estrangement and distrust: see Alexander Afinogenov's diary as analyzed in ibid., 300, 314–315.
88. RGALI, f. 1702, op. 10, d. 83, l. 202–204 (Volchansk, Sverdlovsk region, registered 16 May 1963).
89. Ibid., l. 202.

90. Ibid., l. 203.
91. Ibid., l. 202; RGALI, f. 1204, op. 2, d. 2642, ll. 47ob–48. The names of the stages come from Peter H. Solomon, *Soviet Criminal Justice under Stalin* (Cambridge: Cambridge University Press, 1996), 15. On the mechanism of repression, see Hagenloh, *Stalin's Police*, 202–209, 227–287; Shearer, *Policing Stalin's Socialism*, 285–370. On the grassroots foundations for the purges, specifically support for reprisals against local bosses, see Sheila Fitzpatrick, "How the Mice Buried the Cat: Scenes from the Great Purges of 1937 in the Russian Provinces," *Russian Review* 52 (July 1993): 299–320; Goldman, *Terror and Democracy*, esp. 163, 184–185, 187.
92. RGALI, f. 1702, op. 10, d. 82, l. 79 (town of Arsen'ev, 14 February 1963).
93. Ibid. Long after, in 1957, Semenov's parents were posthumously rehabilitated. In 1960 *Novyi mir* even published Maxim Gorky's sketch about Semenov's father: Gorky, "O edinittse," *NM*, no. 11 (1960), 57.
94. Hannah Arendt, *The Origins of Totalitarianism* [1951] (San Diego: Harcourt Brace, 1973), 317, 323.
95. RGALI, f. 1702, op. 10, d. 83, ll. 202–203.
96. Ibid., l. 220.
97. Ibid., ll. 92ob–93ob (February 1963); also RGALI, f. 1204, op. 2, d. 2642, ll. 49ob–50. On the continuing repression after Yezhov's removal, see Hagenloh, *Stalin's Police*, 288–323; Shearer, *Policing Stalin's Socialism*, 405–440.
98. RGALI, f. 1702, op. 8, d. 735, ll. 3–7 (Tarasenko, Zaporozh'e, 4 January 1962); ibid., ll. 69–72 (Anatolii Khiir, Kemerovo, 19 April 1962); ibid., op. 10, d. 83, l. 192 (Samarina, 9 March 1963); RGALI, f. 1204, op. 2, d. 2642, l. 21 (Petr Arkhipov, Evdokiia Arkhipova, 1963?).
99. On this, see Hellbeck, *Revolution on My Mind*.
100. RGALI, f. 1702, op. 10, d. 82, ll. 23–25, here 23 (Marton Lovas, Hungarian communist since 1922, who had witnessed the purges in Voronezh in 1937; Budapest, 15 February 1963).
101. Ibid., ll. 17–21, 18 (quotation) (9 February 1963); see also RGALI, f. 1204, op. 2, d. 2642, ll. 64–73.
102. RGALI, f. 1702, op. 10, d. 82, l. 20.
103. RGALI, f. 1204, op. 2, d. 2644, ll. 55–67, here 64–66 (Nikolai Tuchnin, associate professor, Kostroma Pedagogical Institute, 10 February 1963).
104. On this, see Hellbeck, *Revolution on My Mind*, esp. 103–106.
105. Leo Tolstoy, "Ne mogu molchat'," in *Polnoe sobranie sochinenii*, vol. 37 (Moscow, 1957): 83–96; V. S. Spiridonov, "'Ne mogu molchat': Istoriia pisaniia i pechataniia," ibid., 425–427.
106. RGALI, f. 1702, op. 10, d. 82, ll. 19–20.
107. See also Vladislav Zubok, *Zhivago's Children: The Last Russian Intelligentsia* (Cambridge, Mass.: Harvard University Press, 2009).

108. RGALI, f. 1702, op. 10, d. 83, ll. 91–95, here 92, 94ob–95; ibid., ll. 240–241 (Vasilii Kolokolov, sixty-one, Donetsk, registered 11 February 1963); RGALI, f. 1204, op. 2, d. 2642, ll. 27–52ob, here 32ob–39ob.
109. RGALI, f. 1702, op. 10, d. 83, l. 94ob (original emphasis).
110. Ibid., ll. 217–218.
111. Ibid., l. 214.
112. On denial, see Michael Shermer and Alex Grobman, *Denying History: Who Says the Holocaust Never Happened and Why Do They Say It?* (Berkeley: University of California Press, 2009), esp. 231–256.
113. RGALI, f. 1204, op. 2, d. 2643, l. 76ob (Neverov, 6 February 1963); RGALI, f. 1702, op. 10, d. 83, l. 191 (Samarina); ibid., op. 8, d. 735, ll. 13–14 (Popov, journalist, Ukraine, 18 January 1962).
114. RGALI f. 1702, op. 8, d. 631, l. 61 (Moscow).
115. Ibid., op. 10, d. 82, l. 92 (Sarbala, Kemerovo region, February 1963); also RGALI, f. 1204, op. 2, d. 2643, ll. 41–42ob (Valerii Buskis, twenty-four, Kishinev, 5 February 1963).
116. RGALI, f. 1702, op. 8, d. 735, l. 13–14 (Chortkov, Ukraine, 18 January 1962).
117. RGALI, f. 1204, op. 2, d. 2643, l. 76ob (6 February 1963).
118. RGALI, f. 1702, op. 10, d. 83, l. 185 (20 March 1963); RGALI, f. 1204, op. 2, d. 2634, ll. 53–54ob (Droznikas, Chita, 14 January 1962).
119. RGALI, f. 1702, op. 10, d. 83, l. 104 (registered 25 February 1963, original emphasis).
120. Ibid., ll. 7–8 (registered 7 January 1963).
121. Ibid., l. 8; also RGALI, f. 1204, op. 2, d. 2643, l. 83 (Ivan Reznin, Dnepropetrovsk, 7 February 1963).
122. RGALI, f. 1702, op. 8, d. 735, ll. 103–104 (5 June 1962).
123. Ibid., l. 104.
124. Ibid., op. 10, d. 83, l. 94ob.
125. Also RGALI, f. 1204, op. 2, d. 2643, ll. 151ob (Antonina Vainer, sixty, Moscow, 9 February 1963).
126. RGALI, f. 1702, op. 8, d. 735, l. 103.
127. *LGZh* 2:162 *(rokovoi udar)*.
128. Literature on this topic abounds. For a brief discussion, see the introduction to this volume; for the German case, see, e.g., Jeffrey Herf, *Divided Memory: The Nazi Past in the Two Germanys* (Cambridge, Mass.: Harvard University Press, 1997).

7. *Finding New Words*

1. Aleksandr Solzhenitsyn, "Odin den' Ivana Denisovicha," *Novyi mir*, no. 11 (1962): 8–74.

2. On the writing and publication of *One Day*, see Liudmila Saraskina's comprehensive *Aleksandr Solzhenitsyn* (Moscow: Molodaia gvardiia, 2008), 287–322. On Tvardovskii's efforts to publish *One Day* (including negotiations with Khrushchev's assistant on cultural affairs, Vladimir Lebedev, and his meeting with Khrushchev on 21 October 1962), see Tvardovskii, "Rabochie tetradi 60-kh godov" (hereafter *RT-60*), *Znamia*, no. 7 (July 2000): 116 (3 July 1962); 118–119 (26 July 1962); 129 (16 September 1962); 130–131 (20 and 21 September 1962); 135–137 (19 and 21 October 1962). See also Vladimir Lakshin, *Golosa i litsa* (Moscow: Geleos, 2001), 210–221; Lakshin, *Solzhenitsyn i koleso istorii* (Moscow: Veche, 2008), 192–214. Lakshin's memoirs and diary generally match the story of the publication of *One Day* as it stands in Tvardovskii's diary. Unlike with the other texts I discuss in this book, the story of the publication of *One Day*—the most famous text *Novyi mir* ever published—is fairly well known and thoroughly studied. In this chapter, I opt to focus on another, less well studied but equally important issue—the reception of Solzhenitsyn's novella.
3. RGALI, f. 1702, op. 9, d. 80, l. 70 (Tvardovskii to Solzhenitsyn, 8 November 1962), original emphasis.
4. Ibid., d. 81, l. 73 (Tvardovskii to Solzhenitsyn, 25 December 1962).
5. RGALI, f. 1702, op. 10, d. 75, ll. 5–6 (Kuzanova, Baku, registered 30 January 1963); ibid., d. 78, ll. 9–12 (Bazhanov, Kalinin, 5 March 1963); ibid., d. 166, ll. 138–150 (Zinchenko, Kiev, 15 May 1964), 152–158 (Kolotusha, Muukachevo, 16 May 1964), 166–174 (Bashlakov, Grodno region, 10 July 1964).
6. "Young" here and elsewhere refers to ages eligible for Komsomol membership (through twenty-eight). Rather than stating their exact age, most young people identified themselves as "students." "Older" refers to individuals who had reached a standard retirement age by the time of writing. Established in the 1920s and confirmed by the law on pensions in 1956, this age was fifty-five for women and sixty for men. See Cynthia Buckley, "Obligations and Expectations: Renegotiating Pensions in the Russian Federation," *Continuity and Change* 13, no. 3 (1998): 317–338. Most of the older letter writers did not state their exact age either, identifying themselves as "pensioners."
7. Shoshana Felman and Dori Laub, *Testimony: Crises of Witnessing in Literature, Psychoanalysis, and History* (New York: Routledge, 1992), 57–59, 68, 70–71.
8. In his discussion of memory as an analytical tool, Kerwin Lee Klein dismisses the idea of therapeutic writing, finding it depressing. I, on the other hand, accept therapeutic writing as a valid way to interpret eyewitness accounts of the terror. Kerwin Lee Klein, "On the Emergence of *Memory* in Historical Discourse," *Representations* 69 (Winter 2000): 136, 148 (n. 24).
9. On citizenship as a paradigm of letter writing in the 1930s, see Sheila Fitzpatrick, "Supplicants and Citizens: Public Letter-Writing in Soviet Russia in the 1930s," *Slavic Review* 55, no. 1 (Spring 1996): 78–105.

10. RGALI f. 1702, op. 10, d. 78, ll. 38–46ob (pensioner); d. 2, ll. 81–81ob (pensioner), 16–17 (pensioner); d. 1, ll. 34–36 (age sixty-seven), 75 (pensioner); d. 2, ll. 18–22 (age sixty-six); d. 75, ll. 69–70ob (age 66), 88–91 (Grinberg, pensioner); d. 76, ll. 69–70 (pensioner), 76–77ob (age sixty), 82–83ob (pensioner), 94–96 (World War I veteran and party member since 1918); d. 78, ll. 49–60 (Civil War veteran); d. 76, ll. 86–93ob (party member since 1927); d. 79, ll. 55–70ob (pensioner), 76–77 (pensioner, plus three other signatories); d. 166, ll. 76–77ob (pensioner); d. 76, ll. 97–98 (pensioner); d. 173, ll. 87–87ob; d. 76, ll. 80–81 (pensioner); d. 3, ll. 60–61 (pensioner); d. 1, ll. 115–117 (pensioner); d. 74, ll. 7–8ob (pensioner); d. 76, ll. 78–79 (age sixty-seven). The writers of the remaining quarter of the letters were as follows: one letter came from a fifty-two-year-old man: RGALI f. 1702, op. 10, d. 76, l. 65. Three letter writers were in their forties: ibid., d. 76, ll. 74–75ob (age forty-seven); ibid., d. 79, ll. 82–83ob (age forty-four); ibid., d. 76, ll. 57–57ob (age forty to forty-two). Two were in their thirties: RGALI f. 1702, op. 10, d. 76, ll. 53–56 (approx. thirty-five); d. 78, ll. 1–2 (thirty-five to forty). Only one letter writer was in her twenties: RGALI f. 1702, op. 10, d. 1, l. 70 (age twenty-five).
11. See Solzhenitsyn, "Odin den'," 9; Vladimir Voinovich, *Portret na fone mifa* (Moscow, 2002), 17, 29.
12. Vera V. Carpovich, *Solzhenitsyn's Peculiar Vocabulary: Russian-English Glossary* (New York: Technical Dictionaries, 1976), 3.
13. Carpovich, *Solzhenitsyn's Peculiar Vocabulary,* 3 (quotation); Nivat, *Solzhenitsyn,* 175–191; Leonid Rzhevsky, *Solzhenitsyn: Creator and Heroic Deed* (Tuscaloosa: University of Alabama Press, 1978), 19–32.
14. Vasilii Aksenov, "Na polputi k Lune," *Novyi mir,* no. 7 (1962).
15. The publication of *One Day* shortly preceded Khrushchev's December 1962 well-known visit to the Manège, where his reaction to an exhibition of contemporary art became the epitome of similarly critical reactions against nonfigurative art. See Susan E. Reid, "In the Name of the People: The Manège Affair Revisited," *Kritika: Explorations in Russian and Eurasian History* 6, no. 4 (2005): 673–716.
16. RGALI f. 1702, op. 8, d. 731, ll. 2–4, 11–12, 16, 20, 24–25, 32, 38–39, 41–42; ibid., op. 10, d. 76, ll. 100–110 (simultaneous criticism of Aksenov and Solzhenitsyn by Oksamytnyi, literature teacher, Tiraspol', 14 January 1963).
17. Maurice Friedberg, *Russian Classics in Soviet Jackets* (New York: Columbia University Press, 1962), esp. 156–166; Boris Grois, *The Total Art of Stalinism: Avant-garde, Aesthetic Dictatorship, and Beyond* (Princeton: Princeton University Press, 1992); Vladimir Papernyi, *Kul'tura Dva* (Moscow: Novoe literaturnoe obozrenie, 1996); Leonid Heller, "A World of Prettiness: Socialist Realism and Its Aesthetic Categories," in *Socialist Realism without Shores,* ed. Thomas Lahusen and Evgeny Dobrenko (Durham: Duke University Press,

1997), 51–75, esp. 54–59; Dobrenko, *Formovka sovetskogo pisatelia: Sotsial'nye i esteticheskie istoki sovetskoi literaturnoi kul'tury* (Saint Petersburg: Akademicheskii proekt, 1999), 390–396.

18. RGALI f. 1702, op. 10, d. 73, ll. 75, 76 (Sorokin, Moscow, 8 March 1963); d. 78, ll. 38–46ob (Kuz'min, pensioner, Orel, 20 March 1963), 1–2 (Negreus, thirty-five to forty, Leningrad, 11 March 1963); d. 76, ll. 53–56 (Lappo, approx. thirty-five, Severomorsk, registered 16 January 1963); d. 2, ll. 81–81ob (Mel'nikov, pensioner, Moscow, 6 December 1962), 16–17 (Naumova, pensioner, Kaluga, 30 December 1962), 63–63ob (anonymous, registered 22 December 1962); d. 77, l. 50 (Tarasov, Ivanovo, 4 February 1963).
19. Ibid., d. 76, ll. 122–123 (E. A. Tepper, 12 January 1963).
20. Carpovich, *Solzhenitsyn's Peculiar Vocabulary*, 5.
21. The term "continuum of crisis" comes from Peter Holquist, *Making War, Forging Revolution: Russia's Continuum of Crisis, 1914–1921* (Cambridge, Mass.: Harvard University Press, 2002).
22. RGALI, f. 1702, op. 10, d. 1, ll. 13–13ob (anonymous, registered 4 December 1962), 34–36 (Leikand, sixty-seven, registered 7 December 1962), 75 (Petrovskii, pensioner, no date); d. 2, ll. 18–22 (Golikov, sixty-six, 21 December 1962); d. 75, ll. 69–70ob (Gorshunov, sixty-six, 8 January 1963), ll. 88–91 (Grinberg, pensioner, registered 16 January 1963); d. 77, ll. 52–69 (Konstantinov, 10 February 1963); d. 76, ll. 69–70 (Chatskii, pensioner, registered 28 January 1963), 76–77ob (Artamonov, sixty, registered 15 January 1963), 82–83ob (Grigor'ev, pensioner, 20 January 1963), 94–96 (Leizin, 9 January 1963), 113–114ob (Shabalina, 18 January 1963), 115–117 (Rudinskaia, 14 January 1963); d. 78, ll. 49–60 (Kol'tsov, 25 January 1963). Among Solzhenitsyn's older critics, nearly half had gone through the camps: Petrovskii, Kol'tsov, Grinberg, Golikov, Artamonov, Leikand, Gorshunov, Chatskii, Leisin, Grigor'ev.
23. For a different interpretation of readers' responses, see Miriam Dobson, "Contesting the Paradigms of De-Stalinization: Readers' Responses to "One Day in the Life of Ivan Denisovich," *Slavic Review* 64, no. 3 (Autumn 2005): 580–600; Dobson, *Khrushchev's Cold Summer: Gulag Returnees, Crime, and the Fate of Reform after Stalin* (Ithaca: Cornell University Press, 2009), 215–228, esp. 219–223. Dobson argues that negative reactions to Solzhenitsyn's language revealed society's concern about the danger the Gulag returnees might pose to Soviet culture: "If millions of prisoners released from the Gulag spoke and thought in the same way as Ivan Denisovich, the cultured behaviour that the party had fought so hard to inculcate was at risk" (Dobson, *Khrushchev's Cold Summer*, 221). However, many of those who criticized Solzhenitsyn's language were themselves former Gulag prisoners. Among others were older émigrés who lived abroad and had nothing to do with any Soviet fear of the returning

inmates. Thus I doubt that negative reactions to Solzhenitsyn's language had much to do with anxieties about Gulag returnees.

24. RGALI, f. 1702, op. 10, d. 78, l. 62 (Krasnoiarsk, registered 3 January 1963).
25. Ibid., d. 1, l. 42 (Lipshits, 2 December 1962); d. 75, l. 19 (Tikhonov, registered 1 March 1963); d. 1, l. 77 (Khmel'nitskii, 12 December 1962); d. 76, ll. 44–46ob (Vasilii Chubar', 15 January 1963).
26. Ibid., d. 76, ll. 44–46ob (Chubar', 15 January 1963).
27. Ibid., d. 75, l. 66 (3 January 1963).
28. Ibid., l. 67 (11 April 1963).
29. See Dobrenko, *Formovka*, 390–396, 118, 125–126.
30. RGALI, f. 1702, op. 10, d. 75, l. 67 (Kondratovich to Bliuman, 11 April 1963).
31. Georges Nivat, *Solzhenitsyn* (London: Overseas Publications Interchange, 1984), 57–99; on *One Day*, see 82–85.
32. Thomas Lahusen, *How Life Writes the Book: Real Socialism and Socialist Realism in Stalin's Russia* (Ithaca: Cornell University Press, 1997), 173 (a facsimile of the telegram).
33. RGALI, f. 1702, op. 10, d. 74, ll. 75–75ob (Kuliab, Tadzhikistan, 30 December 1962). Original style and punctuation preserved, as best as possible.
34. On Azhaev, see Lahusen, *How Life Writes the Book*; on "montage of life," see 46–47, 178.
35. Ibid., 163.
36. RGALI, f. 1702, op. 10, d. 75, l. 100 (Penza, registered 30 January 1963), original emphasis.
37. E.g., RGALI f. 1702, op. 10, d. 2, ll. 154–159ob (Markelov, 15 December 1962); d. 77, ll. 72–80 (Barbon, 22 February 1963); d. 75, ll. 66–66ob (Bliuman, 3 January 1963), 19 (Tikhonov, registered 1 March 1963); d. 1, ll. 42 (Lipshits, 2 December 1962), 77 (Khmel'nitskii, registered 12 December 1962); d. 76, ll. 44–46ob (Chubar', 15 January 1963); d. 1, ll. 50–51 (Pronman, 26 November 1962); d. 78, l. 37 (Latyshev, 17 March 1963); d. 1, ll. 103–104 (Stashevich, Vilnius, 12 December 1962); d. 166, ll. 32–36 (Fedin, 7 March 1964); d. 75, l. 32 (Radzinskaia, 6 March 1963); d. 78, l. 27 (Vasil'eva, 6 June 1963); d. 75, l. 22 (Rudkovskii, reg. 23 February 1963); d. 74, ll. 75–75ob (Korolev, 30 December 1962); d. 2, ll. 166–168 (Borisov, 14 December 1962); d. 76, ll. 82–83ob (Grigor'ev, 20 January 1963); d. 78, l. 19 (Gress, 26 June 1963); d. 75, ll. 94ob–94 (Solomakha, 29 December 1962); d. 78, ll. 62–63 (Golitsyn, registered 3 January 1963); d. 3, ll. 48–49 (Ignatenkov, registered 18 December 1962), 69–78ob (Einer-Biener, 20 December 1962), 10–14 (Zhevtun, registered 12 December 1962), 4–7 (Kolpakov, registered 22 December 1962); d. 1, l. 94 (Rakovskii, registered 12 December 1962); d. 74, ll. 76–77ob (Tomashevskaia, 30 December 1962); d. 2, ll. 18–22 (Golikov, 21 December 1962); d. 172, ll. 12–13 (Ivanov, no date); d. 1, ll. 126–127 (Dokuchaev, registered 22 December 1962); d. 166, ll. 37–44 (Pupyshev, 12

March 1964), 8–9 (Baranovskii, registered 13 February 1964); d. 397, ll. 1–2ob (Lisiutin, 28 February 1967).

38. RGALI f. 1702, op. 10, d. 3, ll. 10–14 (Zhevtun, registered 12 December 1962), 48–49 (Ignatenkov, registered 18 December 1962); d. 79, l. 54 (Lisiutin, 27 March 1963); d. 78, l. 19 (Gress, 26 June 1963).
39. Ibid., d. 2, l. 159ob (15 December 1962), original emphasis. See also "Bezhavshie iz fashistskogo plena sovetskie ofitsery o svoem prebyvanii v Shveitsarii," *Izvestiia*, 15 April 1945.
40. RGALI, f. 1702, op. 10, d. 2, l. 154.
41. Mikhail Sholokhov, "Sud'ba cheloveka," in Sholokhov, *Sobranie sochinenii v vos'mi tomakh*, vol. 8 (Moscow: Pravda, 1962), 22–54 (first published in *Pravda*, 31 December 1956 and 1 January 1957).
42. RGALI, f. 1702, op. 10, d. 2, ll. 159–159ob.
43. Ibid., d. 74, l. 14ob (Murmansk, 27 December 1962).
44. Ibid., d. 3, ll. 45–46 (Arzamas, registered 18 December 1962).
45. Ibid., ll. 54–55ob (Gelendzhik, 10 December 1962).
46. Ibid., d. 1, ll. 98–98ob (registered 1 December 1962); ibid., op. 9, d. 82, ll. 127–128.
47. Ibid., op. 10, d. 74, ll. 78–79ob (31 December 1962).
48. Ibid., d. 1, ll. 13–13ob (anonymous, former prisoner, registered 4 December 1962); d. 77, ll. 1–4 (Efim Kondratenko, an Old Bolshevik who spent 1937–1956 in the camps. Krivoi Rog, 5 February 1963).
49. Ibid., d. 75, l. 101.
50. Michael Scammell, *Solzhenitsyn: A Biography* (New York: W. W. Norton, 1984), 554, 559–560, 835. See also RGALI f. 1702, op. 10, d. 77, ll. 40–49ob (Ramm, pensioner, registered 2 February 1963), 29–30ob (Kruglov, party member since 1917, 21 February 1963), 52–69 (Konstantinov, 10 February 1963); d. 76, ll. 39–41ob (Kolendovskii, seventy-one, 20 January 1963); d. 74, ll. 64–66ob (Luk'ianov, twenty-four, 30 December 1962), 49–53 (Galitskii, 16 January 1963); d. 73, ll. 80–93ob (Vakhrameev, pensioner, 24 December 1962).
51. Scammell, *Solzhenitsyn*, 510–511, 542–543, 621–622.
52. Leopold Labedz, ed., *Solzhenitsyn: A Documentary Record* (Harmondsworth: Penguin Books, 1972; first published by Allen Lane, Penguin Press, 1970), 44–62. For the story of this chapter's publication, see Scammell, *Solzhenitsyn*, 621–622. On *The Gulag Archipelago* as a collective historical enterprise, see ibid., 560.
53. Labedz, *Solzhenitsyn*, 44 (Markelov), 45 (Golitsyn), 48 (Lilenkov), 49 (Vilenchik; Solzhenitsyn spelled his name "Vilenchuk"). When quoting from their letters, Solzhenitsyn stayed true to the original texts and kept the letter writers' original names.
54. RGALI f. 1702, op. 10, d. 1, ll. 130–131; d. 79, ll. 76–77; d. 166, ll. 76–77ob; d. 79, ll. 8–8ob; d. 75, l. 65; d. 74, ll. 35–39; d. 1, ll. 115–117, 99; d. 73, ll. 36–37; d. 248,

ll. 89–94; d. 74, ll. 4–6ob; d. 79, ll. 79ob–89ob; d. 78, ll. 132–135, 49–60, 62–63; d. 3, ll. 69–78ob; d. 74, ll. 15–22; d. 78, ll. 94–113; d. 73, ll. 80–93ob. Of the remaining five letters, four came from people in their forties; one person was thirty-eight: ibid., d. 2, ll. 6–15ob; d. 79, ll. 82–83ob; d. 76, ll. 74–75ob; d. 78, ll. 33–34; d. 79, ll. 9–19ob.

55. On a military mentality as a legacy of the Civil War and World War I, see Sheila Fitzpatrick, "The Legacy of the Civil War," in *Party, State, and Society in the Russian Civil War: Explorations in Social History*, ed. Diane Koenker, William Rosenberg, and Ronald Grigor Suny (Bloomington: Indiana University Press, 1989), 385–398; Moshe Lewin, "The Civil War: Dynamics and Legacy," in ibid., 399–423; Leopold Haimson, "Civil War and the Problem of Social Identities in Early Twentieth-Century Russia," in ibid., 24–47; Holquist, *Making War, Forging Revolution*.
56. RGALI f. 1702, op. 10, d. 1, l. 99; d. 73, ll. 36–37; d. 74, ll. 4–6ob; d. 78, ll. 49–60, 33–34, 62–63; d. 3, ll. 69–78ob; d. 74, ll. 15–22; d. 78, ll. 94–113; d. 73, ll. 80–93ob; d. 76, ll. 132–142ob, 44–46ob; d. 74, ll. 87–87ob; d. 79, ll. 9–19ob; d. 76, ll. 118–121ob. See esp. ibid., op. 10, d. 74, ll. 4–6ob (Evgenii Grachev, party member since 1918, prisoner in 1936–1956, Bugul'ma, registered 28 January 1963).
57. On the importance of World War II and individual wartime records in defining postwar legitimacies, see Amir Weiner, *Making Sense of War: The Second World War and the Fate of the Bolshevik Revolution* (Princeton: Princeton University Press, 2001), 314, 322–331, 378–380.
58. Solzhenitsyn, *Odin den' Ivana Denisovicha* (Moscow: Sovetskii pisatel', 1963), 59.
59. RGALI, f. 1702, op. 10, d. 79, ll. 79–79ob (11 April 1963), original emphasis.
60. Ibid., d. 76, l. 75 (registered 15 January 1963). Stoliarov refers to the teenage character Gopchik in *One Day*, imprisoned for bringing food to the woods for Banderovite guerrillas.
61. Ibid., d. 75, l. 33 (Kimovsk, Tula Oblast, registered 13 March 1963); Labedz, *Solzhenitsyn*, 58.
62. Ibid., d. 78, ll. 104ob, 106, 110 (Gomel', 8 March 1963).
63. Ibid., d. 3, l. 18 (Moscow, 8 December 1962).
64. Ibid., d. 166, ll. 198–199 (21 September 1964).
65. Ibid., d. 73, ll. 72–73 (Moscow, 8 March 1963).
66. Also ibid., d. 75, ll. 49–51 (Sykchin, former schoolteacher, at the time a collective-farm party organizer, Novosibirsk Oblast, 9 February 1963); d. 75, ll. 82–83ob (Astaf'ev, 44, mining technician, Irkutsk Oblast, 25 March 1963); d. 76, ll. 58–64 (L'vova, engineer-geologist, Irkutsk, 7 January 1963); d. 178, ll. 84–84ob (anonymous World War II veteran, 1965).
67. Ibid., d. 2, ll. 8ob–9 (Kotlas, 7 December 1962).

68. See, e.g., Stanislaw Swianiewicz, *In the Shadow of Katyn: Stalin's Terror* (Pender Island, B.C.: Borealis, 2002).
69. RGALI, f. 1702, op. 10, d. 2, l. 14.
70. Ibid., l. 15.
71. Ibid., d. 76, l. 35 (Cherepovets, 7 January 1963).
72. Ibid., d. 2, l. 12.
73. Ibid., d. 248, ll. 89–94; d. 2, ll. 6–15ob; d. 76, ll. 58–64; d. 79, ll. 71–74ob; d. 166, l. 109–129ob; d. 76, ll. 34–36; d. 79, ll. 20–25ob, 39–45; d. 75, l. 33; d. 78, ll. 14–14ob. The total number of letters from former camp officers, guards, and free hires was larger, about 15, but the other letter writers in this group did not explicitly advance the enemy thesis.
74. Ibid., op. 10, d. 74, l. 14ob; d. 248, ll. 89–94 (Kasatskii, Govorko).
75. Ibid., d. 2, l. 13.
76. Ibid., ll. 14–14ob.
77. Ibid., d. 79, ll. 41, 44.
78. E.g., ibid., op. 10, d. 166, ll. 76–77ob (E. F. Krasikova, an old propagandist and party member for forty years, who also argued that a camp was "not a health resort"—Moscow, registered 7 April 1964); d. 78, l. 14 (Nesterov, L'vov, 29 December 1962); d. 79, ll. 73ob–74 (V. V. Samatskin, a war veteran and former MVD officer who had also served in the camps, Karaganda, 23 March 1963). A few such letters (Panchuk's and Samatskin's among them) were initially sent to *Pravda*, whose editors forwarded them to *Novyi mir*, possibly with the maliciously joyful intent to present the journal's editors with a few negative reader responses to *Novyi mir*'s publications. Ibid., d. 79, ll. 39, 71.
79. E.g., ibid., d. 1, l. 38 (Golovin, 27, journalism student, Kurgan, registered 7 December 1962).
80. Ibid., op. 9, d. 81, l. 73.
81. Ibid., op. 10, d. 1, ll. 112 (registered 22 December 1962); d. 2, l. 1 (registered 27 December 1962), 63–63ob (reg. 22 December 1962); d. 76, ll. 126–127 (20 February 1963).
82. Ibid., d. 78, l. 59.
83. Ibid., d. 76, l. 74ob (registered 15 January 1963).
84. Ibid., d. 75, l. 51 (9 February 1963). Original punctuation preserved as best as possible.
85. Ibid., d. 75, l. 55 (1–5 April 1964).
86. Ibid., d. 166, ll. 32–36 (village of Rozhdestveno, Tatar ASSR, 7 March 1964).
87. Ibid., l. 29 (19 March 1964).
88. Ibid., ll. 109–129ob (25 March 1964).
89. Ibid., ll. 111ob–117ob, 110 (quotation).
90. Ibid., ll. 111–111ob, 117ob.
91. Ibid., d. 73, ll. 80–93ob (24 December 1962); for the quotation see l. 80.

92. Ibid., ll. 81, 81ob, 93.
93. In parentheses he used a Russian idiom, "*kukish v karmane*," of which this is an approximate translation.
94. RGALI, f. 1702, op. 10, d. 73, ll. 83ob–84.
95. Ibid., l. 87ob.
96. Ibid., d. 2, l. 18 (Vladimir Ivanovich Golikov, sixty-six, prisoner from 1938 to 1946, Gor'kii, 21 December 1962); d. 78, l. 118 (Rakhil' Meerovna Gor, pensioner, former camp prisoner, Vilnius, 23 February 1963).
97. Ibid., d. 2, l. 82 (Filippov, economist, Petropavlovsk, 14 December 1962), 39 (Zabelkin, pensioner, Vladimir-Volynskii, registered 22 December 1962).
98. Ibid., d. 76, ll. 39, 40–40ob, 41ob (20 January 1963).
99. Ibid., d. 166, ll. 42ob, 43–43ob (12 March 1964). For his first letter, see ibid., d. 2, l. 114ob (registered 22 December 1962).

8. *Discovering Human Rights*

1. For Siniavskii and Daniel's Western publications, see "Le réalisme socialiste," *Esprit*, no. 2 (February 1959): 335–366; Abram Terc, *Sąd idzie*. Anonim, *Co to jest realism socjalistyczny?* (Paris: Instytut Literacki, 1959); Mikołaj Arżak, "Ręce," *Kultura* (September 1961): 83–87; for a list, see Margaret Dalton, *Andrei Siniavskii and Julii Daniel': Two Soviet "Heretical" Writers* (Würzburg: Jal-Verlag, 1978), 189–190. See also Catharine Theimer Nepomnyashchy, *Abram Tertz and the Poetics of Crime* (New Haven: Yale University Press, 1995), 365–367; Andrei Siniavskii, *127 pisem o liubvi*, 3 vols. (Moscow: Agraf, 2004), 1:13–14; Hoover Institution Archives, Andrei Siniavskii Papers (hereafter ASP), Box 4, Folder 12 (Siniavskii's interrogations of 11 September, 21 September, and 26 October 1965).
2. In 1988 Soviet literary periodicals began publishing Daniel's writings, and the journalist Elena Platonova once interviewed him. Iulii Daniel', "Iskuplenie," *Iunost'*, no. 11 (1988): 8–21; Daniel', ". . . A nuzhno l' bylogo churat'sia?" *Druzhba narodov*, no. 9 (1988): 111–113; "Ia chist pered sobstvennoi sovest'iu," in Daniel', *Govorit Moskva: Proza, poeziia, perevody* (Moscow: Moskovskii rabochii, 1991), 293–298.
3. Olga Matich, "*Spokoinoj noči*: Andrei Siniavskij's Rebirth as Abram Terc," *Slavic and East European Journal* 33, no. 1 (1989): 60; Boris Shragin, "Iskuplenie Iuliia Danielia," in Daniel', *Govorit Moskva*, 315; Nepomnyashchy, *Abram Tertz and the Poetics of Crime*, 4; Leonid Zorin, *Avanstsena: Memuarnyi roman* (Moscow: Slovo, 1997), 190; Aleksandr Daniel', "Predislovie," in Iulii Daniel', *"Ia vse sbivaius' na literaturu . . .": Pis'ma iz zakliucheniia* (Moscow: Zven'ia, 2000), 7; Lazar Fleishman, "Muzhskoe pis'mo," in Siniavskii, *127 pisem*, 1:8–9.
4. Pasternak to Siniavskii, 29 June 1957, in Aleksandr Ginzburg, ed., *Belaia kniga o dele Siniavskogo i Danielia* (Frankfurt am Main: Possev-Verlag, 1967), 144–145; Fleishman, "Muzhskoe," 8.

5. Daniel', *Govorit Moskva*, 288–289 (illustration).
6. RGALI, f. 1702, op. 9, d. 47, l. 10. Also Aleksandr Tvardovskii, "Po sluchaiu iubileia," *NM*, no. 1 (January 1965): 17.
7. Aleksandr Tvardovskii, *RT-60*, *Znamia*, no. 4 (April 2002): 137 (12 January 1966), 143 (18 January), 146 (15 February), 150 (17 February), 154 (4 March 1966).
8. Tvardovskii, *RT-60*, *Znamia*, no. 4 (April 2002): 154 (2 March 1966), 150 (17 February 1966).
9. Ibid., 153 (1 March 1966), 154 (4 March), 155 (5 March).
10. RGANI, f. 5, op. 36, d. 156, l. 197. I thank Eleonory Gilburd for drawing my attention to this document.
11. RGALI, f. 1702, op. 9, d. 220, ll. 17, 18–31.
12. Ibid., l. 32 (11 August 1967).
13. For details, see Denis Kozlov and Eleonory Gilburd, "The Thaw as an Event in Russian History," in *The Thaw: Soviet Society and Culture during the 1950s and 1960s*, ed. Kozlov and Gilburd (Toronto: University of Toronto Press, 2013): 18–81; Denis Kozlov, "'I Have Not Read, but I Will Say': Soviet Literary Audiences and Changing Ideas of Social Membership, 1958–1966," *Kritika: Explorartions in Russian and Eurasian History* 7, no. 3 (2006): 557–597. On the late Soviet idea of rights, see Benjamin Nathans, "The Dictatorship of Reason: Aleksandr Vol'pin and the Idea of Rights under 'Developed Socialism,'" *Slavic Review* 66, no. 4 (2007): 630–663; Nathans, "Soviet Rights-Talk in the Post-Stalin Era," in *Human Rights in the Twentieth Century*, ed. Stefan-Ludwig Hoffmann (Cambridge: Cambridge University Press, 2011), 166–190. On contemporary concerns with legality in Western Europe, see Jan-Werner Müller, *A Dangerous Mind: Carl Schmitt in Post-War European Thought* (New Haven: Yale University Press, 2003), 63–68; Jeffrey Herf, *Divided Memory: The Nazi Past in the Two Germanys* (Cambridge, Mass.: Harvard University Press, 1997), 334–342; Rebecca Wittmann, *Beyond Justice: The Auschwitz Trial* (Cambridge, Mass.: Harvard University Press, 2005), 48–53; Sarah Farmer, *Martyred Village: Commemorating the 1944 Massacre at Oradour-sur-Glane* (Berkeley: University of California Press, 1999), 135–170; Samuel Moyn, *A Holocaust Controversy: The Treblinka Affair in Postwar France* (Waltham: Brandeis University Press, 2005), 142–149; Henry Rousso, *The Vichy Syndrome: History and Memory in France since 1944* (Cambridge, Mass.: Harvard University Press, 1991), 96–97.
14. Vladimir Kudriavtsev and Aleksei Trusov, *Politicheskaia iustitsiia v SSSR* (Saint Petersburg, 2002), 263–264, 351; Mikhail Strogovich, *Uchenie o material'noi istine v ugolovnom protsesse* (Moscow, 1947), 227–259; Harold J. Berman, "The Presumption of Innocence: Another Reply," *American Journal of Comparative Law* 28, no. 4 (1980): 615–623; "Postanovlenie Plenuma Verkhovnogo Suda SSSR ot 16 iiunia 1978 g. no. 5 'O praktike primeneniia

sudami zakonov, obespechivaiushchikh obviniaemomu pravo na zashchitu'," *Biulleten' Verkhovnogo Suda SSSR*, no. 4 (1978): 9; L. V. Boitsova, "Tolkovanie somnenii v pol'zu podsudimogo v sudebnom poriadke," *Pravovedenie*, no. 3 (1989): 94–99.

15. Andrei Vyshinskii, *Teoriia sudebnykh dokazatel'stv v sovetskom prave* (Moscow, 1941), 180–181; Kudriavtsev and Trusov, *Politicheskaia iustitsiia v SSSR*, 247–259, 340–341; "The Code of Criminal Procedure of the RSFSR," articles 74, 77, in Harold J. Berman, ed., *Soviet Criminal Law and Procedures: The RSFSR Codes* (Cambridge, Mass.: Harvard University Press, 1966), 280–281.
16. Peter H. Solomon, *Soviet Criminal Justice under Stalin* (Cambridge, Mass.: Harvard University Press, 1996), 360–364; D. Karev, "Likvidirovat' posledstviia kul'ta lichnosti v sovetskoi pravovoi nauke," *Sotsialisticheskaia zakonnost'*, no. 2 (1962): 54–62; "Do kontsa likvidirovat' vrednye posledstviia kul'ta lichnosti v sovetskoi iurisprudentsii," *Sovetskoe gosudarstvo i pravo*, no. 4 (1962): 3–16; N. V. Zhogin, "Ob izvrashcheniiakh Vyshinskogo v teorii sovetskogo prava i praktike," *Sovetskoe gosudarstvo i pravo*, no. 3 (1965): 22–31; Mikhail Strogovich, ed., *Problemy sudebnoi etiki* (Moscow, 1974), 124–126, 146.
17. "Criminal Code of the RSFSR," article 3, in *Soviet Criminal Law*, 145.
18. Peter H. Solomon, "Judicial Reform under Gorbachev and Russian History," in *The Impact of Perestroika on Soviet Law*, ed. Albert J. Schmidt (Dordrecht: M. Nijhoff, 1990), 18.
19. I have eighty-five letters responding to the Siniavskii-Daniel' affair, either specifically or in other contexts. Of these, forty-two come from a file that the Letters Group at the Komsomol CC put together in 1966 when preparing a note on responses to the affair for the Party Central Committee: RGASPI f. M-1, op. 45, d. 18. Another twenty-three letters, dated 1965–1968, are in the Siniavskii-Daniel' investigation file: Hoover Institution Archives, ASP, Box 5, Folders 7, 9. Twenty more letters come from *Novyi mir's* archive for 1966–1969: RGALI f. 1702, op. 9, d. 220, ll. 2–3ob, 4–6, 7–13, 14–16ob, 17, 18–31, 32; d. 222, ll. 22–23; d. 223, ll. 28–32, 51–51ob; d. 255, l. 10; d. 260, ll. 40–41; d. 263, ll. 31–34; d. 324, ll. 37–44; d. 325, ll. 25–28ob, 70–71; d. 326, ll. 79–85; d. 328, ll. 56–57; d. 330, ll. 58–59, 84–87 ob; d. 331, ll. 87–96.
20. E.g., RGASPI f. M-1, op. 45, d. 18, ll. 88, 89, 9, 10–11.
21. Ibid., ll. 92–93, 94.
22. Hoover Institution Archives, ASP, Box 5, Folder 9. Filippova wrote to the court, while Litvinova addressed her letter to the editors of the newspaper *Sel'skaia zhizn'*, who forwarded her letter to the Procuracy. Another such letter appeared in print shortly before the trial: the agronomist Z. Gulbis (Latvia) described the moment when, during World War II, she and a few other women, older men, and children had managed to escape Nazi deportation. It occurred to her then what a precious blessing it was to be in her home country.

Remembering this twenty years later, she was appalled to read how Siniavskii and Daniel' "slandered" their motherland: Z. Gulbis, "Ikh udel—prezrenie," *Izvestiia*, 18 January 1966. Yet another such censure came from Siniavskii's own elder sister, Veviia Donatovna (1919–2001), who, having learned of his publications abroad and the trial, broke all ties with her brother, considering him a traitor. Notably, she did so in a private letter. Siniavskii, *127 pisem*, 1:42, 148, 152–153.

23. Iurii Feofanov, "Tut tsarit zakon," *Izvestiia*, 11 February 1966; Feofanov, "Izoblichenie," *Izvestiia*, 12 February 1966; Feofanov, "Pora otvechat'," *Izvestiia*, 13 February 1966; "Litso klevetnikov," *Komsomol'skaia Pravda*, 11 February 1966; "Tsena podlosti," *Komsomol'skaia Pravda*, 12 February 1966; "Postavshchiki antisovetskoi kukhni," *Komsomol'skaia Pravda*, 13 February 1966; "Klevetnikam—po zaslugam!" *Komsomol'skaia Pravda*, 15 February 1966; B. Krymov, "Sud prodolzhaetsia," *Literaturnaia gazeta*, 12 February 1966; M. Il'in, "Klevetniki," *Sovetskaia Rossiia*, 11 February 1966; I. Kotenko, "Fakty oblichaiut," *Sovetskaia Rossiia*, 12 February 1966; A. Nabokov, "Liudi s dvoinym dnom," *Vecherniaia Moskva*, 14 February 1966. The best-known articles are Dmitrii Eremin, "Perevertyshi," *Izvestiia*, 13 January 1966, and Zoia Kedrina, "Nasledniki Smerdiakova," *Literaturnaia gazeta*, 22 January 1966.
24. RGASPI f. M-1, op. 45, d. 18, ll. 3, 10–10ob, 19, 96. Concerns of brevity do not allow me to illustrate fully this analysis of the condemnations. For examples, see Kozlov, "The Readers of *Novyi mir*, 1945–1970: Twentieth-Century Experience and Soviet Historical Consciousness," PhD diss., University of Toronto, 2005, 365–375. On the Soviet intelligentsia's open protests, see L. S. Eremina, ed., *Tsena metafory ili Prestuplenie i nakazanie Siniavskogo i Danielia* (Moscow: Kniga, 1989), 498–500, 502–506. Ludmilla Alexeyeva counted twenty-two open letters of protest against the trial, twenty of them written by Muscovites. See Alexeyeva, *Istoriia inakomysliia v SSSR. Noveishii period* (Moscow: Vest', 1992), 205.
25. Hoover Institution Archives, ASP, Box 5, Folders 10 and 11. The Politburo, at its 19 May 1971 meeting, sanctioned Siniavskii's pardon and release.
26. Ibid., Folder 11 (KGB *svodki* of 19 February, 15 March, and 22 March 1966).
27. RGANI, f. 5, op. 30, d. 490, ll. 31, 32, 34.
28. In the Komsomol archive, twenty-seven letters largely condemn Siniavskii and Daniel, thirteen largely support them, and two are undecided. In the investigation file, ten letters condemn the writers, eleven are on their side, and two are undecided. Letters to *Novyi mir* were often more ambivalent (see below), but it is possible to see that ten letters largely sympathize with the writers and another ten reject their literary-political undertaking.
29. RGALI f. 1702, op. 9, d. 220, ll. 4–6 (17 February, hereafter 1966), 7–13 (19 January), 14–16ob (18 February); RGASPI f. M-1, op. 45, d. 18, ll. 58–61

(15 February), 63–66 (16 February), 77–78 (February); Hoover Institution Archives, ASP, Box 5, Folder 7 (18 January 1966), Folder 9 (four letters, filed, respectively, on 25 December 1965, 28 February, 4 February, and 2 March 1966).

30. Nine of the thirty-four defense letters (26.5 percent) and seven of the forty-seven condemnation letters (14.9 percent) came from Moscow and Leningrad.
31. My conclusion is mainly based on declared occupations, although a few people did indicate their age.
32. Zorin, *Avanstsena*, 213.
33. RGASPI f. M-1, op. 45, d. 18, l. 69.
34. Ibid., l. 68.
35. Ibid., l. 67 (no date but apparently early to mid-February 1966).
36. Ibid., ll. 65–66. Also RGALI, f. 1702, op. 10, d. 83, ll. 240–241. On the revival of the Lenin cult during the Thaw, see Nina Tumarkin, *Lenin Lives! The Lenin Cult in Soviet Russia* (Cambridge, Mass.: Harvard University Press, 1997), 257–261.
37. Esenin may have ended up in the same row, thanks to his widespread image as a people's poet and a simple freedom-loving martyr. On the popular cult of Esenin, see Varlam Shalamov, "Sergei Esenin i vorovskoi mir," in Shalamov, *Sobranie sochinenii v chetyrekh tomakh*, vol. 2 (Moscow: Vagrius, 1998), 86–92. It also might be that the letter writer meant not the poet but his son, Aleksandr Esenin-Vol'pin, who actively participated in organizing protests against the persecution of Siniavskii and Daniel'. The letter is not clear on which of the Esenins it meant. See also Nathans, "The Dictatorship of Reason," 658. As Nathans suggests, Esenin-Vol'pin was alive and under arrest, unlike his poet father, who was long dead and never arrested. However, Pasternak, too, was dead by 1966, and had never been arrested, either. It is hardly possible to arrive at a perfect interpretation in this case.
38. RGASPI f. M-1, op. 45, d. 18, l. 63.
39. Ibid., ll. 64, 66. The Third Party Program was adopted in 1961.
40. For a (relatively rare) expression of self-congratulatory Russianness, see ibid., ll. 77–78 (no date, but apparently between 10 and 14 February 1966).
41. Ibid.
42. Ibid., ll. 55–56.
43. Ibid., ll. 71–72 (apparently between 12 and 14 February 1966); also RGALI f. 1702, op. 9, d. 220, ll. 7–13 (Ernst Orlovskii, patent law expert, Leningrad, 19 January 1966). On Orlovskii, a well-known human rights activist, see his "Moi put' v dissidenty," *Neva*, no. 6 (2002): 166–187; *Biographical Dictionary of Dissidents in the Soviet Union, 1956–1975*, ed. S. P. de Boer et al. (The Hague: Martinus Nijhoff, 1982), 407. I thank Benjamin Nathans for referring me to the entry on Orlovskii.
44. RGASPI f. M-1, op. 45, d. 18, ll. 70, 72.

45. Ibid., l. 70.
46. Ibid., l. 71.
47. Ibid., l. 72.
48. Hoover Institution Archives, ASP, Box 5, Folder 7 (Sinitsyn, 18 January 1966), Folder 9 ("Murat," filed 25 December 1965; Bukreev, 4 February 1966; Popkov, filed 2 March 1966; illegible name, 1 March 1966; Nikolaenko, 20 February 1968; Orion Kvachevskii, 26 February 1968; anonymous, filed 4 March 1968).
49. See, e.g., Daniel', *Govorit Moskva.*
50. Albert P. van Goudoever, *The Limits of Destalinization in the Soviet Union: Political Rehabilitations in the Soviet Union since Stalin,* trans. Frans Hijkoop (London: Croom Helm, 1986), 127.
51. Raisa Orlova and Lev Kopelev, *My zhili v Moskve: 1956–1980 gg.* (Ann Arbor: Ardis, 1988), 27–29, 43, 46, 56–60; Ludmilla Alexeyeva and Paul Goldberg, *The Thaw Generation: Coming of Age in the Post-Stalin Era* (Pittsburgh: University of Pittsburgh Press, 1990), 68–71, 76–77, 83–84.
52. Katerina Clark, "Changing Historical Paradigms in Soviet Culture," in *Late Soviet Culture: From Perestroika to Novostroika,* ed. Thomas Lahusen and Gene Kuperman (Durham: Duke University Press, 1993), 289–306, esp. 300; Olga Velikanova, *Making of an Idol: On Uses of Lenin* (Göttingen: Muster-Schmidt Verlag, 1996), 127–133; Velikanova, *The Public Perception of the Cult of Lenin Based on Archival Materials* (Lewiston, N.Y.: Edwin Mellen Press, 2001), 251–252.
53. Elena Zubkova, *Obshchestvo i reformy: 1945–1964* (Moscow: Rossiia molodaia, 1993); Elena Seniavskaia, *Psikhologiia voiny v XX veke: Istoricheskii opyt Rossii* (Moscow: ROSSPEN, 1999), 171–190.
54. Hoover Institution Archives, ASP, Box 5, Folder 9.
55. On reinforced practices of social exclusion after World War II, see Amir Weiner, *Making War, Forging Revolution: The Second World War and the Fate of the Bolshevik Revolution* (Princeton: Princeton University Press, 2001), esp. 82–126.
56. Lidiia Chukovskaia, "Protsess iskliucheniia: Ocherk literaturnykh nravov," in *Izbrannoe* (Moscow: Gorizont; Minsk: Aurika, 1997), 410.
57. Hoover Institution Archives, ASP, Box 5, Folder 9 (anonymous, filed 12 March 1966; original emphasis and capitalization).
58. For an argument about the overall persistence of (modified) enemy imagery in the 1960s, see Miriam Dobson, *Khrushchev's Cold Summer: Gulag Returnees, Crime, and the Fate of Reform after Stalin* (Ithaca: Cornell University Press, 2009). I argue that, despite the common persistence of enemy imagery, the Thaw-era intellectual shifts portended a gradual decline in the use of exclusionary paradigms of social membership.
59. On national reconciliation, see, e.g., Henry Carey, ed., *National Reconciliation in Eastern Europe* (Boulder: East European Monographs, 2003).

60. See also Nathans, "Dictatorship of Reason"; Vladislav Zubok, *Zhivago's Children: The Last Russian Intelligentsia* (Cambridge, Mass.: Harvard University Press, 2009). The famous rally of Moscow's intelligentsia in support of Siniavskii and Daniel', at which participants demanded respect for the law and an open trial, was held on Constitution Day, 5 December 1965. Aleksandr Esenin-Vol'pin, a principal organizer of the rally, actively insisted on the strict legality of all court proceedings. See Esenin-Vol'pin, *Filosofiia. Logika. Poeziia. Zashchita prav cheloveka: Izbrannoe* (Moscow: RGGU, 1999), 313, 319–320. For criticism of the intelligentsia's legalistic *fronde* of the 1960s as futile, see Petr Vail' and Aleksandr Genis, *60-e: mir sovetskogo cheloveka* (Moscow: Novoe literaturnoe obozrenie, 2001), 177–178.
61. According to the official statistics, 28.8 million people in the USSR were "engaged in intellectual labor" in 1968, compared with 2.6 million in 1926 and 20.5 million in 1959. In 1939 there were 8 persons with higher education per 1,000 people over age 10 in the USSR. In 1959 the ratio was 23:1,000. By 1970 it had gone up to 42:1,000. In 1967 the country had 6.4 million individuals with higher education, compared with 1.2 million in 1939 and 3.8 million in 1959. There were more than 4.1 million college students in the academic year 1966–67, as opposed to 812,000 in 1940–41 and 2.4 million in 1960–61. *Narodnoe khoziaistvo SSSR v 1967 g* (Moscow: Statistika, 1968), 34, 35, 788; *Narodnoe khoziaistvo SSSR v 1970 g.* (Moscow: Statistika, 1971), 23, 637.
62. For positive mentions of Siniavskii and Daniel' in letters on Kardin, see RGALI f. 1702, op. 9, d. 260, ll. 40–41 (Zakharov, Gorodok, Lviv Oblast); d. 263, ll. 31–34 (engineer D'iakov, Zavodskoi, Rostov Oblast).
63. Ibid., d. 222, ll. 22–22ob (24 April 1966, age and place not identified).
64. Ibid., d. 223, ll. 31–32 (V. Ivanov, apparently from Kazakhstan, 5 May 1966).
65. RGALI f. 1702, op. 9, d. 328, l. 54 (25 August 1969; letter to the journal *Ogonek*); d. 325, l. 70ob (A. Filipchenko, Gatchina, 7 August 1969, letter to *Ogonek*).
66. Ibid., d. 330, l. 58 (Baidov, Abgarian, Galogre, Shavshivili, Kizirian, Todua, 25 September 1969); also d. 331, ll. 87–96 (Lokalova, village schoolteacher, Kukoboi, Iaroslavl' Oblast, August–September 1969).
67. RGASPI f. M-1, op. 45, d. 18, l. 41 (Sergeant Vladislav Zolotarev, military unit 73638, Ussuriisk).
68. For analyses of this mentality in the 1920s and 1930s, see Sheila Fitzpatrick, "The Foreign Threat during the First Five-Year Plan," *Soviet Union/Union Soviétique* 5, no. 1 (1978): 26–35; Fitzpatrick, *Everyday Stalinism: Ordinary Life in Extraordinary Times: Soviet Russia in the 1930s* (New York: Oxford University Press, 1999), 203; Katerina Clark, "The 'Quiet Revolution' in Intellectual Life," *Russia in the Era of NEP: Explorations in Soviet Society and Culture*, ed. Sheila Fitzpatrick, Alexander Rabinowitch, and Richard Stites (Bloomington: Indiana University Press, 1991), 210–227, esp. 226; Olga Velikanova, *The Myth*

of the Besieged Fortress: Soviet Mass Perception in the 1920s–1930s* (Toronto: Centre for Russian and East European Studies, 2002), esp. 19–28.

69. Hoover Institution Archives, ASP, Box 5, Folder 9 (court sentence); *Siniavskii i Daniel' na skam'e podsudimykh* (New York: Inter-Language Literary Associates, 1966), 54–57, 95–98, 103–104.
70. Hoover Institution Archives, ASP, Box 4, Folder 12 (Siniavskii's letter to the KGB, 9 October 1965); Box 5, Folder 8 (his deposition, 16 December 1965); *Siniavskii i Daniel' na skam'e,* 55–58, 102, 104.
71. *Siniavskii i Daniel' na skam'e,* 128. Daniel' did argue, earlier, that publishing in the West did not make a book anti-Soviet. Ibid., 103.
72. Daniel', "*Ia vse sbivaius' na literaturu. . . ,*" 25 (letter of 2 March 1966, original emphasis).
73. Thirty years later Iurii Feofanov, the journalist who covered the Siniavskii-Daniel' trial for *Izvestiia* in 1966, remembered: "I was sincerely convinced at the time that sending literature to 'white emigrant' publishers was a crime." Yuri Feofanov and Donald D. Barry, *Politics and Justice in Russia: Major Trials of the Post-Stalin Era* (Armonk: M. E. Sharpe, 1996), 40, also 38–49.
74. E.g., Robert D. English, *Russia and the Idea of the West: Gorbachev, Intellectuals, and the End of the Cold War* (New York: Columbia University Press, 2000), 63.
75. Aleksandr Tvardovskii, *RT-60, Znamia,* no. 2 (February 2002): 154 (entry of 13 November 1965).
76. Ibid., *Znamia,* no. 4 (February 2002): 143 (18 January 1966), 146 (13 February 1966).
77. Ibid., 145 (15 February 1966).
78. Ibid., 152 (1 March 1966); 156 (5 March 1966).
79. Ibid., 149, 150–151, 169 (16, 17, 27 February, 6 April 1966); no. 9 (September 2002), 188 (3 June 1967).
80. Harriet Murav, "The Case against Andrei Siniavskii: The Letter and the Law," *Russian Review* 53, no. 4 (October 1994): 549–560; Nepomnyashchy, *Abram Tertz and the Poetics of Crime,* particularly 1–39, esp. 34, 38 (quotation).
81. At the trial of Siniavskii and Daniel', the judge, Lev Nikolaevich Smirnov, repeatedly stated this point. See *Siniavskii i Daniel' na skam'e,* 52, 74.

9. *In Search of Authenticity*

1.. V. Kardin [the pseudonym of Emil' Vladimirovich Kardin], "Legendy i fakty," *Novyi mir,* no. 2 (February 1966): 237–250.
2. Aleksandr Krivitskii, "Fakty i legendy," *Literaturnaia gazeta,* 19 March 1966.
3. F. Petrov, K. Rokossovskii, I. Baikov, and N. Khlebnikov, "Legendarnoe ne zacherknut'!" *Krasnaia zvezda,* 21 April 1966, reprinted in *Literaturnaia gazeta,* 26 April 1966.

4. E.g., Iurii Molok, *Pushkin v 1937 godu: Materialy i issledovaniia po ikonografii* (Moscow: NLO, 2000).
5. Albert van Goudoever, *The Limits of Destalinization in the Soviet Union: Political Rehabilitations in the Soviet Union since Stalin* (London: Croom Helm, 1986), 127.
6. RGANI, f. 5. op. 58, d. 46, ll. 78, 80–81, 94, 88, 85, 92–93, and esp. 83–84, 95; "Dogovarivaiutsia do togo, chto ne bylo zalpa 'Avrory'," *Istochnik*, no. 2 (1996): 112–121, esp. 112.
7. Aleksei Isaev, *Kotly 41-go: Istoriia VOV, kotoruiu my ne znali* (Moscow: Iauza, Eksmo, 2005), 251–255, 324–327. For a recent examination of the actual circumstances of the battle, see Alexander Statiev, " 'La Garde meurt mais ne se rend pas!' Once Again on the 28 Panfilov Heroes," *Kritika: Explorations in Russian and Eurasian History* 13, no. 4 (Fall 2012): 769–798.
8. V.[asilii] Koroteev, "Gvardeitsy Panfilova v boiakh za Moskvu," *Krasnaia zvezda* (hereafter *KZ*), 27 November 1941.
9. [Aleksandr Krivitskii,] "Zaveshchanie 28 pavshikh geroev," *KZ*, 28 November 1941.
10. David Brandenberger, *National Bolshevism: Stalinist Mass Culture and the Formation of Modern Russian National Identity* (Cambridge, Mass.: Harvard University Press, 2002).
11. Order no. 308 of the People's Commissar of Defense [Stalin], 18 September 1941, in *Russkii arkhiv: Velikaia Otechestvennaia: Prikazy narodnogo komissara oborony SSSR 22 iiunia 1941 g.–1942 g.*, vol. 13 (2-2) (Moscow: Terra, 1997), 84–85; "O pereimenovanii 100, 127, 153, 161, 64, 107, 120 i 316 strelkovykh divizii, 1 Moskovskoi strelkovoi divizii v gvardeiskie divizii," *KZ*, 18 November 1941.
12. Aleksandr Krivitskii, "O 28 pavshikh geroiakh," *KZ*, 22 January 1942.
13. Aleksandr Krivitskii, *Geroi* (Cheliabinsk: Cheliabgiz, 1942); Krivitskii, *28 geroev-gvardeitsev* (Moscow: Pravda, 1942); Krivitskii, *O 28 pavshikh geroiakh* (Moscow: Pravda, 1942, 1944, 1945); Krivitskii, *28 geroev-panfilovtsev* (Moscow: Politizdat, 1943).
14. Mikhail Svetlov, *Dvadsat' vosem'* (Moscow: Molodaia gvardiia, 1942); Nikolai Tikhonov, *Slovo o 28 gvardeitsakh* (Moscow: Voenizdat NKO SSSR, 1942).
15. "We will remember the severe autumn, / The rattle of tanks and glitter of bayonets, / And in the hearts will live the twenty-eight / Of your very best sons," Mark Lisianskii and Sergei Agranian, "Dorogaia moia stolitsa."
16. See, e.g., Ernle Bradford, *Thermopylae: The Battle for the West* (Cambridge, Mass.: Da Capo Press, 1980), which *The Economist* praised as "a gripping story." Witness also the commercial success of the movie 300, directed by Zack Snyder (2006), about the Battle of Thermopylae.

17. E.g., RGALI, f. 3126, op. 1, d. 400, ll. 7–7ob (Batishcheva, Kostroma, 31 May 1962); ibid., ll. 4–4ob (9 October 1964), 27 (7 May 1965).
18. E.g., Benedikt Sarnov, *Nash sovetskii novoiaz: Malen'kaia entsiklopediia real'nogo sotsializma* (Moscow: Materik, 2002); Sarnov, *Skuki ne bylo*, 2 vols. (Moscow: Agraf, 2004–2005); Alexei Yurchak, *Everything Was Forever, until It Was No More: The Last Soviet Generation* (Princeton: Princeton University Press, 2006).
19. Thomas C. Wolfe, *Governing Soviet Journalism: The Press and the Socialist Person after Stalin* (Bloomington: Indiana University Press, 2005), 26, 28, 50–51, 70, 117–118, 133. In its appreciation of veracity, Soviet journalism was not far from the universal principles of propaganda. Modern theorists of mass persuasion everywhere—in Russia, in the West, in Nazi Germany—have insisted on the maximum possible accuracy and verisimilitude in propagandistic texts. Jacques Ellul, *Propaganda: The Formation of Men's Attitudes* (New York: Vintage Books, 1965), xv, 36–39, 43, 52–61; Leonard W. Doob, "Goebbels' Principles of Propaganda" [1950], in *Propaganda*, ed. Robert Jackall (Houndmills, Basingstoke: Palgrave Macmillan, 1995), 190–216, esp. 199–200, 214–215; Stanley B. Cunningham, "Smoke and Mirrors: A Confirmation of Jacques Ellul's Theory of Information Use in Propaganda," in *Propaganda: A Pluralistic Perspective*, ed. Ted J. Smith III (New York: Praeger, 1989), 151–164, esp. 152–153; Douglas Walton, *Media Argumentation: Dialectic, Persuasion, and Rhetoric* (Cambridge: Cambridge University Press, 2007), 91–92, 124–125; Frank Luntz, *Words That Work: It's Not What You Say, It's What People Hear* (New York: Hyperion, 2007), 92–94, 136.
20. ORF GLM, f. 468, op. 1, d. 30, ll. 97, 36; Nikita Petrov and Ol'ga Edel'man, "Novoe o sovetskikh geroiakh," *Novyi mir*, no. 6 (June 1997), 146; Viacheslav E. Zviagintsev, *Tribunal dlia geroev* (Moscow: OLMA-Press, 2005), 265–266.
21. "Spravka-doklad 'O 28 Panfilovtsakh,'" signed by the chief military prosecutor of the Armed Forces of the USSR, Lieutenant General N. Afanas'iev, 10 May 1948, published in Nikita Petrov and Ol'ga Edel'man, "Novoe o sovetskikh geroiakh," *Novyi mir*, no. 6 (June 1997): 143–149, esp. 143–144, 146; Georgii Kumanev, *Podvig i podlog: Stranitsy Velikoi Otechestvennoi voiny 1941–1945 gg.* (Moscow: Russkoe slovo, 2005), 135.
22. "Spravka-doklad," 146–148.
23. Petrov and Edel'man, "Novoe o sovetskikh geroiakh," 149; David Ortenberg, *Vremia ne vlastno* (Moscow: Sovetskii pisatel', 1975), 303. On Ortenberg, see Jeffrey Brooks, *Thank You, Comrade Stalin! Soviet Public Culture from Revolution to Cold War* (Princeton: Princeton University Press, 2000), esp. 167–172.
24. Ortenberg, *Vremia ne vlastno*, 300.
25. See Brandenberger, *National Bolshevism*.

26. Aleksandr Krivitskii, *Traditsii russkogo ofitserstva* (Moscow: Voennoe izdatel'stvo Narodnogo komissariata oborony, 1945).
27. RGALI, f. 3126, op. 1, d. 339, l. 9 (Simonov to Krivitskii, 13 May 1955).
28. Aleksandr Krivitskii, "Elka dlia vzroslogo, ili povestvovanie v razlichnykh zhanrakh," in Krivitskii, *Sobranie sochinenii*, vol. 1 (Moscow: Khudozhestvennaia literatura, 1984), 323.
29. Lidiia Chukovskaia, "Polgoda v 'Novom mire'," in *Sochineniia v dvukh tomakh*, vol. 2 (Moscow: Gud'ial Press, 2000), e.g., diary entries of 14 and 17 December 1946, 25 January 1947, 7 and 29 February 1947, 7, 10, 12, 18, 20, and 27–28 March 1947, 1, 4, 10, 12, 17, 26–28, and 30 April 1947, 4 and 7 May 1947.
30. ORF GLM, f. 168, op. 1, d. 44, l. 1 (Simonov to Krivitskii, 23 April 1957); RGALI, f. 3126, op. 1, d. 339, ll. 7, 9, 11–13 (Simonov to Krivitskii, 1955–56), esp. l. 11; ibid., d. 340, ll. 1, 5, 8, 10, 12, 14–16, 19, 23, 31 (1957); ibid., d. 341, ll. 4–12, 14, 16, 18 (Simonov to Krivitskii, 1957–58); ibid., d. 342, ll. 4, 10–12, 30, 31, 38–41.
31. RGALI, f. 3126, op. 1, d. 342, l. 8 (no date).
32. ORF GLM, f. 168, op. 1, d. 26, l. 1 (Simonov to Krivitskii, 26 July 1957); RGALI, f. 3126, op. 1, d. 341, l. 14 (Simonov to Krivitskii, 21 July 1957).
33. RGALI, f. 3126, op. 1, d. 343, l. 18 (Simonov to Krivitskii, 18 April 1978). Konstantin Simonov, *Tak nazyvaemaia lichnaia zhizn'* (Moscow: Khudozhestvennaia literatura, 1979); Simonov, *Zhivye i mertvye* (Moscow: Khudozhestvennaia literatura, 1989).
34. RGALI, f. 3126, op. 1, d. 341, ll. 14 (Simonov to Krivitskii, 21 July 1957), 11 (Simonov to Krivitskii, 24 July 1957); ORF GLM, f. 168, op. 1, d. 26, l. 1 (Simonov to Krivitskii, 26 July 1957).
35. Boris Pankin, *Chetyre Ia Konstantina Simonova* (Moscow: Voskresen'e, 1999), 152.
36. Aleksandr Karaganov, *Konstantin Simonov vblizi i na rasstoianii* (Moscow: Sovetskii pisatel', 1987), 109.
37. Konstantin Simonov, "Dym otechestva," *Novyi mir*, no. 11 (November 1947): 1–123.
38. On the novella, see Lazar' Lazarev, *Konstantin Simonov: Ocherk zhizni i tvorchestva* (Moscow: Khudozhestvennaia literatura, 1985), 156–165; Karaganov, *Konstantin Simonov vblizi i na rasstoianii*, 109–115; Orlando Figes, *The Whisperers: Private Life in Stalin's Russia* (New York: Metropolitan Books, 2007), 503–505.
39. ORF GLM, f. 168, op. 1, d. 7, ll. 1–4, 8–9.
40. Lazarev, *Konstantin Simonov*, 156–165; Karaganov, *Konstantin Simonov vblizi i na rasstoianii*, 109–115; Konstantin Simonov, *Glazami cheloveka moego pokoleniia: razmyshleniia o I. V. Staline* (Moscow: APN, 1988), 144.
41. Lazarev, *Konstantin Simonov*, 158; Karaganov, *Konstantin Simonov vblizi i na rasstoianii*, 109.

42. Katerina Clark, *The Soviet Novel: History as Ritual* (Bloomington: Indiana University Press, 2000), 136–152, esp. 136 and 142, 207–209, 215–217, 223–224, 231.
43. See also Thomas Lahusen, *How Life Writes the Book: Real Socialism and Socialist Realism in Stalin's Russia* (Ithaca: Cornell University Press, 1997).
44. "O povesti K. Simonova 'Dym otechestva,'" *Literaturnaia gazeta*, 7 December 1947; N. Maslin, "Zhizni vopreki," *Kul'tura i zhizn'*, 30 November 1947; Simonov, *Glazami cheloveka moego pokoleniia*,145–148.
45. Simonov, *Glazami cheloveka*, 130–133, 148–158; Simonov, *Dym otechestva* (Moscow: Sovetskii pisatel', 1956). For a later edition, see, e.g., Konstantin Simonov, "Dym otechestva," in *Tam, gde my byvali* (Moscow: Moskovskii rabochii, 1964).
46. RGALI, f. 3126, op. 1, d. 340, ll. 12–13; d. 341, ll. 5–6; see also d. 340, l. 10
47. E.g., Aleksandr Krivitskii, *Bessmertie* (Moscow: Moskovskii rabochii, 1950); Krivitskii, *Krasnoe chislo v kalendare: Dokumental'nyi rasskaz* (Moscow: Sovetskaia Rossiia, 1963); Krivitskii, *Ne zabudu vovek: Zapiski voennogo korrespondenta* (Moscow: Voenizdat, 1964).
48. Boris Efimov, "On zaikalsia, no ego vnimatel'no slushali," *Lechaim* (May 2000), http://www.lechaim.ru/ARHIV/97/efimov.htm (accessed 10 March 2009).
49. Chukovskaia, "Polgoda v 'Novom mire'," e.g. diary entries of 14 and 17 December 1946; 25 January 1947; 7 and 29 February 1947; 7, 10, 12, 18, 20, and 27–28 March 1947; 1, 4, 10, 12, 17, 26–28, and 30 April 1947; 4 and 7 May 1947. Also see Lidiia Chukovskaia, *Zapiski ob Anne Akhmatovoi* (Moscow: Soglasie, 1997), vol. 2, 739–740; Krivitskii, "Elka dlia vzroslogo," 338, 344–345; Natalia Bianki, *K. Simonov, A. Tvardovskii v "Novom mire"* (Moscow: Violanta, 1999), 16–17, 20–21, 30.
50. Aleksandr Krivitskii, "O 28 pavshikh geroiakh," *KZ*, 22 January 1942.
51. Krivitskii, *Bessmertie*, 24.
52. Krivitskii, *Ne zabudu vovek*, 64.
53. RGALI, f. 3126, op. 1, dd. 251, 271; Aleksandr Krivitskii, "Raz'ezd Dubosekovo," in *Gody velikoi bitvy*, ed. Georgii Gaidovskii (Moscow: Sovetskii pisatel', 1958): 375–383, here 381.
54. El'vira Popova, "Mir veshchei i mir chelovecheskoi dushi," *Komsomol'skaia pravda*, 11 October 1959.
55. Ilya Ehrenburg, "Otvet na odno pis'mo," *Komsomol'skaia pravda*, 2 September 1959; Boris Slutskii, "Fiziki i liriki," *Literaturnaia gazeta*, 13 October 1959.
56. C. P. Snow, *The Two Cultures* (Cambridge: Cambridge University Press, 2008), first published as *The Two Cultures and the Scientific Revolution* (Cambridge: Cambridge University Press, 1959); in Russian as Charl'z Persi Snou [Charles Percy Snow], *Dve kul'tury: Sbornik publitsisticheskikh rabot* (Moscow: Progress, 1973). See also George Steinmetz, "Positivism and Its Others in the Social Sciences," in *The Politics of Method in the Human Sciences: Positivism and Its*

Epsitemological Others, ed. Steinmetz (Durham: Duke University Press, 2005), 1–43, here 16; Guy Ortolano, *The Two Cultures Controversy: Science, Literature, and Cultural Politics in Postwar Britain* (Cambridge: Cambridge University Press, 2009).

57. On this, see also Vladislav Zubok, *Zhivago's Children: The Last Russian Intelligentsia* (Cambridge, Mass.: Harvard University Press, 2009), 134–140.

58. Slava Gerovitch, *From Newspeak to Cyberspeak: A History of Soviet Cybernetics* (Cambridge, Mass.: MIT Press, 2002), 153–198, esp. 162–163. On other aspects of the physicists-lyricists debate, particularly the role of emotions in private and collective life, see Susan Costanzo, "The 1959 *Liriki-Fiziki* Debate: Going Public with the Private?" in *Borders of Socialism: Private Spheres of Soviet Russia*, ed. Lewis H. Siegelbaum (New York: Palgrave Macmillan, 2006), 251–268. While she focuses on the issues of private versus public as discussed in the press, Costanzo does not emphasize the epistemological aspect of the physicists-lyricists polemic.

59. I regard the resilience and revival of positivism in Soviet culture as a phenomenon similar (but not identical, as it was guided by the Russian epistemological tradition originating in the imperial period) to the post-Stalin search for a "universal language" of scientific accuracy, rationality, and logic. At the heart of Soviet cybernetics, this search was also a factor in the emergence of the Soviet human rights movement (at least in the conception of its early activist, Aleksandr Esenin-Vol'pin). See Gerovitch, *From Newspeak to Cyberspeak*, and Benjamin Nathans, "The Dictatorship of Reason: Aleksandr Vol'pin and the Idea of Rights under "Developed Socialism," *Slavic Review* 66, no. 4 (Winter 2007): 630–663, esp. 644–647. See also Petr Vail and Aleksandr Genis, *60-e: Mir sovetskogo cheloveka* (Moscow: NLO, 2001), 100–112.

60. This image was perpetuated, for example, in one of the most popular films of the epoch—Mikhail Romm's *Nine Days of One Year* (1962), a movie about nuclear physicists that was seen by 23.9 million viewers. *Nashe kino* portal, http://www.nashekino.ru/data.movies?id=1339 (accessed 28 November 2012); Mark Zak, *Mikhail Romm i ego fil'my* (Moscow: Iskusstvo, 1988), 188–221; Josephine Woll, *Real Images: Soviet Cinema and the Thaw* (London: I. B. Tauris, 2000), 127–133. See also Iu. Konobeev et al., eds., *Fiziki shutiat: Sbornik perevodov* (Moscow: Mir, 1966); V. F. Turchin, ed., *Fiziki prodolzhaiut shutit': Sbornik perevodov* (Moscow: Mir, 1968); Vail and Genis, *60-e*, 100–112.

61. Zubok, *Zhivago's Children*, 137–139; Svetlana Kovaleva, ed., *Ty pomnish', fizfak? Neformal'nye traditsii fizfaka MGU* (Moscow: Pomatur, 2003); Veniamin Tsukerman and Zinaida Azarkh, *Arzamas-16: Soviet Scientists in the Nuclear Age: A Memoir*, trans. Timothy Sergay (Nottingham: Bramcote Press, 1999), 68.

62. Ethan Pollock, *Stalin and the Soviet Science Wars* (Princeton: Princeton University Press, 2006), 72–103, esp. 92–93, 96–103. Note Pollock's nuanced

discussion of the complex relationship between ideology and state necessity in the epistemological debates within physics in the late 1940s. Particularly interesting is the prominence of the issue of objective knowledge in the polemics on such Western developments as quantum mechanics and the theory of relativity. Ibid., 77–83, 87–88. Also Douglas Weiner, *A Little Corner of Freedom: Russian Nature Protection from Stalin to Gorbachev* (Berkeley: University of California Press, 1999); Josephson, *New Atlantis Revisited,* 31–32; Josephson, *Red Atom: Russia's Nuclear Power Program from Stalin to Today* (Pittsburgh: University of Pittsburgh Press, 2000, 2005), 4, 184–185.

63. E.g, Nathans, "The Dictatorship of Reason."
64. Norman Pereira, *The Thought and Teachings of* N. G. Černyševskij (The Hague: Mouton, 1975), 35–41; Irina Paperno, *Chernyshevsky and the Age of Realism: A Study in the Semiotics of Behavior* (Stanford: Stanford University Press, 1988), 10–11, 65–67; S. S. Gusev, "Ot 'zhivogo opyta' k 'organizatsionnoi nauke'," in *Russkii pozitivizm: Lesevich, Iushkevich, Bogdanov,* ed. S. S. Gusev (Saint Petersburg: Nauka, 1995), 287–353; N. N. Nikitina, *Filosofiia kul'tury russkogo pozitivizma nachala veka* (Moscow: Aspekt Press, 1996); Barbara Olaszek, *Russkii pozitivizm: Idei v zerkale literatury* (Lodz: Wydawnictwo Uniwersytetu Łódźkiego, 2005), esp. 11–82.
65. Igor S. Narskii, *Marksistskoe ponimanie predmeta filosofii i pozitivizm* (Moscow: Izdatel'stvo VPSh i AON pri TsK KPSS, 1959), esp. 16–32; Narskii, *Sovremennyi pozitivizm: Kriticheskii ocherk* (Moscow: Izdatel'stvo Akademii nauk SSSR, 1961).
66. Roger Markwick, *Rewriting History in Soviet Russia: The Politics of Revisionist Historiography,* 1956–1974 (Houndmills, Basingstoke: Palgrave, 2001), 12–13, 15, 18, 68.
67. See, e.g., Aron Ia. Gurevich, "Chto takoe istoricheskii fakt?" in *Istochnikovedenie: Teoreticheskie i metodologicheskie problemy,* ed. Sigurd O. Shmidt (Moscow: Nauka, 1969): 59–88, esp. 74–82, 84, 86.
68. Gerovitch, *From Newspeak to Cyberspeak,* esp. 1, 6, 293.
69. On these issues, see Denis Kozlov, "The Historical Turn in Late Soviet Culture: Retropsectivism, Factography, Doubt," in *Kritika; Explorations in Russian and Eurasian History* 2, no. 3 (2001): 577–600; Kozlov, "Athens and Apocalypse: Writing History in Soviet Russia," in *Oxford History of Historical Writing,* vol. 5, ed. Daniel Woolf and Axel Schneider (Oxford: Oxford University Press, 2011): 375–398.
70. Kozlov, "Athens and Apocalypse"; Vladimir Lakshin, "Professor Gudzii," *Golosa i litsa* (Moscow: Geleos, 2004), 6–7; B. S. Itenberg, "Polveka s uchitelem," in *P. A. Zaionchkovskii,* 1904–1983 *gg. Stat'i, publikatsii i vospominaniia o nem,* ed. L. G. Zakharova et al. (Moscow: ROSSPEN, 1998), 102, 106; D. I. Budaev, "Vospominaniia aspiranta-zaochnika," ibid., 110; T. Emmons,

"P. A. Zaionchkovskii—nauchnyi rukovoditel' inostrannykh stazherov," ibid., 117–118; Iu. D. Margolis, "Petr Andreevich Zaionchkovskii i Semen Bentsianovich Okun'," ibid., 125; M. O. Chudakova, "Vospominaniia o Petre Andreeviche," ibid., 135; Thomas Sanders, "Introduction: A Most Narrow Present," in *Historiography of Imperial Russia: The Profession and Writing of History in a Multinational State*, ed. Thomas Sanders (Armonk: M. E. Sharpe, 1999), 3–13, here 10–12; Marc Raeff, "Remembrance of Things Past: Historians and History in Russia Abroad," ibid., 188–211, esp. 197–199; Raeff, "Toward a New Paradigm?" ibid., 481–491, esp. 483–485.

71. In this respect, I do not share Roger Markwick's view that "Stalin's war on historians destroyed the great traditions of Russian historical writing" (Markwick, *Rewriting History*, 39). Although not denying the impact of politics on the twentieth-century historical profession, I suggest viewing late-imperial, Stalin-era, and late Soviet (post-1953) historical writing and teaching as sharing crucial elements of the same epistemological culture.
72. Kozlov, "Athens and Apocalypse"; Liubov' Sidorova, *Ottepel' v istoricheskoi nauke: Sovetskaia istoriografiia pervogo poslestalinskogo desiatiletiia* (Moscow: Pamiatniki istoricheskoi mysli, 1997), 12, 18–19, 63, 121, 172–175.
73. V. Kardin, *Segodnia o vcherashnem: Memuary i sovremennost'* (Moscow: Voennoe izdatel'stvo Ministerstva oborony SSSR, 1961), 17–18, 33, 70, 96, 175–190; *Marshal Tukhachevskii. Vospominaniia druzei i soratnikov.* Literaturnaia podgotovka teksta V. Kardina (Moscow: Voennoe izdatel'stvo Ministerstva oborony, 1965), 18, 21, 30, 110, 128–129, 133–134, 160–161, 170, 191, 215, 220–221, 234; V. Kardin, "'Legendy i fakty'. Gody spustia," *Voprosy literatury* 6 (2000): 3–28.
74. Roland Barthes, "Myth Today" [1956], in *A Barthes Reader*, ed. Susan Sontag (New York: Hill and Wang, 1982), 93–147, here 115; see also 114–118, 147.
75. Bianki, *K. Simonov, A. Tvardovskii*, 34.
76. ORF GLM, f. 468, op. 1, d. 3, ll. 2–5.
77. For details, see John Garrard and Carol Garrard, *The Bones of Berdichev: The Life and Fate of Vasily Grossman* (New York: Free Press, 1996), 260–262.
78. See Edith Rogovin Frankel's interview with Grigorii Svirskii, spring 1974, in Frankel, *Novy mir: A Case Study in the Politics of Literature, 1952–1958* (Cambridge: Cambridge University Press, 1981), 173n5.
79. Lazar' Lazarev, *Zapiski pozhilogo cheloveka: Kniga vospominanii* (Moscow: Vremia, 2005), 371.
80. In 1964, another writer and war veteran, Rudol'f Bershadskii, published a story about one of the twenty-eight Panfilovites who had survived—the soldier Illarion Vasil'ev. Bershadskii bitterly criticized Krivitskii (whom he described as "equally inventive and merciless, in anything that worked for his newspaper") for concealing the survivors' names and profiting on the soldiers' blood.

Rudol'f Bershadskii, "Smert' schitat' nedeistvitel'noi," in *Smert' schitat' nedeistvitel'noi* (Moscow: Voenizdat, 1964), 38–49, here 38. Bershadskii was not entirely precise, as in 1958 Krivitskii had admitted that two soldiers, Shemiakin and Vasil'ev, had survived. As Vasil'ev figured in both Krivitskii's and Bershadskii's accounts, there may have been an element of personal tension between the two writers. Unlike Kardin, Bershadskii did not doubt the battle of the twenty-eight itself.

81. Interview wth Elena Vladimirovna Pasternak and Evgenii Borisovich Pasternak, 2 June 2002. Voice emphasis recorded.
82. RGALI, f. 1702, op. 9, d. 212, ll. 29–38; d. 221, ll. 1–73; d. 222, ll. 1–109; d. 223, ll. 2–61; d. 224, ll. 1–69; d. 225, ll. 1–41ob; d. 259, l. 29; d. 330, ll. 64–68, 84–87ob; d. 331, ll. 65–66, 124–147. These files contain eighty-six letters from more than ninety-six individuals; 96.5 percent of the letters were fully signed.
83. Ibid., d. 225, l. 1 (illegible signature, 8 December 1966).
84. Ibid., d. 223, l. 50ob (28 April 1966).
85. Ibid., l. 20b (5 May 1966).
86. Ibid., ll. 28–32 (V. Ivanov, 5 May 1966).
87. Ibid., d. 222, ll. 36–39 (General V. F. Ryzhikov, in 1945 chair of the tribunal of the Kiev Military District, Moscow, 21 April 1966).
88. Ibid., d. 224, l. 27 (10 May 1966).
89. E.g., ibid., d. 221, ll. 61–61ob, 32–33; d. 223, ll. 2–6ob.
90. Clark, "Changing Historical Paradigms in Soviet Culture," in *Late Soviet Culture: From Perestroika to Novostroika*, ed. Thomas Lahusen and Gene Kuperman (Durham: Duke University Press, 1993): 289–306.
91. RGALI, f. 1702, op. 9, d. 221, ll.61–61ob, 32–33; d. 223, ll. 2–6ob.
92. Ibid., d. 223, ll. 49–49ob (Moscow, 21 March 1966); original emphasis.
93. Ibid., d. 224, l. 43 (Leningrad, 17 May 1966).
94. Ibid., d. 221, l. 57 (Moscow); also d. 224, l. 24 (registered 31 May 1966).
95. Ibid., d. 222, l. 102 (Kiev, 22 March 1966).
96. Ibid., d. 224, l. 21 (Leningrad, 16 May 1966).
97. Kardin, "Legendy i fakty. Gody spustia," 6.
98. RGALI, f. 634, op. 5, d. 1116, ll. 10–11. Ianskaia later became Kardin's wife.
99. Ibid., l. 12.
100. Ibid. Rumer's words are all the more valuable since the archive does not have those responses.
101. Valerii Agranovskii, *Poslednii dolg: Zhizn' i sud'ba zhurnalistskoi dinastii Agranovskikh s prologom i epilogom: V vospominaniiakh, svidetel'stvakh, pis'makh s kommentariiami, dokumentakh, fotografiiakh*, 1937–1953 (Moscow: Academia, 1994), 66–67.
102. Vladimir Radzishevskii, "Baiki staroi 'Literaturki,'" *Znamia*, no. 6 (2004): 141–142.

103. Agranovskii, *Poslednii dolg*, 67 (first quotation), 73.
104. Zalman Rumer, *Kolymskoe ekho: Dokumental'noe povestvovanie* (Magadan: Gobi, 1991), 36.
105. Ibid., 37.
106. Ibid., 38. For a different interpretation of remembering the terror during the Thaw, see Orlando Figes, *The Whisperers: Private Life in Stalin's Russia* (New York: Metropolitan Books, 2007), 597–656.
107. RGALI, f. 634, op. 5, d. 1116, ll. 13–14, 17, 20–21 (Naum Mar, A. Bel'skaia, B. Krymov, B. Galanov).
108. Ibid., ll. 14, 18–20, 20–21 (quotations).
109. RGALI, f. 634, op. 5, d. 1116, ll. 15–17.
110. A. Belyshev and B. Burkovskii, "Nedostoinaia zadacha," *Ogonek*, no. 13 (March 1966): 32.
111. RGALI, f. 1702, op. 9, d. 223, l. 60 (Ivan Antipin, thirty-eight, driver, the Siberian town of Divnogorsk, 21 April 1966).
112. Interview with Andrei Borisovich Burkovskii, Saint Petersburg, recorded 9 June 2006.
113. My evidence comes from the dispersed Burkovskii family archive and from interviews and conversations with his former colleagues and family: Andrei Borisovich Burkovskii, Saint Petersburg, recorded 9 June 2006; Tamara Iarmeevna Burkovskaia, Saint Petersburg, recorded 11 June 2006; Irina Aleksandrovna Mach and Pavel Pavlovich Mach, Saint Petersburg, recorded 12 June 2006. Burkovskii's wife Irina Vladimirovna Sakharova left a brief memoir about her husband: see her "Zhena kavtoranga," *Neva*, no. 11–12 (1991): 263–267.
114. Interview with Liubov' Stepanovna Petrova aboard the *Aurora* cruiser, Saint Petersburg, 13 May 2006.
115. V. Pallon, "Zdravstvuite, kavtorang," *Izvestiia*, 15 January 1964.
116. Unfortunately, this correspondence does not seem to have survived. Interview with Andrei Borisovich Burkovskii, Saint Petersburg, 9 June 2006; Sakharova, "Zhena kavtoranga," 267.
117. Tvardovskii, *RT-60*, *Znamia*, no. 11 (2000): 145, 168 (30 January 1964), 158, 172 (31 March 1964). Promoting Solzhenitsyn's nomination for the prize, Samuil Marshak also mentioned Burkovskii on the basis of the *Izvestiia* article. Marshak, "Pravdivaia povest'," *Pravda*, 30 January 1964.
118. RGALI, f. 1702, op. 9, d. 135, l. 4.
119. Ibid., ll. 15, 16–17.
120. Tvardovskii believed that the article was written by the *Ogonek* journalist V. V. Arkhipov (1913–1977) and "signed" by Belyshev and Burkovskii from Leningrad, over the telephone. Aleksandr Tvardovskii, *Novomirskii dnevnik* (Moscow: PROZAiK, 2009), vol. 1, 454 (28 March 1966).

121. Burkovskii to Natalia Sakharova and Aleksandr Gurvich, 20 March 1955. Burkovskii family archive.
122. Interview with Andrei Borisovich Burkovskii, 9 June 2006; interview with Irina Aleksandrovna Mach and Pavel Pavlovich Mach, 12 June 2006.
123. Aleksandr Solzhenitsyn, *The Gulag Archipelago, 1918–1956: An Experiment in Literary Investigation* (New York: Harper and Row, 1974–78), vol. 1, 8, and vol. 3, 54, 76, 487.
124. Dimitrii Panin, *Lubianka—Ekibastuz: Lagernye zapiski* (Moscow: Obnovlenie, 1990), 493–494; Ruf' Tamarina, *Shchepkoi—v potoke . . .* (Alma Ata: Zhazushi, 1991), 184–185.
125. Interview with Andrei Borisovich Burkovskii, 9 June 2006.
126. Conversation with Elena Evgen'evna Golovko, Naval Museum, Saint Petersburg, 10 May 2006; Valentin Ivanov, "Grustnye muzy Soiuza," *Lebed'*, no. 403 (28 November 2004).

10. *Last Battles*

1. Aleksei Kondratovich, *Novomirskii dnevnik (1967–1970)* (Moscow: Sovetskii pisatel', 1990), 381.
2. Aleksandr Tvardovskii, *Novomirskii dnevnik* (hereafter *ND*), vol. 1 (Moscow: PROZAiK, 2009), 522–524 (entries of 18 and 21 December 1966), vol. 2, 7–14 (4, 5, 6, 8, and 9 January 1967).
3. "Kogda otstaiut ot vremeni," *Pravda*, 27 January 1967.
4. Regina Romanova, *Aleksandr Tvardovskii: Trudy i dni* (Moscow: Vodolei, 2006), 669–683 (partly published transcript of the discussion); Tvardovskii, *ND*, 2:19 (16 March 1967).
5. Vladislav Zubok, *Zhivago's Children: The Last Russian Intelligentsia* (Cambridge: Harvard University Press, 2009), 294–299, 307, 351, 428, 435.
6. Tvardovskii, *ND*, 2:206 (5 August 1968); see also 2:205 (19 July 1968), 209–210 (11 August 1968), 215 (16 August 1968).
7. Ibid., 219–220 (29 August 1968).
8. Ibid., 221 (5 September 1968); Vladimir Lakshin, *Solzhenitsyn i koleso istorii* (Moscow: Veche-Az, 2008), 347; Romanova, *Aleksandr Tvardovskii*, 712.
9. "Poluchili reshenie TsK s razresheniem na vypusk romana v svet," interview with Al'bert Beliaev, *Kommersant. Vlast'*, 28 September 2009, http://www.kommersant.ru/doc.aspx?DocsID=1239513 (accessed 2 February 2011).
10. Nikolai Voronov, "Iunost' v Zheleznodol'ske," *NM*, no. 11 (November 1968): 3–95; no. 12 (December 1968): 31–110.
11. Nikolai Voronov, "Ognennaia kovka," *Voprosy literatury*, no. 1 (2005): 213–246.
12. Ibid., 245.
13. M. Sinel'nikov, "Pravde vopreki," *LG*, 5 March 1969.

14. *LG*, 5 March 1969.
15. Tvardovskii, *ND*, 2:297–300, here 299 (8 March 1969); see also 282 (19 February 1969).
16. RGALI, f. 1702, op. 9, d. 328, ll. 102–103 (Semen Samuilovich Gorelik, Moscow, 23 August 1969).
17. Zubok, *Zhivago's Children*, 236–245, 251, 258, 306–308, 317; Denis Kozlov, "The Historical Turn in Late Soviet Culture: Retrospectivism, Factography, Doubt, 1953–91," *Kritika: Explorations in Russian and Eurasian History* 2, no. 3 (2001): 577–600; Yitzhak Brudny, *Reinventing Russia: Russian Nationalism and the Soviet State, 1953–1991* (Cambridge, Mass.: Harvard University Press, 1998).
18. Nikolai Mitrokhin, *Russkaia partiia: Dvizhenie russkikh natsionalistov v SSSR, 1953–1985 gody* (Moscow: Novoe literaturnoe obozrenie, 2003).
19. RGALI, f. 1702, op. 9, d. 86, l. 17 (8 December 1961).
20. Tvardovskii, *ND*, 1;411–412 (12 January 1966).
21. V. Chalmaev, "Velikie iskaniia," *Molodaia gvardiia*, no. 3 (1968): 270–295; Chalmaev, "Neizbezhnost'," *Moodaia gvardiia*, no. 9 (1968): 259–289, esp. 263, 267–268; M. Lobanov, "Prosveshchennoe meshchanstvo," *Molodaia gvardiia*, no. 4 (1968): 294–306; see also Vadim Kozhinov, "O realizme 30-kh godov XIX veka," *Voprosy literatury*, no. 5 (1968): 60–82.
22. Aleksandr Dement'ev, "O traditsiiakh i narodnosti," *NM*, no. 4 (1969): 215–235, here 216.
23. Ibid., 230.
24. Ibid., 219, 221, 230–233.
25. Dement'ev, "O traditsiiakh i narodnosti," 217–218, 225; Iurii Surovtsev, "Pridumannaia neizbezhnost'," *Literaturnaia Rossiia*, no. 45 (1968).
26. The eleven were Mikhail Alekseev, Sergei Vikulov, Sergei Voronin, Vitalii Zakrutkin, Anatolii Ivanov, Sergei Malashkin, Aleksandr Prokof'ev, Petr Proskurin, Sergei Smirnov, Vladimir Chivilikhin, and Nikolai Shundik; Alekseev et al., "Protiv chego vystupaet *Novyi mir*," *Ogonek*, no. 30 (26 July 1969): 26–29.
27. Viktor Petelin, *Schast'e byt' samim soboi: Zhizneopisanie v vospominaniiakh, pis'makh, interv'iu, fotografiiakh* (Moscow: Golos, 1999), 194–195; Mitrokhin, *Russkaia partiia*, 356.
28. Alekseev et al., "Protiv chego vystupaet," 27.
29. Ibid. The Dement'ev publication to which they referred was "Protiv antipatrioticheskogo estetizma and formalizma v poezii," *Zvezda*, no. 3 (1949): 205–206. For a similar anti-Dement'ev diatribe, which inspired the letter writers, see Dmitrii Moldavskii, "A literaturnaia kritika—tvorchestvo!" *Oktiabr'*, no. 10 (1966).
30. RGASPI, f. M-73, op. 1, d. 168, ll. 16–19 (Vasilii Evseenkov, printer, Rostov-on-Don).

31. See Polly Jones, "The Personal and the Political: Opposition to the 'Thaw' and the Politics of Literary Identity in the 1950s and 1960s," in *The Thaw: Soviet Society and Culture during the 1950s and 1960s*, ed. Denis Kozlov and Eleonory Gilburd (Toronto: University of Toronto Press, 2013): 231–265.
32. Alekseev et al., "Protiv chego vystupaet," 27, 29.
33. Ibid., 27. On Dement'ev and the *Ogonek* letter, see Valentina Tvardovskaia, "A. G. Dement'ev protiv 'Molodoi gvardii' (Epizod iz ideinoi bor'by 60-kh godov)," *Voprosy literatury*, no. 1 (2005): 178–212.
34. Tvardovskii, *ND*, 2:354 (27 July 1969); "Ot redaktsii," *NM*, no. 7 (1969): 285–286. For details, see Tvardovskaia, "A. G. Dement'ev protiv 'Molodoi gvardii'."
35. M. E. Zakharov, "Otkrytoe pis'mo Glavnomu redaktoru zhurnala *Novyi mir* Tvardovskomu A.T.," *Sotsialisticheskaia industriia*, 31 July 1969.
36. *Sotsialisticheskaia industriia*, 9 August 1969.
37. Ibid.
38. RGASPI, f. 638, op. 1, d. 20, l. 4. For the casting of some of these clichés, see Matthew Lenoe, *Closer to the Masses: Stalinist Culture, Social Revolution, and Soviet Newspapers* (Cambridge, Mass.: Harvard University Press, 2004), 38–45.
39. RGALI, f. 1702, op. 9, d. 324, ll. 1–101; d. 325, ll. 2–103; d. 326, ll. 1–94; d. 327, ll. 4–107; d. 328, ll. 9–141; d. 329, ll. 1–91; d. 330, ll. 5–117; d. 331, ll. 1–147. For Voronov, see ibid., op. 10, d. 479, ll. 1–128.
40. RGASPI, f. M-73, op. 1, d. 168, ll. 16–19 (Evseenkov); RGASPI, f. M-1, op. 45, d. 117, ll. 11–15 (teachers, village of Kez, Udmurtiia; some signatures are repeated several times, suggesting an awkward "self-multiplication" for the sake of enhancing the argument), 16–22 (Aleksandr Govorov, member of the Writers' Union). The three letters condemned Dement'ev and *Novyi mir.*
41. RGALI, f. 1702, op. 9, d. 324, ll. 1–4, 5–6 (registered 8 and 13 August 1969).
42. Ibid., ll. 3, 5.
43. Ibid., l. 4.
44. Ibid., d. 326, l. 37 (Anatolii Shishkov, 13–14 August 1969).
45. Ibid., ll. 24–25 (14 August 1969).
46. Ibid., d. 327, l. 43 (Mikhail Tomshin, 10–14 August 1969); also d. 324, ll. 61–61ob (Iu[rii] Papuda).
47. Ibid., op. 10, d. 479, ll. 24–31.
48. Ibid., op. 9, d. 324, ll. 78–79 (4 August 1969).
49. Ibid., d. 327, l. 40. See also ibid., op. 10. d. 479, ll. 12–13 (Marianna Vekhova).
50. Ibid., op. 9, d. 325, l. 17 (7 August 1969); also ibid., d. 327, l. 41 (Tomshin); d. 328, l. 135 (Litvinova).
51. Ibid., d. 327, l. 30 (N. Ialonov, Leningrad)
52. Ibid., ll. 30–31; d. 325, ll. 34–46 (Kryzhanovskii, Moscow, 10 August 1969); d. 326, ll. 37ob (Shishkov, Tula Oblast); d. 327, ll. 4, 6 (Viktor Ladygin, Irkutsk);

d. 329, l. 56 (Aleksandr Mikhailov, Magnitogorsk); d. 330, ll. 5–6 (Dmitrii Piatakov, Nikolaev, 29 September 1969); d. 331, l. 61 (Konovalov, Moscow).

53. Ibid., d. 324, l. 62.
54. Ibid., d. 325, l. 74 (20 August 1969); for the students' letter, see l. 76 (V. Romanov, O. Galkin, K. Lisovskii, 11 August 1969). Also ibid., d. 327, l. 36.
55. Ibid., d. 327, ll. 96–97 (Vladimir Gavriushov, worker, Leningrad Gorky drama theater, July 1969); for Tvardovskii's reply see l. 98.
56. Tvardovskii, *ND*, 2:401 (13 September 1969).
57. Kondratovich, *Novomirskii dnevnik*, 406–413 (14–29 May, 2–6 June 1969).
58. Bernard Gwertzman, "11 Soviet Conservatives, in Sharp Attack on Novy Mir, Warn of Dangers from Bourgeois Ideology," *New York Times*, 27 July 1969.
59. D. Ivanov, "Po povodu vystupleniia Niu Iork Taims," *Sovetskaia Rossiia*, 3 August 1969. See also Tvardovskaia, "A. G. Dement'ev protiv 'Molodoi gvardii'."
60. See, e.g., Tvardovskii, *ND*, 2:431 (14 November 1969).
61. RGALI, f. 1702, op. 9, d. 323, ll. 30–31.
62. Aleksandr Iakovlev, "Protiv antiistorizma," *LG*, 15 November 1972.
63. Aleksandr Iakovlev, *Omut pamiati* (Moscow: Vagrius, 2001), 173–181; Tvardovskaia, "A. G. Dement'ev protiv 'Molodoi gvardii' "; Mitrokhin, *Russkaia partiia*, 368.
64. "Leninskaia partiinost'—znamia revolioutsionnogo iskusstva," *Pravda*, 12 September 1969; Tvardovskii, *ND*, 2:401 (13 September 1969).
65. Tvardovskii, *ND*, 2:324–328 (30 April, 3–10 June 1969).
66. Sources on this abound. See, e.g., Vladimir Lakshin, *Solzhenitsyn i koleso istorii* (Moscow: Veche, 2008); Lakshin, *Solzhenitsyn, Tvardovsky and* Novy Mir, trans. and ed. Michael Glenny (Cambridge, Mass.: MIT Press, 1980); Solzhenitsyn, *Bodalsia telenok s dubom: Ocherki literaturnoi zhizni* (Paris: YMCA Press, 1975).
67. For the two quotes, see, respectively: Tvardovskii, *ND*, 2:432 (2 December 1969) and 421 (5 November 1969).
68. Ibid., 423–425 (7 November 1969).
69. Ibid., 434 (6 December 1969).
70. Stalin uttered these words at a conference of combine-harvester operators in Moscow on 1 December 1935. The phrase was his reply to the statement by a collective farmer, A. G. Til'ba, who began his speech by saying: "Comrades, I am the son of a kulak." See "Rech' tov. A. G. Til'by," *Pravda*, 2 December 1935.
71. Translated from: Aleksandr Tvardovskii, "Po pravu pamiati," http://www.lib.ru/POEZIQ/TWARDOWSKIJ/memory.txt (accessed 23 February 2011).
72. Tvardovskii, *ND*, 2:320 (24 April 1969).
73. See, e.g., "Spravka Glavlita o zamechaniiakh k materialam, podgotovlernnym k opublikovaniiu v 1966 g." (15 March 1967), in *Istoriia sovetskoi politicheskoi*

tsenzury: Dokumenty i kommentarii, ed. T. M. Goriaeva (Moscow: ROSSPEN, 1997), 558–559; Al'bert Beliaev, "Na Staroi ploshchadi," *Voprosy literatury*, no. 3 (2002): 243–270, esp. 244–256.

74. Tvardovskii, *ND*, 2:312, 317–319, 329–342, 355, 357, 393, 432 (23 March, 20–21 April, 14–30 June, 29 July, 3 August, 31 August, 2 December 1969). On Simonov's later years, see also Orlando Figes, *The Whisperers: Private Life in Stalin's Russia* (New York: Metropolitan Books, 2007), 621–629.
75. RGALI, f. 3133, op. 1, d. 169, l. 17 (Vitalii Semin to Aleksandr Mariamov, 30 December 1969).
76. Tvardovskii, *ND*, 2:439 (19 December 1969).
77. Ibid., 452–453, 459–460 (16, 27 January 1970); Tsentral'nyi arkhiv Soiuza Pisatelei SSSR, op. 37, d. 361, pub.: Romanova, *Aleksandr Tvardovskii*, 740; Al'bert Beliaev, *Literatura i labirinty vlasti: ot "ottepeli" do perestroiki* (Moscow, 2009).
78. A. Petrov and I. Brainin, eds., "Osada 'Novogo mira'" Iz khroniki odnogo goda po dokumentam arkhiva TsK KPSS," *LG*, 21 June 1995; Tvardovskii, *ND*, 2:465 (4 February 1970).
79. Tvardovskii, *ND*, 2:466–468 (quotation) (6–8 February 1970); Romanova, *Aleksandr Tvardovskii*, 741–743.
80. Tsentral'nyi arkhiv Soiuza Pisatelei SSSR, op. 37, d. 363, published: Romanova, *Aleksandr Tvardovskii*, 744; *LG*, 11 Feb. 1970.
81. Tvardovskii, *ND*, 2:469 (12 February 1970); Tsentral'nyi arkhiv Soiuza Pisatelei SSSR, op. 37, d. 364, published in Romanova, *Aleksandr Tvardovskii*, 745–746.
82. Tvardovskii, *ND*, 2:475 (22 February 1970); Romanova, *Aleksandr Tvardovskii*, 748–749.
83. Interview with Igor' Ivanovich Vinogradov, recorded 19 July 2002.
84. Tvardovskii, *ND*, 2:471, 479, 602 (13, 17 February and 21 March 1970).
85. Translated from Aleksandr Tvardovskii, "Rabochie tetradi 60-kh gg.," in *Znamia*, no. 10 (2005), http://magazines.russ.ru/znamia/2005/10/tv11.html.

Epilogue

1. Aleksandr Tvardovskii to Konstantin Tvardovskii, 31 March 1970, in *Sibirskie ogni*, no. 2 (1988): 175.
2. RGALI, f. 1702, op. 9, d. 349, l. 11; also RGALI, f. 3133, op. 1, d. 169, l. 18 (Vitalii Semin to Aleksandr Mariamov, 27 February 1970).
3. Aleksandr Tvardovskii, *Novomirskii dnevnik* (Moscow: PROZAiK, 2009), vol. 2, 491 (17 May 1970).
4. The term comes from Ludmilla Alexeyeva, *The Thaw Generation: Coming of Age in the Post-Stalin Era* (Boston: Little, Brown, 1990).

5. Sergei Nekhamkin, "Zolotoi mig 'tolstykh' zurnalov," *Izvestiia*, 2 August 2005, http://www.izvestia.ru/archive/02–08–05/?5 (accessed 10 March 2011).
6. RGAE, f. 3527, op. 27, d. 1416, ll. 43–44.
7. Natal'ia Ivanova, "Nostal'iashchee," *Znamia*, no. 9 (1997), http://magazines.russ.ru/znamia/dom/ivanova/ivan0019.html (accessed 10 October 2010); N. N. Shneidman, *Russian Literature, 1988–1994: The End of an Era* (Toronto: University of Toronto Press, 1995), 26.
8. E.g., http://echo.msk.ru/programs/personalno/531398-echo/comments.html#comments; http://echo.msk.ru/news/531936-echo.html (accessed 20 March 2010).

ACKNOWLEDGMENTS

Over the years of research and writing, I have accumulated many intellectual debts, and it is with pleasure that I now thank the people who made this book possible.

I am grateful first of all to Lynne Viola at the University of Toronto. For years, and long after graduate school, Lynne gave me invaluable professional advice and human support. Conveying the highest standards of our discipline, she introduced me to the field and wisely guided me through the many complex stages of research and writing. She encouraged me to think about my work broadly and was always (without exaggeration, always) willing to help, whether it came to reading various drafts and proposals—more than I can remember now—or discussing academic life. To a great extent, it is to Lynne's guidance that the book owes its existence.

Thomas Lahusen has, from the first time we met in Toronto, responded with enthusiasm to my interest in ties between history and literature. His numerous insights broadened my knowledge and did much to inspire and improve the book. Derek Penslar taught me a lot about European intellectual history and was extremely supportive of this project, offering comparative perspectives that helped me place my work in a broader context. Robert Johnson conveyed to me his knowledge of historical statistics and suggested important improvements for my approach to mass sources.

The book benefited immeasurably from the time I spent as a Social Sciences and Humanities Research Council of Canada postdoctoral fellow at the University of California, Berkeley, and as a postdoctoral fellow at the Davis Center for Russian and Eurasian Studies at Harvard University. Yuri Slezkine welcomed me to Berkeley, responded to my project with great interest, and read several drafts of my work, as well as the final book manuscript, offering invaluable conceptual comments and suggestions. Terry Martin was always keenly interested in the book, made me feel welcome me at the Davis Center, and created an excellent working environment full of the lively exchange of ideas. A year spent on an Andrew W. Mellon Fellowship for assistant professors at the School of Historical Studies of the Institute for Advanced Study in Princeton was most beneficial for the final stages of writing, as was the support from the National Council for Eurasian and East European Research. The company of fellow historians at the Institute, exploring a variety of fields and epochs, broadened my perspective substantially.

Acknowledgments

I wish to thank the organizers of and participants at a number of conferences and workshops, for stimulating discussions that gave me valuable food for thought. My thanks in particular go to the participants in the 2004 Maryland-Harvard Workshop on New Approaches to Russian and Soviet History; the 2005 conference "The Thaw: Soviet Society and Culture during the 1950s and 1960s" at Berkeley; the 2006 conference "The Relaunch of the Soviet Project, 1945–1964" at the School of Slavonic and East European Studies, University College London; the 2006 "History and Legacy of the GULAG" conference at the Davis Center at Harvard; the 2008 conference "The Pain of Words: Narratives of Suffering in Slavic Cultures" at Princeton; the 2010 conference "After the War, after Stalin" at the University of Saint Petersburg, Russia; and the 2012 conference "Trust/Distrust in the USSR" at the School of Slavonic and East European Studies, University College London. I am also grateful to the participants in the University of Chicago European history workshop, the Russian history workshop at Berkeley, the Stanford University Russian history workshop, the Russian and Eastern European history workshop at Harvard, the University of Pennsylvania history workshop, and the community of fellow Russianists at Princeton for their numerous productive ideas and comments.

My colleagues in the History Department and the Department of Russian Studies at Dalhousie University have responded with great interest to my research, offering many helpful suggestions and generous support. Conversations with Gregory Hanlon, Shirley Tillotson, Ruth Bleasdale, Norman Pereira, Yuri Leving, and John Barnstead were always enjoyable and constructive, as was the feedback from the participants in the Lawrence D. Stokes Seminar in the History Department.

While on research trips, I met many people who became interested in my work and helped me. I thank Natal'ia Borisovna Volkova, Tatiana Mikhailovna Goriaeva, Galina Iur'evna Drezgunova, Natal'ia Alekseevna Strizhkova, and Elena Evgen'evna Chugunova at the Russian State Archive of Literature and Art; Liudmila Gennad'evna Kiseleva at the State Archive of the Russian Federation; Andrei Vital'evich Vasilevskii at the journal *Novyi mir*; and Sergei Ivanovich Chuprinin at the journal *Znamia* for their help. I am grateful to Valentina Aleksandrovna Tvardovskaia, Evgenii Borisovich Pasternak, Natalia Fedorovna Dudintseva, Ivan Vladimirovich Dudintsev, Yulia Borisovna Zaks, Andrei Borisovich Burkovskii, Tamara Iarmeevna Burkovskaia, Nadezhda Andreevna Lisina, and Pavel Pavlovich Mach for fascinating conversations and for generously granting me access to their family archives.

At Harvard University Press, I am grateful to my editor, Kathleen McDermott, who saw early promise in the book manuscript and offered numerous valuable suggestions for improving it. Andrew Kinney provided expert assistance with preparing the manuscript for publication. I also thank the readers, who invested much of their time and thought in the manuscript. The book has greatly benefited from their comments.

During these years, and in a variety of professional settings, I have exchanged ideas with many fellow historians whose work helped me rethink and improve my own approaches. In addition to the colleagues mentioned above, I would like to thank Steven

Barnes, Glen Bowersock, Heather Coleman, Michael David-Fox, Heather DeHaan, Evgeny Dobrenko, Mikhail Dolbilov, Sheila Fitzpatrick, Michael Gordin, Loren Graham, Jochen Hellbeck, Paul Hollander, Peter Holquist, Geoffrey Hosking, Polly Jones, Jean Levesque, Stephen Lovell, Tracy McDonald, Mie Nakachi, Benjamin Nathans, Sergei Oushakine, Irina Paperno, Benjamin Tromly, Amir Weiner, Serhy Yekelchyk, and Vladislav Zubok.

Portions of Chapter 3 were previously published as "Naming the Social Evil: The Readers of *Novyi mir* and Vladimir Dudintsev's *Not by Bread Alone*, 1956–1959 and Beyond," in *The Dilemmas of De-Stalinization: Negotiating Cultural and Social Change in the Khrushchev Era*, ed. Polly A. Jones (London: Routledge, 2006), 80–98. Portions of Chapters 4 and 8 were published as "'I Have Not Read, but I Will Say': Soviet Literary Audiences and Changing Ideas of Social Membership, 1958–1966," *Kritika: Explorations in Russian and Eurasian History* 7, no. 3 (Summer 2006): 557–597. Portions of Chapter 7 were published as "Otzyvy sovetskikh chitatelei 1960-kh gg. na povest' A. I. Solzhenitsyna 'Odin den' Ivana Denisovicha': Svidetel'stva iz arkhiva 'Novogo mira'," in *Noveishaia istoriia Rossii*, no. 1 (2011): 178–200, and no. 2 (2011): 192–200. Excerpts from Aleksandr Tvardovskii's poetry published in Tvardovskii, "Rabochie tetradi," *Znamia*, no. 7 (1989): 143–144 (entry of 5 October 1954), 167 (entry of 22 April 1955), 178 (entry of 6 January 1956); Tvardovskii, "Rabochie tetradi 60-kh godov," *Znamia*, no. 10 (2005), http://magazines.russ.ru/znamia/2005/10/tv11.html; and Tvardovskii, "Rabochie tetradi 60-kh godov," *Znamia*, no. 5 (2004), http://magazines.russ.ru/znamia/2004/5/tvar8.html), are my translations from the original Russian, published here with permission from Valentina Aleksandrovna Tvardovskaia, Ol'ga Aleksandrovna Tvardovskaia, and the journal *Znamia*.

My family offered the greatest support on my long path toward completing this book. I am grateful to my parents, to Eleonor, who has always been my most careful reader and demanding critic, and to Anthony Kozlov, who appeared at the concluding stages of this work and has not yet had a chance to read it, but whose help in life cannot be measured.

INDEX

Abetz, Otto, 176, 382n13
Abramov, Fedor, 44, 49, 73
Agapov, Boris, 17, 40, 112
Akhmatova, Anna, 6, 13, 80, 160
Aksakova, Tat'iana Aleksandrovna, 158–159
Aksenov, Vasilii, 138, 161, 163, 214
Aleksandrov, Georgii, 31, 38
Alexander II, 5
Andropov, Iurii, 246
Anticosmopolitan campaigns, 40–41, 205, 302–303, 306–307
Anti-Semitism, 174, 176, 205. *See also* Jews
Antistatism, of the intelligentsia, 62
Arakcheev, Aleksei Andreevich, 81
Arendt, Hannah, 197
Arkhangel'sk, 33
Astrakhan', 33
Aurora (Avrora), cruiser, 263, 288, 290, 307
Authenticity, 53, 68–71, 135, 155, 159, 162–166, 201, 209, 215–216, 219–220, 263–294, 299, 327

Babaevskii, Semen, 44, 49, 54, 81
Babel', Isaac, 80, 92, 154, 178–180
Banderovites, 223, 225, 227–228
Basov, Vladimir, 185
BBC radio broadcasts, 315
Bek, Aleksandr, 92
Belarus (Belorussia), 28–29, 227
Beliaev, Al'bert, 298, 300, 320
Belief, 13, 46–47, 54, 68–70, 82, 98, 100, 104, 114, 120, 130, 142, 156, 184–207, 233–235, 243, 251, 258–261, 270, 282, 287, 297, 299, 308, 315, 328, 386n85
Belinsky, Vissarion, 61
Berggol'ts, Olga, 44, 47, 241
Beria, Lavrenty, 104, 149, 198, 284
Berzin, Ian, 181, 383n41
Black Sea Fleet, 288
Bliukher, Vasilii Konstantinovich, Marshal of the Soviet Union, 204
Bogoraz, Larisa, 242
Bol'shov, D. G., 320
Borshchagovskii, Aleksandr, 40
Brezhnev, Leonid, 188, 239, 246, 264, 297, 314, 320, 325
Bryansk, 33
Bukharin, Nikolai, 177
Bulgaria, 55
Burkovskii, Boris Vasil'evich, 287–292

Central Committee (CC) of the Communist Party of the Soviet Union (until October 1952 CC of the All-Union Communist Party [Bolshevik]): Department (Board) of Propaganda and Agitation, 27, 31, 38, 315; Department of Culture, 53, 112–113, 295, 298–299; Department of Science and Culture, 54, 57, 77; Orgburo, 26; Politburo, 26, 245; as a political force, 19, 28–30, 33, 38, 40, 44, 49, 54, 73, 75–76, 78, 80, 91, 99, 104, 110, 119, 143, 155, 160, 169, 188, 192, 246, 248, 268–269, 296, 298, 300, 303, 308, 314–317, 320; Presidium, 74, 77, 241, 260; Russian Federation Bureau, 34; Secretariat, 26, 29, 75–77, 245
Chalmaev, Viktor, 303–306
Chekhov, Anton Pavlovich, 15–16, 60, 63, 184
Chernyshevsky, Nikolai Gavrilovich, 2, 276
Chlenov, Semen, 179
Chudakova, Marietta, 82

Chuev, Feliks, 304
Chukovskaia, Lidiia Korneevna, 114, 124, 164–166, 170, 173, 254, 302, 327
Chukovskii, Kornei Ivanovich, 66–67
Civil War, Russian, 2, 6, 96, 110, 114, 153–154, 196, 224, 234–235, 238, 245, 252, 278, 292; atrocities in, 121–125
Civil War, Spanish, 179, 182
Clark, Katerina, 271
Code of Criminal Procedure of the Russian Federation, 243
Cold War, 11, 113, 125, 259, 315
Collectivization, 6, 45, 141–142, 144–145, 278, 318; as an underrepresented theme in writings about Soviet political violence, 162–163, 172–173
COMES (European Community of Writers), 241
Cosmopolitanism, 174–175, 301. *See also* Anticosmopolitan campaigns
Council of Ministers of the USSR, 31
Countryside, 35, 41, 45, 49, 53, 58, 80–81, 138–139, 144, 147, 232, 303, 305. *See also* Collectivization; Kulaks; Peasantry; Village prose
Criminal Code of the Russian Federation, 243
Cruelty, perceptions of, 121–125, 229–230, 248
Czechoslovakia, 55, 239, 297–298. *See also* Prague Spring

Dal', Vladimir, 63, 213
Daniel', Iulii Markovich, 240–242, 249, 259. *See also* Siniavskii-Daniel' affair
Deliberative democracy, 18–19
Dement'ev, Aleksandr Grigor'evich, 73–75, 77, 113, 153–154, 158, 161, 165–166, 175, 288, 295–296, 302–308, 312–314, 317
District Routine (sketch), 41–42, 49, 53, 62
Doctors' Plot, 178
Doctor Zhivago (novel), 110–133, 169, 242, 252, 279, 326. *See also* Pasternak, Boris Leonidovich
Dolinina, Natalia, 82–83
Dostoevsky, Fedor Mikhailovich, 15–16, 62
Druzhba narodov (journal), 28, 326–327
Dudintsev, Vladimir Dmitrievich, 21, 88–109, 127, 133, 135, 152–153, 169, 190, 209, 271, 326. See also *Not by Bread Alone*
Dunaevskii, Isaak, 266

Eastern Europe, reactions to the Thaw in the Soviet Union, 55–57
Ehrenburg, Ilya Grigor'evich, 72; and memories of the terror, 171–208, 209–211, 215, 224, 230, 234–235, 237–238; memoir *People, Years, Life*, 7, 8, 107, 130–131, 171–208, 209–211, 215, 224, 230, 234–235, 237–238, 248, 253, 259, 262, 281, 282, 327; novella *Thaw*, 44; reactions to Konstantin Simonov's work, 270; representation of Boris Pasternak, 130–131; role in the "physicists-lyricists" polemic, 274–275
Eikhenbaum, Boris, 82
Émigrés, 1, 2, 215
Enemies, as a notion and image, 8, 17, 73, 89, 95–98, 100–102, 104, 105, 107, 117, 140, 168, 174, 178, 188, 192, 194–199, 204, 206, 220, 222–231, 233, 235–236, 248, 255, 259–261, 265–266, 282–285, 401n58
Ermilov, Vladimir, 60, 73–74, 187–194, 196–199, 201, 207, 234, 282
Esenin, Sergei, 80, 249
Estonia, 36, 225
Ethics, and Soviet intellectual change, 4, 7, 9, 15, 43, 47, 50, 66, 71, 85, 86, 89–90, 93, 96, 98, 103, 108, 110, 125, 127–129, 132, 135, 152, 160, 164, 167, 183, 185, 188–190, 199, 201, 204, 206, 208, 209, 214–215, 230, 237, 251, 260, 272, 277, 279, 283, 293–294, 297, 301, 307, 324
Experience, as a paradigm, 21–22

Facts, as a notion and its significance in Soviet culture, 52–53, 69, 129, 155–159, 264, 267, 271, 273–283, 293–294, 304, 326–327
Fadeev, Aleksandr, 39, 41, 73, 75–76, 140, 149, 176–177, 180
Far East, 104, 138, 197, 216–217
Far North, 233, 286
Fascism, 207. *See also* Nazi Germany and Nazism
Fear, 7–8, 14, 20, 42, 125–126, 130, 179, 184, 193–194, 197–198, 200–202, 236, 266, 299, 310, 324

Fedin, Konstantin, 75, 112, 113
Fet, Afanasii, 61
Fin-de-siècle, 61, 215, 276, 303, 305
Finland and the Winter War of 1939–1940, 141, 176, 231
France, 9, 115, 155, 174, 181, 182, 220, 240, 243, 250
French Revolution, 172
Furtseva, Ekaterina, 109, 143, 152

Gagen-Torn, Nina Ivanovna, 159–160, 162, 283
Generations, in language and arguments on the Thaw, 129, 130, 132, 185–186, 192, 202–203, 205, 206, 285, 325
Georgia, 257, 272
Germany, East, 55. *See also* Nazi Germany and Nazism
Germany, West, 9, 242–243. *See also* Nazi Germany and Nazism
Ginzburg, Evgeniia, 161–164, 170, 173, 179
Gladkov, Fedor, 67
Glavlit, 296
Gogol, Nikolai Vasil'evich, 61, 66, 96, 214
Gorbachev, Mikhail, 15, 33, 81, 108, 172, 315, 325. *See also* Perestroika
Goslitizdat, 111
Graphomania, 26
Great Patriotic War. *See* World War II and its legacies
Great Reforms, 5–6, 304
Great Turn, 29, 45
Gribachev, Nikolai, 73, 296
Grossman, Vasilii, 42–43, 167–170, 176, 279–280, 326
Gulag: and former camp guards, 227–231; and former prisoners, 7, 8, 13, 21, 103–104, 107, 145, 179, 196, 199, 211–236, 283–292; and long-term impact of literature about, 7, 8, 13, 21, 212, 239, 243, 252–254, 325–326; and Solzhenitsyn, 209–238; Tvardovskii and survivors' writings, 145–148, 151–164, 168, 209–210. *See also* Burkovskii, Boris Vasil'evich; Rumer, Zalman Afroimovich; Terror
Gulag Archipelago (book), 19, 222, 291, 327
Gwertzman, Bernard, 315

Historical consciousness, as a paradigm, 21–23, 107, 132
Historical turn, in late Soviet culture, 152, 301
Hitler, Adolf, 177, 195
Holocaust, 146, 148, 212
Human documents, as a notion, 155–156, 379n68
Human rights movement and activism, 8, 79, 239–262, 408n59
Hungarian Revolution, 98–99

Iakovlev, Aleksandr, 315–316
Iashvili, Paolo, 179
Il'f, Ilya, and Petrov, Evgenii, 66, 80
Il'ichev, Leonid, 188
Inostrannaia literatura (journal), 28, 53
Intellectual change in societies, as a mechanism, 1–23, 237, 293–294, 328–329
Intelligentsia, 3–4, 6, 9, 39, 50, 59, 62, 64, 74, 113–114, 116–117, 119–125, 128–130, 154, 161–164, 172–174, 178, 182, 188, 200–201, 213, 221, 245, 256, 259, 271, 276, 297, 302, 304–305, 310, 312, 325, 329, 402n61
Internationalism, 302, 305, 312
Iron Curtain, 9, 11, 243
Istochnikovedenie (source study), 277
Italy, 111, 250
Iunost' (journal), 28, 109
Izvestiia (newspaper), 19, 32–33, 93, 179, 183–186, 187–188, 190, 220, 246, 288

Jasieński, Bruno, 205
Jews, 178. *See also* Anti-Semitism

Kardin, Emil' Vladimirovich, 257, 263–264, 273, 278, 280, 282–288, 291–292, 294, 296, 307, 327
Kataev, Valentin, 40, 75, 108
Katyn massacre, 227
Kazakhstan, 157, 180, 215–216, 242, 281
Kazan, 80–81, 83, 281
KGB (Committee for State Security), 93, 111, 126, 148, 169, 240, 246, 280. *See also* Gulag; NKVD; Police; Terror; Violence
Khabarovsk, 58–59, 257

Khrushchev, Nikita, 6–8, 32–33, 56, 75–78, 91, 98, 101, 117, 132, 143, 148, 154–155, 177, 183, 187–188, 193, 198, 209, 222, 239, 314. *See also* Secret Speech
Kiev (Kyiv), 32, 40, 61, 205, 282
Kochetov, Vsevolod, 34, 115
Kol'tsov, Mikhail, 179
Kolyma, 151, 216, 220, 285–286. *See also* Gulag
Komsomol, 19, 25–26, 30, 51, 113, 117, 197, 211, 244–249, 300
Komsomol'skaia Pravda (newspaper), 25, 32, 56–57, 249, 284
Kondratovich, Aleksei Ivanovich, 84–85, 106, 216, 232, 295, 305, 317, 320–321
Korolenko, Vladimir Galaktionovich, 15
Kosolapov, Valerii Alekseevich, 115, 320–321
Kostomarov, Nikolai, 151
Kotov, Anatolii, 111
Krasnaia nov' (journal), 37
Krasnaia zvezda (Red Star) (newspaper), 40, 264–268, 279
Krest'ianka (journal), 36
Krivitskii, Aleksandr Iur'evich, 40, 109, 112, 264–274, 278–284, 286–287, 294
Krokodil (journal), 183
Kulaks, 105, 139–140, 143–144, 270, 318. *See also* Collectivization; Countryside; Peasantry
Kuznetsov, Anatolii, 257–258

Lakshin, Vladimir Iakovlevich, 16, 113, 288, 295, 305, 317, 320–321
Language: conservatism and resistance to linguistic innovation, 213–215; and the emergence of modern Russian ideology and culture, 2; evolution and diversification during the Thaw, 6–9, 14–15, 20, 43, 65–68, 79–84, 86, 132, 145–152, 166–167, 210–220; 222–231, 233, 235–236, 248, 255, 259–261, 265–266, 282–285, 328, 341n37, 359n93, 391n23, 401n58, 408n59; and experience, 21; and generations, 129, 130, 132, 185–186, 192, 202–203, 205, 206, 285, 325; and jargon/slang, 67–68, 210–219; and legality, 243–244, 250–253, 256; and mass political violence, 6–9, 96–104, 145–152, 166–167, 170–173, 183–187, 207–208, 210–219, 222–231, 233, 235–236, 248, 255, 259–261, 265–266, 282–287, 290–292, 401n58, 408n59; and the memory of the Revolution, 124–127; and neologisms/neo-archaisms, 213–219; and the notion of "enemies," 8, 17, 73, 89, 95–98, 100–102, 104, 105, 107, 117, 140, 168, 174, 178, 188, 192, 194–199, 204, 206, 220, 222–231, 233, 235–236, 248, 255, 259–261, 265–266, 282–285, 391n23, 401n58; and positivism/facts, 276–279; and Russian nationalism, 304–305; and silence, 183–187; and sincerity, 53–54, 65–72, 79–84; and Solzhenitsyn's prose, 210–219, 223–224, 234, 237–238, 304, 391n23; and the Soviet media/officialdom, 6–8, 53–54, 65–72, 79–84, 96, 118, 124, 126–127, 129, 132, 145–152, 166–167, 184, 208, 218, 244–247, 261, 273, 276–279, 282, 307, 310–311; Stalin-era paradigms and their disintegration during the Thaw, 6–9, 14–15, 20, 43, 64, 79–84, 86–87, 90, 96–103, 107, 124, 126–127, 129, 132, 190, 210–219, 223–224, 230, 234, 237–238, 256, 276–279, 282, 286–287, 289, 307, 310–311, 341n37, 359n93, 391n23, 401n58, 408n59; and swear words, 210–219; and Tvardovskii's efforts at linguistic innovation, 145–152, 166–167, 170
Latvia, 55, 93, 225
Lavrenev, Boris, 112–113
Law and legality, in the Soviet Union and postwar Europe, 8–9, 229, 243–244, 250–253, 256, 340n29, 397n13, 402n60
"Legends and Facts," article, 263–294
Lenin, Vladimir, 29, 52, 97, 128–129, 150, 182, 184, 194, 195, 248–250, 253, 264, 276, 288, 305, 386n82
Leningrad (city), 3, 28, 32, 38–39, 51, 58, 88, 95, 101, 126, 128–129, 159, 179–180, 182, 192, 205, 246, 282, 288–289, 302, 311. *See also* Saint Petersburg
Leningrad (journal), 26, 28, 38–40, 76
Lenin Mausoleum, 154, 284
Lenin Prize in literature, 288
Leonov, Leonid, 44
Leont'ev, Boris, 115
Leont'ev, Konstantin, 304
Lesiuchevskii, Nikolai, 60, 73
Letter of the Eleven Writers, 257, 306–308

Letters, significance in Russian/Soviet history and culture, 15–21
Lifshits, Mikhail, 44, 54, 73
Literature-centrism, 2–6, 24–25, 58, 92, 100, 204
Literaturnaia gazeta (newspaper), 17, 41, 52–53, 55–58, 75, 78, 93, 108, 112–118, 121, 126, 190, 248, 282–287, 300, 320, 323
Literaturnaia Moskva (almanac), 111
Lithuania, 36
Litvinov, V. M., 115
Liubarskii, Kronid, 79–83
Living word, concept of, 67
Lobanov, Mikhail, 303, 306
Lozovskii, Solomon, 181, 383n41
L'vovskaia Pravda (newspaper), 161
Lyrical poetry, 44, 67, 110
Lyricists, 274–276
Lysenko, Trofim, 108

Machado, Antonio, 181, 383n41
Magnitogorsk, 298, 300, 311
Makedonov, Adrian Vladimirovich, 140, 145, 148
Malenkov, Georgii, 27, 29, 38, 41, 91, 357n62
Malokartin'e (scarcity of feature films), 28
Mal'tsev, Elizar, 81
Mandel'shtam, Osip, 179–180
Manège exhibition, 187
Mar'enkov, Efrem, 148
Mariamov, Aleksandr Moiseevich, 295, 320
Markish, Perets, 179
Marqué, Albert, 181, 383n41
Marxism, 73, 81, 276
Mayakovskii, Vladimir, 63–64, 66
Memory, as a paradigm, 22
Meyerhold, Vsevolod, 178–179
Mikhailov, Oleg, 306
Molodaia gvardiia (journal), 28, 303, 307, 314, 316
Moscow, 3, 12, 24, 28, 31, 32, 34–35, 51, 55, 56, 58, 60, 63–64, 75, 78–81, 89, 90, 92, 97, 99, 104–106, 110, 112, 127, 140, 143–145, 146, 154, 161, 176–178, 185, 187, 191, 196, 204, 210, 226, 240, 246, 250, 263–268, 302, 308, 315, 319, 323, 330
Moscow Does Not Believe in Tears (film), 185
Moscow Institute of Philosophy, Literature, and History (MIFLI), 140
Moscow Institute of World Literature, 240
Moskatov, P., 143
Moskva (journal), 28
Mukhina-Petrinskaia, Valentina Mikhailovna, 151–152, 156, 158
MVD (Ministry of the Interior), 228–229, 232. *See also* Gulag; KGB; NKVD; Police

Nabokov, Vladimir Vladimirovich, 1–2, 11, 23
Nash sovremennik (journal), 28
Nationalism, Russian, 301–306, 312, 316
Nazaretskaia, K. A., 81–82
Nazi Germany and Nazism, 68–69, 130, 146, 148, 168, 200, 212, 279
Nazi-Soviet pact of August 1939, 174, 176–177
Nekrasov, Nikolai Alekseevich, 4, 37, 58, 60, 64
Neva (journal), 28, 326–327
New Economic Policy (NEP), 5, 54
New York Times, 315
Nicholas I, 304
Nikolaeva, Galina, 49, 81
Nikonov, Anatolii, 316
NKVD (People's Commissariat of Internal Affairs), 140, 191, 197, 222, 227. *See also* Gulag; KGB; MVD; Police; Terror
Nobel Prize, 110, 112–114, 117, 124
Not by Bread Alone (novel), 21, 88–109, 127, 133, 135, 152–153, 169, 190, 209, 271

Ogonek (journal), 32, 36, 287, 306–307, 310, 314
Oktiabr' (journal), 6, 26–29, 31–32, 34, 38, 108, 326
Okudzhava, Bulat Shalvovich, 301
Old Bolsheviks, 200, 221, 224, 235
One Day in the Life of Ivan Denisovich (novella), 7, 10, 12, 21, 34, 36, 93, 105, 107, 125, 155, 158–159, 161, 163–164, 166, 169–170, 171, 187, 209–238, 288–292, 317
Otechestvennye zapiski (*Notes of the Fatherland*) (journal), 5, 313
Ovechkin, Valentin, 41–43, 49, 53–54, 62, 113, 135, 143–144

Panferov, Fedor, 25, 27, 71, 81
Panfilov, Ivan, general, 263, 265
Panfilovites, 263–268, 273–274, 278–282

Party Congresses: Twelfth, 194; Nineteenth, 41; Twentieth, 6, 89, 91, 101, 103–104, 110, 132, 148–149, 198–199 (*see also* Secret Speech); Twenty-Second, 7, 154, 158, 171, 230; Twenty-Third, 308
Pasternak, Boris Leonidovich, 110–133, 135, 140, 154, 169, 174, 180, 205, 236, 240, 242, 244–249, 251–252, 257, 261, 272, 287, 318, 326; and the Pasternak affair, 110–133, 240, 242, 244–249, 251–252, 257, 261. See also *Doctor Zhivago*
Pasternak, Elena Vladimirovna, 280
Pasternak, Evgenii Borisovich, 132
Paustovskii, Konstantin Georgievich, 89, 99, 153–154, 158, 166
Pavlov, Dmitrii, general, 181
Peasantry, 45, 68, 84, 123–124, 135, 139, 143, 162–163, 172–173, 208, 286, 305, 307, 318–319, 322. *See also* Collectivization; Countryside; Kulaks; Village prose
People, Years, Life (memoir), 7–8, 107, 130–131, 171–208, 215, 224, 230, 234–235, 237–238, 248, 253, 259, 262, 281, 282, 327. *See also* Ehrenburg, Ilya Grigor'evich
People's Commissariat of Posts and Telegraphs (after 1932 People's Commissariat of Communications, after 1946 Ministry of Communications), 30
Perestroika, 15, 37, 81, 108, 172, 240, 315; as a continuation of the Thaw, 325–328
Petelin, Viktor, 306
Physicists-lyricists polemic, 274–277
Poland, 55–56
Polevoi, Boris, 54–55, 73, 80
Police, 1, 11, 30, 89, 191, 227–231, 279. *See also* Gulag; KGB; MVD; NKVD
Polikarpov, Dmitrii, 113
Polizei, 225, 228, 267, 273
Pomerantsev, Vladimir Mikhailovich, 44–87, 89, 90, 92–93, 98, 100, 115, 127, 132–133, 135, 143–144, 165, 170, 187, 190, 205, 214
Positivism, 271, 274–279, 282, 293–294, 304, 408n59
Pospelov, Petr, 54, 73–75, 78
POWs, 45, 219, 220, 225, 265
Prague Spring, 297, 239, 297–298
Pravda (newspaper), 19, 32, 33–34, 42, 73–74, 78–79, 113, 117, 128, 129, 178, 189, 192, 193, 205, 296, 316
Provinces, 3, 15, 35, 58, 60
Purges. *See* Terror
Pushkin, Aleksandr, 60, 62, 214
Pushkin Theater, 51

Rabotnitsa (journal), 32, 36
Ramsin, F., 31
Raskol'nikov, Fedor, 181, 383n41
Razgovorov, Nikita, 115
Readers of *Novyi* mir, statistical and social analysis, 336
Reading and readers, general significance in Russian and Soviet history, 1–23, 323–332
Realism, 21, 100, 165, 216, 218–219, 228, 259, 299. *See also* Socialist realism
Reconciliation, national, 255
Red Army, 223, 226, 265, 268
Red Army Theater, 51
Re-education, of Gulag prisoners, 291
Repentance, as a paradigm, 203
Representativeness, as a category in intellectual history, 14–15
Revolution, Russian, 1–2, 5–7, 10, 110–133, 135, 139, 147, 152–154, 158, 186, 200–201, 224, 236, 238, 245, 252–253, 263, 264, 276–278, 288–290, 292
Riurikov, Boris Sergeevich, 53, 55–57, 60, 75, 80, 115
Rokossovskii, Konstantin Konstantinovich, Marshal of the Soviet Union, 264, 283
Roman-gazeta (journal), 36
Rostov-on-Don, 319
Rudenko, Roman, 111
Rumer, Zalman Afroimovich, 284–287
Rumiantsev, I. P., 139–140
Russian Association of Proletarian Writers (RAPP), 140
Russian Soviet Federative Socialist Republic (RSFSR), 308
Russian State Archive of Literature and Art (RGALI), 12
Russkii vestnik (Russian Messenger), 5
Rybakov, Anatolii, 327
Ryklin, Grigorii, 183

Saint Petersburg, 247, 330
Samizdat (clandestinely published literature), 112, 222
Sats, Igor, 147, 295, 320
Savich, Ovadii, 182, 383n42
Secret Speech, 6, 89, 91, 101, 103–104, 110, 132, 148–149, 154, 183, 198–199, 252–253
Self-absolution, 202–203
Semichastnyi, Vladimir, 113
Severyanin, Igor, 61
Sevrikov, Konstantin, 183–184
Shaginian, Marietta, 44, 246
Shauro, Vasilii, 295
Shcheglov, Mark, 44, 73
Shcherbina, Vladimir, 38
Shepilov, Dmitrii, 27
Shestidesiatniki, 186, 259
Sholokhov, Mikhail, 157, 220
Silence: during the terror and in memories about the terror, 177–178, 183–201, 204, 285; in the media about the terror, 152, 180, 292; proverbial in the provinces, 58, 60
Simonov, Konstantin Mikhailovich, 10–12, 27, 29, 32, 34, 35, 37, 73, 75, 77–78, 80, 81, 85, 88, 92, 108–109, 111–113, 153, 318–319; editorial strategies, 39–42, 268–274, 294
Sincerity, as a paradigm, 44–87, 100, 135, 144, 205
Siniavskii, Andrei Donatovich, 240. *See also* Siniavskii-Daniel' affair
Siniavskii-Daniel' affair, 239–262, 282, 287, 295, 302–303, 318
Skorino, Liudmila, 51, 53, 56, 60–62, 355n42
Slavophilism, 304, 312
Slutskii, Boris, 275
Smirnov, Sergei Sergeevich, 73, 75
Smoke of the Fatherland (novella), 40–41, 270–272
Smushkevich, Iakov, 181, 383n41
Snow, C. P. (Charles Percy), 275. See also *Two Cultures*
Socialist realism, 2–3, 16, 41, 44, 57, 62, 68, 71–73, 81–82, 214–216, 234, 270–274, 293
Socialist Revolutionaries, 182
Sofia Petrovna (novella), 164–166, 327
Sofronov, Anatolii, 306
Soiuzpechat' (Central Directorate for the Distribution and Expedition of the Press), 29–34
Sokol'nikov, Grigorii, 177
Sokolov-Mikitov, Ivan, 137
Soloukhin, Vladimir, 115
Solzhenitsyn, Aleksandr Isaevich, 7, 10, 12, 21, 34, 36, 67, 93, 105, 107, 125, 155, 158–159, 161, 163–164, 166–170, 171, 173, 187, 189, 208, 209–238, 252, 254, 259, 262, 281, 282, 288–292, 299, 304, 317, 327, 330. See also *One Day in the Life of Ivan Denisovich*
"Son Does Not Answer for His Father," 318
Sotsialisticheskaia industriia (newspaper), 308–310, 314
Soviet Literature in Foreign Languages (journal), 321
Sovnarkhozy (councils of the economy), 91
Sovremennik (*Contemporary*) (journal), 37, 304, 313
Stalin, Joseph, 6–8, 24, 26–28, 37–43, 48, 67, 77, 81–83, 91, 101, 102–104, 107–108, 125, 130, 154, 171–174, 178, 182–184, 188, 223, 268, 272, 281, 284, 286, 304, 314, 318, 319, 321, 327, 330, 416n70; in readers' letters, 190–191, 193–195, 198, 200, 202, 235, 248, 251–252; Tvardovskii's ideas about, 140–142, 148–150, 318. *See also* Stalin cult
Stalin cult ("cult of personality"), 54, 67, 101, 104, 142, 180, 182, 184, 186, 202, 205, 217, 232–233, 282, 356n43
Stalin Prize in literature, 24, 39, 41, 140–141
Statistics of readership, *Novyi mir*, 336
Stavskii, Vladimir, 38
Subscription to Soviet periodicals, 28–35, 264, 327
Supreme Soviet of the RSFSR, 308
Supreme Soviet of the USSR, 40, 248, 266
Surkov, Aleksei, 51, 60, 73, 75, 80, 143, 241–242, 296
Surov, Anatolii, 51
Suslov, Mikhail, 169, 246, 295
Sutotskii, Sergei, 73
SVAG (Soviet military administration in Germany), 45
Sverdlovsk, 32, 118, 190, 311
Svodki, 246

Tabidze, Titsian, 179
Tägliche Rundschau (newspaper), 45
Terror: as a concept and term, 171–173; experiences in memories, writings, and interpretations during the Thaw, 152–166, 171–262, 282–294, 299, 312; and language, 6–9, 96–104, 145–167, 170–173, 183–187, 207–208, 209–219, 222–231, 233, 235–236, 248, 255, 259–261, 265–266, 282–287, 290–292, 401n58, 408n59; logic of, in readers' behavior during the early Thaw, 96–98, 101–104; and long-term impact of literature and reading about, 2, 6–9, 13–15, 20–21, 43, 86, 104, 107, 170, 173–174, 203–204, 207–208, 210–224, 230–238, 239, 243, 248–254, 256, 262, 281–287, 289–294, 310–312, 325–326, 330, 341n37, 401n58; and Tvardovskii's ideas and literary strategies, 141–167, 170, 208, 297. *See also* Gulag; MVD; NKVD; Police; Secret Speech; Thaw; Violence
Terterian, Artur Sergeevich, 115
Thaw (historical epoch): and the evolution in thought and language, disintegration of Stalin-era paradigms, 6–9, 13–15, 20–21, 43, 64–68, 79–84, 86–87, 90, 96–104, 107, 124, 126–127, 129, 132, 145–152, 166–167, 170, 173–174, 190, 203–204, 207–208, 210–231, 233–239, 243, 248–256, 259–262, 276–279, 281–287, 289–294, 307, 310–312, 325–326, 328, 330, 341n37, 359n93, 391n23, 401n58, 408n59
Thaw (novella), 171
Thick journals as a concept, 4–6; during the perestroika and the post-Soviet years, compared to the Thaw, 325–329; under Stalin, 26–28, 37–39
Third Party Program, 249
Tikhookeanskaia zvezda (Pacific Star) (newspaper), 59
Tiutchev, Fedor, 61
Tolstoy, Leo, 3, 15–16, 48, 62, 72, 156, 164–165, 190, 200–201, 214, 304
Trifonov, Yuri, 24–25, 42, 79
Truth, 1, 15, 25, 46–48, 50, 53–54, 59, 63–65, 70, 86, 100, 127, 148–149, 157, 169–170, 191, 198, 201, 203, 210–220, 222, 232, 234, 236, 266–274, 276–282, 285, 288–289, 292, 310, 312, 319, 327; conceptual evolution of, and Soviet intellectual change, 293–294; in socialist realism, 271–274. *See also* Authenticity; Facts; Positivism
Tsvetaeva, Marina, 131, 180
Tukhachevskii, Mikhail Nikolaevich, Marshal of the Soviet Union, 196, 248–249, 283
Tvardovskaia, Maria Illarionovna, 75, 136, 138
Tvardovskaia, Olga Aleksandrovna, 136
Tvardovskaia, Valentina Aleksandrovna, 420
Tvardovskii, Aleksandr Trifonovich, 10–12, 24, 32, 35, 39, 41–42, 44–45, 50–52, 58, 72, 85, 88, 109, 115, 130, 133, 211–212, 232, 318–322; and Aleksandr Fadeev, 73–76, 149; and Aleksandr Solzhenitsyn, 158–159, 161, 163–164, 166, 173, 209–210, 213, 231, 317; approach to memoirs, 153–164, 212; attitudes to Stalin, 140–142, 148–150, 235, 318; and C. P. Snow, 275; editorial strategies, literary and political views, 16, 34, 37, 39, 43, 49, 67, 72–78, 84, 106–108, 112–113, 134–170, 209–210, 213, 218, 239–242, 263–264, 278, 282, 288–289, 293–322, 323–331; efforts at linguistic innovation, 145–152, 166–167, 170, 237; and Emil' Kardin, 278, 282; and Evgeniia Ginzburg, 161–164, 170; experiences of the 1930s, 139–141, 143–144, 317–318, 322; family, 139, 143–144, 317–318, 322; and Gulag survivors' writings, 145–148, 151–164, 168, 209–210, 212; ideas and literary strategies of representing the terror, 141–167, 170, 208, 237, 259–261, 297, 318; and Ilya Ehrenburg, 175–177; and Konstantin Paustovskii, 153–154; and Konstantin Simonov, 318–319; lasting impact, 170, 314, 323–331; and Lidiia Chukovskaia, 164–166, 170; and Nikolai Voronov, 298–300; poetry, 73, 75, 77, 80, 135–136, 138, 145–146, 148, 317–318, 322; policy on keeping readers' letters in the journal's archive, 12, 158–159, 212; and the Siniavskii-Daniel' affair, 239–242, 259–261; and Vasilii Grossman, 167–170
Two Cultures, lecture/book and polemic on, 275. *See also* Snow, C. P.
Two Thousand Words (manifesto), 297
Tynianiov, Iurii, 80

Ukraine, 28, 51, 61, 100, 106, 129, 205, 225, 227, 267, 310

Union of Soviet Writers (Writers' Union), 26, 38–39, 45, 51, 59–60, 73, 76–78, 111, 113, 128, 140, 143, 148, 241, 260, 317, 296, 298, 300, 314, 317, 320–321
United States, 137, 270, 288

Varnishing of reality, 46–47, 54, 271
Vasilevskii, Andrei, 52
Vasilevskii, Vitalii, 52–54, 56–57, 60
Vestnik Evropy (*Messenger of Europe*) (journal), 5
Village prose, 49, 303–305
Vinogradov, Igor' Ivanovich, 295, 298, 317, 320–321
Violence, political, 6–9, 13, 96–104, 107, 123, 141–262, 265–266, 280–294, 299, 312, 327–328, 342n37, 401n58, 408n59. *See also* Gulag; MVD; NKVD; Police; Secret Speech; Terror
Virgin Lands campaign, 354n21
Virta, Nikolai, 81
Vlasov, Andrei, general, 225
Vlasovites, 223, 225, 227–228
Vologda, 33
Voronkov, Konstantin, 241, 298, 317, 320
Voronov, Nikolai Pavlovich, 298–300, 306–309, 311–312
Vyshinskii, Andrei, 243

Warsaw Pact, 297
Weblogs, 18
White Army, 121–122
World War II and its legacies, 24, 27, 28–30, 38, 45, 66, 68–70, 122, 141, 174, 177, 196, 207, 219, 224–227, 229, 231, 238, 243, 254, 263–271, 273–275, 278–280, 281–283, 288, 292, 298–299, 304, 318–319. *See also* POWs

Yezhov, Nikolai, 195, 197–198
Youth in Zheleznodol'sk (novel), 298–300, 306–309, 311–312

Zakharov, Mikhail Egorovich, 308–312
Zaks, Boris, 113, 175, 295–296
Zalygin, Sergei, 326–327
Zaslavskii, David, 113, 128–129, 205
Zhdanov, Andrei, 27, 38, 40
Znamia (journal), 26, 28–29, 31, 32, 38, 53, 111, 169, 279, 326
Zolotusskii, Igor', 81, 83
Zorin, Leonid, 247
Zoshchenko, Mikhail, 40, 66, 80
Zvezda (journal), 6, 26, 28–29, 31, 32, 38–40, 76, 326

www.ingramcontent.com/pod-product-compliance
Lightning Source LLC
Chambersburg PA
CBHW030828310726
48980CB00006B/686/J
* 9 7 8 0 6 7 4 0 7 2 8 7 9 *